Welcome to MODERN CURRICULUM PRESS Phonics

Celebrating More Than 50 Years of Success!

Creating successful readers has been the goal of Modern Curriculum Press Phonics for over fifty years. Since its early beginnings, this tried and true program has helped over 55 million children learn how to read. Today, MCP Phonics is ready to give our next generation of learners the solid foundation they need to become lifelong readers. Teachers can rely on MCP Phonics as a proven program based on current research and best practices for teaching phonics in today's classroom.

The tools that help children learn to read . . .

- **Student books** for kindergarten–third grade.
- A comprehensive **Teacher's Resource Guide** for each level.
- **Phonics Picture Cards** for kindergarten and first/second grade.
- **Phonics Word Cards** for first–third grade.
- A **Phonics and Reading Library** for each level featuring books from MCP Ready Readers and Early Chapter Books programs.
- A complete set of **assessment** tools including pretests and posttests and a direct connection to MCP's new assessment tool, Phonemic Awareness and Phonics Assessment (PAPA).

Teachers want to know . . .

How does MCP Phonics deliver systematic and explicit phonics instruction? T2

What is the research base that supports MCP Phonics? T6

What phonics skills do I need to teach? T8

How does MCP Phonics make planning a lesson easy? T10

How does MCP Phonics fit into my classroom reading instruction? T12

How does MCP Phonics help my students apply their skills to reading, writing, and language arts? T13

How does MCP Phonics incorporate high-frequency word instruction? T15

How will MCP Phonics help my English Language Learners? T16

How do I assess my students' needs in phonics? T18

How can I adapt MCP Phonics for summer school? T19

How can MCP Phonics help struggling readers in an after-school program? T20

LEVEL K

How does MCP Phonics deliver systematic and explicit phonics instruction?

Level K of MCP Phonics presents the letters and sounds of the alphabet in a systematic sequence of instruction that fosters strong phonemic awareness, phonics, and early literacy skills.

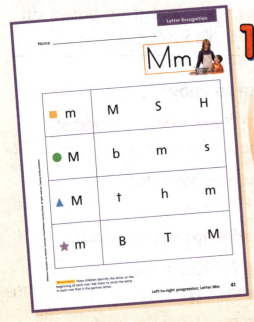

1 Start each lesson with **letter recognition** activities to strengthen alphabetic awareness.

2 Reinforce letter recognition with **handwriting** activities to develop understanding that print conveys meaning.

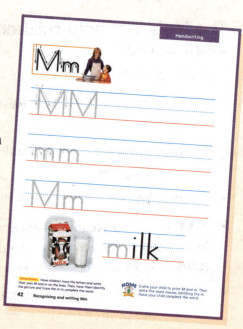

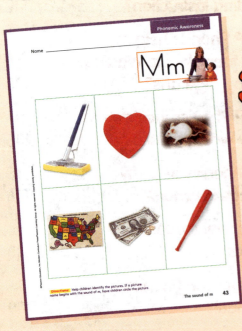

3 Develop students' ability to hear, focus on, and recognize phonemes in spoken words with **phonemic awareness** activities.

4 Help students make connections between spoken sounds and their corresponding printed symbols with **sound to symbol** activities.

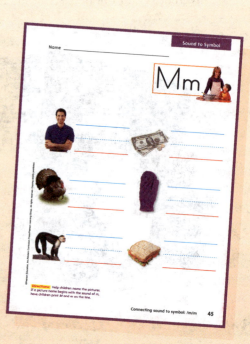

 Apply newly learned phonemic awareness and phonics concepts to reading with fun and decodable **Take-Home Books**.

7 Improve reading fluency with practice in key **high-frequency** words.

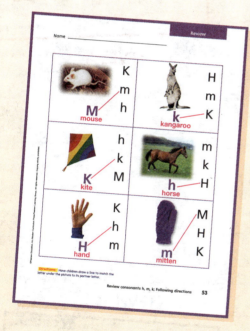

6 Measure students' understanding of skills and concepts with **review** pages.

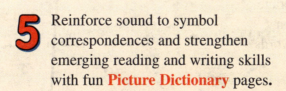 Reinforce sound to symbol correspondences and strengthen emerging reading and writing skills with fun **Picture Dictionary** pages.

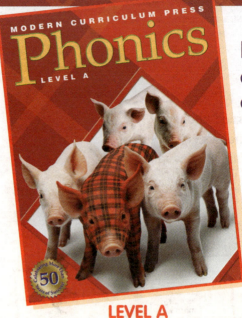

LEVEL A

MCP Phonics Level A focuses on explicit and systematic instruction in consonants, short and long vowels, and high-frequency words.

1 Begin instruction with **phonemic awareness** activities to teach children the sound a vowel makes.

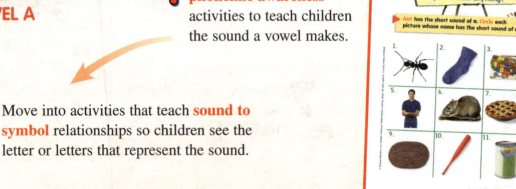

LEVEL A

2 Move into activities that teach **sound to symbol** relationships so children see the letter or letters that represent the sound.

3 Provide essential practice in combining phonemes and phonograms into words with **blending** lessons.

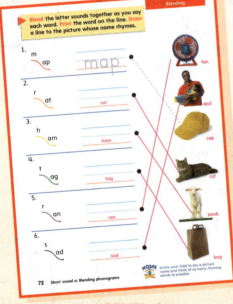

LEVEL A

4 Continue with **spelling** activities that target specific skills and encourage children to make the connection between hearing and reading words.

5 Practice high-frequency words (highlighted in the Teacher's Resource Guide) and newly learned decoding skills to read sentences in **words in context** activities.

LEVEL B

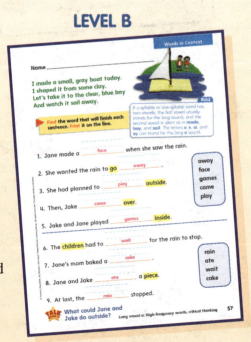

MCP Phonics LEVELS B and C focus on long and short vowels, vowel pairs, diphthongs, and digraphs, as well as compound words, prefixes, and suffixes. High-frequency word instruction continues in Level B.

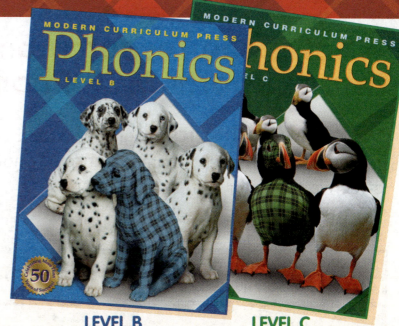

LEVEL B　　**LEVEL C**

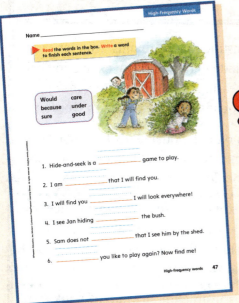

LEVEL B

9 Continue instruction in selected **high-frequency words** to provide children with the tools they need to be successful readers.

8 Provide opportunities for individual reading success with highly decodable **Take-Home Books**.

LEVEL A

7 Apply newly learned phonics skills to make new words with fun **Word Building** activities.

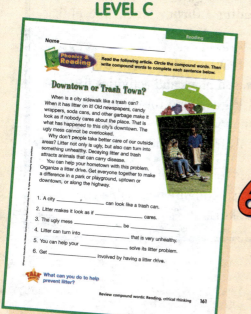

LEVEL C

6 Encourage fluency and build comprehension while providing skills practice with engaging **Phonics & Reading** passages.

T5

What is the research base that supports MCP Phonics?

The new **MCP Phonics** program is based on current research that stresses the importance of phonics and effective teaching methods for phonics.

The National Reading Panel and Put Reading First say...	The new MCP Phonics provides...
• Phonemic awareness instruction is most effective when children are taught to manipulate phonemes by using the letters of the alphabet.	• sound to letter instruction, beginning with letter recognition in kindergarten that moves in a logical sequence from hearing the sounds letters make to associating the sounds with the letters in words.
• Children with phonological and phonemic awareness skills are likely to have an easier time learning to read and spell.	• series of lessons on individual skills that first focus on phonemic awareness, then give a broader emphasis on phonological awareness.
• Systematic and explicit phonics instruction improves kindergarten and first-grade children's word recognition, spelling, and reading comprehension.	• systematic and explicit instruction and practice in phonemic and phonological awareness, sound to symbol relationships, blending, syllabication, and other phonics and word study skills.
• Systematic and explicit phonics instruction is most effective when introduced early.	• complete phonics instruction in **student books** beginning with kindergarten and continuing through third grade.
• Phonics instruction is not an entire reading program for beginning readers. Children also need to work on their knowledge of the alphabet, listen to stories and informational texts read aloud, read texts both out loud and silently, and write letters, words, and stories.	• a variety of activities that help children transition from phonics to reading, including read-aloud fiction and nonfiction **unit openers** that encourage oral language, **reading passages** with comprehension questions, decodable **Take-Home Books** for group and independent reading, instruction on different **types of writing**, and a **Phonics and Reading Library** for each level that includes little books and chapter books.
• Systematic and explicit phonics instruction is particularly beneficial for children who are having difficulty learning to read.	• a comprehensive **Teacher's Resource Guide** for each level with lesson plans and activities for different types of learners and for children who need additional support, as well as a complete set of **assessment tools** for each unit.
• Repeated and monitored oral reading improves reading fluency and overall reading achievement.	• many opportunities for children to read aloud with teacher guidance using highly decodable text targeting phonics skills.

Listed here are some of the resources used to develop the new edition of MCP "Plaid" Phonics.

Research Resources

Adams, Marilyn Jager. *Beginning to Read.* 1990. Cambridge, MA: Massachusetts Institute of Technology.

Allington, Richard L., editor. *Teaching Struggling Readers.* 1998. Newark, DE: International Reading Association.

Ambruster, Bonnie and Jean Osborn. *Put Reading First: The Research Building Blocks for Teaching Children to Read.* 2001. Developed by the Center for the Improvement of Early Reading Achievement (CIERA) from the findings of the National Reading Panel. Washington D.C. Partnership for Reading. National Institute for Literacy. www.nifl.gov

Baumann, J.F., J.V. Hoffman, A.M. Duffy-Hester, and J.M. Ro. "The First R Yesterday and Today: U.S. Elementary Reading Instruction Practices Reported by Teachers and Administrators." *Reading Research Quarterly* 35: 343–353, 2000.

Beck, Isabel and Connie Juel. "The Role of Decoding in Learning to Read" in *What Research Has To Say About Reading Instruction.* Samuels, S. Jay and Alan E. Farstrup, editors. 1992. Newark, DE: International Reading Association.

Ericson, Lita, and Moira Fraser Juliebö. *The Phonological Awareness Handbook for Kindergarten and Primary Teachers.* 1998. Newark, DE: International Reading Association.

Hiebert, E.H. *Text Matters in Learning to Read.* November 1, 1998. CIERA Report #1-001. Ann Arbor, MI: Center for the Improvement of Early Reading Achievement, University of Michigan.

Juel, Connie, and Cecilia Minden-Cupp. *Learning to Read Words: Linguistic Units and Strategies.* September 30, 1998. CIERA Report #1-008. Ann Arbor, MI: Center for the Improvement of Early Reading Achievement, University of Michigan.

Morrow, L.M. *Literacy Development in the Early Years: Helping Children Read and Write,* 4th ed., 2001. Needham Heights, MA: Allyn & Bacon.

Preventing Reading Difficulties in Young Children, National Research Council. 1998. Washington, D.C.: National Academy Press.

Report of the National Reading Panel: Teaching Children to Read. An Evidence-Based Assessment of the Scientific Research Literature on Reading and Its Implications for Reading Instruction. Reports of the Subgroups. December 2000. National Reading Excellence Initiative, an activity of the National Institute for Literacy. www.nationalreadingpanel.org

Samuels, S. Jay, Nancy Schermer, and David Reinking. "Reading Fluency: Techniques for Making Decoding Automatic" in *What Research Has To Say About Reading Instruction.* Samuels, S. Jay and Alan E. Farstrup, editors. 1992. Newark, DE: International Reading Association.

Strickland, Dorothy S., and Lesley Mandel Morrow, editors. *Beginning Reading and Writing.* 2000. New York, NY: Teachers College Press.

Strickland, Dorothy S. *Teaching Phonics Today: A Primer for Educators.* 1998. Newark, DE: International Reading Association.

Yopp, H. "Developing Phonemic Awareness in Young Children," *The Reading Teacher* 45: 696–703, 1992.

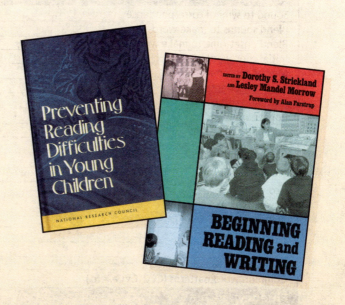

What phonics skills do I need to teach?

MCP Phonics Scope and Sequence

	Kindergarten (Level K)	Grade 1 (Level A)	Grade 2 (Level B)	Grade 3 (Level C)
Phonemic Awareness				
Identify and isolate initial and final consonant sounds of spoken words	♦	♦	♦	♦
Identify and isolate initial vowel sounds of spoken words	♦	♦	♦	♦
Identify and isolate medial consonant and vowel sounds of spoken words	♦	♦	♦	♦
Segment phonemes in words	♦	♦	♦	♦
Blend phonemes into words	♦	♦	♦	♦
Phonological Awareness				
Recognize and produce rhyming words	♦	♦	♦	♦
Blend onset-rimes into words	♦	♦		♦
Understand that spoken words are composed of sounds which are represented by alphabetic letters	♦	♦	♦	♦
Print Knowledge and Concepts of Print				
Develop concept of letter, word	♦	♦		♦
Develop concept of sentence, paragraph	♦	♦	♦	
Track print left to right, top to bottom on page, front to back of book	♦	♦		
Match spoken to printed words	♦	♦		
Develop awareness that print conveys meaning	♦	♦		
Alphabetic Awareness				
Know the order of the alphabet	♦	♦		♦
Know capital and lowercase letter names and distinguish between the two	♦	♦		
Know letter/sound relationships	♦	♦		
Write letters of the alphabet, both capitals and lowercase	♦	♦		
Emerging Reading/Writing Skills				
Print own name	♦	♦		♦
Write using pictures, some letters	♦	♦		
Oral language development	♦	♦		
Visual discrimination	♦	♦		
Phonics Decoding Strategies				
Use phonics and structural analysis to decode words	♦	♦	♦	♦
Use semantic, syntactic, and graphophonic clues to identify words and their meanings	♦	♦	♦	♦
Phonics and Decoding Skills				
Sound to symbol correspondence	♦	♦	♦	♦
Blend sounds to make words	♦	♦		
Blend onset-rime to make words	♦	♦		
Initial consonants	♦	♦	♦	♦
Medial consonants		♦	♦	♦
Final consonants	♦	♦	♦	♦
Hard and soft c and g			♦	♦
Consonant blends		♦	♦	♦
Consonant digraphs		♦	♦	♦
Short vowels	♦	♦	♦	♦
Long vowels	♦	♦	♦	♦
Y as a vowel		♦	♦	♦
r-controlled vowels		♦	♦	♦
Vowel pairs		♦	♦	♦
Vowel digraphs		♦	♦	♦
Vowel diphthongs		♦	♦	♦
Words ending in le			♦	♦
Phonograms (word families)	♦	♦	♦	♦
Common word patterns (CVC, CVCe, etc.)		♦	♦	♦
Fluency				
Repeated readings	♦	♦	♦	♦

MCP Phonics provides instruction in

- ★ Alphabetic awareness
- ★ Phonological awareness, phonemic awareness, phonics
- ★ Decoding strategies and skills
- ★ High-frequency words
- ★ Spelling
- ★ Vocabulary
- ★ Comprehension
- ★ Writing
- ★ Study Skills
- ★ Fluency

	Kindergarten (Level K)	Grade 1 (Level A)	Grade 2 (Level B)	Grade 3 (Level C)
Word Analysis				
Plural endings			◆	◆
Base words		◆	◆	◆
Inflectional endings		◆	◆	◆
Suffixes			◆	◆
Prefixes			◆	◆
Contractions		◆	◆	◆
Compound words			◆	◆
Syllabication and common syllable patterns for word identifications			◆	◆
Spelling				
Building words (phonograms)		◆	◆	
Vowels: short, long, r-controlled, digraphs, diphthongs, unusual vowel spellings		◆	◆	◆
Consonants: single, double, blends, digraphs, silent, unusual consonant spellings		◆	◆	◆
Endings on nouns and verbs		◆	◆	◆
Syllable constructions		◆	◆	◆
Affixes		◆	◆	◆
Apostrophes in contractions		◆	◆	◆
Vocabulary				
Picture clues	◆	◆	◆	
High-frequency words	◆	◆	◆	
Synonyms			◆	◆
Antonyms			◆	◆
Homonyms			◆	◆
Multiple-meaning words (homographs)				◆
Comprehension				
Reading words in context	◆	◆	◆	◆
Critical thinking	◆	◆	◆	◆
Speaking and listening skills	◆	◆	◆	◆
Writing				
A sentence		◆		
Description: an event, a place, a picture		◆	◆	◆
Diary entry				◆
Directions			◆	
e-mail message				◆
Friendly letter		◆	◆	
Informative paragraph				◆
Interview				◆
Journal entry				◆
Letter to the editor				◆
Lists		◆		
Log entry			◆	
Main idea and details				◆
Narrative paragraph				◆
News story			◆	
Postcard		◆	◆	◆
Poem			◆	
Report (preparation for)				◆
Story				◆
Study Skills				
Dictionary alphabetical order				◆
Dictionary guide words				◆
Locating words in the dictionary				◆

How does MCP Phonics make planning a lesson easy?

Identifies the skill-driven learning goals for the lesson, providing direction and structure, as well as a measure for meeting state standards

Features research-based, built-in activities in each lesson that target, teach, and build phonemic and phonological awareness skills

Provides an array of multisensory teaching options and activities to address different learning styles

Offers unparalleled on-the-spot support for English language learners with a specially designed instructional model that provides tips, suggestions, and activities

Provides additional suggestions for practicing skills with the student book, and **applying** them to immediate reading opportunities

---

Lesson 31   Pages 69–70

Short Vowel a

Skill Focus
Children will
★ recognize the short sound of *a*.
★ understand that *a* stands for /a/.
★ write uppercase and lowercase *Aa*.
★ apply what they have learned by reading and writing.

Teach

Phonemic Awareness: Phoneme Categorization Say the word *map*, elongating the medial short *a* sound: *maaaap*. Then say the word naturally. Encourage children to repeat the word. Review that the sound they hear in the middle of *map* is short *a*. Next, say groups of three words. Ask children to clap each time they hear a word that has the sound of short *a*.

- hat   pan   pin
- map   mop   mat

Sound to Symbol Write the words *bat, can,* and *pan* on the board. Read each word slowly, blending the individual phonemes before saying the words naturally: *bbbaaattt, cccaaannn, pppaaannn*. Discuss how the words are the same. (*The letter* a *stands for the short* a *sound.*)

Distribute copies of Blackline Master 13 and have children select the *a* letter card. As you read the following words, have children listen for short *a* and identify the position in which they hear the sound by placing their *a* card in the correct box on the blackline master. Use the following words: *rag, hat, apple, cap, ax.*

	a	

Handwriting Write *Aa* on the chalkboard and use the models on page 70 to review how to form the letters. Have children follow along with their fingers on their desktops.

Practice and Apply

Sound to Symbol As children complete page 69, encourage them to say the correct picture name softly to themselves by blending the phonemes.

Writing Note short *a* words in children's writing and check for correct spelling.

Reading Use *Haddie's Caps*, MCP Phonics and Reading Library, Level A, to provide additional practice in reading words with the short *a* sound.

69

Sound to Symbol

Name _____

▶ Say the name of each picture. Circle its name.

1. (bat) bad bag   2. ant wax (ax)   3. nap (can) ca
4. cab (cap) nap   5. man bag (band)   6. (tag) rag ta
7. fat (fan) tan   8. had (hand) land   9. tap lap la
10. (van) had ran   11. bad cab (dad)   12. pat (pan) ra

Short vowel a: Sound to symbol

FOCUS ON ALL LEARNERS

ESL/ELL ENGLISH LANGUAGE LEARNERS

Use everyday objects whose names contain the sound of short *a* to identify children's comprehension of and ability to identify the sound of short *a*.

- Display an object. Ask a volunteer to name it and the vowel sound. Provide assistance naming objects if necessary.
- When all objects have been named, choose one and write its name plus two other words on the chalkboard. Have a volunteer underline the correct word and tell why the word was chosen.

AUDITORY/KINESTHETIC LEARNERS

Write these word pairs on the board: *fat, bag; pat, cat; wag, sap; fan, man;* and *tap, lap*. Read them aloud. When you say a rhyming pair, the children pantomime the action.

VISUAL LEARNERS

Materials: chart paper, drawing paper, crayons or marke

Draw a hat, a fan, and a cap at the top of a chart. Label the pictures. Touch a word and ask if children can make a rhymin word by changing the beginning letter. As children suggest words, write them in a list.

MCP Phonics Teacher's Resource Guides provide research-based methods for teaching skills and strategies along with a wide variety of activities that address diverse learning styles and connections to other areas of the curriculum.

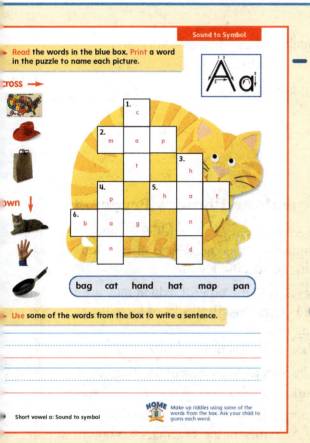

CURRICULUM CONNECTIONS

SPELLING
Materials: index cards.

Have children copy one of the list words *bag, can, cat, fan, ham,* and *map* onto one side of each index card. Then have them draw a picture of the word on the back of the card. Have them show one picture at a time to a partner, who should say and spell the word.

WRITING

Have children write two sentences that tell about a cat that has a cap. Ask them to include some other short *a* words in their sentences.

TECHNOLOGY   **AstroWord** Short vowel *a*

Provides opportunities to tap other areas of the curriculum through a wide variety of activities

Connects teachers and students to phonics instruction on CD-ROM

KINESTHETIC LEARNERS PARTNERS
Materials: Phonics Picture Cards: apple (45), bag (47), cap (48), cat (49), ham (50), hand (51), hat (52), pig (59), sun (67), ox (70), boat (108), broom (123)

Shuffle the Picture Cards. Have partners work together to remove any cards with names lacking the short *a* sound.

CHALLENGE
Materials: paper ruled into 1-inch squares

Children can work in pairs to make word chains. Have one child write the letters for a short *a* word in the squares on the paper. Then have the partner write another word, using a letter from the first word as its first or last letter. Have them continue, taking turns.

EXTRA SUPPORT/INTERVENTION
Materials: Letter Cards: Aa, Bb, Cc, Hh, Ff, Mm, Pp, Tt

Write *cat* on the board and have children make the word with letter cards. Have them change the first letter to make new words and read each word. See Daily Phonics Practice, page 312.

Integrating Phonics and Reading

Guided Reading
Draw children's attention to the cover of the book and ask them what they think the book will be about. You may wish to use the activity in the English Language Learners section below.
First Reading Ask children to identify each hat and what Haddie does as she wears it.
Second Reading Ask children to identify the short *a* words in the story. You may want to add these words to the classroom Word Wall.
Comprehension
After reading, ask children the following questions:
• How does each of Haddie's caps fit the action she is doing? *Inference/Comparisons*
• Which of Haddie's caps is your favorite? Why? *Reflective Analysis/Personal Response*

ESL/ELL English Language Learners
After children have looked through the book, ask them what is on Haddie's head in each picture.(*A hat*) Explain that *cap* means almost the same thing as *hat*.

Presents a guided or shared reading mini-lesson that enables students to apply newly learned skills to decodable text and build fluency

How does MCP Phonics fit into my classroom reading instruction?

The new **MCP Phonics** offers more meaningful skills practice and activities to address the needs of all learners.

Flexible Choices

One of the most outstanding features of MCP Phonics, and one that makes MCP Phonics a very easy program to use, is its flexibility. MCP Phonics can be quickly incorporated into class reading time…

★ to support phonics instruction in any basal reading or guided reading program.

★ independently as a stand-alone phonics program.

Using MCP Phonics . . .

to support core reading programs

- Teach lessons from MCP Phonics as the phonics component of your reading program.
- Assign practice pages to reinforce phonics concepts presented in your program.
- Use Words in Context pages, Phonics and Reading, and Take-Home Books for practice in applying newly learned skills to decodable texts.
- Enhance instruction for all learning types by using suggested activities presented in Focus on All Learners in the Teacher's Resource Guide.
- Assess knowledge of skills and concepts with built-in assessment tools, review lessons, and unit checkups.

as a stand-alone Phonics Program

- Use the Assessment Tools in MCP Phonics to determine students' needs and then match instruction to specific lessons.
- Teach lessons in the order in which they are presented or select skill blocks of lessons according to teacher preference to provide basic phonics instruction.
- Assign lessons as independent practice or for homework.
- Enhance instruction with Daily Phonics Practice Activities in the Teacher's Resource Guide.
- Use Words in Context pages, Phonics and Reading, and Take-Home Books for practice in applying newly learned skills to decodable texts.

Technology

Teachers who want to move beyond the workbook and reinforce specific phonics skills may choose to use a technology program called AstroWord*, featuring in-depth phonics instruction on CD-ROM. This tool is especially helpful in tailoring lessons for children who need help and those who have different learning styles.

*AstroWord Copyright ©1998 Pearson Education, Inc.

How does MCP Phonics help my students apply their skills to reading, writing, and language arts?

From Phonics to Reading and Writing

By taking full advantage of the features offered in **MCP Phonics**, teachers can move children from phonics instruction into authentic reading and a variety of language arts activities to build fluency.

LEVEL B (Grade 2)

Apply newly learned phonics skills to reading stories and nonfiction passages in **Phonics and Reading** activities, Levels A, B, C.

LEVEL B

LEVEL A

LEVEL C

In all levels **Unit Openers** provide opportunities for children to read and talk about poems by well-known poets or high-interest nonfiction articles.

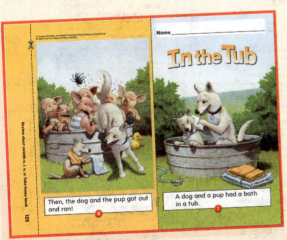

LEVEL A (Grade 1)

Reinforce targeted skills and high-frequency words with beautifully illustrated, decodable **Take-Home Books** at all levels.

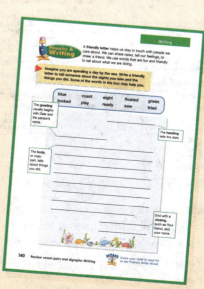

LEVEL C (Grade 3)

Provide more opportunities for children to build words and extend practice to writing activities with special **Phonics and Writing** pages, Levels A, B, C.

The new MCP Phonics and Reading Libraries for Grades K-3

The **Phonics and Reading Library** for grades K–3 features collections of titles from MCP's *Ready Readers* and *Early Chapter Books* programs. All the titles are featured at point-of-use in the MCP Phonics Teacher's Resource Guide and provide essential application of skills to reading. Titles can be used in a variety of ways to support balanced literacy: as part of a classroom independent reading library or reading center, or to foster early literacy skills with guided and shared reading activities that develop confidence, fluency, and comprehension.

These books may be used . . .
★ with the lessons in the Teacher's Resource Guide.
★ as part of a classroom independent reading library or reading center.
★ to reinforce selected phonics skills.

Teachers also have the option to purchase multiple copies of each book to guide reading with a group of children.

Guiding Students' Reading

In addition to thematic unit introductions, Take-Home Books, and engaging reading passages, MCP Phonics offers more choices for reading with a unique feature called **Integrating Phonics and Reading** that uses books from MCP Phonics and Reading Libraries.

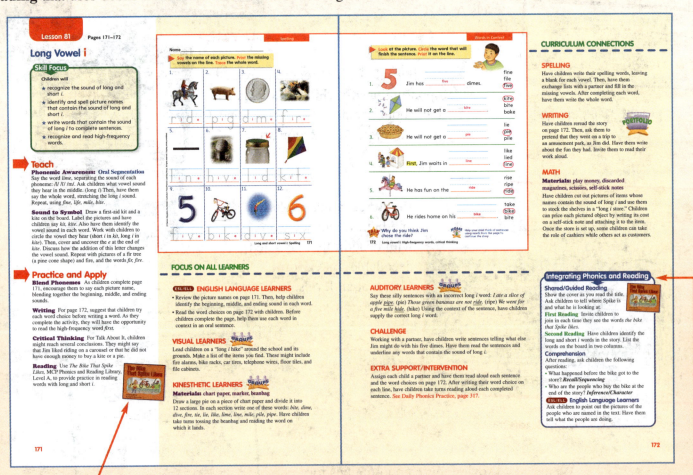

At the end of each lesson in the Teacher's Resource Guide, a book from the **MCP Phonics and Reading Library** is recommended for practice in applying the phonological awareness, phonics, or word study skill taught in the lesson.

Integrating Phonics and Reading enhances instruction and builds fluency with a small-group reading activity that reinforces the specific skills presented in the lesson. This mini-lesson describes how to use each little book or chapter book with children in multiple readings. An activity is also suggested for English language learners.

How does MCP Phonics incorporate high-frequency word instruction?

As children begin to read, they will often encounter words they cannot decode using phonics skills they know. These words are commonly called "high-frequency words." Many state guidelines now require that as early as kindergarten, children memorize and read selected high-frequency words.

MCP Phonics . . .

★ teaches the most common high-frequency words beginning at Level K.
★ builds a comprehensive and cumulative list by the end of Level B.
★ teaches and provides practice for words individually and in context.
★ reinforces high-frequency words in reading passages.
★ assesses selected high-frequency words in Pretests, Posttests, and Unit Checkups.
★ helps to build fluency through repeated readings of high-frequency words.

Level K	Level A			Level B		
a	about	I	saw	about	girl	saw
are	after	in	says	after	go	scare
at	are	into	sees	again	good	see
can	as	is	she	along	grow	she
do	because	it	some	always	has	should
for	blue	just	takes	any	have	some
go	by	knows	that	anywhere	her	something
have	called	like	the	around	here	song
here	come	little	their	because	his	sure
I	could	live	them	before	holding	that
is	do	long	then	began	house	their
it	does	look	there	behind	inside	then
like	down	love	they	believe	into	there
look	each	made	time	beyond	laugh	these
me	finds	make	to	bought	likes	they
my	first	many	too	boy	listen	things
not	for	more	trees	build	little	this
on	friend	most	two	buy	look	today
see	from	my	under	care	loved	together
the	get	no	up	children	might	too
to	glad	not	use	choose	my	two
we	go	now	very	climb	near	under
with	goes	of	want	come	new	usually
you	going	off	was	could	nice	very
	got	on	water	decided	often	wants
	grow	one	were	different	once	was
	have	only	when	does	one	watch
	he	other	where	down	only	water
	help	our	which	edge	other	we
	her	out	why	enough	our	were
	here	over	with	even	outside	what
	his	people	you	ever	over	when
	home	runs	your	every	own	where
	how	said		everything	people	with
				favorite	piece	would
				finally	pours	you
				find	probably	your
				first	said	
				friends		

How will MCP Phonics help my English Language Learners?

ESL/ELL **English language learners** need additional support and alternative teaching methods to help them succeed.

Each lesson in the MCP Phonics Teacher's Resource Guides provides flexible strategies for adapting the pages for native-English speakers and English language learners in the same classroom. These strategies incorporate recommendations from SDAIE (Specially Designed Academic Instruction in English) and CALLA (Cognitive Academic Language Learning Approach), which include:

1. Analyze material from the student's point of view.
2. Provide background experience and personalize the lesson.
3. Identify and teach essential vocabulary.
4. Present lesson orally.
5. Use a variety of visuals.
6. Simplify grammatical structures and paraphrase.
7. Reinforce language learning while teaching content.
8. Teach study skills text aids.
9. Use manipulative materials and hands-on activities.
10. Monitor student's progress.

Four Stages of Language Acquisition

Language learners move through a series of predictable stages as they acquire a new language. Although the terminology and number of stages vary among language professionals, most recognize four stages. Individual language acquisition will vary as language learners develop. The strategies provided for MCP "Plaid" Phonics take into account the following stages.

Pre-Production Stage

Children at this stage of language acquisition have an extremely limited command of English, although they understand more English than they can produce. They often use gestures, yes or no answers, nods or shakes of their heads to communicate. At this stage, instruction may be most effective in native-language or formal English classes.

Early Production Stage

Children at this stage comprehend more spoken English, but they still are unable to respond fluently. Communication is beginning, but responses are likely to be of the short-answer variety and may be awkward in grammar and structure.

Speech Emergence Stage

Children at this stage can follow along for most classroom and daily routines, but they are limited by vocabulary and inconsistent grammatical structures. There's an emphasis on acquiring verbal fluency.

Intermediate Fluency Stage

Children at this stage are well on their way to achieving dual-language fluency. They can comprehend more, can respond more fluently using the conventions of English, and can make themselves understood in a variety of settings, social and academic.

Strategies for the English-Speaking Classroom

Try these language acquisition strategies with your English language learners.

Gestures

★ Limit unconscious, random hand movements. For example, a hand gesture or symbol such as the "V" (peace sign) can be confusing to some children, and, in some cultures, may have different linguistic or cultural connotations.

★ Do use gestures to act out what you are trying to communicate.

Repetition and Consistency

★ Children at the pre-production and early production stages thrive on repetition to familiarize themselves with classroom rhythms.

★ When comprehension fails, class routines and activity formats give ELLs contextual clues on how to proceed.

Visuals

★ Use pictures, objects, and realia, or real-world clues, to convey meaning; to name an object; to indicate color, size, and shape.

★ Pantomime or bring videos to illustrate conceptualized vocabulary such as verbs and adjectives.

High-frequency Vocabulary

★ ELLs acquire everyday words before specialized or content vocabulary. Bring in familiar household objects and use items in the classroom to model lesson content.

★ Take advantage of other high-frequency vocabulary, such as sight words and proper names, to illustrate target sounds.

★ Look for good sources of daily vocabulary that use target sounds in your classroom and school community and from the children.

Encouraging Input

★ Support all response and oral input.

★ Model native pronunciation naturally and indirectly by repeating the target word(s) in context after the speaker has finished.

★ If additional pronunciation practice is needed, set aside small group time to reinforce this area.

Adapting Conceptual Activities

★ Activities such as word searches, crossword puzzles, mazes, and so on, contain words printed in vertical or diagonal patterns that may confuse the letter-order patterns children are learning.

★ Incorporate conceptual activities after children master the concepts to reinforce word recognition, comprehension, or pronunciation.

Peer Practice

★ Have ELLs work in pairs with more English-proficient children to afford one-on-one learning.

★ Have ELLs cooperate on worksheet activities and read stories aloud in small groups.

★ Monitor pair work for participation.

How do I assess my students' needs in phonics?

Today's teachers know that ongoing assessment is the key to identifying students' strengths, teaching to their needs, and measuring their progress in acquiring phonics skills. **MCP Phonics** provides several ways to assess students' reading skills that can be used as a guide to meaningful, effective instruction.

Formal Assessment Tools

★ **Pretests** identify each student's strengths and needs, allowing teachers to structure lesson plans.

★ **Posttests** evaluate a student's overall mastery of skills and identify specific areas that require reteaching.

★ The **Performance Assessment Profile** identifies the specific skills on the pre- and posttests and provides suggestions for reteaching activities in the Teacher's Resource Guide.

Informal Assessment Tools

★ **Review pages** can be found at different points within a series of lessons to help check mastery of skills.

★ **Take-Home Books** provide reading practice targeted to specific skills.

★ A two-page **Unit Checkup** at the end of each unit can be used as a quick assessment.

★ Suggestions for **Student Portfolios** are provided with the lessons in the Teacher's Resource Guide.

★ A **Student Progress Checklist** is provided with each unit to keep track of each student's mastery of skills.

Phonemic Awareness and Phonics Assessment (PAPA)

This normed, standardized tool enables teachers to

★ Analyze each student's phonemic awareness and phonics skills.

★ Administer assessment in only 30 minutes to individuals, groups, or the entire class.

★ Raise standardized test scores by driving effective instruction.

Once skills have been assessed, the PAPA Teacher's Resource Guide provides a correlation of results to MCP Phonics lessons.

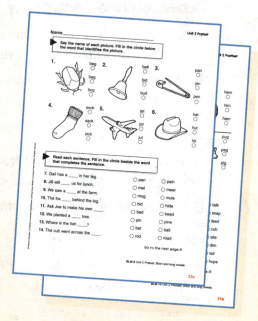

A **pretest** and a **posttest** are provided at the beginning of each unit.

How can I adapt MCP Phonics for summer school?

To easily adapt MCP Phonics for summer school students who need help with reading…

★ assess student needs using unit reviews in the MCP Phonics student books, pretests in the Teacher's Resource Guides, and the PAPA program.

★ target instruction to specific skills using the student book table of contents to select one or two two-page lessons for each day.

★ plan for 20 minutes of a 90-minute block for reading and language arts to do a quick review and additional instruction in phonics.

Following is a chart that outlines suggested basic skills to cover in MCP Phonics, Levels A through C (Grades 1–3), during each week of a six-week summer school program.

WEEK	LEVEL A (GRADE 1)	LEVEL B (GRADE 2)	LEVEL C (GRADE 3)
1	**Unit 1**	**Unit 2**	**Unit 2**
Day 1	Initial Consonants	Short Vowel a	Short Vowel a
Day 2	Initial Consonants	Short Vowel a	Short Vowel i
Day 3	Initial Consonants	Short Vowel i	Short Vowel o
Day 4	Medial Consonants	Short Vowel i	Short Vowel u
Day 5	Final Consonants	Short Vowel o	Short Vowel e
2	**Unit 1**	**Unit 2**	**Unit 2**
Day 1	Short Vowel a	Short Vowel o	Long Vowel a
Day 2	Short Vowel a	Short Vowel u	Long Vowel i
Day 3	Short Vowel a	Short Vowel u	Long Vowel o
Day 4	Short Vowel i	Short Vowel e	Long Vowel u
Day 5	Short Vowel i	Short Vowel e	Long Vowel e
3	**Unit 2**	**Unit 3**	**Unit 3**
Day 1	Short Vowel i	Long Vowel a	Consonant Blends
Day 2	Short Vowel o	Long Vowel a	Consonant Blends
Day 3	Short Vowel o	Long Vowel i	Consonant Digraphs
Day 4	Short Vowel o	Long Vowel i	Consonant Digraphs
Day 5	Short Vowel u	Long Vowel o	R-Controlled Vowels
4	**Unit 2**	**Unit 3**	**Units 4 and 5**
Day 1	Short Vowel u	Long Vowel o	R-Controlled Vowels
Day 2	Short Vowel u	Long Vowel u	Vowel Digraphs
Day 3	Short Vowel e	Long Vowel u	Vowel Digraphs
Day 4	Short Vowel e	Long Vowel e	Vowel Diphthongs
Day 5	Short Vowel e	Long Vowel e	Vowel Diphthongs
5	**Unit 3**	**Unit 4**	**Units 4 and 6**
Day 1	Long Vowel a	Consonant Blends	Plurals
Day 2	Long Vowel a	Consonant Blends	Endings
Day 3	Long Vowel i	Consonant Digraphs	Endings
Day 4	Long Vowel i	Consonant Digraphs	Suffixes
Day 5	Long Vowel o	R-controlled Vowels	Suffixes
6	**Unit 3**	**Units 4 and 6**	**Unit 5**
Day 1	Long Vowel o	R-controlled Vowels	Prefixes
Day 2	Long Vowel u	Vowel Digraphs	Prefixes
Day 3	Long Vowel u	Vowel Digraphs	Base Words/Syllables
Day 4	Long Vowel e	Diphthongs	Syllables
Day 5	Long Vowel e	Diphthongs	Syllables

How can MCP Phonics help struggling readers in an after-school program?

MCP Phonics can be used in a variety of ways to provide instruction and additional practice. This flexibility makes it a perfect tool for teachers who want to give students additional support in reading skills.

Reinforce phonics in 15 minutes after school

★ Assess students to determine in which skills they need additional instruction. Use the pretests and posttests in the Teacher's Resource Guide, review lessons and Unit Checkups in the student books, and PAPA (Phonemic Awareness and Phonics Assessment).

★ Select lessons to target specific reading skills by using the detailed table of contents in the student book.

★ Adapt MCP Phonics to any basal reading program to give students additional practice. Again, use the table of contents as a guide for selecting specific lessons that correlate to the day's lessons.

★ Use MCP Phonics as a stand-alone program for students who need additional phonics instruction. Present skills in the order shown in the table of contents, or rearrange them. The two-page lesson format will provide as much or as little instruction as time allows.

Select skills to correlate to basal reading lessons taught during class time.

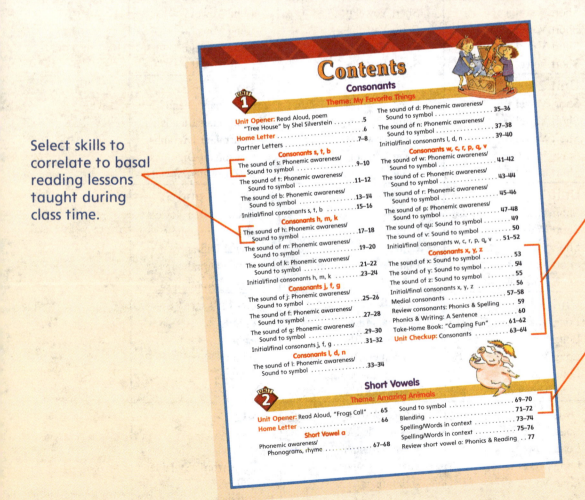

Use MCP Phonics as a stand-alone phonics program. Use lessons in order, or present lessons in an order that best fits with classroom reading instruction.

Pull out lessons to target skills for extra instruction. For example, these lessons will help a student who needs practice with short vowel *a* sound to symbol and blending.

MODERN CURRICULUM PRESS
Phonics
LEVEL A

ELWELL • MURRAY • KUCIA

TEACHER ADVISORY BOARD

Dr. Elsie Dabbs Heller
Kennett, MO

Emily Hendricks
Lafayette, IN

Debie Jarvie
Montville Township, NJ

Ellen Johnston
Dallas, TX

Meg Kouretsos
Chicago, IL

Cindy O'Linn
Hollywood, FL

Sr. Mary Jean Raymond, O.S.U.
Cleveland, OH

Frank Russomanno
Newark, NJ

Patricia Sears
Virginia Beach, VA

Ann E. Straw
Los Altos, CA

Fran Threewit
Kenwood, CA

Sonjia M. Wilson
Portland, OR

MODERN CURRICULUM PRESS
Pearson Learning Group

The following people have contributed to the development of this product:
Art and Design: Lisa Arcuri, Stephen Barth, Dorothea Fox, Sherri Hieber-Day, Denise Ingrassia, Judy Mahoney, Karen Mancinelli, Elbaliz Méndez, Terry Taylor, Dan Thomas, Daniel Trush, Heather Wendt-Kemp
Editorial: Leslie Feierstone Barna, Teri Crawford Jones, Cindy Kane
Manufacturing: Lori Servidio, Cristina Tamen
Marketing: Alison Bruno
Production: Irene Belinsky, Alan Dalgleish, Lissy Díaz, Suellen Leavy, Susan Levine
Publishing Operations: Thomas Daning, Vince Esterly, Magali Iglesias, Kate Matracia

PHOTOGRAPHS: All photos © Pearson Learning unless otherwise noted.
Cover: *t.* Siede Preis/PhotoDisc/Getty Images. *b.* Francois AEF D'Elbee/The Image Bank/Getty Images. Page 65: Digital Vision. 79: *t.* © Merlin Tuttle/Photo Researchers, Inc., *b.* © Merlin D. Tuttle/Bat Conservation International. 80: *t., b.* © Merlin D. Tuttle/Bat Conservation International. 95: *t.* The Image Bank/Getty Images, *b.* Tony Freeman/PhotoEdit. 96: *t.* Tony Freeman/PhotoEdit, *b.* AP Photo/Danny Johnston. 111: *t.* Gay Baumgarner/Stone, *b.* Dorey A. Sparre/Parker-Boon Productions for Silver Burdett Ginn. 112: *t., b.* Dorey A. Sparre/Parker-Boon Productions for Silver Burdett Ginn. 123: Diana L. Stratton/Tom Stack & Associates, Inc. 141: *t.* Marc Chamberlain/Stone, *b.* Dave B. Fleetham/Tom Stack & Associates, Inc. 142: *t.* A. & J. Visage/Peter Arnold, Inc., *b.* Norbert Wu/Stone. 146: *t.r.* Abbe Boon for Silver Burdett Ginn. 175: © Orion Press/Pacific Stock. 180: Spencer Grant/PhotoEdit. 213: *b.* Richard Hutchings/PhotoEdit. 214: *t.* © Wesley Bocxe/Photo Researchers, Inc., *b.* Jeff Greenberg/PhotoEdit. 239: © Stock Food America/Robert Kaufman. 269: © Martha Cooper/The Viesti Collection. 291: *t.* Lorentz Gullachsen/Stone, *b.* Hank Morgan/Rainbow. 292: *t.* © Doug Millar; Science Source/Photo Researchers, Inc., *b.* Lewis Kemper/Stone.

REBUS PHOTOS: All photos © Pearson Learning unless otherwise noted.
Ant: Raymond A. Mendez/Animals Animals. *Baby:* Don Mason/Corbis Stock Market. *Band:* © Lawrence Migdale/Photo Researchers, Inc. *Barn:* Jeff Gnass/Corbis Stock Market. *Beak:* Harvey Lloyd/Corbis Stock Market. *Bee:* SuperStock, Inc. *Bird:* ZEFA Germany/Corbis Stock Market. *Boat:* SuperStock, Inc. *Bride:* Naideau/Corbis Stock Market. *Bridge:* Susan Van Etten/PhotoEdit. *Bug:* Imagery. *Camel:* Four by Five/SuperStock, Inc. *Car:* Tony Freeman/PhotoEdit. *Chick:* Tim Davis/Stone. *Chicks:* David A. Wagner/Corbis Stock Market. *Chimney:* Harvey Lloyd/Corbis Stock Market. *Clown:* Alan Epstein/FPG International. *Cow:* James Marshall/Corbis Stock Market. *Crab:* R. Calvert/Stone. *Cry:* Norbert Shafer/Corbis Stock Market. *Cub:* Jeanne Drake/Stone. *Deer:* SuperStock, Inc. *Dive:* David Madison/Stone. *Door:* SuperStock, Inc. *Duck:* S. Nielsen/Imagery. *Fence:* Michael P. Gadomski/Earth Scenes. *Fin:* Jack Grove/PhotoEdit. *Fire:* Mats Lindgren/Stone. *Fish:* Zig Leszczynski/Animals Animals. *Fishing:* Norbert Shafer/Corbis Stock Market. *Fly:* Rod Planck/Stone. *Fox:* Darrell Gulin/Stone. *Gate:* Elena Rooraid/PhotoEdit. *Goat:* James Marshall/Corbis Stock Market. *Goose:* Bill Ivy/Stone. *Grasshopper:* SuperStock, Inc. *Hen:* D. MacDonald/PhotoEdit. *Hide:* Dorey Sparre/Parker-Boon Productions for Silver Burdett Ginn. *Hill:* SuperStock, Inc. *Hive:* Edward C. Cohen/SuperStock, Inc. *Horse:* Robert Maier/Animals Animals. *Hump:* Mickey Gibson/Animals Animals. *Hut:* Ralph A. Reinhold/Earth Scenes. *Jet:* Brian Parker/Tom Stack & Associates, Inc. *Kangaroo:* Fritz Prenzel/Stone. *Kitchen:* Dorey Sparre/Parker-Boon Images for Silver Burdett Ginn. *Kitten:* ZEFA Germany/Corbis Stock Market. *Lake:* Dennis MacDonald/PhotoEdit. *Lamb:* Renee Lynn/Stone. *Lion:* David A. Northcott/SuperStock, Inc. *Mice:* Terry G. Murphy/Animals Animals. *Monkey:* Zig Leszczynski/Animals Animals. *Moon:* SuperStock, Inc. *Mouse:* Gérard Lacz/Animals Animals. *Mule:* Robert Maier/Animals Animals. *Nurse:* George W. Disario/Corbis Stock Market. *Ox:* Michael Francis/The Wildlife Collection. *Pig:* Don Mason/Corbis Stock Market. *Pony:* Robert Maier/Animals Animals. *Puppy:* Tim Davis/Stone. *Ram:* Thomas Kitchin/Tom Stack & Associates. *Rat:* Breck P. Kent/Animals Animals. *Roof:* Bo Saunders/Corbis Stock Market. *Row:* Ariel Skelley/Corbis Stock Market. *Sail:* Robert Pearcy/Earth Scenes. *Seal:* Dan Guravich/Corbis. *Sheep:* Ralph A. Reinhold/Animals Animals. *Ship:* SuperStock, Inc. *Skunk:* D. Robert Franz/Masterfile. *Sky:* John Lemker/Earth Scenes. *Smoke:* Francis Lepine/Earth Scenes. *Snail:* F.E. Unverhau/Animals Animals. *Snake, Snowman, Spider:* SuperStock, Inc. *Squirrel:* E.R. Degginger/Animals Animals. *Steps:* Peter Gridley/FPG International. *Stop:* Daphne Godfrey Trust/Earth Scenes. *Store:* Dorey A. Cardinale/Parker-Boon Productions for Silver Burdett Ginn. *Street:* Jeff Greenberg/PhotoEdit. *Swim:* Pete Saloutos/Corbis Stock Market. *Swing:* Dorey A. Cardinale/Parker-Boon Productions for Silver Burdett Ginn. *Team:* SuperStock, Inc. *Tiger:* Zig Leszczynski/Animals Animals. *Tim:* Dorey Sparre/Parker-Boon Productions for Silver Burdett Ginn. *Train:* Walter C. Lankenau/Evergreen Graphics. *Tree:* Jack Wilburn/Earth Scenes. *Trunk:* Art Wolfe/Stone. *Tub:* David Young-Wolff/PhotoEdit. *Tune:* Dorey Sparre/Parker-Boon Productions for Silver Burdett Ginn. *Tusk:* Stone. *Volcano:* Robert Reiff/FPG International. *Wave:* Warren Bolster/Stone. *Web:* J.C. Stevenson/Animals Animals. *Whale:* Fred Felleman/Stone. *Wheat:* Kevin Morris/Stone. *Windmill:* John Nees/Earth Scenes. *Wing:* SuperStock, Inc. *Yard:* Dorey A. Cardinale/Parker-Boon Productions for Silver Burdett Ginn. *Zebra:* Patti Murray/Animals Animals. Rebus art: Stephen Clarke, P.T. Pie Illustrations, Pearson Learning.

ILLUSTRATIONS: Page 249, 294: Anthony Accardo. 4, 215, 277: Elizabeth Allen. 156: Bob Berry. 274: Gary Bialke. 172: Chi Chung. 99: Genevieve Claire. 1, 7, 9, 53, 63, 122: Lynn Cravath. 86, 165, 208: Molly Delaney. 1, 83, 296: Chris Demarest. 289: Karen Dugan. 19, 21, 49, 297, 298: Julie Durrell. 202, 295: Len Ebert. 145: Alan Eitzen. 284, 304: Kate Flanagan. 35, 37: Brian Floca. 259: Toni Goffe. 113: Linda Graves. 5: Shelly Hehenberger. 54, 64, 184, 245, 293: Meryl Henderson. 17, 285: Dennis Hockerman. 159: Joan Holub. 16, 40, 42, 55, 65, 152, 174, 190: Ann Iosa. 29, 45, 92, 163, 226, 273: Meredith Johnson. 261: Wallace Keller. 216, 283: Anne Kennedy. 3, 7, 109, 192, 257: Jeff Le Van. 50, 164, 217: Anthony Lewis. 125, 126: Brian Lies. 300: Diana Magnuson. 235, 236: Maurie Manning. 288: Claude Martinot. 25, 33, 41, 97, 98, 179, 180, 253: Anni Matsick 11: Erin Mauterer. 188, 224, 248: Kathleen McCarthy. 106, 136: Patrick Merrell. 144: Susan Miller. 90: Cheryl Kirk Noll 193: Christina Ong. 240: Pearson Learning. 220, 275: Mick Reid. 17, 19, 108, 129, 135, 279: Francesc Rovira. 43, 49: Ellen Sasaki. 299: Stacey Schuett. 93: Janet Skiles. 138: Susan Spellman. 177, 178: Nicole Tadgell. 76, 233: Terry Taylor. 99: Lynn Titleman. 13, 150, 211: George Ulrich. 181, 183, 197, 241, 271, 281: Gary Undercuffler. 27: Baker Vail. 102: Teri Weidner. 286: Thor Wickstrom. 301, 302: Fred Willingham. 158, 206, 252: Amy Wummer. 272: Lane Yerkes.

ACKNOWLEDGMENTS: Excerpt titled "Tree House" from *Where The Sidewalk Ends* by Shel Silverstein. Copyright © 1974 by Evil Eye Music, Inc. Used by permission of HarperCollins for the World excluding UK and British. Edite Kroll Literary Agency for the UK and British. "Play" by Frank Asch from *Country Pie* by Frank Asch. Copyright 1979 by Frank Asch. Greenwillow Books (A division of William Morrow & Co.)

ZB Font Method Copyright © 1996 Zaner-Bloser

NOTE: Every effort has been made to locate the copyright owner of material reprinted in this book. Omissions brought to our attention will be corrected in subsequent printings.

Copyright © 2003 by Pearson Education, Inc., publishing as Modern Curriculum Press, an imprint of Pearson Learning Group, 299 Jefferson Road, Parsippany, NJ 07054. All rights reserved. No part of this book may be reproduced or transmitted in any form or by any means, electronic, or mechanical, including photocopying, recording, or by any information storage and retrieval system, without permission in writing from the publisher, except for the Blackline Masters which may be reproduced for classroom use only. For information regarding permission(s), write to Rights and Permissions Department. This edition is published simultaneously in Canada by Pearson Education Canada.

Printed in the United States of America

6 7 8 9 10   11 10 09 08 07

ISBN 0-7652-2625-1 (Teacher Resource Guide)
ISBN 0-7652-2514-X (Full Color Edition - Pupil)
ISBN 0-7652-2619-7 (Black and White Edition - Pupil)

This work is protected by United States copyright laws and is provided *solely for the use of teachers and administrators* in teaching courses and assessing student learning in their classes and schools. Dissemination or sale of any part of this work (including on the World Wide Web) will destroy the integrity of the work and is *not* permitted.

1-800-321-3106
www.pearsonlearning.com

Contents

Overview	T1
Level K Student Edition	T2
Levels A, B, and C Student Editions	T4
Research-based Resources	T6
Scope and Sequence	T8
Teacher's Resource Guide	T10
Using MCP Phonics in the Classroom	T12
High-frequency Word Instruction	T15
English Language Learners	T16
Assessment Tools	T18
MCP Phonics in Summer School	T19
MCP Phonics After School	T20

UNIT 1

Consonants
Theme: My Favorite Things

Student Performance Objectives ... 5a
Overview of Resources ... 5b
Assessment Options ... 5c
- Formal Assessment • Informal Assessment • Student Progress Checklist • Portfolio Assessment • PAPA
- Administering & Evaluating the Pretest/Posttest ... 5d
- Assessment Blackline Masters ... 5e

English Language Learners ... 5j

Phonics Games, Activities, and Technology ... 5l
- Activity Blackline Master ... 5p

Home Connections ... 5q

LESSON PLANS
Unit Opener ... 5
- Unit Focus
- Theme Focus
- Bulletin Board Suggestion
- Home Connections
- Learning Center Activities

Lessons 1-28 ... 7-62
- Skill Focus
- Teach/Practice and Apply
- Focus on All Learners
  - English Language Learners • Visual Learners • Kinesthetic Learners • Auditory Learners • Challenge • Extra Support/Intervention
- Curriculum Connections
- Integrating Phonics and Reading

Lesson 29: Unit Checkup ... 63
- Skill Focus
- Teach/Practice and Apply
- Focus on All Learners
- Assess Understanding of Unit Skills

Short Vowels
Theme: Amazing Animals

Student Performance Objectives . . . 65a
Overview of Resources 65b
Assessment Options 65c
  Formal Assessment • Informal Assessment • Student Progress Checklist • Portfolio Assessment • PAPA
  Administering & Evaluating the Pretest/Posttest. 65d
  Assessment Blackline Masters 65e
English Language Learners 65j
Spelling Connections 65k
  Spelling Blackline Master 65l
Phonics Games, Activities, and Technology 65m
  Activity Blackline Master 65p
Home Connections 65q

LESSON PLANS
Unit Opener 65
  Unit Focus
  Theme Focus
  Bulletin Board Suggestion
  Home Connections
  Learning Center Activities
Lessons 30-67 67-142
  Skill Focus
  Teach/Practice and Apply
  Focus on All Learners
    English Language Learners • Visual Learners • Kinesthetic Learners • Auditory Learners • Challenge • Extra Support/Intervention
  Curriculum Connections
  Integrating Phonics and Reading
Lesson 68: Unit Checkup 143
  Skill Focus
  Teach/Practice and Apply
  Focus on All Learners
  Assess Understanding of Unit Skills

Long Vowels
Theme: Let's Play

Student Performance Objectives . . 145a
Overview of Resources 145b
Assessment Options 145c
  Formal Assessment • Informal Assessment • Student Progress Checklist • Portfolio Assessment • PAPA
  Administering & Evaluating the Pretest/Posttest. 145d
  Assessment Blackline Masters 145e
English Language Learners 145j
Spelling Connections 145k
  Spelling Blackline Master 145l
Phonics Games, Activities, and Technology 145m
  Activity Blackline Master 145p
Home Connections 145q

LESSON PLANS
Unit Opener 145
  Unit Focus

Unit 3 continued

    Theme Focus
    Bulletin Board Suggestion
    Home Connections
    Learning Center Activities

Lessons 69-113 147-236

    Skill Focus
    Teach/Practice and Apply
    Focus on All Learners

English Language Learners • Visual Learners • Kinesthetic Learners • Auditory Learners • Challenge • Extra Support/ Intervention

        Curriculum Connections
        Integrating Phonics and Reading

Lesson 114: Unit Checkup 237

    Skill Focus
    Teach/Practice and Apply
    Focus on All Learners
    Assess Understanding of Unit Skills

UNIT 4 — Consonant Blends, Y as a Vowel
Theme: Everybody Eats

Student Performance Objectives . . 239a
Overview of Resources 239b
Assessment Options 239c

    Formal Assessment • Informal Assessment • Student Progress Checklist • Portfolio Assessment • PAPA
    Administering & Evaluating the Pretest/Posttest. 239d
    Assessment Blackline Masters 239e

English Language Learners 239j
Spelling Connections 239k

    Spelling Blackline Master 239l

Phonics Games, Activities, and Technology 239m

    Activity Blackline Master 239p

Home Connections 239q

LESSON PLANS

Unit Opener 239

    Unit Focus
    Theme Focus
    Bulletin Board Suggestion
    Home Connections
    Learning Center Activities

Lessons 115-127 241-266

    Skill Focus
    Teach/Practice and Apply
    Focus on All Learners

        English Language Learners • Visual Learners • Kinesthetic Learners • Auditory Learners • Challenge • Extra Support/Intervention

    Curriculum Connections
    Integrating Phonics and Reading

Lesson 128: Unit Checkup 267

    Skill Focus
    Teach/Practice and Apply
    Focus on All Learners
    Assess Understanding of Unit Skills

Endings, Digraphs, Contractions
Theme: Whatever the Weather

Student Performance Objectives . . 269a
Overview of Resources 269b
Assessment Options 269c
  Formal Assessment • Informal Assessment • Student Progress Checklist • Portfolio Assessment • PAPA
  Administering & Evaluating the Pretest/Posttest. 269d
  Assessment Blackline Masters 269e
English Language Learners 269j
Spelling Connections 269k
  Spelling Blackline Master 269l
Phonics Games, Activities, and Technology 269m
  Activity Blackline Master 269p
Home Connections 269q

LESSON PLANS
Unit Opener 269
  Unit Focus
  Theme Focus
  Bulletin Board Suggestion
  Home Connections
  Learning Center Activities

Lessons 129-144 271-302
  Skill Focus
  Teach/Practice and Apply
  Focus on All Learners
    English Language Learners • Visual Learners • Kinesthetic Learners • Auditory Learners • Challenge • Extra Support/Intervention
  Curriculum Connections
  Integrating Phonics and Reading

Lesson 145: Unit Checkup 303
  Skill Focus
  Teach/Practice and Apply
  Focus on All Learners
  Assess Understanding of Unit Skills

Daily Phonics Practice. 308

UNIT 1

Consonants
THEME: MY FAVORITE THINGS

CONTENTS

UNIT 1 RESOURCES 5b
Assessment Options 5c
Administering & Evaluating the Pretest/Posttest 5d
   Unit 1 Pretest 5e–5f
   Unit 1 Posttest 5g–5h
   Unit 1 Student Progress Checklist 5i
English Language Learners 5j–5k
Phonics Games, Activities, and Technology 5l–5o
BLM Unit 1 Activity 5p
Home Connections 5q

TEACHING PLANS
   Unit 1 Opener/ Home Letter 5–6
   Lesson 1: Partner Letters 7–8
   Lesson 2: The sound of *s* 9–10
   Lesson 3: The sound of *t* 11–12
   Lesson 4: The sound of *b* 13–14
   Lesson 5: Review consonants *s, t, b* 15–16
   Lesson 6: The sound of *h* 17–18
   Lesson 7: The sound of *m* 19–20
   Lesson 8: The sound of *k* 21–22
   Lesson 9: Review consonants *h, m, k* 23–24
   Lesson 10: The sound of *j* 25–26
   Lesson 11: The sound of *f* 27–28
   Lesson 12: The sound of *g* 29–30
   Lesson 13: Review consonants *j, f, g* 31–32
   Lesson 14: The sound of *l* 33–34
   Lesson 15: The sound of *d* 35–36
   Lesson 16: The sound of *n* 37–38
   Lesson 17: Review consonants *l, d, n* 39–40
   Lesson 18: The sound of *w* 41–42
   Lesson 19: The sound of *c* 43–44
   Lesson 20: The sound of *r* 45–46
   Lesson 21: The sound of *p* 47–48
   Lesson 22: The sound of *qu* 49
               The sound of *v* 50
   Lesson 23: Review consonants *w, c, r, p, q, v* 51–52
   Lesson 24: The sound of *x* 53
               The sound of *y* 54
   Lesson 25: The sound of *z* 55
               Review consonants *x, y, z* 56
   Lesson 26: Medial consonants 57–58
   Lesson 27: Review consonants:
               Phonics & Spelling 59
               Phonics & Writing: A Sentence 60
   Lesson 28: Take-Home Book: "Camping Fun" 61–62
   Lesson 29: Unit Checkup: Consonants 63–64

Student Performance Objectives

In Unit 1, children will be introduced to the sound associations for the consonant letters within the context of the theme "My Favorite Things." As children begin to understand and learn to apply the concept that letters represent the sounds we hear in spoken words, they will be able to

▶ Recognize partner letters

▶ Associate the consonants *s, t, b, h, m, k, j, f, g, l, d, n, w, c, r, p, q, v, x, y,* and *z* with the sounds they stand for

▶ Identify consonant sounds in the initial, medial, and final positions in words

Overview of Resources

LESSON	MCP PHONICS AND READING LIBRARY, LEVEL A			LETTER CARDS/ WORD CARDS	DAILY PHONICS PRACTICE
	TITLE	PRACTICE	PICTURE CARDS		
1: Partner Letters	RR, Stg One Bk 4	A Mess		Ss, Tt, Bb, Hh, Mm, Kk, Jj, Ff, Gg, Ll, Dd, Nn, Ww, Cc, Rr, Pp, Qq, Vv, Xx, Yy, Zz	308–311
2: The sound of s	RR, Stg One Bk 7	We Are Singing	33–35, 37, 43–44, 60, 67	Ss	308
3: The sound of t	RR, Stg One Bk 8	Terrific Shoes	7–9, 36–37, 68, 71, 75, 82–83, 101–102, 153		308
4: The sound of b	RR, Stg One Bk 9	One Bee Got on the Bus	1–3, 28–29, 47, 54, 59, 61–62, 76, 100		308
5: Review consonants s, t, b	RR, Stg One Bk 10	Six Go By	49, 61–62, 67–68, 82	Ss, Tt, Bb	308
6: The sound of h	RR, Stg One Bk 36	Where Can a Hippo Hide?	10, 16–18, 27, 45–46, 50–53, 81, 98		308
7: The sound of m	RR, Stg One Bk 6	My Monster and Me	16, 23–27, 73, 81, 103, 127		308
8: The sound of k	RR, Stg One Bk 38	Too Much Ketchup	2, 13, 17, 20, 56, 59, 98		308
9: Review consonants h, m, k	RR, Stg One Bk 33	Kangaroo in the Kitchen	16–18, 20, 23–25, 50, 56, 98		308
10: The sound of j	RR, Stg One Bk 35	Jump Right In			309
11: The sound of f	RR, Stg One Bk 29	As Fast as a Fox	10–12, 28, 38–39, 59, 94–95	Ff	309
12: The sound of g	RR, Stg One Bk 20	Goose Chase	5–6, 13–15, 86, 89, 112, 129, 138		309
13: Review consonants j, f, g	RR, Stg One Bk 21	Nanny Goat's Nap	10–15, 19	Jj, Ff, Gg	309
14: The sound of l	RR, Stg One Bk 17	Where Do They Live?	16, 21–22, 26–27, 31–32, 53, 57		309
15: The sound of d	RR, Stg One Bk 15	Who Made That?	1, 7–9, 34, 36–37, 68, 71–72, 79, 83		309
16: The sound of n	RR, Stg One Bk 21	Nanny Goat's Nap	3, 18, 26–27, 53, 57, 65, 90, 99		309
17: Review consonants l, d, n	RR, Stg One Bk 3	The Party	7–8, 21–22, 27		309
18: The sound of w	RR, Stg One Bk 32	Wilma's Wagon	38–41, 84, 92, 172		310–311
19: The sound of c	RR, Stg One Bk 23	I Like to Count	5–6, 13, 15, 48–49, 63, 86		310–311
20: The sound of r	RR, Stg One Bk 11	Who Is Ready?	21–22, 25, 31–32, 53, 66, 91, 104		310–311
21: The sound of p	RR, Stg One Bk 14	Pat's Perfect Pizza	2–3, 10–11, 28–29, 59, 100		310–311
22: The sound of qu, v	RR, Stg One Bk 41	Quack!	30, 38–41, 92, 172	Qq, Vv	310–311
23: Review consonants w, c, r, p, q, v	RR, Stg One Bk 30	Night Animals	4–5, 28–32, 38–41, 73	Ww, Cc, Rr, Qq, Vv	310–311
24: The sound of x, y	RR, Stg One Bk 49	Fix It, Fox	42, 46, 70, 74		311
25: The sound of z	RR, Stg 0/1 Bk 42	At the Zoo	42–44, 46, 60, 70	Xx, Yy, Zz	311
26: Medial consonants	RR, Stg One Bk 34	Funny Faces and Funny Places		Bb, Dd, Ff, Gg, Kk, Ll, Mm, Nn, Pp, Rr, Tt	308–311
27: Review consonants	RR, Stg One Bk 50	Let's Go Marching!	3, 10, 22, 25, 35	Bb, Mm, Ss	308–311
28: Review consonants; Take-Home Book: "Camping Fun"				Complete Set	308–311
29: Unit Checkup			3, 5, 10, 47–49, 57, 59, 62–63, 68, 76	Dd, Ll, Pp, Tt, Ww	308–311

RR–Ready Readers Stg–Stage Bk–Book

Assessment Options

In Unit 1, assess children's ability to identify and write consonants that represent beginning and ending sounds. Use the Unit Pretest and Posttest for formal assessment. For ongoing informal assessment, you may wish to use children's work on the Review pages, Take-Home Books, and Unit Checkups. You may also want to encourage children to evaluate their own work and to participate in setting goals for their own learning.

ESL/ELL Some children may require additional assessment strategies to meet their special language needs. For additional support for English language learners, see pages 5j and 5k.

FORMAL ASSESSMENT

Use the Unit 1 Pretest, on pages 5e–5f, to help assess a child's knowledge at the beginning of the unit and to plan instruction.

ESL/ELL Before administering the Pretest, gather in a paper bag items (or pictures of them) that match the visuals on page 5e–5f. Have volunteers select an item, then name it. Ask other children to tell you what sound the beginning letter of that word name makes.

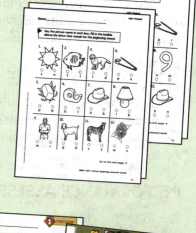

Use the Unit 1 Posttest, on pages 5g–5h, to help assess mastery of unit objectives and to plan for reteaching, if necessary.

ESL/ELL Some children may understand a concept but have difficulty with directions. Read the directions aloud and model how to complete the worksheets.

INFORMAL ASSESSMENT

Use the Review pages, Unit Checkup, and Take-Home Books in the student book to provide an effective means of evaluating children's performance.

Unit 1 Skills	Review pages	Checkups	Take-Home Books
Letters s, t, b, h, m, k	15–16, 23–24	63–64	61–62
Letters j, f, g, l, d, n	31–32, 39–40	63–64	61–62
Letters w, c, r, p, q, v	51–52	63–64	61–62
Letters x, y, z	55–56	63–64	61–62
Medial Consonants	57–58	63–64	61–62

STUDENT PROGRESS CHECKLIST

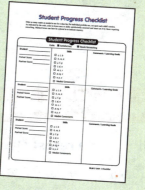

Use the checklist on page 5i to record children's progress. You may want to cut the sections apart to place each child's checklist in his or her portfolio.

PORTFOLIO ASSESSMENT

This logo signals opportunities for collecting student work for individual portfolios. You may also want to include the Pretest and Posttest, the Review pages, the Unit Checkup, Phonics & Reading, and Phonics & Writing pages.

PHONEMIC AWARENESS AND PHONICS ASSESSMENT

Use PAPA to obtain an itemized analysis of children's decoding skills.

PAPA Skills	MCP Phonics Lessons in Unit 1
Beginning sounds	Lessons 1–29
Ending sounds	Lessons 1–29
Deleting sounds	Lessons 2–21, 25–27, 29
Letter sounds	Lessons 1–29

Pretest and Posttest

DIRECTIONS

To help you assess children's progress in learning Unit 1 skills, tests are available on pages 5e–5h.

Administer the Pretest before children begin the unit. The results of the Pretest will help you identify each child's strengths and needs in advance, allowing you to structure lesson plans to meet individual needs. Administer the Posttest to assess children's overall mastery of skills taught in the unit and to identify specific areas that will require reteaching.

ESL/ELL Note that the objective of both the Unit 1 Pretest and Posttest is sound identification, not vocabulary recognition, with which children may be unfamiliar. To ensure that vocabulary comprehension does not interfere with sound recognition, name each of the items aloud as children move from item to item in the tests.

PERFORMANCE ASSESSMENT PROFILE

The following chart will help you identify specific skills as they appear on the tests and enable you to identify and record specific information about an individual's or the class's performance on the tests.

Depending on the results of each test, refer to the Reteaching column for lesson-plan pages where you can find activities that will be useful for meeting individual needs or for daily phonics practice.

Answer Keys

Unit 1 Pretest, page 5e (BLM 1)
1. s
2. f
3. d
4. p
5. b
6. t
7. h
8. l
9. m
10. g
11. z
12. w

Unit 1 Pretest, page 5f (BLM 2)
b = beginning; e = ending
13. b
14. e
15. b
16. b
17. e
18. b
19. e
20. e
21. b
22. e
23. e
24. b

Unit 1 Posttest, page 5g (BLM 3)
1. f
2. d
3. v
4. p
5. r
6. k
7. y
8. n
9. c
10. j
11. q
12. h

Unit 1 Posttest, page 5h (BLM 4)
13. c
14. n
15. b
16. t
17. j
18. g
19. l
20. f
21. b
22. x
23. r
24. n

Performance Assessment Profile

Skill	Pretest Questions	Posttest Questions	Reteaching Focus on All Learners	Daily Phonics Practice
s, t, b	1, 5, 6, 14, 15, 17, 22	15, 16, 21	9–16	308
h, m, k	7, 9, 13	6, 12	17–24	308
j, f, g	2, 10, 19, 20, 24	1, 10, 17, 18, 20	25–32	309
l, d, n	3, 8, 16, 18	2, 8, 14, 19, 24	33–40	309
w, c, r	12	5, 9, 13, 23	41–46, 51–52	310–311
p, q, v	4, 23	3, 4, 11	47–52	310–311
x, y, z	11, 21	7, 22	53–56	311

Unit 1 Pretest

Name _____

Say the picture name in each box. Fill in the bubble above the letter that stands for the beginning sound.

Go to the next page. →

BLM 1 Unit 1 Pretest: Beginning consonant sounds

Unit 1 Pretest

Name _____

▶ Say the name of each picture. If the name begins with the sound of the letter in the box, print it on the first line. If it ends with that sound, print it on the second line.

Possible score on Unit 1 Pretest is 24. Number correct _____

BLM 2 Unit 1 Pretest: Beginning and ending consonant sounds

Unit 1 Posttest

Name _____

▶ Say the picture name in each box. Fill in the bubble under the letter that stands for the beginning sound.

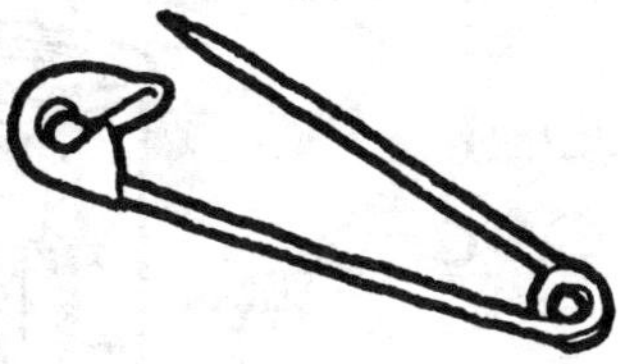

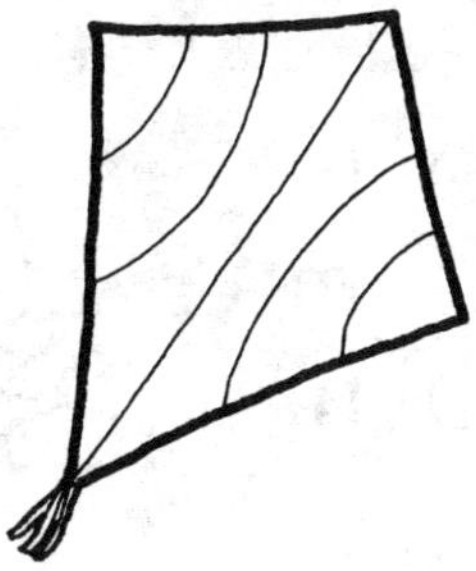

1.	2.	3.	4.
f d	d b	v w	p r
○ ○	○ ○	○ ○	○ ○

5.	6.	7.	8.
m r	k r	y g	n m
○ ○	○ ○	○ ○	○ ○

9.	10.	11.	12.
c d	p j	q g	h n
○ ○	○ ○	○ ○	○ ○

Go to the next page. →

BLM 3 Unit 1 Posttest: Beginning consonant sounds

Unit 1 Posttest

Name _____

▶ Say each picture name. Fill in the bubble by the letter that stands for the beginning sound. Fill in the bubble next to the letter that stands for the ending sound.

13.
○ p
○ r
○ c

14.
○ f
○ n
○ b

15.
○ p
○ d
○ b

16.
○ t
○ f
○ d

17.
○ e
○ r
○ j

18.
○ p
○ g
○ j

19.
○ l
○ m
○ n

20.
○ v
○ f
○ c

21.
○ p
○ g
○ b

22.
○ x
○ c
○ b

23.
○ v
○ r
○ w

24.
○ m
○ d
○ n

Possible score on Unit 1 Posttest is 24. Number correct _____

BLM 4 Unit 1 Posttest: Beginning and ending consonant sounds

Student Progress Checklist

Make as many copies as needed to use for a class list. For individual portfolio use, cut apart each child's section. As indicated by the code, color in boxes next to skills satisfactorily assessed and insert an *X* by those requiring reteaching. Marked boxes can later be colored in to indicate mastery.

Student Progress Checklist

Code: ■ Satisfactory ☒ Needs Reteaching

Student: _____

_____

Pretest Score: _____

Posttest Score: _____

Skills
- ☐ s, t, b
- ☐ h, m, k
- ☐ j, f, g
- ☐ l, d, n
- ☐ w, c, r
- ☐ p, q, v
- ☐ x, y, z
- ☐ Medial Consonants

Comments / Learning Goals

Student: _____

_____

Pretest Score: _____

Posttest Score: _____

Skills
- ☐ s, t, b
- ☐ h, m, k
- ☐ j, f, g
- ☐ l, d, n
- ☐ w, c, r
- ☐ p, q, v
- ☐ x, y, z
- ☐ Medial Consonants

Comments / Learning Goals

Student: _____

_____

Pretest Score: _____

Posttest Score: _____

Skills
- ☐ s, t, b
- ☐ h, m, k
- ☐ j, f, g
- ☐ l, d, n
- ☐ w, c, r
- ☐ p, q, v
- ☐ x, y, z
- ☐ Medial Consonants

Comments / Learning Goals

BLM 5 Unit 1 Checklist

ESL/ELL English Language Learners

Throughout Unit 1 there are opportunities to assess English language learners' ability to identify and write consonants that represent beginning and ending sounds. Certain consonants may be especially problematic for English language learners. Some may be learning the Roman alphabet for the first time. Take note of difficulties, but assess children based on their ability to distinguish consonant sounds when pronounced by a native speaker.

Lesson 1, pages 7–8; 7, pages 19–20 Some children may be learning the Roman alphabet for the first time. Stress that certain uppercase letters differ from their lowercase partners in both size and form.

Lesson 2, pages 9–10 Native speakers of Spanish may introduce an *e* sound when pronouncing English words that begin with *s* blends, like *snow, step*. Provide oral practice with English words if this is an issue.

Lesson 3, pages 11–12 Children who speak Spanish, French, Russian, or Haitian Creole may pronounce the *t* softly. Tapping your tongue against your teeth offers an accurate approximation of the sound.

Lesson 4, pages 13–14 Some children may have trouble with initial /b/ and /p/ or /d/. Model the different pronunciation of the sounds with *bay, pay,* and *day; big, pig,* and *dig;* and so on.

Lessons 5, pages 15–16; 9, pages 23–24; 13, pages 31–32 Native speakers of Spanish and Hmong may have difficulty pronouncing *t, b, m, k, j, f,* and *g* at the ends of words, since words ending in these consonants are not a common occurrence in these languages.

Lesson 6, pages 17–18 Some children who speak Middle Eastern languages or Russian may pronounce /h/ with a throaty sound. In Spanish, French, Hmong, and Haitian Creole, the *h* is silent.

Lesson 8, pages 21–22 Native speakers of Spanish may be familiar with the sound of *k* (which is the same as the sounds of hard *c, que,* and *qui*) but not recognize the written letter, which is not used as commonly in Spanish. Model with *king, key,* and *kite*.

Lesson 10, pages 25–26 Native speakers of Spanish may pronounce the sound of *j* as *y,* saying *Yimmy* instead of *Jimmy,* and so on.

Lesson 11, pages 27–28 Native speakers of Spanish may have trouble distinguishing between /f/ and /v/ or /p/. Practice with words like *fan, van,* and *pan*.

ESL/ELL English Language Learners

Lesson 12, pages 29–30 Some children may have difficulty distinguishing between the voiced /g/ and the unvoiced /k/. Clearly model the different initial sounds in *good, go,* and *get* versus *king, key,* and *kite.*

Lesson 14, pages 33–34; 20, pages 45–46 Native speakers of Vietnamese, Hmong, Korean, and Cantonese may confuse /l/ and /r/. Help them distinguish the difference between these sounds by practicing with *lock, rock; lid, red; light, right,* and so on.

Lesson 15, pages 35–36 Native speakers of Vietnamese might have difficulties discriminating between /d/ and /b/ or /p/ in English. Assist them by practicing *duck, buck, puck; dig, big, pig,* and so on.

Lesson 16, pages 37–38 Some children may have difficulty discriminating between the English sounds of *n* and *l*. Help children differentiate between these sounds by practicing *nine, line; night, light, net, let;* and so on.

Lesson 18, pages 41–42 Many English language learners will confuse both the sound and the form of *w* with those of *v* because *w* may be an uncommon letter and sound in their native language. Practice *wet, vet; well, veil; west, vest;* and so on.

Lesson 19, pages 43–44 Native speakers of Asian languages, especially Korean, may not discriminate /k/ from /g/. Practice *coat, goat; cold, gold.* In Russian, the written *Cc* is equivalent to the English *Ss*. Reinforce the *k* sound of *c* with *cat, sat; can, sand.*

Lesson 20, pages 45–46 Spanish and Tagalog speakers might trill initial *r* or pronounce "tap r" (similar to *tt* in *better*).

Lesson 21, pages 47–48 To distinguish initial /p/ from /f/ or /v/, practice *pine, fine, vine; pan, fan, van.* Speakers of Korean may confuse initial /p/ with /b/; practice *pig, big; pie, bye;* and *pat, bat.*

Lesson 22, pages 49–50 Native speakers of Spanish may pronounce *qu* like the sound of *k* instead of *kw*. Practice with *queen, key; quarter, kangaroo;* and *quiet, kite.* Spanish speakers will also pronounce /v/ as /b/.

Lesson 24, pages 53–54 Children who speak Spanish or Tagalog may pronounce initial /y/ like *g* in *genre* or like *j* in *joy*. Those who speak Cambodian or Vietnamese may pronounce it like *ny* in *canyon*.

Lesson 25, pages 55–56 Speakers of Spanish, Tagalog, Korean, or Hmong may not distinguish /z/ from /s/. Practice *zip, sip; zoo, soon; zigzag, sag.*

Phonics Games, Activities, and Technology

The following collection of ideas offers a variety of opportunities to reinforce phonics skills while actively engaging children. The games, activities, and technology suggestions can easily be adapted to meet the needs of your group of learners. They vary in approach so as to consider children's different learning styles.

PICK A MATCH

Duplicate Blackline Master 6 on tagboard or construction paper and cut apart to make letter cards with blank backs. Place the capital letters and small letters in separate containers. Have children choose a letter from each container. If the letters match, the child keeps the pair. If the letters do not match, they are both returned to the containers. You may want to limit the sets to six or eight letters at a time.

CONSONANT CONCENTRATION

Duplicate Blackline Master 6 on tagboard or construction paper and cut apart to make pairs of letter cards. Using sets of capital and lowercase of eight letters (16 cards) at a time, have children place the cards in a grid of four cards by four cards. Then have children take turns turning over two cards at a time to find the matching capital and lowercase letter. Matched pairs are picked up, unmatched pairs are returned to their original positions. When children become proficient with the game, the number of cards can be increased to 20, then 24.

ESL/ELL This activity as well as Pile Up can be simplified by reducing the number of letter cards or objects used to play the games. When children become more familiar with the game, increase the number of items to be identified.

MYSTERY SOUND BOXES

Place small objects whose names begin with the same sound, such as a button, a bell, and a balloon, in a box or other container. Set up several boxes in this way. Children select a box, look at the objects, and write the letter that stands for the beginning sound. Number the boxes and let children keep track of the sounds they have guessed.

PILE UP

Have each child select any five consonant letter cards from his or her set, and place the cards in a row. As you pronounce words that begin with consonant sounds, children listen for the sounds of their letters. When a child hears a word that begins with one of his or her letters, the card is moved to a pile. When all five cards are placed in the pile, the child may say "Pile up!" and the game is over. Repeat, having children choose five new cards.

QUICK DRAW

Provide each child with a slate or have players stand at the chalkboard. Place a consonant letter card in a bag or box, shake it, and dump the card onto the floor. If the capital letter faces up, the children must write the matching lowercase letter. If the lowercase letter faces up, the children must write the capital form. Continue, placing one letter card in the box at a time.

BEGINNING, MIDDLE, OR END?

Draw three empty, connected boxes on the chalkboard. Explain that these boxes represent the beginning, middle, and end of a word. Call on a child to stand by the boxes. Say a word and name a consonant that is heard in the word. Have the child touch the box that shows where the consonant is heard in the word. For example, if you say *mop, p*, the child should touch the last box to show that the sound of *p* is at the end of *mop*.

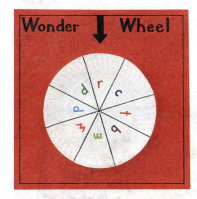

WONDER WHEEL

Mark a paper plate into sections and write a consonant in each section. Place a brad through the center of the plate to mount it to posterboard. Mark an arrow on the posterboard. Children take turns spinning the plate and naming a word that begins with the sound of the consonant that lands by the arrow.

SLIDE IT DOWN

Specify five or six consonants and have children place those letter cards across the top of their desks. As you say a word, have the children slide the card with the letter that stands for the initial sound down to a position in front of them. After checking their response, have the card returned to the row at the top and repeat.

Variation: When children are ready for increased difficulty, give two, then three words at once and have children slide down the corresponding initial letters in order.

ESL/ELL This activity as well as Sorting Sounds and Consonant Catch relies on natural pronunciation. Be sure to say each word clearly and distinctly, but be aware of overexaggeration or a heavy regional accent, which can distort the sound of a letter or word.

SORTING SOUNDS

Gather a collection of small objects. Have children sort the names for the objects according to sound, and then ask them to explain why they sorted the objects as they did. For example, they may sort by beginning sound or by ending sound.

CONSONANT CATCH

Have children stand in a circle with you in the center. Say a word as you toss a foam ball to a child. The child who catches the ball must repeat the word and name the consonant he or she hears at the beginning (or end), then toss the ball back to you. Repeat with a new word. Continue until all children have had a chance to catch the ball.

TARGET TOSS

Place consonant letter cards in a container. Provide children with a beanbag and a box or bucket for a target. Have a child toss the beanbag at the target. When the beanbag lands in the container, the child selects a letter card and gives a word that begins with the letter sound.

5m

MOVE ALONG

Have children stand behind a chalk or tape line on one side of the room. Make a second line at the other side of the room. Have one child select a card from a pile of consonant letter cards. The child must name the letter and then can take one step forward for each word he or she can name that begins with the consonant sound. The child must stop when no new word can be given. Then, the next child chooses a card, and the game continues.

ESL/ELL This activity and Listen for Sounds (page 5o) are individual activities that can be modified by dividing the class into teams of three or more children. This allows children to participate when they can and eliminates peer pressure focusing on one person.

FIRST OR LAST

Prepare a chart as shown, with three sandwich bags attached. Label one bag first and another bag last. The third bag is for letter cards. Have available a set of pictures or objects that contain the target consonant sound. Children name each picture or object and place it in the bag according to whether the sound is the first or last sound heard in the name. Change the target sound by placing a different letter card in the bag.

WHO IS IT?

Make sure each child has a name card. Then give consonant-letter hints for a child's name. When the name is guessed, have that child come to the front to show his or her name card and to identify the consonants. For example, you might say, "I'm thinking of a name that has two *s*'s. It begins with *J*. It also has a *c*." (Jessica)

ESL/ELL This activity and My Favorite Letter assume your English language learners know, can pronounce, and can spell their classmates' names. Boost self-concept by asking children to decorate their own name tags and attach them to their desks with clear tape before you conduct these activities.

MY FAVORITE LETTER

Suggest that children each choose a favorite letter, perhaps the first letter of their name or a letter they feel they can form particularly well. Let each child draw a large letter and cut it out. Provide paints, markers, tissue paper, glitter, and glue and invite children to decorate their letters. Have each child display his or her letter and name at least three things that begin with the letter sound.

SECRET CONSONANT

Before children arrive for the day, write a consonant on the board and cover it with a sheet of construction paper. Tell children that you have written a secret letter on the board and that you will give hints from time to time for them to guess the letter. Give several hints throughout the day, but don't let children tell what letter they guess. At the end of the day, reveal the letter. Hints may refer to the letter's shape, its formation, its uppercase or lowercase partner, or its sound; for example, hints for *M* might be *This letter is made with all straight lines. To make this letter, start with a straight line down. This letter's partner has two humps. You hear the sound for this letter at the end of* gum.

CONSONANT CATERPILLARS

Make available a supply of circles cut from different colors of construction paper. Give each child two circles. On one circle, have them draw a smiling caterpillar face. They may want to paste on paper antennae. On the second circle, have them write a consonant. You may assign the consonant or have them choose it. Children make caterpillars by drawing objects that begin with the consonant sound on separate circles. They can paste the circles together to form long caterpillars.

LISTEN FOR SOUNDS

Have children respond to letter questions asked in the following format: *What letter do you hear at the beginning of* dog *and at the end of* mud? Challenge children to choose a letter and to ask some similar questions.

The following software products reinforce children's understanding of letter recognition and consonant sounds.

Reader Rabbit's® 1st Grade–Capers on Cloud Nine!™

This product, part of a series, is designed to teach first graders core skills including spelling, phonics, and phonemic awareness through fun activities. Several skill levels are available.

** Riverdeep The Learning Company
500 Redwood Blvd.
Novato, CA 94947
(800) 825-4420
www.learningcompanyschool.com

JumpStart Phonics™

Children from PreK to first grade learn reading skills, phonics, and letter recognition through lessons and activities. The program contains speech-recognition technology so that children can interact with the computer.

** Sunburst Technology
1900 South Batavia Ave.
Geneva, IL 60134
(800) 321-7511
www.sunburst.com

B	C	D	F	G	H
J	K	L	M	N	P
Q	R	S	T	V	W
X	Y	Z	b	c	d
f	g	h	j	k	l
m	n	p	q	r	s
t	v	w	x	y	z

Home Connections

The Home Connections features of this program are intended to involve families in their children's learning and application of phonics skills. Three effective opportunities to make connections between home and school include the following.

- **HOME LETTER**
- **HOME NOTES**
- **TAKE-HOME BOOKS**

HOME LETTER

A letter is available to be sent home at the beginning of Unit 1. This letter informs family members that children will be learning to identify consonant sounds within the context of the unit theme, "My Favorite Things." The suggested home activity focuses on making a Letter Book, which groups pictures according to the beginning consonant sounds of their names. This activity promotes interaction between child and family members while supporting children's learning of consonant letters and their sounds. The letter, which is available in both English and Spanish, also suggests books about favorite subjects that family members can look for in a local library and enjoy reading together.

HOME NOTES

Whenever the Home logo appears within the student book, a phonics activity is suggested to be done at home. The activities are simple to do, requiring little or no preparation or special materials, and are meant to reinforce the targeted phonics skill.

TAKE-HOME BOOKS

Within the student book are Take-Home Books that can be cut out and assembled. The story language in each book reinforces the targeted phonics skills. The books can be taken home and shared with family members. In Unit 1, one Take-Home Book is available. It focuses on consonant sounds as well as the unit theme, "My Favorite Things."

Home Notes in Spanish are also available for both teachers and parents to download and use from our website, www.PlaidPhonics.com.

UNIT 1

Pages 5–6

Consonants

Skill Focus

Assess Prior Knowledge
To assess children's prior knowledge of consonants, use the pretest on pages 5e–5f.

Unit Focus

▶ Build Background

- Write the theme "My Favorite Things" on the board. Read the words and help children find them on page 5. Invite children to name some of their favorite things. To get them started, you might wish to list categories such as animals, foods, and games, and have them name favorites within each category.

- Read the poem aloud and then discuss it. Explain to children that when the poet says "Spring's on parade," he means that the springtime plants and animals are as fun to look at as a parade. Ask what things the children in the poem might see from the tree house.

▶ Introduce Consonants

- Ask children to tell anything they know about letters that are called consonants, how they look, and the sounds they stand for. Write any letters that the children name on the board.

- Write *H* on the board and have children find the word in the title of the poem that begins with this letter. Help them read the word *House* aloud. Then, have them find the word *house* in the poem. Tell children that the letters *H* and *h* stand for the same sound.

- Write the letters *Tt* and *Ss* on the board. Ask children to find words beginning with these consonants in the poem. Discuss the sounds children hear at the beginning of *Tree*, *two*, *Seats*, and *sit*.

Critical Thinking Read aloud the Talk About It question at the bottom of page 5. As children name their favorite places, invite them to tell what it is they like about them.

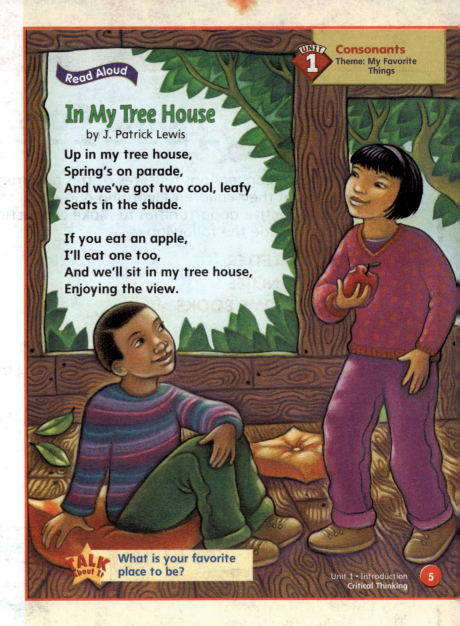

THEME FOCUS

FAVORITE BOOKS

Materials: picture books

Display a variety of books and invite children to look through them. Ask each child to choose one book that he or she likes best and to tell why. Then, have children look through the books again and identify any letters or words they know.

CONSONANT GRAB BAG

Materials: slips of paper, paper bag

Write each consonant on a separate slip of paper or use Blackline Master 6 (page 5p) and put the slips in the bag. Have children take turns drawing letters. Challenge children to name as many of their favorite things as they can that begin with that letter.

NAME GAME

Materials: oak tag strips printed with children's first names

Remind children that some of their favorite people, namely friends and classmates, are with them at school each day. Have children trace their own names and identify letters they know. Then, display all the names. Pair children and have them work together to pick out their names. Have pairs display each other's names and tell something special about their partner.

Dear Family,

In this unit about "My Favorite Things," your child will be learning about consonants and the sounds they make. Many of your child's favorite things begin with consonants, such as home, pets, music, fun, and books. As your child becomes familiar with consonant sounds, you might try these activities together.

▶ Help your child make a Letter Book. Your child can print a letter on each page, then tape or glue on pictures that begin with that letter.

▶ Read the poem on page 5 aloud. Help your child to identify the consonants at the beginning of words such as house and secret.

▶ Your child might enjoy reading these books with you. Look for them in your local library.

The Very Hungry Caterpillar
by Eric Carle

A Pocket for Corduroy
by Don Freeman

Sincerely,

Estimada familia:

En esta unidad, titulada "Mis cosas favoritas" ("My Favorite Things"), su hijo/a estudiará las consonantes y sus sonidos. Muchas de las cosas favoritas de su hijo/a comienzan con consonantes, como home (juegos), pets (mascotas), music (música), fun (diversión) y books (libros). A medida que su hijo/a se vaya familiarizando con los sonidos de las consonantes, pueden hacer las siguientes actividades juntos.

▶ Ayuden a su hijo/a a hacer un Libro de letras. Su hijo/a puede escribir una letra en cada página y después unir con cinta adhesiva o pegamento dibujos que comiencen con esa letra.

▶ Lean en voz alta el poema en la página 5. Ayuden a su hijo/a a identificar las consonantes al principio de palabras como house (casa) y secret (secreto).

▶ Ustedes y su hijo/a disfrutarán leyendo estos libros juntos. Búsquenlos en su biblioteca local.

The Very Hungry Caterpillar de Eric Carle
A Pocket for Corduroy de Don Freeman

Sinceramente,

Unit 1 • Introduction

HOME CONNECTIONS

- The Home Letter on page 6 is intended to acquaint family members with the phonics skills children will be studying in the unit. Children can tear out page 6 and take it home.
- You may want to suggest that children complete the activities on the page with a family member. Encourage them to look in the library for the books suggested and read them with family members.

LEARNING CENTER ACTIVITIES

WRITING CENTER

Invite children to draw a picture of themselves in their own tree house. Then, have them write or dictate one or more sentences telling how they would spend their time there.

SCIENCE CENTER

Materials: a variety of tree leaves, paper, crayons, scissors

Take children out to gather leaves from different trees, or bring in a variety of leaves for children to examine. Have them describe the different shapes, colors, and textures that they see and feel. Then, have children trace the leaves, color, and cut to make their own leaf cutouts.

ART CENTER

Materials: paints, markers, or crayons

Have each child choose his or her favorite color and paint or draw favorite things and animals using that color. Help children caption their artwork with a sentence that names their favorite color.

BULLETIN BOARD

Prepare a bulletin board that has a large tree with leaves big enough to frame children's drawings. Ask children to draw pictures showing a favorite family activity. Display these drawings on the leaves of the tree with the title "Our Favorite Things."

Lesson 1 Pages 7–8

Partner Letters

Skill Focus

Children will

★ recognize and match beginning consonant sounds.

★ identify by name the uppercase and lowercase forms of consonants *s, t, b, h, m, k, j, f, g, l, d, n, w, c, r, p, q, v, x, y,* and *z.*

ESL/ELL Some English language learners may be learning the Roman alphabet for the first time. Stress that certain uppercase letters differ from their lowercase partners in both size and form.

Teach

Phonological Awareness: Blending Onsets and Rimes Tell children that you will say a beginning sound and then the rest of a word: /b/ox. Then, model how to blend the parts together to say the whole word: *box.* Continue by asking children to blend together the following word parts.

- /b/us   /h/ill   /k/at
- /t/en   /f/ace   /l/id
- /n/et   /r/un   /w/et

Sound to Symbol
Materials: letter cards *Bb, Cc, Dd, Ff, Gg, Hh, Jj, Kk, Ll, Mm, Nn, Pp, Qq, Rr, Ss, Tt, Vv, Ww, Xx, Yy, Zz*

Write the letters *Bb* on the board. Tell children that these letters are partners because they both stand for the same sound, /b/. Then, invite volunteers to tell how the uppercase and lowercase forms of *Bb* differ. To reinforce these differences, have children trace their letter cards for *Bb*. Repeat with the other consonants.

Practice and Apply

Sound to Symbol Help children identify the letters on pages 7 and 8. As they begin page 8, suggest that they look at the first letter in each word to see if it is a partner letter to the one in the box.

Reading Use *A Mess*, MCP Phonics and Reading Consonant Skills Library, Level A, to provide practice in reading words with beginning consonants *m, s, t, b,* and *r.*

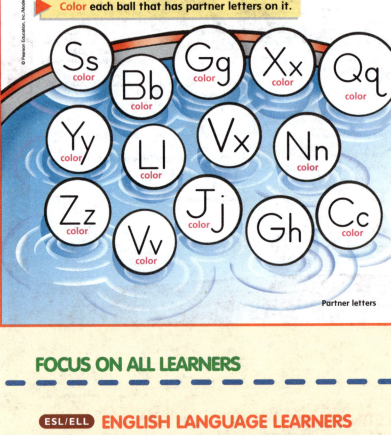

FOCUS ON ALL LEARNERS

ESL/ELL ENGLISH LANGUAGE LEARNERS

Materials: letter cards *Bb, Cc, Gg, Jj, Ll, Nn, Qq, Ss, Vv, Xx, Yy, Zz ; Ff, Dd, Hh, Kk, Mm, Tt, Pp, Rr, Ww*

- To complete the activity on page 7 in a more structured format, draw the 14 balls on the chalkboard as they appear on the page. Then, hold up cards for *Bb*. Have children shade the appropriate ball on the board, then repeat with the remaining letters shown on the page.

- Prepare children for page 8 by dividing the uppercase and lowercase letters shown on the page among the children. Ask a volunteer to name a letter held by one child. Then ask, "Who is (child)'s partner?" The volunteer must pair the child holding the uppercase letter with the child who has the lowercase one.

KINESTHETIC LEARNERS   INDIVIDUAL

Materials: clay

After rolling clay snakes, have children shape them to form the uppercase and lowercase consonant letters. Circulate, asking children to name the letters they have formed.

Partner Letters

▶ **Look** at the letter above each picture. **Circle** each word that begins with its partner letter.

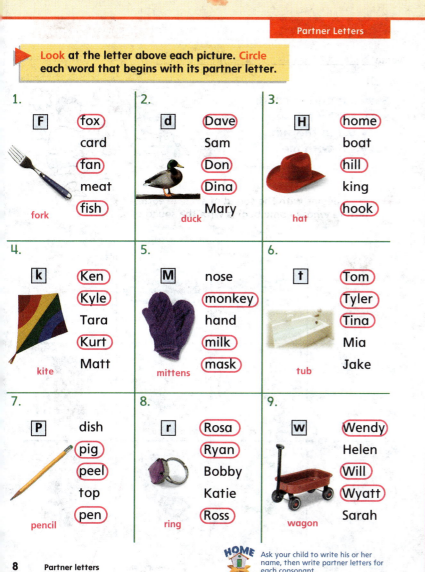

1. F — (fox), card, (fan), meat, (fish) — fork
2. d — (Dave), Sam, (Don), (Dina), Mary — duck
3. H — (home), boat, (hill), king, (hook) — hat
4. k — (Ken), (Kyle), Tara, (Kurt), Matt — kite
5. M — nose, (monkey), hand, (milk), (mask) — mittens
6. t — (Tom), (Tyler), (Tina), Mia, Jake — tub
7. P — dish, (pig), (peel), top, (pen) — pencil
8. r — (Rosa), (Ryan), Bobby, Katie, (Ross) — ring
9. w — (Wendy), Helen, (Will), (Wyatt), Sarah — wagon

HOME Ask your child to write his or her name, then write partner letters for each consonant.

8 Partner letters

CURRICULUM CONNECTIONS

WRITING
Materials: drawing paper, crayons, markers, toothpicks, paste, yarn

Have children use many different materials to explore writing uppercase and lowercase consonants. Possibilities include using crayons and markers as well as forming letters from toothpicks or yarn.

SOCIAL STUDIES
Materials: chart paper, crayons

Invite children to dictate names of friends and family members for you to record on chart paper. Have volunteers underline and identify the uppercase consonant letters.

 **AstroWord** Consonant Sounds and Letters

AUDITORY/KINESTHETIC LEARNERS

Materials: two sets of letter cards: *Bb, Ss, Tt, Hh, Mm, Kk; Jj, Ff, Gg, Ll, Dd, Nn; Ww, Cc, Rr, Pp, Qq, Vv*

Beginning with the first group of six letters, give each of 12 children one letter card. Invite them to pretend they are taxis. Call the "cars" by naming a letter and directing the two children who have it to a spot in the room. Children can match their cards when they reach the spot. The activity can be repeated with the other groups of letters.

CHALLENGE
Materials: picture books

Have partners scan books for words that begin with consonants and take turns reading the words aloud.

EXTRA SUPPORT/INTERVENTION

Ask children to watch carefully as you write a letter on the chalkboard. Then, have them take turns erasing the letter with finger-tracing as they pronounce its name. **See Daily Phonics Practice, page 308.**

Integrating Phonics and Reading

Guided Reading
Show children the cover as you read the title. Have them use the illustration to tell who is making a mess and how.

First Reading Have children look at the illustrations and point out the characteristics named for each group of animals, such as *ten tiny* toads or *round red* rabbits.

Second Reading Ask children to find words beginning with the uppercase and lowercase forms of *m, s, t, b,* and *r*.

Comprehension
After reading, ask children these questions:
• What do the messy monkeys see? *Recall/Details*
• What kind of mess do the round red rabbits see at the end? *Inference/Details*

ESL/ELL English Language Learners
Review the number words *seven* and *ten*. Then, have children draw pictures to show *one* of an item, *two* of an item, and so on up to *ten*.

Lesson 2 Pages 9–10

The Sound of s

Skill Focus

Children will

★ recognize the sound of s.

★ identify pictures whose names begin with the sound of s.

★ print the lowercase form of the letter s to complete words.

ESL/ELL Native speakers of Spanish may introduce an e sound when pronouncing English words that begin with s blends, like *snow*, *step*. Provide oral practice with English words.

▶ Teach

Phonemic Awareness: Phoneme Categorization Draw a sun on the board as you say the word and ask children to repeat *sun*, emphasizing the beginning sound. Explain that the sound heard at the beginning of *sun* is *s*. Then, say the following groups of words. Ask children to repeat the two words in each group that begin with the sound of *s*.

- soap   sand   dog
- silly   moon   sister
- man   sat   sing
- book   soup   seal

Sound to Symbol Write *sun* under the picture you drew on the board. Have children read it with you, emphasizing the initial sound. Ask them to identify the initial lowercase *s*. Then, write the name *Suzy* and have children identify the initial uppercase *S*. Point out that the *s* in *sun* and the *S* in *Suzy* stand for the same sound, /s/. Ask volunteers to underline the letter that stands for the sound of *s* at the beginning of each word. Then, model how to write uppercase and lowercase *s*.

▶ Practice and Apply

Phonemic Awareness Read aloud the rhyme on page 9. Have children listen for and name words that begin with the sound of *s*. Write the words on the board.

Sound to Symbol Help children identify the pictures on pages 9 and 10. Suggest that they listen for the beginning sound as they say each picture name. For page 10, remind children to trace the word if they print *s* for the beginning sound.

Reading Use *We Are Singing*, MCP Phonics and Reading Consonant Skills Library, Level A, to provide practice in reading words that begin with the sound of *s*.

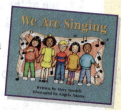

Phonemic Awareness

Name _____

Suzy sat on the sand.
Suzy sat by the sea.
Suzy sat in the sun.
Suzy sat with me.

▶ **Sand** begins with the sound of s. Circle each picture whose name begins with the sound of s.

1. sun
2. soap
3. bed
4. six
5. bell
6. saw
7. sandwich
8. door
9. sink
10. two
11. sock
12. suit

The sound of s: Phonemic awareness

FOCUS ON ALL LEARNERS

ESL/ELL ENGLISH LANGUAGE LEARNERS

- Before children complete page 9, practice distinguishing between /s/ and /z/. Ask children to repeat these word pairs: *sip, zip; sap, zap; supper, zipper*.
- Read the directions for the activity on page 10 aloud. Complete items 1 to 3 with children. Ask children to work in pairs to complete items 4 to 12. Review the answers.

VISUAL LEARNERS GROUPS

Materials: Phonics Picture Cards: scissors (33), seven (34), soap (35), turkey (37), zebra (43), zipper (44), six (60), sun (67); paper bag

To make "S soup," draw a soup kettle on the bag. Then, display each picture card and have children take turns saying the picture name. If the picture name begins with /s/, have them place the card in the bag.

KINESTHETIC LEARNERS

Materials: letter card Ss; small sand trays

Have children trace the letters on the cards. Then, say these words and have them trace Ss's in the sand if the word begins like *sand*: *sat, mitt, Suzy, salad, sun, sofa, Sam, dog, zipper, silly, suit, sandwich, sub*.

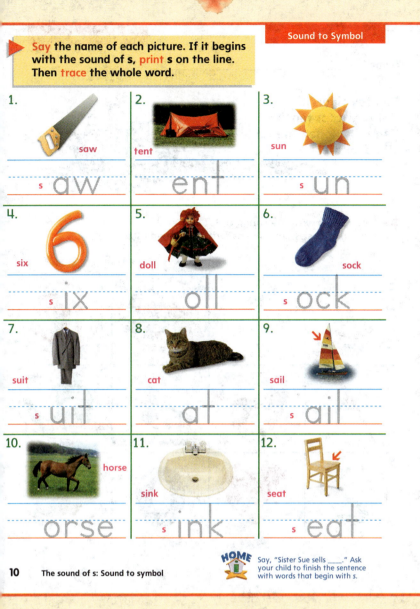

Sound to Symbol

Say the name of each picture. If it begins with the sound of s, print s on the line. Then trace the whole word.

1. saw — s aw
2. tent — ent
3. sun — s un
4. six — s ix
5. doll — oll
6. sock — s ock
7. suit — s uit
8. cat — at
9. sail — s ail
10. horse — orse
11. sink — s ink
12. seat — s eat

10 The sound of s: Sound to symbol

HOME Say, "Sister Sue sells ____." Ask your child to finish the sentence with words that begin with s.

CURRICULUM CONNECTIONS

WRITING
Materials: index cards, crayons

Invite children to draw large picture postcards of themselves at the seashore to send to a classroom partner. Encourage them to include objects whose names begin with the sound of *s*; for example, sea, sand, sand castle, seals, sun, sandwiches, sand pail. On each item, have them write the letters *Ss*. Some may be able to write labels for the sand, the sun, and the sea.

SCIENCE
Materials: sand, hand lenses, soft rocks, cloth bag, hammer

Invite children to use a hand lens to examine sand. Discuss what they discover. Explain that sand is made up of rocks that have been broken into tiny pieces. If you wish to demonstrate this process, pulverize some small rocks in a bag as children watch. Then, invite children to examine this "sand" with their hand lenses.

 TECHNOLOGY   **AstroWord** Phonemic Awareness

AUDITORY LEARNERS **GROUPS**
Sing a nonsense song to the tune of "Twinkle, Twinkle, Little Star." *Seven silly seals have fun sitting in the sunny sun. One seal says, "It's hot today." Six seals say, "Let's surf and play." Seven silly seals to see, surfing in the sunny sea.* As children listen, have them clap as they say words that begin with /s/.

CHALLENGE
Challenge children to make up oral riddles whose answers are words that begin with the sound of *s*. As an example, you might begin with one or two clues for a riddle with the answer as *soap*.

EXTRA SUPPORT/INTERVENTION
Materials: Phonics Picture Cards: scissors (33), seven (34), soap (35), tiger (37), zebra (43), zipper (44)

Ask the child to sort the picture cards into two piles: those whose picture names begin with the sound of *s* and those that do not. Have the child test each beginning sound by saying the word *sun* and the picture name. **See Daily Phonics Practice, page 308.**

Integrating Phonics and Reading

Shared/Guided Reading
Show the cover as you read the title. Invite children to name their favorite songs and tell what the songs are about.

First Reading Invite children to read the second line in each rhyme on pages 2–7. Point to the picture of the item to help them.

Second Reading Ask children to identify the initial *s* words in the story. You might want to add these to the classroom Word Wall.

Comprehension
After reading, ask children the following questions:
- What kind of song do the children in the story sing? *Recall/Summarize*
- What would you like to write a song about? *Creative/Personal Experience*

ESL/ELL English Language Learners
Point to each sign that the children in the story hold up. Have volunteers name the item and tell about it in a sentence. For example: *socks: You wear socks on your feet.*

10

Lesson 3 Pages 11–12

The Sound of t

> **Skill Focus**
>
> Children will
> - ★ recognize the sound of t.
> - ★ identify pictures whose names begin with the sound of t.
> - ★ print the lowercase form of the letter t to complete words.
>
> **ESL/ELL** Children who speak Spanish, French, Russian, or Haitian Creole may pronounce /t/ softly.

▶ Teach

Phonemic Awareness: Initial Sound Isolation Say the word *toy*, emphasizing the beginning sound, and have children repeat the word. Then, say *toy*, /t/. Explain that the sound children hear at the beginning of *toy* is the sound of t. Repeat, using the words below. Ask children to repeat each word and say the first sound in each word.

- ten   tap   toes
- tank   tip   top

Tell children that the sound at the beginning of each word is the sound of t.

Sound to Symbol Draw a picture of a tiger on the board. Say and write the word *tiger*. Have children repeat the word with you and ask them to identify the initial lowercase letter *t*. Then, tell children that the tiger you drew is named Tina. Write *Tina* on the board. Help children identify the uppercase letter *T*. Point out that both letters stand for the same sound, /t/. Ask children to name other words that begin with /t/. Write each word on the board and ask volunteers to underline the letter that stands for the sound of *t* at the beginning of each word. Then, model for children how to write uppercase and lowercase *t*.

▶ Practice and Apply

Phonemic Awareness Read aloud the rhyme on page 11. Have children listen for and name words that begin with the sound of *t*. Write the words on the board.

Sound to Symbol Help children identify the pictures on pages 11 and 12. After they have completed the pages, encourage them to name some words that begin with the letter *t*.

Reading Use *Terrific Shoes*, MCP Phonics and Reading Consonant Skills Library, Level A, to provide practice in reading words that begin with the sound of *t*.

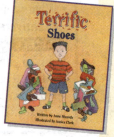

Phonemic Awareness

Name_____

Ten toy tigers
Sat down for tea.
Ten tails tipped the table—
Oh, dear me!

▶ **Tea** begins with the sound of **t**. **Circle** each picture whose name begins with the sound of **t**.

1. top	2. sink	3. toys	4. ten
5. bat	6. tail	7. duck	8. tape
9. two	10. heart	11. tire	12. tag

The sound of t: Phonemic awareness

FOCUS ON ALL LEARNERS

ESL/ELL ENGLISH LANGUAGE LEARNERS

- Before children complete page 11, help them identify objects around the room whose names begin with *t*, such as *table, toy, tape*.
- To prepare for page 12, model the sound of *t* by reviewing the words on Phonics Picture Cards for tiger (36), ten (82), tie (101), and teeth (153).

VISUAL LEARNERS GROUPS

Materials: self-stick notes, pencils

Have each child write the letters *Tt* on several self-stick notes. Then, have them "tag the *t*'s" by affixing the notes to objects in the classroom whose names begin with the sound of *t*, such as *tape, tables, tacks, terrarium*.

KINESTHETIC/VISUAL LEARNERS GROUPS

Materials: Phonics Picture Cards: daisy (7), dinosaur (8), tiger (36), turkey (37), tub (68), dog (71), top (75)

Display each picture card. Have children tap the table when the picture name begins with the sound of t. End the activity by asking children to form living *Tt*'s with their bodies.

Sound to Symbol

▶ **Say** the name of each picture. If it begins with the sound of **t**, *print* **t** on the line. Then *trace* the whole word.

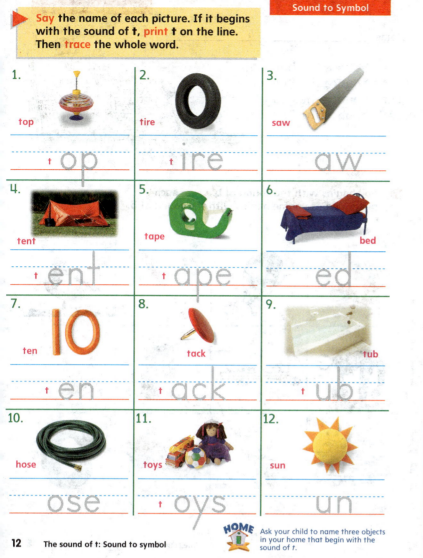

1. top — t op
2. tire — t ire
3. saw — aw
4. tent — t ent
5. tape — t ape
6. bed — ed
7. ten — t en
8. tack — t ack
9. tub — t ub
10. hose — ose
11. toys — t oys
12. sun — un

HOME Ask your child to name three objects in your home that begin with the sound of *t*.

12   The sound of t: Sound to symbol

CURRICULUM CONNECTIONS

WRITING
Materials: drawing paper, crayons

Invite children to draw pictures of toys they'd enjoy sharing with a friend. Under each toy that begins with the sound of *t*, have them write the letters *Tt*. These might include a train, a teddy bear, a turtle, a tuba, a top, or a tiger. Encourage children to write any words that they can.

SOCIAL STUDIES
Materials: picture of Theodore Roosevelt

Display the picture of Theodore Roosevelt and explain that he was president of the United States about a hundred years ago. Mention that Teddy is a nickname for Theodore, and tell children that the first teddy bear was named in honor of President Roosevelt. Use this opportunity to discuss nicknames and invite volunteers to share their family nicknames. Have children identify any that begin with /t/.

 TECHNOLOGY   **AstroWord** Phonemic Awareness

AUDITORY/KINESTHETIC LEARNERS *GROUPS*
Invite children to act out this rhyme: *Touch your nose. Touch your toes. Turn around. Touch the ground.* As children chant and act it out, have them emphasize words that begin with /t/.

CHALLENGE
Present children with this rhyme: *Tiny Tony taps his nose ten times. Tiny Tony taps his toes ten times.* After chanting the rhyme, challenge children to change the rhyme using a different name and some new words beginning with /t/.

EXTRA SUPPORT/INTERVENTION
Materials: toy telephone; Phonics Picture Cards: daisy (7), door (9), tiger (36), turkey (37), tub (68), top (75), tent (83), tire (102)

Partners take turns acting as customer and order clerk. The customer holds up a picture card. If the picture name begins with the sound of *t*, the order clerk can write the letters *Tt*. If it does not, the order clerk writes nothing. **See Daily Phonics Practice, page 308.**

Integrating Phonics and Reading

Guided Reading
Show the cover as you read the title. Then, flip through the pages to preview the illustrations. Ask children where they think the story takes place.

First Reading Have children look at the illustrations and use their own words to describe the different shoes they see.

Second Reading Ask children to identify the initial *t* words in the story. List the words on the board or add them to the classroom Word Wall.

Comprehension
After reading, ask children the following questions:
• What were the shoes that the boy tried on like? *Recall/Details*
• What kinds of shoes do you like best? *Reflective Analysis/Personal Experience*

ESL/ELL English Language Learners
Have children retell the events on pages 4 to 10 using complete sentences. For example: *The blue shoes were too tiny.*

Lesson 4 Pages 13–14

The Sound of b

Skill Focus

Children will

★ recognize the sound of *b*.

★ identify pictures whose names begin with the sound of *b*.

★ print the lowercase form of the letter *b* to complete words.

ESL/ELL Some English language learners may have difficulty distinguishing initial /b/ from /p/ and /d/. Model the different pronunciations of the sounds with *bay, pay, day; big, pig, dig;* and so on.

Teach

Phonemic Awareness: Phoneme Substitution Say the word *tall*. Then, tell children that they can change the first letter of *tall* to *b* to make a new word: *ball*. Next, have children change the first letters of these words to make more words that begin with the sound of *b*: *red, fox, dig, lake, dark, see, toy*.

Sound to Symbol Draw a ball on the board and write *ball* under it. Have children read the word with you, emphasizing the initial sound. Ask them to identify the initial lowercase letter *b*. Then, write a child's name beginning with *B* and have children identify the uppercase letter. Explain that the *b* in *ball* and the *B* in the name stand for the same sound, /b/. Invite children to think of other words that begin with the sound of *b*. Write them on the board and ask volunteers to underline the letter that stands for the sound of *b* at the beginning of each word. Then, model for children how to write uppercase and lowercase *b*.

Practice and Apply

Phonemic Awareness Read aloud the rhyme on page 13. Have children listen for and name words that begin with the sound of *b*. Write the words on the board.

Sound to Symbol Help children identify the pictures on pages 13 and 14. After they have completed the pages, encourage them to name some words beginning with the letter *b*.

Reading Use *One Bee Got on the Bus*, MCP Phonics and Reading Consonant Skills Library, Level A, to provide practice in reading words that begin with the sound of *b*.

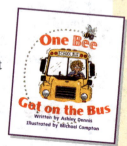

Phonemic Awareness

Name _____

Let's bounce the ball high,
Let's bounce the ball low.
Let's bounce the ball fast,
Let's bounce the ball slow.

▶ **Ball** begins with the sound of **b**. **Circle** each picture whose name begins with the sound of **b**.

1. ball
2. bug
3. bat
4. duck
5. monkey
6. bus
7. bag
8. bell
9. boat
10. saw
11. bed
12. tire

The sound of b: Phonemic awareness

FOCUS ON ALL LEARNERS

ESL/ELL ENGLISH LANGUAGE LEARNERS

Materials: Phonics Picture Cards: balloon (1), basket (2), book (3), bag (47), bug (61), bus (62), bed (76)

- Model the sound of *b* by reviewing the appropriate words and picture clues on pages 13 and 14. Continue by saying and having children repeat the words represented on the picture cards.

- Before children complete page 14, use an alphabet chart to verify whether children can identify the uppercase and lowercase forms of the letter *b*. Ask volunteers to point to the letter *b* and to write it on the chalkboard.

KINESTHETIC LEARNERS

Materials: Phonics Picture Cards: balloon (1), basket (2), book (3), pillow (28), popcorn (29), bag (47), pig (59), bug (61), bus (62), bed (76)

Place picture cards on a chalkboard ledge. Invite children to take turns pretending to be bees by stopping and *buzzing* at each picture whose name begins with /b/.

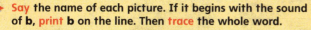

Sound to Symbol

Say the name of each picture. If it begins with the sound of **b**, print **b** on the line. Then trace the whole word.

1. bag — b ag
2. boat — b oat
3. ball — b all
4. belt — b elt
5. sock — ock
6. box — b ox
7. bat — b at
8. sun — un
9. bus — b us
10. bed — b ed
11. toys — oys
12. bug — b ug

 Say "Buddy bought a ___." Ask your child to add a word that begins with the sound of b.

14   The sound of b: Sound to symbol

CURRICULUM CONNECTIONS

WRITING
Materials: chart paper, marker, crayons

Draw the outline of a large bus on chart paper and have children identify it. Working together, have children dictate sentences telling about a bus ride. Suggest they illustrate their sentences. Then, help individual children read aloud their contributions. Invite children to point out any words that begin with *b*.

MATH
Materials: round counters

Invite children to pretend the counters are balls. Working with partners, have them use the counters to make up and solve oral word problems. Encourage them to use words that begin with /b/; for example:

Betsy had 3 balls.
Then, 1 ball rolled under the bed.
How many balls did Betsy have left?

 **AstroWord** Phonemic Awareness

AUDITORY LEARNERS
Materials: index cards, crayons

Have each child draw a ball with *Bb* inside it on an index card. Then, say these words and have children hold up the ball when they hear a word that begins with /b/: *boy, cat, balloon, basket, banana, apple, sock, barn, paper, big, pencil, bat.*

CHALLENGE
Share the first line of the traditional tongue twister "Betty Botter bought some butter." Then, challenge children to make up and share tongue twisters of their own with words that begin with /b/.

EXTRA SUPPORT/INTERVENTION
Materials: Phonics Picture Cards: balloon (1), basket (2), book (3), bib (54), pig (59), bus (62), pie (100); string

Give the child picture cards and a piece of string. Have the child lay the string on a table. Then, have the child "string a set of beads" by placing those pictures whose names begin with /b/ on the string. **See Daily Phonics Practice, page 308.**

Integrating Phonics and Reading

Shared/Guided Reading
Show the cover as you read the title. Then, flip through the pages to preview the illustrations. Ask children who else will get on the bus.

First Reading As you read, have children join in for each initial *b* word.
Second Reading Ask children to repeat the initial *b* words in the story. List the words on the board or add them to the classroom Word Wall.

Comprehension
After reading, ask children the following questions:
• What happens when one bee gets on the bus? *Recall/Plot*
• Why does this happen? *Inference/Plot*

ESL/ELL English Language Learners
Have children retell the story, using different animal names. For example: *Six dogs got on the bus.*

Lesson 5 Pages 15–16

Review Consonants s, t, b

Skill Focus

Children will

★ identify pictures whose names begin or end with the sounds of s, t, and b.

★ print the initial or final consonant for picture names that begin or end with the sounds of s, t, and b.

ESL/ELL Native speakers of Spanish and Hmong may have difficulty pronouncing t and b at the ends of words, since words ending in these consonants are not a common occurrence in these languages.

Teach

Phonemic Awareness: Phoneme Blending
Say the word *tub*, separating the sound of each phoneme: /t/ /u/ /b/. Have children repeat the segmented word. Then, ask them to identify the word. Ask what sound is heard at the beginning (the sound of *t*) and the end (the sound of *b*). Repeat the procedure using these words: *sit, bus, bat*.

Sound to Symbol Write the uppercase and lowercase forms of *s, t,* and *b* in three columns on the board. Ask children to name words that begin with each letter sound. Record each word under the letter that stands for its beginning sound.

Next, challenge children to name other words that end with the same letter sounds. Possibilities include *bus, his, sat, pot, tub, job*.

Practice and Apply

Sound to Symbol Help children identify the pictures on pages 15 and 16. Point out that they will be listening for beginning and ending sounds as they say the picture names on page 15. For page 16, they will be listening for words that have the same beginning sound. You may want to review the game of tic-tac-toe before children begin page 16.

Reading Use *Six Go By*, MCP Phonics and Reading Consonant Skills Library, Level A, to provide practice in reading words that begin with the sounds of *s* and *b* and words that end with *s*.

Name _____

Initial/Final Consonants

▶ **Say** the name of each picture. If the name **begins** with the sound of the letter in the box, **print** it on the first line. If it **ends** with that sound, **print** it on the second line.

1. b ball — b	2. t net — t	3. s bus — s	4. b box — b
5. t tie t —	6. b web — b	7. s saw s —	8. b bat — b
9. b crib — b	10. s seven s —	11. t ten — t	12. s lips — s

Initial/final consonants s, t, b   **15**

FOCUS ON ALL LEARNERS

ESL/ELL ENGLISH LANGUAGE LEARNERS

Materials: Phonics Picture Cards: bug (61), bus (62), sun (67), tub (68), ten (82), cat (49)

To prepare children for the activities on pages 15 and 16, demonstrate words that begin and end with the target sounds.

• Hold up the picture card for *sun* and ask a volunteer to name it. Write *sun* on the board, then ask children to identify the first letter and the sound it stands for. Then, hold up the card for *bus* and have a volunteer name it. Under the word *sun*, write *bus*, and ask children to identify the letter at the end of the word and the sound it stands for. Model the pronunciation of initial *s* in *sun* and final *s* in *bus*, and explain that the letter *s* stands for the same sound at the beginning or the end of a word.

• Repeat, using *ten* and *cat* for the letter *t* and *bug* and *tub* for the letter *b*.

KINESTHETIC LEARNERS

Materials: masking tape, chalk, beanbags

Using tape and chalk, create a target on the floor with sections for the letters *s, t,* and *b*. Have children take turns tossing the beanbag on a letter. Have them name the letter and give a word that begins or ends with that letter sound.

Initial Consonants

▶ **Say** each picture name. **Draw** a line through the pictures in a row that begin with the same letter sound. **Write** the letter that wins in each game.

1.
2.
3.

HOME Ask your child to name each picture, then say the beginning consonant for the picture name.

16 Initial consonants s, t, b

CURRICULUM CONNECTIONS

WRITING
Materials: drawing paper, crayons

Using these sentence frames, children can write letter poems by filling in the frame with rebus pictures or words that begin with the designated letter.

S is for _____.
T is for _____.
B is for _____.

Suggest that they share their finished poems with a partner.

MATH
Materials: picture books with minimal text, paper, pencils

Working with a partner, have children tally the number of times the letters *s, t,* and *b* appear on several pages. Before children begin to count, have them make predictions about which letter will appear most and least frequently.

TECHNOLOGY **AstroWord** Phonemic Awareness

AUDITORY LEARNERS *INDIVIDUAL*

Present these oral riddles for the child to answer.

• What word rhymes with *mop* and begins with the sound of *t*?
• What word rhymes with *clock* and begins with the sound of *s*?
• What word rhymes with *mat* and begins with the sound of *b*?

CHALLENGE

Have children fold their papers into thirds and head each column with *Ss, Tt,* or *Bb*. Have them look around the classroom for words that begin or end with these letters and record them in the correct column.

EXTRA SUPPORT/INTERVENTION

Materials: letter cards: *Ss, Tt, Bb*

Give each child the letter cards. Say these words and ask the child to show the letter that stands for the initial sound: *sand, tie, boat, bush, tub, seat, tin*. Repeat, focusing on ending sounds with the words *nut, web, hat, rib, gas*. See Daily Phonics Practice, page 308.

Integrating Phonics and Reading

Shared/Guided Reading
Show the cover as you read the title. Ask children what the man in the illustration is holding and have them count the balloons.

First Reading As you read, have children join in each time they see the word *six*.

Second Reading Ask children to find the initial *b* and *s* words in the story. Then, have them find the words that end in *s*. Point out that the *s* at the ends of these words tells them that there is more than one.

Comprehension
After reading, ask children the following questions:

• What are the things that go by in the story? *Recall/Details*
• What is the surprise at the end? How do you know? *Inference/Details*

ESL/ELL **English Language Learners**
Ask children questions that can be answered with story words, such as, "What went by on a birthday cake?" (*candles*)

Lesson 6 — Pages 17–18

The Sound of h

Skill Focus

Children will

★ recognize the sound of *h*.

★ identify pictures whose names begin with the sound of *h*.

★ print the lowercase form of the letter *h* to complete words.

ESL/ELL Some English language learners who speak Middle Eastern languages or Russian may pronounce /h/ with a throaty sound. In Spanish, French, Hmong, and Haitian Creole, the *h* is silent.

Teach

Phonemic Awareness: Phoneme Categorization Hop on one foot and then say *hop*. Have children repeat after you: *hop*, /h/. Explain that the sound heard at the beginning of *hop* is the sound of *h*. Then, say the following groups of words. Ask children to repeat the two words in each group that begin with the sound of *h*.

- toe   head   hair
- hen   met   house
- hope   hip   sock

Sound to Symbol Point to the hamster on page 17 and write the word on the board. Help children read *hamster* aloud, emphasizing the initial *h* sound. Ask them to identify the initial lowercase letter *h*. Then, ask children to think of a name for the hamster that also begins with the sound of *h*. Write the name on the board and explain that the *h* in *hamster* and the *H* in the name both stand for the same sound, /h/. Ask volunteers to underline the letter that stands for the sound of *h* at the beginning of each word. Then, model for children how to write uppercase and lowercase *h*.

Practice and Apply

Phonemic Awareness Read aloud the rhyme on page 17. Have children name words that begin with the sound of *h*. Write them on the board.

Sound to Symbol Help children identify the pictures on pages 17 and 18. Read the directions for both pages with them. Make sure that children understand that on page 17 they should circle only the pictures whose names begin with *h*.

Reading Use *Where Can a Hippo Hide?*, MCP Phonics and Reading Consonant Skills Library, Level A, to provide practice in reading words that begin with the sound of *h*.

Name _____

Phonemic Awareness

My hamster has been running
On his wheel since half past five.
He's gone a hundred miles by now,
So when will he arrive?

▶ **Hamster** begins with the sound of **h**. **Say** the name of each picture. **Circle** the beginning letter of the picture name. Then **circle** each picture whose name begins with the sound of **h**.

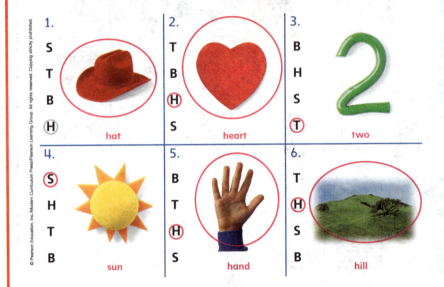

1. S T B **(H)** — hat
2. T B **(H)** S — heart
3. B H S **(T)** — two
4. **(S)** H T B — sun
5. B T **(H)** S — hand
6. T **(H)** S B — hill

The sound of h: Phonemic awareness   17

FOCUS ON ALL LEARNERS

ESL/ELL ENGLISH LANGUAGE LEARNERS

- Have children work in pairs to complete page 17. Review the answers by asking them to identify the beginning letters and pictures they circled.
- Before children complete page 18, practice listening for and pronouncing words with initial *h*. Say these words as you point to each body part; have children repeat after you: *head, hair, hand, heart, heel*.

VISUAL/KINESTHETIC LEARNERS *INDIVIDUAL*

Materials: drawing paper, crayons

Help each child trace around a hand. At the tip of each finger, have the child draw a picture of an object whose name begins with /h/. On the hand itself, have the child write *Hh*.

KINESTHETIC LEARNERS *GROUPS*

Materials: Phonics Picture Cards: heart (16), horn (17), horse (18), apple (45), ax (46), ham (50), hat (52), lamp (53)

Ask a volunteer to hold up one card at a time. Ask the other children to clap their hands each time the picture name begins with the sound of *h*.

17

CURRICULUM CONNECTIONS

WRITING
Materials: drawing paper, crayons

Invite children to draw and label a picture called "Home." Suggest that they include objects or people whose names begin with the sound /h/. Under each one, have them write the letters *Hh*. Some children may be able to write labels. Invite children to share their writing with the class by posting it on a bulletin board titled "Home, Sweet Home."

FINE ARTS
Materials: paper plates, hole puncher, yarn, drawing paper, crayons

Invite children to decorate paper plate hats with pictures whose names begin with the same sound as *hat*. Help them punch holes in their hats and attach yarn ties; then, hold a hat parade in which children model their hats and name the pictures used to decorate them.

TECHNOLOGY AstroWord Phonemic Awareness

Integrating Phonics and Reading

Guided Reading
Show the cover as you read the title. Ask children to tell what they know about hippos.
First Reading Ask children to identify the house, the horse, and the hill.
Second Reading Ask children to identify the initial *h* words in the story. You might want to add these to the classroom Word Wall.

Comprehension
After reading, ask children the following questions:
- Where does the hippo hide at the end of the story? Why is this a good place for it to hide? *Inference/Cause and Effect*
- Where else could a hippo hide? *Creative/Personal Experience*

ESL/ELL English Language Learners
Ask children to think of a phrase that means the opposite of *behind*. Then, have them give and follow directions using *behind* and *in front of*. For example: *Stand in front of the desk.*

AUDITORY LEARNERS
Play a game of Simon says, using as many words as possible that begin with /h/. Use commands such as: *Simon says hold your head. Simon says touch your heel.* After each command, have children identify words with /h/.

CHALLENGE
Teach children this chant: *Humpty Dumpty sat on his hat. Now Humpty Dumpty's hat is flat.* Then, suggest children provide another line for these Humpty Dumpty chants: *Humpty Dumpty has a hat. Humpty Dumpty feels so hot. Humpty Dumpty sees a hen.*

EXTRA SUPPORT/INTERVENTION
Materials: hat; Phonics Picture Cards: fan (10), heart (16), horn (17), horse (18), nurse (27), ham (50), hand (51), hat (52), hen (81), kite (98)

Give children the picture cards and have them take turns saying each picture name. Have them place the card in the hat if the picture name begins with /h/. See Daily Phonics Practice, page 308.

Lesson 7   Pages 19–20

The Sound of m

Skill Focus

Children will

★ recognize the sound of *m*.

★ identify pictures whose names begin with the sound of *m*.

★ print the lowercase form of the letter *m* to complete words.

ESL/ELL Some English language learners may be learning the Roman alphabet for the first time; stress the differences between uppercase and lowercase *m*.

Teach

Phonemic Awareness: Phoneme Identity
Tell children that you will say a sentence for them to repeat after you. Then say: *Maria munched mini muffins*. Ask children what is the same about all the words in the sentence. (All begin with the same sound, /m/.) Explain that the sound heard at the beginning of each word in the sentence is the sound of *m*. Then, tell children you will say part of a sentence. Ask them to finish it with a word that begins with /m/. Use this sentence: *Mike makes marvelous _____*.

Sound to Symbol Write the word m*uffin* and have children say it several times, emphasizing the initial sound. Ask them to identify the initial lowercase letter *m*. Then, write the name *Mike*. Have children say the word with you and identify the uppercase *M*. Point out that the *m* in *muffin* and the *M* in *Mike* both stand for the same sound, /m/. Ask volunteers to underline the letter that stands for the sound of *m* at the beginning of each word. Then, model for children how to write uppercase and lowercase *m*.

Practice and Apply

Phonemic Awareness Read aloud the rhyme on page 19. Have children listen for and name words that begin with the sound of *m*. Write the words on the board.

Sound to Symbol Help children identify the pictures on pages 19 and 20. Suggest that they listen for the beginning sound as they say each picture name. For page 20, remind children to trace the word if they print *m* for the beginning sound.

Reading Use *My Monster and Me*, MCP Phonics and Reading Consonant Skills Library, Level A, to provide practice in reading words that begin with the sound of *m*.

Phonemic Awareness

Name _____

Mom gave me a muffin for lunch.
Mom gave me a muffin to munch.
The muffin I munched was yummy.
The muffin is in my tummy.

▶ **Mom** begins with the sound of **m**. **Circle** each picture whose name begins with the sound of **m**.

1. mop
2. heel
3. money
4. mouse
5. sandwich
6. man
7. mitten
8. map
9. mitt
10. moon
11. bug
12. milk

The sound of m: Phonemic awareness   19

FOCUS ON ALL LEARNERS

ESL/ELL ENGLISH LANGUAGE LEARNERS

• Before children begin page 19, build vocabulary using household objects that begin with the sound of *m*, such as *mop, mitten, milk*. Include some objects that do not begin with *m* such as *pencil, book, cup*. On the board draw the outline of a house and write *Mm* on the roof. Mix up the objects, display them one at a time, and ask volunteers to name them. Ask, *Does it begin with the sound of* m? *If it does, write the word on the board inside the "m house."*

• Read aloud the directions for the activity on page 20. Complete items 1 to 3 together. Have children complete items 4 to 12 in small groups.

VISUAL LEARNERS

Materials: discarded magazines, scissors, paste, drawing paper

Have each child find pictures whose names begin with /m/. Have them use the pictures to create a collage in the shape of a large *M*.

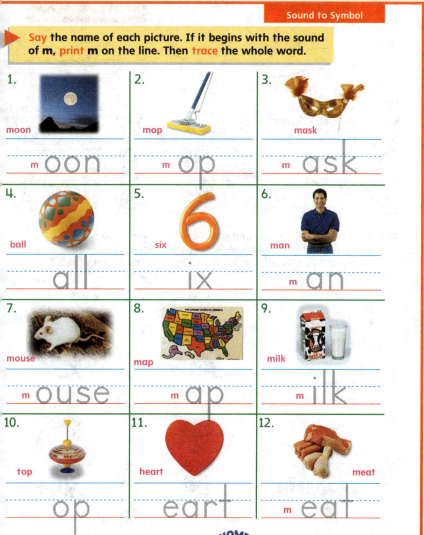

Sound to Symbol

Say the name of each picture. If it begins with the sound of **m**, print **m** on the line. Then trace the whole word.

1. moon — m oon
2. mop — m op
3. mask — m ask
4. ball — all
5. six — ix
6. man — m an
7. mouse — m ouse
8. map — m ap
9. milk — m ilk
10. top — op
11. heart — eart
12. meat — m eat

The sound of m: Sound to symbol

Point to a picture. Have your child say its name and then think of a word that begins with the same sound.

CURRICULUM CONNECTIONS

WRITING

Materials: box decorated to look like a mailbox, drawing paper, crayons, old envelopes

Assign each child a partner. Have children draw or write the names of things they like that begin with the sound of *m*. Help children address their envelopes to their partners and then mail their letters by dropping them in the mailbox for delivery.

SOCIAL STUDIES/FINE ARTS
Materials: drawing paper, crayons

Have children talk about mothers and how they look when they are having fun. Then, invite them to draw laughing portraits with the words *My mom* printed beneath them.

TECHNOLOGY   **AstroWord** Phonemic Awareness

AUDITORY LEARNERS
Say some words that begin with initial *m* and some that do not, such as *milk, sit, monkey, mine, balloon, map, paper, mask*. Ask children to moo like cows each time they hear the sound of *m*.

CHALLENGE
Challenge children to draw and then label as many foods as they can that begin with the sound of *m*. Possibilities include *milk, meat, muffins, melons,* and *maple syrup*.

EXTRA SUPPORT/INTERVENTION
Materials: Phonics Picture Cards: heart (16), monkey (23), mittens (24), moon (25), newspaper (26), nurse (27), mop (73), hen (81), mule (103), drum (127)

Place the cards face down. Have children take turns turning over two cards. If both picture names begin with /m/, the cards match and are removed. If a match is not made, children should turn the cards face down and continue the game. See Daily Phonics Practice, page 308.

Integrating Phonics and Reading

Shared/Guided Reading

Show the cover as you read the title. Ask children to describe the monster in the illustration and tell if it looks friendly or unfriendly.

First Reading Read aloud the sentences that begin with the words *My monster*. Help students read aloud the sentences that begin with *I*.

Second Reading Ask children to identify the initial *m* words in the story. List the words on the board or add them to the classroom Word Wall.

Comprehension
After reading, ask children the following questions:
- What things do the girl and her monster do in the same way? *Recall/Comparison*
- What do they do differently at the end? *Recall/Comparison*

ESL/ELL English Language Learners
Explain that *munch* is another word for *eat*. Then, have students finish this sentence in different ways: *I munch ___ for lunch*.

Lesson 8 Pages 21–22

The Sound of k

Skill Focus

Children will

★ recognize the sound of *k*.

★ identify pictures whose names begin with the sound of *k*.

★ print the lowercase form of the letter *k* to complete words.

ESL/ELL Native speakers of Spanish may be familiar with the sound of *k* (which is the same as the sounds of hard *c*, *que*, and *qui*) but not recognize the written letter, which is not used as commonly in Spanish.

▶ Teach

Phonemic Awareness: Phoneme Blending
Say the word *kite*, separating the sound of each phoneme: /k/ /ī/ /t/. Have children repeat the segmented word and then say it naturally. Repeat with *key*. Tell children that the sound they hear at the beginning of these words is the sound of *k*.

Sound to Symbol
Materials: key

Hold up a key and have children identify it. Then, write *key* on the board, and help children read the word aloud, emphasizing the initial sound. Ask them to identify the initial lowercase letter *k*. Next, write the name *Katy* and help children read it aloud and identify the uppercase letter. Help children conclude that the *k* in *key* and the *K* in *Katy* stand for the same initial sound, /k/. Then, say and write other words that begin with *k*, such as *kite, kitten,* and *kangaroo*. Ask volunteers to underline the letter that stands for the sound of *k* at the beginning of each word. Then, model for children how to write uppercase and lowercase *k*.

▶ Practice and Apply

Phonemic Awareness Read aloud the rhyme on page 21. Have children listen for and name words that begin with the sound of *k*. Write the words on the board.

Sound to Symbol Help children identify the pictures on pages 21 and 22. Read the directions for both pages with them. Make sure they understand that on page 21 they should circle only the pictures whose names begin with *k*. On page 22, they should trace only the words that begin with *k*.

Reading Use *Too Much Ketchup*, MCP Phonics and Reading Consonant Skills Library, Level A, to provide practice in reading words that begin with the sound of *k*.

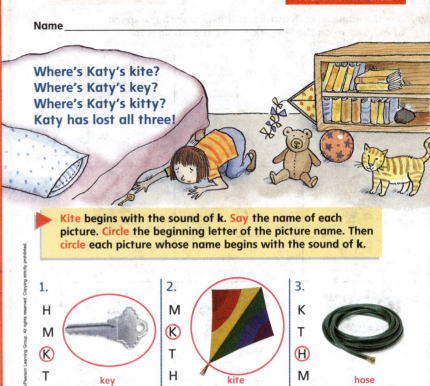

Phonemic Awareness

Name _____

Where's Katy's kite?
Where's Katy's key?
Where's Katy's kitty?
Katy has lost all three!

▶ **Kite** begins with the sound of k. **Say** the name of each picture. **Circle** the beginning letter of the picture name. Then **circle** each picture whose name begins with the sound of k.

1. H M (K) T — key
2. M (K) T H — kite
3. K T (H) M — hose
4. T (K) M H — kitten
5. H (M) K T — mitten
6. T H M (K) — kangaroo

The sound of k: Phonemic awareness 21

FOCUS ON ALL LEARNERS

ESL/ELL ENGLISH LANGUAGE LEARNERS

- As you read the rhyme on page 21, have children point to the kite, key, and kitten. Write these words on the board, then model pronunciation and have children repeat.

- Have children take turns naming the pictures on page 22. Then, complete items 1 to 3 as a group. Have children complete items 4 to 10 individually.

VISUAL LEARNERS

Materials: bag, marker, Phonics Picture Cards: girls (13), key (20), king (56), pig (59), kite (98)

Write a large *Kk* on the bag and explain that it is for keeping things that begin with the sound of *k*. Have children place the card in the bag if the picture name begins with /k/.

KINESTHETIC/VISUAL LEARNERS

Materials: Phonics Picture Cards: basket (2), horn (17), key (20), king (56), kite (98); index cards

Place picture cards so they are partially visible. Have pairs of children hunt for the cards. When they find one that begins with /k/, have them write *Kk* on their index cards.

Sound to Symbol

▶ **Say** the name of each picture. If it begins with the sound of **k**, **print k** on the line. Then **trace** the whole word.

1. key — k ey
2. bike — ___ ike
3. king — k ing
4. book — ___ ook
5. kite — k ite
6. fork — ___ ork
7. milk — ___ ilk
8. kitten — k itten
9. kitchen — k itchen
10. ketchup — k etchup

HOME Taking turns with your child, think of more words that begin with the sound of k, such as *keep* and *kind*.

22 The sound of k: Sound to symbol

CURRICULUM CONNECTIONS

WRITING

Materials: drawing paper, crayons

Invite children to draw a picture of a kitchen. In the kitchen, have them show different objects and animals whose names begin with the same sound as *kitchen*. Under each of these objects, have them write the letters *Kk*. Encourage children who are able to write captions for their kitchen pictures. Others may wish to dictate captions for you to record.

SCIENCE
Materials: photo of a kangaroo

Display the photo and have a volunteer identify the animal. Have children name the letter that stands for the sound heard at the beginning of *kangaroo*. Talk with children about the distinctive features of a kangaroo. Discuss that it has strong legs and a large tail that helps it balance while it jumps. Take children to an open space and invite them to hop like kangaroos.

TECHNOLOGY  **AstroWord** Phonemic Awareness

AUDITORY/KINESTHETIC LEARNERS
Invite children to stand in a circle. Say these words and have them make a loud kiss each time they hear a word that begins with /k/: *kitchen, bedroom, kitten, puppy, kangaroo, king, mustard, ketchup, kite, hug, kick.*

CHALLENGE
Working with a partner, challenge children to think of words that begin with /k/ whose meanings can be pantomimed. They might use pictures from pages 21 to 22. Have them pantomime each word for others to guess.

EXTRA SUPPORT/INTERVENTION
Materials: fingerpaints, paper

Invite children to print *Kk* and create a picture of a king. Then, suggest they create other pictures whose names or actions begin with *k*. Help them recall words such as *key, kangaroo, kiss, kite*. **See Daily Phonics Practice, page 308.**

Integrating Phonics and Reading

Guided Reading
Show the cover as you read the title. Ask children to tell what they know about ketchup.
First Reading Have children point out each food item that Hank is putting ketchup on.
Second Reading Ask children to identify the initial *k* words in the story. If necessary, help them distinguish these from the initial *h* words.

Comprehension
After reading, ask children these questions:
- Do you think that Hank used too much ketchup? Why or why not? *Reflective Analysis/Opinion*
- Do you think mustard is a good choice to use instead? Why or why not? *Reflective Analysis/Opinion*

ESL/ELL English Language Learners
Have children practice using the word *instead*. Ask them to reread pages 2 to 5, saying: *Hank puts mustard on hot dogs instead*, and so on.

Lesson 9 Pages 23–24

Review Consonants h, m, k

Skill Focus

Children will

★ identify pictures whose names begin or end with the sounds of *h*, *m*, and *k*.

★ print the initial or final consonant for picture names that begin or end with the sounds of *h*, *m*, and *k*.

ESL/ELL Native speakers of Spanish and Hmong may have difficulty pronouncing *m* and *k* at the ends of words, since words ending in these consonants are not a common occurrence in these languages.

▶ Teach

Phonemic Awareness: Phoneme Substitution Remind children that they can sometimes make a new word by changing a word's first letter. Then, present these riddles.

- What word rhymes with *top* and begins with the sound of *m*? (*mop*)
- What word rhymes with *ring* and begins with the sound of *k*? (*king*)
- What word rhymes with *bug* and begins with the sound of *h*? (*hug*)

Sound to Symbol
Materials: letter cards *Hh, Mm, Kk*

Tell children that you will say some words; they will hold up the card that stands for the beginning sound as you say each one. Use such words as *hen, key, hop, man, mine, keep, hot*. Invite children to suggest other words.

Next, have children identify the sound they hear at the end of a word. Have them hold up the correct card as you say *swim, talk, make, him*.

▶ Practice and Apply

Sound to Symbol Help children identify the pictures on pages 23 and 24. Point out that they will be listening for beginning sounds as they say the picture names on page 23. For page 24, they will be listening for both beginning and ending sounds.

Reading Use *Kangaroo in the Kitchen*, MCP Phonics and Reading Consonant Skills Library, Level A, to provide practice in reading words that begin with the sounds of *h*, *m*, and *k* and words that end with *m* and *k*.

Initial Consonants

Name _____

▶ Say the name of each picture. Find the beginning letter of each picture name. Circle that letter.

1. hen	2. kite	3. moon
(H) M K	M (K) H	K H (M)
4. mop	5. key	6. hand
H (M) K	(K) M H	M (H) K
7. man	8. kitten	9. heart
H K (M)	(K) M H	M (H) K
10. kitchen	11. hill	12. mitt
H (K) M	K M (H)	(M) H K

Initial consonants h, m, k   23

FOCUS ON ALL LEARNERS

ESL/ELL **ENGLISH LANGUAGE LEARNERS**

Materials: Phonics Picture Cards: heart (16), horn (17), horse (18), monkey (23), mittens (24), moon (25), key (20), king (56), kite (98)

- To prepare children for page 23, hold up the cards one at a time at random and ask a volunteer to say the picture name, then identify the letter that stands for the beginning sound. Write the words on the board under these headings: *Words that begin with k, Words that begin with h, Words that begin with m*.

- Prepare for page 24 by focusing on the difference between beginning and ending sounds. Say and write the words *hook, Kim, Mark, hum, mask,* and *him*, emphasizing the beginning sound. Ask volunteers to underline the letter that stands for the beginning sound. Repeat, emphasizing the ending sound, and have children circle the letter that stands for that sound.

KINESTHETIC LEARNERS

Materials: wooden block, masking tape, marker

Using tape, have children transform the block into a letter cube with *H, h, M, m, K, k*, one letter on each face. Have them roll the cube and say a word or name that begins or ends with the displayed letter.

Initial/Final Consonants

Say the name of each picture. If the name **begins** with the sound of the letter in the box, print it on the first line. If it **ends** with that sound, print it on the second line.

1. k — beak — k
2. h — heel — h
3. m — gum — m
4. m — man — m
5. k — key — k
6. m — swim — m
7. k — kite — k
8. h — hand — h
9. h — heart — h
10. k — fork — k
11. m — milk — m
12. k — kitten — k

24 Initial/final consonants h, m, k

HOME Ask your child to name two pictures that begin with the same sound and two that end with the same sound.

CURRICULUM CONNECTIONS

WRITING
Materials: drawing paper, crayons

Brainstorm a list of names beginning with *H*, *M*, or *K*. Then, have children write sentences with the names and rebus pictures or words that begin with the designated letter. They can also add other words to the sentences. Use these sentence frames.

H____ hides h____.
M____ mixes m____.
K____ keeps k____.

SOCIAL STUDIES
Materials: map of the United States

Display the map and help children identify it as a U.S. map. Discuss that the United States is made up of 50 states and help children find and name their state. Then, have volunteers point to other states that begin with the letters *H*, *M*, or *K*. Possibilities include: Minnesota, New Hampshire, Kansas, Michigan, Maine, and Kentucky. As each state is indicated, have children repeat its name.

TECHNOLOGY **AstroWord** Phonemic Awareness

AUDITORY LEARNERS GROUPS *Friday*

Read these silly sentences, emphasizing the underlined word. Ask children to name a word that begins with the same letter so that the sentence makes sense.

- A <u>kitten</u> is the ruler of a country. (*king*)
- You catch a ball with a baseball <u>mat</u>. (*mitt*)
- You wear a hat on your <u>hand</u>. (*head*)

CHALLENGE *Friday - food and animals*
Materials: writing paper, pencil

After folding their papers into thirds, have children head each column with the letters *Hh*, *Mm*, or *Kk*. Have them look at classroom displays or books for words that begin or end with these letters and record them in the correct column. Ask them to circle words they can read.

EXTRA SUPPORT/INTERVENTION
Materials: three bags; marker; Phonics Picture Cards: heart (16), horn (17), horse (18), key (20), mittens (24), ham (50), kite (98)

Label each bag with the letters *Hh*, *Mm*, or *Kk*. Have the children say each picture name, and sort each card into the correct bag. **See Daily Phonics Practice, page 308.**

Integrating Phonics and Reading

Guided Reading
Show the cover as you read the title. Invite children to tell what they know about kangaroos.

First Reading Have children look at the pictures and describe what Kim, Mom, and Dad are thinking and feeling.

Second Reading Have children identify words in the story that begin with the sounds of *h*, *m*, and *k* and words that end with *m* and *k*.

Comprehension
After reading, ask children these questions:
- What surprising people or animals does Kim find in the kitchen? *Recall/Plot*
- Do you think Mom and Dad are surprised at the end of the story? What makes you think so? *Inference/Details*

ESL/ELL English Language Learners
Explain that *there's* is a contraction, or short form, for *there is*. Then, help children form sentences beginning with *there's*; for example, *There's a book on my desk.*

Lesson 10   Pages 25–26

The Sound of j

Skill Focus

Children will

★ recognize the sound of *j*.

★ identify pictures whose names begin with the sound of *j*.

★ print the lowercase form of the letter *j* to complete words.

ESL/ELL Native speakers of Spanish may pronounce the sound of *j* as *y*, saying *Yimmy* instead of *Jimmy*, and so on. Offer practice with the picture clues on pages 25–26.

Teach

Phonological Awareness: Blending Onsets and Rimes Say the following word parts. Have children orally blend the parts to say the words.

- /j/une   /j/et   /j/ames
- /j/oke   /j/uice   /j/ump

Repeat each word once more with children. Explain that the sound heard at the beginning of each one is the sound of *j*.

Sound to Symbol Ask children to jump up. Then, write the word *jump* on the board. Have children read it with you, emphasizing the beginning sound. Ask them to identify the initial lowercase letter *j*. Next, write the name *Joy* on the board. Encourage children to read the word aloud and identify the uppercase letter. Point out that the *j* in *jump* and the *J* in *Joy* stand for the same sound, /j/. Ask volunteers to underline the letter that stands for the /j/ sound at the beginning of each word. Then, model for children how to write uppercase and lowercase *j*.

Practice and Apply

Phonemic Awareness Read aloud the rhyme on page 25. Have children listen for and name words that begin with the sound of *j*. Write the words on the board.

Sound to Symbol Help children identify the pictures on pages 25 and 26. Read the directions for both pages with them. Make sure that they understand that on page 25 they should circle only the pictures whose names begin with *j*. On page 26, they should trace only the words that begin with *j*.

Reading Use *Jump Right In*, MCP Phonics and Reading Consonant Skills Library, Level A, to provide practice in reading words that begin with the sound of *j*.

25

Phonemic Awareness

Name _____

Joy can pick a prize.
It will be hers to keep.
Will she take the jacks or the jet,
The jump rope or the jeep?

▶ **Jeep** begins with the sound of **j**. **Circle** each picture whose name begins with the sound of **j**.

1. jeep   2. bird   3. jack
4. kite   5. jump   6. jar
7. jack-in-the-box   8. jet   9. hand

The sound of j: Phonemic awareness   25

FOCUS ON ALL LEARNERS

ESL/ELL ENGLISH LANGUAGE LEARNERS

- To prepare for the activity on page 25, say a series of words, such as *Jack, chip, jeep, jet, house, jar, jump, hump, chin,* and *Jim*. Have children repeat a word only if it has the sound of *j*.
- Read aloud the directions for the activity on page 26. Model the activity by completing the first two items aloud. Have children complete the rest individually or in pairs, then review answers.

VISUAL LEARNERS

Materials: magazines, picture books, scraps of paper for place markers

Have children work in pairs to find two or more pictures whose names begin with /j/. Ask them to mark the places in the books or magazines with scrap-paper markers. Later, have them show and describe what they found to the rest of the class.

KINESTHETIC/AUDITORY LEARNERS

Have children pretend to be jack-in-the-boxes. Say these words and have them jump to their feet when they hear a word that begins with /j/: *jam, milk, jet, joke, kite, jump, jar, job, bike, jeep*.

Sound to Symbol

▶ **Say** the name of each picture. If it begins with the sound of **j**, **print j** on the line. Then **trace** the whole word.

1. jeep
2. leaf
3. jug
4. tent
5. heel
6. jump
7. jet
8. mouse
9. sun
10. bug
11. jack
12. jar

Help your child think of sentences using words that begin with *j*, such as *Joe juggled the jacks.*

26 The sound of j: Sound to symbol

CURRICULUM CONNECTIONS

WRITING
Materials: drawing paper, crayons

Have children brainstorm a list of toys whose names begin with /j/. These might include a jeep, a jack-in-the-box, a jet, a jump rope, and some jacks. Have children draw or write an invitation to a friend to play with one of these toys. They might use a sentence frame such as *We can play with a _____*. Children can share their finished invitations with a partner.

SOCIAL STUDIES
Materials: photos of various modes of transportation, including a jeep, a jet, a train, a car, a helicopter, a bus, a subway, a boat

Display the photos and talk with children about how people get from one place to another. Encourage children to share ways they have traveled. Then, have children categorize the pictures as ways to travel on land, in the air, and by water.

TECHNOLOGY AstroWord Phonemic Awareness

AUDITORY LEARNERS

Share some traditional nursery rhymes such as "Jack and Jill," "Jack Be Nimble," and "Jumping Joan." Have children clap each time they hear a word that begins with the sound of *j*.

CHALLENGE
Have children work in pairs to think of as many words as possible that begin with *j*. Then, have them see how many of these words they might fit into one realistic or nonsense sentence or a story.

EXTRA SUPPORT/INTERVENTION
Materials: fingerpaints, paper

Have children recall any words they know that begin with *j*. Have them make *Jj*'s on their papers and illustrate any words they can. See Daily Phonics Practice, page 309.

Integrating Phonics and Reading

Shared/Guided Reading
Show the cover as you read the title. Ask children if they jump rope and invite them to tell what they enjoy about this game.

First Reading After you read the four lines on each spread, invite children to repeat the text. Point out that jump-rope rhymes have a special rhythm.

Second Reading Ask children to identify the initial *j* words in the story. List the words on the board or add them to the classroom Word Wall.

Comprehension
After reading, ask children these questions:
- Are the children in the story having fun? How can you tell? *Inference/Details*
- Do you know any other jump-rope rhymes? What are they? *Reflective Analysis/Personal Experience*

ESL/ELL English Language Learners
Point out the sentence *Jump right in*. Explain that it is a command, or sentence that tells someone to do something.

26

Lesson 11 — Pages 27–28

The Sound of f

Skill Focus

Children will
- ★ recognize the sound of f.
- ★ identify pictures whose names begin with the sound of f.
- ★ print the lowercase form of the letter f to complete words.

ESL/ELL Native speakers of Spanish may have trouble distinguishing between /f/ and /v/ or /p/. Practice with words like *fan*, *van*, and *pan*.

Teach

Phonemic Awareness: Phoneme Categorization Use a sheet of paper to fan yourself as you repeat the word *fan* with children several times, emphasizing the initial sound. Tell children that the sound they hear at the beginning of *fan* is the sound of f. Then, say the following groups of words. Ask children to repeat the two words in each group that begin with the sound of f.

- four   ten   five
- fit   fell   sank
- fold   say   fill
- bus   foot   fun

Sound to Symbol Write the numeral 5 and the word *five* on the board. Have children read the word with you, emphasizing the initial sound. Ask them to identify the initial lowercase letter f. Then, write a child's name beginning with F and have children identify the capital letter. Explain that the f in *five* and the F in the name stand for the same sound, /f/. Ask volunteers to underline the letter that stands for the sound of f at the beginning of each word. Then, model for children how to write uppercase and lowercase f.

Practice and Apply

Phonemic Awareness Read aloud the rhyme on page 27. Have children listen for and name words that begin with the sound of f. Write the words on the board.

Sound to Symbol Help children identify the pictures on pages 27 and 28. Read the directions for both pages with them. Make sure that they understand that on page 27 they should circle only the pictures whose names begin with f. On page 28, they should trace only the words that begin with f.

Reading Use *As Fast as a Fox*, MCP Phonics and Reading Consonant Skills Library, Level A, to provide practice in reading words that begin with the sound of f.

27

Phonemic Awareness

Name _____

Five furry foxes
Fanning in the heat.
They all run away
On furry fox feet.

▶ **Five** begins with the sound of **f**. Circle each picture whose name begins with the sound of f.

1. fox
2. fire
3. saw
4. four
5. fan
6. five
7. fork
8. hat
9. box
10. fish
11. fence
12. feet

The sound of f: Phonemic awareness   **27**

FOCUS ON ALL LEARNERS

ESL/ELL ENGLISH LANGUAGE LEARNERS

- Before children begin page 27, practice differentiating between the sounds of *f*, *v*, and *p*. Have children repeat these word groups and identify the word that begins with *f*: *fat, vat, pat; pin, fin; peel, feel, veal; fan, pan, van*. Talk about the meanings of the different words.

- Read aloud the directions for the activity on page 28. Complete items 1 and 2 together. Have children complete items 3 to 12 individually. Review all items aloud to check comprehension.

VISUAL LEARNERS

Materials: Phonics Picture Cards: fan (10), fork (11), fox (12), vegetables (38), violin (39), fire (94)

Draw a fence on the board. Tape the cards on the fence. Have children take turns selecting a card. Ask them to say the picture name and tell whether or not it begins with /f/.

Sound to Symbol

> Say the name of each picture. If it begins with the sound of **f**, print **f** on the line. Then trace the whole word.

1. fish — **f** ish
2. leaf — eaf
3. four — **f** our
4. feet — **f** eet
5. five — **f** ive
6. fan — **f** an
7. sail — ail
8. fork — **f** ork
9. fence — **f** ence
10. lamp — amp
11. fox — **f** ox
12. fire — **f** ire

HOME Make up riddles for your child to answer with words from the page, such as *What rhymes with box?* (fox)

28 The sound of f: Sound to symbol

AUDITORY LEARNERS

Have children stand in a circle. Say these words and have children fan themselves with their fingers when they hear a word that begins with the same sound as *fan* and *fingers*: *basket, fire, five, box, fan, sun, fish, match, four, fat, hat, finger.*

CHALLENGE

Have children count to 60 and identify the numbers that start with the sound of *f*.

EXTRA SUPPORT/INTERVENTION

Materials: letter card *Ff*; Phonics Picture Cards: fork (11), fox (12), pillow (28), vegetables (38), violin (39), pig (59), five (95)

Display the picture cards. Ask volunteers to say the picture names. Have children hold up their letter card if the picture name begins with /f/.
See Daily Phonics Practice, page 309.

CURRICULUM CONNECTIONS

WRITING

Materials: drawing paper, crayons

Ask children to draw a picture of a funny face, funny feet, funny boy or girl, or funny animal. Have them write or dictate sentences about the picture. Encourage them to use words beginning with the *f* sound in their sentences. Then, have them share their work with their partners. Encourage them to observe if their partner makes a funny face as they read it.

MATH

Materials: counters

Reread the rhyme at the top of page 27 and have children use their counters to represent what happens in it. Then, invite children to make up word problems about a fox family. Here is an example.

Four foxes sat in the sun.

Two more foxes came.

How many foxes were there in all?

As children share their problems, have the rest of the class solve them with counters.

TECHNOLOGY   AstroWord Phonemic Awareness

Integrating Phonics and Reading

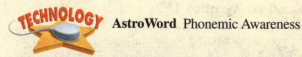

Shared/Guided Reading
Show the cover as you read the title. Ask children to predict whether the girl will run as fast as the fox.

First Reading Invite children to help you read aloud the words that answer each question: *super fox*, *super fish*, and so on.

Second Reading Ask children to identify the initial *f* words in the story. List the words on the board or add them to the classroom Word Wall.

Comprehension
After reading, ask children the following questions:
- Who is asking and answering the questions in this story? *Inference/Character*
- Can this girl really do all the things she says she can? Why or why not? *Inference/Fantasy and Realism*

ESL/ELL English Language Learners
Explain that a superhero is a character who has special abilities. Point to each superhero in the story and ask: *Who is this? What does (name) do?*

Lesson 12   Pages 29–30

The Sound of g

Skill Focus

Children will
* recognize the sound of g.
* identify pictures whose names begin with the sound of g.
* print the lowercase form of the letter g to complete words.

ESL/ELL Some English language learners may have difficulty distinguishing between the voiced /g/ and the unvoiced /k/. Clearly model the different initial sound in *good*, *go*, and *get* versus *king*, *key*, and *kite*.

Teach

Phonemic Awareness: Phoneme Identity
Tell children that you will say a sentence for them to repeat after you. Then say, *Good gardeners get good gardens.* Ask children what is the same about all the words in the sentence. (All begin with the same sound, /g/) Explain that the sound heard at the beginning of each word in the sentence is the sound of g. Then, tell children you will say part of a sentence. Ask them to finish it with a word that begins with /g/. Use this sentence: *Grandma gave Gary a ___.*

Sound to Symbol Draw a gift box on the board and write the word *gift*. Have children read it with you, emphasizing the initial sound. Ask them to identify the initial lowercase letter g. Then, ask children to imagine that the gift is from a girl named Gail. Write *Gail* and have children identify the uppercase G. Point out that the g in *gift* and the G in *Gail* stand for the same sound, /g/. Ask volunteers to underline the letter that stands for the sound of g at the beginning of each word. Then, model for children how to write uppercase and lowercase g.

Practice and Apply

Phonemic Awareness Read aloud the rhyme on page 29. Have children listen for and name words that begin with the sound of g. List the words on the board.

Sound to Symbol Help children identify the pictures on pages 29 and 30. Read the directions for both pages with them. Make sure that they understand that on page 29 they should circle only the pictures whose names begin with g. On page 30, they should trace only the words that begin with g.

Reading Use *Goose Chase*, MCP Phonics and Reading Consonant Skills Library, Level A, to provide practice in reading words that begin with the sound of g.

Phonemic Awareness

Name _____

Get the gifts.
Do not be late.
Run to the garden,
And open the gate.

▶ **Garden** begins with the sound of g. **Circle** each picture whose name begins with the sound of g.

1. goat 2. hand 3. girl
4. gift 5. fork 6. gum
7. duck 8. game 9. gate

The sound of g: Phonemic awareness   29

FOCUS ON ALL LEARNERS

ESL/ELL ENGLISH LANGUAGE LEARNERS

* Before children begin page 29, practice differentiating initial /g/ from /k/. Say these word pairs and have children identify the word in each one that begins with /g/: *get, kit; cold, gold; game, come; coat, goat.* Talk about the meanings of the words.

* Have children say the names of the pictures on page 30. Correct pronunciation as needed. Read the directions aloud and have the children complete the page in pairs. Review answers aloud.

VISUAL LEARNERS

Materials: discarded catalogs or magazines, scissors, gift box

Have each child cut out pictures of objects whose names begin with /g/ and place them in a gift box. Ask children to take turns picking a "gift" and saying its name.

KINESTHETIC LEARNERS

Have children form a line. Ask two children to join hands to form a gate. To open the gate and pass through it, each child must say a word that begins with /g/.

Sound to Symbol

▶ **Say** the name of each picture. If it begins with the sound of g, **print** g on the line. Then **trace** the whole word.

1. gum — g um
2. girl — g irl
3. five — ive
4. gold — g old
5. game — g ame
6. dog — og
7. gate — g ate
8. gift — g ift
9. goat — g oat
10. bag — ag
11. pig — ig
12. goose — g oose

HOME Invite your child to think of more words that begin with g such as go, get, good, give.

The sound of g: Sound to symbol

CURRICULUM CONNECTIONS

WRITING
Materials: drawing paper, crayons

Assign partners and have children talk about games they like to play. Then, have them work cooperatively to draw a picture of themselves playing this game. Write this sentence frame on the board and have children copy and complete it to caption their pictures: _____ and _____ like to play the game ____. Display the pictures and label them *Go, Games, Go!*

FINE ARTS/SOCIAL STUDIES
Materials: fingerpaints and paper

Ask children to name and show some things they are good at. Some may want to demonstrate jumping, singing, making a face, writing, reading, telling a funny story, pretending. Then, have children fingerpaint themselves doing their special activity. Have them title their painting, *I am good.*

TECHNOLOGY **AstroWord** Phonemic Awareness

AUDITORY LEARNERS
Invite children to pretend to be geese. Then, say these words and have children honk like geese each time they hear a word that begins with /g/: *girl, gift, dog, gather, camera, gas, lemon, gate.*

CHALLENGE
Have children look at the pictures on page 30. Challenge them to identify those picture names where the sound of g is heard at the end of the word.

EXTRA SUPPORT/INTERVENTION
Materials: Phonics Picture Cards: car (5), cookies (6), girls (13), glove (14), goose (15), cake (86), gate (89), goat (112), grapes (129), glass (138)

Display each picture and have children say aloud its name as they listen for the beginning sound. Have them giggle and then write *Gg* if the picture name begins with the sound of g. See Daily Phonics Practice, page 309.

Integrating Phonics and Reading

Guided Reading
Show the cover as you read the title. Invite children to make predictions about what will happen in the story.

First Reading Have children use the illustrations to tell who is chasing the goose at each point in the story.

Second Reading Ask children to identify the initial *g* words. List the words on the board or add them to the classroom Word Wall.

Comprehension
After reading, ask children these questions:
- Who first chases the goose? Who chases it next? *Recall/Sequencing*
- Why did the goose go back inside the gate? *Recall/Details*

ESL/ELL English Language Learners
Explain that the phrase *was on the loose* means "was running away." Then, help children make up other sentences to show the phrase's meaning. For example: *The snake escaped from the zoo. Now it is on the loose.*

Lesson 13 Pages 31–32

Review Consonants j, f, g

Skill Focus

Children will

★ identify pictures whose names begin or end with the sounds of *j, f,* and *g.*

★ print the initial or final consonant for picture names that begin or end with the sounds of *j, f,* and *g.*

ESL/ELL Native speakers of Spanish and Hmong may have difficulty pronouncing words that begin or end with *j, f,* and *g,* since these consonants are not a common occurrence in these languages.

Teach

Phonemic Awareness: Phoneme Blending

Say the word *fog,* separating the sound of each phoneme: /f/ /o/ /g/. Have children repeat the segmented word, then identify the whole word. Ask what sound is heard at the beginning. (the sound of *f*) Then, say the following words, again separating phonemes: *give, jacks, fan, Jim, fish, gas.* Have children repeat each word, say the whole word, and identify the beginning sound.

Sound to Symbol

Materials: letter cards: *Jj, Ff, Gg*

Write on the board: *Begins with J, Begins or Ends with F, Begins or Ends with G.* Next, say initial *j, f,* and *g* words, such as *just, fix,* and *give.* Have children hold up the card that stands for the beginning sound. Write each word on the board and ask volunteers to underline the letter that stands for the beginning sound. Repeat activity, having children listen for the sound at the ends of words such as *leaf, leg, roof,* and *dog* and hold up a letter card for each ending sound. After recording these words on the board, ask volunteers to circle the letter that stands for the ending sound.

Practice and Apply

Sound to Symbol Help children identify the pictures on pages 31 and 32. Point out that they will be listening for beginning and ending sounds as they work through each page. As they complete page 32, they will also be printing the letter that stands for each sound.

Reading Use *Nanny Goat's Nap,* MCP Phonics and Reading Consonant Skills Library, Level A, to provide practice in reading words that begin or end with the sound of *g.*

FOCUS ON ALL LEARNERS

ESL/ELL ENGLISH LANGUAGE LEARNERS

- Prepare for page 31 by focusing on the difference between beginning and ending sounds. Say and write the words *fog, golf, Jeff, jug,* emphasizing the beginning sound. Ask volunteers to underline the letter that stands for the beginning sound. Repeat, emphasizing the ending sounds, and have children circle the letter that stands for that sound.

- Read the directions for page 32 aloud. Ask children to name the objects shown in the pictures. Monitor their work as they decide which letter is missing and write it in the correct position.

VISUAL LEARNERS

Materials: Phonics Picture Cards: fan (10), fork (11), fox (12), girls (13), glove (14), goose (15), jack-in-the-box (19); three bags; marker

Have partners write the letters *Jj, Ff,* or *Gg* on the bags. Have them take turns saying each picture name, identifying its beginning sound, and placing the card in the correct bag.

31

Initial/Final Consonants

▶ **Say** the name of each toy. **Print** a letter to finish the word on each sign. Then **trace** the word.

1. j et
2. f ish
3. g oat
4. bu g
5. do g
6. g ame
7. j eep
8. f arm

32 Initial/final consonants j, f, g

Ask your child to finish sentences using words from the page, such as *Cows and ducks live on a ___.* (farm)

CURRICULUM CONNECTIONS

WRITING

Materials: drawing paper, crayons

Ask children to imagine that they are car salespersons, trying to sell cars that can go anywhere. Have them draw pictures and write a short ad selling this car. Children can form small groups of "customers" to view the ads. Invite them to comment on whether they would buy such a car.

SOCIAL STUDIES
Materials: globe, piece of masking tape

Point out the picture of the jet on page 31 and invite children to describe plane rides they have taken. Then, display a globe and explain that it is a model of the earth. Use masking tape to mark your approximate location on the globe. Ask volunteers to spin the globe and with closed eyes, point to a location. Have them tell if they would go by jet, by boat, or by car to travel to this spot.

TECHNOLOGY  **AstroWord** Phonemic Awareness

---

AUDITORY LEARNERS
Materials: letter cards: *Jj, Ff, Gg*

Children take turns holding up a letter card while others call out words that begin with the letter. Ask children to see how many words they can think of for each letter.

CHALLENGE
Materials: books of nursery rhymes and other poetry books

Have children locate rhymes that illustrate the use of *j, f, g* such as "Jack and Jill," "Five Little Monkeys," "Here We Go." They can plan and present a lively recitation for the class.

EXTRA SUPPORT/INTERVENTION
Materials: Phonics Picture Cards: fan (10), fork (11), fox (12), girls (13), glove (14), goose (15), jack-in-the-box (19); letter cards *Jj, Ff, Gg*

Place the letter cards on a desk. Have children select a picture, say its name, and place it on the letter that stands for the beginning sound. **See Daily Phonics Practice, page 309.**

Integrating Phonics and Reading

Shared/Guided Reading
Show the cover as you read the title. Then, preview the illustrations and ask children who the characters in the story will be.

First Reading Invite children to read each animal's reply to Nanny Goat's question, using a different voice for each character.

Second Reading Ask children to find four words that begin with *g* and one word that ends with *g* in the story.

Comprehension
After reading, ask children these questions:
- Why does Nanny Goat have trouble finding a place to take a nap? *Recall/Cause and Effect*
- Why is the laundry basket a good place for Nanny Goat to take her nap? *Inference/Details*

ESL/ELL English Language Learners
Explain that *May I . . . ?* means *Do I have permission to. . . ?* Then, help children ask and answer questions beginning with *May I?* For example: *May I use the telephone?*

32

Lesson 14 Pages 33–34

The Sound of l

Skill Focus

Children will

★ recognize the sound of *l*.

★ identify pictures whose names begin with the sound of *l*.

★ print the lowercase form of the letter *l* to complete words.

ESL/ELL Native speakers of Vietnamese, Hmong, Korean, and Cantonese may confuse /l/ and /r/. Help them distinguish these sounds by practicing words such as *rock, lock*.

Teach

Phonemic Awareness: Phoneme Categorization Point to your eyes as you say the word *look*. Repeat the word with children several times, emphasizing the initial sound. Tell children that the sound they hear at the beginning of *look* is the sound of *l*. Then, say the following groups of words. Ask children to repeat the two words in each group that begin with the sound of *l*.

- list   heart   lace ✓
- lunch laugh   pack ✓
- leap   learn   dance ✓
- gate   late   last ✓

Sound to Symbol Write the word *look* on the board. Have children read it with you, emphasizing the initial sound. Ask them to identify the initial lowercase letter *l*. Then, write the name *Lizzy*. Have children identify the capital letter. Point out that the *l* in *look* and the *L* in the name both stand for the same sound, /l/. Ask volunteers to underline the letter that stands for the sound of *l* at the beginning of each word. Then, model for children how to write uppercase and lowercase *l*.

Practice and Apply

Phonemic Awareness Read aloud the rhyme on page 33. Have children listen for and name words that begin with the sound of *l*. Write the words on the board.

Sound to Symbol Help children identify the pictures on pages 33 and 34. Suggest that they listen for the beginning sound as they say each picture name. For page 34, remind children to trace the word if they print *l* for the beginning sound.

Reading Use *Where Do They Live?*, MCP Phonics and Reading Consonant Skills Library, Level A, to provide practice in reading words that begin with the sound of *l*.

Phonemic Awareness

Name _____

Look, look, Lizzy!
Quick, come and see.
A lovely little ladybug
Just landed on me.

▶ **Ladybug** begins with the sound of **l**. **Circle** each picture whose name begins with the sound of **l**.

1. lamp
2. lion
3. bug
4. log
5. lock
6. horse
7. leaf
8. leg
9. hand
10. lake
11. lid
12. ladder

The sound of l: Phonemic awareness 33

FOCUS ON ALL LEARNERS

ESL/ELL ENGLISH LANGUAGE LEARNERS

Materials: Phonics Picture Cards: heart (16), lion (22), nurse (27), ribbon (31), rooster (32); photos or realia of a lamp, a leaf, a lid, and lips

- Before children begin page 33, say the following words one at a time as you show the picture card or the photo/realia of each: *lamp, heart, lion, leaf, rooster, lid, nurse, lips, ribbon*. Have children clap when they hear a word that begins with the sound of *l*. Ask them to repeat the word. Then, write the *l* words on the board. Tape the picture cards or draw a sketch next to each word.

- Before children begin page 34, review the sound of *l* and the picture names together. Then, read the directions aloud and complete items 1 to 3 as a group. Have children work in pairs to complete items 4 to 12, then review the answers.

KINESTHETIC LEARNERS

Have children arrange their chairs in a long line to form a log. To sit on the log, ask each child to give a word that begins with /l/.

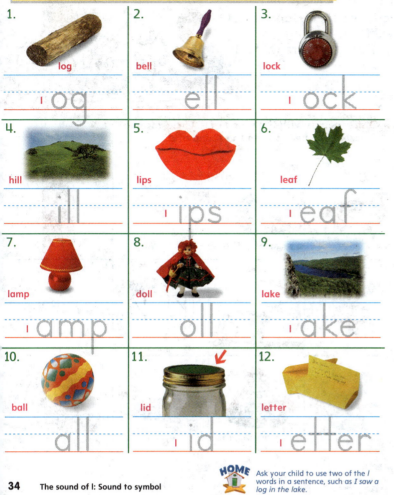

Sound to Symbol

Say the name of each picture. If it begins with the sound of l, print l on the line. Then trace the whole word.

1. log
2. bell
3. lock
4. hill
5. lips
6. leaf
7. lamp
8. doll
9. lake
10. ball
11. lid
12. letter

HOME Ask your child to use two of the l words in a sentence, such as *I saw a log in the lake.*

34 The sound of l: Sound to symbol

CURRICULUM CONNECTIONS

WRITING
Materials: lemon juice, cotton swabs, lamp

Using lemon juice, have children write a secret message to a partner about a visit to a lake. Explain that when the lemon juice dries, their letter will be invisible. Brainstorm a list of things they might see, including words like *leaves, ladybugs,* and *logs.* Have children exchange their finished notes. To make the letters reappear, have children hold the paper near a warm light bulb.

SCIENCE
Materials: leaves, hand lenses, drawing paper, crayons

Point out the picture of the leaf on page 33. Explain that leaves help plants and trees produce the food they need to live. Have children use a hand lens to examine leaves, describing what they see. Point out that the raised veins they see carry water and food. Talk with students about what happens to the leaves of many trees during each season. Invite them to draw four pictures showing these changes in the leaves.

TECHNOLOGY AstroWord Phonemic Awareness

AUDITORY LEARNERS
Divide the children into two groups: the lions and the lambs. Say some words and have the lions roar if the word begins like *lion*. Have the lambs say *baaa* if the word ends like *doll*. Use these and other words: *ladder, hotel, list, lost, fall, lipstick, lemon, lime, pal, bell.*

CHALLENGE
Working with a partner, have children make up riddle clues for the pictures on pages 33 and 34. Have them take turns giving clues and then guessing the mystery picture.

EXTRA SUPPORT/INTERVENTION
Materials: Phonics Picture Cards: ladder (21), lion (22), newspaper (26), nurse (27), lamp (53), lid (57)

Draw a ladder on the board for each child. Display the picture cards and have children say the picture name. Have them write *Ll* on a rung each time they identify a picture name that begins with /l/. **See Daily Phonics Practice, page 309.**

Integrating Phonics and Reading

Shared/Guided Reading
Show the cover as you read the title. Ask children if they think this book will tell facts or a made-up story, and why.
First Reading As you read, point to each animal name and invite children to read it with you.
Second Reading Ask children to identify the initial *l* words in the story. List the words on the board or add them to the classroom Word Wall.

Comprehension
After reading, ask children these questions:
- What other kinds of animal homes do you know about? *Reflective Analysis/Prior Knowledge*
- How are animal homes like human homes? *Reflective Analysis/Comparison*

ESL/ELL English Language Learners
Explain that *let's* is a contraction, or short way of saying *let us.* Have children make up oral sentences beginning with *let's,* such as *Let's read this book together.*

Lesson 15 Pages 35–36

The Sound of d

Skill Focus

Children will

★ recognize the sound of *d*.

★ identify pictures whose names begin with the sound of *d*.

★ print the lowercase form of the letter *d* to complete words.

ESL/ELL Vietnamese English language learners may have difficulty discriminating between /d/ and /p/ or /b/. Clearly model the different initial sounds in such words as *day, bay,* and *pay*.

► Teach

Phonemic Awareness: Initial Sound Isolation Hold up the Phonics Picture Card for dog (71) and say the word *dog*, stressing the beginning sound. Have children repeat the word. Then, explain that the sound heard at the beginning of *dog* is the sound of *d*, /d/. Next, hold up these picture cards: daisy (7), balloon (1), dinosaur (8), door (9), seven (34), doll (72), tiger (36). Ask children to name the pictures, then name the sound they hear at the beginning of each picture name.

Sound to Symbol Draw a circle representing a dish on the board and write the word *dish* inside. Have children repeat the word with you, emphasizing the initial sound. Ask them to identify the initial lowercase letter *d*. Then, write the name *Denny* and have children identify the uppercase letter. Point out that the *d* is *dishes* and the *D* in *Denny* stand for the same sound, /d/. Ask volunteers to underline the letter that stands for the sound of *d* at the beginning of each word. Then, model for children how to write uppercase and lowercase *d*.

► Practice and Apply

Phonemic Awareness Read aloud the rhyme on page 35. Have children listen for and name words that begin with the sound of *d*. Write the words on the board.

Sound to Symbol Help children identify the pictures on pages 35 and 36. Read the directions for both pages with them. Make sure that children understand that on page 35 they should circle only the pictures whose names begin with *d*.

Reading Use *Who Made That?*, MCP Phonics and Reading Consonant Skills Library, Level A, to provide practice in reading words that begin with the sound of *d*.

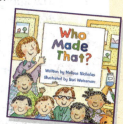

Phonemic Awareness

Name _____

Denny does the dishes.
Dori does them, too.
Dad feeds the dog,
And soon they are through.

▶ **Dishes** begins with the sound of **d**. **Circle** each picture whose name begins with the sound of **d**.

1. dog ⭕	2. duck ⭕	3. bat	4. door ⭕
5. top	6. deer ⭕	7. desk ⭕	8. key
9. dive ⭕	10. doll ⭕	11. bed	12. dime ⭕

The sound of d: Phonemic awareness   35

FOCUS ON ALL LEARNERS

ESL/ELL ENGLISH LANGUAGE LEARNERS

- Before children begin page 35, practice differentiating initial /d/, /b/, and /p/. Say these words and have children repeat them after you, raising their hands when they hear a word that begins with /d/: *dad, bad, pad; puck, duck, buck; big, dig, pig*.

- Read the directions for page 36 aloud. Complete items 1 to 3 aloud together. Have the children work in pairs or small groups to complete the page. Review the answers together.

VISUAL LEARNERS

Materials: flower-petal cutouts, crayons, construction paper, paste

Give each child in the group a daisy petal. Have them draw a picture whose name begins with /d/. Then, have the group work together to assemble a daisy from the decorated petals.

KINESTHETIC LEARNERS

Invite children to pretend to be dogs, donkeys, deer, or ducks and have them line up outside the classroom door. Explain that to pass through the door, they need to give a word that begins with /d/. Then, call on each animal and have those children give their words.

35

Sound to Symbol

Say the name of each picture. If it begins with the sound of **d**, print **d** on the line. Then trace the whole word.

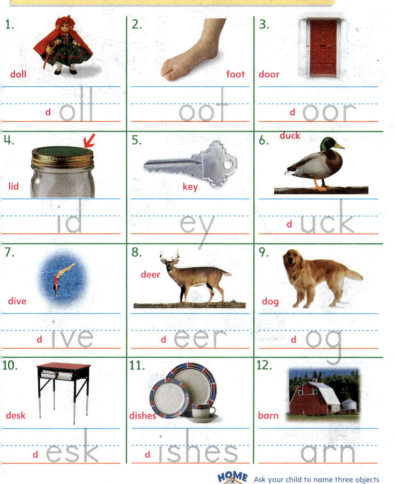

1. doll — d oll
2. foot — oot
3. door — d oor
4. lid — id
5. key — ey
6. duck — d uck
7. dive — d ive
8. deer — d eer
9. dog — d og
10. desk — d esk
11. dishes — d ishes
12. barn — arn

36 The sound of d: Sound to symbol

HOME Ask your child to name three objects in your home that begin with the *d* sound.

CURRICULUM CONNECTIONS

WRITING

Ask children to pretend their birthdays are coming up. Have them write a wish list of favorite things that they'd like to receive. Encourage them to include at least one thing whose name begins with /d/ in their lists. Have children compare their completed lists with a partner's list and circle any items that are the same on both lists.

SOCIAL STUDIES

Materials: tape player, dance music from various cultures

Play some lively music and invite children to dance to the beat. If you have children from other cultures in your class, invite them to demonstrate traditional dances. You might consider inviting family members to talk about traditional dances they learned as children. Some may be willing to demonstrate these dances in traditional dress.

 **AstroWord** Phonemic Awareness

AUDITORY LEARNERS

Say these words and have children bark like dogs each time they hear a word that begins with /d/: *daisy, tulip, door, doughnut, bagel, dirt, diamond, table, doll, wagon, lid, ladder, dish.*

CHALLENGE

Working with a partner, give children categories such as toys, animals, or action words. Have them list words beginning with /d/ that belong in each category.

EXTRA SUPPORT/INTERVENTION

Materials: Phonics Picture Cards: daisy (7), dinosaur (8), door (9), tiger (36), turkey (37), tub (68), dog (71), doll (72), desk (79), tent (83)

Display the pictures. Then, invite children to pretend to be ducks going for a walk. To join the duck parade, have each child select a picture whose name begins with /d/ and identify the letter that stands for this sound. See **Daily Phonics Practice, page 309.**

Integrating Phonics and Reading

Shared/Guided Reading
Show the cover as you read the title. Ask children where they think the story takes place, based on the illustration.

First Reading As you come to each animal name that begins with *d*, point to the picture and have children supply the word.

Second Reading Ask children to repeat the initial *d* words. List the words on the board or add them to the classroom Word Wall.

Comprehension
After reading, ask children these questions:
- Who makes the picture on the last page? How? *Recall/Details*
- What kind of picture would you like to make? *Creative/Personal Experience*

ESL/ELL English Language Learners
Point out that the students in the story made pictures of different animals. Then, point to the illustrations and ask questions that can be answered with story words, such as *What did this girl make? What did this boy make?*

Lesson 16 Pages 37–38

The Sound of n

Skill Focus

Children will

★ recognize the sound of *n*.

★ identify pictures whose names begin with the sound of *n*.

★ print the lowercase form of the letter *n* to complete words.

ESL/ELL Some English language learners may have difficulty discriminating between the English sounds of *n* and *l*. Help children differentiate between these sounds by practicing such words as *nine*, *line* and *net*, *let*.

► Teach

Phonemic Awareness: Phoneme Blending
Say the word *no*, separating the individual phonemes: /n/ /ō/. Have children repeat the segmented word and then say the word naturally. Tell children that the sound they hear at the beginning of *no* is the sound of *n*. Repeat with *nap*, *nice*, *neck*, *new*, *nose*. Have children identify the sound at the beginning of each word as /n/.

Sound to Symbol Write the word *no* on the board and have children read it with you, emphasizing the initial sound. Ask them to identify the initial lowercase letter *n*. Next, write the name *Nellie*. Help children read it aloud and identify the uppercase letter. Point out that the *n* in *no* and the *N* in *Nellie* stand for the same sound, /n/. Ask volunteers to underline the letter that stands for the sound of *n* at the beginning of each word. Then, model for children how to write uppercase and lowercase letter *n*.

► Practice and Apply

Phonemic Awareness Read aloud the rhyme on page 37. Have children listen for and name words that begin with the sound of *n*. Write the words on the board.

Sound to Symbol Help children identify the pictures on pages 37 and 38. Suggest that they listen for the beginning sound as they say each picture name. For page 38, remind children to trace the word if they print *n* for the beginning sound.

Reading Use *Nanny Goat's Nap*, MCP Phonics and Reading Consonant Skills Library, Level A, to provide practice in reading words that begin with the sound of *n*.

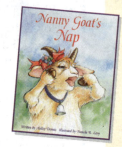

Phonemic Awareness

Name _____

No, no, Nellie.
No, no, Ned.
Do not jump up
On my nice neat bed.

▶ **No** begins with the sound of **n**. **Circle** each picture whose name begins with the sound of **n**.

1. net   2. nail   3. leaf   4. nine
5. nose 6. nest   7. dog   8. nut
9. door 10. needle 11. nurse 12. newspaper

The sound of n: Phonemic awareness   **37**

FOCUS ON ALL LEARNERS

ESL/ELL ENGLISH LANGUAGE LEARNERS

• For page 37, invite volunteers to name the picture clues one at a time. Then, read the directions aloud. Verify comprehension by completing items 1 to 3 together with children. Have them work in pairs to complete items 4 to 12. Review answers aloud.

• Use page 38 to assess children's level of mastery of the letter *n*. Read the directions aloud. Model items 1 and 2 if necessary. Have children complete the activity individually.

VISUAL LEARNERS

Materials: newspapers, scissors, paste, drawing paper

Have each child draw a net. Then, have the child scan the headlines for words containing *Nn*. After cutting out the words and pasting them on the net, have the child circle words he or she can read.

KINESTHETIC LEARNERS

Materials: Phonics Picture Cards: newspaper (26), horse (18), nurse (27), book (3), nuts (65), nails (90), lid (57)

Hold up the picture card for newspaper and say, *newspaper*, /n/. Ask children to pretend to read a newspaper if they hear a picture name that begins with the sound of *n*. Then, hold up the cards one at a time and have volunteers identify each picture name.

Sound to Symbol

Say the name of each picture. If it begins with the sound of n, print n on the line. Then trace the whole word.

1. nest
2. ten
3. nose
4. nut
5. bus
6. nine
7. baby
8. pan
9. nurse
10. mop
11. net
12. nail

38 The sound of n: Sound to symbol

With your child, take turns naming as many words that begin with n as you can.

CURRICULUM CONNECTIONS

WRITING
Talk with children about the purpose of a newspaper. Elicit that newspapers have pictures and articles that tell about things that happen. Work with the class to cooperatively write a news article that describes something that the class has recently done. Duplicate the article and have children add pictures with original captions. Suggest that children take the news article home to share with family members.

FINE ARTS/SOCIAL STUDIES
Materials: burlap or mesh, marker, colorful yarn, blunt needles

Tell children that many years ago, samplers were stitched by children who were learning the alphabet. Distribute large mesh or burlap squares with the letters *Nn* drawn on them in marker. Have children stitch their own *Nn* samplers, using colorful yarn and blunt needles.

TECHNOLOGY AstroWord Phonemic Awareness

AUDITORY LEARNERS
Have children sit in a circle. Then, say these words and ask children to nod each time they hear a word that begins with /n/: nickel, note, bike, lake, no, notice, pat, nice, never, bat, nut, name.

CHALLENGE
Display a nickel and discuss that a nickel is worth five pennies. Using manipulatives, challenge children to figure out how much nine nickels are worth.

EXTRA SUPPORT/INTERVENTION
Materials: index cards; markers; Phonics Picture Cards: newspaper (26), nurse (27), lamp (53), nuts (65), nails (90), nine (99)

Have each child write the letters *Nn* on an index card. Children can take turns displaying a picture and saying its name. Others in the group should display their letter card if the picture name begins with /n/. See **Daily Phonics Practice, page 309.**

Integrating Phonics and Reading

Guided Reading
Show the cover as you read the title. Based on the illustration, ask children to describe the story's main character and predict what might happen to her.

First Reading Have children use the illustrations to point out each animal that Nanny Goat meets and describe its home.

Second Reading Ask children to identify the initial *n* words in the story. List these on the board or add them to the classroom Word Wall.

Comprehension
After reading, ask children the following questions:
- Why is Nanny Goat happy at the end of the story? *Inference/Cause and Effect*
- Where do you like to go to take a nap? Why? *Reflective Analysis/Personal Experience*

ESL/ELL English Language Learners
Explain that a nanny goat is a female goat. Then, encourage children to retell what Nanny Goat did and said, using the words *she* and *her*.

38

Lesson 17 — Pages 39–40

Review Consonants l, d, n

Skill Focus

Children will
- identify pictures whose names begin or end with the sounds of *l*, *d*, and *n*.
- print the initial or final consonant for picture names that begin or end with the sounds of *l*, *d*, and *n*.

Teach

Phonemic Awareness: Phoneme Substitution Remind children that they can sometimes make a new word by changing a word's first letter. Then, present these riddles.

- What word rhymes with *wish* and begins with the sound of *d*? (*dish*)
- What word rhymes with *sock* and begins with the sound of *l*? (*lock*)
- What word rhymes with *shine* and begins with the sound of *n*? (*nine*)

Sound to Symbol Write on the board and have children say the letter names *Ll, Dd, Nn*. Then, point to and name objects in the classroom whose names begin with /l/, /d/, and /n/, such as a light, a desk, a door, and a notebook. Write the words on the board, and ask volunteers to underline the letter that stands for the beginning sound.

Repeat the activity, focusing on ending sounds. Possible objects to use include a curtain, a pencil, a pen, and a card. Write the words on the board and ask volunteers to underline the letter that stands for the ending sound of each word.

Practice and Apply

Sound to Symbol Help children identify the pictures on pages 39 and 40. Point out that they will be listening for beginning and ending sounds as they say the picture names on page 39. For page 40, they will be listening for beginning sounds.

Reading Use *The Party*, MCP Phonics and Reading Consonant Skills Library, Level A, to provide practice in reading words that begin with the sounds of *l*, *d*, and *n*.

FOCUS ON ALL LEARNERS

ESL/ELL ENGLISH LANGUAGE LEARNERS

- Prepare for page 39 by clarifying the difference between beginning and ending sounds. Have children say words like *lid, nod, doll, load, nail, need, led,* and *den*, emphasizing the beginning sound and then identifying the letter that stands for the sound. Repeat, emphasizing the ending sounds.
- Assist children with the activity on page 40. To simplify the picture search, children can talk about the illustration or point to items as you name them.

VISUAL LEARNERS

Materials: Phonic Picture Cards: daisy (7), dinosaur (8), ladder (21), lion (22), nurse (27)

Place the cards face down on a table. Before turning over a card, have the child guess with what letter the picture name begins. If correct, the child keeps the card. If not, the card is turned face down and play passes to the next child.

KINESTHETIC LEARNERS

Have children take turns tracing the letters *Ll, Dd,* and *Nn* on each other's palms for their partners to guess, then take turns giving a word that begins or ends with the letter's sound.

Initial Consonants

Say the names of the pictures in the boxes. Look for these pictures in the big picture. Circle each one. Write the letter of each beginning sound.

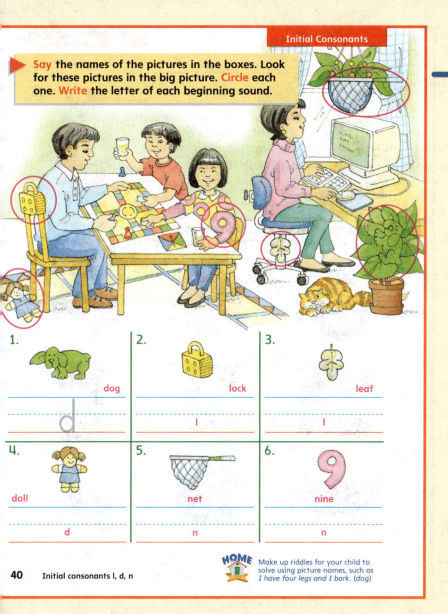

1. dog — d
2. lock — l
3. leaf — l
4. doll — d
5. net — n
6. nine — n

 Make up riddles for your child to solve using picture names, such as *I have four legs and I bark.* (dog)

40 Initial consonants l, d, n

CURRICULUM CONNECTIONS

WRITING
Ask each child to write a short note to tell about a favorite book or story. Invite children to illustrate their notes. Have children get together with partners and read aloud and discuss their book notes.

SCIENCE
Materials: drawing paper, crayons

Point out the picture of the nest on page 39. Then, ask children to scan the other pictures on the page to find the animal that makes its home in a nest. After the bird is identified, talk about other places where animals make their homes. Ask children to look at the pictures on page 39 once more and identify the log as another spot where animals could make their homes. Then, have children draw a large log and show animals that might live there.

TECHNOLOGY — AstroWord Phonemic Awareness

AUDITORY LEARNERS
Read these questions. Have children respond orally and identify the first letter in each answer.
- Is a **leaf** or a **ladder** something you climb?
- Is a **dog** or a **duck** a kind of bird?
- Is **nine** or **ninety** the number before ten?

CHALLENGE
Materials: timer

Have partners set the timer for five minutes and list words or draw pictures whose names begin with the sound of *d*. Repeat for words beginning with the sounds of *n* and *l*. Have children count the words and compare the totals.

EXTRA SUPPORT/INTERVENTION
Materials: used envelopes, marker, discarded magazines, scissors

Print the letters *Ll, Dd, Nn* on each envelope. Have children cut out words and pictures whose names begin with each letter sound and place these words and pictures in the appropriate envelopes. **See Daily Phonics Practice, page 309.**

Integrating Phonics and Reading

Guided Reading
Show the cover as you read the title. Invite children to say who some of the guests at the party will be.

First Reading Have children look at the pictures and point out details, such as balloons, that show the animals are at a party.

Second Reading Have children identify words in the story that begin with the sounds of *l*, *d*, and *n*. List the words under separate headings.

Comprehension
After reading, ask children the following questions:
- What are all the animals except the newts doing? *Recall/Summarize*
- What kinds of things do you like to do at a party? *Reflective Analysis/Personal Experience*

ESL/ELL English Language Learners
Point out the word *But* on page 7. Discuss that this word signals that the newts are doing something different from the rest of the animals.

Lesson 18   Pages 41–42

The Sound of w

> **Skill Focus**
>
> Children will
> * recognize the sound of w.
> * identify pictures whose names begin with the sound of w.
> * print the lowercase form of the letter w to complete words.
>
> **ESL/ELL** Many English language learners will confuse both the sound and the form of w with those of v because w may be an uncommon letter and sound in their native language.

▶ Teach

Phonemic Awareness: Phoneme Categorization Point to a window and have children name it, emphasizing the initial sound. Tell children that the sound they hear at the beginning of *window* is the sound of *w*. Then, say the following groups of words. Ask children to repeat the two words in each group that begin with the sound of *w*.

- lift   win   watch
- wave   safe   well
- fix   wish   wash
- we   bake   woke

Sound to Symbol Write *wind* on the board. Have children read the word with you, emphasizing the initial sound. Ask them to identify the initial lowercase letter *w*. Then, write a child's name beginning with *W* and have children identify the uppercase letter *W*. Point out that the *w* in *wind* and the *W* in the name stand for the same sound, /w/. Ask volunteers to underline the letter that stands for the sound of *w* at the beginning of each word. Then, model for children how to write uppercase and lowercase *w*.

▶ Practice and Apply

Phonemic Awareness Read aloud the rhyme on page 41. Have children listen for and name words that begin with the sound of *w*. Write the words on the board.

Sound to Symbol Help children identify the pictures on pages 41 and 42. Read the directions for both pages with them. Make sure they understand that on page 41 they should circle only the pictures whose names begin with *w*.

Reading Use *Wilma's Wagon*, MCP Phonics and Reading Consonant Skills Library, Level A, to provide practice in reading words that begin with the sound of *w*.

41

Name _____

> We watch from the window
> As winter winds blow.
> We watch from the window,
> And wish it would snow.

▶ **Window** begins with the sound of **w**. **Circle** each picture whose name begins with the sound of **w**.

1. web
2. heart
3. wagon
4. moon
5. wave
6. window
7. watermelon
8. wallet
9. sock

The sound of w: Phonemic awareness   41

FOCUS ON ALL LEARNERS

ESL/ELL ENGLISH LANGUAGE LEARNERS

- Before children begin page 41, practice differentiating /w/ from /v/. Ask children to pronounce these word pairs with you and identify the words that begin with /w/: *vet, wet; wig, vine; well, veil; vest, west; velvet, watch*.

- Before beginning page 42, review the sound of *w* and the picture names. Read the directions aloud and complete items 1 and 2 together. Have children complete items 3 to 9 in pairs, then review answers as a group.

VISUAL LEARNERS

Materials: Phonics Picture Cards: vegetables (38), violin (39), wagon (40), windmill (41), web (84), vase (92), watch (172); masking tape

Draw a large web on the board. Distribute the picture cards and ask children to name the picture on each card. Those holding pictures whose names begin with /w/ can tape them on the web.

KINESTHETIC/AUDITORY LEARNERS

Explain the two meanings of the word *wave*. Then, say these words and have them wave when they hear one that begins with /w/: *wallet, boat, window, wall, bed, kitten, wife, wade, well*.

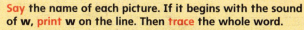

Sound to Symbol

▶ **Say** the name of each picture. If it begins with the sound of **w**, **print w** on the line. Then **trace** the whole word.

1. wagon — w agon
2. heel — eel
3. wing — w ing
4. watch — w atch
5. wave — w ave
6. dog — og
7. key — ey
8. wallet — w allet
9. web — w eb

HOME Ask your child to choose two pictures whose names begin with the sound of *w* and use the words in a sentence.

42 The sound of w: Sound to symbol

CURRICULUM CONNECTIONS

WRITING
Materials: slips of paper, modeling dough, fortune cookie (optional)

Ask children if they have ever eaten fortune cookies. If possible, display one, break it open, and read the fortune. Have children write their own cookie messages that are wishes for good fortune. Suggest they make a "cookie" of modeling dough and fold it with the message inside to exchange with a partner.

SCIENCE
Materials: photos of spiders in their webs, chalk, black construction paper

Display the photos and talk with children about how spiders use webs to catch food. Explain that spiders produce a sticky thread inside their bodies that they use to make their webs. Different spiders spin webs of different designs. Using chalk, have children draw different styles of webs on black paper. Invite them to write or dictate captions for their drawings.

TECHNOLOGY  **AstroWord** Consonant Sounds and Letters

---

AUDITORY LEARNERS
Draw a wishing well and explain that it can only be used for wishes whose names begin with /w/. Share these clues to help children guess each wish.
- something that tells time (*watch*)
- a juicy red fruit (*watermelon*)
- something that holds money (*wallet*)

CHALLENGE
Have children draw a house with six large windows. In each window, have them draw a shade with a picture of something that begins with the sound of *w*. Challenge them to label each picture.

EXTRA SUPPORT/INTERVENTION
Materials: Phonics Picture Cards: vegetables (38), violin (39), wagon (40), windmill (41), web (84), watch (172); self-stick notes

Number the picture cards 1 to 6 with the self-stick notes and have children number their papers. Display the picture cards on the chalkboard ledge, have the picture identified, and have children write *Ww* by the number on their papers if the picture name starts with /w/.

See Daily Phonics Practice, pages 310–311.

Integrating Phonics and Reading

Shared/Guided Reading
Show the cover as you read the title. Have children point out Wilma and tell what she is putting in her wagon.

First Reading Invite children to join in for the exclamations "Wait!" and "Wow!"
Second Reading Ask children to identify the initial *w* words in the story. List the words on the board or add them to the classroom Word Wall.

Comprehension
After reading, ask children the following questions:
- What happens after Wilma and Anna push the wagon up the hill? *Recall/Sequencing*
- What happens after the wagon goes into the water? *Inference/Sequencing*

ESL/ELL English Language Learners
Explain that the apostrophe and *s* in *Wilma's* make the word mean "belonging to Wilma." Then, help children form oral sentences using the possessive form of their names; for example: *This is Maria's book.*

42

Lesson 19 Pages 43–44

The Sound of c

Skill Focus

Children will

★ recognize the sound of c.

★ identify pictures whose names begin with the sound of c.

★ print the lowercase form of the letter c to complete words.

ESL/ELL Native speakers of Asian languages, especially Korean, may not discriminate /k/ from /g/. In Russian, the written Cc is equivalent to the English Ss.

Teach

Phonological Awareness: Blending Onsets and Rimes Tell children that you will say a beginning sound and then the rest of a word: /k/all. Then, model how to blend the parts together to say the whole word: call. Continue by asking children to blend together the following word parts.

- /k/ape   /k/at
- /k/up   /k/oat

Explain that the sound heard at the beginning of each word is the sound of c.

Sound to Symbol
Materials: coat

Put the coat on and say *coat*, then write the word on the board. Have children read it with you, emphasizing the beginning sound. Ask them to identify the initial lowercase letter c. Next, write the name *Carla* on the board and have children identify the uppercase letter C. Pont out that the c in *coat* and the C in *Carla* stand for the same sound, /k/. Ask volunteers to underline the letter that stands for the /k/ sound of c at the beginning of each word. Then, model for children how to write uppercase and lowercase letter c.

Practice and Apply

Phonemic Awareness Read aloud the rhyme on page 43. Have children listen for and name words that begin with the sound of c.

Sound to Symbol Help children identify the pictures on pages 43 and 44. Suggest that they listen for the beginning sound as they say each picture name. For page 44, remind children to trace the word if they print c for the beginning sound.

Reading Use *I Like to Count*, MCP Phonics and Reading Consonant Skills Library, Level A, to provide practice in reading words that begin with the sound of c.

Phonemic Awareness

Name_____

Carla has a cape.
She's carrying a cane.
Cory has her dad's coat
To play a dress-up game.

▶ **Cape** begins with the sound of c. **Circle** each picture whose name begins with the sound of c.

1. cat   2. cone   3. duck
4. heart   5. can   6. cup
7. cake   8. coat   9. game

The sound of c: Phonemic awareness   43

FOCUS ON ALL LEARNERS

ESL/ELL ENGLISH LANGUAGE LEARNERS
Materials: index cards, small self-stick notes

- Adapt page 43 to provide additional practice with the sound of c. Write the words *cat, cone, can, cup, cake, coat* on index cards. As you hold up each word card, say the word and have children repeat it. Then, ask children to cover the matching picture clue on their papers with the self-stick notes. When you have reviewed all the words with children, have them remove the notes. Then, read the directions aloud and have children complete the page individually.

- Review the picture names on page 44 as a group. Read the directions aloud and complete items 1 and 2 together. Then, have children of varying proficiency levels work in pairs to complete the activity. Review the answers together.

VISUAL LEARNERS GROUPS
Materials: drawing paper, crayons, discarded magazines, scissors, paste

Have children draw a picture of a car. Then, have them cut out pictures of things they might see on a car trip whose names begin with /k/. Have them paste the pictures around the car.

43

Sound to Symbol

Say the name of each picture. If it begins with the sound of **c**, **print** c on the line. Then **trace** the whole word.

1. can
2. cap
3. watch
4. cane
5. dog
6. cake
7. cow
8. car
9. cup
10. cage
11. gum
12. comb

Ask your child to pick three words from the page that begin with c, then draw a picture showing them.

44 The sound of c: Sound to symbol

CURRICULUM CONNECTIONS

WRITING
Materials: drawing paper, crayons

Have children write a note to a family member, asking to borrow something to use when playing dress-up. Suggest that they illustrate their notes with a picture showing how they might look when dressed up.

SCIENCE
Materials: pictures showing the stages of moth or butterfly metamorphosis

Display the picture of a caterpillar and have children identify it. Ask children if they know what a caterpillar becomes. Display and discuss the pictures showing the process of metamorphosis. Then, have children create their own sequence of drawings showing eggs, a caterpillar, a cocoon or chrysalis, and a moth or butterfly. If possible, purchase a butterfly kit from a science supply house and allow children to observe this transformation process.

TECHNOLOGY **AstroWord** Consonant Sounds and Letters

AUDITORY LEARNERS
Say these food names and have children clap each time they hear a food name that begins with /k/: *carrots, cake, apples, cauliflower, cupcakes, corn, beans, sandwich, caramels, cookies.*

CHALLENGE
Explain that the letter *c* can have two sounds. Write *cat* and *city* on the board. Read them aloud and have children identify the two sounds of *c* as /k/ and /s/. Repeat the procedure with these words: *coat, circle, cow, cap, circus, cent, cave, cook, cell.*

EXTRA SUPPORT/INTERVENTION
Materials: Phonics Picture Cards: car (5), cookies (6), girls (13), goose (15), cap (48), cat (49), cup (63), cake (86); paper bag, marker

Decorate the bag to look like a cookie jar. Display each picture card and ask a volunteer to say the picture name. Have a child place the card in the cookie jar if the picture name begins with /k/. **See Daily Phonics Practice, pages 310–311.**

Integrating Phonics and Reading

Shared/Guided Reading
Show the cover as you read the title. Ask children what is on the girl's T-shirt. Then, have them look at the pictures in the border and name some things she might count.

First Reading As you read each page, point to the object illustrated at the top and have children supply the word.

Second Reading Ask children to identify the initial *c* words in the story. List the words on the board or add them to the classroom Word Wall.

Comprehension
After reading, ask children the following questions:
- What does the girl in the story like to do? *Recall/Summarize*
- What is one thing she never counts? Why? *Inference/Cause and Effect*

ESL/ELL **English Language Learners**
Have children count from one to ten. Then, have them use each number word in a sentence, for example: *I have one sister.*

Lesson 20

Pages 45–46

The Sound of r

Skill Focus

Children will

★ recognize the sound of *r*.

★ identify pictures whose names begin with the sound of *r*.

★ print the lowercase form of the letter *r* to complete words.

ESL/ELL Spanish and Tagalog speakers might trill initial *r* or pronounce "tap *r*" (similar to *tt* in *better*). Native speakers of languages such as Vietnamese, Hmong, Korean, and Cantonese may confuse /r/ and /l/.

Teach

Phonemic Awareness: Phoneme Identity
Tell children that you will say a sentence for them to repeat after you. Then say: *Rushing rivers run rapidly*. Ask children what is the same about all the words in the sentence. (All begin with the same sound, /r/.) Explain that the sound heard at the beginning of each word in the sentence is the sound of *r*. Then, tell children you will say part of a sentence. Ask them to finish it with a word that begins with /r/. Use this sentence: *Rita's robot repairs _____*.

Sound to Symbol Write *red* on the board. Have children repeat the word with you, emphasizing the initial sound. Ask them to identify the initial lowercase letter *r*. Then, write a child's name beginning with *R* and have children identify the uppercase letter *R*. Point out that the *r* in *red* and the *R* in the name stand for the same sound. Ask volunteers to underline the letter that stands for the sound of *r* at the beginning of each word. Then, model for children how to write uppercase and lowercase letter *r*.

Practice and Apply

Phonemic Awareness Read aloud the rhyme on page 45. Have children listen for and name words that begin with the sound of *r*. Write the words on the board.

Sound to Symbol Help children identify the pictures on pages 45 and 46. Read the directions for both pages with them. Make sure they understand that on page 45 they should circle only the pictures whose names begin with *r*.

Reading Use *Who Is Ready?*, MCP Phonics and Reading Consonant Skills Library, Level A, to provide practice in reading words that begin with the sound of *r*.

Name _____

The roses are red.
The ribbon is, too.
I ran over to bring
These red roses to you.

▶ *Roses* begins with the sound of **r**. Circle each picture whose name begins with the sound of **r**.

1. rake
2. robot
3. rat
4. kite
5. cup
6. rain
7. jack-in-the-box
8. radio
9. ring

The sound of r: Phonemic awareness **45**

FOCUS ON ALL LEARNERS

ESL/ELL ENGLISH LANGUAGE LEARNERS

• Before children begin page 45, practice the sound of *r*. Say the following words one at a time: *row, red, lake, rake, radio, rat, wet, rabbit, wing, ring, rain, star, ribbon, let, rug*. Ask children to stand when they hear a word that begins with the sound of *r*.

• You may wish to work with individual children to model the sound of *r*, using the picture clues on page 46. Point to a clue and have the child name the object. Model the sound of *r* as needed, having children watch the way your mouth looks while producing the sound.

VISUAL LEARNERS

Materials: discarded catalogs or magazines, scissors, ribbon, paste

Have each child cut out pictures of objects whose names begin with /r/ and paste them on lengths of ribbon to make "Ribbons of *r*'s."

KINESTHETIC LEARNERS

Have children join hands and act out the nursery rhyme "Ring Around the Rosie." After they've all fallen down, go around the circle and ask each child to stand and say a word that begins with /r/ like *ring* and *rosie*.

Sound to Symbol

▶ **Say** the name of each picture. If it begins with the sound of **r**, **print r** on the line. Then **trace** the whole word.

1. ring
2. lake
3. rip
4. rat
5. cat
6. ten
7. radio
8. lips
9. rain
10. rug
11. rake
12. web

 Point to the ring picture and ask your child, *What rhymes with king?* Repeat with rhymes for *rip*, *rat*, and *rug*.

46 The sound of r: Sound to symbol

CURRICULUM CONNECTIONS

WRITING
Materials: bottle-shaped cutouts

Distribute the bottle cutouts and have children write a short message on their bottles telling where they would row in a red rowboat. Have them toss their bottles into a paper bag. Then, pass the bag around and have each child select a bottle and read the message.

MATH
Materials: manipulatives

Ask children to make up word problems about red roses, for example: *If I have 5 red roses and Ben gives me 2 more, how many red roses do I have in all?* Children can use the manipulatives to check their answers.

 **AstroWord** Consonant Sounds and Letters

AUDITORY LEARNERS
Show children how to make a rainbow by arching their arms above their heads. Then, say these words and have children make the rainbow sign when they hear a word that begins with /r/: *robot, rabbit, juggler, rose, windmill, ribbon, lake, rake, rug, look, run, ruler.*

CHALLENGE
Have children look at the pictures on pages 45 and 46. Challenge them to come up with rhyming words to describe some of the pictures; for example: *fat rat, Jake's rake, snug rug.*

EXTRA SUPPORT/INTERVENTION
Materials: Phonics Picture Cards: ladder (21), lion (22), moon (25), ribbon (31), rooster (32), lamp (53), run (66), rake (91), ruler (104)

Display the cards on the chalkboard ledge. Then, invite children to walk like robots. Have them walk to the board, select a picture, and say the picture name in a robot voice. Have them raise up the picture if it begins with /r/. **See Daily Phonics Practice, pages 310–311.**

Integrating Phonics and Reading

Shared/Guided Reading
Show the cover as you read the title. Ask children what time of day they think it might be and where they think the bus is going.

First Reading Invite children to join in each time this sentence appears: *Robert is not.*
Second Reading Ask children to identify the initial *r* words. List the words on the board or add them to the classroom Word Wall.

Comprehension
After reading, ask children the following questions:
- Where is the bus taking the children? *Inference/Setting*
- Were you ever late for a bus? What happened? *Reflective Analysis/Personal Experience*

ESL/ELL English Language Learners
Help children to find three different punctuation marks in the story (period, question mark, exclamation point). Have them repeat story sentences after you that demonstrate how to read each punctuation mark.

Lesson 21
Pages 47–48

The Sound of p

Skill Focus

Children will

★ recognize the sound of *p*.

★ identify pictures whose names begin with the sound of *p*.

★ print the lowercase form of the letter *p* to complete words.

ESL/ELL Speakers of Korean may confuse initial /p/ with /b/; practice *pig, big; pie, bye,* and *pat, bat*. Other English language learners may confuse /p/ with /f/ or /v/; practice *pine, fine, vine; pan, fan, van*.

Teach

Phonemic Awareness: Phoneme Substitution Say the word *tie*. Then, tell children that they can change the first letter of *tie* to make a new word: *pie*. Point out that *pie* begins with the sound of *p*, and have children say the word. Next, have children change the first letters of these words to make more words that begin with the sound of *p*: *hot, can, niece, last, cat, day*.

Sound to Symbol On the board, draw a circle divided into eight sections and tell children that it is a peach pie. Write the word *pie* and have children read it with you, emphasizing the beginning sound. Ask them to identify the initial lowercase letter *p*. Then, write the name *Penny* and have children identify the uppercase letter *P*. Point out that the *p* in *pie* and the *P* in *Penny* stand for the same sound, /p/. Ask volunteers to underline the letter that stands for the sound of *p* at the beginning of each word. Then, model for children how to write uppercase and lowercase letter *p*.

Practice and Apply

Phonemic Awareness Read aloud the rhyme on page 47. Have children listen for and name words that begin with the sound of *p*. Write the words on the board.

Sound to Symbol Help children identify the pictures on pages 47 and 48. After they have completed the pages, encourage them to name some words beginning with the letter *p*.

Reading Use *Pat's Perfect Pizza*, MCP Phonics and Reading Consonant Skills Library, Level A, to provide practice in reading words that begin with the sound of *p*.

Phonemic Awareness

Name _____

Penny passed the peach pie,
Peach pie, peach pie.
Penny passed the peach pie,
Till not a piece was left.

▶ **Peach** begins with the sound of **p**. **Circle** each picture whose name begins with the sound of **p**.

1. pig
2. pie
3. bird
4. pot
5. pen
6. puppet
7. mouse
8. pillow
9. purse

The sound of p: Phonemic awareness   47

FOCUS ON ALL LEARNERS

ESL/ELL ENGLISH LANGUAGE LEARNERS
Materials: pennies

• You may use the picture clues on page 47 to model the sound of *p*. Point to the picture clue for one of the words beginning with *p*. Help children name the object, then make the initial consonant sound. Ask children to watch how you position your lips as they pronounce the *p*. You may wish to complete the page aloud as a group.

• Hand out several pennies to each child. Say the name of one of the pictures on page 48 whose name begins with the sound of *p*. Instruct children to cover the picture with a penny. After practicing a few more words in this way, read the directions aloud. Have children complete the page individually.

VISUAL LEARNERS *INDIVIDUAL*
Materials: drawing paper, crayons

Have each child draw an outline of a large purse. Then, have him or her draw things inside the purse whose names begin with the same sound as *purse*.

Sound to Symbol

Say the name of each picture. If it begins with the sound of **p**, print **p** on the line. Then trace the whole word.

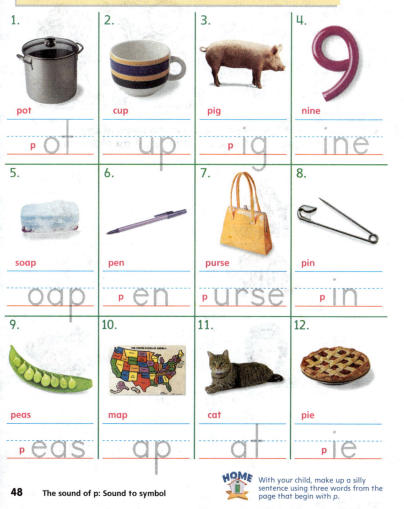

1. pot — p ot
2. cup — _ up
3. pig — p ig
4. nine — _ ine
5. soap — _ oap
6. pen — p en
7. purse — p urse
8. pin — p in
9. peas — p eas
10. map — _ ap
11. cat — _ at
12. pie — p ie

 With your child, make up a silly sentence using three words from the page that begin with *p*.

48   The sound of p: Sound to symbol

CURRICULUM CONNECTIONS

WRITING

Materials: drawing paper, crayons

Ask children who have pets to tell how they care for them. Use their suggestions to make a list of things that must be done for pets, such as feeding, cleaning, brushing, and petting them. Invite each child to select a pet that he or she would like to have. Show children how to fold their paper to make a booklet. Then, have them draw pictures and write a sentence telling how they would care for their pet.

SCIENCE

Materials: popcorn, hot plate, pan, napkins

Display some unpopped popcorn and have children describe the kernels. Then as children observe, pop the corn. Invite them to describe what they see, hear, and smell. As children enjoy the popcorn, ask them why they think the corn pops. Children may be interested to learn that the popcorn kernels contain moisture. When the kernels get hot, the moisture expands; this causes the kernels to explode, or pop.

 **AstroWord** Consonant Sounds and Letters

AUDITORY LEARNERS

Recite some nursery rhymes such as "Pease Porridge Hot," "Peter, Peter, Pumpkin Eater," and "Polly Put the Kettle On." Ask children to raise their hands each time they hear a word that begins with /p/.

CHALLENGE

Teach children the tongue twister "Peter Piper." Review the words with them and have them repeat it several times. Challenge them to count the uppercase and lowercase *Pp*'s in the first sentence. Some may be able to count the number in the entire rhyme.

EXTRA SUPPORT/INTERVENTION

Materials: Phonics Picture Cards: basket (2), book (3), fan (10), fork (11), pillow (28), popcorn (29), pig (59), pie (100)

Draw a large pizza on the board and divide it into slices. Tape a picture in each slice and have children say its name. If it begins with /p/, have a volunteer write the letters *Pp* on the slice. **See Daily Phonics Practice, pages 310–311.**

Integrating Phonics and Reading

Guided Reading
Show the cover as you read the title. Ask children to look closely at the illustration and tell what toppings they see on the pizza.

First Reading Have children use the illustrations to point out each topping Pat is adding to her pizza.

Second Reading Ask children to identify the initial *p* words in the story. List the words on the board or add them to the classroom Word Wall.

Comprehension
After reading, ask children the following questions:
- What does Pat put in the pizza pan? *Recall/Details*
- Do you think Pat's pizza is perfect? Why or why not? *Reflective Analysis/Details*

ESL/ELL English Language Learners
Have children list the silly toppings Pat put on her pizza. Then say, *Pat puts ___ in the pan.* Ask children to finish the sentence with story words.

48

Lesson 22
Pages 49–50

The Sound of qu and the Sound of v

Skill Focus

Children will

★ recognize the sounds of qu and v.

★ identify pictures whose names begin with the sounds of qu and v.

★ print the uppercase and lowercase forms of the letters q and v.

ESL/ELL Native speakers of Spanish may pronounce qu like /k/ instead of /kw/. Practice with *queen, key; quarter, kangaroo;* and *quiet, kite.* Spanish speakers may also pronounce /v/ as /b/.

Teach

Phonemic Awareness: Phoneme Blending

Say the word *quack*, separating the individual phonemes: /kw/ /a/ /k/. Have children repeat the segmented word and then say the word naturally. Tell children that the sound they hear at the beginning of *quack* is the sound of *qu*. Then, help them think of other words that begin with this sound, for example, *queen, quilt, quite*. Repeat the procedure for the sound of *v*, using the segmented word /v/ /ī/ /n/, *vine*.

Sound to Symbol Write *q*uack and *Q*uinn on the board. Help children read the words with you, emphasizing the beginning sound. Then, underline *qu* in *quack* and *Qu* in *Quinn*. Explain that the letter *q* is usually followed by the letter *u* in words and together they make the sound of /kw/. Help children identify the partner letters *Qq*, and model how to write uppercase and lowercase *Qq*.

Next, write *valentine* and *Viv* on the board. Say each word and have children repeat it, emphasizing the initial sound. Ask children to identify the initial lowercase letter *v* in *valentine* and the uppercase *V* in *Viv*. Underline the letters and explain that they stand for the same sound, /v/. Then, model for children how to write uppercase and lowercase letter *v*.

Practice and Apply

Phonemic Awareness Read aloud the rhymes on pages 49 and 50. Have children listen for and name words that begin with the sound of *qu* and the sound of *v*. Write the words on the board.

Sound to Symbol Help children identify the pictures on pages 49 and 50. Read the directions for both pages with them. Make sure children understand that they should only print the letters on the line if a picture name begins with the sound of that letter.

Reading Use *Quack!*, MCP Phonics and Reading Consonant Skills Library, Level A, to provide practice in reading words that begin with the sound of *qu*.

49

Sound to Symbol

Name _____

Quinn's toy duck said,
"Quack, quack, quack!"
"Quiet!" said Quincy.
But the duck quacked back!

Quack begins with the sound of **qu**. **Say** the name of each picture. If it begins with the sound of **qu**, **print qu** on the line.

1. queen
2. purse
3. fish
4. qu — question mark
5. qu — quiet
6. qu — quilt
7. pencil
8. qu — quarter

The sound of qu: Sound to symbol **49**

FOCUS ON ALL LEARNERS

ESL/ELL ENGLISH LANGUAGE LEARNERS

Materials: letter cards *Qq, Vv*

- Before children begin page 49, practice differentiating /kw/ from /k/. Say these words and have children hold up their *Qq* letter cards when they hear a word that begins with *qu*: *kick, quick, quiet, cat, kite, queen, kit, quit*.

- Before beginning page 50, have children practice differentiating /v/ from /b/. Say these words and have children hold up their *Vv* letter cards when they hear a word that begins with *v*: *valentine, batter, vest, best, vegetable, banana, bed, very*.

VISUAL LEARNERS *INDIVIDUAL*

Materials: drawing paper, crayons, tape

Give each child two sheets of drawing paper. Have the child draw on one sheet pictures whose names begin with /kw/ and on the other sheet pictures whose names begin with /v/. Assemble pictures from everyone in the class to form *q* and *v* quilts for display.

Sound to Symbol

Viv has a valentine.
Val has one, too.
Vic makes a valentine
To give to you.

▶ **Valentine** begins with the sound of **v**. Say the name of each picture. If it begins with the sound of **v**, print **Vv** on the line.

1. vase — Vv
2. cake —
3. vest — Vv
4. volcano — Vv
5. question mark —
6. vegetables — Vv
7. van — Vv
8. pillow —
9. valentine — Vv
10. vine — Vv
11. vacuum — Vv
12. pot —

50 The sound of v: Sound to symbol

HOME With your child, make up a story using some of the words from the page that begin with *v*.

CURRICULUM CONNECTIONS

WRITING
Materials: construction paper, crayons

Invite children to share what they know about Valentine's Day. Discuss that this is a day when we tell friends that we care about them. Assign each child a partner in the class. Have children make a friendship card to send to their partners. The card should include a message that tells something special about the friend.

FINE ARTS
Materials: paper bags, crayons, scraps of fabric, glue, scissors

Talk with children about how quilts are made. Point out that quilts are a good way to recycle old clothing. Children can make quilted vests out of paper bags, crayons, and scraps of fabric. Help them cut neckholes and armholes and open the front of the bags to make their vests. Then, have them glue on fabric patches to decorate their vests. Consider holding a fashion show in which children model their quilted creations.

TECHNOLOGY AstroWord Consonant Sounds and Letters

AUDITORY/KINESTHETIC LEARNERS
Say these words and have children make a V sign with their fingers whenever they hear a word that begins with /v/: *vacuum, velvet, juice, wagon, vase, violets, village, wax, volcano, vest.*

CHALLENGE
Show children the symbol for a question mark and explain that it is used at the end of a sentence to indicate a question. Have children write a question for a partner to answer.

EXTRA SUPPORT/INTERVENTION
Materials: Phonics Picture Cards: queen (30), vegetables (38), violin (39), wagon (40), windmill (41), vase (92), watch (172)

Display the picture cards on the chalkboard ledge. Then, write *Qq* and *Vv* in two columns on the board. Have children say each picture name and place the card under the letter that stands for the beginning sound or off to the side if it belongs to neither group. **See Daily Phonics Practice, pages 310–311.**

Integrating Phonics and Reading

Shared/Guided Reading
Show the cover as you read the title. Ask children to identify the animals in the illustration and imitate the sound they make.

First Reading As you read, invite children to join in as you come to each initial *q* word.

Second Reading Ask children to repeat the initial *q* words in the story. List these on the board or add them to the classroom Word Wall.

Comprehension
After reading, ask children the following questions:
- Who is watching the ducks as they play in the grass? *Recall/Details*
- Who tells the little ducks to "swim here to me"? *Inference/Character*

ESL/ELL English Language Learners
Ask children to show you how they can be *quiet* and *quick*. Encourage them to use the words *quiet* and *quick* to describe their actions.

50

Lesson 23

Pages 51–52

Review Consonants w, c, r, p, q, v

Skill Focus

Children will

★ identify pictures whose names begin or end with the sounds of w, c, r, p, q, and v.

★ print the initial or final consonant for picture names that begin or end with the sounds of w, c, r, p, q, and v.

Teach

Phonemic Awareness: Phoneme Categorization Say these groups of words and ask children to identify the word that does not contain the same beginning consonant sound.

- rain   rice   wake
- quite   cat   comb
- pie   pipe   vine
- win   pop   west
- quilt   quiet   kite
- van   sun   vain

Sound to Symbol

Materials: letter cards *Ww, Cc, Rr, Pp, Qq, Vv*

Ask six children to hold up the letter cards. Go around the class and ask each child to say a word that begins with the sound represented by one of the letters. Next, say these words: *pour, camp, rap, pop, quarter, vinegar*. Have children point to the letter cards that stand for the beginning and ending sound of each word. Then, write each word on the board. Have volunteers underline the letters that stand for the beginning and ending sounds.

Practice and Apply

Sound to Symbol Help children identify the pictures on page 51. Point out that they will be listening for beginning and ending sounds as they say the picture names. Read aloud the directions for page 52. Make sure children understand that they will read the letters inside the box from top to bottom to find the secret message.

Reading Use *Night Animals*, MCP Phonics and Reading Consonant Skills Library, Level A, to provide practice in reading words that begin with the sounds of *c* and *r*.

Initial/Final Consonants

Name_____

Say the name of each picture. Print the letter for its beginning sound on the first line. Then print the letter for its ending sound on the second line.

1. rain — r n	2. cup — c p	3. pin — p n	4. quarter — q r
5. car — c r	6. wagon — w n	7. vacuum — v m	8. rip — r p
9. quilt — q t	10. van — v n	11. web — w b	12. pot — p t

Initial/final consonants w, c, r, p, q, v   51

FOCUS ON ALL LEARNERS

ESL/ELL ENGLISH LANGUAGE LEARNERS

Materials: Phonics Picture Cards: camel (4), popcorn (29), wagon (40), rooster (32), queen (30), vegetables (38), car (5), mop (73)

- Write the letters *w, c, r, p, q,* and *v* on the board. Write *r* and *p* twice (in two columns): once as an initial consonant and once in the final position. Then, hold up each picture card. Ask volunteers to name the objects and their beginning sound. For *car* and *mop*, ask children to name the ending sound. Add each word to the appropriate column and have volunteers underline the target letters.

- Have children work in pairs or small groups to complete the puzzle on page 52. Help them identify the pictures before they begin. If children have difficulty reading the secret message vertically, rewrite the message for them from left to right.

KINESTHETIC LEARNERS

Materials: butcher paper, marker

Draw six lily pads and print one set of these partner letters on each: *Ww, Cc, Rr, Pp, Qq, Vv*. Have children pretend to be frogs. As they hop on each pad, have them give a word that begins or ends with each letter sound.

Initial/Final Consonants

▶ Say each picture name. Write the word that names each picture. What is the secret message?

1. h o p
2. c a r
3. v a n
4. w e b
5. f i v e
6. q u e e n
7. n e t

HOME Ask your child what the secret message is.

52 Initial/final consonants w, c, r, p, q, v

CURRICULUM CONNECTIONS

WRITING
Materials: construction-paper strips, crayons, paste

Write the letters *w, c, r, p, q,* and *v* on the board and explain to children that they will make sentence chains. Have them work with a partner to make up a sentence with at least one word that begins with a letter on the chalkboard. Have them write one word from the sentence on each strip. Then, have them paste the strips together to form a sentence chain. Have children exchange chains with another pair and talk about the sentences they have written.

MATH
Materials: counters

Using the pictures on pages 51 and 52, have children make up simple oral math problems to share with a partner. For example:

I saw 1 red van.

Tom saw 3 blue vans.

How many more vans did Tom see?

Have partners take turns solving each other's problems by using counters or other manipulatives.

TECHNOLOGY AstroWord Consonant Sounds and Letters

Integrating Phonics and Reading

Guided Reading
Show the cover as you read the title. Explain that night animals are animals that come out at night. Invite children to discuss any night animals they know about.

First Reading Point to the picture of each night animal, and have children supply the name.

Second Reading Have children identify words in the story that begin with the sounds of *c* and *r*. List the words on the board.

Comprehension
After reading, ask children these questions:
- What night animals does the girl read about? *Recall/Summarize*
- How is the girl different from the night animals? *Recall/Comparison*

ESL/ELL English Language Learners
Encourage children to complete each of these sentence frames in different ways: I ___ at night. I ___ during the day. For example: *I eat dinner at night. I eat lunch during the day.*

AUDITORY LEARNERS GROUPS
Materials: Phonics Picture Cards: camel (4), car (5), pillow (28), popcorn (29), ribbon (31), rooster (32), vegetables (38), violin (39), wagon (40), windmill (41)

Place the cards face down on a table. Have children take turns turning over two cards. If the picture names begin with the same sound, the child may keep the cards.

CHALLENGE
Materials: drawing paper, crayons

Have children draw pictures of people or foods whose names begin with *w, c, r, p, q,* or *v*. Help them label the pictures.

EXTRA SUPPORT/INTERVENTION

Write *w, c, r, p, q, v* on the board. Then, say and write these words, leaving off the first letter. Have children supply the missing letter: *pan (can, ran, van), violin, wet (pet), quarter, cup (pup).* See Daily Phonics Practice, pages 310–311.

Lesson 24   Pages 53–54

The Sound of x and the Sound of y

Skill Focus

Children will

★ recognize the sounds of *x* and *y*.

★ identify pictures whose names end with the sound of *x* and *y*.

★ print the uppercase and lowercase forms of the letters *x* and *y*.

ESL/ELL Native speakers of Spanish may need extra pronunciation practice with the sound of *x*. Children who speak Spanish or Tagalog may pronounce initial /y/ like *g* in *genre* or like *j* in *joy*. Those who speak Cambodian or Vietnamese may pronounce it like *ny* in *canyon*.

Teach

Phonological Awareness: Blending Word Parts Tell children that you will say the beginning sound and then the rest of a word: /fi/ks/. Then, model how to blend the parts together to say the whole word: *fix*. Explain that the sound heard at the end of *fix* is the sound of *x*. Then, ask children to blend together the following word parts: /si/ks/, /o/ks/, /a/ks/.

Follow the same procedure for /y/es, calling children's attention to the sound of *y* at the beginning of each word. Ask children to blend together these word parts: /y/ard, /y/ellow, /y/ell.

Sound to Symbol Draw a box and write *box* on the board. Have children read the word with you, emphasizing the ending sound. Help children identify the letter *x* and explain that this letter stands for the sound of *x*. Then, model for children how to write uppercase and lowercase letter *x*. Repeat, yawning as you write *yawn* on the board. Identify the *y* as the /y/ sound, and model for children how to write uppercase and lowercase letter *y*.

Practice and Apply

Phonemic Awareness Read aloud the rhymes on pages 53 and 54. Have children listen for and name words that end with the sound of *x* and begin with the sound of *y*. Write the words on the board.

Sound to Symbol Help children identify the pictures on pages 53 and 54. Remind them to write the partner letters only if the word ends with the sound of *x* (page 53) or begins with the sound of *y* (page 54).

Reading Use *Fix It, Fox*, MCP Phonics and Reading Consonant Skills Library, Level A, to provide practice in reading words that end with the sound of *x*.

Sound to Symbol

Name _____

Will Foxie Fox and Oxie Ox
Fit inside our big toy box?
Mix things up and push and pull.
Fox and Ox make the toy box full!

▶ *Box* ends with the sound of **x**. **Say** the name of each picture. If it ends with the sound of **x**, print **Xx** on the line.

1. box — Xx	2. ball	3. ax — Xx
4. top	5. six — Xx	6. fox — Xx
7. cow	8. star	9. ox — Xx

The sound of x: Sound to symbol   53

FOCUS ON ALL LEARNERS

ESL/ELL ENGLISH LANGUAGE LEARNERS

• Have children practice final consonant sounds before they begin page 53. Say these sentences and ask children to repeat them, placing emphasis on the final sounds: *The fox is in the box. The ox will pull the box. I will mix for six minutes.*

• Before beginning page 54, have children practice differentiating /y/ from /j/. Say these words and have children clap when they hear a word that begins with *y*: *yet, yak, joy, yell, June, judge, yellow, yes.*

VISUAL LEARNERS   GROUPS

Materials: box, yogurt container, marker, discarded magazines, scissors

Label the box *Xx* and the yogurt container *Yy*. Ask children to cut out pictures whose names end with the sound /ks/ and pictures whose names begin with the sound /y/. Invite children to share their pictures as they put them in the containers.

Sound to Symbol

Yesterday I went shopping
With my Grandma Lin.
I got a yellow yo-yo.
You can watch it spin.

▶ **Yo-yo** begins with the sound of **y**. **Say** the name of each picture. If it begins with the sound of **y**, print **Yy** on the line.

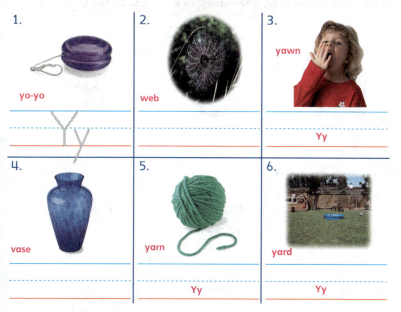

1. yo-yo
2. web
3. yawn — Yy
4. vase
5. yarn — Yy
6. yard — Yy

 Say, "In my yard, I have a ___." Ask your child to finish the sentence with words that begin with *y*.

54 The sound of y: Sound to symbol

CURRICULUM CONNECTIONS

WRITING
Invite children to pretend that the letter *x* can talk. Ask them to think about how letter *x* feels to usually be found at the end of a word. Have children work with a partner to write a question to ask the letter *x*. Then, have them write *x*'s answer. Have the pair read aloud their question and answer.

FINE ARTS
Materials: yarn, glue, fabric or paper squares

Introduce the term *tapestry* and explain that tapestries are created by stitching or embroidering with colored yarn or thread on cloth. Using yarn and glue, children can create their own tapestry pictures on cloth or paper squares. Some may even wish to work the letters *x* and *y* into their designs.

TECHNOLOGY AstroWord Consonant Sounds and Letters

AUDITORY LEARNERS
Say these words and have children use their arms and legs to form *X* and *Y* to represent the ending or beginning sounds: *fox, yellow, yard, ox, six, yes, mix, yell, yawn, yesterday.*

CHALLENGE
Invite partners to make up nonsense rhymes to share with the class. Have them see how many of these word pairs they can include in their rhymes: *six, mix; ox, fox; ax, wax; yarn, barn; yell, fell; you, too.*

EXTRA SUPPORT/INTERVENTION
Materials: Phonics Picture Cards: yo-yo (42), ax (46), box (70), ox (74); index cards; markers

Have children write the letters *Xx* and *Yy* on index cards. Place the picture cards face up on a table. Have children say each picture name and place the letter card that stands for the beginning or ending sound on the picture. **See Daily Phonics Practice, page 311.**

Integrating Phonics and Reading

Guided Reading
Show the cover as you read the title. Help children read the signs in the illustration. Ask where they think the story will take place.

First Reading Invite children to use the illustrations to tell what they think is wrong with the items Fox is asked to fix.

Second Reading Ask children to identify the words ending in *x* in the story. List these on the board or add them to the classroom Word Wall.

Comprehension
After reading, ask children these questions:
- How does Fox feel about having so many things to fix? *Inference/Character*
- Why does Fox change the name of his shop? *Inference/Cause and Effect*

ESL/ELL English Language Learners
List and review the objects that fox and his friends fixed. Then, ask children to use the list and the pictures to complete sentences as you say, *Pig asked Fox to fix the ___* (pot), *Mouse asked Fox to fix the ___* (pan), and so on.

54

Lesson 25   Pages 55–56

The Sound of z and Review Consonants x, y, z

Skill Focus

Children will

★ recognize the sound of z.

★ identify pictures whose names begin with the sound of z.

★ print the uppercase and lowercase forms of the letter z.

★ print the initial or final consonant for picture names that begin or end with the sounds of x, y, and z.

ESL/ELL Speakers of Spanish, Tagalog, Korean, or Hmong may not distinguish /z/ from /s/. Practice with words such as *zip, sip*.

Teach

Phonemic Awareness: Phoneme Categorization Write and say *zoo* and have children repeat the word several times. Explain that the sound heard at the beginning of *zoo* is the sound of *z*. Then, say these words. Ask children to repeat the two words that begin with the sound of *z*.

- zero   yes   zap
- zone   zip   sit
- zigzag   zipper   scissors

Sound to Symbol Write *zoo* on the board. Have children repeat the word with you, emphasizing the initial sound. Ask them to identify the initial lowercase letter *z*. Then, write the name *Zelda* and have children identify the uppercase letter *Z*. Point out that the *z* in *zoo* and the *Z* in *Zelda* stand for the same sound, /z/. Ask volunteers to underline the letter that stands for the sound of *z* at the beginning of each word. Then, model for children how to write uppercase and lowercase *z*.

Practice and Apply

Phonemic Awareness Read aloud the rhyme on page 55. Have children name words that begin with /z/. Write the words on the board.

Sound to Symbol Help children identify the pictures on pages 53 and 54. Make sure children understand that for page 53, they will listen for the beginning sound of the word. For page 54, they will listen for the sounds of *x*, *y*, or *z* at the beginning or ending of each word.

Reading Use *At the Zoo*, MCP Phonics and Reading Consonant Skills Library, Level A, to provide practice in reading words that end with the sound of *x* and words that begin with the sound of *z*.

55

Sound to Symbol

Name _____

Zelda and Zena
Went to the zoo.
There they saw zebras
And lions, too.

▶ **Zoo** begins with the sound of z. **Say** the name of each picture. If it begins with the sound of z, **print** Zz on the line.

1. zebra	2. zero	3. sun
Zz	Zz	

4. zoo	5. nest	6. zigzag
Zz		Zz

The sound of z: Sound to symbol   55

FOCUS ON ALL LEARNERS

ESL/ELL ENGLISH LANGUAGE LEARNERS

Materials: Phonics Picture Cards: yo-yo (42), zebra (43), zipper (44), ax (46), six (60), box (70); letter cards *Xx, Yy, Zz*

- Before children begin page 55, practice differentiating /z/ from /s/. Have children repeat these words, raising their hands when they hear a word that begins with z: *zing, sing, sap, zap, zero, so, sip, zip*.

- To prepare children for the activity on page 56, place the letter cards face up in front of children. Then, hold up each picture card. Have a volunteer identify the letter sound with which the word begins or ends.

VISUAL LEARNERS

Materials: Phonics Picture Cards: yo-yo (42), zebra (43), zipper (44), ax (46), six (60), box (70)

Working in pairs, have children place the cards face down in two piles. Have both children turn over a card. If the picture names contain the same sound, the first child to clap gets both cards. Continue until all the pictures have been identified.

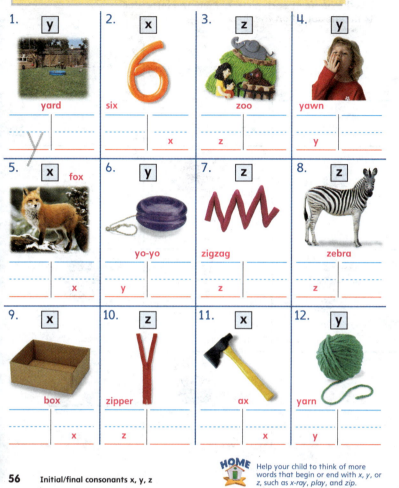

CURRICULUM CONNECTIONS

WRITING

Materials: drawing paper, crayons

Ask children to imagine that they work for a zoo. Have them create a poster advertising the zoo. They might wish to focus on interesting or unusual animals, including zebras, that live in the zoo. Children can share their posters by creating a zoo display on a bulletin board.

MATH

Materials: drawing paper, crayons, two classroom objects

Hold up the objects and ask children to count how many objects they see. (*two*) Then, hide the objects behind your back and ask how many they see. (*zero*) Distribute drawing paper and have children fold the sheet in half. On one half, have them draw a picture that illustrates a number, such as five eggs in a nest. Have them label the picture with the number of objects. Then, have them illustrate zero objects, such as the nest with no eggs, on the other half. They should label this side with the word *zero*.

 **AstroWord** Consonant Sounds and Letters

56 Initial/final consonants x, y, z

Integrating Phonics and Reading

Guided Reading
Show the cover as you read the title. Ask children if they have ever visited a zoo and invite them to share their experiences.

First Reading Point to the picture of each animal and have children supply the name.

Second Reading Ask children to identify the words that begin with *z* and the words ending in *x* in the story. List the words on the board.

Comprehension
After reading, ask children the following questions:
- What did the boy see at the zoo? *Recall/Summarize*
- What happened in the picture on the last page? Did you think it was funny? *Reflective Analysis/Opinion*

ESL/ELL English Language Learners
Point out that *saw* is the past tense of *see*. Read the book again, substituting *see* for *saw*. Have the children repeat each sentence after you.

AUDITORY LEARNERS

Have children answer these oral riddles with rhyming words that begin with /z/.
- This word rhymes with *hero* and names a number. (*zero*)
- This word rhymes with *rip* and names a code that is part of your address. (*zip*)

CHALLENGE

Materials: picture and other dictionaries

Challenge children to find words containing *x*, *y*, and *z* in the dictionaries. Ask which of these letters begin the greatest and least number of entries and how they compare with other letters in the alphabet.

EXTRA SUPPORT/INTERVENTION

Materials: Phonics Picture Cards: yo-yo (42), zebra (43), zipper (44), ax (46), six (60), box (70); letter cards *Xx, Yy, Zz*

Display the picture cards and have children name them. Then, ask children to take turns matching a picture card with a letter card. **See Daily Phonics Practice, page 311.**

Lesson 26   Pages 57–58

Medial Consonants

Skill Focus

Children will

★ identify pictures whose names contain medial consonant sounds.

★ print the consonants that stand for the medial sounds.

ESL/ELL Words in Hmong, Vietnamese, Cantonese, Korean, and Khmer are monosyllabic. Prolonging the medial consonant sound may cause children to say each word as two.

Teach

Phonemic Awareness: Medial Sound Isolation

Materials: ruler, cookie, lemon

Hold up the ruler and have children identify it. Have them repeat the word with you several times, stretching the middle sound: *rullller*. Help children identify the medial sound as the sound of *l*. Repeat the procedure for *cookie* and *lemon*.

Sound to Symbol Display the ruler again and have it identified. Say the word *ruler*, emphasizing the middle sound. Elicit that the letter *l* stands for this middle sound, /l/. Write *ruler* on the board and ask a volunteer to underline the letter that stands for the middle sound. Repeat the procedure for *cookie* and *lemon*.

Then, write the numeral 7 and the word *seven* on the board. Have children say the word *seven* and finger-write the letter that stands for the middle sound. Repeat this procedure, drawing a peanut and a wagon and writing each word on the board.

Practice and Apply

Sound to Symbol Help children identify the pictures on pages 57 and 58. Make sure that they understand that on page 57 they are to write the letter that stands for each middle sound. On page 58, they should write the letter and then trace the word.

Reading Use *Funny Faces and Funny Places*, MCP Phonics and Reading Consonant Skills Library, Level A, to provide practice in reading words with medial consonants.

Medial Consonants

Name _____

▶ **Say** the name of each picture. **Print** the letter for its middle sound on the line.

1. mitten	2. ruler	3. tiger
___	l	g
4. peanut	5. balloon	6. ladder
n	l	d
7. camel	8. zipper	9. robot
m	p	b
10. hammer	11. cookies	12. kitten
m	k	t

Medial consonants   57

FOCUS ON ALL LEARNERS

ESL/ELL ENGLISH LANGUAGE LEARNERS

Materials: letter cards *Bb, Dd, Gg, Kk, Ll, Mm, Nn, Pp, Tt*

- Before beginning page 57, review the letter cards and have children pronounce the sound of each. Preview the names of the picture clues. Read the directions aloud and model the first item for the group. Then, complete items 1 to 3 together. You may want to have children work in pairs to complete items 4 to 12.

- Read the directions for page 58 aloud and ask children to name each picture. Then, model the first item by writing *ba_y* on the board. Complete the item with children and model, writing the medial *b* in *baby* as you repeat the directions. Assist children as they complete items 2 to 9 individually or in pairs.

KINESTHETIC LEARNERS

Materials: three classroom chairs arranged in a row, letter cards

Say these words: *drummer, button, lemon, dipper, butter, ruler, mitten, tiger, kitten*. Ask three children to select cards for the letters heard at the beginning, middle, and end of a word. Have them sit in the three chairs.

Medial Consonants

Say the name of each picture. Print the letter for its middle sound on the line. Trace the whole word.

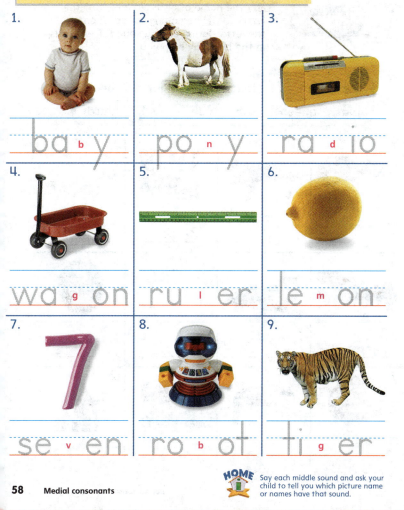

1. ba b y
2. po n y
3. ra d io
4. wa g on
5. ru l er
6. le m on
7. se v en
8. ro b ot
9. ti g er

HOME Say each middle sound and ask your child to tell you which picture name or names have that sound.

CURRICULUM CONNECTIONS

WRITING
Materials: drawing paper, crayons

Ask children to look at the pictures of the animals on pages 57 and 58. Have each child select one as a mystery animal and draw its picture on one side of the paper. On the other side, have them write or dictate a clue about the animal's identity. Children can share their riddles with the class and take turns guessing the mystery animals.

SCIENCE/ART
Materials: boxes, tubes, egg cartons, construction paper, glue, crayons

Write the word *robot* on the chalkboard and help children read it aloud. Talk about jobs that robots do in real life on assembly lines. Then, invite children to describe jobs that they'd like a robot to do. Working in small groups, have children construct robots out of recyclable materials. When the robots are finished, invite children to write or dictate labels that describe the jobs that they'd like to program their robot to do.

TECHNOLOGY AstroWord Consonant Sounds and Letters

Integrating Phonics and Reading

Guided Reading
Show the cover as you read the title. Invite children to get ready for the story by making funny faces.
First Reading Invite children to describe the funniest face on each page.
Second Reading Point out the word *funny* and write it on the board. Have children identify the medial consonant sound and the letter *n*.
Comprehension
After reading, ask children the following questions:
- What do you call people who make funny faces like the ones in the story? *Reflective Analysis/Prior Knowledge*
- What are some places you might see clowns? *Reflective Analysis/Personal Experience*

ESL/ELL English Language Learners
Use the photos to extend children's vocabulary. Point to a photo and ask: *What is behind the clowns?* (balloons); *What will the clowns drive?* (cars), etc.

AUDITORY LEARNERS — INDIVIDUAL
Present these oral riddles and ask children to identify the new word.
- Change the middle sound of *lesser* to /t/. (*letter*)
- Change the middle sound of *fuzzy* to /n/. (*funny*)
- Change the middle sound of *ruder* to /l/. (*ruler*).

CHALLENGE
Materials: letter cards: *Bb, Dd, Ff, Gg, Mm, Pp, Rr, Tt*

Have partners write three words for each letter card. Challenge them to write words in which each letter appears at the beginning, middle, or end of a word.

EXTRA SUPPORT/INTERVENTION
Materials: balloon, ruler, mitten, peanut, toy tiger, toy baby doll

Display two of the objects, such as the mitten and the baby. Ask children to name the objects and then select the object whose name has the sound /t/ in the middle. Repeat with other pairs of objects and other medial sounds. **See Daily Phonics Practice, pages 308–311.**

Lesson 27   Pages 59–60

Phonics and Spelling / Phonics and Writing

Consonants

Skill Focus
Children will
★ write beginning and ending consonants to complete words.
★ write a sentence about a picture of themselves and their friends.

Teach

Phonics and Spelling Draw a bat on the board and have children name it. Under the picture draw a blank with the letter *a* in the center. Tell children they can help you spell the word *bat*. Ask what sound children hear at the beginning of *bat* and what letter stands for the sound. When children respond correctly, write *b* in front of the *a*. Repeat for the ending sound/letter *t*.

Practice and Apply

Phonics and Spelling Help children name each picture on page 59. Have children read the list words aloud to hear the beginning and ending sounds before they print the letters that stand for those sounds.

Phonics and Writing
Materials: a picture with a caption

Display the picture and read the caption. Explain that a caption tells about a picture. Then, tell children that on page 60 there is room to draw a picture of themselves and their friends. Point out the lines under the box and explain that they can write a sentence about their picture on these lines. Remind children that a sentence begins with a capital letter and ends with a period.

Reading Use *Let's Go Marching!*, MCP Phonics and Reading Consonant Skills Library, Level A, to review initial and final consonants.

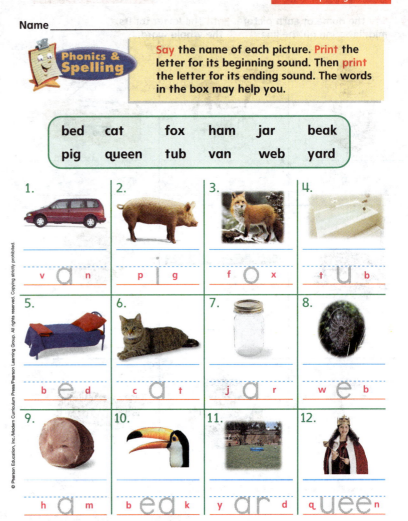

FOCUS ON ALL LEARNERS

ESL/ELL ENGLISH LANGUAGE LEARNERS

- Before children begin page 59, review beginning and ending sounds. Say and write words such as *hat, big, hop, net, sand, wig*. Have children identify each beginning and ending sound.
- For page 60, model the activity by drawing a simple picture, such as a group of children jumping rope, and writing a sentence about it. Remind children to begin the sentence's first word with an uppercase letter and to end the sentence with a period.

VISUAL/AUDITORY LEARNERS
Materials: letter cards: *b, m, s*

Tell children you will say a word that has a *b* sound. Have them place the *b* card on the left side of their desk if the *b* is at the beginning of the word or on the right side if the *b* is at the end. Repeat with other letters, using *map, tub, sad, bus,* and *Tom*.

KINESTHETIC/AUDITORY LEARNERS
Materials: trays of sand or salt

Have children trace a line in the sand to divide the tray into two parts. Then, say these words and have children finger-write the letters that stand for the beginning and ending sounds: *big, hid, gas, ham, sad, tap, wag, lip, net, pen, bed, fox*.

Phonics & Writing

Writing

Draw a picture of yourself with your friends. Write a sentence about the picture.

60 Review consonants: Writing

CURRICULUM CONNECTIONS

WRITING
 PORTFOLIO

Materials: drawing paper, crayons

Lead a discussion in which you introduce the term *keepsake* and give several examples such as a book, a piece of jewelry, a special piece of furniture, or china. Explain that keepsakes are often passed down from older members of a family to younger members of a family. Invite children to draw pictures of items that are special to their family that they think are keepsakes. Suggest that they write a sentence under the picture telling why this item is special to their family.

MATH

Materials: small dolls or other figures

Model how to make up an oral word problem that deals with friends by sharing the following. *Sam invited 4 friends over to play. His sister Pam invited 3 friends. How many children came over to play?* Help children make up similar math problems and act them out with small dolls.

TECHNOLOGY **AstroWord** Consonant Sounds and Letters

AUDITORY/VISUAL  GROUPS

Materials: Phonics Picture Cards: book (3), fan (10), moon (25), soap (35)

Have children place the picture cards face up on the table. Then, have them take turns giving clues about the beginning and ending sound of a mystery picture for others to guess. For example, *My mystery picture starts with /b/ and ends with /k/.* (book)

CHALLENGE

Materials: drawing paper, crayons

Write these letter pairs on the board: *p, g; t, p; b, g; h, t.* Challenge children to select two letter pairs and write words that begin and end with the sounds that the letters stand for.

EXTRA SUPPORT/INTERVENTION

Materials: Phonics Picture Cards: book (3), lion (22), moon (25), soap (35); self-stick notes

Using the self-stick notes, have children label each picture with two letters, one for the beginning sound and one for the ending sound.

See Daily Phonics Practice, pages 308–311.

Integrating Phonics and Reading

Guided Reading
Show the cover and read the title. Ask children whom they see in the illustration and have them tell why they might be marching.

 LET'S GO MARCHING!

First Reading Have children point out each object or sight named in the story.

Second Reading Point out these words in the story: *box, cap, dog, jet, top, van.* Have children identify the beginning and ending sound/letter in each word.

Comprehension
After reading, ask children these questions:
- What are the most unusual things that can be seen at the parade? *Reflective Analysis/Judgments*
- Have you ever been to a parade? What did you see? *Reflective Analysis/Personal Experience*

ESL/ELL English Language Learners
With children, find the contractions in the story: *let's, there's, I'm, they're.* Write each one on the board and help children to identify the words each one stands for.

Lesson 28 **Pages 61–62**

Take-Home Book

Review Consonants

Skill Focus
Children will
★ read words with initial and final consonant sounds in the context of a story.
★ reread for fluency.

Teach
Build Background
Materials: backpack containing a flashlight, bottle of water, and a hat or cap

Unpack the backpack and have children identify each object. Explain that these are all things they might bring along if they were going camping. Ask what kind of shelter they might be able to bring along, set up, and stay in while camping. Then, invite children to share any experiences they have had with tents and camping.

Phonological Awareness: Blending Onsets and Rimes
Say /t/ent. Then, together with children, blend the beginning and ending parts to say the word *tent*. Next, ask children to blend these word parts to make words: /r/ent, /b/ent, /w/ent. After children have pronounced the words, help them notice that the words rhyme. Explain that rhyming words sound alike except for the beginning sounds.

Practice and Apply
Read the Book Help children tear out and fold the pages to make their Take-Home Books. Then, read the book together. Invite children to describe the tents they see in the photos.

Sound to Symbol Read aloud or have volunteers read the book. Have children identify the beginning and ending consonant sounds in words such as *fun, camp, yard,* and *dog* and the beginning sounds in *woods* and *little*. Invite volunteers to write the words on the board and underline the letters that stand for these consonant sounds.

Reread for Fluency Have children reread the book to increase their fluency and comprehension. Children can take their books home to read and share with family members.

Review consonants: Take-home book   61

FOCUS ON ALL LEARNERS

ESL/ELL ENGLISH LANGUAGE LEARNERS
Assist children with making the Take-Home Book and read the text together. Then, read the story again one page at a time. Assign children specific tasks, such as:

- Listen for a word that ends with the sound of *p* and circle it. (*camp*)
- Listen for a word that has the middle sound of *t* and draw a box around it. (*little*)
- Listen for a word that rhymes with *hog*. Circle the beginning and ending letters. (*dog*)

VISUAL/AUDITORY LEARNERS
Materials: Take-Home Books

Children can play "I Spy" with a partner. Have them take turns challenging each other to point to words that begin or end with a specified consonant.

VISUAL/KINESTHETIC LEARNERS
Materials: letter cards

Give children letter cards that spell story words such as *tent* and *yard* in scrambled order. Have children line up and hold up the cards in the correct order to spell each word.

2 A tent can go in the woods or in a yard.

3 A tent can be big or little.

62 Review consonants: Take-home book

CURRICULUM CONNECTIONS

HEALTH
Remind children that when they eat snacks, they should pick foods that are good for them. Help children to brainstorm a list of healthful snacks that might be good to take along on a camping trip, such as fruit, vegetables, and popcorn. Have children work together to make a poster or bulletin board showing the healthful snacks, and assist them in creating labels for each food.

SCIENCE
Materials: nonfiction books about woodland animals

Remind children that they might see or hear different animals if they went camping in the woods. Invite them to look through the books to learn about some of these animals. Suggest children share what they learned by choosing one animal to show pictures of and tell about.

ART
Materials: crayons, paper

Invite children to draw pictures of a tent they would like to use if they went camping. Help caption their pictures with simple sentences that tell about their tents.

 AstroWord Consonant Sounds and Letters

AUDITORY LEARNERS
Materials: Take-Home Book

Write one of these consonants on the board: *c, d, f, t, w, y*. Tell children to listen for the sound of this letter as you read the story aloud. Have them bark like dogs when they hear a word that begins with the letter sound. Repeat with the other letters.

CHALLENGE
Challenge students to write or dictate an adventure story about something that might happen while they are camping. On the board, list words from the Take-Home Book that they might use, such as *tent, big, little, yard, woods,* and *dog*. Encourage them to add titles and illustrate their stories.

LEARNERS WHO NEED EXTRA SUPPORT
Materials: Take-Home Books, tape player, audiotape

Tape-record the Take-Home Book. Then, invite children to listen to the tape several times as they follow along in their books. Help them use a finger to track the text on each page as they listen to the story. **See Daily Phonics Practice, pages 308–311.**

Lesson 29   Pages 63–64

Unit Checkup

Consonants

Skill Focus

Children will

★ identify and print the consonant that stands for the sound heard at the beginning or end of a picture name.

Teach

Phonemic Awareness: Phoneme Substitution Have children answer these questions.

- What word rhymes with *mitten* and begins like *king*? (*kitten*)
- What word rhymes with *ten* and begins like *peanut*? (*pen*)
- What word rhymes with *fall* and begins like *box*? (*ball*)

Sound to Symbol On the board, draw write-on lines similar to those on page 63. Then, draw a sad face and say *sad*. Have the children repeat the word as you write the letters *ad* on the lines. Talk with children about the placement of the *s* on the line. Then, add *s* to the beginning of the word. Repeat with *bug*. First, draw a simple bug on the board and say the word for children to repeat. Then, write the word part on the board.

Next, change the activity so the target letter is the ending sound. Use the words *mug* and *pen*.

Practice and Apply

Assess Skills Help children identify the pictures on pages 63 and 64. Make sure they understand that on page 63 they will be writing the consonant that is missing from each word. You may wish to demonstrate how to fill in the bubble to mark the correct answer on page 64. Remind children that for the first six items they will listen for beginning sounds, and on the last six items they will listen for ending sounds.

UNIT 1 CHECKUP

Name _____

▶ **Say** the name of each picture. **Print** the letter for the missing sound to finish each word. **Trace** the whole word.

1. y arn
2. bu s
3. v ase
4. ha t
5. f ire
6. h eart
7. j ug
8. z ebra
9. pe n
10. q ueen
11. w agon
12. tu b

Consonants: Assessment   63

FOCUS ON ALL LEARNERS

ESL/ELL ENGLISH LANGUAGE LEARNERS

Materials: Phonics Picture Cards: bag (47), cap (48), lid (57), pig (59), cup (63), bed (76)

- Display the picture cards face up on a desk. Together with the group, say the picture names, emphasizing the ending sounds.
- Ask children to name each picture. Then, have them match the pictures whose names end with the same sound.

VISUAL/AUDITORY LEARNERS

Materials: Phonics Picture Cards: book (3), car (5), fan (10), cat (49), pig (59), bus (62), tub (68); paper bag

Place the cards in the bag and have children take turns selecting a card. Have them say the picture name and identify the letters that stand for the beginning and ending sounds.

KINESTHETIC/AUDITORY LEARNERS

Materials: letter cards: Dd, Ll, Pp, Tt, Ww

Have children place the letter cards in a row. Say a word and either *beginning* or *end*. Have students touch the letter they hear at the beginning or end as specified. Some words to use are *dog*, *cat*, *wagon*, *lamp*, *doll*, and *hop*.

UNIT 1 CHECKUP

▶ **Say** the name of each picture. **Fill in** the bubble next to the letter or letters that stand for the beginning sound.

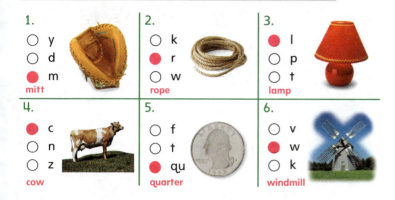

1. ○ y ○ d ● m — mitt
2. ○ k ● r ○ w — rope
3. ● l ○ p ○ t — lamp
4. ● c ○ n ○ z — cow
5. ○ f ○ t ● qu — quarter
6. ○ v ● w ○ k — windmill

▶ **Say** the name of each picture. **Fill in** the bubble next to the letter that stands for the ending sound.

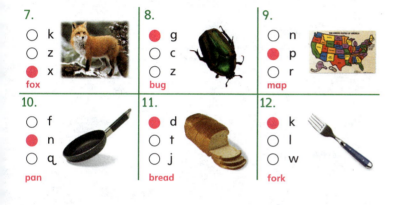

7. ○ k ○ z ● x — fox
8. ● g ○ c ○ z — bug
9. ○ n ● p ○ r — map
10. ○ f ● n ○ q — pan
11. ● d ○ t ○ j — bread
12. ● k ○ l ○ w — fork

64 Consonants: Assessment

ASSESS UNDERSTANDING OF UNIT SKILLS

STUDENT PROGRESS ASSESSMENT

You may wish to review the observational notes you made as children worked through the activities in the unit. Your notes will help you evaluate the progress children make with identifying consonant letters and their sounds.

PORTFOLIO ASSESSMENT

Review the materials children have collected in their portfolios. You may wish to have interviews with children to discuss the progress they have made since the beginning of the unit. As you review children's work, evaluate how well they use phonics skills.

DAILY PHONICS PRACTICE

For children who need additional practice identifying consonant and consonant sounds, quick reviews are provided on pages 308–311 in Daily Phonics Practice.

PHONICS POSTTEST

To assess children's mastery of consonants, use the posttest on pages 5g–5h.

AUDITORY LEARNERS

Say names such as *Ken, Pam, Meg, Bob, Lynn,* and *Ned*. Have children identify the beginning and ending sound in each name.

CHALLENGE

Materials: strips of paper

Using the paper, have children cover the pictures in one row on page 63. Challenge them to try to read each word in the row. Then, have them check their responses by uncovering the pictures.

EXTRA SUPPORT/INTERVENTION

Materials: Phonics Picture Cards: bag (47), cap (48), lid (57), pig (59), cup (63), bed (76)

Mix up the cards and place them face up on a desk. Have children say each picture name, emphasizing the beginning sound. Ask them to identify the letter that stands for this sound. Repeat for ending sounds.
See Daily Phonics Practice, pages 316–320.

64

Teacher Notes

UNIT 2

Short Vowels
THEME: AMAZING ANIMALS

CONTENTS

UNIT 2 RESOURCES 65b
Assessment Options 65c
Administering & Evaluating the Pretest/Posttest 65d
    Unit 2 Pretest 65e–65f
    Unit 2 Posttest 65g–65h
    Unit 2 Student Progress Checklist 65i
English Language Learners 65j
Spelling Connection 65k–65l
Phonics Games, Activities, and Technology 65m–65o
BLM Unit 2 Activity 65p
Home Connections 65q

TEACHING PLANS

Unit 2 Opener/ Home Letter		65–66
Lessons 30–34:	Short vowel *a*	67–76
Lesson 35:	Review short *a*: Phonics & Reading	77
	Phonics & Writing: Building Words	78
Lesson 36:	Take-Home Book: "Bats"	79–80
Lesson 37:	High-frequency words	81–82
Lessons 38–39:	Short vowel *i*	83–86
Lesson 40:	Short vowels *a, i*	87–88
Lessons 41–42:	Short vowel *i*	89–92
Lesson 43:	Review short *i*: Phonics & Reading	93
	Phonics & Writing: Building Words	94
Lesson 44:	Take-Home Book: "Fast Pig"	95–96
Lesson 45:	High-frequency words	97–98
Lessons 46–47:	Short vowel *u*	99–102
Lesson 48:	Short vowels *a, i, u*	103–104
Lessons 49–50:	Short vowel *u*	105–108
Lesson 51:	Review short *u*: Phonics & Reading	109
	Phonics & Writing: Building Words	110
Lesson 52:	Take-Home Book: "Lunch in a Jug"	111–112
Lessons 53–54:	Short vowel *o*	113–116
Lesson 55:	Short vowels *a, i, u, o*	117–118
Lessons 56–57:	Short vowel *o*	119–122
Lesson 58:	Review short *o*: Phonics & Reading	123
	Phonics & Writing: Building Words	124
Lesson 59:	Take-Home Book: "In the Tub"	125–126
Lesson 60:	High-frequency words	127–128
Lessons 61–62:	Short vowel *e*	129–132
Lesson 63:	Short vowels *a, i, o, u, e*	133–134
Lessons 64–65:	Short vowel *e*	135–138
Lesson 66:	Review short vowels: Phonics & Reading	139
	Phonics & Writing: A Postcard	140
Lesson 67:	Take-Home Book: "Fish Food"	141–142
Lesson 68:	Unit Checkup: Short vowels, High-frequency words	143–144

Student Performance Objectives

In Unit 2, children will be introduced to the short vowel sound associations for *a, e, i, o,* and *u* within the context of the theme "Amazing Animals." As children begin to understand and learn to apply the concept that consonant and vowel sounds can be blended together to form words, they will be able to

▶ Recognize the vowels *a, e, i, o,* and *u* by name

▶ Associate the vowels *a, e, i, o,* and *u* with the short sounds they stand for

▶ Distinguish among the short sounds for *a, e, i, o,* and *u*

▶ Blend the sounds vowels and consonants stand for

▶ Apply the short vowel rule as an aid to decoding words

▶ Learn and read high-frequency words in context

Overview of Resources

LESSON	MCP PHONICS AND READING LIBRARY, LEVEL A			PICTURE CARDS	LETTER CARDS/ WORD CARDS	DAILY PHONICS PRACTICE
	TITLE	PRACTICE				
30: Short vowel *a*	RR, Stg One Bk 19	Sandy		45–47, 49, 51–52, 58, 63, 73, 76	Aa, Ff, Mm, Pp, Rr, Tt, Vv	312
31: Short *a*: Sound to symbol	RR, Stg One Bk 39	Haddie's Caps		45, 47–52, 59, 67, 70, 108, 123	Aa, Bb, Cc, Hh, Ff, Mm, Pp, Tt	312
32: Short *a*: Blending phonemes	RR, Stg 0/1 Bk 10	Look at That!		46–52, 59, 62, 70, 77	Bb, Hh, Mm, Pp, Ss	312
33: Short *a*: Spelling	RR, Stg One Bk 12	That Fly			Complete Set	312
34: Short *a*: Words in context	RR, Stg One Bk 24	Bags, Cans, Pots, and Pans		48–49, 51	16–17, 28	312
35: Review Short *a*	RR, Stg Two Bk 10	It's Hot		47, 49, 52	Aa, Bb, Cc, Nn, Pp, Tt	312
36: Review short *a*; Take-Home Book: "Bats"				9, 10, 12	Aa, Nn, Dd, Bb, Ss, Hh, Mm, Pp, Cc, Rr, Tt	312
37: High-frequency words	RR, Stg One Bk 13	My Cat			Complete Set/*here, I, my, said, the, with*	
38: Short vowel *i*	RR, Stg One Bk 16	Stop That!		46–48, 51–52, 54, 57–60		312–313
39: Short vowel *i*: Sound to symbol	RR, Stg Two Bk 2	The Big Cat		46, 48, 51, 54, 56–60	34–36, 38–40, 43, 49–50, 56	312–313
40: Short vowels *a, i*: Blending	RR, Stg Two Bk 6	My Hamster, Van		47–49, 52–54, 56, 59–60, 124, 136, 149, 152, 163	Complete Set	312–313
41: Short vowel *i*: Spelling	RR, Stg One Bk 28	Mr. Fin's Trip		47–49, 54, 57–60	Ff, Ll, Pp, Ss/34–35, 38–39, 46, 53	312–313
42: Short vowel *i*: Words in context	RR, Stage Two Bk 16	I Can Swim		47–49, 54–60	Ii/34–35, 38, 46, 53, 57	312–313
43: Review short *i*	RR, Stage Two Bk 7	Three Little Pigs and One Big Pig			Ff, Hh, Mm, Pp, Rr, Ww/8, 18–19, 27, 34–37, 40–43, 50, 56, 58–59	312–313
44: Take-Home Book: "Fast Pig"					Aa, Ii/ 12, 52, 58	312–313
45: High-frequency words	RR, Stg One Bk 34	Funny Faces and Funny Places			*are, do, down, for, like, you*	
46: Short vowel *u*	RR, Stg Two Bk 14	Just Like Us		61, 63–64, 68		313–314
47: Short vowel *u*: Sound to symbol	RR, Stg One Bk 42	Good Night, Little Bug		47, 49, 59–64, 66–68	Bb, Gg, Aa, Ii, Uu 61, 63, 67, 71, 78–80	313–314
48: Short vowels *a, i, u*	RR, Stg Two Bk 50	Cat's Trip		45, 47–49, 52, 57–59, 60–63	Aa, Ii, Uu, Bb, Gg, Ss, Cc, Pp, Dd, Rr, Mm, Tt, Nn	312–314
49: Short vowel *u*: Spelling	RR, Stg One Bk 43	A Nut Pie for Jud			Aa, Ii, Uu	313–314
50: Short vowel *u*: Words in context	RR, Stg Two Bk 8	Night and Day		45, 48, 52, 54, 56, 58–59, 61–63, 67–68		313–314
51: Review short vowel *u*	RR, Stg Two Bk 48	Mr. Wink			8–9, 34, 60–63, 66–67, 71, 80	313–314
52: Take-Home Book: "Lunch in a Jug"						313–314
53: Short vowel *o*	RR, Stg Two Bk 12	Little Frog's Monster Story			Aa, Cc, Hh, Nn, Oo, Pp, Tt	314–315
54: Short vowel *o*	RR, Stg Two Bk 3	"POP" Pops the Popcorn		70–75		314–315
55: Short vowels *a, i, u, o*: Blending	RR, Stg One Bk 27	Can a Cow Hop?		49, 52, 54, 61, 64, 66–67, 73, 75, 124, 133–134	13, 27, 52, 55, 61, 67, 86, 90, 94	312–315
56: Short vowel *o*	RR, Stg One Bk 25	Lost in the Fog		70–75		314–315
57: Short vowel *o*	RR, Stg Two Bk 11	What Is at the Top?		46–48, 54, 56–57, 61–63, 70–75	Complete Set	314–315
58: Review short *o*	RR, Stg One Bk 46	The Merry-Go-Round			83, 85–86, 89	314–315
59: Take-Home Book: "In the Tub"						312–315
60: High-frequency words	RR, Stg One Bk 24	Bags, Cans, Pots, and Pans			*come, have, her, of, one, our*	
61: Short vowel *e*	RR, Stg Two Bk 13	What Do We Have to Get?			Ee, Hh, Tt, Bb, Gg, Ll, Vv, Ww	315
62: Short vowel *e*	RR, Stg One Bk 31	Ben's Pets		46, 51, 53, 58–59, 61, 68, 72, 74, 76–84	96, 98, 100, 103, 113–114	315
63: Short vowel *a, i, o, u, e*: Blending	RR, Stg Two Bk 49	The Apple Farm		47, 49, 52, 56, 59, 61, 64, 66–67, 71, 73, 75, 81–82	13–14, 49, 51, 68, 79, 90, 95, 99, 113	312–315
64: Short vowel *e*: Spelling	RR, Stg One Bk 40	Ted's Red Sled			96, 99, 102, 103, 111, 113	315
65: Short vowel *e*: Words in context	RR, Stg Two Bk 4	The Best Places		77–79, 81–82, 84	96, 98, 100, 103, 113–114	315
66: Review short vowels	RR, Stg Two Bk 20	When We Are Big		47, 57, 59, 62–63, 175	Aa, Bb, Cc, Ff, Gg, Ii, Oo, Pp, Tt, Uu/ 8, 46, 52, 63, 67	312–315
67: Take-Home Book: "Fish Food"					Aa, Ee, Ii, Oo, Uu, Bb, Cc, Hh, Nn, Pp, Tt	312–315
68: Unit Checkup				45–84	27, 33, 48, 58, 61, 76, 85, 90, 96, 102	312–315

RR–Ready Readers Stg–Stage Bk–Book

Assessment Options

In Unit 2, assess children's ability to read and write words with short vowel sounds. Use the Unit Pretest and Posttest for formal assessment. For ongoing informal assessment you may wish to use children's work on the Review pages, Take-Home Books, and Unit Checkups. You may also want to encourage children to evaluate their own work and to participate in setting goals for their own learning.

ESL/ELL Short vowel sounds may be especially problematic for English language learners. Note pronunciation difficulties, but assess based upon children's ability to distinguish short vowel sounds when pronounced by a native speaker. For additional support for English language learners, see page 65j.

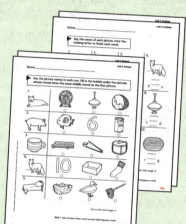

FORMAL ASSESSMENT

Use the Unit 2 Pretest, on pages 65e–65f, to help assess a child's knowledge at the beginning of the unit and to plan instruction.

ESL/ELL Before administering the Pretest, gather in a paper bag a variety of items (or pictures of them) that match the visuals on pages 65e–65f. Have volunteers select an item and then name it. Ask other children in the group to identify the vowel sound.

Use the Unit 2 Posttest, on pages 65g–65h, to help assess mastery of unit objectives and to plan for reteaching, if necessary.

ESL/ELL Some children may have difficulty with direction. Read the directions aloud and model how to complete the worksheets.

INFORMAL ASSESSMENT

Use the Review pages, Unit Checkup, and Take-Home Books in the student book to provide an effective means of evaluating children's performance.

Unit 2 Skills	Review pages	Checkups	Take-Home Books
Short vowel *a*	77–78	143–144	79–80
Short vowel *i*	93–94	143–144	95–96
Short vowel *u*	109–110	143–144	111–112
Short vowel *o*	123–124	143–144	125–126
Short vowel *e*	139–140	143–144	141–142

STUDENT PROGRESS CHECKLIST

Use the checklist on page 65i to record children's progress. You may want to cut the sections apart to place each child's checklist in his or her portfolio.

PORTFOLIO ASSESSMENT

This logo appears throughout the teaching plans. It signals opportunities for collecting student work for individual portfolios. You may also want to include the Pretest and Posttest, the Review pages, the Unit Checkup, Phonics & Reading, and Phonics & Writing pages.

PHONEMIC AWARENESS AND PHONICS ASSESSMENT

Use PAPA to obtain an itemized analysis of children's decoding skills.

PAPA Skills	MCP Phonics Lessons in Unit 2
Blending sounds	Lessons 32, 40, 48, 55, 63
Deleting sounds	Lessons 32, 33, 40, 48, 49, 55, 56, 63, 64
Short vowels	Lessons 30–67

65c

Pretest and Posttest

DIRECTIONS

To help you assess children's progress in learning Unit 2 skills, tests are available on pages 65e–65h.

Administer the Pretest before children begin the unit. The results of the Pretest will help you identify each child's strengths and needs in advance, allowing you to structure lesson plans to meet individual needs. Administer the Posttest to assess children's overall mastery of skills taught in the unit and to identify specific areas that will require reteaching.

ESL/ELL Note that the objective of both the Unit 2 Pretest and Posttest is identification of short vowel sounds, not vocabulary recognition, with which children may be unfamiliar. To ensure that vocabulary comprehension does not interfere with sound recognition, name each of the items aloud as children move from item to item in the tests.

To assess the high-frequency words for Unit 2, have a child read orally each word on the Pretest and the Posttest as you point to it. Then have the child check each word read.

PERFORMANCE ASSESSMENT PROFILE

The following chart will help you identify specific skills as they appear on the tests and will enable you to identify and record specific information about an individual's or the class's performance on the tests.

Depending on the results of each test, refer to the Reteaching column for lesson-plan pages where you can find activities that will be useful for meeting individual needs or for daily phonics practice.

Answer Keys

Unit 2 Pretest, page 65e (BLM 7)
1. fan, ham
2. fish, six
3. bus, drum
4. box, sock
5. nest, net

Unit 2 Pretest, page 65f (BLM 8)
6. fan
7. ham
8. bed
9. rug
10. bat
11. dog
12. tent
13. pig
14. pen

Unit 2 Posttest, page 65g (BLM 9)
1. bed, e
2. ham, a
3. pig, i
4. fox, o
5. bus, u
6. mop, o
7. sun, u
8. top, o
9. bag, a
10. web, e
11. pin, i
12. rug, u

Unit 2 Posttest, page 65h (BLM 10)
13. map
14. pig
15. nest
16. dog

Performance Assessment Profile

Skill	Pretest Questions	Posttest Questions	Reteaching Focus on All Learners	Daily Phonics Practice
Short vowel *a*	1, 6, 7, 10	2, 9, 13	67–80, 87–88, 95–96, 103–104, 117–118	312
Short vowel *i*	2, 13	3, 11, 14	83–96, 103–104, 117–118	312–313
Short vowel *u*	3, 9	5, 7, 12	99–112, 104, 117–118	313–314
Short vowel *o*	4, 11	4, 6, 8, 16	113–126, 133–134	314–315
Short vowel *e*	5, 8, 12, 14	1, 10, 15	129–138	315

Unit 2 Pretest

Name _____

> Say the picture names in each row. Fill in the bubble under the pictures whose names have the same middle sound as the first picture.

1.    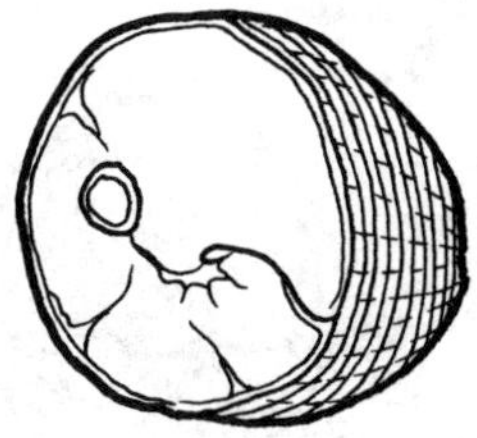
2.    
3.   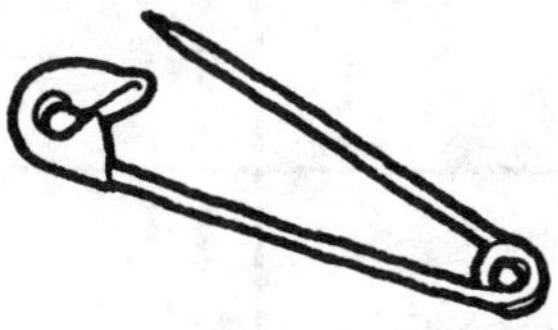 
4.  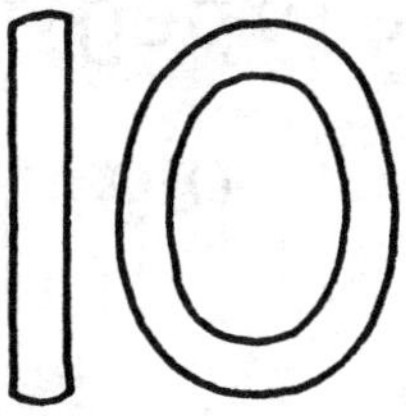 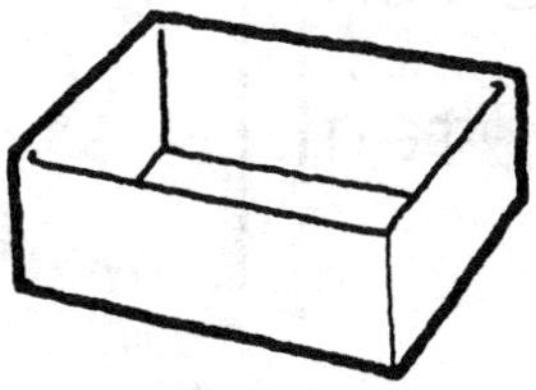 
5.

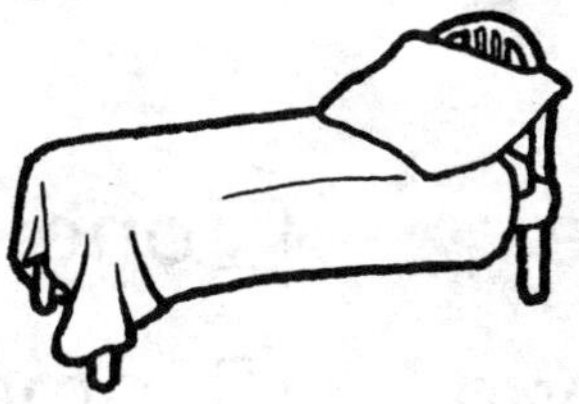

Go to the next page. →

BLM 7 Unit 2 Pretest: Short vowel sounds, high-frequency words

65e

Unit 2 Pretest

Name _____

▶ Say the name of each picture. Fill in the bubble beside the picture name.

6.  ○ fun
○ fin
○ fan

7. 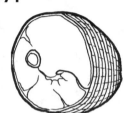 ○ hum
○ ham
○ him

8.  ○ bed
○ bud
○ bid

9. 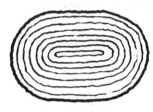 ○ rag
○ rug
○ rig

10.  ○ but
○ bit
○ bat

11.  ○ dig
○ dog
○ dug

12.  ○ tint
○ ten
○ tent

13.  ○ pug
○ peg
○ pig

14.  ○ pin
○ pan
○ pen

▶ Check ☑ each word you can read.

☐ I   ☐ are   ☐ of   ☐ here   ☐ like   ☐ one
☐ for   ☐ my   ☐ her ☐ with   ☐ down   ☐ come
☐ the   ☐ you   ☐ our ☐ said   ☐ have   ☐ do

Possible score on Unit 2 Pretest is 14. Number correct _____

BLM 8 Unit 2 Pretest: Short vowel sounds, high-frequency words

Unit 2 Posttest

Name _____

▶ Say the name of each picture. Print the missing letter to finish each word.

1.
b _ d

2.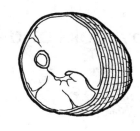
h _ m

3.
p _ g

4.
f _ x

5.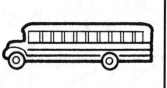
b _ s

6.
m _ p

7.
s _ n

8.
t _ p

9.
b _ g

10.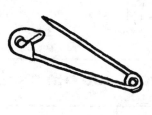
w _ b

11.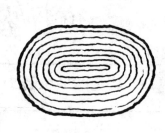
p _ n

12.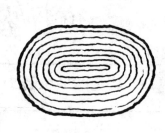
r _ g

Go to the next page. →

BLM 9 Unit 2 Posttest: Short vowel sounds, high-frequency words

65g

Unit 2 Posttest

Name _____

▶ Follow the boy on his walk. Look at each picture. Fill in the bubble by the word that finishes each sentence.

13.  The boy looks at a ____.
○ mop
○ map
○ mat

14.  He walks by a ____.
○ pin
○ pat
○ pig

15.  He looks at a hen in a ____.
○ nest
○ net
○ nut

16.  The boy pets a ____.
○ dog
○ dig
○ dug

▶ Check ✓ each word you can read.

☐ I ☐ are ☐ of ☐ here ☐ like ☐ one
☐ for ☐ my ☐ her ☐ with ☐ down ☐ come
☐ the ☐ you ☐ our ☐ said ☐ have ☐ do

Possible score on Unit 2 Posttest is 16. Number correct _____

BLM 10 Unit 2 Posttest: Short vowel sounds, high-frequency words

Student Progress Checklist

Make as many copies as needed to use for a class list. For individual portfolio use, cut apart each child's section. As indicated by the code, color in boxes next to skills satisfactorily assessed and insert an *X* by those requiring reteaching. Marked boxes can later be colored in to indicate mastery.

Student Progress Checklist

Code: ■ Satisfactory ☒ Needs Reteaching

Student: _____

Pretest Score: _____

Posttest Score: _____

Skills
- ☐ Short *a*
- ☐ Short *i*
- ☐ Short *u*
- ☐ Short *o*
- ☐ Short *e*

High-Frequency Words
- ☐ I ☐ are ☐ of
- ☐ for ☐ my ☐ her
- ☐ the ☐ you ☐ our
- ☐ like ☐ here ☐ one
- ☐ down ☐ with ☐ come
- ☐ have ☐ said ☐ do

Comments / Learning Goals

Student: _____

Pretest Score: _____

Posttest Score: _____

Skills
- ☐ Short *a*
- ☐ Short *i*
- ☐ Short *u*
- ☐ Short *o*
- ☐ Short *e*

High-Frequency Words
- ☐ I ☐ are ☐ of
- ☐ for ☐ my ☐ her
- ☐ the ☐ you ☐ our
- ☐ like ☐ here ☐ one
- ☐ down ☐ with ☐ come
- ☐ have ☐ said ☐ do

Comments / Learning Goals

Student: _____

Pretest Score: _____

Posttest Score: _____

Skills
- ☐ Short *a*
- ☐ Short *i*
- ☐ Short *u*
- ☐ Short *o*
- ☐ Short *e*

High-Frequency Words
- ☐ I ☐ are ☐ of
- ☐ for ☐ my ☐ her
- ☐ the ☐ you ☐ our
- ☐ like ☐ here ☐ one
- ☐ down ☐ with ☐ come
- ☐ have ☐ said ☐ do

Comments / Learning Goals

Student: _____

Pretest Score: _____

Posttest Score: _____

Skills
- ☐ Short *a*
- ☐ Short *i*
- ☐ Short *u*
- ☐ Short *o*
- ☐ Short *e*

High-Frequency Words
- ☐ I ☐ are ☐ of
- ☐ for ☐ my ☐ her
- ☐ the ☐ you ☐ our
- ☐ like ☐ here ☐ one
- ☐ down ☐ with ☐ come
- ☐ have ☐ said ☐ do

Comments / Learning Goals

BLM 11 Unit 2 Checklist

ESL/ELL English Language Learners

Throughout Unit 2 there are opportunities to assess English language learners' ability to read and write words with short vowel sounds. Short vowel sounds may be especially problematic for English language learners. The home languages spoken by English language learners vary from five pure vowel sounds in Spanish to 35 syllabic vowels in Cantonese. English language learners will need lots of opportunities to listen to English vowel sounds before being expected to produce them without error. Take note of difficulties with pronunciations, but assess children based on their ability to distinguish short vowel sounds when pronounced by a native speaker.

Lesson 30, pages 67–68 Speakers of Spanish, Tagalog, or Russian may pronounce *a* /ah/ as in father. Speakers of Asian languages may make a tonal or nasal *a*. Koreans and Russians may say /ya/ after some consonant sounds, making *ga* of *gamble* sound like *gya* in *big yam*.

Lesson 35, pages 77–78 Many languages other than English, including Spanish, do not discriminate between long and short vowel sounds. Provide frequent opportunities for English language learners to hear and say words containing short vowels.

Lesson 38, pages 83–84 Children who speak a language other than English may pronounce *i* like the *e* in *me*. Practice *sit, seat*; *fit, feet*; *bin, bean*; and so on.

Lesson 46, pages 99–100 Children who speak Spanish, Tagalog, or some Asian languages may have problems with short *u* as they did with short *a*, pronouncing it like *o* in *hot* or *a* in *father*. Spanish speakers might pronounce short *u* like *oo* in *foot*. Russian speakers might pronounce short *u* like *ee* in *feet*.

Lesson 53, pages 113–114 Native speakers of Spanish, Tagalog, and some Asian languages may not distinguish between the sounds of short *o*, short *a*, and short *u*. Practice *hot, hut* and *lock, lack, luck*.

Lesson 54, pages 115–116 Native speakers of Spanish and Russian may confuse the sound of short *u* or *o* with the sound of *oo* in *foot*. Assess English language learners' ability to discriminate and pronounce these sounds. Provide individualized practice with word pairs as necessary.

Lesson 61, pages 129–130 Native speakers of Tagalog might pronounce written *e* like the *ay* in *say*. Practice *let, late*; *pen, pain*; and so on. Since no similar vowel sound exists in Korean, offer additional practice and support for native speakers of Korean.

Spelling Connections

INTRODUCTION

The Unit Word List is a comprehensive list of spelling words drawn from this unit. The words are grouped by short vowel patterns. To incorporate spelling into your phonics program, use the activity in the Curriculum Connections section of each teaching plan.

Spelling

Name________________

Phonics & Spelling — Say the name of each picture. Circle the vowel you hear in its name. Print the word.

1. a e i o u — bag
2. a e i o u — cup
3. a e i o u — pig
4. a e i o u — jet
5. a e i o u — map
6. a e i o u — sock
7. a e i o u — bus
8. a e i o u — lid

bag
bus
lid
map
pig
jet
cup
sock

Review short vowels: Spelling 139

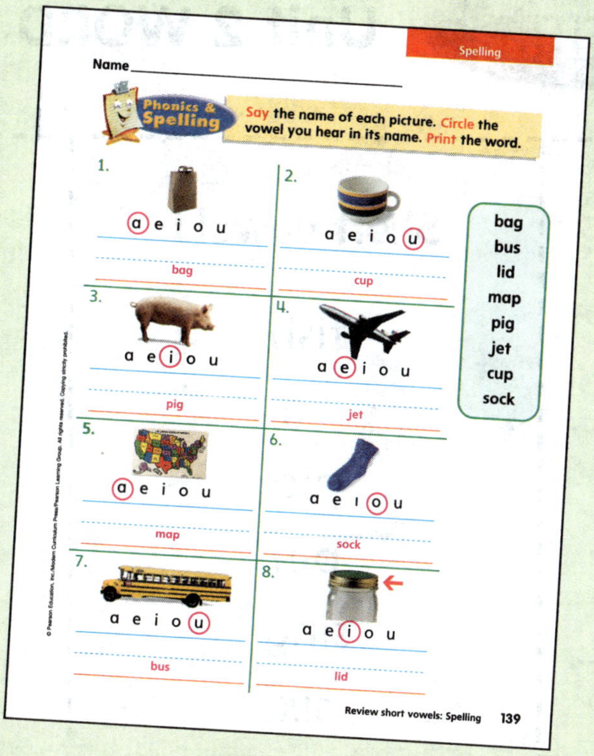

ESL/ELL It is recommended that English language learners reach the intermediate fluency level of English proficiency before focusing on spelling. For English language learners introduce 8–10 words at a time and their meanings through visuals or realia.

The spelling lessons utilize the following approach for each short vowel sound.

1. Administer a pretest of six words that have not yet been introduced. Dictation sentences are provided.
2. Provide practice.
3. Reassess. Dictation sentences are provided.

A final review that covers short vowel words is provided at the end of the unit, on page 140.

DIRECTIONS

Make a copy of Blackline Master 12 for each child. After administering the pretest for each short vowel, give children a copy of the appropriate word list.

Children can work with a partner to practice spelling the words orally and identifying the vowel sound in each word. They can also use their letter cards to form the words on the list. You may want to challenge children to make new words by substituting the vowel sounds. Children can write words of their own on My Own Word List (See Blackline Master 12).

Have children store their list words with the letter cards in the envelope in the back of their books. You may want to suggest that students keep a spelling notebook, listing words with similar patterns. Another idea is to build Word Walls with children and display them in the classroom. Each section of the wall could focus on words with a single phonics element. The walls will become a good resource for spelling when children are engaged in writing.

Unit Word List

Short Vowel *a*
bag
can
cat
fan
ham
map

Short Vowel *i*
fish
lid
pig
pin
sing
six

Short Vowel *u*
bug
bus
cup
drum
tub
sun

Short Vowel *o*
dog
rock
fox
pot
sock
top

Short Vowel *e*
bed
jet
nest
bell
ten
web

Name _____

 Unit 2 WORD LIST

Short Vowel a	Short Vowel i	Short Vowel u
bag	fish	bug
can	lid	bus
cat	pig	cup
fan	pin	drum
ham	sing	tub
map	six	sun

Short Vowel o	Short Vowel e	My Own Word List
dog	bed	
rock	jet	
fox	nest	
pot	bell	
sock	ten	
top	web	

BLM 12 Unit 2 Spelling Words

Phonics Games, Activities, and Technology

The following collection of ideas offers a variety of opportunities to reinforce phonics skills while actively engaging children. The games, activities, and technology suggestions can easily be adapted to meet the needs of your group of learners. They vary in approach so as to consider children's different learning styles.

SHORT VOWEL BINGO

Provide children with blank bingo game boards and markers for covering. Have children fill the board by randomly writing the vowels *a, e, i, o, u* in the spaces, or have them write words given by you. The words you choose may already appear on a Word Wall in your classroom. To play, call out a word slowly and have children repeat it. They can cover the letter whose vowel sound is heard in the word or the word itself, depending on the version you've chosen. Play until someone has bingo!

HOW MANY SOUNDS?

Provide partners with a set of counters and picture cards whose names have short vowel sounds. Partners can say the picture name together, decide how many sounds they hear in the word, and indicate that number by placing the corresponding number of counters on the picture card. Observe children as they work. Eventually provide children with letter cards as well, to build the picture names.

ANIMAL TIC-TAC-TOE

Each pair of players will need a nine-square-grid playing board and two sets of vowel playing cards. The playing cards will feature vowels and animals in place of X's and O's. The playing cards for short *a* can feature a cat, for short *i* a fish, for short *o* a fox, for short *u* a duck, and for short *e* a hen. Each set of five cards should be in a distinct color, and the cards should fit in the squares of the grid. Each player chooses one set of vowel cards. Players take turns picking one of their cards and saying a word that contains the short vowel sound represented on the playing cards. If the player is correct, the card may be placed on the game board. Players continue taking turns until one wins in a tic-tac-toe pattern or until the board is filled.

Variation: Another version requires use of phonogram cards. To make a move, players must say and spell a word that ends with the phonogram. Then the card can be placed on the tic-tac-toe board.

ESL/ELL This activity can be adapted for English language learners by reducing the number of cards or objects used to play the games.

OH, A-HUNTING WE WILL GO

Place around the room pictures whose names contain short vowel sounds. Have children form teams of two or three and present each team with a list of picture names. At your signal, team members must read the words on the list and go in search of the corresponding pictures. When the hunt is over, have each team match its words and pictures for the group.

Variation: Place word cards around the room and provide lists of words that rhyme for students to match.

ESL/ELL For this activity and for Word Finger-Puppets (page 65o), pair English language learners with more English-proficient peers. To ensure that all children participate actively, assign tasks to each child.

WORD SLIDES

Make word slides featuring words with each of the short vowel sounds. Working alone or with a partner, children can pull the word strip through the slide, reading the word that appears in the window. To focus on the theme "Amazing Animals," you may want to make the slide in the shape of an animal whose name features the vowel sound in the words featured on the strip.

Variation: Provide a slide with a blank strip for children to write their own words. Then they can trade slides with a partner and read the words.

ESL/ELL This activity as well as Word Flip Books, Word Wheels (page 65o), and Change-a-Letter (page 65o) are fun ways to introduce the Unit Word List on page 65k. Have children prepare their own word strips or wheels for each of the vowels you identify. Select phonograms representing each of the short vowels for the flip books or letter cards.

ISOLATING VOWEL SOUNDS

Display a set of word cards featuring words with short vowel sounds. Say a word from one of the cards. Ask a volunteer to repeat the word, isolate the medial vowel sound, and find the word card. Continue in the same manner until each child has had a turn.

WORD FLIP BOOKS

Make flip books that feature a short vowel phonogram. As the letter pages are flipped, each new word that is formed is read. Make several books with phonograms representing each of the short vowels.

CIRCLE RHYME

Have children form a circle. Give a word card featuring a short vowel to one child. Have the child read the word on the card and say another word that rhymes. The word card is then passed on to the next child in the circle and the procedure continues. Once several words have been given, or the card has traveled around the circle, begin again with a new word card.

Variation: Have children read the word on the card and say another word that has the same short vowel sound.

ESL/ELL This activity can be played in two teams, rather than individually, to alleviate English language learners' insecurity over participating alone. Allow the teams the opportunity to brainstorm their responses, then respond chorally as a group, with all children participating.

NAME A WORD THAT RHYMES

Use words related to the "Amazing Animals" theme to present this phonemic awareness activity that focuses on words with short vowels that rhyme. Ask children to respond to questions such as *What rhymes with dog? pig? fox? cat? fish? hen? duck?*

WORD WHEELS

A word wheel is another variation of a flip book. A phonogram is written on the left side of the top wheel. Consonants that represent initial sounds are written on the bottom wheel. As the bottom wheel is turned, children can read each word that is formed. Use a paper plate as the bottom wheel and use a brad or paper fastener to attach a circle cut from tagboard for the top wheel.

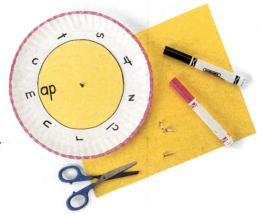

CHANGE-A-LETTER

Provide children with letter cards to build and read a word such as *hat*. Then, have them replace the vowel *a* with *o* and read the new word, *hot*. Follow the same procedure to build and read the words *hut* and *hit*. Follow the same vowel substitution procedure, using other words with short vowel sounds.

WORD FINGER-PUPPETS

Write short vowel words on small strips of paper. Bring together the edges of each strip and tape to form a cylinder shape that can be slipped over a child's finger. Invite each child to read the word on his or her word finger-puppet. As you say words, children with finger-puppets featuring words with the same short vowel sound should wiggle the puppets.

TECHNOLOGY

The following software products reinforce children's understanding of short vowels.

Reader Rabbit's® I Can Read! with Phonics™
Beginning readers (grades 1–3) learn basic phonics skills through lessons and interactive storybooks designed to build phonemic awareness, reading comprehension, and vocabulary skills.

** Riverdeep The Learning Company
500 Redwood Blvd.
Novato, CA 94947
(800) 825-4420
www.learningcompanyschool.com

Reading Who? Reading You!
Children learn letter and sound correspondence for 250 words through a variety of games and puzzles. Video clips featuring words of encouragement and sports highlights provide reinforcement.

** Sunburst Technology
1900 South Batavia Ave.
Geneva, IL 60134
(800) 321-7511
www.sunburst.com

Name _____

Building Words

BLM 13 Unit 2

Home Connections

The Home Connections features of this program are intended to involve families in their children's learning and application of phonics skills. Three effective opportunities to make connections between home and school include the following.

- **HOME LETTER**
- **HOME NOTES**
- **TAKE-HOME BOOKS**

HOME LETTER

A letter is available to be sent home at the beginning of Unit 2. This letter informs family members that children will be learning to read and write words with short vowel sounds within the context of the unit theme, "Amazing Animals." The suggested home activity focuses on making a collage showing animals whose names have a short vowel sound. This activity promotes interaction between child and family members while supporting children's learning of short vowel sounds. The letter, which is available in both English and Spanish, also suggests animal-theme books family members can look for in a local library and enjoy reading together.

HOME NOTES

Whenever the Home logo appears within the student book, a phonics activity is suggested to be done at home. The activities are simple to do, requiring little or no preparation or special materials, and are meant to reinforce the targeted phonics skill.

TAKE-HOME BOOKS

Within the student book are Take-Home Books that can be cut out and assembled. The story language in each book reinforces the targeted phonics skill. The books can be taken home and shared with family members. In Unit 2, five Take-Home Books are available, focusing on each of the short vowels *a*, *e*, *i*, *o*, and *u* as well as the unit theme, "Amazing Animals."

Home Notes in Spanish are also available for both teachers and parents to download and use from our website, www.PlaidPhonics.com.

UNIT 2

Pages 65–66

Short Vowels

Skill Focus

Assess Prior Knowledge
To assess children's prior knowledge of short vowels and high-frequency words, use the pretest on pages 65e–65f.

Unit Focus

Build Background

- Write the theme "Amazing Animals" on the board, read the words, and help children find them on page 65. Talk with children about how animals might be amazing.

- Point to the picture on the page and ask if anyone can identify the animals. Explain that they are a special kind of frog called a red-eyed tree frog. They are found in the rain forests of Costa Rica in Central America as well as in South America.

- Read the text aloud. Then, tell children that there are many kinds and colors of tree frog. These small frogs peep loudly during summer rains. Their sticky toes help them to walk and climb on trees. Many brightly colored tree frogs excrete a substance on their skin that is poisonous to people and other animals.

Introduce Vowels

- Print the vowels *a, e, i, o, u* on the chalkboard. Help children identify each letter, and tell them that these letters are called vowels. Remind them that all letters in the alphabet are either vowels or consonants.

- Read the text "Frogs Call" again. Then, read the words *can, wet, sick, hop, jump* slowly, emphasizing the short vowel sound: *caaan, weeet, siiick, hooop, juuump*. Explain to children that they will learn more about vowel sounds as they work in this unit.

Critical Thinking Ask children to think about what the article tells us about the things that tree frogs can do, such as sing, hop, and jump.

UNIT 2 Short Vowels
Theme: Amazing Animals

Read Aloud

Frogs Call

Little frogs call.
They sing a song.
Soon the rain will fall.
Tree frogs like wet places.
They hop and jump.
Some tree frogs are green.
Some are red.
Others are blue or yellow.
You can not touch some tree frogs.
The wet skin can make you sick!

TALK About It! What can tree frogs do?

THEME FOCUS

AMAZING ANIMALS
Read the text "Frogs Call" again, inviting children to pay special attention to what they learn about tree frogs. Have children describe any experiences they have had with frogs. Encourage them to tell if there was anything amazing about those experiences.

ANIMAL MASKS
Materials: paper plates, construction paper, yarn, scissors, glue

Have children make masks of their favorite animals. Encourage children to either use their imaginations or look at photographs in reference books to design their masks. After the masks have been made, children may want to put on their masks and introduce themselves to the class as their chosen animal.

ANIMAL SONGS AND POEMS
Invite children to bring in favorite poems about animals or recordings of animal songs. You may also wish to provide some examples. Read aloud poems or play recordings. If the songs are familiar to children, invite them to sing along. If the song or poem is about an animal whose name has a short vowel sound, encourage children to listen for the sound.

Dear Family,

In this unit about "Amazing Animals," your child will learn about the vowels **a, e, i, o,** and **u** and the sounds they make. Many animal names contain short vowels such as cat, hen, pig, fox, and duck. As your child becomes familiar with short vowel sounds, you might try these activities together.

▶ Make a collage of animals whose names have the same short vowel sound. With your child, draw pictures or cut pictures from magazines and glue them on paper, one sheet for each vowel.

▶ Your child might enjoy reading these books with you. Look for them in your local library.
Pet of a Pet by Marsha Hayles
How Chipmunk Got His Stripes by Joseph Bruchac

Sincerely,

Estimada familia:

En esta unidad, que trata de "Animales asombrosos," su hijo/a aprenderá las vocales **a, e, i, o, u** y los sonidos que éstas hacen. Los nombres de muchos animales contienen vocales con sonidos breves, como por ejemplo, cat (gato), hen (gallina), pig (cerdo), fox (zorro), y duck (pato). A medida que su hijo/a se vaya familiarizando con las vocales de sonidos breves, podrían hacer las siguientes actividades juntos.

▶ Hagan un collage de fotos o dibujos de animales cuyos nombres contienen vocales con sonidos breves. Junto con su hijo/a, dibujen o recorten fotos de revistas y péguenlos en hojas de papel—una hoja por vocal.

▶ Quizás a su hijo/a le gustaría leer con ustedes los siguientes libros que podrían buscar en su biblioteca local.
Pet of a Pet de Marsha Hayles
How Chipmunk Got His Stripes de Joseph Bruchac

Sinceramente,

66 Unit 2 • Introduction

HOME CONNECTIONS

- The Home Letter on page 66 is intended to acquaint family members with the phonics skills children will be studying in the unit. Children can tear out page 66 and take it home.
- You may want to suggest that they complete the activities on the page with a family member. Encourage children to look in the library for the books suggested and read them with family members.

LEARNING CENTER ACTIVITIES

WRITING CENTER
Provide materials for children to write a story about a favorite animal. Have them make a cover that has the shape of the animal.

SCIENCE CENTER
Provide reference picture books about backyard animals, a magnifying glass, and writing and drawing materials. Encourage children to draw or trace and write about animals that interest them.

MATH CENTER
Provide pattern blocks or paper cutouts of circles, squares, rectangles, and triangles for children to design animals out of the shapes.

BULLETIN BOARD

Display letter cards of the vowels *a, e, i, o, u*. Invite children to draw and label a picture of an animal with a short vowel sound in its name. Display the pictures on a bulletin board entitled "Amazing Animals." Link each picture to its appropriate short vowel sound card with pieces of yarn.

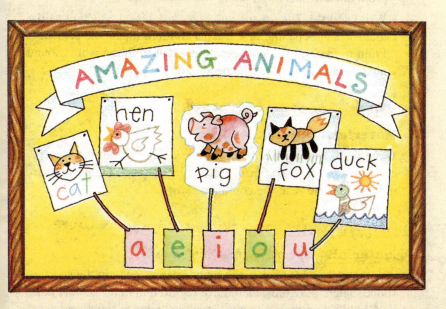

Lesson 30 Pages 67–68

Short Vowel a

Skill Focus

Children will

★ recognize the sound of short vowel *a*.

★ identify picture names and words that contain the sound of short vowel *a*.

★ identify rhyming short vowel *a* words.

ESL/ELL Speakers of Spanish, Tagalog, or Russian may pronounce *a* /ah/ as in *father*. Speakers of Asian languages may make a tonal or nasal *a*. Koreans and Russians may say /ya/ after some consonant sounds (*gyamble* for *gamble*).

▶ Teach

Phonological Awareness: Blending Onsets and Rimes Explain to children that you will say the parts of a word. Children should repeat the parts after you, orally blending the parts to make the word.

- /m/an (*man*)
- /l/ap (*lap*)
- /k/at (*cat*)
- /b/ag (*bag*)

Explain that the sound heard in the middle of each word is short vowel *a*.

Phonological Awareness: Rhyme Say *cat, hat*. Point out that these words rhyme. Then, read aloud the groups of words below. Ask children to say the two words in each group that rhyme.

- back   tack   bag
- lamp   dad   camp
- ant   pan   tan

Sound to Symbol Write the word *ant* on the board and underline the *a*. Explain that this letter represents the short *a* sound heard at the beginning of *ant*.

▶ Practice and Apply

Phonemic Awareness Read aloud the rhyme on page 67. Have children listen for and name words with the short *a* sound.

Sound to Symbol Help children identify the pictures on pages 67 and 68. Suggest that they say the picture names quietly to themselves as they complete each page.

Reading Use *Sandy*, MCP Phonics and Reading Short Vowel Skills Library, Level A, to provide practice in reading words with the short vowel *a* sound.

FOCUS ON ALL LEARNERS

ESL/ELL ENGLISH LANGUAGE LEARNERS

Materials: Phonics Picture Cards: cat (49) and hat (52); letter card *Aa*

- Display letter card *Aa*. Have children name the letter and pronounce the sound of short vowel *a*.
- Write and say *The fat cat sat on my hat*. Use the picture cards to ensure understanding and have children repeat the sentence. Point to *fat, cat, sat, hat*, explaining that rhyming words sound alike except for the beginning sound.

VISUAL LEARNERS

Materials: letter card *Aa*

Write the following words on the board, leaving out the vowel: *bad, tap, sad, bag, had, ran*. Have children place their letter card in the word and read the completed word.

AUDITORY/KINESTHETIC LEARNERS

Materials: tape player, marching music

Ask the class to draw pictures whose names contain the short *a* sound. Then, play music and have children march like ants in a line, holding up their pictures. Stop the music at times and ask several children to name their pictures.

Say the names of the pictures in each row.
Color the pictures whose names rhyme.

Phonograms/Rhyme

1. pan, rat (color), ax, cat (color)
2. man (color), can (color), fan (color), lamp
3. tag (color), tack, bag (color), bug
4. ram (color), dad, ham (color), lamb (color)
5. bat, cap (color), map (color), hand

HOME Help your child use rhyming words from the page to make up silly sentences such as *The rat chased the cat.*

68 Short vowel a: Phonograms/rhyme

CURRICULUM CONNECTIONS

SPELLING
Dictate the following words and sentences. Have children write the words as a spelling pretest.
1. **bag** — Fill the **bag** to the top.
2. **can** — I like peaches that come in a **can**.
3. **cat** — The **cat** plays with a ball.
4. **fan** — The **fan** makes the room cooler.
5. **ham** — Martha will bake a **ham**.
6. **map** — Did you find our town on a **map**?

WRITING
Write *band* on the board. Erase *b*, replace it with *s*, and read *sand*. Use both words in a short rhyme, such as *The band played on the sand.* Then, ask children to write or say aloud five words that rhyme with *cat, fan,* or *tap.* Have them use some of their words to write a simple rhyme. You may also wish to refer to *The Write Direction Big Book of Writing Models,* Teacher Resource Guide, Grade 1, page 126.

PORTFOLIO

TECHNOLOGY **AstroWord** Short Vowels: *a, i*

KINESTHETIC LEARNERS *PARTNERS*
Materials: Phonics Picture Cards: apple (45), ax (46), bag (47), cat (49), hand (51), hat (52), mitt (58), cup (63), mop (73), bed (76)

Shuffle the cards and fan them out face down. Have partners take turns drawing a card and saying the picture name. If the name has the short *a* sound, the child draws another card. Continue until all the cards have been drawn.

CHALLENGE
Have children complete a sentence by adding a word that rhymes with the underlined word.
1. The <u>cat</u> is ___.
2. It makes me <u>sad</u> when you act ___.
3. Pat the <u>sand</u> with your ___.

Children can make up additional rhyming sentences of their own.

EXTRA SUPPORT/INTERVENTION
Materials: letter cards *Ff, Mm, Pp, Rr, Tt, Vv*

Write *can* on the board and have children make the word with letter cards. Have them change the first letter to make new words and read each word. See Daily Phonics Practice, page 312.

Integrating Phonics and Reading

Guided Reading
Show children the cover illustration as you read the title. Ask who has a cat and what things might make a cat want to run.

First Reading Ask children who is running past Sandy in each picture.

Second Reading Ask children to identify the short *a* words. You may want to add these to the classroom Word Wall.

Comprehension
After reading, ask children the following questions:
• Who ran past Sandy? *Recall/Sequencing*
• Why did Sandy run after the dog ran by? *Inference/Cause and Effect*

ESL/ELL English Language Learners
Say *Jan ran past Sandy.* Ask two students to act out the action in the sentence. You may want to explain that *past* can also mean a former time.

Lesson 31   Pages 69–70

Short Vowel a

Skill Focus

Children will
★ recognize the short sound of a.
★ understand that a stands for /a/.
★ write uppercase and lowercase Aa.
★ apply what they have learned by reading and writing.

Teach

Phonemic Awareness: Phoneme Categorization Say the word *map*, elongating the medial short a sound: *maaaap*. Then say the word naturally. Encourage children to repeat the word. Review that the sound they hear in the middle of *map* is short *a*. Next, say groups of three words. Ask children to clap each time they hear a word that has the sound of short *a*.

- hat   pan   pin
- map   mop   mat

Sound to Symbol Write the words *bat*, *can*, and *pan* on the board. Read each word slowly, blending the individual phonemes before saying the words naturally: *bbbaaattt, cccaaannn, pppaaannn*. Discuss how the words are the same. (*The letter* a *stands for the short* a *sound.*)

Distribute copies of Blackline Master 13 and have children select the *a* letter card. As you read the following words, have children listen for short *a* and identify the position in which they hear the sound by placing their *a* card in the correct box on the blackline master. Use the following words: *rag, hat, apple, cap, ax*.

Handwriting Write *Aa* on the chalkboard and use the models on page 70 to review how to form the letters. Have children follow along with their fingers on their desktops.

Practice and Apply

Sound to Symbol As children complete page 69, encourage them to say the correct picture name softly to themselves by blending the phonemes.

Writing Note short *a* words in children's writing and check for correct spelling.

Reading Use *Haddie's Caps*, MCP Phonics and Reading Short Vowel Skills Library, Level A, to provide additional practice in reading words with the short *a* sound.

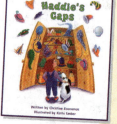

FOCUS ON ALL LEARNERS

ESL/ELL ENGLISH LANGUAGE LEARNERS

Use everyday objects whose names contain the sound of short *a* to identify children's comprehension of and ability to identify the sound of short *a*.

- Display an object. Ask a volunteer to name it and the vowel sound. Provide assistance naming objects if necessary.
- When all objects have been named, choose one and write its name plus two other words on the chalkboard. Have a volunteer underline the correct word and tell why the word was chosen.

AUDITORY/KINESTHETIC LEARNERS

Write these word pairs on the board: *fat, bag; pat, cat; wag, sap; fan, man;* and *tap, lap*. Read them aloud. When you say a rhyming pair, the children pantomime the action.

VISUAL LEARNERS

Materials: chart paper, drawing paper, crayons or markers

Draw a hat, a fan, and a cap at the top of a chart. Label the pictures. Touch a word and ask if children can make a rhyming word by changing the beginning letter. As children suggest words, write them in a list.

Sound to Symbol

► Read the words in the blue box. Print a word in the puzzle to name each picture.

Across →
2.
5.
6.

Down ↓
1.
3.
4.

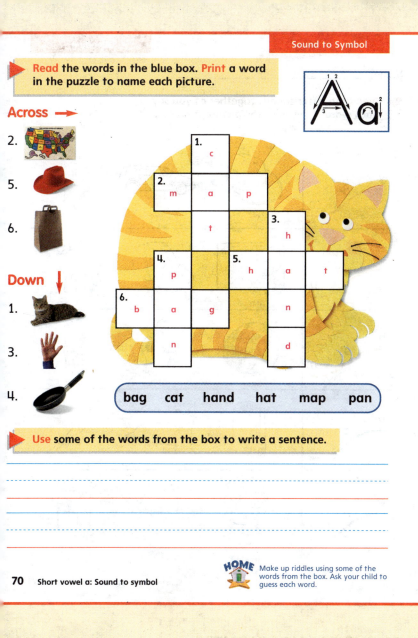

Across: 2. map 5. hat 6. bag
Down: 1. cat 3. hand 4. pan

| bag | cat | hand | hat | map | pan |

► Use some of the words from the box to write a sentence.

 Make up riddles using some of the words from the box. Ask your child to guess each word.

70 Short vowel a: Sound to symbol

CURRICULUM CONNECTIONS

SPELLING
Materials: index cards

Have children copy one of the list words *bag, can, cat, fan, ham,* and *map* onto one side of each index card. Then have them draw a picture of the word on the back of the card. Have them show one picture at a time to a partner, who should say and spell the word.

WRITING

Have children write two sentences that tell about a cat that has a cap. Ask them to include some other short *a* words in their sentences.

PORTFOLIO

TECHNOLOGY AstroWord Short Vowels: *a, i*

KINESTHETIC LEARNERS PARTNERS

Materials: Phonics Picture Cards: apple (45), bag (47), cap (48), cat (49), ham (50), hand (51), hat (52), pig (59), sun (67), box (70), boat (108), broom (123)

Shuffle the picture cards. Have partners work together to remove any cards with names lacking the short *a* sound.

CHALLENGE

Materials: paper ruled into 1-inch squares

Children can work in pairs to make word chains. Have one child write the letters for a short *a* word in the squares on the paper. Then have the partner write another word, using a letter from the first word as its first or last letter. Have them continue, taking turns.

EXTRA SUPPORT/INTERVENTION

Materials: letter cards: *Aa, Bb, Cc, Hh, Ff, Mm, Pp, Tt*

Write *cat* on the board and have children make the word with letter cards. Have them change the first letter to make new words and read each word. **See Daily Phonics Practice, page 312.**

Integrating Phonics and Reading

Guided Reading
Draw children's attention to the cover of the book and ask them what they think the book will be about. You may wish to use the activity in the English Language Learners section below.

First Reading Ask children to identify each hat and what Haddie does as she wears it.

Second Reading Ask children to identify the short *a* words in the story. You may want to add these words to the classroom Word Wall.

Comprehension
After reading, ask children the following questions:
• How does each of Haddie's caps fit the action she is doing? *Inference/Comparisons*
• Which of Haddie's caps is your favorite? Why? *Reflective Analysis/Personal Response*

ESL/ELL English Language Learners
After children have looked through the book, ask them what is on Haddie's head in each picture. (*A hat*) Explain that *cap* means almost the same thing as *hat*.

70

Lesson 32 Pages 71–72

Short Vowel a

Skill Focus

Children will
★ orally blend phonemes.
★ orally blend word parts.
★ identify picture names and spell words that contain the sound of short *a*.

Teach

Phonological Awareness: Rhyme
Say these groups of words and ask children to identify the two rhyming words:

- man ran pen
- nut cat pat
- land bend sand
- sat bit pat

Phonological Awareness: Blending Onsets and Rimes Tell children that you will say the parts of a word. Children should blend the parts together to say the word.

- /b/at *(bat)*
- /d/ad *(dad)*
- /f/an *(fan)*
- /k/amp *(camp)*

Explain that the sound heard in the middle of each word is short *a*.

Sound to Symbol Display and identify the picture cards for bag (47), cap (48), and hat (52). Then, write the words on the board and have children say them, blending the individual phonemes (/b/ /a/ /g/). Ask volunteers to underline the letter that stands for the short *a* sound in each word.

Practice and Apply

Phonological Awareness: Blending
Before children begin page 71, write *van* on the board, spacing the letters out, and draw the curving arrow underneath. Model how to blend the letters by running your hand under the arrow and saying *van*. For page 72, use *map* to model how to blend the initial *m* with the phonogram *ap*.

Sound to Symbol Point out the sample answer on page 72 and write *map* on the board. Ask children what letter stands for the sound of short *a*. Then underline the *a* in *map*.

Reading Use *Look at That!* MCP Phonics and Reading Short Vowel Skills Library, Level A, to provide additional practice in reading words with the short *a* sound.

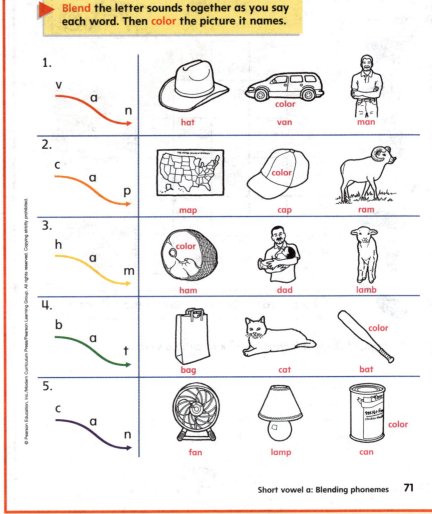

FOCUS ON ALL LEARNERS

ESL/ELL ENGLISH LANGUAGE LEARNERS
Materials: a cap and a can

- Before beginning page 71, show children a cap and a can. Ask a volunteer to name each object and the vowel sound he or she hears. Then, review the picture names on page 71. You may need to explain that the car in item 1 is called a van, and that the animal in item 2 is a ram, or male sheep.

- Before beginning page 72, review picture names with children (*fan, dad, cap, cat, lamb, bag*). To model a rhyme, read a rhyming sentence, such as *The fat cat chased the rat*. Then, ask children to explain what rhyming words are by giving examples from the rhyme. Complete the first item together to make sure children understand they will draw a line to the picture with a rhyming name.

VISUAL LEARNERS GROUPS
Materials: paper bag, index cards
Have each child in the group write five short *a* words on separate index cards and place the cards in the bag. Ask children to take turns picking a card, reading the word aloud, and using it in a sentence.

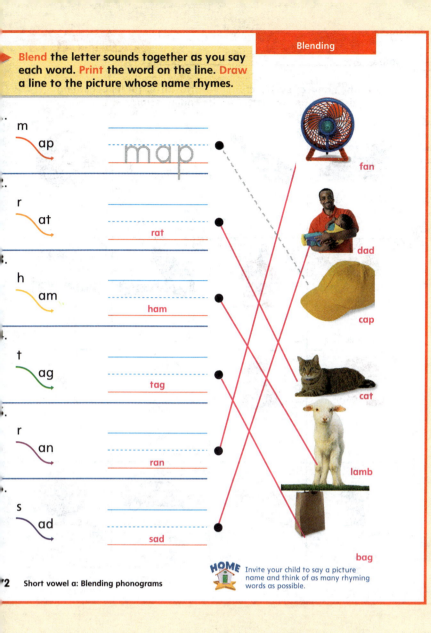

CURRICULUM CONNECTIONS

SPELLING
Write the spelling words *bag, cat, fan, ham,* and *map* on the board and read them aloud with the children. Then, say each of the following words and invite children to write the spelling word that rhymes with it: *man, tag, ram, cap, sat.*

WRITING

Write the words *I can* on the board and have children read. Ask children to describe or act out things they are good at doing. Then, have them write and illustrate an "I Can" poster.

SOCIAL STUDIES
Write the short *a* word *sad* on the board and tell children that everyone feels sad sometimes. Remind them that being silly can help. Ask children to look again at the words on pages 71 and 72. Have them use one or more of these words in a silly sentence that might make a sad person want to laugh.

 **AstroWord** Short Vowels: *a, i*

VISUAL LEARNERS
Materials: Phonics Picture Cards: cat (49), ax (46) pig (59), bell (77), ham (50), bag (47), bus (62), hat (52), box (70), hand (51)

Have one child take turns saying the picture names. The other child claps if the word has a short *a*.

CHALLENGE
Challenge children by having them write as many rhyming words as they can for each word on page 72.

EXTRA SUPPORT/INTERVENTION
Materials: letter cards Bb, Hh, Mm, Pp, Ss

Use letter cards to make word families with short *a*. For example, use the cards to spell *bad*. Ask children to change the *b* to *h* (*had*), the *h* to *m* (*mad*), and so on. See Daily Phonics Practice, page 312.

Integrating Phonics and Reading

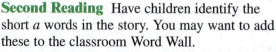

Guided Reading
Show children the cover illustration as you read the title. Ask what the boy and girl might be pointing at.
First Reading Ask children to use the pictures to point out the object the child is asking about on each page.
Second Reading Have children identify the short *a* words in the story. You may want to add these to the classroom Word Wall.
Comprehension
After reading, ask children the following questions:
• What do the children point to on the last page? *Recall/Description*
• What was surprising about it? *Inference/Drawing Conclusions*

ESL/ELL English Language Learners
Point to various objects in the classroom as you say *Look at that! Is that a . . .?* Have children complete the question by naming the object.

Lesson 33 Pages 73–74

Short Vowel a

Skill Focus

Children will

★ recognize the sound of short *a*.

★ identify and spell picture names that contain the sound of short *a*.

★ write words that contain the sound of short *a* to complete sentences.

★ recognize and read high-frequency words.

Teach

Phonemic Awareness: Phoneme Blending
Say the word *man*, separating the sound of each phoneme: /m/ /a/ /n/. Ask what vowel sound is heard in the middle. (short *a*) Have children say the word, stretching the medial sound: *maaan*.

Sound to Symbol Say the word *ram*, stretching the sound of each letter: *rrraaammm*. Ask children what letter stands for each sound. Write the word on the board.

Distribute Blackline Master 13. Have children place the *a* letter card on the middle box. Say the words *bag, fan, hat*. Have children listen for the initial and final sounds, then select the letters for each sound and place them in the correct boxes.

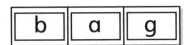

Practice and Apply

Blend Phonemes As children complete page 73, encourage them to say each picture name, blending together the three phonemes in each consonant-vowel-consonant word.

Writing For page 74, suggest that children try each word choice before writing a word. As they complete the activity, they will have the opportunity to read the following high-frequency words: *is, my, he, on, with*.

Critical Thinking For Talk About It, point out that the girl enjoys the things that Max does.

Reading Use *That Fly*, MCP Phonics and Reading Short Vowel Skills Library, Level A, to provide practice in reading words with the short *a* sound.

Spelling

Name _____

▶ **Say** the name of each picture. **Print** the letter for its beginning sound. Then **print** the letter for its ending sound.

1. c a t
2. p a n
3. t a g
4. h a m
5. m a p
6. d a d
7. r a m
8. r a t
9. h a t
10. b a g
11. c a n
12. b a t
13. m a n
14. c a p
15. v a n
16. f a n

Short vowel a: Spelling 73

FOCUS ON ALL LEARNERS

ESL/ELL ENGLISH LANGUAGE LEARNERS

- Before beginning page 73, have children look at the picture clues and raise a hand if they need help naming them. Then, explain that you will name each object. Children are to write the word you say under the picture. Repeat each word twice. Review after children have completed 5–6 target words; then continue.

- Help children understand the vocabulary on page 74 by asking them to identify the pertinent word for each picture. Say: *What animal is that?* and *Where is the cat sitting?*

VISUAL LEARNERS

Materials: paper bag, index cards or slips of paper

Have each child in the group write three short *a* words on separate cards or slips of paper and place the words in the bag. Ask children to take turns picking a card, reading the word aloud, and using it in a sentence.

KINESTHETIC LEARNERS

Have children say a sentence, leaving out a short *a* word which they can pantomime for others to guess. They might suggest *cat, sat, nap, lap, pan,* or *man*.

Words in Context

▶ **Look** at the picture. **Circle** the word that will finish the sentence. **Print** it on the line.

1. Max is my ___cat___ .
   cat (circled) / sat / can

2. He licks my ___hand___ .
   land / hand (circled) / ham

3. Max sits on my ___lap___ .
   pad / rap / lap (circled)

4. He likes my ___dad___ .
   sad / dad (circled) / bad

5. He plays with a ___bag___ .
   bat / rag / bag (circled)

6. Max takes a ___nap___ .
   nap (circled) / cap / cab

TALK About It Why does the girl like Max?

HOME Help your child think of sentences using words from the page to continue the story.

74 Short a: High-frequency words, critical thinking

CURRICULUM CONNECTIONS

SPELLING
Write the words *bag, can, cat, fan, ham,* and *map* on the board and read them with children. Give clues for each word, such as *It is an animal.* Have volunteers touch and spell the word that goes with the clue.

WRITING
Have children reread the story about Max on page 74. Then, suggest that they write and draw their own stories that tell more about Max. Brainstorm a list of short *a* words and write them on the board for children to use in their stories. Encourage them to use the high-frequency words *is, my, he, on, with.* Invite volunteers to share their stories with the class.

MATH
Invite children to name pets they have or would like to have. List the kinds of pets, such as gerbils, fish, cats, and dogs. Record the names of children who have or would like to have each kind of pet on a chart under the pet name. Have children count the names to determine which pets are the most popular and which are the most unusual.

TECHNOLOGY **AstroWord** Short Vowels: *a, i*

Integrating Phonics and Reading

Guided Reading
Have children look at the cover illustration as you read the title. Ask them what they think the book will be about.

First Reading Ask children where the fly is and what it is doing in each picture.

Second Reading Encourage children to identify the short *a* words in the story. You may want to add these to the classroom Word Wall.

Comprehension
After reading, ask children the following questions:
* What does the fly do after it comes in the window? *Recall/Sequence*
* Why does the fly go back out the window at the end of the story? *Reflective Analysis/Inference*

ESL/ELL English Language Learners
Draw an exclamation point on the board and make sure that children understand it is used to express strong feeling. Read the sentence *Look at that fly!* with expression, then ask children how the girl feels about the fly in her room.

AUDITORY/KINESTHETIC LEARNERS
GROUPS

Materials: fingerpaints, paper

Have children listen to words and paint a picture for each one with a name that contains a short *a.* They can write *a*'s under the pictures. Use *apple, ant, dog, cat, dad.*

CHALLENGE
Challenge children by having them think of a new song for a familiar tune. Encourage them to use short *a* rhyming words. As an alternate, you might have them listen to and identify short *a* words in a familiar song. In addition, have them use or listen for the high-frequency words *is, my, he, on, with.*

EXTRA SUPPORT/INTERVENTION
Materials: letter cards

Use letter cards to make groups of words with the same phonogram. For example, use cards to spell *bat.* Ask children to change the *b* to *c* to make *cat,* the *c* to *s* to form *sat,* the *s* to *h* to make *hat,* and so on. See **Daily Phonics Practice, page 312.**

74

Lesson 34 Pages 75–76

Short Vowel a

Skill Focus

Children will

★ identify picture names and spell words that contain the sound of short *a*.

★ write words that contain the sound of short *a* to complete sentences.

★ recognize and read high-frequency words.

Teach

Phonemic Awareness: Phoneme Substitution Tell children that they are going to make new words by changing the first letter in some words that you say; for example: *man*—change *m* to *v*. (*van*)

- *lap*—change *l* to *c* (*cap*)
- *rat*—change *r* to *s* (*sat*)
- *tack*—change *t* to *p* (*pack*)

Sound to Symbol Display word cards for *rag (28), ham (17),* and *pad (16).* Say *rrraaaggg*, stretching out the sound of each letter. Have one child take the word card and write the word on the board, then underline the letter *a*. Continue with *ham* and *pad*.

Words in Context: Decodable Words Write these words on the board: *lap, nap*. Then, write and read the sentence below. Have children select the word that completes the sentence.

- The cat sat on my ____. (*lap*)

Practice and Apply

Sound to Symbol As children complete page 75, encourage them to say each picture name, stretching out the sound of each letter.

Writing For page 76, suggest that children try each word choice before writing a word. As they complete the activity, they will have the opportunity to read the following high-frequency words: *got, in, the, it, was, time, to, go, made*.

Critical Thinking For Talk About It, discuss Jan playing and making a mask at camp.

Reading Use *Bags, Can, Pots, and Pans,* MCP Phonics and Reading Short Vowel Skills Library, Level A, to provide practice in reading words with the short *a* sound.

Spelling

Name _____

▶ Say the name of each picture. Print the name on the line. In the last box, draw a picture of a short *a* word. Print the word.

1. fan
2. cap
3. bag
4. dad
5. rat
6. can
7. ram
8. man
9. hand
10. map
11. ant
12.

Short vowel a: Spelling **75**

FOCUS ON ALL LEARNERS

ESL/ELL ENGLISH LANGUAGE LEARNERS

- For page 75, explain that you will name the first object. Have children write the word you say under the picture. Repeat each word twice. Complete 5 to 6 of the target words, then verify that children have correctly written the dictated words.

- Before beginning page 76, discuss summer camp and what happens there. Then, talk about the plot of the story told in the worksheet. Include vocabulary needed to complete the activity, such as talking about what a van is. Read the directions aloud and ask children to explain the activity to you in their own words. Model the first item for the group.

VISUAL LEARNERS

Materials: mural paper, paints or markers

Have small groups of children work together to create a mural that focuses on things with names containing the short *a* sound. You might brainstorm a list, such as *cat, hat, sand,* etc. Encourage children to make a list of all the items in the mural whose names have the short sound of *a*.

Words in Context

Read the sentences. Circle the word that will finish each sentence. Print it on the line.

1. Jan got in the _____ van _____.
   can / (van) / cat

2. It was time to go to _____ camp _____.
   cap / lamp / (camp)

3. In the van, Jan had a _____ nap _____.
   tap / (nap) / sat

4. At camp, Jan made a name _____ tag _____.
   (tag) / rag / tan

5. Jan made a mask with a _____ bag _____.
   wag / bad / (bag)

6. Jan played in the _____ band _____.
   (band) / can / hand

 Do you think Jan had fun at camp? Why?

 Ask your child questions that can be answered with words on the page, such as *Jan was sleepy so she took a ____.* (nap)

Short a: High-frequency words, critical thinking

CURRICULUM CONNECTIONS

SPELLING
Write the list words on the board. Have partners play "spell and mix." One partner selects the letters for a list word and mixes them up. The other partner tries to put them back together to make the list word.

WRITING
Have the children reread the story about Jan on page 76. Then, suggest that they write about something else Jan did at camp. Brainstorm a list of short *a* words and write them on the board for children to use in their stories. Add the high-frequency words *to, in, the, got, go, it, was, time, made* as a separate list for children to use. Encourage them to add titles and illustrate their stories. Invite volunteers to read their stories aloud.

SOCIAL STUDIES
Talk about what it might be like to stay over one night at a camp. Where do people sleep? How do they feel? What can they do to help others who might be homesick? Then, have small groups act out a "First Night at Camp" scene.

 **AstroWord** Short Vowels: *a, i*

Integrating Phonics and Reading

Guided Reading
Show children the cover as you read the title. Invite them to predict what people might do with bags, cans, pots, and pans.

First Reading Ask children to use the illustrations to point out the object or objects named on each page.

Second Reading Have children identify the short *a* words in the story.

Comprehension
After reading, ask children the following questions:
- What is the family doing? *Recall/Drawing Conclusions*
- Why do they need a big new van? *Inference/Cause and Effect*

ESL/ELL English Language Learners
Draw children's attention to the word *get* on page 3. Explain that because *get* is a command, the word *you* is understood. Reread pages 4 and 5 to make sure that children understand the use of *get* on these pages.

AUDITORY LEARNERS
Materials: a tape of songs for children

Have children listen to a song and write down any words they hear that have the short *a* sound.

CHALLENGE
Challenge children to make up riddles that can be answered with the picture names on page 75. For example, a child might say, *This could hold soup or vegetables.* (can)

EXTRA SUPPORT/INTERVENTION
Materials: Phonics Picture Cards: cap (48), cat (49), hand (51)

Ask children to form a circle and distribute the pictures. When you say *Go*, have children start passing the picture cards around the circle. When you say *Stop*, children with cards name them and say a word that rhymes with the picture name. See Daily Phonics Practice, page 312.

Lesson 35 Pages 77–78

Phonics and Reading / Phonics and Writing

Short Vowel a

Skill Focus

Children will

★ Read words that contain the sound of short *a*.

★ write short *a* words to finish sentences.

★ build words with short *a* phonograms -an, -ap.

★ recognize and read high-frequency words

ESL/ELL Many languages other than English do not discriminate between long and short vowel sounds. Provide opportunities for children to hear and say short-vowel words.

Teach

Phonemic Awareness: Phoneme Categorization Display the picture cards for hat (52), cat (49), bag (47). Have children name each picture. Then, ask which two picture names sound the same. (*hat, cat*) Talk about how the words are the same (rhyme, short *a* sound, same ending consonant), and how they are different (different beginning consonant).

Sound to Symbol Have children use their letter cards to form -at. Then have them take out the *c, d, f, h, l,* and *m* cards. Ask them which real words they can make. (*cat, fat, hat, mat*)

Read Words in Sentences Write this sentence on the board.

• The ant ran fast.

Help children read the sentence. Then, ask them to circle the words that have the short *a* sound.

Practice and Apply

Phonics and Reading After children have read the story, have them identify words that have the short *a* sound. As children are reading, they will have the opportunity to read the following high-frequency words: *takes, runs, up, not, get.*

Critical Thinking To discuss the Talk About It question, ask what the cat was doing before the ant came and what the ant did.

Phonics and Writing For page 78, tell children to try each letter at the top to make a word with -an or -ap. Remind them that not every letter will make a real word.

Reading Use *It's Hot,* MCP Phonics and Reading Short Vowel Skills Library, Level A, to provide practice in reading words with short *a*.

Read the story. Use short *a* words to finish the sentences.

Go, Ant!

The cat **takes** a nap.
The ant **runs** fast.
The ant is on the cat.
The cat is **up**!

The cat taps the ant.
Go, ant, go!
The cat can **not get** the ant.

1. The _____ant_____ runs fast.

2. The ant is on the _____cat_____.

3. The cat _____taps_____ the ant.

Talk About It Why does the cat want to catch the ant?

Review short vowel a: Reading, critical thinking   77

FOCUS ON ALL LEARNERS

ESL/ELL ENGLISH LANGUAGE LEARNERS

Use the following activities to teach English language learners.

• Read "Go, Ant!" aloud to children. As you read the story a second time, ask children to underline all the words that contain short *a*.

• Read the story again, asking children to read one line at a time.

• Assist children who need support in making the sound of *a* to pronounce each word.

VISUAL/KINESTHETIC LEARNERS

Materials: black construction paper, white chalk, glue

Write short *a* words on the chalkboard, such as *cat, nap, taps, can*. Have children cut out oval shapes from black construction paper and glue these shapes together, then use chalk to copy a short *a* word on each part of their "ant." Illustrate an anthill on a bulletin board, and have children attach their ants to the board.

77

Phonics & Writing

Building Words

Use one of the letters to make a word with **an** or **ap**. Write each real word on the lines.

r y c m p — an

1. ran
2. can
3. man
4. pan

c l b n t — ap

5. cap
6. lap
7. nap
8. tap

▶ Write a sentence using one of the words you made.

_____
_____
_____

HOME Invite your child to think of more words that end with *an* or *ap* such as *fan, tan, gap, map, rap, zap*.

78 Review short vowel a: Phonograms

KINESTHETIC LEARNERS
Materials: letter cards *Aa, Bb, Cc, Nn, Pp, Tt*

Have children use letter cards to make the word *ant*. Then have them change one letter at a time to make new words. When a child has made a word, have him or her read and spell it for the group. Possible words are *an, tan, can, tap, nap*.

CHALLENGE
Write the words *black ants* on the board. Challenge children to make as many short *a* words as they can from the letters in these words. Possible words include *at, sat, cat, tan, tank, lab, back, blast, last*.

EXTRA SUPPORT/INTERVENTION
Write the words *cat, ant, fast, nap* on the board. Have children look at the picture on page 77. Point to one word at a time and help children read it. Then, invite a volunteer to use the word in a sentence that tells something about the picture. See Daily Phonics Practice, page 312.

CURRICULUM CONNECTIONS

SPELLING
For the spelling posttest, dictate a word and then read it in context in the sentence.
1. **cat** My **cat** says meow.
2. **can** I **can** sing.
3. **ham** One kind of meat is **ham**.
4. **nap** The cat takes a **nap**.
5. **bag** I have an apple in the **bag**.
6. **ant** The **ant** runs fast.

WRITING

Have children reread the story about the ant and the cat on page 77. Then, suggest that they write about what the ant and the cat might be thinking as the story unfolds. Encourage children to share their ideas with the class.

SCIENCE
Materials: picture books about ants

Challenge children to find out three interesting facts about ants. Help them gather and bind the pages into an ant book to share.

TECHNOLOGY **AstroWord** Short Vowels: *a, i*

Integrating Phonics and Reading

Shared/Guided Reading
Have children look at the cover while you read the title. Explain that they will read about what the boy and mother do when it's hot.

First Reading Have children read the boy's words as you read the mother's.

Second Reading Help children identify words with the short *a* vowel sound.

Comprehension
After reading, ask children the following questions:
• Why does the boy say no to all of his mother's suggestions? *Recall/Character*
• Why won't the boy's idea work? *Reflective Analysis/Cause and Effect*

ESL/ELL English Language Learners
Review the story with children, asking *Do you want ___ ?* Have children use the pictures to complete each question. Children should point to the object and say the short *a* word.

Lesson 36 **Pages 79–80**

Take-Home Book

Review Short Vowel a

> **Skill Focus**
>
> Children will
> ★ read short *a* words in the context of a story.
> ★ reread for fluency.

Teach

Build Background

- Recall with children that the theme of this unit is "Amazing Animals." Ask children to name some of the animals they have read about in this unit.

- Print the word *bat* on the chalkboard and read it aloud. Ask what children know about bats. If necessary, explain that a bat looks something like a mouse, has wings, and can fly. Explain that they will be reading a book about bats.

Phonemic Awareness: Phoneme Substitution Point to the word *bat* written on the board. Invite children to read it aloud and identify the vowel sound they hear. (short vowel *a*) Then, have children delete the *b* at the beginning of the word and add other consonants to form words that rhyme with *bat*, such as *rat, hat, sat, cat, mat, pat.*

Sound to Symbol Display the word cards for *bat* (9), *has* (10), and *can* (12) on the chalkboard ledge. Then, write these word forms on the board: *b_t, h_s, c_n.* Pick a word card and ask a volunteer to read the word, then use the letter card *Aa* to complete the word on the board.

Practice and Apply

Read the Book Help children tear out and fold the pages to make their Take-Home Books. Encourage children to look through the book and talk about the pictures. Then, read the story together. Discuss what children learned about bats.

Sound to Symbol Read aloud or have volunteers read the book. Ask children what words have the short *a* sound: *bat, has, can, fast.* Invite volunteers to write the words on the board and read them aloud. You may want to point out that *far* is not a short *a* word, because the *r* changes the sound of the *a*.

Reread for Fluency Have children reread the book to increase their fluency and comprehension. Children can take their books home to read and share with family members.

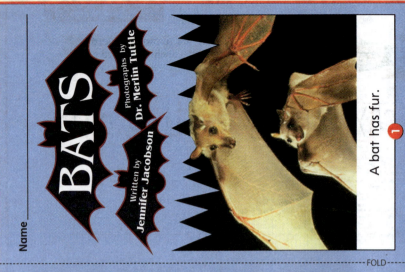

FOCUS ON ALL LEARNERS

ESL/ELL ENGLISH LANGUAGE LEARNERS
After assisting children with making the Take-Home Book, use the following activities to teach English language learners.

- Tell children to look at the photos and begin a discussion about bats. You may wish to make a word web to organize information about bats.
- Read the story together.
- Have children look through the story for familiar words that contain the sound of short *a*. Keep a list on the chalkboard of all the words they find, and read the list aloud to children.

KINESTHETIC/AUDITORY LEARNERS

Materials: letter cards *Aa, Nn, Dd, Bb, Ss, Hh, Mm, Pp, Cc, Rr, Tt*

Have children work with a partner to create short *a* words with the phonograms *-ad* and *-an*. Encourage partners to read the words aloud.

2. This bat has a bug.

3. A bat can go far.

80 Review short vowel a: Take-home book

CURRICULUM CONNECTIONS

SCIENCE
Materials: chart paper, felt-tip marker

Invite children to share reasons why they think a story about bats is good for a unit about amazing animals. Brainstorm a list with children about why they think bats are amazing. Record the reasons on chart paper. You may wish to provide additional information about bats to add to the chart. For example: Most of the 850 different kinds of bats eat insects. A few kinds of bats eat fruit, fish, or other small animals. Bats use echolocation when they fly in the dark: They make high-pitched sounds, which bounce off objects. Bats listen to find out how far away they are from the objects.

SOCIAL STUDIES
Materials: modeling clay, construction paper

Children can use materials to begin work on a class zoo. On construction paper they can make paths and designate areas for the animals. Have them begin by making animals whose names contain the short *a* sound, such as *bat, bobcat, camel.*

LANGUAGE ARTS

Materials: crayons, construction paper

Invite children to make up animal rhymes using as many short *a* words as possible. You may wish to share this example.

  A cat with a fan.
  A cat on a mat.
  A cat in a band.
  Imagine that!

 **AstroWord** Short Vowels: *a, i*

KINESTHETIC LEARNERS GROUPS
Play a game called "Bats in a Cave." Mark one corner of the room Bat Cave and the opposite corner Bat Tree. Have children stand in the "cave." Explain that they are to listen for words that have the short sound of *a*. If they hear a word that has the short sound of *a*, they can fly from the cave to the tree or from the tree to the cave. Then, give words such as *snack, run, fast, hop,* and *hand*.

CHALLENGE
Materials: picture books about bats

Challenge children to find out more about bats. Encourage them to look through picture books for facts and then to write and illustrate what they learn.

EXTRA SUPPORT/INTERVENTION
Materials: Take-Home Books

Read the story aloud to children as they follow along in their books. Then, invite them to reread each page of the story with you. **See Daily Phonics Practice, page 312.**

Lesson 37 Pages 81–82

High-Frequency Words

Skill Focus

Children will

★ recognize and write the high-frequency words *I, my, here, the, with, said*.

★ use the high-frequency words to complete sentences.

★ begin to recognize irregular spelling patterns.

Teach

Analyze Words Write the words *I, my, here, the, with, said* on the board. Slowly point to each letter as you read each word aloud. Then:

- Have children use letter cards to spell each word.

- Repeat each word by stretching each sound. Encourage children to point to each letter in the word as they hear its sound.

- Help children associate the sounds they hear in each word with a familiar word.

- Have children say each word, blending the sounds.

- You may wish to make a class Word Wall so that children can use the words they learn to find similar spelling patterns and phonemic elements in new words.

Read Words in Sentences Write the following sentences on the board. Invite volunteers to underline the high-frequency words. Then, help children read the sentences.

Pat is <u>here</u> <u>with</u> Jan.

"<u>I</u> like <u>my</u> friend Pat," <u>said</u> Jan.

Pat and Jan ran to <u>the</u> van.

Practice and Apply

Write Words Have children turn to page 81. Read the directions aloud and make sure children understand what to do. Do the same for page 82. Encourage them to use the strategies they have learned to associate sounds with letters and blend words to help them read. Children can work with a partner to complete Checking Up.

Reading You may wish to use *My Cat*, MCP Phonics and Reading Library, High Frequency Word Collection, Level A, to reinforce some of the high-frequency words.

High-Frequency Words

Name _____

▶ Read the words in the box. Write a word to finish each sentence.

I	the
My	with
here	said

1. Pal got ____the____ ball.

2. "Run," ____said____ Dan to Pal.

3. Pal ran ____with____ the ball.

4. "Now run ____here____, Pal," said Dan.

5. "____My____ dog runs fast," Dan said.

6. "____I____ like to play with my dog."

High-frequency words 81

FOCUS ON ALL LEARNERS

ESL/ELL ENGLISH LANGUAGE LEARNERS

Some children whose first language is not English may have difficulty pronouncing /th/ and the *y* that has a long *i* sound.

- Write each word on an index card.

- As you show children a word, read it aloud and have children repeat it. Then, ask them to use the word in a sentence.

AUDITORY LEARNERS

Materials: high-frequency word cards

Provide each group with a set of the high-frequency word cards *I, my, here, the, with, said*. Have one child in each group select a word card, read the word, then create an oral sentence or phrase using the word. Have groups continue until everyone has had a chance to create a sentence and all words have been used.

High-Frequency Words

> **Unscramble** the letters to **write** a word from the box. The word shapes will help you print the words.

here	my
said	with
	the

1. asdi — s a i d
2. eth — t h e
3. hree — h e r e
4. hwit — w i t h
5. ym — m y

> Put a ✔ next to each word you can read.

☐ with   ☐ said   ☐ my   ☐ here   ☐ the   ☐ I

HOME Using any two words on the page, help your child make up a sentence, then draw a picture to go with it.

82 High-frequency words

CURRICULUM CONNECTIONS

SOCIAL STUDIES
Review the story about the boy throwing a ball to his dog on page 81. Call on volunteers to describe games people like to play with their pets. Encourage them to use the high-frequency words to tell about their pets.

ART/WRITING
Encourage children to write a complete sentence using as many high-frequency words as possible. For example, children might write *A cat is with my dog.* Then have them illustrate their sentence. You may also wish to refer to *The Write Direction Big Book of Writing Models*, Teacher Resource Guide, Grade 1, page 183.

KINESTHETIC LEARNERS — PARTNERS
Materials: letter cards
Make sure children have the letter cards to spell the high-frequency words, including three *e*'s and three *h*'s. Have partners mix up the cards, then unscramble them to spell *my, here, the, with, said.* You may want to write the words on the board to provide a reference.

CHALLENGE
Invite children to write a sentence using one or more of the high-frequency words. Encourage them to cut apart the individual words. Then have them put the parts together to make the original sentence. They can also try leaving out a word or rearranging the words to try to make a new sentence that makes sense.

EXTRA SUPPORT/INTERVENTION
Materials: letters card *Mm, Ss, Hh, Tt, Ww*
Print the word parts __ere, __y, __aid, __he, __ith on the chalkboard. Call on volunteers to select a letter card to place in front of a word part to make a high-frequency word. If the word is correct, have the child write the letter to complete the word. Then have children copy each word to make their own list for reference. Ask them to read each word as they complete it.

Integrating Phonics and Reading

Shared/Guided Reading
Ask children to share their experiences with pet cats. Invite them to tell what they know about how cats behave.

First Reading Have children read the sentences beginning *I love* as you read the other sentences.

Second Reading Ask children to identify the words that are repeated in the story and what's different about the last page.

Comprehension
After reading, ask children the following questions:

- What does the boy in the story do after he plays with blocks? *Recall/Sequence*
- What was funny about the last page of the story? *Reflective Analysis/Understanding Humor*

ESL/ELL English Language Learners
Make sure that children understand that the words *I* and *my* refer to the boy who is telling the story. Invite children to read the text as if they were the main character telling a story about themselves.

82

Lesson 38 Pages 83–84

Short Vowel i

Skill Focus

Children will

★ recognize the sound of short *i*.

★ identify picture names and words that contain the sound of short *i*.

★ identify rhyming short *i* words.

ESL/ELL Children who speak a language other than English may pronounce *i* like the *e* in *me*. Practice *sit/seat*; *fit/feet*; *bin/bean*; etc.

Teach

Phonemic Awareness: Phoneme Categorization Say the word *lid*, elongating the medial short *i* sound. Then say the word naturally. Have children repeat the word. Tell children that the sound they hear in the middle of *lid* is short *i*. Next, say these groups of words. Ask children to clap when they hear a word that has the sound of short *i*.

- pin   six   mat
- crib cap   skin
- bat   fit   list

Phonological Awareness: Rhyme Say *Jill, will*. Point out that these words rhyme. Then, read aloud the sentences below. Ask children to tell you which two words in each sentence rhyme.

- Kit made a fish dish. (*fish, dish*)
- Jim had a quick swim. (*Jim, swim*)
- Rick has a bib and a crib. (*bib, crib*)

Sound to Symbol Write the word *pig* on the board and underline the *i*. Explain that this letter represents the short *i* sound heard in the middle of *pig*. Then, write these words on the board: *pink, sit, will*. Ask volunteers to underline the letter that makes the short *i* sound in each word.

Practice and Apply

Phonemic Awareness Read aloud the rhyme on page 83. Have children listen for and name the words that have the sound of short *i*. (*big, pink, pig, fig, wig, did, jig*)

Sound to Symbol Help children identify the pictures on pages 83 and 84. Suggest that they say the picture names softly to themselves as they complete each page.

Reading Use *Stop That!* MCP Phonics and Reading Short Vowel Skills Library, Level A, to provide practice in reading words with the short *i* sound.

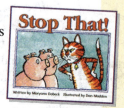

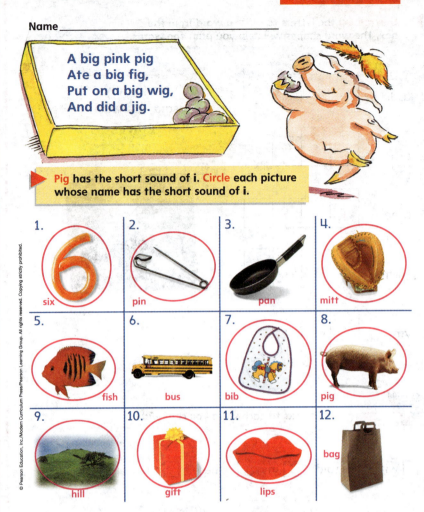

A big pink pig
Ate a big fig,
Put on a big wig,
And did a jig.

Pig has the short sound of **i**. **Circle** each picture whose name has the short sound of **i**.

1. six
2. pin
3. pan
4. mitt
5. fish
6. bus
7. bib
8. pig
9. hill
10. gift
11. lips
12. bag

Short vowel i: Phonemic awareness 83

FOCUS ON ALL LEARNERS

ESL/ELL ENGLISH LANGUAGE LEARNERS

- Before beginning page 83, pantomime actions for *ate a big fig*, *put on a big wig*, and *did a jig*, using props to clarify meaning if necessary.

- Read aloud the directions for page 84 and remind children that rhyming words sound alike except for the beginning sound. You may want to offer examples, such as *dim-him* and *pink-sink*. Then, ask a volunteer to name the pictures in item 1. Assist children in determining which picture names rhyme, and have them color the pictures (*bib* and *crib*). Have children work in pairs to complete items 2 to 5, then review answers aloud.

VISUAL/KINESTHETIC LEARNERS

Materials: Phonics Picture Cards: ax (46), bag (47), cap (48), hand (51), hat (52), bib (54), lid (57), mitt (58), pig (59), six (60)

Place the picture cards along the chalkboard ledge. Have one child at a time select a card that has a short *i* sound and say its name.

83

Phonograms/Rhyme

▶ **Say** the names of the pictures in each row.
Color the pictures whose names rhyme.

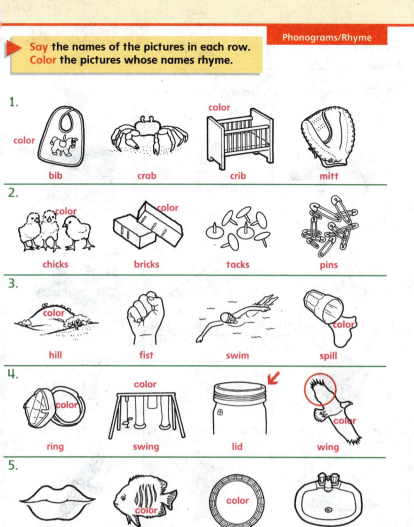

1. bib, crab, crib, mitt
2. chicks, bricks, tacks, pins
3. hill, fist, swim, spill
4. ring, swing, lid, wing
5. lips, fish, dish, sink

84 Short vowel i: Phonograms/rhyme

HOME With your child, make up silly sentences using the rhyming words from each row.

CURRICULUM CONNECTIONS

SPELLING
For the spelling pretest, dictate a list word and then read it in context in the sentence.
1. **fish** A **fish** swims in the pond.
2. **lid** A **lid** is a cover for a jar.
3. **pig** A **pig** is an animal that lives on a farm.
4. **pin** I have a round **pin** with a smiling face on it.
5. **sing** We'll **sing** a new song.
6. **six** The number **six** is one more than five.

WRITING
Have pairs of children work together to write and illustrate a silly sentence about a pig in a wig. Encourage them to share their sentence with other pairs.

 **AstroWord** Short Vowels: a, i

---

AUDITORY LEARNERS
Materials: plastic lid

Write *i* on one side of a lid and *a* on the other. Have children take turns flipping the lid. The child who flips must say a word with the short sound of the letter that lands face up.

CHALLENGE
Materials: index cards or slips of paper, margarine tub or small box

Label the box or margarine tub Short *i* Word Bank. Have children write words that have /i/ on index cards and put them in the container.

EXTRA SUPPORT/INTERVENTION
Materials: Phonics Picture Cards: bib (54), lid (57), mitt (58), pig (59), six (60)

Place the picture cards along the chalkboard ledge. Say a word and have children repeat it. Then, have a volunteer select the picture whose name rhymes with the word you said. Words to use are *kid, sit, wig, mix,* and *rib*. See Daily Phonics Practice, pages 312–313.

Integrating Phonics and Reading

Guided Reading
Show children the cover illustration as you read the title. Ask children who in the story will be saying these words.

First Reading Ask children what the cat wants the pigs to stop doing on each page.

Second Reading Ask children to identify the words that rhyme with *pig* or *pigs*.

Comprehension
After reading, ask children the following questions:
• Why do the pigs say "Scat, cat!" at the end?
  Inference/Character
• Were you surprised by the story's ending?
  Reflective Analysis/Cause and Effect

ESL/ELL English Language Learners
Review the story with children, having them pantomime the actions of the pigs. Children should stop when you say, *Stop that!*

Lesson 39 — Pages 85–86

Short Vowel i

Skill Focus

Children will

* recognize the short sound of *i*.
* understand that *i* stands for /i/.
* write uppercase and lowercase *Ii*.
* apply what they have learned by reading and writing.

Teach

Phonological Awareness: Blending Onsets and Rimes Say /h/id. Have children blend the sounds together to say the word *hid*. Then, say these words. Ask children to repeat the parts after you, then orally blend the parts to make the word:

* /l/ip (*lip*)
* /d/id (*did*)
* /r/ib (*rib*)
* /p/ig (*pig*)

Explain that the sound heard in the middle of each word is short *i*.

Sound to Symbol Write the words *hit, pin,* and *fish* on the board and read each one aloud. Ask what is the same about all the words. Help children conclude that the letter *i* stands for the short *i* sound in each word. Have children reread the words and suggest others with the sound of short *i*. Write the words on the board and ask volunteers to underline the letter that stands for the short *i* sound.

Handwriting Write *Ii* on the chalkboard and use the models on page 86 to review how to form the letters. Have children use their fingers to trace the letters in the air.

Practice and Apply

Phonemic Awareness Help children identify the pictures on page 85. Have them say each picture name, emphasizing the vowel sound.

Writing Note the short *i* words that children write on page 86 and check for correct spelling.

Reading Use *The Big Cat*, MCP Phonics and Reading Short Vowel Skills Library, Level A, to provide practice in reading words with the short *i* sound.

Say the name of each picture. Circle its name.

1.	pin wig (pig)
2.	(six) ax mix
3.	hid (lid) did
4.	(bib) bit bad
5.	fin (pin) pan
6.	fill (hill) bill
7.	mix mat (mitt)
8.	sing sank (sink)
9.	will (milk) mitt
10.	win (fin) fan
11.	(fist) fish fast
12.	win (wing) ring

Short vowel i: Sound to symbol 85

FOCUS ON ALL LEARNERS

ESL/ELL ENGLISH LANGUAGE LEARNERS

* Before beginning page 85, help children identify the pictures on the page. Have them say each picture name, emphasizing the vowel sound. After children have completed the page, review answers aloud as a group.

* For page 86, display picture card 59 or a toy pig. Discuss what children know about pigs.

VISUAL LEARNERS

Materials: Phonics Word Cards: *big* (34), *dip* (35), *did* (36), *fill* (38), *fin* (39), *fit* (40), *hill* (43), *mix* (49), *pick* (50), *six* (56)

Have children stand in a circle. Display a card and ask children to say the word aloud. Have a volunteer name a rhyming word and then sit down. Repeat until everyone is sitting.

KINESTHETIC LEARNERS

Materials: Phonics Picture Cards: *ax* (46), *cap* (48), *hand* (51), *king* (56), *lid* (57), *mitt* (58), *pig* (59)

Have children name the pictures. Place the cards face down. Children can pick a card and dance a jig if the picture shows an object whose name contains the sound of short *i*.

Sound to Symbol

▶ Farmer Jill's pigs have short **i** words on them. Help Farmer Jill catch her pigs. **Circle** the short **i** words.

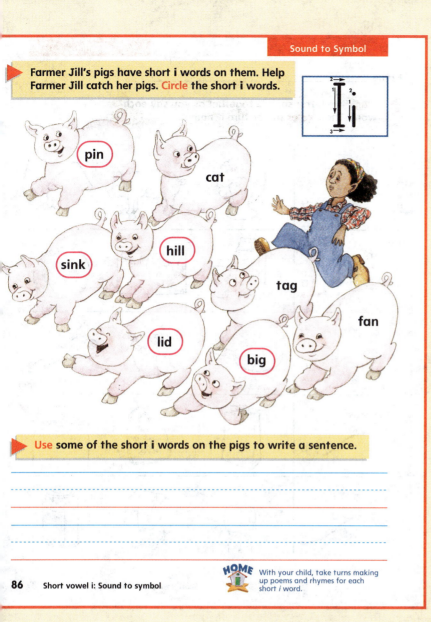

▶ **Use** some of the short **i** words on the pigs to write a sentence.

_____
_____

86 Short vowel i: Sound to symbol

HOME With your child, take turns making up poems and rhymes for each short *i* word.

CURRICULUM CONNECTIONS

SPELLING
Write the list words *fish, lid, pig, pin, sing,* and *six* on the board and read them with the children. Give an oral hint for each word, and when children guess the word, have them spell it.

WRITING
Have children choose a picture on page 85 and list several rhyming words. Ask them to write a pair of their rhyming words. For example, children might write *six mix.* Suggest they illustrate their rhyme and show a labeled picture to the group.

PORTFOLIO

SCIENCE/FINE ARTS
Tell children that fish have fins to help them move in the water. Help children find pictures of different kinds of fish, such as a goldfish, a trout, a tuna, etc. Encourage them to draw or paint small pictures of each fish they find. Staple the children's pictures together in a class book labeled *Fish Have Fins.*

TECHNOLOGY **AstroWord** Short Vowels: *a, i*

AUDITORY/KINESTHETIC LEARNERS

Have children play "Giant Steps." Ask everyone to stand in a line across the back of the room. Explain that each time they hear a word that has the same vowel sound as in *win,* they should take a giant step forward. Use the following words: *king, fill, fast, kind, must, sink, rat, pin, rain, milk, suit, mile, bit, bike, fin.*

CHALLENGE
Have children write about a fish with six silver fins, then have them draw a picture.

EXTRA SUPPORT/INTERVENTION
Materials: Phonics Picture Cards: bib (54), lid (57), mitt (58), pig (59), six (60)

Write the words *mitt, pig, bib, lid,* and *six* on the board. Give each child one picture card. Have each child name the picture and match the picture to the word on the board. Remind them to use the beginning and ending sound of each picture name to help them find the words. **See Daily Phonics Practice, pages 312–313.**

Integrating Phonics and Reading

Guided Reading

Show children the cover as you read the title. Ask what the big cat is. (*a tiger*) Have children share what they know about tigers.
First Reading Have children explain what the animals are doing on each page.
Second Reading Have children point out two rhyming short *i* words. (*slid, hid*)
Comprehension
After reading, ask children the following questions:
• How do the other animals feel about the big cat? *Inference/Drawing Conclusions*
• Did the ending surprise you? Why or why not? *Reflective Analysis/Personal Response*

ESL/ELL English Language Learners
Point out that *hid, slid,* and *sat still* are action words. Have children act out these actions.

Lesson 40 Pages 87–88

Short Vowels a, i

Skill Focus
Children will
★ orally blend phonemes.
★ orally blend word parts.
★ identify picture names and spell words that contain the sound of short *i* and short *a*.

Teach

Phonological Awareness: Rhyme Say these groups of words and ask the children to identify the two rhyming words. Then, help children to identify the sound heard in the middle of the rhyming words.

- can   man   pen   (short *a*)
- hill   fell   pill   (short *i*)
- sat   sit   bat   (short *a*)
- win   won   tin   (short *i*)

Phonological Awareness: Blending Onsets and Rimes Tell children that you will say the parts of a word. Have them blend the parts together to say the word. Then, help them identify the sound heard in the middle of each word.

- /f/ish (short *i*) /t/ag (short *a*)
- /b/at (short *a*) /h/ill (short *i*)

Sound to Symbol Display and identify picture cards for bib (54), cat (49), six (60), and bag (47). Then, write the words on the board and have children say them. Ask volunteers to come to the board and underline the letter that stands for the short *i* or short *a* sound in each word.

Practice and Apply

Phonological Awareness: Blending Before children begin page 87, write *wig* on the board, spacing the letters out, and draw the curving arrow underneath. Model how to blend the letters by running your hand under the arrow and saying *wig*. For page 88, model how to blend the initial *p* with the phonogram *-ig* to say *pig*.

Sound to Symbol Write *pig* on the board. Ask children what letter stands for the sound of short *i*. Repeat with *pan* and sound of short *a*. Point out that children will be writing both short *i* and *a* words on page 88.

Reading Use *My Hamster, Van*, MCP Phonics and Reading Short Vowel Skills Library, Level A, to provide practice in reading words with the short *a* and short *i* sound.

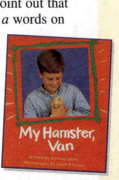

Blending

Name _____

▶ **Blend** the letter sounds together as you say each word. Then, **color** the picture it names.

1. w↘i↘g   color — wig   pig   tag
2. m↘a↘p   milk   map color   ham
3. p↘i↘n   pan   rip   pin color
4. b↘i↘b   bag   bib color   lid
5. m↘a↘n   man color   mitt   can

Short vowels a, i: Blending phonemes 87

FOCUS ON ALL LEARNERS

ESL/ELL ENGLISH LANGUAGE LEARNERS

- To teach children to differentiate words following the consonant-vowel-consonant (c-v-c) pattern by identifying the vowel and consonant sounds, write a series of c-v-c patterns on the board, omitting vowels: p_t, b_g, d_d, h_t, p_n. Ask volunteers to fill in the letter *i* and say the word. Then, ask them to erase the *i*, fill in the letter *a*, and say the word.

- Before beginning pages 87 and 88, read the directions aloud. Work with children to complete the first item on the page and verify understanding of the task.

KINESTHETIC LEARNERS

Materials: Phonics Picture Cards: bag (47), cap (48), cat (49), hat (52), king (56), pig (59), six (60), fish (163); 8 envelopes; 8 index cards

Play "Mail Call." Put one picture card and one index card in each envelope. Deliver the envelopes to eight children. Have these children write each picture name on an index card, then put the cards back in the envelopes and deliver the letter to a classmate. The recipient adds a rhyming word to the card and passes it along.

Blending

▶ **Blend** the letter sounds together as you say each word.
Print the word on the line. **Draw** a line to the picture it names.

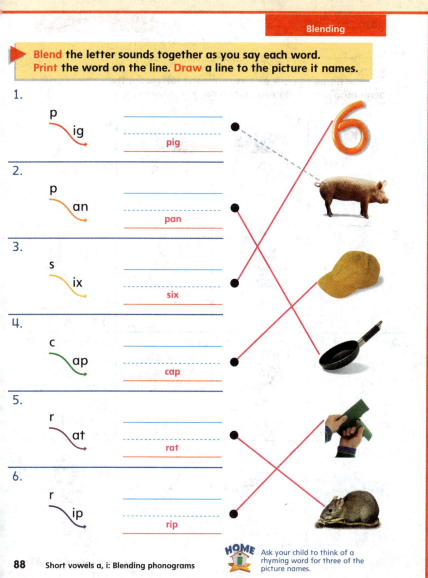

1. p / ig — pig
2. p / an — pan
3. s / ix — six
4. c / ap — cap
5. r / at — rat
6. r / ip — rip

HOME Ask your child to think of a rhyming word for three of the picture names.

Short vowels a, i: Blending phonograms

CURRICULUM CONNECTIONS

SPELLING
Materials: letter cards

Write the list words *fish, lid, pig, pin, sing,* and *six* on the board and read them aloud with children. Have children select one word and spell it with letter cards. Then, have them mix up the letters, exchange them with a partner, and unscramble them.

WRITING

Have children fold a piece of paper in thirds and draw the head of a pig, a bat, or a cat on the top third. Then, fold the paper so that the head is hidden and pass the paper to a classmate. This time each child draws the body of one of the animals and folds the page again. A third child draws the legs. Have children write a sentence about the animal.

SCIENCE
Prepare a chart about fish with the following headings: What We Know, What We Want to Know, and What We Learned. As children discuss, have them dictate facts for the chart.

TECHNOLOGY
AstroWord Short Vowels: *a, i*

Integrating Phonics and Reading

Guided Reading
Show the cover as you read the title. Ask if the book will tell a true story or a made-up story.
First Reading Ask children to use the photos to retell what is happening on each page.
Second Reading Have children identify the short *a* and *i* words in the story.
Comprehension
After reading, ask children the following questions:
• What makes Van a good pet? *Recall/Details*
• Would you like to have a hamster? *Reflective Analysis/Personal Response*

ESL/ELL English Language Learners
Ask children if they have pets. Have volunteers tell how they take care of them.

AUDITORY/KINESTHETIC LEARNERS
Have children put their fingertip to their lips if they hear a word that has the short sound of *i* or clap their hands if they hear a word that has the short sound of *a*. Use the following words: *hit, lap, six, cap, can, rib, man, sit, bag, sag, fix, bib*.

CHALLENGE
Challenge children to illustrate and write a sentence about a fat pig or a big cat.

EXTRA SUPPORT/INTERVENTION
Materials: Phonics Picture Cards: bag (47), cat (49), hat (52), lamp (53), bib (54), king (56), crib (124), flag (136), stamp (149), swing (152)

Make sure children know the name of each picture. Place the pictures face down. Have children turn over two cards at a time to try to match pairs of rhyming words. See Daily Phonics Practice, pages 312–313.

Lesson 41   Pages 89-90

Short Vowel i

Skill Focus

Children will

★ identify picture names and words that contain the sound of short *i*.

★ identify initial and final consonants in words that contain the sound of short *i*.

★ write words that contain the sound of short *i* to complete sentences.

★ recognize and read high-frequency words.

Teach

Phonemic Awareness: Phoneme Blending
Say the word *wig*, separating the sound of each phoneme: /w/ /i/ /g/. Ask what vowel sound is heard in the middle. (short *i*) Have children say the word, stretching the medial sound: *wiiig*. Repeat with *win*, *wink*, *lip*, *flip*, *bib*, *crib*.

Sound to Symbol After children say each segmented word, ask them what letter stands for each sound. Write the word on the board.

Words in Context: Decodable Words Write these words on the board: *dish*, *fish*. Then, write and read the sentence below. Have children select the word that completes the sentence.

• Jim can swim as fast as a ___! (*fish*)

Practice and Apply

Sound to Symbol As children complete page 89, encourage them to say each picture name, stretching out its beginning and ending sound. Point out that they will finish each word by writing the letters that stand for these sounds.

Writing For page 90, suggest that children try each word choice before writing a word. As they complete the activity, they will have the opportunity to read the high-frequency word *does*.

Critical Thinking For Talk About It, encourage children to tell what kind of pet they received and how they learned to take care of it.

Reading Use *Mr. Fin's Trip*, MCP Phonics and Reading Short Vowel Skills Library, Level A, to provide practice in reading words with phonograms *-ip*, *-in*, and *-it*.

Spelling

Name _____

▶ **Say** the name of each picture. **Print** the letters for its beginning and ending sounds. **Trace** the whole word.

1. w i g
2. l i d
3. p i g
4. s i x
5. p i n
6. r i p
7. b i b
8. g i f t
9. s i n k
10. m i l k
11. l i p s
12. c r i b
13. f i n
14. s i t
15. l i s t
16. f i s t

Short vowel i: Spelling   89

FOCUS ON ALL LEARNERS

ESL/ELL ENGLISH LANGUAGE LEARNERS

• For page 89, ask children to listen to and identify the beginning and ending sound of each picture name. Assist with items 1 to 3 to verify comprehension.

• Briefly summarize the plot of the "story" on page 90. Incorporate vocabulary words needed to complete the activity, such as *gift*, not *present*, and *dish*, not *bowl*. Then, read the directions and ask children to explain in their own words what they are to do. Model item 1 with children.

KINESTHETIC LEARNERS

Materials: Phonics Word Cards: *big* (34), *dip* (35), *hit* (38), *fin* (39), *lid* (46), *pill* (53)

Play "Sit Down." Have children stand in a circle and close their eyes. Quietly place the word cards on the floor in front of several children. Ask children to open their eyes. The children with cards read their word and use it in a sentence. Then, they may sit down. Play until everyone is sitting down.

Words in Context

▶ **Look** at the picture. **Circle** the word that will finish the sentence. **Print** it on the line.

1. I got a ___gift___.
   gap / **(gift)** / gum

2. Is it a ___mitt___?
   milk / **(mitt)** / tip

3. **Does** it drink ___milk___?
   (milk) / mitt / mat

4. Will it fit in a ___dish___?
   damp / dig / **(dish)**

5. Can it swim in the ___sink___?
   sick / **(sink)** / sank

6. It is a ___fish___!
   fist / fast / **(fish)**

TALK About It Did you ever get a pet as a gift? Tell about it.

HOME With your child, pick a word on the page and take turns changing the first letter to make new words, such as *dish—fish*.

90 Short i: High-frequency words, critical thinking

CURRICULUM CONNECTIONS

SPELLING
Materials: Letter Cards *Ff, Ll, Pp, Ss*

Have children locate their letter cards. List *-ish, -id, -ig, -in, -ing,* and *-ix* on the board. Invite volunteers to point out a word on the spelling list, while others locate and hold up the initial consonant for the word.

WRITING

Have children draw a fish swimming. Then, suggest that they trade pictures with a classmate and write a caption for the picture.

FINE ARTS
Children can make a print of a pig. Have them first draw an outline of a pig, then trace over it with a thin line of glue. When the glue is dry, children can use ink, paint, or colored chalk to cover the raised pig outline. They can make a print by placing the pig face down on a piece of colored construction paper and rubbing over the back of the pig.

TECHNOLOGY **AstroWord** Short Vowels: *a, i*

AUDITORY/KINESTHETIC LEARNERS
Have children make a fist when they hear a word that rhymes with *fist*. Use the following words: *kiss, kick, list, win, mist, gift, fit, pig, pick, six, wrist, miss.*

CHALLENGE
Challenge children to write and illustrate a sentence that uses at least three short *i* words, such as *Six fish swim.*

EXTRA SUPPORT/INTERVENTION
Materials: Phonics Picture Cards: bag (47), cap (48), cat (49), bib (54), lid (57), mitt (58), pig (59), six (60)

Shuffle the cards. Have a child select a card and name the picture. If the picture has a short *i* sound, have the child finger-write an *i* on the tabletop. If not, put the picture card aside. **See Daily Phonics Practice, pages 312–313.**

Integrating Phonics and Reading

Shared/Guided Reading
Show children the cover as you read the title. Invite them to predict where Mr. Fin will go on his trip.
First Reading Invite children to join in as you read the repeating text on pages 2, 4, 6, and 8.
Second Reading Have children identify the short *i* words in the story. You may want to add these to the classroom Word Wall.

Comprehension
After reading, ask children the following questions:
- What problem did Mr. Fin have? *Recall/Problem and Solution*
- How else could Mr. Fin have solved his problem? *Creative/Problem and Solution*

ESL/ELL English Language Learners
Have children make labeled pictures for these words from the story: *ship, grin, pants, rip, sit,* and *pin.*

Lesson 42 Pages 91–92

Short Vowel i

Skill Focus

Children will

★ identify picture names and spell words that contain the sound of short *i*.

★ write words that contain the sound of short *i* to complete sentences.

★ recognize and read high-frequency words.

◆ Teach

Phonemic Awareness: Phoneme Substitution Tell children that they will make rhyming sentences by changing the first letter in a word you say. Give this example: "A pink ___. Change *p* to *s: sink*. A pink sink." Then, give them these items.

1. A big ___: Change *b* to *w*. (wig)
2. A tin ___: Change *t* to *p*. (pin)
3. A quick ___: Change *qu* to *p*. (pick)

Sound to Symbol Put the following picture cards on the chalkboard ledge so that only the backs show: bib (54), lid (57), pig (59), six (60). Invite volunteers to pick a "mystery card" and write the picture name on the board.

Words in Context: Decodable Words Write these words on the board: *dig*, *big*. Then, write and read the sentence below. Have children select the word that completes the sentence.

• Kim has a ___ cat. (*big*)

◆ Practice and Apply

Sound to Symbol As children complete page 91, encourage them to say each picture name, stretching out each sound.

Writing For page 92, suggest that children try each word choice before writing a word. As they complete the activity, they will have the opportunity to read the following high-frequency words: *going, they, saw, that, just, she, glad, help*.

Critical Thinking For Talk About It, discuss how shovels, hands, and spoons can be used to dig.

Reading Use *I Can Swim*, MCP Phonics and Reading Short Vowel Skills Library, Level A, to provide practice in reading words with short *i*.

Spelling

Name_____

▶ Say the name of each picture. Print the name on the line. In the last box, draw a picture of a short i word. Print the word.

1. lid
2. six
3. pig
4. pin
5. bib
6. rip
7. wig
8. sink
9. hill
10. milk
11. gift
12.

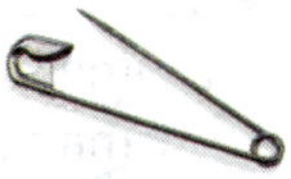

Short vowel i: Spelling 91

FOCUS ON ALL LEARNERS

ESL/ELL ENGLISH LANGUAGE LEARNERS

• You can use the worksheet on page 91 as a spelling and vocabulary test. Have children look at the picture clues. Name one of the objects on the page and ask children to write the word you say under the picture. When children have completed the worksheet, review the dictated words together.

• Before beginning page 92, ask children if they have ever seen real machines like the toys in the picture. Talk about what these big machines can do. Use words such as *dig, lift, move,* and *help*.

VISUAL/KINESTHETIC LEARNERS

Materials: Phonics Word Cards: *big-Rick* (34), *Bill-dip* (35), *fill-hit* (38), *it-lid* (46), *pill-quit* (53), *tip-tin* (57)

Distribute the cards to pairs of children. Have each child read the word and use it in a sentence. Then, ask the child to give the card to his or her partner. The second child can turn the card over, read the word, and use it in a sentence. Continue with new cards.

Words in Context

Read the sentences. Circle the word that will finish each sentence. Print it on the line.

1. Jim and Linda were going to ___dig___ . dog / (dig) / pig
2. They went to the top of the ___hill___ . bill / hit / (hill)
3. Jim saw a rock that was ___big___ . rig / (big) / bag
4. He could just see the ___tip___ . (tip) / tap / rip
5. Linda's truck moved ___it___ . at / (it) / if
6. She was glad to help ___him___ . (him) / her / rim

TALK What other things can be used to dig?

HOME With your child, make up sentences with short *i* words such as "With a shovel, I can ___."

Short i: High-frequency words, critical thinking

CURRICULUM CONNECTIONS

SPELLING
Write the list words *fish, lid, pig, pin, sing,* and *six* on the board. Have children pick a secret word and give an oral clue for another child to guess the word. When the word is guessed, have the child spell it.

WRITING
Materials: picture of a big truck

Display the picture and ask children to write about what the truck can do. Suggest that they use some short *i* words.

SCIENCE
Materials: informational picture books or encyclopedia articles about rocks; pictures or different examples of rocks

Make available several pictures of rocks or types of rocks. Discuss the ways in which the rocks are different: size, texture, color, shape, shiny or not shiny, etc. On the board, make a list of the characteristics of rocks.

TECHNOLOGY
AstroWord Short Vowels: *a, i*

AUDITORY/KINESTHETIC LEARNERS
Materials: letter card *Ii*

Have children trace over the letter *i* on the card when they hear a word that has the short sound of *i*. Use the following words: *list, win, mask, mist, gift, fit, stop, pig, lamp, pick, six, wrist, cold, miss.*

CHALLENGE
Have children each work with a partner to make a list of short *i* words. Have them write three sentences about a hill, using some words from their list. Ask them to illustrate their work.

EXTRA SUPPORT/INTERVENTION
Materials: Phonics Picture Cards: bag (47), cap (48), cat (49), bib (54), igloo (55), king (56), lid (57), mitt (58), pig (59), six (60)

Have a child select a card and name the picture. If the picture has a short *i* sound, have the child say the word and finger-write an *i* on the tabletop. If not, put the card aside. **See Daily Phonics Practice, pages 312–313.**

Integrating Phonics and Reading

Shared/Guided Reading
Show the cover as you read the title. Invite children to talk about different places to swim.

First Reading Have the children finish each sentence after you read, *I can swim with* (or *as*) . . .

Second Reading Write *swim* in the center of a word web. Have children fill in the web with other short *i* words from the story.

Comprehension
After reading, ask children the following questions:
- How does the girl feel about swimming? *Inference/Drawing Conclusions*
- What words might you add to the last page? *Creative/Point of View*

ESL/ELL English Language Learners
Help children think of other ways to say *I bet I can . . .*, such as *I think I can . . .* or *I'm sure I can . . .*

Lesson 43   Pages 93–94

Phonics and Reading / Phonics and Writing

Short Vowel i

Skill Focus

Children will

★ read words that contain the sound of short *i*.

★ write short *i* words to finish sentences.

★ build words with short *i* phonograms *-ig*, *-ing*.

★ recognize and read high-frequency words.

Teach

Phonemic Awareness: Medial Sound Isolation Say *hill*, then /i/. Tell children that you are saying a word and then its middle vowel sound. Model the procedure again, using *big*, then /i/. Then, have children say these words and follow each one with its middle vowel sound: *win, bit, wig, fill, miss*. Explain that the sound heard in the middle of each word is short *i*.

Sound to Symbol Have children use their letter cards to form the phonogram *-in*. Then, have them take out the *Ff, Hh, Mm, Pp, Rr*, and *Ww* cards. Ask them which real words they can make with the cards. (*fin, pin, win*)

Read Words in Sentences Write these sentences on the board.

- The big fish has fins.
- The little fish likes to swim.

Help children read the sentences. Then, ask them to circle the words with the short *i* sound.

Practice and Apply

Phonics and Reading After children have read the story, encourage them to identify words that begin with the short *i* sound. As children are reading, they will have the opportunity to read the following high-frequency words: *little, likes, friend*.

Critical Thinking For Talk About It, encourage children to tell how the two fish are friends because they have fun together.

Phonics and Writing For page 94, encourage children to say each word they can make softly to themselves to see if it is a real word.

Reading Use *Three Little Pigs and One Big Pig*, MCP Phonics and Reading Short Vowel Skills Library, Level A, to provide practice in reading words with short *i*.

Name_____

 **Read** the story. **Print** short **i** words to finish the sentences.

Fish Tale

The big fish has **little** fins.
The little fish has big fins.
The big fish **likes** to sing.
The little fish likes to swim.
The big fish sings to his **friend**.
The little fish waves a fin.

1. The _____**big**_____ fish has little fins.

2. The big fish likes to _____**sing**_____.

3. The little fish waves a _____**fin**_____.

TALK about it Why might the big and little fish be friends?

Review short i: Reading, critical thinking   93

FOCUS ON ALL LEARNERS

ESL/ELL ENGLISH LANGUAGE LEARNERS

- Before reading the story on page 93, have children tell what they see in the illustration. Encourage them to use these words: *big, little, fish, fin, sing, swim*. Read the story aloud several times. On the third reading, ask children to underline all the words that contain a short *i*.

- For page 94, read the directions aloud and ask children to explain in their own words what they are to do. Complete the first item together to verify understanding.

KINESTHETIC/VISUAL LEARNERS

Materials: Phonics Word Cards: *bag* (8), *hand* (18), *hat* (19), *pan* (27), *big* (34), *did* (36), *dig* (37), *fix* (41), *hill* (43), *lift* (48), *mix* (49), *win* (58), *will* (59); chalk or masking tape

Make one line for children to stand behind. Make a second line about 15 feet from the first. Shuffle the cards and show one word at a time. Have children read the word and take a step forward if it has the short *i* sound. Continue until children reach the finish line.

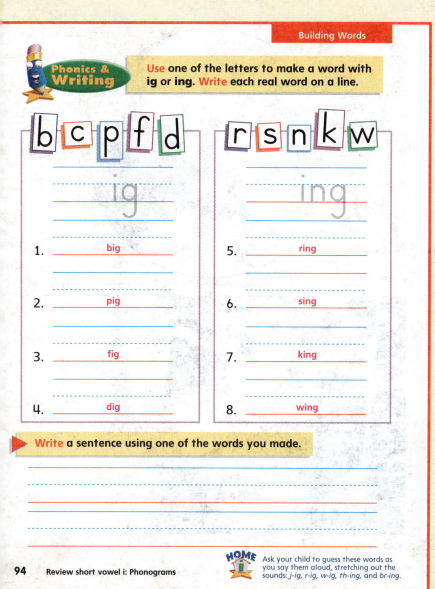

Phonics & Writing

Building Words

Use one of the letters to make a word with **ig** or **ing**. Write each real word on a line.

b c p f d — ig
1. big
2. pig
3. fig
4. dig

r s n k w — ing
5. ring
6. sing
7. king
8. wing

Write a sentence using one of the words you made.

94 Review short vowel i: Phonograms

HOME Ask your child to guess these words as you say them aloud, stretching out the sounds: *j-ig, r-ig, w-ig, th-ing,* and *br-ing.*

CURRICULUM CONNECTIONS

SPELLING
Dictate these spelling words and sentences and have children write the words as a spelling posttest.
1. **pig** — Can a **pig** run a race?
2. **six** — **Six** crayons are lost.
3. **fish** — A **fish** lives in water.
4. **sing** — We like to **sing** folk songs.
5. **lid** — Put the **lid** on the box.
6. **pin** — A **pin** has a sharp point.

SOCIAL STUDIES
Suggest that your class plan a class fair to show some of the work children have done. They may include stories they have written or artwork they have made.

WRITING
Have children make cartoon strips showing the big fish and the little fish. Ask them to draw speech balloons and write what the fish might say to each other.

 PORTFOLIO

 **TECHNOLOGY** **AstroWord** Short Vowels: *a, i*

Integrating Phonics and Reading

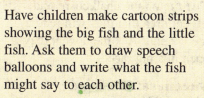

Shared/Guided Reading
Show the cover as you read the title. Invite children to predict what the pigs will be like.

First Reading Invite children to join in as you read the repeating text on pages 7, 9, 11, and 13.

Second Reading Have children identify the short *i* words in the story.

Comprehension
After reading, ask children the following questions:
- How is the big pig different from the little pigs? *Recall/Comparison*
- What words would you use to describe the big pig? Why? *Inference/Drawing Conclusions*

ESL/ELL English Language Learners
Explain that *trip* can mean "to fall down." To *trip* someone means "to make him or her fall." Have children use *trip* to tell what the big pig does to the wolf on pages 14–15.

AUDITORY LEARNERS
Draw a large circle on the board. Tell children it is a short *i* pond. Only fish whose names have the sound of short *i* can swim in it. Then say: *big fish, small fish, red fish, pink fish, silly fish, long fish, little fish.* Have children tell you which fish can swim in the pond. Have a volunteer write the short *i* words inside the pond.

CHALLENGE
Put these word cards in a paper bag: *big-Rick* (34), *Bill-dip* (35), *did-gift* (36), *fit-in* (40), *hid-Jill* (42), *hill-kick* (43), *miss-pick* (50), *six-Tim* (56). Have children pick a card and use both words in a sentence.

EXTRA SUPPORT/INTERVENTION
Before children complete page 93, write these rebus sentences on the board:
- The big (fish rebus) likes to sing.
- The little (fish rebus) likes to swim.
- One (fish rebus) waves a fin.

Read the sentences aloud with children. Then, have volunteers write the word *fish* above each rebus.

94

Lesson 44 Pages 95–96

Take-Home Book

Review Short Vowels a, i

Skill Focus

Children will

★ read short *a* and short *i* words in the context of a story.

★ review selected high-frequency words in the context of a story.

★ reread for fluency.

Review short vowels a, i: Take-home book 95

Teach

Build Background

• Remind children that the theme of this unit is "Amazing Animals." Help them recall that they read a book about bats when they were learning words with short *a*.

• Write the title *Fast Pig* on the chalkboard and read it aloud. Tell children that they will read a book about a race for pigs. Ask them what they think might happen in a pig race.

Phonemic Awareness: Phoneme Categorization
Ask children to raise their hands when they hear the word in each group that does not have the sound of short *i*. Then say these groups of words.

• pig   quick   fast
• little   thin   flat
• hill   race   swift

Practice and Apply

Read the Book Help children tear out and fold the pages to make their Take-Home Books. Encourage them to look through the book and talk about the pictures. Then, read the story together. Ask children if they guessed which pig would win the race.

Sound to Symbol Read aloud or have volunteers read the book. Have children identify the short *i* and short *a* words. (*this, pig, in, pink, is, pigs, zip, ring, wins; can, has, fast, catch*) Invite volunteers to write the words on the board and read them aloud.

Review High-Frequency Words Write the words *with* and *the* on the board. Have the children spell the words, then say them.

Reread for Fluency Have children reread the book to increase their fluency and comprehension. Children can take their books home to read and share with family members.

FOCUS ON ALL LEARNERS

- -

ESL/ELL ENGLISH LANGUAGE LEARNERS

• Before reading *Fast Pig*, have children tell what a race is. Explain that pig races are sometimes held at fairs or carnivals. Ask children what types of fairs and carnival celebrations they have attended.

• Read one page of the story at a time. Ask children to listen for and circle words with the sound of short *a*. (*can, has, fast, catch*) Then, read the story a second time, asking children to listen for and underline words with the sound of short *i*. (*this, pig, in, pink, is, pigs, zip, ring, wins*) Write the words from the story on the board under the headings *Short a* and *Short i*.

VISUAL/KINESTHETIC LEARNERS

Materials: letter cards *Aa, Ii*

Write these incomplete words on the board: *p_g, r_ng, b_g, f_st, c_n, h_s*. Have children choose a letter card, place the letter in the middle of each word, and read the completed word. Point out that four of the incomplete words can be completed with either vowel: *r_ng, b_g, f_st, h_s*.

2. The race has started. The pig in pink is fast.

3. The pigs zip around the ring. These pigs can not catch the pig in pink.

96 Review short vowels a, i: Take-home book

CURRICULUM CONNECTIONS

ART/MATH
Have children design a board game that looks like a racetrack. Explain that they can write a short *i* or short *a* word in each space. Players read each word they land on as they roll a die and advance around the track. The first player to reach the "finish line" wins.

SOCIAL STUDIES
Encourage children to think of rules for a pig race. Write their ideas on chart paper. Underline the short *i* and short *a* words that you used.

WRITING
Have children pretend to have a pig that can do amazing tricks. Ask them to write about the pig and draw a picture of its trick.

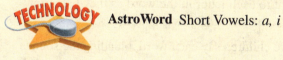

AstroWord Short Vowels: *a, i*

AUDITORY/VISUAL LEARNERS
Materials: Take-Home Books

Read aloud sentences from the story, pausing as you omit a short *i* or short *a* word. For example, say: *The pigs ____ around the ring.* Ask children to find the sentence in their books and supply the missing word.

CHALLENGE
Ask children to draw a prize they might give to the pig that is the winner. Have them write a sentence saying why this would be a good prize for the pig.

EXTRA SUPPORT/INTERVENTION
Materials: Take-Home Books, tape recorder

Record the story. Suggest that children listen to the tape and follow along in their books. See Daily Phonics Practice, pages 312–313.

Lesson 45 Pages 97–98

High-Frequency Words

Skill Focus

Children will

★ recognize and read the high-frequency words *you, for, like, down, are, do.*

★ use the high-frequency words to complete sentences.

★ begin to recognize irregular spelling patterns.

Teach

Analyze Words Write the words *you, for, like, down, are, do* on the board. Point to each word as you read it aloud. Have children repeat each word after you. Then:

- Have children use letter cards to spell each word.
- Slowly say each word. Encourage children to point to each letter in the word as they listen for the consonant and vowel sounds.
- Have children say each word, blending the sounds.
- Help children associate the sounds they hear in each word with a familiar word.
- You may wish to add these words to the class Word Wall so that children can use the words they learn to find similar spelling patterns and phonemic elements in new words.

Read Words in Sentences Write the following sentences on the board. Invite volunteers to read the sentences and underline the high-frequency words.

- Do you like to run for fun?
- We can run up and down the hill.
- We are at the top.

Practice and Apply

Write Words Before children complete page 97, read the directions aloud. Then, read each word in the box. Encourage children to read each sentence with their word choice to make sure it makes sense.

For page 98, point out that children will be finishing a word that reads across and a word that reads down. Children can work with a partner to complete Checking Up.

Reading You may wish to use *Funny Faces and Funny Places,* MCP Phonics and Reading Library, High Frequency Word Collection, Level A, to provide practice in reading some of the high-frequency words.

High-Frequency Words

Name _____

▶ **Read** the words in the box. **Write** a word to finish each sentence.

you	for
like	down
are	do

1. Min and Tim ____are____ playing in the sand.

2. Min says, "What did I ____do____ with my ring?"

3. "I will help look ____for____ it," Tim says.

4. Min and Tim look ____down____ in the sand.

5. "This looks ____like____ the ring," says Tim.

6. "Tim, ____you____ are my friend," says Min.

High-frequency words **97**

FOCUS ON ALL LEARNERS

ESL/ELL ENGLISH LANGUAGE LEARNERS

Use each of the high-frequency words in a simple sentence, making gestures as appropriate to communicate the meaning of the sentence. For example: *I sit down. I like the book. We are friends. Do you see that pencil? Is it for me?* Then ask children to use each word in a sentence.

VISUAL/AUDITORY LEARNERS

Materials: Storybooks on audiotape; tape player

Have partners select a favorite recording of a storybook and play it. Have them listen for the words *you, for, like, down, are,* and *do* and write the words they hear.

KINESTHETIC LEARNERS

Materials: sheets of paper, marker, tape

Write each of the high-frequency words on a sheet of paper and tape the sheets to the floor so that they are about a foot apart. Have children take turns walking the path you have made, reading aloud the words as they go along.

97

High-Frequency Words

▶ Write the letter to finish each word.
Then print the words on the lines.

down   are   for   do   like   you

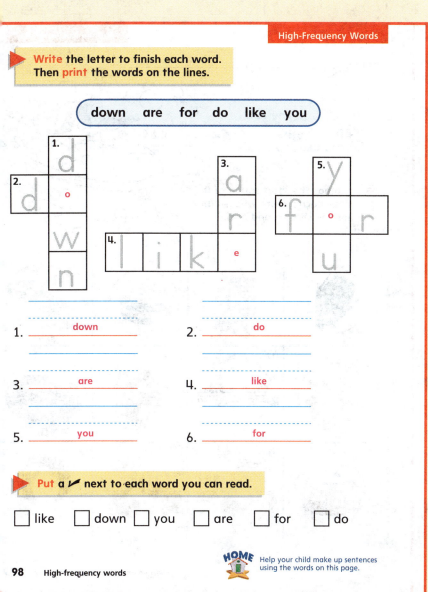

1. down
2. do
3. are
4. like
5. you
6. for

▶ Put a ✔ next to each word you can read.

☐ like   ☐ down   ☐ you   ☐ are   ☐ for   ☐ do

 Help your child make up sentences using the words on this page.

98 High-frequency words

CURRICULUM CONNECTIONS

SOCIAL STUDIES
Encourage children to write sentences about their communities using the high-frequency words. Have them draw pictures to illustrate their sentences. Then, post the children's work on a bulletin board under the heading Where We Live.

WRITING/ART

Review the story on page 97. Then, have children draw a picture showing something that Min and Tim built in the sand. Tell them that they can use speech balloons to show what each child is saying. Encourage them to use as many high-frequency words as possible.

VISUAL LEARNERS
Materials: oak tag, markers
Write each high-frequency word on an oak tag strip and give one strip to each child. Have each child write a sentence containing the word on the other side of the strip.

CHALLENGE
Challenge children to construct word-search puzzles using the high-frequency words.

EXTRA SUPPORT/INTERVENTION
Materials: high-frequency word cards
Ask children to hold up the correct card as you say each word. Then, help them use the word in a sentence.

Integrating Phonics and Reading

Shared/Guided Reading
Show the cover as you read the title. Ask children what they think the book will be about. You may wish to use the activity in the English Language Learners section, below.

First Reading Encourage children to look for the word *are*. Have them join in each time the words *There are* appear.

Second Reading Ask children to identify the rhyming words on pages 2–3, 4–5, 6–7, and 8. List them on the board or the Word Wall.

Comprehension
After reading, ask children the following questions:
- Whose funny faces do we see in this book?
  Recall/Connect to Experience
- Did you like the book? Why or why not?
  Reflective Analysis/Personal Response

ESL/ELL English Language Learners
Explain that funny can mean "humorous," as it does in *funny faces*. It can also mean "odd or unexpected," as in *funny places*.

Lesson 46
Pages 99–100

Short Vowel u

Skill Focus

Children will

★ recognize the sound of short *u*.

★ identify picture names and words that contain the sound of short *u*.

★ identify rhyming short *u* words.

ESL/ELL Speakers of Spanish, Tagalog, or some Asian languages may pronounce short *u* like *o* in *hot* or *a* in *father*. Spanish speakers may pronounce it like *oo* in *foot*. Russian speakers may pronounce short *u* like *ee* in *feet*.

► Teach

Phonemic Awareness: Phoneme Categorization Draw a bug on the board and say *bug*. Have children repeat the word. Explain that the sound heard in the middle of *bug* is short *u*. Next, say groups of words. Ask children to raise a hand when they hear a word that has the sound of short *u*.

- van   flat   bud
- jump pin   trip
- sit   hug   spin

Phonological Awareness: Rhyme Tell children that you are going to say two rhyming short *u* words: *cub, tub*. Next say each group of words below. Ask children to identify the two words that rhyme.

- drum plum bin
- sun   clap bun
- bug   tap   rug

Sound to Symbol Write *sun* on the board and read it aloud. Underline the *u*. Tell children that *u* stands for the short *u* sound. Then, write *hum, fun,* and *rug*. Have volunteers come up, read each word, and underline the letter that stands for the short *u* sound.

► Practice and Apply

Phonemic Awareness Read aloud the rhyme at the top of page 99. Have children listen for and identify the real short *u* words. (*rub, cub, tub, scrub*) List the words on the board. You might point out that *dub* is a nonsense word.

Sound to Symbol Help children identify the pictures on pages 99 and 100. Suggest that they say the picture names softly to themselves as they complete each page.

Reading Use *Just Like Us*, MCP Phonics and Reading Short Vowel Skills Library, Level A, to provide practice in reading words with the short *u* sound.

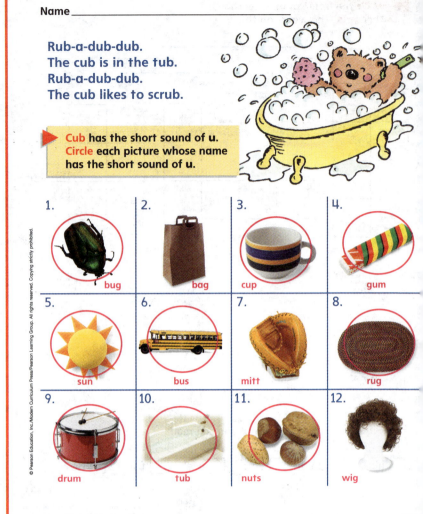

Phonemic Awareness

Name _____

Rub-a-dub-dub.
The cub is in the tub.
Rub-a-dub-dub.
The cub likes to scrub.

▶ **Cub** has the short sound of **u**. **Circle** each picture whose name has the short sound of **u**.

1. bug
2. bag
3. cup
4. gum
5. sun
6. bus
7. mitt
8. rug
9. drum
10. tub
11. nuts
12. wig

Short vowel u: Phonemic awareness   99

FOCUS ON ALL LEARNERS

ESL/ELL ENGLISH LANGUAGE LEARNERS

- Read the directions on page 99 aloud and model item 1. Ask children to complete the page in pairs. Review the answers.
- Before children complete page 100, reread the rhyme at the top of page 99. Point out that because *tub, cub, scrub, rub* all end in the same sound, they rhyme. Then, identify the pictures on page 100 with children. Remind them that they will be listening for words that rhyme.

VISUAL LEARNERS

Materials: chart paper

At the top of a chart, draw and label pictures of a bug, a cub, and a drum. Write the rhyming word *rug* under *bug*. Help children compare the words. List other rhyming words under the picture. Then, continue with *cub, tub* and *drum, gum*.

VISUAL/KINESTHETIC LEARNERS

Materials: Phonics Picture Cards: tub (68), jug (64)

Ask the partners to name each picture. Then, have them draw one or more pictures that rhyme with each picture name, such as cub or rug.

Phonograms/Rhyme

▶ **Say** the names of the pictures in each row.
Color the pictures whose names rhyme.

1. bat / can / cut (color) / hut (color)
2. hug (color) / bug (color) / rug (color) / pig
3. gum (color) / ham / swim / drum (color)
4. cub (color) / tub (color) / bib / club (color)
5. fan / pin / run (color) / sun (color)

Help your child think of more words that rhyme with the ones on this page.

100 Short vowel u: Phonograms/rhyme

CURRICULUM CONNECTIONS

SPELLING
For the spelling pretest, dictate a word and then read it in context in the sentence.
1. **bug** — The **bug** flies fast.
2. **bus** — Did you ride on the **bus**?
3. **cup** — I had milk in a **cup**.
4. **drum** — Sam can play a **drum**.
5. **tub** — The **tub** is full of water.
6. **sun** — The **sun** is hot.

WRITING
Have children suggest rhyming word pairs for *bug* and other short *u* words and then work in pairs to write rhyming sentences about a bug. Have them illustrate their sentences and share them with the group.

SCIENCE
Have children keep a bug log. Encourage them to draw bugs they see.

AstroWord Short Vowels: *e, u*

AUDITORY/KINESTHETIC LEARNERS
Materials: Phonics Picture Cards: bug (61), cup (63), tub (68)

Place one picture at one end of the chalkboard ledge, one in the middle, and one at the other end. Name each picture. Say some words and have children point to the picture whose name rhymes with each word. Use *hug, up, rub, cub, snug, pup, dug,* and *stub*.

CHALLENGE
Challenge children to write the names of the rhyming pictures on page 100.

EXTRA SUPPORT/INTERVENTION
Write the word *bug* on the board. Have children take turns changing the beginning or the ending letter to make new words. Have each new word read aloud. Possible words are *bun, sun, run, rug, tug, hug,* and *hum*.
See Daily Phonics Practice, pages 313–314.

Integrating Phonics and Reading

Shared/Guided Reading
Show children the cover as you read the title. Ask who they think the "us" in the title will be.
First Reading Have children join in each time they see "just like us."
Second Reading Ask children to identify the short *u* words.

Comprehension
After reading, ask the following questions:
- Do the children all live in the same place? How do you know? *Inference/Drawing Conclusions*
- How are the children just like us? *Recall/Comparison*

ESL/ELL English Language Learners
Say and write *children* and explain that this is the plural form of the word *child*. Then, help children say other plural words that name people: *girl/s, boy/s, woman/women,* etc.

Lesson 47 Pages 101–102

Short Vowel u

Skill Focus
Children will
★ recognize the sound of short u.
★ understand that u stands for /u/.
★ write uppercase and lowercase Uu.
★ apply what they have learned by reading and writing.

Teach

Phonological Awareness: Blending Onsets and Rimes Tell children that you will say the parts of a word. Children should blend the parts together to say the word.

- /dr/um (*drum*)
- /f/un (*fun*)
- /m/ug (*mug*)
- /pl/ug (*plug*)

Sound to Symbol Distribute copies of Blackline Master 13 and have children select these letter cards: *Bb, Gg, Aa, Ii,* and *Uu.* Then, have them form the word *bag* and read it aloud. Have them change the *a* in the middle to *i* and read the new word. (*big*) Finally, have them change the *i* to *u* and read the word. (*bug*) Ask children what sound they hear in the middle of *bug* and what letter stands for the sound. (short *u, u*)

Handwriting Write *Uu* on the chalkboard and use the models on page 102 to review how to form the letters. Have children practice writing the letters on their own paper.

Practice and Apply

Sound to Symbol Help children identify the pictures on page 101. Suggest that they say the words quietly to themselves, stretching out the beginning, middle, and ending sounds.

For page 102, remind children that they will be looking for words with the short *u* sound. Suggest that they listen for the middle sound as they softly say each word.

Writing Note the short *u* words in children's writing and check for correct spelling.

Reading Use *Good Night, Little Bug,* MCP Phonics and Reading Short Vowel Skills Library, Level A, to provide practice in reading words with the short *u* sound.

Sound to Symbol

Name _____

▶ **Say** the name of each picture. **Circle** its name.

1. Sun	2. Gum	3. Cup
suds sand (sun)	(gum) mug gust	cut cap (cup)
4. Bus	5. Bug	6. Tub
bun (bus) sun	bag (bug) big	but tab (tub)
7. Jug	8. Nuts	9. Duck
(jug) jack gum	huts mugs (nuts)	tuck (duck) luck
10. Rug	11. Club	12. Drum
mug (rug) rag	cub cup (club)	(drum) dip mad

Short vowel u: Sound to symbol 101

FOCUS ON ALL LEARNERS

ESL/ELL ENGLISH LANGUAGE LEARNERS

- To prepare English language learners to do page 101, hold up a familiar short *u* item, such as a cup. Have the group say its name. Then, write the name plus two other words on the chalkboard, such as *cap, cup, cub.* Ask a volunteer to circle the correct word.

- For page 102, read the directions aloud with children. Have volunteers identify the first three short *u* words in the path.

AUDITORY LEARNERS

Ask children to choose the word that goes with each sentence. Then, have them identify the vowel.

- You can do this with a rope. (*jam, jump, Jim*)
- You can blow bubbles with this. (*guppy, gum, give*)
- This shines in the sky during the day. (*supper, sun, sip*)

KINESTHETIC LEARNERS

Materials: Phonics Picture Cards: bag (47), cat (49), pig (59), six (60), bug (61), bus (62), cup (63), jug (64), sun (67)

Ask children to stand in a circle. Pass out the picture cards. Have each child name his or her picture. If the picture name has the sound of short *u*, the group can all jump once.

Sound to Symbol

Help the cub get home. **Draw a line** from the cub to the first word with the short **u** sound. **Draw** a line to each short **u** word.

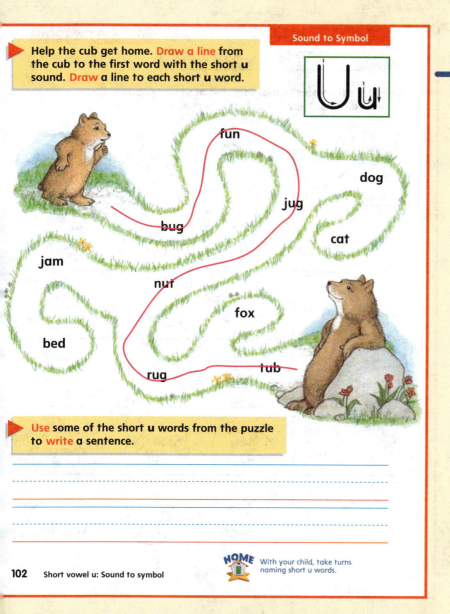

Use some of the short **u** words from the puzzle **to write** a sentence.

_____
_____
_____

With your child, take turns naming short u words.

102 Short vowel u: Sound to symbol

CURRICULUM CONNECTIONS

SPELLING
Write the list words *bug, bus, cup, drum, tub,* and *sun* on the board and read them with the children. Have volunteers select a secret word and name the beginning and ending sounds. When another child guesses the word, have him or her spell it.

WRITING
Have children illustrate and write about a duck, a cub, or a bug on a bus. Ask them to use short *u* words in their sentences.

ART
Materials: paper plates, craft sticks

Have children make a bear mask out of a paper plate. Help them cut eye holes. They can paste or staple the mask to a craft stick. Then, have partners act out what the cub and the mother bear on page 102 might have said to each other when the cub came home.

  AstroWord Short Vowels: *e, u*

AUDITORY/KINESTHETIC LEARNERS
Materials: drawing paper, crayons, scissors, chart paper, tape

Ask children to draw two objects, one that contains the short sound of *u* and another that does not. Then, have them exchange pictures with a partner. The partner should cut out the picture whose name has the sound of short *u* and tape it to a class chart.

CHALLENGE
Have partners write a rhyme using short *u* words from pages 101 and 102.

EXTRA SUPPORT/INTERVENTION
Materials: Phonics Picture Cards: bug (61), bus (62), cup (63), jug (64), run (66), sun (67), tub (68); Phonics Word Cards, Set 1: *bug* (61), *bus* (63), *cup* (67), *jug* (71), *run* (78), *sun* (79), *tub* (80)

Give each child one card. Then, have each child find the person with the matching picture or word. When all the cards have been matched, have the pairs display their cards, name the pictures, and read the words aloud. **See Daily Phonics Practice, pages 313–314.**

Integrating Phonics and Reading

Shared/Guided Reading
Show children the cover as you read the title. Ask children to describe the main character, based on the illustration.

First Reading Let half the class read aloud the words said by the little bug, while the other reads the words said by the mother.

Second Reading Have children find the rhyming short *u* words in the story. (*run, fun, bug, hug, snug, rug*)

Comprehension
After reading, ask children the following questions:
• What does the little bug want to do? *Recall/Details*
• Why does the mother say *no* at the end? *Inference/Cause and Effect*

ESL/ELL English Language Learners
Insert the words "Please" and "Okay" to help children understand the little bug's requests and the mother's responses.

102

Lesson 48
Pages 103–104

Short Vowel a, i, u

Skill Focus

Children will
- ★ orally blend phonemes.
- ★ orally blend word parts.
- ★ identify picture names and spell words that contain the sound of short *u*.

▶ Teach

Phonemic Awareness: Phoneme Blending
Say /s/ /u/ /n/. Have children repeat the phonemes, then say the complete word, *sun*. Next ask children to repeat these sounds after you, then blend the sounds together make a word.

- /r/ /u/ /g/ (*rug*)
- /p/ /a/ /t/ (*pat*)
- /w/ /i/ /n/ (*win*)
- /k/ /u/ /b/ (*cub*)

Help children to identify the sound heard in the middle of each word.

Phonemic Awareness: Medial Sound Isolation Say these words: *bus, ran, rip, can, sun, did*. Ask children what sound they hear in the middle of each word. (short vowel *u, a, i, a, u, i*) Encourage children to repeat each word, isolating the short vowel sound, as in /b/ /u/ /s/.

Sound to Symbol Display the picture cards for lid (57), bug (61), sun (67), bag (47), six (60), hat (52) on the chalkboard ledge. Ask a volunteer to come up, find a picture that shows a short *u* word, and say and write the picture name. Repeat with short *a* and short *i* words until all the cards have been used.

▶ Practice and Apply

Phonological Awareness: Blending
Before children begin page 104, practice blending initial sounds and phonograms. Say /f/an. Ask children to blend the word parts together to say the word. (*fan*)

Continue with these initial sounds:

- /f/un (*fun*)
- /k/an (*can*)
- /p/in (*pin*)
- /r/un (*run*)

Reading Use *Cat's Trip*, MCP Phonics and Reading Short Vowel Skills Library, Level A, to provide practice in reading words with the short *u* sound.

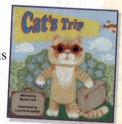

103

Blending

Name _____

▶ Blend the letter sounds together as you say each word. Then, color the picture it names.

1. b u g		bag	bug (color)	bib
2. c a n		can	cut	fan
3. p i n		mug	pan	pin (color)
4. t u b		bus	tag	tub (color)
5. r a t		rat (color)	rip	hut
6. w i g		six	wig (color)	pig

Short vowels a, i, u: Blending phonemes 103

FOCUS ON ALL LEARNERS

ESL/ELL ENGLISH LANGUAGE LEARNERS

- Before children begin page 103, help them name the objects pictured. If necessary, pantomime the pictured verbs (*cut, rip*).
- For page 104, read the directions and name the objects pictured. Ask children to complete item 1 and check their work to verify understanding of the task.

VISUAL LEARNERS

Materials: drawing paper, animal picture books

Have pairs of children look in books to find animals whose names have a short *a, i,* or *u* sound in them. Children may record what they find by writing the name of the animal and by drawing a picture of it.

KINESTHETIC LEARNERS

Materials: Phonics Picture Cards: apple (45), bag (47), cap (48), lid (57), mitt (58), pig (59), bug (61), bus (62), cup (63); masking tape

Write the vowels *a, i,* and *u* on the board and draw a large circle beneath each letter. Ask volunteers to choose a picture, say its name, and tape it in the circle for the appropriate vowel sound.

Blending

Blend the letter sounds together as you say each word. Print the word on the line. Draw a line to the picture it names.

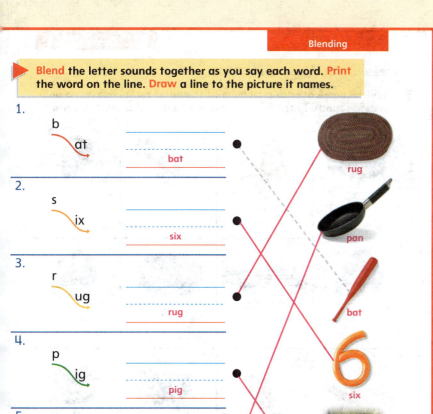

1. b-at — bat
2. s-ix — six
3. r-ug — rug
4. p-ig — pig
5. p-an — pan
6. c-ub — cub

Help your child make up silly rhymes for these picture names, such as *a cub in a tub*.

104 Short vowels a, i, u: Blending phonograms

CURRICULUM CONNECTIONS

SPELLING
Write the list words *bug, bus, cup, drum, tub,* and *sun* on the board and read them aloud with children. Have children select a word and spell it with letter cards. Have them scramble the letter cards and exchange them with a partner. Then have children unscramble the words.

WRITING
Have children draw a picture of a bear cub and write a caption or sentence for their picture.

SCIENCE
Materials: informational picture books about insects

Explain that most of the animals we call bugs are called insects by scientists. Help children make a chart of the characteristics of insects: six legs, antennae, three body parts. The chart might note that many, but not all, insects have wings. Help them use the books to find out why some insects are truly bugs. Children might like to draw insects and label their body parts.

 **AstroWord** Short Vowels: *e, u*

Integrating Phonics and Reading

Shared/Guided Reading
Show the cover as you read the title. Have children name different ways Cat might travel.
First Reading Each time an animal shares news about Cat's trip, have children read the words aloud with you.
Second Reading Write the headings *Short a, Short i,* and *Short u* on chart paper. Have children list words from the story under each heading.
Comprehension
After reading, ask children the following questions:
• What happens each time an animal passes on the news about Cat? *Recall/Summarize*
• Do you know any games that remind you of this story? *Reflective Analysis/Personal Experience*

ESL/ELL English Language Learners
Explain that *pass it on* means "tell it to someone." Have children think of something to say and then show how they pass on their statements.

AUDITORY/KINESTHETIC LEARNERS

Materials: letter cards *Aa, Ii, Uu*

Ask children to listen for the short sound of *a, i,* and *u* in words and wave the appropriate letter card in the air as they say the sound of the vowel they hear. Some words to use are *fast, fit, fun, tip, sack, list, duck, sad,* and *sun*.

CHALLENGE
Challenge children to illustrate and write about a sad duck, a fast fish, or a bad bug.

EXTRA SUPPORT/INTERVENTION
Materials: Phonics Picture Cards: cap (48), cat (49), pig (59), six (60), bug (61), bus (62)

Mix up the pictures on a table. Have children take a card, say its name, then find another picture with the same vowel sound. Have children identify the vowel sound in each pair. See Daily Phonics Practice, pages 312–314.

Lesson 49   Pages 105-106

Short Vowel u

Skill Focus

Children will

★ identify and spell picture names that contain the sound of short *u*.

★ identify initial and final consonants in words that contain the sound of short *u*.

★ write words that contain the sound of short *u* to complete sentences.

★ recognize and read high-frequency words.

Teach

Phonemic Awareness: Phoneme Substitution Tell children that they are going to make new words by changing the first letter in some words that you say. For example: *Rug*: change *r* to *b*. (*bug*)

- bun: change *b* to *r* (*run*)
- gum: change *g* to *h* (*hum*)
- nut: change *n* to *c* (*cut*)

Sound to Symbol Write the word *bud* on the board. Underline the *u* and ask children what sound it stands for. Then erase the *b* and the *d*. Have two volunteers come up to the board. As you say these new words, have one child write the letter that stands for the beginning sound and the other write the letter that stands for the ending sound. Use *fun, cub, tug,* and *pup*.

Practice and Apply

Blend Phonemes As children complete page 105, encourage them to say each picture name, blending together the three phonemes in each word. For item 16, ask children to print the word that names their picture.

Writing For page 106, suggest that children try each word choice before writing a word. As they complete the activity, they will have the opportunity to read the following high-frequency words: *his, sees*.

Critical Thinking For Talk About It, encourage children to tell what happens after a bus gets stuck in the mud.

Reading Use *A Nut Pie for Jud*, MCP Phonics and Reading Short Vowel Skills Library, Level A, to provide practice in reading words with phonograms -*ud* and -*ut*.

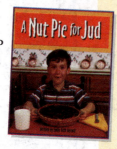

Spelling

Name _____

▶ **Say** the name of each picture. **Print** the letter for its beginning and ending sounds. In the last box, **draw** a picture of a short u word.

1. cup	2. s_n	3. g_m	4. b_g
5. h_t	6. b_s	7. r_g	8. h_g
9. t_b	10. j_g	11. c_b	12. b_n
13. r_n	14. c_t	15. n_t	16.

Short vowel u: Spelling   105

FOCUS ON ALL LEARNERS

ESL/ELL ENGLISH LANGUAGE LEARNERS

Before beginning page 105, read the directions aloud. Have children tell in their own words what they will do. Name the pictured objects, if necessary.

- Before starting page 106, review and reinforce the words *plays, soon, sees,* and *stuck,* using pantomime gestures if needed for the verbs. Then, ask a volunteer to read the first part of item 1 on page 106. Tell children to circle the word that finishes the sentence. Verify and reinforce correct answers. Continue for items 2 to 6. Read the entire story when finished. Ask children to think about what happens next.

VISUAL/KINESTHETIC LEARNERS

Materials: Letter Cards *Aa, Ii, Uu*

Write the following word forms on the board: b_g, c_p, r_g, r_n, l_mp. Have one child at a time use a letter card to insert a vowel in a word form, read the completed word, and decide if it is a real word. Have the group use the real word in a sentence.

Words in Context

Look at the picture. Circle the word that will finish the sentence. Print it on the line.

1. Gus sits on the __rug__.
   - rub
   - (rug)
   - jug

2. He plays with his __pup__.
   - (pup)
   - up
   - cup

3. Soon Gus sees the __bus__.
   - bud
   - bug
   - (bus)

4. He jumps __up__.
   - hug
   - (up)
   - cup

5. Gus has to __run__.
   - rub
   - fun
   - (run)

6. The bus is stuck in the __mud__!
   - (mud)
   - mug
   - hum

Talk about it: What do you think will happen next?

Home: Ask your child to raise a hand for the short *u* words as you say, *But the bus was just stuck in the mud for an hour.*

106 High-frequency words, critical thinking

CURRICULUM CONNECTIONS

SPELLING
Write the list words *bug, bus, cup, drum, tub,* and *sun* on the board and read them aloud with children. Have children make up an oral clue for each word. Ask partners to exchange papers, guess each word, and spell it.

WRITING

Have children write about a bus ride, telling where they might like to go if they could go on a ride with their friends. Ask them to illustrate their work.

MATH
Have children draw a school bus. Then, have them decide what parts to count on their bus, such as windows, wheels, or doors. Help them make a chart that tells how many of each part their bus has.

TECHNOLOGY **AstroWord** Short Vowels: *e, u*

AUDITORY/KINESTHETIC LEARNERS

Materials: letter card *Uu*

Tell children that you will say some words. If they hear a word that has the sound of short *u*, they are to hold up the letter card. Words to use are *bus, bug, bat, bun, pig, rug, pin,* and *gum.*

CHALLENGE
Challenge children to hunt for objects in the room whose names have the sound of short *u*. Have each child list the objects he or she finds, then compare the list with a partner.

EXTRA SUPPORT/INTERVENTION
Write the word *bug* on the board. Give directions for changing one letter at a time to make new words. Have a volunteer make each change and read the word. Directions to give are *Change* b *to* n; *change* g *to* t, *change* n *to* r, *change* t *to* n, *change* s *to* c. **See Daily Phonics Practice, pages 313–314.**

Integrating Phonics and Reading

Guided Reading
Show children the cover as you read the title. Invite them to tell if they have ever tasted nut pies.

First Reading Ask children to describe each picture. Encourage them to point out details.

Second Reading Have children identify the short *u* words in the story. You may want to add these to the classroom Word Wall.

Comprehension
After reading, ask children the following questions:
- How does Jud's pie come from a tree? *Recall/Sequencing*
- How does the picture on page 7 help you understand why Mom said no? *Inference/Details*

ESL/ELL English Language Learners
Say *This is* and point to an item on each page. Have children tell what they see. For example: *This is a nut pie. This is a glass of milk.*

Lesson 50 Pages 107–108

Short Vowel u

Skill Focus

Children will

★ identify picture names and spell words that contain the sound of short *u*.

★ write words that contain the sound of short *u* to complete sentences.

★ recognize and read high-frequency words.

Teach

Phonemic Awareness: Phoneme Blending
Say the word *rug*. Then, repeat the word, separating the phonemes: /r/ /u/ /g/. Ask children what sound they hear in the middle. (short *u*) Say the segmented word twice more, asking children what sound they hear at the beginning (*r*) and the end (*g*). Continue with *cup, mud, tug,* and *gum*.

Sound to Symbol Write the following sentences on the board, leaving a blank for the letter *u*.

- A p_p is a little dog.
- A h_t is a little house.
- A c_b is a little bear.

Ask volunteers to come up to the board and write the letter *u* to complete each word. Then, read the sentences aloud with children.

Words in Context: Decodable Words Write these words on the board: *fun, sun*. Then, write and read the sentence below. Have children select the word that completes the sentence.

- I like to run in the ___. (*sun*)

Practice and Apply

Blend Phonemes As children complete page 107, encourage them to say each picture name, stretching out the beginning, middle, and ending sounds.

Writing For page 108, suggest that children try each word choice before writing a word. As they complete the activity, they will have the opportunity to read the following high-frequency words: *our, look, under, trees*.

Critical Thinking For Talk About It, encourage children to use short *u* words such as *run, jump, sun,* and *fun* as they tell what they might do at a farm.

Reading Use *Night and Day*, MCP Phonics and Reading Short Vowel Skills Library, Level A, to provide practice in reading words with short *a*, short *i*, and short *u*.

107

Name _____ Spelling

> Say the name of each picture. Print the picture name on the line. In the last box, draw a picture of a short *u* word. Print the word.

1. tub
2. bug
3. cut
4. hug
5. cup
6. sun
7. cub
8. bus
9. rug
10. hut
11. run
12.

Short vowel u: Spelling 107

FOCUS ON ALL LEARNERS

ESL/ELL ENGLISH LANGUAGE LEARNERS

- To monitor auditory comprehension and spelling for the activity on page 107, explain that you will name the objects on the page one at a time. Ask children to write each word you say under the matching picture. After children have completed three target words, verify that they have written the words correctly, then continue with the rest.

- For page 108, invite children to talk about what they know about farms. Give a brief overview of the story told on the page so children can anticipate the action. Then, read the directions and ask children to explain the activity to you.

KINESTHETIC LEARNERS

Materials: Phonics Picture Cards: bib (54), pig (59), bug (61), bus (62), cup (63), sun (67), tub (68); sand trays

Children can work in pairs and share a sand tray. Have one child hold up a picture card. If the picture name contains the short sound of *u*, as in *cup*, the other child can trace the letter *u* in the sand. Then, have the partners exchange roles.

Words in Context

Read the sentences. Circle the word that will finish each sentence. Print it on the line.

1. Our farm is __fun__.
   - fan
   - fin
   - (fun)

2. I look under trees for __nuts__.
   - (nuts)
   - rugs
   - suns

3. Bugs buzz and __hum__.
   - hut
   - hand
   - (hum)

4. The pigs dig in the __mud__.
   - must
   - (mud)
   - mug

5. My dog jumps and __runs__.
   - (runs)
   - rings
   - cuts

6. He likes the warm __sun__.
   - gum
   - (sun)
   - hum

TALK about it What are some things you might do at a farm?

HOME Help your child to make up a sentence using the words *fun* and *sun*, then draw a picture to go with it.

108 Short vowel u: High-frequency words, critical thinking

CURRICULUM CONNECTIONS

SPELLING
Write the list words *bug, bus, cup, drum, tub,* and *sun* on the board. Have a child name two words for a partner to spell.

WRITING
Have children draw a picture of a farm and write about fun things they might do on a farm.

SCIENCE
Have children find pictures of different kinds of nuts. They might use print or CD-ROM encyclopedias. If possible, bring in some nuts and ask children to describe them.

TECHNOLOGY **AstroWord** Short Vowels: *e, u*

AUDITORY/KINESTHETIC LEARNERS **GROUPS**
Materials: Phonics Picture Cards: apple (45), cap (48), hat (52), bib (54), king (56), mitt (58), bug (61), cup (63), tub (68)

Have children sit in a circle and take turns picking a card. If they get one that shows something whose name has the short *u* sound, they say the word, then walk around the outside of the circle and return to their place.

CHALLENGE
Challenge children to write a series of simple instructions for a partner to follow using short vowel words such as *hug, jump, run, sit,* and *clap*.

EXTRA SUPPORT/INTERVENTION
Materials: magazines, paper, glue

Ask children to go through magazines to find pictures of things with names containing the sound of short *u*. Have them cut out the pictures and glue them to a paper labeled *u*. See Daily Phonics Practice, pages 313–314.

Integrating Phonics and Reading

Shared/Guided Reading
Show children the cover as you read the title. Invite them to look at the illustration and tell what happens at night and what happens during the day.

First Reading Invite groups of children to join in as you read the words spoken by the sun, the flowers, the animals, and the children.

Second Reading Have children identify the short *u* words in the story. Have volunteers list these on the board.

Comprehension
After reading, ask children the following questions:
- What happens after the sun goes to sleep? *Recall/Sequencing*
- Is this a true story or a made-up story? How do you know? *Reflective Analysis/Fantasy and Reality*

ESL/ELL English Language Learners
Help children find another way to say these expressions: *Stay up. Get up. I'll be back.*

Lesson 51 Pages 109–110

Phonics and Reading / Phonics and Writing

Short Vowel u

Skill Focus

Children will

★ read words that contain the sound of short *u*.

★ write short *u* words to finish sentences.

★ build words with short *u* phonograms *-ug*, *-un*.

Teach

Phonemic Awareness: Medial Sound Isolation Say *hut*, then /u/. Tell children that you are saying a word and then its middle vowel sound. Then, have children say these words and follow each one with its middle vowel sound: *nut, bug, cut, mud, bud*. Explain that the sound heard in the middle of each word is short *u*.

Sound to Symbol Display the following word cards: *gum* (66), *cup* (67), *jug* (71), *just* (71), *tub* (80). Say each word in random order. Have a volunteer choose the correct card, write the word on the board, and underline the letter *u*.

Read Words in Sentences Write these sentences on the board, leaving blank spaces as shown:

- G_s r_ns _p the hill.
- G_s j_mps on the b_s.

Have volunteers write the letter *u* in each blank and read the short *u* word aloud. Then, help children read the sentences.

Practice and Apply

Phonics and Reading After children have read the story, ask them to identify words that have the short *u* sound. You may want to explain the meaning of *fuss* (something that bothers or worries people). As children are reading, they will have the opportunity to read the high-frequency word *make*.

Critical Thinking For Talk About It, discuss what the bug, the pup, and the cub were doing to cause a fuss.

Phonics and Writing For page 110, tell children to try each letter at the top to make a word with *-un* or *-ug*. Remind them that not every letter will make a real word.

Reading Use *Mr. Wink*, MCP Phonics and Reading Short Vowel Skills Library, Level A, to provide practice in reading words with short vowels.

Dylan   A.J.   Robbie!

Reading

Name _____

Phonics & Reading ▶ **Read** the story. **Use** short *u* words to finish the sentences.

A Fuss in a Bus

The bug jumps in the bus.
The pup hums in the bus.
The cub runs in the bus.
"Sit down!" says the driver.
"Do not <mark>make</mark> such a fuss!"
The bug sits.
The cub sits.
The pup does not hum.
No more fuss in the bus!
Now it can go.

1. The ____bug____ jumps in the bus.

2. The pup hums in the ____bus____.

3. The ____cub____ runs in the bus.

TALK About It Why did the bus driver say, "Do not make such a fuss"?

Review short u: Reading, critical thinking   109

FOCUS ON ALL LEARNERS

ESL/ELL ENGLISH LANGUAGE LEARNERS

- Before beginning page 109, display or draw pictures of a bug, a pup, and a cub. Help children identify each animal. Write the words on the board. Review *bus* by asking a volunteer to draw a bus and write the word on the board. Then, write and read the phrase *make a fuss*. Discuss its meaning with children.

- For page 110, read the directions aloud. Complete the first item together to verify understanding of the activity.

KINESTHETIC/VISUAL LEARNERS

Write the words *jump, tug, run, bump, hug, rub,* and *puff* on the board. Touch one word and call on a child to pantomime the action. Continue with other children and words. Then, call on a child and touch two words to be pantomimed.

VISUAL LEARNERS

Materials: Phonics Word Cards: *bag* (8), *bat* (9), *big* (34), *bun* (60), *bug* (61), *bump* (62), *bus* (63)

Mix up the cards and show a word to one child. Have the child read the word and pretend to drive a bus if it has the short *u* sound. Continue showing words to others in the group.

109

Building Words

Use one of the letters to make a word with *un* or *ug*. Write each real word on a line.

b r f s l   l m b k j t

_un_   _ug_

1. bun   5. mug
2. run   6. bug
3. fun   7. jug
4. sun   8. tug

▶ Write a sentence using one of the words you made.

Help your child think of other *un* and *ug* words.

110 Review short vowel u: Phonograms

CURRICULUM CONNECTIONS

SPELLING
For the spelling posttest, dictate a list word and then read it in context in the sentence.
1. **bug** The **bug** sat on the flower.
2. **bus** I rode the **bus** home.
3. **cup** He had a **cup** of cocoa.
4. **drum** Can you play a **drum**?
5. **tub** Fill the **tub** with water.
6. **sun** The **sun** is shining.

SCIENCE
Materials: informational picture books about bears

Explain that a *cub* is a baby bear. Ask children to pick a kind of bear, draw a picture of it, and write a sentence about it.

MATH
Have children make counting books featuring short *u* words, such as *One bus, Two pups, Three ducks,* and so on.

 **AstroWord** Short Vowels: *e, u*

AUDITORY/KINESTHETIC LEARNERS
Have children read the story on page 109 aloud, one sentence at a time. Tell readers to add actions as they read.

CHALLENGE
Write this list of words on the board: *bug, cup, cut, drum, dug, fuss, Gus, hum, hut, pup.* Challenge children to use the list to write five sentences that have rhyming short *u* words; for example: *The bug dug a hole in the sand.*

EXTRA SUPPORT/INTERVENTION
Draw a large outline of a bus on the chalkboard. Say the following words and have children write them inside the picture: *bug, bus, pup, hum, cub, run, jump, fuss.* **See Daily Phonics Practice, pages 313–314.**

Integrating Phonics and Reading

Shared/Guided Reading

Show the cover as you read the title. Tell them that Mr. Wink has a problem. Then, flip through the illustrations and have them predict what the problem will be.

First Reading Invite children to make the Hoot! Tap! and Buzz! sounds on pages 3, 5, and 7.

Second Reading Write the word *muffs* on the board and help children read it aloud. Have them point out the earmuffs in the book.

Comprehension
After reading, ask children the following questions:
- What was Mr. Wink's problem? *Recall/Problem and Solution*
- How else could Mr. Wink have solved his problem? *Creative/Problem and Solution*

ESL/ELL English Language Learners
Say these sentences from the story: *Mr. Wink fell asleep. Mr. Wink woke up.* Help children say each one in the present tense.

Lesson 52   Pages 111–112

Take-Home Book

Review Short Vowel u

Skill Focus
Children will
★ read short *u* words in the context of a story.
★ review selected high-frequency words in the context of a story.
★ reread for fluency.

Teach
Build Background Remind children that the theme of this unit is "Amazing Animals." Tell them you will give some hints about a kind of animal. Have them raise their hands when they know what the animal is.

- They have tails.
- They have two legs.
- They have feathers.
- They have wings.

When most children have raised their hands, ask for their response. (*birds*)

Phonological Awareness: Rhyme Say this sentence: *We will crunch a bunch of nuts for lunch.* Then, repeat it. Ask children to identify the words that rhyme. (*crunch, bunch, lunch*) Ask what vowel sound is heard in the middle of each one. (short *u*) Finally, say the sentence once more and ask children to name one more short *u* word. (*nuts*)

Practice and Apply
Read the Book Help children tear out and fold the pages to make their Take-Home Books. Then, read the book together. Explain that a book that tells how to do or make something is called a "how-to book." Ask children what they learned to make from this book. (*a bird feeder*)

Sound to Symbol Read aloud or have volunteers read the book. Have children identify the short *u* words. (*jug, scrub, cut, up, nuts, fun*) Invite volunteers to write the words on the board and read them aloud.

Review High-Frequency Words Write the word *the* on the board. Have children spell the word, then say it, blending /th/e.

Reread for Fluency Have children reread the book to increase their fluency and comprehension. Children can take their books home to read and share with family members.

FOCUS ON ALL LEARNERS

ESL/ELL ENGLISH LANGUAGE LEARNERS
After reading, talk about steps in making this bird feeder. Help children retell the directions on each page using the clue words *first, next, then,* and *last.*

VISUAL/AUDITORY LEARNERS
Materials: bird cutouts, crayons
Give children bird cutouts and have them write a word that contains the short *u* sound on each bird. Help children fasten the birds to a bulletin board, chalkboard, or string. Have them read each word as they attach the bird.

KINESTHETIC/AUDITORY LEARNERS
Have children pantomime bird actions, such as flying, hopping on two feet, or pecking. Let them choose their favorite action. Say some words. Ask children to pantomime their bird action if a word has a short *u* sound. Some words to use are *snug, drum, stump, lamp, crumb, pond,* and *plum.*

2. Scrub a milk jug. Cut a hole in the jug.

3. Put a string on the jug. Hang the jug up.

112 Review short vowel u: Take-home book

CURRICULUM CONNECTIONS

LANGUAGE ARTS
Materials: Take-Home Books, plastic milk jug, scissors, string, birdseed

Have children use the Take-Home Books to give you instructions for making a bird feeder. If possible, place the feeder in the schoolyard and observe it.

SCIENCE
Materials: picture books about birds

Ask children to look through picture books to identify birds they have seen in your area. Challenge children to find pictures of various kinds of bird beaks, such as the long beak of an insect-eater or the sharp, curved beak of a bird of prey. Have children find out what birds eat with each kind of beak.

WRITING
Materials: drawing paper, crayons

Have children draw an amazing bird that might come to the most fantastic bird feeder ever. Have them write about the bird, including where it lives and what it eats.

PORTFOLIO

TECHNOLOGY **AstroWord** Short Vowels: *e, u*

AUDITORY/VISUAL LEARNERS
Materials: Take-Home Books

Read aloud the first part of a sentence from the story. Ask children to find the sentence and to read the complete sentence.

CHALLENGE
Have children illustrate and write about the birds they might see at the bird feeder from the story.

EXTRA SUPPORT/INTERVENTION
Materials: Take-Home Books, tape recorder, audiotape

Record the story and have children listen to the tape as they follow along in their books. See Daily Phonics Practice, pages 313–314.

Lesson 53 — Pages 113–114

Short Vowel o

Skill Focus

Children will

★ recognize the sound of short o.

★ identify picture names and words that contain the sound of short o.

★ identify rhyming short o words.

ESL/ELL Native speakers of Spanish and some Asian languages may not distinguish between the sound of short o, short a, and short u. Practice *hot, hat, hut* and *lock, lack, luck*.

Teach

Phonological Awareness: Blending Onsets and Rimes Tell children that you will say the parts of a word; then say /h/ot. Have children repeat the parts, then blend the word: hot. Continue by having children repeat the parts of the following words after you, orally blending the parts to make the word.

- /j/ob (*job*)
- /f/ox (*fox*)
- /p/ot (*pot*)
- /l/og (*log*)

Ask children if all the words have the same middle sound. Tell them that the sound they hear is the sound of short o.

Phonological Awareness: Rhyme Say *hot, pot*. Point out that these words rhyme. Then, read aloud the groups of words below. Ask children to name the two words in each group that rhyme.

- hot   got   sock
- job   box   cob
- hop   hog   dog

Sound to Symbol Draw a box on the board and write *box* inside. Say *box* and underline the *o*. Point out that the letter *o* stands for the short *o* sound heard in the middle of *box*.

Practice and Apply

Phonemic Awareness Read aloud the rhyme on page 113. Have children listen for and name words with the short *o* sound.

Sound to Symbol Help children identify the pictures on pages 113 and 114. Suggest that they say the picture names softly to themselves as they complete each page.

Reading Use *Little Frog's Monster Story*, MCP Phonics and Reading Short Vowel Skills Library, Level A, to provide practice in reading words with short *a, i,* and *o*.

Phonemic Awareness

Name_____

My dog has lots of spots.
My dog's spots look like dots.
My dog's spots are on his hair.
My dog's spots are everywhere!

► *Spot* has the short sound of **o**. Circle each picture whose name has the short sound of **o**.

1. top
2. pop
3. cup
4. lock
5. sock
6. tack
7. box
8. pot
9. rock
10. knot
11. mop
12. mitt

Short vowel o: Phonemic awareness   113

FOCUS ON ALL LEARNERS

ESL/ELL ENGLISH LANGUAGE LEARNERS

- Before beginning page 113, give children index cards. Assist them in drawing and coloring stop signs and writing *STOP* on each card. Then, read the rhyme aloud. Tell children to listen for words with the sound of short *o* and to hold up their stop signs when they hear one.

- For page 114, read the directions aloud and have a volunteer name the pictures in item 1. Assist children in determining which picture names rhyme, then have children color them. You may wish to have children complete items 2 to 5 in pairs. Review answers aloud.

VISUAL LEARNERS

Materials: chart paper

At the top of a chart, draw pictures of a pot, a sock, and a mop. Label the pictures. Write the word *hot* under *pot* and have children read the words with you. Help children note the difference in the initial sound of the words, then ask the children to name other words that rhyme with *pot*, such as *cot, dot, lot*. Repeat for words that rhyme with *sock* and *mop*, such as *lock, rock, clock* and *hop, pop, stop*. Display the chart.

Phonograms/Rhyme

Say the names of the pictures in each row.
Color the pictures whose names rhyme.

114 Short vowel o: Phonograms/rhyme

With your child, make up action rhymes using short o words from the page, such as *hop with a mop*.

CURRICULUM CONNECTIONS

SPELLING

For the spelling pretest, dictate a list word and then read it in context in the sentence.
1. **dog** You can pet the **dog**.
2. **rock** I found a **rock** in the sand.
3. **fox** The **fox** is a small, wild animal.
4. **pot** Heat the soup in the **pot**.
5. **sock** Max lost one **sock**.
6. **top** Put the **top** on the box.

WRITING

Have children work with a partner to write a short rhyme about a dog. Encourage them to begin by listing several rhyming words. Invite them to read their rhymes to the class.

SOCIAL STUDIES

Have children learn about how guide dogs help the visually impaired. If possible, invite a guide dog and its master to visit your class.

TECHNOLOGY AstroWord Short Vowels: *i, o*

AUDITORY/KINESTHETIC LEARNERS

Materials: letter cards *Aa, Cc, Hh, Nn, Oo, Pp, Tt*

Have children form the word *cat* with their cards. Then, have them change the word to *hat*, to *hot*, to *pot*, to *cot*, to *cop*, and to *not*.

CHALLENGE

Challenge children to write about a frog who hops in socks with spots.

EXTRA SUPPORT/INTERVENTION

On page 113, if children have difficulty determining which pictures have the short sound of *o*, tell them that *spot* has the short *o* sound, and ask them to repeat the word. Have them say the name of each picture and the word *spot* together and listen for the vowel sound. **See Daily Phonics Practice, pages 314–315.**

Integrating Phonics and Reading

Shared/Guided Reading
Read the title and preview the illustrations. Ask children who Little Frog will be telling his story to.
First Reading Whenever a sentence has words with all uppercase letters, invite children to read along with you. Have them read with appropriate expression.
Second Reading Ask children to identify the short *o* words in the story.
Comprehension
After reading, ask children the following questions:
• Why did Little Frog think the hog was a monster? *Recall/Details*
• Which clue helped Big Frog guess that the monster was really a hog? *Inference/Making Judgments*

ESL/ELL English Language Learners
Point out the contractions *couldn't*, *I'll*, and *that's*. Help children identify the two words that make up each one.

Lesson 54
Pages 115–116

Short Vowel o

Skill Focus

Children will
- ★ recognize the sound of short o.
- ★ understand that o stands for /o/.
- ★ write uppercase and lowercase Oo.
- ★ apply what they have learned by reading and writing.

ESL/ELL Native speakers of Spanish and Russian may confuse the sound of short o with the sound of oo in *foot*. Assess children's ability to discriminate and pronounce these sounds. Provide individualized practice with word pairs as needed.

Teach

Phonemic Awareness: Phoneme Categorization Say the words *pot, lock,* and *box*. Have children repeat the words, then identify the sound in the middle of each word. (short *o*) Then, have children tell which two words in each group have the short *o* sound.

- hop   mitt   sock
- doll   log   pad
- nut   pond   Bob

Sound to Symbol Write these word forms on the board: d_g, f_x, p_p, and h_t. Call on volunteers to come up and write an *o* in the middle of each one. Have children read the completed words. Point out that all the words have the sound of short *o* in the middle.

Next, call on other volunteers to make new words by changing the first letter in each word. Possibilities include *log, box, hop,* and *pot*.

Handwriting Write Oo on the chalkboard and use the models on page 116 to review how to form the letters. Have children follow along with their fingers on their desktops.

Practice and Apply

Sound to Symbol Encourage children to say each picture name on page 115 softly to themselves, stretching out each sound, before circling the correct word.

For page 116, encourage children to stretch out the middle sound to see if each word on the page is a short *o* word or not.

Writing Note the short *o* words that children write on page 116 and check for correct spelling.

Reading Use *"POP" Pops the Popcorn,* MCP Phonics and Reading Short Vowel Skills Library, Level A, to provide practice in reading words with the short *o* sound.

115

Sound to Symbol

Name_____

▶ **Say** the name of each picture. **Circle** its name.

1. pot — top (pot) pack
2. fox — box (fox) fog
3. log — (log) dog lot
4. mop — nap map (mop)
5. top — tap tip (top)
6. hot — hat (hot) hit
7. dog — (dog) dig dug
8. box — bat (box) bug
9. doll — fill duck (doll)
10. ox — (ox) sock ax
11. rock — rip rack (rock)
12. pop — (pop) pup pat

Short vowel o: Sound to symbol   **115**

FOCUS ON ALL LEARNERS

ESL/ELL ENGLISH LANGUAGE LEARNERS

- One at a time, display the picture cards for box (70), dog (71), doll (72), mop (73), ox (74), and top (75). Ask a volunteer to say each picture name and identify the short vowel sound.
- Ask another volunteer to write the picture name on the chalkboard and underline the letter that stands for short *o*.

AUDITORY LEARNERS

Materials: small rock

Have children sit in a circle. Give one child a rock. Say the word *rock* and ask the child to say a rhyming word. Have the child pass the rock to the next child to say another rhyming word. When the children cannot think of new rhyming words, give another word, such as *pot* or *stop*.

KINESTHETIC LEARNERS

Materials: Phonics Picture Cards: dog (71), doll (72), mop (73), ox (74), top (75)

Mix up the cards and pass them out. Have one child at a time act out the picture. Let the others guess what the picture is. When the name is guessed, have a volunteer write the word.

Sound to Symbol

▶ Color each short o word red. What do you see?

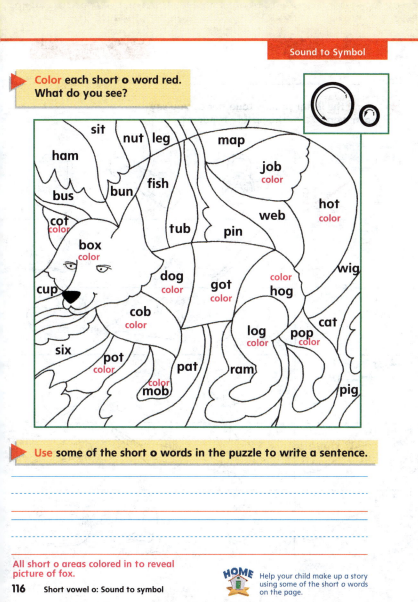

▶ Use some of the short o words in the puzzle to write a sentence.

All short o areas colored in to reveal picture of fox.

116 Short vowel o: Sound to symbol

HOME Help your child make up a story using some of the short o words on the page.

CURRICULUM CONNECTIONS

SPELLING
Write the list words *dog, rock, fox, pot, sock,* and *top* as column heads on the board and read them aloud with children. Have children put together the two words that rhyme. Then, have them name other rhyming words for each list word.

WRITING

Have children draw a picture of an animal whose name contains the sound of short *o*, such as *fox, ox, otter, octopus, dog,* or *hog.* Then, have them write one or more sentences about the picture.

MATH
Talk with children about the size of a frog, a dog, and an ox. Ask them to write or dictate sentences comparing the sizes. For example, *A dog is bigger than a frog.*

 AstroWord Short Vowels: *i, o*

AUDITORY/KINESTHETIC LEARNERS **GROUPS**
Materials: chart paper, tape, crayons, paper, scissors

Title a chart "Bob's Short *O* Shop" and draw shelves on the chart. Explain that Bob only sells things whose names contain the short *o* sound. Have children draw and cut out things that Bob can sell, and tape them to the shelves.

CHALLENGE
Have children fold a paper into fourths. Ask them to write a letter *a, i, u,* or *o* in each box. Ask them to look for c-v-c word patterns, such as *hat, hit, hot,* and *hut,* that are the same except for the vowel. Have them write each word in the correct box. Tell them they can also use patterns that appear in only three boxes, such as *rib, rub, rob.*

EXTRA SUPPORT/INTERVENTION
Work with children to name each picture on page 115. Have them identify the beginning and ending sounds of each picture name before they look for the word that names the picture. **See Daily Phonics Practice, pages 312–315.**

Integrating Phonics and Reading

Guided Reading
Show children the cover as you read the title. Ask them to share what they know about popcorn.

First Reading Have children look at the illustrations. Invite them to point out the items with short *o* names, such as popcorn and the pot.

Second Reading Have children find the rhyming short *o* words in the story. (*pot, lot; pop, stop, top, mop*)

Comprehension
After reading, ask children the following questions:
- Why does the popcorn pop over the top? *Inference/Cause and Effect*
- Could the events in this story really happen? Why or why not? *Reflective Analysis/Opinion*

ESL/ELL English Language Learners
List all the words from the story that contain *pop.* (*popcorn, pop, pops, popping*) Help children use each word in a sentence.

Lesson 55   Pages 117–118

Short Vowels a, i, u, o

Skill Focus
Children will
- ★ orally blend phonemes.
- ★ orally blend word parts.
- ★ identify picture names and spell words that contain the sound of short *a, i, u,* and *o*.

Teach

Phonological Awareness: Blending Onsets and Rimes Say /d/ot. Then, help children blend the sounds together to say the word *dot*. Ask them what vowel sound they hear in the middle of *dot*. (short *o*) Then, have children blend the following and identify the short vowel in the middle of each word: /g/um, /b/ad, /d/ip, /j/am, /m/ud, /l/id, /t/op.

Phonological Awareness: Rhyme Say the following groups of words. Ask children to name the two words that rhyme in each group.

- map   pot   cap
- sit   fit   sat
- rag   rug   tug
- lock   rack   rock

After children have identified the rhyming words, ask them to name the sound they hear in the middle of both rhyming words.

Sound to Symbol Write the words *map, lid, mud,* and *lot* on the board. Ask volunteers to come up and point to the letter that stands for the short *a, i, u,* or *o* sound in each word.

Practice and Apply

Phonological Awareness: Blending Before children begin page 117, write *log* on the board, spacing the letters out, and draw the curving arrow underneath. Model how to blend the letters. Have a volunteer write the word on the board. For page 118, model how to blend the initial *b* with the phonogram *-ox* to say *box*.

Sound to Symbol Write *hot* on the board and ask children what letter stands for the short *o* sound. Continue, changing the *o* to *a* (*hat*), *a* to *i* (*hit*), and *i* to *u* (*hut*). Point out that children will be writing short *a, i, u,* and *o* words on page 118.

Reading Use *Can a Cow Hop?* MCP Phonics and Reading Short Vowel Skills Library, Level A, to provide practice in reading words with the phonograms *-op* and *-ot*.

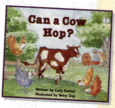

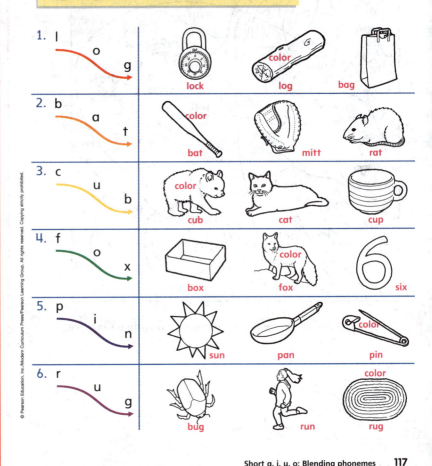

Short *a, i, u, o*: Blending phonemes   117

FOCUS ON ALL LEARNERS

ESL/ELL ENGLISH LANGUAGE LEARNERS
Before English language learners begin pages 117 and 118, review short vowel sounds *a, i, u,* and *o*. Write *stand, hum, hop,* and *sit* on the board. Tell children to act out each word as you say it. Have volunteers identify and circle the vowels.

VISUAL LEARNERS
Write the following words on the chalkboard: *bat, fan, fin, wig, sun, bug, hot, stop*. Have each group of children select two words with different vowel sounds and work together to list as many rhyming words as they can. Have the groups share their lists.

KINESTHETIC LEARNERS
Materials: Phonics Word Cards: *cat* (13), *pan* (27), *pig* (52), *sit* (55), *bug* (61), *cup* (67), *dog* (86), *mop* (90), *rock* (94)

Pass out a word card to each child in the group. Have one child at a time come up to the board to draw a picture of the word. Ask a second child to write the word.

Blending

Blend the letter sounds together as you say each word. Print the word on the line. Draw a line to the picture it names.

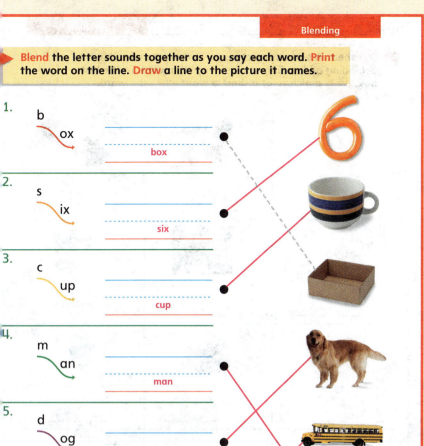

1. b ox — box
2. s ix — six
3. c up — cup
4. m an — man
5. d og — dog
6. b us — bus

 Name the beginning letter of a word. Ask your child to say a word that starts with that letter.

118 Short vowels a, i, u, o: Blending phonograms

CURRICULUM CONNECTIONS

SPELLING
Write the list words *dog, rock, fox, pot, sock,* and *top* on the board and read them with the children. Have a volunteer draw a picture for one of the spelling words. Have another child write the name under the picture. Then ask the group to read and spell the word.

WRITING
Discuss with children the word *odd*. Ask them to illustrate and write about an odd animal.

MATH
Draw an octagon and name it. Explain that it is called an octagon because it has eight sides, and the word part *octo-* or *octa-* means "eight." Ask if children know of anything else whose name has the word part *octo-*. If they suggest octopus, point out that an octopus has eight legs. Ask children to draw an animal such as a dinosaur with eight spines.

 **AstroWord** Short Vowels: *a, i;* Short Vowels: *e, u*

AUDITORY/KINESTHETIC LEARNERS
Have children tap their feet, hold up six fingers, run in place, or put their hands on top of their heads when they hear you say a word that rhymes with *tap, six, run,* or *top*. Use the following words: *fix, cap, bun, lap, mix, hop, chop, gap, sun, nap, fun*.

CHALLENGE
Challenge children to select two words from pages 117 and 118 and to write and illustrate a sentence using the words.

EXTRA SUPPORT/INTERVENTION
Materials: Phonics Picture Cards: cat (49), hat (52), bug (61), jug (64), run (66), sun (67), bib (54), crib (124), mop (73), top (75), block (133), clock (134)

Make sure children can name the pictures. Place the cards face down. Have children turn over two cards at a time to try to find pairs of rhyming words. Have them identify the short vowel sound in the rhyming words. **See Daily Phonics Practice, pages 312–315.**

Integrating Phonics and Reading

Shared/Guided Reading
Show the cover as you read the title. Ask children if they think a cow can hop. Then, have them list some animals that can hop.

First Reading Each time you come to an animal name, such as *cow* or *lion*, pause and point to the word. Let children read the word aloud.

Second Reading Have children find two words that end in *-op* in the story. (*hop, stop*) Then, have them find two other short *o* words. (*not, frogs*)

Comprehension
After reading, ask children the following questions:
- Can you name an animal that can hop and one that can not? **Recall/Comparison**
- How would you finish this sentence? *A cow (lion, snake) can ___.* **Creative/Prior Knowledge**

ESL/ELL English Language Learners
Have children supply different action words to finish this sentence: *I can ___.*

Lesson 56 — Pages 119–120

Short Vowel o

Skill Focus

Children will

★ identify picture names and spell words that contain the sound of short o.

★ identify initial and final consonants in words that contain the sound of short o.

★ write words that contain the sound of short o to complete sentences.

★ recognize and read high-frequency words.

Teach

Phonemic Awareness: Phoneme Substitution Tell children that they can change some words into animal names by changing the vowel sound to the short o sound. Demonstrate by saying *hug, hog.* Use these words to continue: *ax, utter, dig, fix.*

Sound to Symbol Draw a large pond on the board. Write the word *pond*, omitting the letters *p* and *d*. Help children identify the picture. Then, have a volunteer fill in the letters for the beginning and ending sounds. Repeat for *log* (omit the *l* and *g*) and *frog* (omit the *f* and *g*). Ask in what way all the words on the board are alike. (All have the short *o* sound.)

Words in Context: Decodable Words Write these words on the board: *rock, lock*. Then, write and read the sentence below. Have children select the word that completes the sentence.

• We will sit on the big ___. (rock)

Practice and Apply

Sound to Symbol As children complete page 119, encourage them to say each picture name, blending together the beginning, middle, and ending sounds. Point out that they will finish each word by writing the letters that stand for these sounds.

Writing For page 120, suggest that children try each word choice before writing a word. As they complete the activity, they will have the opportunity to read the following high-frequency words: *of, off.*

Critical Thinking For Talk About It, have children review sentences 1 to 6 before predicting what Bob might do next.

Reading Use *Lost in the Fog*, MCP Phonics and Reading Short Vowel Skills Library, Level A, to provide practice in reading words with -og.

Name_____ Spelling

▶ **Say** the name of each picture. **Print** the letters for its beginning and ending sounds. **Trace** the word. In the last box, **draw** a picture of a short **o** word. **Print** the word.

1. mop
2. d o g
3. l o g
4. t o p
5. f o x
6. p o t
7. b o x
8. r o c k
9. p o p
10. o x
11. f r o g
12.

Short vowel o: Spelling 119

FOCUS ON ALL LEARNERS

ESL/ELL ENGLISH LANGUAGE LEARNERS

• Have English language learners work in pairs to complete page 119. First, have them identify the pictures. Then, complete items 1 to 11 together. Children can complete the last item by themselves.

• For page 120, encourage children to talk about the pictures they see. Ask questions such as *Where is Bob?* and *What is in the pond?*

KINESTHETIC/VISUAL LEARNERS GROUPS

Materials: Phonics Picture Cards: box (70), dog (71), doll (72), mop (73), ox (74), top (75); masking tape; small objects for playing pieces

Using masking tape, outline a hopscotch grid. In the corner of each of six boxes, have children tape a picture card. Have children take turns playing the game. As they hop on each square with a card, have them name the picture and identify the vowel.

Words in Context

▶ **Look** at the picture. **Circle** the word that will finish the sentence. **Print** it on the line.

1. Bob is ___hot___ .
   (hot) / got / hop

2. He sits on top of a ___rock___ .
   (rock) / rack / lock

3. He takes off his ___socks___ .
   sacks / (socks) / locks

4. The grass is ___soft___ .
   sack / lift / (soft)

5. He sees a frog in the ___pond___ .
   (pond) / pot / pod

6. The frog hops on a ___log___ .
   lock / lost / (log)

TALK about it What do you think Bob might do next?

HOME With your child, think of silly sentences using the short *o* words, such as *The frog took off its socks*.

120 Short o: High-frequency words, critical thinking

CURRICULUM CONNECTIONS

SPELLING
Materials: index cards or slips of paper

Have children write their spelling words on separate index cards or slips of paper. Then, ask them to sort the words in different ways, such as by ending sound or by words that name living and nonliving things. Have them share each word sort with a partner and explain their sorting criteria.

WRITING
Materials: drawing paper, crayons

PORTFOLIO

Have children recall the story. Ask them to imagine that Bob also took his dog Spot to the pond. What do they think Spot might do when he saw the frog hopping up on the log? Have children draw a picture and write a few sentences showing what might happen.

PHYSICAL EDUCATION
Invite children to pretend to be frogs. Take them to the gym or, if possible, to a grassy spot outdoors. Have them hop and leap high.

TECHNOLOGY **AstroWord** Short Vowels: *i, o*

AUDITORY LEARNERS **GROUPS**
Talk with children about how popcorn looks and sounds when it pops. Ask children to pretend to be popcorn kernels. Read these words and have them "pop" when they hear a word with the short *o* sound: *hop, map, stop, jog, not, cub, sad, lost, rock, hat, top*.

CHALLENGE
Materials: self-stick notes, scissors

Have children cut self-stick notes in narrow strips to cover the words under the pictures on page 119. Then, have them try writing the whole picture name. They can check their spelling by bending back the strip.

EXTRA SUPPORT/INTERVENTION
Have children name the pictures on page 119. Ask them to find pictures whose names rhyme. As they name rhyming pictures, such as *mop, top, pop* and *dog, log*, write the first word on the board. Then, ask volunteers to change the beginning letter to make another word. See **Daily Phonics Practice, pages 314–315.**

Integrating Phonics and Reading

Shared/Guided Reading
Show the cover as you read the title. Ask children to tell who will be lost in the fog, using only short *o* words.

First Reading Each time you come to a short *o* word, pause and have children read it aloud.

Second Reading Have children find five words that end in *-og* in the story.

Comprehension
After reading, ask children the following questions:
- How did the dog, the frog, and the hog feel about being lost? *Inference/Drawing Conclusions*
- What do you think happens on the last page? *Creative/Details*

ESL/ELL English Language Learners
Call children's attention to the exclamations "Lost!" "Oh, no!" and "Help!" Have them talk about the meaning of each one and read the exclamations with appropriate feeling.

120

Lesson 57 Pages 121–122

Short Vowel o

Skill Focus

Children will

★ identify picture names and spell words that contain the sound of short o.

★ write words that contain the sound of short o to complete sentences.

★ recognize and read high-frequency words.

Teach

Phonemic Awareness: Medial Sound Isolation Say *hop*, then /o/. Tell children you are saying a word and then its middle vowel sound. Model the procedure again, using *lot*, then /o/. Then, have children say these words and follow each one with its middle vowel sound: *hog, box, lot, sock, top*. Explain that the sound heard in the middle of each word is short *o*.

Sound to Symbol Jog in place and encourage children to use the word *jog* to name the action. Then, invite them to use short *o* words to name places to which you might jog. Elicit such places as a big *rock*, a *shop*, a *dock*, a *pond*. Record the words on the board and ask volunteers to underline the letter *o* in each word.

Practice and Apply

Blend Phonemes As children complete page 121, encourage them to say each picture name, stretching out the beginning, middle, and ending sounds. Point out that the spelling word *sock* has a sound, /k/, that is made with two letters, *ck*.

Writing For page 122, suggest that children try each word choice before writing a word. As they complete the activity, they will have the opportunity to read the following high-frequency words: *her, very*.

Critical Thinking For Talk About It, encourage children to provide details that explain what they like about their favorite sports.

Reading Use *What Is at the Top?* MCP Phonics and Reading Short Vowel Skills Library, Level A, to provide practice in reading words with phonograms -op and -ot.

Spelling

Name _____

Say the name of each picture. Print the picture name on the line. In the last box, draw a picture of a short o word. Print the word.

1. mop
2. pot
3. fox
4. sock
5. top
6. dog
7. pop
8. log
9. box
10. ox
11. frog
12.

Short vowel o: Spelling 121

FOCUS ON ALL LEARNERS

ESL/ELL ENGLISH LANGUAGE LEARNERS

- Have children work in pairs to complete items 1 to 11 on page 121. Children can complete item 12 independently.
- For page 122, review the words *likes, puts, shoes,* and *very,* using gestures to communicate meaning. Have a volunteer read item 1. Ask children to circle the word at the right that completes the sentence. Continue for items 2 to 6.

VISUAL LEARNERS

Materials: Phonics Picture Cards: ax (46), bag (47), cap (48), bib (54), king (56), lid (57), bug (61), bus (62), cup (63), box (70), dog (71), doll (72), mop (73), ox (74), top (75)

Have children take turns turning over a card. If the picture name contains a short *o* sound, the first person to "bop" or slap the card may keep it.

KINESTHETIC LEARNERS

Materials: letter cards *Bb, Ff, Hh, Oo, Pp, Ss, Tt, Xx*

Say *box, top,* or *hot* and have partners use their letter cards to form the word. Then, have them change one letter to make a new word and read their new word to the group.

Words in Context

Circle the word that will finish the sentence. Print it on the line.

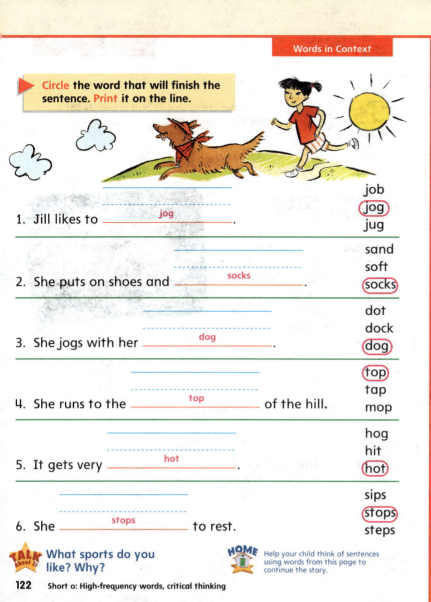

1. Jill likes to __jog__ .
   job
   (jog)
   jug

2. She puts on shoes and __socks__ .
   sand
   soft
   (socks)

3. She jogs with her __dog__ .
   dot
   dock
   (dog)

4. She runs to the __top__ of the hill.
   (top)
   tap
   mop

5. It gets very __hot__ .
   hog
   hit
   (hot)

6. She __stops__ to rest.
   sips
   (stops)
   steps

TALK About It What sports do you like? Why?

HOME Help your child think of sentences using words from this page to continue the story.

122 Short o: High-frequency words, critical thinking

CURRICULUM CONNECTIONS

SPELLING
Materials: letter cards
Write the list words *dog, rock, fox, pot, sock,* and *top* on the board. Have children select a word and spell it with letter cards.

WRITING
Materials: tissue tubes, tape
Have children tape the tubes together to make a pair of play binoculars. Then, have them imagine that they have jogged to the top of Jill's hill. Have them look at the view through the binoculars and write about what they see.

PORTFOLIO

SOCIAL STUDIES
Materials: drawing paper, crayons
Working with partners or in small groups, have children map a jogging route around the school grounds. Have them label landmarks on their maps such as a big rock, a log, the slide, swings, or other playground apparatus.

TECHNOLOGY AstroWord Short Vowels: *i, o*

AUDITORY LEARNERS **GROUPS**
Have children create oral riddles that follow this model to share with the class.
- I'm an animal whose name rhymes with *fog*. I make a good pet. What am I? (a dog)
- You put things inside me. My name rhymes with *fox*. What am I? (a box)

CHALLENGE
Challenge children to write the rhyming words from page 121 in lists. Then, have them add rhyming words to each list.

EXTRA SUPPORT/INTERVENTION
On page 121, suggest that children write the consonants that stand for the beginning and ending sounds first. Then, have them write the letter that stands for the vowel sound. They may need help with the ending sound of *sock*. See Daily Phonics Practice, pages 314–315.

Integrating Phonics and Reading

Shared/Guided Reading
Read the title and preview the illustrations. Have children tell what the animals will climb to the top of.
First Reading Read the part of the narrator and ask volunteers to read the parts of the frog, dog, cat, and pig.
Second Reading Point out the words that describe movements on pages 5, 7, 9, and 11. Have children identify the short vowel sounds.
Comprehension
After reading, ask children the following questions:
- Why did the frog, dog, cat, and pig go to the top of the hill? *Recall/Summarize*
- Did they find what they were looking for? How do you know? *Inference/Details*

ESL/ELL English Language Learners
Call attention to the words *hop, trot, skip,* and *hip-hop*. Have children act out each movement.

Lesson 58   Pages 123-124

Phonics and Reading / Phonics and Writing

Short vowel o

Skill Focus

Children will
* read words that contain the sound of short o.
* write short o words to finish sentences.
* build words with short o phonograms -ot, -og.

Teach

Phonemic Awareness: Phoneme Blending
Tell children to listen as you say the parts of a word: /t/ /o/ /p/. Ask them to put the parts together to say the whole word: *top*. Then, have children repeat these words, stretching the medial sound: *not, lock, job, pop, fox, doll*. Ask them to identify each word and tell what vowel sound is heard. (short o)

Sound to Symbol Display the following Phonics Word Cards on the chalkboard ledge: *dock* (83), *hot* (85), *dog* (86), *hop* (89). Invite volunteers to come up, choose a card, and write the word on the board. Then, have them change the first letter to write as many new words as they can.

Read Words in Sentences Write these sentences on the board.

* The dog is hot.
* The fox is in the box.

Help children read the sentences. Then, ask them to circle the words that have the sound of short *o*.

Practice and Apply

Phonics and Reading After children have read the article, encourage them to identify words that begin with the short *o* sound. As children are reading, they will have the opportunity to read these high-frequency words: *live, some, called*.

Critical Thinking For Talk About It, have children use the sentences and the picture to compare foxes with dogs.

Phonics and Writing For page 124, tell children to try each letter at the top to make a word with -ot or -og. Remind them to write only the real words.

Reading Use *The Merry-Go-Round*, MCP Phonics and Reading Short Vowel Skills Library, Level A, to provide practice in reading words with the phonograms -on, -an, -in, and -un.

123

Reading

Name_____

 Read the story. Print short **o** words to finish the sentences.

F🐾xes

Foxes **live** in many places.
Some foxes live where it is hot.
Some live where it is cold.
Foxes are like dogs.
They have soft fur.
A baby fox is **called** a cub or a pup.

1. ____**Foxes**____ live in many places.

2. Some foxes live where it is ____**hot**____.

3. Foxes are like ____**dogs**____.

🌟 How is a fox like a dog?

Review short o: Reading, critical thinking   123

FOCUS ON ALL LEARNERS

ESL/ELL ENGLISH LANGUAGE LEARNERS
Use the following activities to teach English language learners.

* Ask children to talk about the photo on page 123 and tell what they know about foxes. Then, have children look for short *o* words in the story. Have volunteers write them on the board. Check comprehension by asking, *Where do foxes live? What other animal is like a fox?* and so on.

* For page 124, read the directions aloud. Complete the first item together to verify understanding.

VISUAL/AUDITORY LEARNERS
Write these words on the chalkboard: *fox, stop, hop, hot, top, pot, lot, pond*. Have children stand near the chalkboard. Say a word from the board and have children race to touch the word. The first child to touch the word may erase it. Continue until all the words are erased. Make the game more interesting by occasionally saying a word that is not on the board. Tell children to go to the board if they hear a short *o* word.

Building Words

Use one of the letters to make a word with **ot** or **og**. Write each real word on a line.

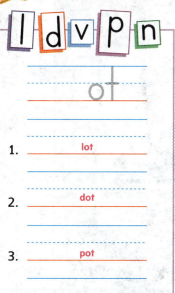

1. lot
2. dot
3. pot
4. not

5. log
6. dog
7. hog
8. fog

Write a sentence using one of the words you made.

  Help your child think of words that end in *on*, *od*, *ox*, and *ob*.

124 Review short vowel o: Phonograms

CURRICULUM CONNECTIONS

SPELLING
For the spelling posttest, dictate a list word and then read it in context in the sentence.
1. **rock**   I found a pretty **rock**.
2. **dog**   Jim's **dog** can do tricks.
3. **pot**   The **pot** is very hot.
4. **fox**   A **fox** hunts for its food.
5. **top**   We climbed to the **top** of the ladder.
6. **sock**   I lost one blue **sock**.

SCIENCE
Materials: picture books about foxes

Help children use the books to identify the foxes shown on page 123. Ask them to write a factual sentence about red foxes.

LANGUAGE ARTS
Have children look for stories that have a fox as a character. Read some of the stories and discuss whether the fox was a good character or a bad character in each story.

   **AstroWord** Short Vowels: *i, o*

Integrating Phonics and Reading

Shared/Guided Reading
Show the cover as you read the title. Invite children to tell what they know about merry-go-rounds.
First Reading Point out the quotation marks. Have half the class join in as you read Ron's words. Have the other half join in as you read Don's.
Second Reading Have children point to each word that contains *on*.
Comprehension After reading, ask children the following questions:
• Do Ron and Don like the merry-go-round? How can you tell? *Inference/Details*
• Would you like to ride on one? Why or why not? *Reflective Analysis/Personal Experience*

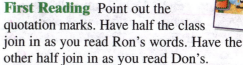

ESL/ELL English Language Learners
Have children find the past form for each of these words in the story: *say, run, spin, stay*. Discuss which is formed by adding *-ed* and which are formed in other ways. Explain that the past form tells about something that has happened.

AUDITORY LEARNERS
Tell children that foxes can bark like dogs. Tell them to bark when they hear a word that rhymes with *fox*. Say: *got, ox, stop, job, docks, box, dot, pond, socks, hop, clocks*.

CHALLENGE
Have children write the word *fox* on a piece of paper. Have them see how many new words they can make by changing one letter of the previous word. For example, *fox* might lead to *fog, dog, dot, hot, hop, top, pot, not, nod, rod,* and *rob*.

EXTRA SUPPORT/INTERVENTION
Read the sentences on page 123 aloud. Then, have children take turns reading a sentence at a time. Ask children to restate what they learned about foxes before they complete the sentences in items 1 to 3. See *Daily Phonics Practice*, pages 314–315.

Lesson 59   Pages 125–126

Take-Home Book

Review Short Vowels a, i, o, u

Skill Focus

Children will
★ read short *a, i, o,* and *u* words in the context of a story.
★ review selected high-frequency words in the context of a story.
★ reread for fluency.

Teach

Build Background Remind children that the theme of this unit is "Amazing Animals." Ask them to tell about favorite stories in which the characters are animals that talk and act like people. Remind them that stories like these are fiction, or make-believe. Then, tell children that they will read a story about a dog, a pup, some bugs, and some pigs.

Phonological Awareness: Rhyme Say groups of three words. Have children identify the words in each group that rhyme. Then, ask volunteers to identify the sound heard in the middle of each pair of rhyming words. Use: *tub, cub, cab* (short *u*); *pan, pop, ran* (short *a*); *hug, jog, fog* (short *o*); *mist, list, dust* (short *i*); *fin, fun, run* (short *u*); *stop, top, pup* (short *o*).

Practice and Apply

Read the Book Help children tear out and fold the pages to make their Take-Home Books. Then, read the book together. Ask children if they thought the story was funny and why.

Sound to Symbol *Use letter cards* Read aloud or have volunteers read the book. Write columns headed *Short a, Short i, Short u, Short o* on the board. Have children identify the short *a, i, u,* and *o* words. (*had, bath, can, ran; in, six, big, pigs; pup, tub, bugs, jump; dog, hot, hop, got*) Invite volunteers to write the words on the board and read the words aloud.

Review High-Frequency Words Write the words *said, the,* and *you* on the board. Have children spell them, then say them.

Reread for Fluency Have children reread the book to increase their fluency and comprehension. Children can take their books home to read and share with family members.

Review short vowels a, i, u, o: Take-home book **125**

FOCUS ON ALL LEARNERS

ESL/ELL ENGLISH LANGUAGE LEARNERS

After assisting children with making the Take-Home book, use the following activities to teach English language learners.

- Discuss the pictures to be sure children can name the animals. Talk about how a pup is different from a dog.
- Discuss the words within quotes. Have children read them after you.
- Encourage children to use their own words to tell what happens at the end and why.

VISUAL LEARNERS

Draw a large tub on chart paper. Have children write short *a, i, u,* and *o* words from the story in the tub. Then, have them add words of their own until the tub is "filled."

KINESTHETIC/AUDITORY LEARNERS

Draw a dog, bug, and pig on the chalkboard. Then, say the following words. Have children repeat each word and point to the picture whose name has the same short vowel sound. Use *pup, rock, stick, pond, shop, fun, sock, win.*

125

Six hot bugs said, "Can we hop in the tub?"
The dog said, "You can."

2

Six big pigs said, "Can we jump in the tub?"
The dog said, "You can."

3

126 Review short vowels a, i, u, o: Take-home book

CURRICULUM CONNECTIONS

SCIENCE

Materials: small plastic tub filled with water; a collection of small objects such as a rag, a bag, a lid, a paper clip, a box, a lock, a stick of gum, and a nut

Help children make a chart with the headings *Sink* and *Float*. Then have them test each object and list it under the appropriate heading. Afterward, have children identify the short *a, i, o,* and *u* words they wrote.

SOCIAL STUDIES

Materials: Books about pet care

Share with children books about taking care of puppies, kittens, or other pets. Then, invite them to make their own how-to books or posters about pet care.

ART/WRITING

Write this rhyme on the board:
 Rub-a-dub-dub,
 ____ in a tub.
Invite children to complete it using characters from the Take-Home Book, such as *a dog* and *a pup*. Then, have them draw a picture to illustrate their rhyme. Suggest that they leave space to write the rhyme underneath.

PORTFOLIO

TECHNOLOGY **AstroWord** Short Vowels: *i, o;*
 Short Vowels: *a, i;*
 Short Vowels: *e, u*

AUDITORY/VISUAL LEARNERS GROUPS

Read aloud sentences from the story, omitting a short vowel word. For example: *The dog said, "You ___."* Ask children to find the sentence in the text and supply the missing word.

CHALLENGE

Challenge children to write another story about the dog, the pup, the bugs, and the pigs. Suggest that they include some words with short *a, i, u,* and *o*.

EXTRA SUPPORT/INTERVENTION

Materials: Take-Home Books, tape recorder, audiotape

Record the story for children to listen to. On a second listening, have them quietly repeat each sentence after the sentence on the tape. See *Daily Phonics Practice, pages 312–315.*

Lesson 60 Pages 127–128

High-Frequency Words

Skill Focus

Children will

★ recognize and read the high-frequency words *of, her, our, have, one, come.*

★ use the high-frequency words to complete sentences.

★ begin to recognize irregular spelling patterns.

Teach

Analyze Words Write the words *of, her, our, have, one, come* on the board. Point to each word as you read it aloud. Have children repeat each word after you. Then:

- Slowly say each word as you point to the letters. Encourage children to listen for the consonant and vowel sounds in the word.
- Help children associate the sounds they hear in each word with a familiar word.
- You may wish to add the words to the class Word Wall so that children can use the words they learn to find similar spelling patterns and phonemic elements in new words.

Read Words in Sentences Write the following sentences on the board. Invite volunteers to read the sentences and underline the high-frequency words.

- We <u>have</u> a friend named Pam.
- Pam is <u>one</u> of <u>our</u> best pals.
- <u>Her</u> cat is black.
- Pam and <u>her</u> cat will <u>come</u> to <u>our</u> yard.

Practice and Apply

Write Words Have children turn to page 127. Read the directions aloud and make sure children understand what to do. Do the same for page 128. Encourage children to use strategies they have learned to associate sounds with letters and blend words to help them read. Children can work with a partner to complete Checking Up.

Reading You may wish to use *Bags, Cans, Pots, and Pans*, MCP Phonics and Reading Library, High Frequency Word Collection, Level A, to reinforce some of the high-frequency words. Invite children to think of a new sentence that uses some of the high-frequency words they have just learned. For example: *We gave her one of our books.*

High-Frequency Words

Name _____

▶ Read the words in the box. Write a word to finish each sentence.

of	her
Our	have
one	come

1. ___Our___ family has a pet.

2. We ___have___ a dog.

3. Molly is ___her___ name.

4. We could not find Molly ___one___ day.

5. I said, "Molly, ___come___ here!"

6. Molly jumped out ___of___ a box!

High-frequency words **127**

FOCUS ON ALL LEARNERS

ESL/ELL ENGLISH LANGUAGE LEARNERS

Materials: high-frequency word cards

English language learners may have difficulty pronouncing words with *r*-controlled vowels (*her, our*) or words with irregular spelling-pronunciation patterns (*of, have, one, come*). To help children with these words, use the high-frequency word cards. Say a word as you display it and have children repeat it. Then, help children use the word in a sentence.

AUDITORY/KINESTHETIC LEARNERS

Write each of the high-frequency words on the chalkboard. Say the words at random. For each one, have a volunteer come up, touch the word, and use it in a sentence.

KINESTHETIC/VISUAL LEARNERS

Write each of the high-frequency words on an index card and hide the cards around the room. Give clues that will help children find each one. When a child finds a card, have him or her say and spell the word.

High-Frequency Words

▶ Unscramble the letters to write a word from the box. The word shapes will help you print the words.

have	one	of
our	come	her

1. fo — **o f**
2. erh — **h e r**
3. uro — **o u r**
4. evha — **h a v e**
5. neo — **o n e**
6. moce — **c o m e**

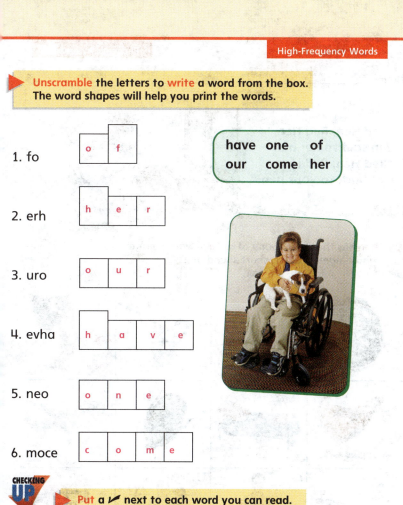

CHECKING UP

▶ Put a ✓ next to each word you can read.

☐ one   ☐ come   ☐ have   ☐ of   ☐ our   ☐ her

128   High-frequency words

 Use some of the words on this page to make up sentences with your child.

VISUAL LEARNERS *PARTNERS*

Write each high-frequency word on two index cards and place the cards face down. Have children take turns flipping over a pair of cards. If the child has a match, he or she reads and spells the word.

CHALLENGE

Write the following story starter on the board:

We have a pet. Her name is ___. You must come to our home to see her. She is one of a kind. You have never seen a ___ like her.

Have children fill in the blanks and underline the high-frequency words. Then, challenge them to continue the story, using as many high-frequency words as possible.

EXTRA SUPPORT/INTERVENTION

Draw word shapes for the high-frequency words on the board, using the ones on page 128 as models. Then, say a word and use it in a sentence. For example: *Come: Please come to the party.* Have a child come to the board and write the word in the correct shape.

CURRICULUM CONNECTIONS

SOCIAL STUDIES

Materials: nonfiction books about animal helpers

Explain that some pets have special jobs. For example, seeing-eye dogs help visually impaired people get around town. Therapy dogs visit people in hospitals and cheer them up. Then, share one or more books about a pet that helps people. Have children note the high-frequency words in the book. Then, have them retell the true story, using as many high-frequency words as they can.

MATH

Invite children to write word problems using the high-frequency words. Suggest that they use pets as a theme. Offer the following example: *Our dog Spot had ten toys. One of her toys was lost. How many toys did she have left?*

Have children exchange problems with a partner. The partners then solve the problems and underline the high-frequency words.

PORTFOLIO

Integrating Phonics and Reading

Shared/Guided Reading
Show the cover as you read the title. Invite children to tell some of the things we can do with bags, cans, pots, and pans.

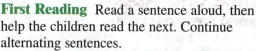

First Reading Read a sentence aloud, then help the children read the next. Continue alternating sentences.

Second Reading Encourage children to look for the word *have*. Let individual children take turns reading the sentences beginning *"I have"* on pages 6–7.

Comprehension
After reading, ask children the following questions:
• Where do you think the family is going? Why? *Inference/Details*
• How do you think they will use the things they are bringing? *Inference/Connect to Experience*

ESL/ELL English Language Learners
Help children understand the different meanings of *can* as a helping verb and a noun. Invite them to use the word in sentences.

128

Lesson 61 Pages 129–130

Short Vowel e

Skill Focus

Children will

★ recognize the sound of short *e*.

★ identify picture names and words that contain the sound of short *e*.

★ identify rhyming short *e* words.

ESL/ELL Native speakers of Tagalog might pronounce written *e* like the *ay* in *say*. No sound similar to short *e* exists in Korean. Offer additional practice and support.

Teach

Phonemic Awareness: Phoneme Categorization Say the word *pen*, elongating the medial short *e* sound. Then, say the word naturally and ask children to repeat the word. Explain that the sound heard in the middle of the word is short *e*. Next, say the following groups of three words. Ask children to write the letter *e* in the air with a pretend pen each time they hear a word with a short *e* sound.

- ran   men   lid
- sit   cup   bed
- wet   pan   sip

Phonological Awareness: Rhyme Tell children you will say pairs of words. If the words rhyme, they should repeat them. If the words do not rhyme, children should remain silent. Say: *let, get; spin, fizz; mask, mess; fell, tell; log, jet; men, pen; tub, tab.*

Sound to Symbol Write *jet* on the board. Read the word with children, emphasizing the middle sound. Underline the *e* and explain that this letter represents the short *e* sound heard in *jet*.

Practice and Apply

Phonemic Awareness Read aloud the rhyme on page 129. Have children listen for and name the short *e* words. You may want to review the spelling of the high-frequency word *said*, underline the *ai*, and explain that it is not a short *e* word.

Sound to Symbol Help children identify the pictures on pages 129 and 130. Suggest that they say the picture names softly to themselves as they complete each page.

Reading Use *What Do We Have to Get?* MCP Phonics and Reading Short Vowel Skills Library, Level A, to provide practice in reading words with short *a* and *e*.

Phonemic Awareness

Name _____

"Red Hen, Red Hen,"
Jen said to her hen.
"Red Hen, Red Hen,
Get back to your pen!"

▶ **Hen** has the short sound of **e**. **Circle** each picture whose name has the short sound of **e**.

1. web   2. ten   3. net   4. heel
5. hen   6. bed   7. bug   8. jet
9. pen   10. man   11. men   12. desk

Short vowel e: Phonemic awareness   129

FOCUS ON ALL LEARNERS

ESL/ELL ENGLISH LANGUAGE LEARNERS

- Read the rhyme on page 129, then write *Jen* and *pen* on the chalkboard. Point out that the girl in the rhyme and the picture is named *Jen*, and discuss the different meanings of *pen*. (It can be a writing instrument or a fenced area to hold animals.) Before beginning the activity, read the directions aloud. Call out item numbers and have children name the picture clues. Provide help as needed, such as *jet*, not *plane*.

- For page 130, read the directions aloud. Ask a volunteer to name the pictures in item 1. Assist children in determining which picture names rhyme and have them color each one. You may wish to pair children to complete items 2 to 5 according to levels of English proficiency. Monitor pairs for equal participation and review orally.

KINESTHETIC LEARNERS

Materials: index cards; letter card *Ee*

Have a child write an *e* on an index card. Write the word forms *m_n, b_d, n_t, r_d, t_n, n_st, t_nt,* on the board. Have each child place his or her letter card on the blank and read the word.

Say the names of the pictures in each row.
Color the pictures whose names rhyme.

Phonograms/Rhyme

130 Short vowel e: Phonograms/rhyme

CURRICULUM CONNECTIONS

SPELLING
For the spelling pretest, dictate a list word and then read it in context in the sentence.
1. **bed** I sleep in a **bed**.
2. **jet** A **jet** is one kind of plane.
3. **nest** The bird makes a **nest** for its babies.
4. **bell** I can hear the **bell** ring.
5. **ten** The number **ten** comes after nine.
6. **web** The spider spins a **web** to catch bugs.

WRITING

Have children illustrate and dictate or write about a wet pet. Encourage them to read their work to a partner.

SCIENCE
Materials: books about dinosaurs and reptiles

Most children know that birds lay eggs. Encourage them to look through books for other animals that lay eggs. Have them draw some of the animals they find and label their illustrations.

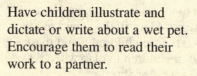 **AstroWord** Short Vowels: e, u

Integrating Phonics and Reading

Shared/Guided Reading
Show the cover and read the title. Ask children where they think the story will take place.

First Reading Have children try to name the items Jan and Ed are supposed to get as you read each page.
Second Reading Ask children to identify the short e words in the story. You might want to add these to the classroom Word Wall.
Comprehension
After reading, ask children the following questions:
- Why did Jan and Ed forget what they were supposed to get? *Inference/Cause and Effect*
- Was going back with a list a good idea? Why? *Reflective Analysis/Cause and Effect*

ESL/ELL English Language Learners
Write *get, met, red, ten, yes* on the board and discuss the meaning of each word. Then erase the letter *e* in the words. Ask volunteers to add the letter that makes the short *e* sound.

AUDITORY/KINESTHETIC LEARNERS GROUPS
Materials: letter cards *Hh, Tt, Bb, Gg, Ll, Vv, Ww*; teacher-made phonogram cards for each child: *-en, -et, -ed, -est,* and *-ell*

Read aloud one rhyming pair at a time: *hen, ten; bet, get; bed, led; best, vest;* and *bell, well.* Have children spell the words with cards.

CHALLENGE
Challenge children to start a Picture Dictionary of short *e* words. Encourage them to look through books and compile a list of the words they find. Then, have them make and label illustrations for as many of the words as they can. Help them bind their pages into a book.

EXTRA SUPPORT/INTERVENTION
Write the word *bell* on the board and read it. Erase the *b* and write *f* in its place. Help children read the new word. Continue changing the first letter to *t, s,* and *w*. Then, write the new word *ten*. Have children change the first letter to make new words. Let the group read each word. **See Daily Phonics Practice, page 315.**

Lesson 62 Pages 131–132

Short Vowel e

Skill Focus

Children will

★ recognize the sound of short e.

★ understand that e stands for /e/.

★ write uppercase and lowercase Ee.

★ apply what they have learned by reading and writing.

Teach

Phonemic Awareness: Blending Onsets and Rimes Say /n/et and have children repeat the sounds. Then, blend the sounds to say *net*. Have children repeat the word. Identify the sound in the middle as short *e*. Next, have children blend these sounds into words. Ask children to clap when they hear a word with the sound of short *e*.

- /l/eg   /b/us   /p/ig
- /h/ad   /r/ed   /t/op
- /j/et   /n/ut   /b/ell

Sound to Symbol Ask volunteers to come up to the board and draw simple pictures to show a net, a pet, an egg, and ten men. Write the words under each picture. Then, have children underline the vowel in each word. Ask what sound this letter stands for. (short *e*)

Handwriting Write *Ee* on the chalkboard and use the models on page 132 to review how to form the letters. Have children follow along on their own paper.

Practice and Apply

Sound to Symbol As children complete page 131, encourage them to say each picture name softly to themselves by blending the sounds. For page 132, read the directions in each box with children. Suggest that they underline key words such as *bed*, *tent*, and *sled* to help them remember what to draw.

Writing Note the short *e* words that children write on page 132 and check for correct spelling.

Reading Use *Ben's Pets*, MCP Phonics and Reading Short Vowel Skills Library, Level A, to provide practice in reading words with phonograms -*et* and -*en*.

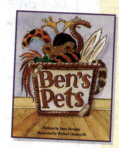

Sound to Symbol

Name_____

▶ Say the name of each picture. Circle its name.

1. (bed)   fed   led
2. bill   sell   (bell)
3. tan   (ten)   tin
4. met   (net)   nut
5. west   well   (web)
6. (jet)   pet   wet
7. went   man   (men)
8. leg   (egg)   beg
9. ten   (tent)   bent
10. (belt)   bell   melt
11. pin   pet   (pen)
12. (nest)   not   just

Short vowel e: Sound to symbol   131

FOCUS ON ALL LEARNERS

ESL/ELL ENGLISH LANGUAGE LEARNERS

- Display real items such as a bell, an egg, a belt, and a pen. Have a volunteer identify each object. Write the word plus two similar words on the board, such as *bell, ball, doll*. Have children identify the object name by circling the correct word choice. Then, have children work in pairs to complete the activity on page 131.

- Before children begin page 132, have four volunteers each read one of the sentences in the boxes. Explain unfamiliar words, if necessary. Have children work individually to complete the page.

KINESTHETIC LEARNERS

Materials: Phonics Picture Cards: ax (46), hand (51), lamp (53), mitt (58), pig (59), bug (61) tub (68), doll (72), ox (74), bed (76), belt (78), desk (79), eggs (80), hen (81), ten (82), tent (83), web (84)

Place the picture card of the hen on the chalkboard ledge. Say *hen* and have children repeat. The, pass out the other picture cards in random order. Have children name their pictures. If they hear the sound of short *e* as in the word *hen*, they put their picture on the chalkboard ledge.

Picture-text Match

▶ Four red hens are missing from their pen. **Draw** a hen in each box. **Follow the directions** below.

1.

   Draw a hen in a bed.

2.

   Draw a hen in a tent.

3.

   Draw a hen on a sled.

4.

   Draw a hen in a nest.

| hen | bed | tent | sled | nest |

▶ **Use** some of the words from the box to **write** a sentence.

 HOME Make up riddles using some of the words from the box. Ask your child to guess each word.

132 Short vowel e: Picture-text match

CURRICULUM CONNECTIONS

SPELLING
Write the list words *bed, jet, nest, bell, ten,* and *web* on the board and read them with children. Ask volunteers to name the beginning and ending sounds. Have volunteers come up and draw a picture for each spelling word and labels for the pictures. As a group, read and spell each word.

WRITING

Have children dictate or write a few sentences about a chick hatching from an egg. Ask them to include a sentence that tells how the chick feels.

FINE ARTS
Read aloud a version of "The Little Red Hen." Have the class act out the story, using props and costumes.

 **AstroWord** Short Vowels: *e, u*

AUDITORY/KINESTHETIC LEARNERS
Materials: crayons, paper, scissors, chart paper, tape

Draw a large web on chart paper. Ask the class to draw two pictures, one whose name contains the short sound of *e*, as in the word *web*, and the other that does not, and give them to a partner. The partner cuts out the picture whose name has the sound of short *e* in it and tapes it to the web.

CHALLENGE
Have children research hens and share the information with classmates through pictures or an oral report.

EXTRA SUPPORT/INTERVENTION
Materials: Phonics Picture Cards: bell (77), belt (78), desk (79), hen (81), ten (82), web (84); Phonics Word Cards, Set 1: bell (96), belt (98), desk (100), hen (103), ten (113), web (114)

Have children name each picture and hold up the word card that names it. See Daily Phonics Practice, page 315.

Integrating Phonics and Reading

Shared/Guided Reading
Show children the cover as you read the title. Ask what they see in the illustration. What kinds of pets might Ben have?

First Reading Have children join in each time the words *Get the vet!* appear.

Second Reading Have children find the words with phonograms *-et* and *-en.* (*pet, get, vet; hen*)

Comprehension
After reading, ask children the following questions:

- Did anything about Ben's pets surprise you? *Reflective Analysis/Plot*
- Were there any clues to the surprise in the pictures? *Inference/Details*

ESL/ELL English Language Learners
Make sure children know that *vet* is short for *veterinarian*, a doctor who treats animals.

Lesson 63   Pages 133–134

Short Vowels a, i, u, o, e

Skill Focus

Children will
- ★ orally blend word parts.
- ★ Identify picture names and spell words that contain the sound of short *a*, *i*, *u*, *o*, or *e*.

Teach

Phonemic Awareness: Phoneme Categorization Tell children that you will say groups of three words. Ask them to identify the two words in each group that have the same short vowel sound.

- list   hand   stick
- hen   hog   pet
- tap   hat   bend
- fill   pot   top
- cut   cap   tub

Phonological Awareness: Blending Onsets and Rimes Tell children that you will say the parts of a word. Children should blend the parts together to say the word. Then, help them identify the sound heard in the middle of each word.

- /c/up   /b/ell   /s/it
- /g/et   /r/ock   /m/ad

Sound to Symbol Display and identify the picture cards for bag (47), bed (76), king (56), dog (71), and sun (67). Write the words on the board and have children say them. Ask volunteers to come up and underline the letter that stands for the short vowel sound in each word.

Practice and Apply

Phonological Awareness: Blending Before children begin page 133, draw three arrows similar to the ones on the page. Write *t-op* along the first arrow, *t-ip* along the second arrow, and *t-ap* along the third arrow. Move your hand along the first arrow as you blend the word *top*. Then, have volunteers move their hands along the second and third arrows as the class blends the words *tip* and *tap*.

For page 134, make sure children understand that they will write each blended word and then draw a line to the correct picture.

Reading Use *The Apple Farm*, MCP Phonics and Reading Short Vowel Skills Library, Level A, to provide practice in reading words with short vowels.

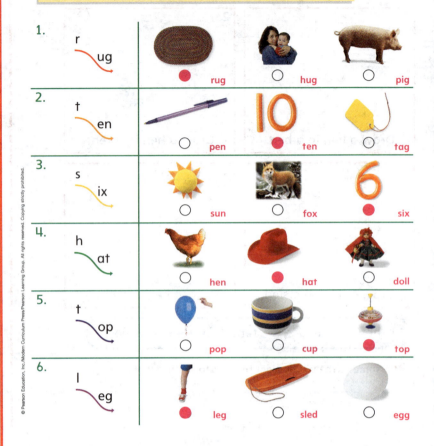

FOCUS ON ALL LEARNERS

ESL/ELL ENGLISH LANGUAGE LEARNERS

Before English language learners begin pages 133 and 134, review short vowel sounds. Have volunteers name a vowel, model the short vowel sound, and say a word containing the sound.

VISUAL LEARNERS

Materials: magazines, scissors, glue, construction paper

Point out that words such as *rug, ten,* and *six* have the c-v-c pattern. Have children look through magazines to find words and pictures of things whose names have this pattern. Encourage children to sort their pictures and words by vowel sound.

KINESTHETIC LEARNERS

Materials: Phonics Picture Cards: cat (49), pig (59), bug (61), dog (71), hen (81); paper and pencil

Pass out a picture card to each child in the group. Ask them to act out the word for their classmates to guess. Guessers write their answers and check them after everyone has had a turn.

Blending

▶ **Blend** the sounds together as you say each word. **Print** the word on the line. **Draw** a line to the picture it names.

1. n-et — **net**
2. m-op — **mop**
3. s-un — **sun**
4. w-ig — **wig**
5. c-at — **cat**
6. p-en — **pen**

Short vowels: Blending phonograms

HOME Name a vowel. Ask your child to read a word that has that vowel.

CURRICULUM CONNECTIONS

SPELLING
Write the following list words on the board: *web, ten, bell, nest, bed, jet.* Ask children to dictate sentences using the words. Record the sentences on the board and draw a box where the spelling word belongs. Have volunteers come up and write the spelling words to complete the sentences.

WRITING
Have the children draw pictures of a hen in a nest and her eggs and other things they might find on a farm with names containing the short sound of *e*. Then, have them label the pictures and circle the words that contain the sound of short *e*.

PORTFOLIO

MATH
Let children explore the number 12 by giving them empty egg cartons and letting them collect 12 objects or pictures of things whose names contain the short vowel sound of *e*.

TECHNOLOGY

AstroWord Short Vowels: *a, i*
Short Vowels: *e, u*
Short Vowels: *i, o*

AUDITORY LEARNERS
Materials: Phonics Word Cards: *map* (13), *fan* (14), *lip* (49), *pin* (51), *dug* (68), *sun* (79), *mop* (90), *socks* (95), *den* (99), *pet* (113)

Pass out a word card to each child. Ask children to make up a question for which their word is the answer and then call on a classmate to answer the question.

CHALLENGE
Challenge children by having them choose a *c-v-c* pattern and write as many words that rhyme as they can think of.

EXTRA SUPPORT/INTERVENTION
Materials: Phonics Picture Cards: *cat* (49), *hat* (52), *bug* (61), *jug* (64), *run* (66), *sun* (67), *mop* (73), *top* (75), *hen* (81), *ten* (82)

Display the pictures in a random order. Ask children to name them. Place the pictures face down. Have children turn over two cards at a time to find pairs of rhyming picture names. **See Daily Phonics Practice, pages 312–315.**

Integrating Phonics and Reading

Shared/Guided Reading
Show the cover as you read the title. Encourage children to describe what the people are doing.

First Reading Each time you come to the word *apple(s)*, point to it and have children read it aloud.

Second Reading Have children find a word in the story for each short vowel sound: *a, i, u, o, e.*

Comprehension
After reading, ask children the following questions:

• Why is everyone picking apples?
Recall/Details

• Would you enjoy picking apples? Why?
Reflective Analysis/Details

ESL/ELL English Language Learners
Make sure children understand that the contraction *everyone's* stands for *everyone is*. Model a sentence using *everyone's*, then have children use the contraction in sentences of their own.

Lesson 64   Pages 135–136

Short vowel e

Skill Focus

Children will
- ★ recognize the sound of short *e*.
- ★ identify and spell picture names that contain the sound of short *e*.
- ★ write words that contain the sound of short *e* to complete sentences.
- ★ recognize and read high-frequency words.

Teach

Phonemic Awareness: Phoneme Substitution Give children a short *e* word followed by a new initial consonant, such as *hen with the sound of t*. Ask children to say the new word. (*ten*) Help then notice that the words rhyme.

Repeat, using these words and initial letters: *net* with *l* (*let*); *red* with *b* (*bed*); *tell* with *s* (*sell*); *neck* with *d* (*deck*).

Sound to Symbol Say a series of words. Have children cluck like hens when they hear a short *e* word. Then, have a volunteer come up and write the word on the board. Use: *step, back, pet, hot, fed, lip, stump, bend, spin, pal, rest.*

Words in Context: Decodable Words Write these words on the board: *bed, red*. Then, write and read the sentence below. Have children select the word that completes the sentence.

- I have a _____ pen. (*red*)

Practice and Apply

Blend Phonemes As children complete page 135, encourage them to say each picture name, blending together the beginning, middle, and ending sounds. For item 16, as children to print the word that names their picture.

Writing For page 136, suggest that children try each word choice before writing a word. As they complete the activity, they will have the opportunity to read the following high-frequency words: *then, by.*

Critical Thinking For Talk About It, have children recall what the girl in the story drew before naming what they like to draw.

Reading Use *Ned's Red Sled*, MCP Phonics and Reading Short Vowel Skills Library, Level A, to provide practice in reading words with the phonogram *-ed*.

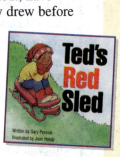

Spelling

Name _____

▶ **Say** the name of each picture. **Print** the letter for its beginning and ending sounds. In the last box, **draw** a picture of a short e word.

1. n e t
2. w e b
3. b e d
4. p e n
5. l e g
6. t e n
7. h e n
8. j e t
9. t e n t
10. s l e d
11. d e s k
12. b e l t
13. n e s t
14. m e n
15. v e s t
16. e

Short vowel e: Spelling   135

FOCUS ON ALL LEARNERS

ESL/ELL ENGLISH LANGUAGE LEARNERS

- Before children begin page 135, encourage them to read the directions aloud and summarize what they are to do. If necessary, help them identify the pictures.
- For page 136, check children's understanding of *picks, draws,* and *hangs*. Make sure children understand that the sentences tell a simple story.

VISUAL LEARNERS

Materials: Phonics Word Cards: *bed-bell* (96), *egg-den* (99), *felt-get* (102), *hen-help* (103), *sell-pen* (111), *ten-pet* (113)

Place the word cards on a table. Encourage pairs of children to take turns choosing a card, reading the words on both sides, and using them in one sentence.

KINESTHETIC LEARNERS

Ask children to form a line to play "Step Forward." Explain that when they hear a word with the same vowel sound as in the word *step*, they are to take a big step forward. Use these words: *dot, jet, lid, best, dad, tent, rug, web.*

Words in Context

▶ **Look** at the picture. **Circle** the word that will finish the sentence. **Print** it on the line.

1. Meg sits at her __desk__.
   - mask
   - (desk)
   - duck

2. She picks up her __pen__.
   - (pen)
   - pet
   - pig

3. Meg draws a __nest__.
   - best
   - (nest)
   - net

4. Then she draws a big __egg__.
   - leg
   - (egg)
   - beg

5. On the nest sits a __hen__.
   - (hen)
   - ten
   - pen

6. Meg hangs it by her __bed__.
   - belt
   - bell
   - (bed)

TALK What kinds of things do you like to draw?

HOME Point to the picture of the pen and ask your child to name as many words that rhyme with *pen* as possible.

136 Short e: High-frequency words, critical thinking

CURRICULUM CONNECTIONS

SPELLING
Write the list words *bell, jet, nest, bed, ten,* and *web* on the board and read them aloud with children. Have children write each word on an index card, cut apart the letters, and mix them up. Then, let children unscramble the words.

WRITING
Have children each draw a picture that they would like to hang by their beds as Meg did. Ask children to title their pictures.

PORTFOLIO

FINE ARTS
Have children make a spiderweb by drawing with white chalk on black construction paper. Encourage them to cut out a spider from colored construction paper and paste it to the web.

TECHNOLOGY **AstroWord** Short Vowels: *e, u*

AUDITORY/KINESTHETIC LEARNERS GROUPS

Materials: paper and pencil

Have children draw pictures of a nest with five large eggs in it. Tell them that you will say some words. When they hear a word with the sound of short *e*, they should write the word in one of the eggs. Words are *bed, tan, net, run, sled, web, pig,* and *pen*.

CHALLENGE
Challenge children to make labels for any objects in the room with names having the sound of short *e*.

EXTRA SUPPORT/INTERVENTION
Have children listen as you say two words. They should repeat the one word that has the short *e* sound. Some word pairs are *ten, top; bug, bed; hat, hen; pet, pin; man, men; will, well.* See Daily Phonics Practice, page 315.

Integrating Phonics and Reading

Shared/Guided Reading
Show the cover as you read the title. Ask children what unusual thing they notice in the illustration.

First Reading Have children join in each time they see this sentence: *But it didn't snow.*

Second Reading Have children find four words in the story that end in *-ed.* (*Ted, red, sled, bed*)

Comprehension
After reading, ask children the following questions:

- What problem does Ted have? *Recall/Problem and Solution*

- Is Ted's problem solved? How? *Inference/Problem and Solution*

ESL/ELL English Language Learners
Call children's attention to the possessive word *Ted's.* Have each child replace *Ted's* with the possessive form of their names in the title _____'s Red Sled.

Lesson 65 Pages 137–138

Short Vowel e

Skill Focus

Children will

★ recognize the sound of short e.

★ identify and spell picture names that contain the sound of short e.

★ write words that contain the sound of short e to complete sentences.

★ recognize and read high-frequency words.

Teach

Phonemic Awareness: Phoneme Blending
Tell children you will say a name. As you do, you will stretch out the sound of each letter: /t/ /e/ /d/. Have children repeat the segmented word, say the word (*Ted*), and identify the vowel sound in the middle. Repeat, using the following names:

- Ken
- Mel
- Ned
- Jen

Sound to Symbol Say the following sentence, then write it on the board: *Meg will get a big bell.* Have volunteers come up and underline each short *e* word and then circle the letter that stands for the short *e* sound. Next, invite children whose names have the short *e* sound to say and write their names. Ask volunteers to circle the letter that stands for short *e* in each name.

Practice and Apply

Blend Phonemes As children complete page 137, encourage them to say each picture name, blending together the beginning, middle, and ending sounds.

Writing For page 138, suggest that children try each word choice before writing a word. As they complete the activity, they will have the opportunity to read the following high-frequency words: *use, as.*

Critical Thinking For Talk About It, have children reread sentences 1 to 6 before telling which sled they would like to use.

Reading Use *The Best Places*, MCP Phonics and Reading Short Vowel Skills Library, Level A, to provide practice in reading words with short *e*.

Spelling

Name_____

▶ Say the name of each picture. Print the picture name on the line. In the last box, draw a picture of a short e word. Print the word.

1. bed
2. ten
3. net
4. men
5. web
6. pen
7. leg
8. desk
9. nest
10. jet
11. hen
12.

Short vowel e: Spelling 137

FOCUS ON ALL LEARNERS

ESL/ELL ENGLISH LANGUAGE LEARNERS

- Help children practice listening comprehension by having a volunteer read aloud the directions for page 137. Then, say each picture name, allowing time for children to write the word under the matching picture. Check children's work as they proceed.

- For page 138, review children's understanding of *have, use,* and *liked.*

VISUAL LEARNERS

Materials: mural paper, paints, brushes

Have children create a mural of children sledding. Encourage them to include and label items whose names contain the short sound of *e*, such as pets and red hats, in addition to sleds.

KINESTHETIC LEARNERS

Materials: paper and pencil

Have children go on a scavenger hunt to collect words or pictures of words that contain the sound of short *e*. Encourage children to write the words or the names of the pictures that they find on their papers.

Words in Context

▶ **Circle** the word that will finish the sentence. **Print** it on the line.

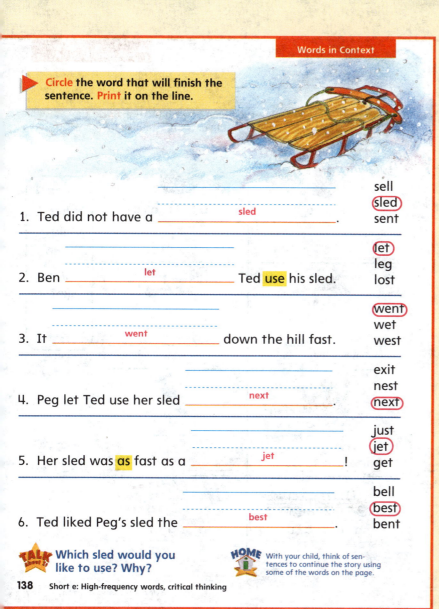

1. Ted did not have a ___sled___.
   - sell
   - (sled)
   - sent

2. Ben ___let___ Ted *use* his sled.
   - (let)
   - leg
   - lost

3. It ___went___ down the hill fast.
   - (went)
   - wet
   - west

4. Peg let Ted use her sled ___next___.
   - exit
   - nest
   - (next)

5. Her sled was *as* fast as a ___jet___!
   - just
   - (jet)
   - get

6. Ted liked Peg's sled the ___best___.
   - bell
   - (best)
   - bent

TALK Which sled would you like to use? Why?

HOME With your child, think of sentences to continue the story using some of the words on the page.

138 Short e: High-frequency words, critical thinking

CURRICULUM CONNECTIONS

SPELLING
For the spelling posttest, dictate a list word and then read it in context in the sentence.
1. **ten**   I have **ten** fingers.
2. **jet**   A **jet** is a very big and fast plane.
3. **bed**   I have a blanket on my **bed**.
4. **bell** I can hear the school **bell** ringing.
5. **nest** There is a bluebird in the **nest**.
6. **web**   I watched the spider spin a **web**.

WRITING
Have the children reread the story about Ted, Ben, and Peg on page 138. Then, suggest that they write an adventure story about Ted, Ben, Peg, and a sled. Encourage them to add titles and illustrate their stories.

SOCIAL STUDIES
Invite children to look through reference books that show and tell about sled dogs. Ask children to share what they find out through pictures, an oral report, or by writing a story.

TECHNOLOGY **AstroWord** Short Vowels: *e, u*

AUDITORY LEARNERS **PARTNERS**
Let partners choose four words from the lesson that contain the short sound of *e* to use in a song or chant they will make up together. Encourage them to perform the song for the class.

CHALLENGE
Materials: a shoe box, magazines, scissors

Have children make a diorama using magazine pictures of things whose names have the short sound of *e*. Ask children to point out all the things in or on the box whose names contain the short sound of e.

EXTRA SUPPORT/INTERVENTION
Materials: Phonics Picture Cards: *bell* (77), *belt* (78), *desk* (79), *hen* (81), *ten* (82), *web* (84); Phonics Word Cards: *bell* (96), *belt* (98), *desk* (100), *hen* (103), *ten* (113), *web* (114)

Display the pictures. Ask children to name them. Hold up the word cards one at a time and have the children read them with you. Ask children to tell you which picture each word names. **See Daily Phonics Practice, page 315.**

Integrating Phonics and Reading

Shared/Guided Reading
Show the cover as you read the title. Ask children to name the best places they can think of and discuss them.

First Reading As you read the word or words that name each best place, have children point to the place in the illustration.

Second Reading Have children identify the short *e* words in the story.

Comprehension
After reading, ask children these questions:
- Why is a mat the best place for the girl's wet boots? *Inference/Details*
- Choose something you see every day. What is the best place for it? *Creative/Relate to Experience*

ESL/ELL English Language Learners
Using common objects, say or write sentences such as: *The best place for a hat is ___*. Ask children to finish the sentences.

Lesson 66
Pages 139–140

Phonics and Reading / Phonics and Spelling

Short Vowels

Skill Focus
Children will
★ spell and write words with short vowels *a, i, u, o, e.*
★ write a postcard using words with short vowels.

Teach

Phonics and Spelling On the chalkboard, write the following headings: *Short a, Short i, Short u, Short o, Short e.* Then, say these words and have a volunteer come up and write each one under the correct heading: *big, pen, tap, mop, mud.* Ask new volunteers to underline the letters that stand for the beginning and ending sounds in each word and to circle the letters that stand for the middle sound. Explain that all these words have a consonant at the beginning, a vowel in the middle, and a consonant at the end.

Next, write the word *lock* on the board. Ask a volunteer to erase the first letter and write a *d*, then name the word. (*dock*) Continue with *r* (*rock*) and *s* (*sock*). Underline the *ck* in *sock* and explain that *c* and *k* together can spell the /k/ sound.

Sound to Symbol One at a time, hold up picture cards for bag (47), cup (63), pig (59), sock (175), bus (62), and lid (57). Ask volunteers to name the picture and write the picture name on the board. Then, ask new volunteers to circle the letter that stands for the short vowel sound in each word.

Practice and Apply

Phonics and Spelling Help children identify the pictures and vowel letters on page 139. Point out that the word list will help them complete each item. Have them read the list words aloud to hear the vowel sounds before they write the words on the page.

Phonics and Writing Before children write a postcard message on page 140, encourage them to recall a recent class trip or family trip. Remind them to start with a greeting and to leave room for their signature. As children prepare to write their own messages, remind them to use some of the words in the box.

Reading Use *When We Are Big*, MCP Phonics and Reading Short Vowel Skills Library, Level A, to review short vowel phonograms.

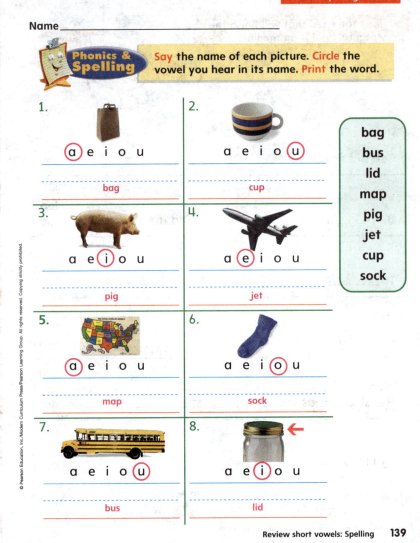

FOCUS ON ALL LEARNERS

ESL/ELL ENGLISH LANGUAGE LEARNERS
- Before children begin page 139, copy the word list onto the chalkboard. Help children read the words aloud.
- For page 140, explain that a postcard is a short letter. Have children work in pairs to write three sentences about a real or imaginary trip. Remind them to use some of the boxed words in their sentences.

VISUAL/AUDITORY LEARNERS
Materials: index cards or slips of paper, marker
Have children write the spelling words from page 139 on cards or slips of paper. Then, have them sort the words into piles according to the short vowel sound.

KINESTHETIC LEARNERS
Have children take turns finger-writing a spelling word from page 139 on the palm of a partner's hand. Once the spelling word is identified, have the partners switch roles. Continue until all the words have been reviewed.

Phonics & Writing

Writing

Write a postcard to tell a friend about a trip. Some of the words in the box may help you.

| cat | map | bed | top | bus |
| dog | six | jet | did | sun |

TO:
My Friend
1 Happy Lane
Yourtown,
USA
12345

HOME Ask your child to use as many of the words in the box as possible in a sentence.

140 Review short vowels: Writing

CURRICULUM CONNECTIONS

SPELLING

Cumulative Posttest Review Unit 2 spelling words by using the following words and dictation sentences.

1. **bag** We put groceries in the **bag**.
2. **can** Mom opened the **can** of soup.
3. **sing** Let's **sing** a song together.
4. **six** **Six** ducks are at the pond.
5. **bus** That **bus** is late.
6. **sun** Clouds covered the **sun**.
7. **dog** Give that **dog** a bone.
8. **pot** The **pot** is on the stove.
9. **bed** My shoes are under my **bed**.
10. **ten** I can count to **ten**.

WRITING

Divide the class into five groups and give each group a list of spelling words for one short vowel. Ask each group to use the words on their list to write sentences about things that might happen at a very unusual zoo.

TECHNOLOGY **AstroWord** Short Vowels: *a, i;* Short Vowels: *i, o;* Short Vowels: *e, u*

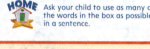

AUDITORY/VISUAL LEARNERS

Materials: list of unit spelling words

Have children take turns giving clues about a spelling word. Once the word is successfully guessed, have each child in the group write the word. Then, have the child giving the clue spell the word aloud so that others can check their spelling.

CHALLENGE

Materials: letter cards *Aa, Bb, Cc, Ff, Gg, Ii, Oo, Pp, Uu, Tt*

Have children use the letter cards to form as many spelling words as they can. Ask them to list the words they make.

EXTRA SUPPORT/INTERVENTION

Materials: Phonics Picture Cards: *bag* (47), *cup* (63), *pig* (59), *bus* (62), *lid* (57); Phonics Word Cards: *bag* (8), *cup* (67), *pig* (52), *bus* (63), *lid* (46)

Display the word cards on the chalkboard ledge. As you hold up each picture card in random order, have children come to the board, touch the word that names the picture, and write the word on the board.

See Daily Phonics Practice, pages 312–315.

Integrating Phonics and Reading

Guided Reading
Show the cover and read the title. Ask children what the boy and girl are thinking of becoming when they are big.

First Reading Have children use the illustrations in the thought bubbles to describe what the people in each one are doing.

Second Reading Have children find words with the phonograms *-ad, -ig, -un, -op, -et*.

Comprehension
After reading, ask children the following questions:
- Which job in the story do you think is the most interesting? Why? *Reflective Analysis/Comparison*
- What would you like to do when you are big? *Creative/Personal Experience*

ESL/ELL English Language Learners
Practice the expression *What about you?* by modeling examples such as *I have a red pen. What about you?* Have children answer each time.

140

Lesson 67   Pages 141–142

Take-Home Book

Review Short Vowels

> **Skill Focus**
>
> Children will
> * read short vowel words in the context of a story.
> * review selected high-frequency words in the context of a story.
> * reread for fluency.

Teach

Build Background Recall with children that the theme of this unit is "Amazing Animals." Explain that they are going to read about some amazing animals that live in the water. Invite them to guess what these animals might be. When someone guesses fish, invite children to tell what they think fish eat. List their ideas on the board. Then explain that they will learn more as they read.

Phonemic Awareness: Medial Sound Isolation Draw a picture of a cat on the board and say *cat*, then /a/. Tell children that you are saying a word and then its middle vowel sound. Help children identify the medial sound as short *a*. Model the procedure again, saying *fish*, then /i/. Help children identify the middle vowel sound as short *i*. Repeat using *pup*, *hog*, and *hen*.

Practice and Apply

Read the Book Help children tear out and fold the pages to make their Take-Home Books. Then, read the book together. Encourage children to tell what they learned about fish.

Sound to Symbol Read aloud or have volunteers read the book. Then, write these headings on the board: *Short a, Short i, Short u, Short o, Short e*. Ask children what words have the short *a* sound (*can, small*). Repeat for short *i* (*fish, this*); short *u* (*bugs, must*); short *o* (*lots, spot*); and short *e* (*best, get*). Ask volunteers to write the words under the correct headings.

Review High-Frequency Words Write the words *do, like, for, you,* and *here* on the board. Have children spell the words, then say them.

Reread for Fluency Have children reread the book to increase their fluency and comprehension. Children can take their books home to read and share with family members.

Review short vowels a, i, u, o, e: Take-home book   141

FOCUS ON ALL LEARNERS

ESL/ELL ENGLISH LANGUAGE LEARNERS

Use the following activities to teach English language learners.

* Ask children to look at the photographs and talk about what they see in each one. Practice reading each page.
* Check children's understanding of these words and phrases: *eat, hide, get away*. Have them act out each one.

VISUAL/LEARNERS

Materials: letter cards *Aa, Bb, Cc, Hh, Ii, Nn, Pp, Oo, Tt*
Have children use the letter cards to form the word *cat* and then change one card at a time. For example: Change *c* to *b*. (*bat*) Change *b* to *h*. (*hat*) Change *a* to *o*. (*hot*) Change *h* to *p*. (*pot*) Change *o* to *a*. (*pat*) Change *t* to *n*. (*pan*) Change *a* to *i*. (*pin*)

AUDITORY/VISUAL LEARNERS

Write a short vowel phonogram, such as *-et*, at the top of a sheet of paper for each group. Have group members pass the sheet around, each adding a word that contains the phonogram. Ask one member of the group to read the list. Continue with other phonograms, such as *-ot, -op, -at,* and *-ub*.

2. This fish likes to eat lots of bugs.

- - - - FOLD - - - -

3. This fish can fish for small fish.

142 Review short vowels a, i, u, o, e: Take-home book

AUDITORY/KINESTHETIC LEARNERS

Have children stand. Say a target word, such as *map*, and then a group of short vowel words, such as *help, hill, fast, spot, drum*. Tell children to take a step forward if a word has the same vowel sound as *map*. Repeat, using a target word for each of the other short vowels and a new group of words each time.

CHALLENGE

Materials: books about tropical fish

Have children look at books about fish to choose another fish that they think is interesting. Have them write one or more sentences telling what the fish they chose can do.

EXTRA SUPPORT/INTERVENTION

Materials: Take-Home Books

Have children discuss the fish and what is happening on each page of the Take-Home Book before they read it independently. **See Daily Phonics Practice, pages 312–315.**

CURRICULUM CONNECTIONS

SCIENCE

Materials: picture books about coral reefs, mural paper, construction paper, crayons or paints

Make available books about life in a coral reef. Help children identify the coral, sea fans, and various kinds of fish that live together in a reef area. Suggest that children make a mural of a coral reef. Have some children draw the coral, sand, and ocean bottom on the mural. Other children can draw and cut out fish from construction paper to attach to the reef.

MATH

Materials: drawing paper, crayons

Have children make a fish counting book. Assign each child a numeral from 1 to 10. Ask each child to illustrate the numeral by drawing the number of fish and decorating them. Also have them write the numeral. Gather the pages and make several counting books, putting one page for each numeral in a book.

WRITING

Materials: drawing paper, crayons

Have children draw an imaginary fish. Ask them to write about what this fish likes to eat.

 **AstroWord** Short Vowels: *a, i;*
Short Vowels: *i, o;*
Short Vowels: *e, u*

142

Lesson 68 Pages 143–144

Unit Checkup

Short Vowels, High-Frequency Words

Skill Focus

Children will
- identify and write picture names and words that contain short vowel sounds.
- read words that contain short vowel sounds.
- read high-frequency words.

Teach

Phonemic Awareness: Phoneme Categorization Say *six, peg, milk*. Have children repeat the words. Ask which two words have the same vowel sound. Then, ask children to identify the vowel sound. Continue with other groups of words, such as *web, ten, trip; pump, bus, jam; pink, clap, spin; fan, just, tag; doll, fox, fix*.

Sound to Symbol Display the following picture cards: hand (51), bib (54), cup (63), dog (71), belt (78). Ask which picture name has the sound of short *u*. Have a volunteer point to the picture, say the word, and write it on the board. Repeat for the other short vowels.

Practice and Apply

Assess Skills Help children identify the pictures on page 143. Have a volunteer read the directions aloud. Suggest that children say each word softly to themselves by stretching out the beginning, middle, and ending sounds.

For page 144, have children tell what they see in each picture. Then, have them read the directions at the top of the page and describe in their own words what they are to do. Suggest that they read each sentence carefully before choosing the answer.

Assess High-Frequency Words Read aloud the directions above the list of high-frequency words. Stress that children should put a check mark in a box only if they can read the word. If they cannot read the word, they should leave the box empty. You may wish to have children work in pairs to complete the exercise, or have individual children read the words aloud to you. The words are also assessed orally on the pretest and posttest for Unit 2, pages 65e–65h.

143

UNIT 2 CHECKUP

Name _____

▶ Say the name of each picture.
Print the picture name on the line.

1. bed	2. bun	3. log
4. pig	5. top	6. tag
7. ten	8. sun	9. gift
10. lamp	11. duck	12. nest

Short vowels: Assessment   143

FOCUS ON ALL LEARNERS

ESL/ELL ENGLISH LANGUAGE LEARNERS

- Practice picture-text matching to prepare children to complete page 143. Display the picture card for cat (49). Print *cat* and *cot* on the board. Ask a volunteer to select the correct word. Continue with pig (59), peg; dog (71), dig; and bug (61), bag.

- For page 144, read the directions with children. Work together to complete item 1. Then, have children complete the other items individually.

VISUAL LEARNERS

Materials: Phonics Picture Cards: bag (47), cat (49), king (56), pig (59), sun (67), dog (71), bed (76)

Place the picture cards face down. Have children take turns drawing a card and giving clues about the letters and sounds in the picture names until someone guesses what the picture is. Have volunteers write the word on the board and have the group read the word.

KINESTHETIC LEARNERS

Materials: Phonics Picture Cards 45–84 for short vowels

Give each child a picture card. Have children come up one at a time, tell what their picture names, and name its vowel sound.

UNIT 2 CHECKUP

▶ **Fill in** the bubble beside the sentence that tells about the picture.

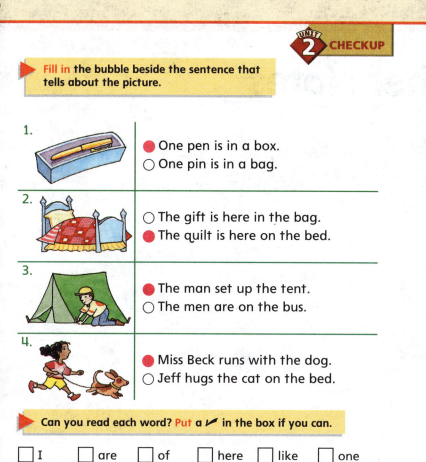

1. ● One pen is in a box.
   ○ One pin is in a bag.

2. ○ The gift is here in the bag.
   ● The quilt is here on the bed.

3. ● The man set up the tent.
   ○ The men are on the bus.

4. ● Miss Beck runs with the dog.
   ○ Jeff hugs the cat on the bed.

▶ Can you read each word? Put a in the box if you can.

☐ I ☐ are ☐ of ☐ here ☐ like ☐ one
☐ for ☐ my ☐ her ☐ with ☐ down ☐ come
☐ the ☐ you ☐ our ☐ said ☐ have ☐ do

Short vowels and high-frequency words: Assessment

ASSESS UNDERSTANDING OF UNIT SKILLS

STUDENT PROGRESS ASSESSMENT
You may wish to review the observational notes you made as children worked through the activities in the unit. Your notes will help you evaluate the progress children made with short vowels.

PORTFOLIO ASSESSMENT
Review the materials children have collected in their portfolios. You may wish to have interviews with children to discuss their written work and the progress they have made since the beginning of the unit. As you review children's work, evaluate how well they apply phonics skills.

DAILY PHONICS PRACTICE
For children who need additional practice with short vowels, quick reviews are provided on **pages 312–315 in Daily Phonics Practice.**

PHONICS POSTTEST
To assess children's mastery of short vowels and high-frequency words, use the posttest on pages 65g–65h.

AUDITORY LEARNERS PARTNERS
Materials: Phonics Word Cards, Set 1, *pan-sat* (27), *lift-milk* (48), *pup-puff* (76), *lock-mop* (90), *bed-bell* (96)

Pass out the cards to pairs of children. The first child reads one word and acts it out for the partner to guess. Then, the partner acts out the other word for the first child to guess. After both words have been guessed, encourage the children to name the short vowel sound heard in both words.

CHALLENGE
Challenge children to write a story that contains five names with short vowel sounds. Have them circle the names and any other short vowel sounds.

EXTRA SUPPORT/INTERVENTION
Materials: Phonics Picture Cards: bag (47), pig (59), jug (64), top (75), belt (78); Phonics Word Cards: *wag* (33), *wig* (58), *bug* (61), *cop* (85), *felt* (102)

Show children a picture and have them name it. Tell children you will read each word card and they will tell you which word rhymes with the picture name. Repeat until all the picture cards have been displayed.
See Daily Phonics Practice, page 312–315.

Teacher Notes

UNIT 3

Long Vowels
THEME: LET'S PLAY

CONTENTS

UNIT 3 RESOURCES 145b
- Assessment Options 145c
- Administering & Evaluating the Pretest/Posttest 145d
  - Unit 3 Pretest 145e–145f
  - Unit 3 Posttest 145g–145h
  - Unit 3 Student Progress Checklist 145i
- English Language Learners 145j
- Spelling Connections 145k–145l
- Phonics Games, Activities, and Technology 145m–145o
- BLM Unit 3 Activity 145p
- Home Connections 145q

TEACHING PLANS

	Unit 3 Opener/Home Letter	145–146
Lessons 69–74:	Long vowel *a*	147–158
Lesson 75:	Review long vowel *a*: Phonics & Reading ..	159
	Phonics & Writing: Building Words	160
Lesson 76:	Take-Home Book: "Make a Face"	161–162
Lesson 77:	High-frequency words	163–164
Lessons 78–82:	Long vowel *i*	165–174
Lesson 83:	Review long vowel *i*: Phonics & Reading ...	175
	Phonics & Writing: Building Words	176
Lesson 84:	Take-Home Book: "Di Tries"	177–178
Lesson 85:	High-frequency words	179–180
Lessons 86–90:	Long vowel *u*	181–190
Lesson 91:	Long and short vowels *a, i, u*	191
	Review long vowels *a, i, u*	192
Lesson 92:	Review long vowel *u*: Phonics & Reading ..	193
	Phonics & Writing: Building Words	194
Lesson 93:	Take-Home Book: "Hand Games"	195–196
Lessons 94–99:	Long vowel *o*	197–209
Lesson 100:	Long vowel *o*	209
	Review long vowels *a, i, u, o*	210
Lesson 101:	Review long vowel *o*: Phonics & Reading ..	211
	Phonics & Writing: Building Words	212
Lesson 102:	Take-Home Book: "Games Around the Globe"	213–214
Lesson 103:	High-frequency words	215–216
Lessons 104–108:	Long vowel *e*	217–226
Lesson 109:	Long vowel *e*	227
	Review long vowels *a, i, u, o, e*	228
Lesson 110:	Review long and short vowels *a, i, u, o, e*	229–230
Lesson 111:	Review long vowels	231
	Review long and short vowels	232
Lesson 112:	Review long vowels: Phonics & Spelling ...	233
	Phonics & Writing: A Friendly Letter	234
Lesson 113:	Take-Home Book: "No Sleep"	235–236
Lesson 114:	Unit Checkup: Long vowels/High-frequency words ...	237–238

Student Performance Objectives

In Unit 3, children will be introduced to the sound associations for the long vowels within the context of the theme "Let's Play." As children begin to understand and learn to apply the concept that vowels can represent a long sound, they will be able to

▶ Associate the vowels, *a, e, i, o,* and *u* with the long sounds they stand for

▶ Identify words in which the vowels *a, e, i, o,* and *u* stand for their long sounds

▶ Distinguish among the long and short vowel sounds of *a, e, i, o,* and *u*

▶ Learn and read high-frequency words in context

145a

Overview of Resources

LESSON	MCP PHONICS AND READING LIBRARY, LEVEL A			LETTER CARDS/ WORD CARDS	DAILY PHONICS PRACTICE
	TITLE	PRACTICE	PICTURE CARDS		
69: Long vowel *a*	RR, Stg Three Bk 14	*Pancakes!*	45–46, 48, 52, 76–77, 81, 85–92		316
70: Long vowel *a*	RR, Stg Three Bk 1	*That Cat!*	48–50, 57–59, 61, 63, 70–72, 81–83, 85–92		316
71: Long and short vowel *a*	RR, Stg Three Bk 33	*Making a Plate*	45–53, 85–90, 92		316
72: Long vowel *a*	RR, Stg Three Bk 15	*My Shadow*	45–53, 85–88	5, 8, 10–11, 16, 25, 33, 119, 122–124, 127–128, 130, 135, 140	316
73: Long vowel *a*	RR, Stg Three Bk 3	*The Best Birthday Mole Ever Had*			316
74: Long vowel *a*	RR, Stg Two, Bk 43	*The Name Is the Same*		119–120, 124–125, 127, 130, 132, 134, 136, 138	316
75: Review long vowel *a*	RR, Stg Three Bk 2	*Save That Trash!*			316
76: Take-Home Book: "Make a Face"			45–46, 52, 89, 90, 91	Aa, Ee, Ii/132, 133, 251	316
77: High-frequency words	RR, Stg One Bk 17	*Where Do They Live?*		Complete Set/*out, they, two, were, where, your*	
78: Long vowel *i*	RR, Stg Three Bk 6	*Jim's Visit to Kim*			317
79: Long vowel *i*	RR, Stg Three Bk 17	*Six Fine Fish*		Ii, Ee, Pp, Ff, Vv, Dd, Mm	317
80: Long and short vowel *i*	RR, Stg Three Bk 4	*Dinner by Five*	54–60, 93–102		317
81: Long vowel *i*	RR, Stg Three Bk 5	*The Bike That Spike Likes*			317
82: Long vowel *i*	RR, Stg Two Bk 44	*Dive In!*		143–144, 146–150, 152, 154–157	317
83: Review long vowel *i*	RR, Stg Three Bk 34	*Flip's Trick*	93, 96, 98–99		317
84: Take-Home Book: "Di Tries"				136–142, 151–157	316–317
85: High-frequency words	RR, Stg Three Bk 16	*Three Little Kittens*		Complete Set/*about, could, little, long, there, why*	
86: Long vowel *u*	RR, Stg Two Bk 47	*True or False?*	85–88, 93–96, 103–107		318
87: Long vowel *u*	RR, Stg Three Bk 12	*Blue Sue*			318
88: Long and short vowel *u*	RR, Stg Three Bk 13	*A Hunt for Clues*	61–65, 67–68, 103–107	Aa, Ii, Uu	318
89: Long vowel *u*	RR, Stg Three Bk 23	*Mrs. Tuck's Little Tune*		Tt, Uu, Bb, Ee/61–62, 65, 67–68, 71–74, 77–80, 158–164	318
90: Long vowel *u*	RR, Stg Three Bk 25	*Who's in the Jungle?*	103	Aa, Ii, Uu/62, 74, 76, 81–82, 158–162, 164	318
91: Long vowel *u*; Reviewing Long vowels *a, i, u*	RR, Stg Three Bk 29	*Blast Off!*	103, 105	Uu, Ee, Bb, Cc, Ll, Mm, Nn, Rr, Tt	318
92: Review long vowel *u*	RR, Stg Three Bk 24	*The Cat That Broke the Rules*	91, 96, 103–106		318
93: Take-Home Book: "Hand Games"				Complete Set	316–318
94: Long vowel *o*	RR, Stg Three Bk 7	*Sparky's Bone*	91, 93–95, 103, 108–115		318–319
95: Long vowel *o*	RR, Stg Three Bk 18	*Lottie Goat and Donnie Goat*	93–95, 103–106, 108–115		318–319
96: Long vowel *o*	RR, Stg Three Bk 8	*When I Go See Gram*	85–92, 103–115	165–168, 174, 176	318–319
97: Long and short vowel *o*	RR, Stg Three Bk 9	*A Stew for Egor's Mom*	70–75, 108–115		318–319
98: Long vowel *o*	RR, Stg Two Bk 45	*When Bob Woke Up Late*	85–115	165–172, 174–179	318–319
99: Long vowel *o*	RR, Stg Three Bk 35	*The Hiccups Would Not Stop*			318–319
100: Long vowel *o*; review long vowels *a, i, u, o*	RR, Stg Three Bk 19	*Grandpa, Grandma, and the Tractor*		Bb, Oo, Nn, Ee, Ww, Rr, Pp, Ss, Aa, Pp, Tt	318–319
101: Review long vowel *o*	RR, Stg Three Bk 32	*The Tale of Cowboy Roy*			318–319
102: Take-Home Book: "Games Around the Globe"				133, 135, 144, 146, 149, 158, 161, 165, 168, 172	316–319
103: High-frequency words	RR, Stg Three Bk 21	*Steve's Room*		Complete Set/*because, from, their, them, want, which*	
104: Long vowel *e*	RR, Stg Three Bk 11	*Dee and Me*	86–87, 93–94, 104, 106, 110–111, 116–120	Ee	319–320
105: Long vowel *e*	RR, Stg Three Bk 22	*Where Is the Queen?*	91, 99, 103, 107 110–111, 116–120		319–320
106: Long and short vowel *e*	RR, Stg Three Bk 20	*Eve Shops*	76–77, 80, 83, 116–119		319–320
107: Long vowel *e*	RR, Stg 2, Bk 46	*Eyes Are Everywhere*	76–77, 79–80, 85, 106, 110, 116–119		319–320
108: Long vowel *e*	RR, Stg Three Bk 21	*Steve's Room*			319–320
109: Long vowel *e*; Review long vowels *a, i, u, o, e*	RR, Stg Three Bk 38	*Ice Fishing*	86, 91, 93, 98, 103, 106, 108, 111, 116, 117	Aa, Ee, Ii, Oo, Uu	316–320
110: Review long and short vowels *a, i, u, o, e*	RR, Stg Two Bk 50	*Cat's Trip*	87, 91–92, 95, 98, 103, 105–106, 108, 110, 115, 117, 119–120	Aa, Ee, Ii, Oo, Uu	316–320
111: Review long and short vowels	RR, Stg Three Bk 27	*Summer at Cove Lake*		Aa, Bb, Cc, Ee, Ii, Kk, Oo, Pp, Rr, Tt, Uu	316–320
112: Review long vowels	RR, Stg Four Bk 20	*Never Say Never*		Aa, Ee, Ii, Oo, Uu	316–320
113: Take-Home Book: "No Sleep"			85–86, 90, 93, 98, 101, 103, 105–106, 108–109, 115, 117, 119, 120	Aa, Ee, Ii, Oo, Uu	316–320
114: Unit Checkup				Aa, Ee, Ii, Oo, Uu/ 126, 152, 158, 165, 185	316–320

RR–Ready Readers   Stg–Stage   Bk–Book

Assessment Options

In Unit 3, assess children's ability to identify and write words with long vowel sounds. Use the Unit Pretest and Posttest for formal assessment. For ongoing informal assessment, you may wish to use children's work on the Review pages, Take-Home Books, and Unit Checkups. You may also want to encourage children to evaluate their own work and to participate in setting goals for their own learning.

ESL/ELL Vowel sounds may be especially problematic for English language learners. Note pronunciation difficulties, but assess based on children's ability to distinguish vowel sounds when pronounced by a native speaker. For additional support for English language learners, see page 145j.

FORMAL ASSESSMENT

Use the Unit 3 Pretest, on pages 145e–145f, to help assess a child's knowledge at the beginning of the unit and to plan instruction.

ESL/ELL Before administering the Pretest, preview the visuals on pages 145e–145f so children are familiar with the picture names.

Use the Unit 3 Posttest, on pages 145g–145h, to help assess mastery of unit objectives and to plan for reteaching, if necessary.

ESL/ELL Some children may understand a concept but have difficulty reading the written directions. Read the directions aloud to the group and model how the Posttest is to be completed.

INFORMAL ASSESSMENT

Use the Review pages, Unit Checkup, and Take-Home Books in the student book to provide an effective means of evaluating children's performance.

Unit 3 Skills	Review pages	Checkups	Take-Home Books
Long vowel *a*	159–160	237–238	161–162
Long vowel *i*	175–176	237–238	177–178
Long vowel *u*	193–194	237–238	195–196
Long vowel *o*	211–212	237–238	213–214
Long vowel *e*	217–218	237–238	235–236
Long and short vowels	227–234	237–238	235–236

STUDENT PROGRESS CHECKLIST

Use the checklist on page 145i to record children's progress. You may want to cut the sections apart to place each child's checklist in his or her portfolio.

PORTFOLIO ASSESSMENT

This logo signals opportunities for collecting student work for individual portfolios. You may also want to include the Pretest and Posttest, the Review pages, the Unit Checkup, Phonics & Reading, and Phonics & Writing pages.

PHONEMIC AWARENESS AND PHONICS ASSESSMENT

Use PAPA to obtain an itemized analysis of children's decoding skills.

PAPA Skills	MCP Phonics Lessons in Unit 3
Deleting sounds	Lessons 73, 75, 81, 83, 90, 92, 99, 101, 108, 111
Long vowels	Lessons 69–76, 78–84, 86–102, 104–114

145c

Pretest and Posttest

DIRECTIONS

To help you assess children's progress in learning Unit 3 skills, tests are available on pages 145e–145h. Administer the Pretest before children begin the unit. The results of the Pretest will help you identify each child's strengths and needs in advance, allowing you to structure lesson plans to meet individual needs. Administer the Posttest to assess children's overall mastery of skills taught in the unit and to identify specific areas that will require reteaching.

ESL/ELL Note that the objective of both the Unit 3 Pretest and Posttest is to read and write words with long vowel sounds. English language learners may find that some sounds in their native languages (especially Vietnamese, Khmer, Hmong, and Spanish) are different than certain long vowel sounds in English. Have children practice saying the picture clues aloud; reinforce with frequent reading and spelling opportunities throughout the unit.

To assess the high-frequency words for Unit 3, have a child read orally each word on the Pretest and Posttest as you point to it. Then, have the child check each word read.

PERFORMANCE ASSESSMENT PROFILE

The following chart will help you identify specific skills as they appear on the tests and enable you to identify and record specific information about an individual's or the class's performance on the tests.

Depending on the results of the tests, refer to the Reteaching column for lesson-plan pages where you can find activities that will be useful for meeting individual needs or for daily phonics practice.

Answer Keys

Unit 3 Pretest, page 145e (BLM 14)
1. (bee) tree, meat
2. (kite) time, pie
3. (cage) gate, rain
4. (boat) snow, road
5. (tube) tune, rule
6. (five) pine, fine
7. (rake) rain, stay
8. (hose) boat, hope

Unit 3 Pretest, page 145f (BLM 15)
9. cube
10. seal
11. goat
12. can
13. tail
14. rain
15. dime
16. pin
17. ten

Unit 3 Posttest, page 145g (BLM 16)
1. long (cake)
2. short (cat)
3. short (bus)
4. long (mule)
5. long (rope)
6. short (rock)
7. long (nail)
8. long (goat)
9. long (leaf)
10. long (kite)
11. short (nest)
12. long (tree)

Unit 3 Posttest, page 145h (BLM 17)
13. seals
14. train
15. ride
16. tune
17. home
18. late

Performance Assessment Profile

Skill	Pretest Questions	Posttest Questions	Reteaching — Focus on All Learners	Daily Phonics Practice
Long *a*	3, 7	14, 18	147–162, 177–178, 192, 195–196, 210, 213–214, 228–236	316
Long and short *a*	12, 13, 14	1, 2, 7	151–152, 229–230, 232	316
Long *i*	2, 6	15	165–178, 192, 195–196, 210, 213–214, 228–236	317
Long and short *i*	15, 16	10	169–170, 229–230, 232	317
Long *u*	5	16	181–196, 210, 213–214, 228–236	318
Long and short *u*	9	3, 4	185, 191, 229–230, 232	318
Long *o*	4, 8	17	197–214, 228–236	318–319
Long and short *o*	11	5, 6, 8	203–204, 229–230, 232	318–319
Long *e*	1	13	217–236	319–320
Long and short *e*	10, 17	9, 11, 12	221, 223, 229–230, 232	319–320

Unit 3 Pretest

Name _____

> Say the name of each picture. Fill in the bubble under each word that has the same vowel sound as the picture name.

#	Picture				
1.	 (bee)	tree ○	net ○	meat ○	tent ○
2.	 (kite)	pin ○	time ○	pie ○	fist ○
3.	 (cage)	gate ○	rain ○	map ○	ran ○
4.	 (boat)	snow ○	pot ○	stop ○	road ○
5.	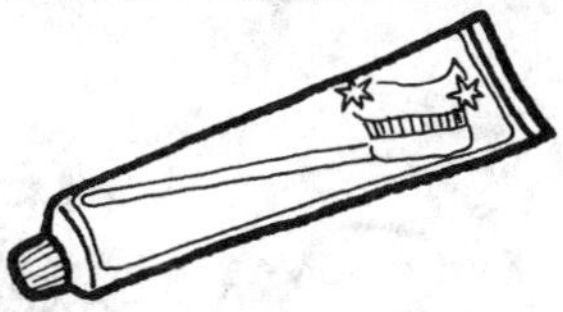 (tube)	tub ○	tune ○	fun ○	rule ○
6.	 (5)	pine ○	fine ○	lid ○	stick ○
7.	 (rake)	rain ○	sad ○	stay ○	last ○
8.	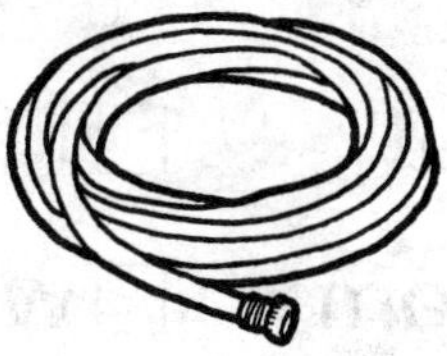 (hose)	hot ○	boat ○	hope ○	hop ○

Go to the next page. →

BLM 14 Unit 3 Pretest: Long and short vowel sounds, high-frequency words

Unit 3 Pretest

Name _____

> Say the name of each picture. Fill in the bubble beside the picture name.

9.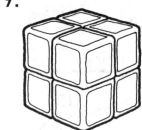
○ cub
○ cube

10.
○ sell
○ seal

11.
○ got
○ goat

12.
○ can
○ cane

13.
○ tall
○ tail

14.
○ ran
○ rain

15.
○ dim
○ dime

16.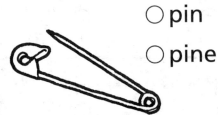
○ pin
○ pine

17.
○ ten
○ teen

> Check ✓ each word you can read.

☐ long   ☐ their   ☐ where   ☐ want   ☐ out   ☐ little
☐ your   ☐ could   ☐ about   ☐ two   ☐ from   ☐ why
☐ they   ☐ which   ☐ them   ☐ were   ☐ there ☐ because

Possible score on Unit 3 Pretest is 17. Number correct _____

BLM 15 Unit 3 Pretest: Long and short vowel sounds, high-frequency words

Unit 3 Posttest

Name _____

> Say the name of each picture. If the vowel sound is short, color the bubble below the word **short**. If the vowel sound is long, color the bubble below the word **long**.

1.	2.	3.	4.
short long ○ ○	short long ○ ○	short long ○ ○	short long ○ ○
5.	6.	7.	8.
short long ○ ○	short long ○ ○	short long ○ ○	short long ○ ○
9.	10.	11.	12.
short long ○ ○	short long ○ ○	short long ○ ○	short long ○ ○

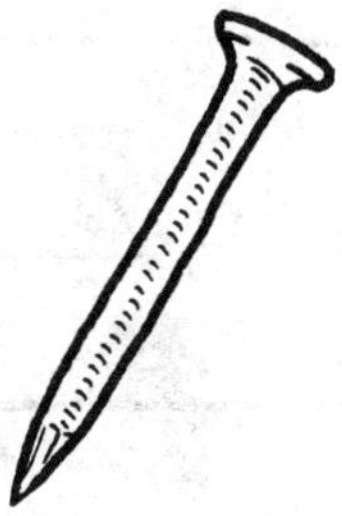

Go to the next page. →

BLM 16 Unit 3 Posttest: Long and short vowel sounds, high-frequency words

Unit 3 Posttest

Name _____

▶ Read each sentence. Fill in the bubble under the word that will finish the sentence.

13. Ben likes to see the _____ at the zoo.	seals ○	sells ○
14. Then Ben hops on the _____.	trick ○	train ○
15. He will _____ to the chimp show.	ride ○	rid ○
16. One chimp plays a _____ with bells.	tube ○	tune ○
17. After the show, Ben must go _____.	home ○	hop ○
18. He must not be _____ for dinner.	lake ○	late ○

▶ Check ✓ each word you can read.

☐ long   ☐ their   ☐ where   ☐ want   ☐ out   ☐ little
☐ your   ☐ could   ☐ about   ☐ two   ☐ from ☐ why
☐ they   ☐ which   ☐ them   ☐ were   ☐ there ☐ because

Possible score on Unit 3 Posttest is 18. Number correct _____

BLM 17 Unit 3 Posttest: Long and short vowel sounds, high-frequency words

Student Progress Checklist

Make as many copies as needed to use for a class list. For individual portfolio use, cut apart each child's section. As indicated by the code, color in boxes next to skills satisfactorily assessed and insert an *X* by those requiring reteaching. Marked boxes can later be colored in to indicate mastery.

Student Progress Checklist

Code: ■ Satisfactory ☒ Needs Reteaching

Student: _____	Skills	High-Frequency Words	Comments / Learning Goals
Pretest Score: _____ Posttest Score: _____	☐ Long *a* ☐ Long *i* ☐ Long *u* ☐ Long *o* ☐ Long *e*	☐ long ☐ their ☐ where ☐ want ☐ out ☐ little ☐ your ☐ could ☐ about ☐ two ☐ from ☐ why ☐ they ☐ which ☐ them ☐ were ☐ there ☐ because	
Student: _____ Pretest Score: _____ Posttest Score: _____	Skills ☐ Long *a* ☐ Long *i* ☐ Long *u* ☐ Long *o* ☐ Long *e*	High-Frequency Words ☐ long ☐ their ☐ where ☐ want ☐ out ☐ little ☐ your ☐ could ☐ about ☐ two ☐ from ☐ why ☐ they ☐ which ☐ them ☐ were ☐ there ☐ because	Comments / Learning Goals
Student: _____ Pretest Score: _____ Posttest Score: _____	Skills ☐ Long *a* ☐ Long *i* ☐ Long *u* ☐ Long *o* ☐ Long *e*	High-Frequency Words ☐ long ☐ their ☐ where ☐ want ☐ out ☐ little ☐ your ☐ could ☐ about ☐ two ☐ from ☐ why ☐ they ☐ which ☐ them ☐ were ☐ there ☐ because	Comments / Learning Goals
Student: _____ Pretest Score: _____ Posttest Score: _____	Skills ☐ Long *a* ☐ Long *i* ☐ Long *u* ☐ Long *o* ☐ Long *e*	High-Frequency Words ☐ long ☐ their ☐ where ☐ want ☐ out ☐ little ☐ your ☐ could ☐ about ☐ two ☐ from ☐ why ☐ they ☐ which ☐ them ☐ were ☐ there ☐ because	Comments / Learning Goals

BLM 18 Unit 3 Checklist

ESL/ELL English Language Learners

Throughout Unit 3 you have opportunities to assess English language learners' ability to read and write words with long vowel sounds. Vowel sounds may be especially problematic for English language learners. In many languages each letter or symbol stands for only one sound; thus, children may need support with pronouncing and spelling long versus short vowel sounds. English language learners will need lots of opportunities to listen to long vowel sounds before being expected to produce them without error. Note pronunciation difficulties, but assess children based on their ability to distinguish long vowel sounds when pronounced by a native speaker.

Lesson 69, pages 147–148 In many languages each letter or symbol stands for only one sound; thus, English language learners may need help in pronouncing and spelling long *a* versus short *a*. Native speakers of Spanish may write *e* instead of long *a* in words.

Lesson 78, pages 165–166 Native speakers of Spanish may spell long *i* as *ai*. Practice with pairs of words like *rain, ride; tail, tire; fair, fire;* and so on.

Lesson 83, pages 175–176 In many languages such as Spanish and Khmer, each letter or symbol stands for one sound. English language learners may need support with pronouncing and spelling long versus short vowel sounds.

Lesson 86, pages 181–182 English language learners who speak Cantonese or Vietnamese may pronounce a "round," French-sounding *u*. Spanish speakers may have trouble with the /yo͞o/ sound of long *u* as in *cube* and *use* (pronouncing *coob, ooze*). Offer additional oral practice.

Lesson 94, pages 197–198 Emphasize the difference between pronouncing and spelling long *o* versus short *o*. Have English language learners say and write *cot, coat; hop, hope; not, note.*

Lesson 95, pages 199–200 English language learners who speak Asian languages may confuse and assimilate long *o* with the sound of *aw* in *awful*. Practice *low, law; so, saw.*

Lesson 104, pages 217–218 English language learners who speak Asian languages or Spanish may confuse long *e* and short *i*. Practice saying *feet, fit; Pete, pit; heal, hill.*

Spelling Connections

INTRODUCTION

The Unit Word List is a comprehensive list of spelling words drawn from this unit. The words are grouped by long vowel patterns. To incorporate spelling into your phonics program, use the activity in the Curriculum Connections section of each teaching plan.

ESL/ELL It is recommended that English language learners reach the intermediate fluency level of English proficiency before focusing on spelling. For English language learners introduce 8 to 10 words at a time and their meanings through visuals or realia.

Spelling

Name ____________

Phonics & Spelling

Say and spell each long vowel word. Print each word on a line in the box that shows its long vowel sound.

fruit rain pie bean bike
bone hay soap seal glue

Long a	hay	rain
Long i	bike	pie
Long u	fruit	glue
Long o	bone	soap
Long e	seal	bean

Review long vowels a, i, u, o, e: Spelling 233

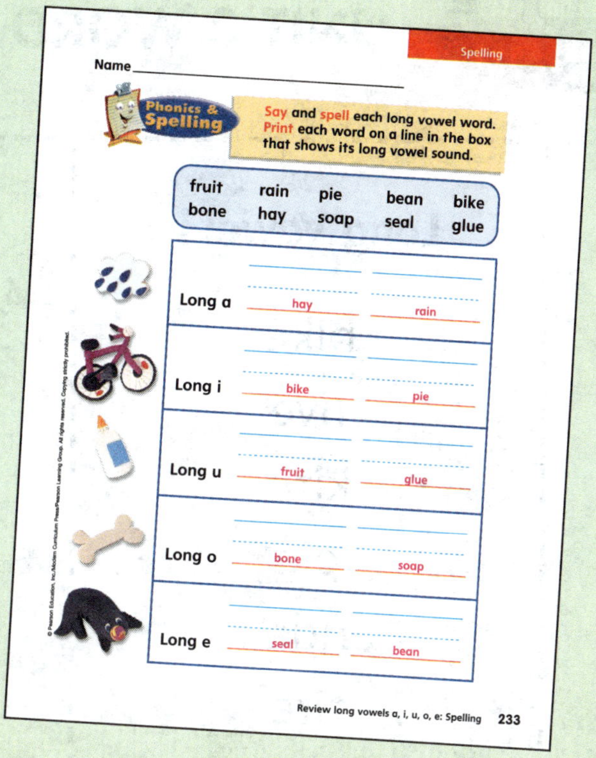

The spelling lessons utilize the following approach for each long vowel sound.

1. Administer a pretest of six words that have not yet been introduced. Dictation sentences are provided.

2. Provide practice.

3. Reassess. Dictation sentences are provided.

A final review that covers long vowel words is provided at the end of the unit, on page 233.

DIRECTIONS

Make a copy of Blackline Master 19 for each child. After administering the Pretest for each long vowel, give children a copy of the appropriate word list.

Children can work with a partner to practice spelling the words orally and identifying the vowel sound in each word. They can also use their letter cards to form the words on the list. You may want to challenge children to make new words by substituting different long vowel sounds. Children can write words of their own on My Own Word List (see Blackline Master 19).

Have children store their list words with the letter cards in the envelope in the back of their books. You may want to suggest that children keep a spelling notebook, listing words with similar patterns. Another idea is to build Word Walls with children for display. Each section of the wall can focus on words with a single long vowel sound. The walls will become a good resource for spelling when children are engaged in writing.

Unit Word List

Long Vowel *a*
cane
hay
lake
rain
tape
vase

Long Vowel *i*
bike
five
kite
pie
ride
tire

Long Vowel *u*
cube
fruit
glue
mule
tube
tune

Long Vowel *o*
bone
bow
robe
rope
soap
toe

Long Vowel *e*
bean
feet
jeep
peel
seal
seat

Name _____

UNIT 3 WORD LIST

Long Vowel a	Long Vowel i	Long Vowel u
cane	bike	cube
hay	five	fruit
lake	kite	glue
rain	pie	mule
tape	ride	tube
vase	tire	tune

Long Vowel o	Long Vowel e	My Own Word List
bone	bean	
bow	feet	
robe	jeep	
rope	peel	
soap	seal	
toe	seat	

BLM 19 Unit 3 Spelling Words

Phonics Games, Activities, and Technology

The following collection of ideas offers a variety of opportunities to reinforce phonics skills while actively engaging children. The games, activities, and technology suggestions can easily be adapted to meet the needs of your group of learners. They vary in approach so as to consider children's different learning styles.

THAT'S MY WORD

Have children sit in a circle. Say a word and indicate one child in the circle to say a rhyming word. Continue clockwise around the circle, each child adding a new rhyming word. If a child hears another child give his or her word, the first child can say, "That's my word" to "catch" the repeater. The "caught" child has one more chance to give a new word. If he or she is unable to do so, say a new word for the "caught" child and continue around with children saying rhymes for the new word.

ESL/ELL This game and Word Clues (page 145n) require that children be familiar with a wide variety of English words and their rhyming patterns. Simplify this activity by having children select words from the Unit 3 Word List, found on pages 145k–145l, or from those of previous units, and match by long or short vowel sounds.

"PUT THE SOUNDS TOGETHER" SONG

Sing the following words to the tune of "Frère Jacques" ("Are You Sleeping?") to help children focus on blending sounds together to form a long vowel word.

> Listen to the sounds I say:
> /f/-/ē/-/t/, /f/-/ē/-/t/
> Put the sounds together,
> And then say the word for
> /f/-/ē/-/t/, /f/-/ē/-/t/

WORD FLIP BOOKS

Make flip books that feature a long vowel phonogram. As the initial letter pages are flipped, children read each new word. Make several books with phonograms for different long vowels, such as *-ain, -ake, -ike, -oat, -ow, -ee.*

LONG VOWEL BOOKS

Have children contribute to a series of class books about imaginary characters with long vowel names. Make a cover with the title for each book, and give an example sentence, such as *Kate and Jake bake a cake* or *Mike and Spike like to hike*. Provide drawing paper for children to write and illustrate a sentence on a page for each book. Possible titles include *Kate and Jake, Mike and Spike, Joe and Flo, Steve and Eve,* and *June and Stu.* Have children place their finished pages inside the correct cover. Then you can bind the pages into books for children to share.

SILLY-SENTENCE GAME

Write the following phrases on index cards, keeping the cards in each group together. Have children select a card from each group and put them together to make a silly sentence. Make available drawing paper for children to write and illustrate their silly sentences.

Group 1
Steve and Kate
Two green beasts
Three goats
The cute mules

Group 2
ride on
take home
smile at
hide in

Group 3
a deep cave.
a sweet treat.
a slow boat.
a fine blue sky.

Two green beasts take home a sweet treat.

WORD RELAYS

Assign children to teams. Write a long vowel word on a sheet of paper for each team. On your signal, have the first team member write a new word by changing one letter of the first word and then pass the paper to the next team member. Each player in turn writes a new word, changing one letter of the preceding word. When the last team member is finished, have the team put their heads down. Award one point to the first team finished and one point for each correct word.

Variation: Put the first word on the chalkboard and have each team member come to the board, write a new word, and then sit down.

ESL/ELL This game requires that children have oral fluency in English in order to participate successfully. Assist English language learners by working with them to create a list or by providing for them a working list of words. Assign children to work in teams; ask them to offer one response per team, on your signal. This allows all children to participate and benefit from the interaction instead of focusing on the speed of the response.

WORD BEADS

Provide large tube-shaped pasta (such as rigatoni), yarn or string, and fine-tipped markers. Have children write different long vowel words on pieces of pasta and string them to make long vowel necklaces. Have them read one another's necklaces.

WORD CLUES

Have children respond to clues for rhyming words given in the following form: *What sounds like* mean *but starts with* b? *What sounds like* lake *but starts with* m?

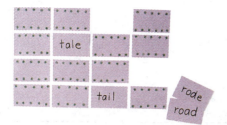

SOUND-ALIKES

Write a number of homophone pairs on cards. Have children play "concentration" to match the homophones. Suggest that children choose a pair of homophones and write and illustrate a sentence using each word correctly.

ZAP WORDS

Duplicate Blackline Master 20 and cut it apart to make the cards for this game. Shuffle the cards and place them face down in a pile. Children play the game by turning over one card at a time and reading the word, placing the words in a row on the table. When the *e* card is chosen, the child who took the card must place the *e* after each exposed card and read the new word. All the cards are then put back in the pile and reshuffled for the next player. Play continues until each child has had a chance to "zap" words.

FEED THE DOG A BONE

Cut bone shapes from construction paper. Write a long vowel word or a short vowel word on each "bone." Display a toy dog or a picture of a dog and tell children the dog only eats bones with long vowel words. Have children read each word and decide which bones can be fed to the dog.

ESL/ELL This game can be more supportive to English language learners by having the class respond whether the card has a long or short vowel word on it. Children respond on the group's cue instead of independent production.

The following software products reinforce children's understanding of long vowels.

Reader Rabbit's® I Can Read! with Phonics™
Beginning readers (grades 1–3) learn basic phonics skills through lessons and interactive storybooks designed to build phonemic awareness, reading comprehension, and vocabulary skills.

** Riverdeep The Learning Company
500 Redwood Blvd.
Novato, CA 94947
(800) 825-4420
www.learningcompanyschool.com

JumpStart 1st Grade®
This CD-ROM uses an interactive classroom setting to help children practice first grade skills, including vowel sounds, vocabulary building, and punctuation.

** Sunburst Technology
1900 South Batavia Ave.
Geneva, IL 60134
(800) 321-7511
www.sunburst.com

Zap Words

e	e	e	e	e
pan	cap	can	hat	at
pin	bit	rid	hid	fin
rip	rob	hop	rod	not
mop	tub	cub	hug	us

Home Connections

The Home Connections features of this program are intended to involve families in their children's learning and application of phonics skills. Three effective opportunities to make connections between home and school include the following.

- **HOME LETTER**
- **HOME NOTES**
- **TAKE-HOME BOOKS**

HOME LETTER

A letter is available to be sent home at the beginning of Unit 3. This letter informs family members that children will be learning to identify long vowel sounds within the context of the unit theme, "Let's Play." The suggested home activity focuses on making collages that group toys, games, sports, etc., whose names have long vowel sounds. This activity promotes interaction between child and family members while supporting children's learning of long vowel sounds. The letter, which is available in both English and Spanish, also suggests books related to the theme of "play" that family members can look for in a local library and enjoy reading together.

HOME NOTES

Whenever the Home logo appears within the student book, a phonics activity is suggested to be done at home. The activities are simple to do, requiring little or no preparation or special materials, and are meant to reinforce the targeted phonics skill.

TAKE-HOME BOOKS

The student book contains a number of Take-Home Books that can be cut out and assembled. The story language in the books reinforces the phonics skills. In each book, children are asked to respond by finishing the book. The books can then be taken home and shared with family members. In Unit 3, five Take-Home Books are available. They focus on long vowel sounds and are related to the theme "Let's Play."

Home Notes in Spanish are also available for both teachers and parents to download and use from our website, www.PlaidPhonics.com.

Pages 145–146

Long Vowels

Skill Focus

Assess Prior Knowledge
To assess children's prior knowledge of long vowels and high-frequency words, use the pretest on pages 145e–145f.

Unit Focus

Build Background

- Write the theme "Let's Play" on the board. Read the words and help children find them on page 145. Talk with children about different ways people can play: games, musical instruments, and so on.

- Point to the picture on the page and ask what the child is doing. Invite children to share their experiences with kites.

- Read the text aloud. Then, discuss the poem with children. Ask them who the "I" in the poem is. Also help them understand that the poet is using his imagination to write what the sun, the earth, and the sky might say to a child about to fly a kite.

Introduce Vowels

- Print the vowels *a, e, i, o, u* on the chalkboard. Ask children to identify each letter. Remind them that these letters are called vowels and that all letters in the alphabet are either vowels or consonants.

- Read the poem "Play" again. Then read the words *play, me, sky, we, I, kite, hold,* emphasizing the long vowel sounds. Tell children that they will learn more about long vowel sounds as they work in this unit.

Critical Thinking Ask children to name some other outdoor games, sports, or activities they enjoy. List their responses on the board.

Read Aloud

Play
by Frank Asch

Come play with me said the sun,
Come play with me said the earth,
Come play with me said the sky.
What shall we play said I?

Let's fly a kite said the sun,
Stand on me said the earth,
I'll bring the wind said the sky,
I'll hold the string said I.

UNIT 3 Long Vowels Theme: Let's Play

Talk About It What are other fun ways to play outdoors?

Unit 3 • Introduction
Critical Thinking

THEME FOCUS

EYE-CATCHING KITES
Materials: paper, crayons, scissors, string, tape

Tell children that some kites are made in geometric shapes, such as diamonds and boxes, and others are made to look like animals, such as bats and birds, or machines, such as planes and rockets. Invite children to draw and cut out shapes for kites of their own. Then, have them tape on string.

NAME THE GAME RIDDLES
Working in small groups, have children play a 20-questions game in which they attempt to identify a mystery sport, game, toy, or instrument by asking yes or no questions.

YEAR-ROUND FUN AND GAMES
Materials: mural paper, paints and brushes

Divide the paper into four parts and label each with a season. Then, assign children to four teams, and have each team create a section of the mural that features sports and games that are especially popular during one of the four seasons.

Dear Family,

In this unit called "Let's Play," your child will learn about the sounds of long vowels. Many words related to play contain long vowels, such as skate, feet, bike, boat, and flute. As your child becomes more familiar with vowel sounds, you might try these activities together.

- Look through old magazines and catalogs to find and cut out pictures of toys, games, musical instruments, sports events, or sports equipment whose names have long vowel sounds. Ask your child to group the pictures according to the long vowel sounds.

- Read the poem on page 145 with your child and help him or her to identify the words with long vowel sounds.
- Your family might enjoy reading these books with you. Look for them in your local library.

Ten Minutes Till Bedtime
by Peggy Rathmann

Lentil by Robert McCloskey

Sincerely,

Estimada familia:

En esta unidad, titulada "Juguemos" ("Let's Play"), su hijo/a estudiará los sonidos de las vocales largas en inglés. Muchas palabras relacionadas con actividades de entretenimiento contienen vocales con sonidos largos, como por ejemplo, skate (patín), feet (pies), bike (bicicleta), boat (bote), y flute (flauta). A medida que su hijo/a se vaya familiarizando con los sonidos de las vocales, pueden hacer las siguientes actividades juntos.

- Busquen y recorten en revistas y catálogos viejos ilustraciones de juguetes, juegos, instrumentos musicales, eventos o equipos deportivos cuyos nombres contengan vocales con sonidos largos. Pidan a su hijo/a que agrupe las ilustraciones de acuerdo a los sonidos largos de las vocales.
- Lean el poema en la página 145 con su hijo/a y ayúdenle a identificar las palabras que contengan vocales con sonidos largos.
- Ustedes y su hijo/a disfrutarán leyendo estos libros juntos. Búsquenlos en su biblioteca local.

Ten Minutes Till Bedtime
de Peggy Rathmann

Lentil de Robert McCloskey

Sinceramente,

HOME CONNECTIONS

- The Home Letter on page 146 is intended to acquaint family members with the phonics skills children will be studying in the unit. Children can tear out page 146 and take it home.
- You may want to suggest that they complete the activities on the page with a family member. Encourage children to look in the library for the books suggested and read them with family members.

LEARNING CENTER ACTIVITIES

WRITING CENTER

Invite children to write and draw to describe a favorite game, sport, or hobby. They might want to include what they found challenging or difficult when they were learning the activity. Suggest that they include an illustration of themselves playing.

SCIENCE CENTER

Materials: balls of different types, such as a tennis ball, Ping-Pong ball, soccer ball, and basketball

Have children use the balls to explore which bounce well and which do not. Can they devise an experiment to find out which ball bounces highest? Have them draw pictures and record their observations under their drawings. Then, have them create a display that shows their findings.

MATH CENTER

Materials: manipulatives

Explain that in certain games, like basketball and football, a goal or basket is worth more than 1 point. If 2 points are scored for each basket, help children develop a table that shows the point values for one, two, three, four, and five baskets. In computing numbers, suggest that they use manipulatives to stand for the points.

BULLETIN BOARD

Have children cut out the shape of something they like to play with. On the cutout, have them write a sentence caption and draw a picture that shows them playing with the item. Children can decide how to group the artwork on the "Let's Play Today" display.

Lesson 69   Pages 147–148

Long Vowel a

Skill Focus

Children will

★ recognize the sound of long *a*.

★ identify picture names and words that contain the sound of long *a*.

★ identify rhyming long *a* words.

ESL/ELL In many languages each letter or symbol stands for only one sound; thus, children may need help in pronouncing and spelling long *a* versus short *a*. Native speakers of Spanish will likely write *e* instead of long *a* in words.

Teach

Phonological Awareness: Blending Onsets and Rimes Say /k/ake and then blend the sounds together to say *cake*. Have children repeat the word. Explain that the sound heard in the middle is long vowel *a*. Then say these word parts. Have children repeat the parts after you, orally blending them to make the word:

- /t/ail (tail)
- /l/ate (late)
- /s/ay (say)
- /r/ain (rain)
- /w/ay (way)
- /sh/ake (shake)

Sound to Symbol Write *cap* and *cape* on the board, say the words, and underline the *a* in each word. Ask children what things sound alike and look alike in the two words. (Both begin with the *c* sound and end with the *p* sound; both words begin with the letters *c-a-p*.) Then, say *cap, cape* again and ask what things sound different and look different in the words. (*Cape* has an *e* at the end. The vowel sounds are different.) Point out that *cap* has the short *a* sound and *cape* has the long *a* sound.

Practice and Apply

Sound to Symbol Read aloud the rhyme on page 147. Have children listen for and point out words that have the same vowel sound as *cape*. (*James, bake, cake, make, Jake*)

Suggest that children say each word softly to themselves as they do the activities on pages 147 and 148.

Reading Use *Pancakes!* MCP Phonics and Reading Long Vowel Skills Library, Level A, to provide practice in reading words with long *a*.

Phonemic Awareness

Name _____

James wants to bake a big birthday cake. He plans to make the cake for Jake.

▶ **Bake** has the long sound of **a**. **Circle** each picture whose name has the long sound of **a**.

1. cake 2. can 3. cane 4. pail
5. nail 6. rain 7. vase 8. bat
9. hand 10. sail 11. pay 12. rake

Long vowel a: Phonemic awareness   **147**

FOCUS ON ALL LEARNERS

ESL/ELL ENGLISH LANGUAGE LEARNERS

- Some children have difficulty differentiating the short *e* and the long *a* vowel sounds. Before beginning page 147, have children repeat these words and clap for the long *a* sound: *nail, net; bet, bait; rest, rate*.

- For page 148, display picture cards for cap (48) and cape (85). Have children name the objects. Ask which different vowel sounds they hear in each word. Have them supply a rhyming word for each.

KINESTHETIC LEARNERS

Materials: Phonics Picture Cards: apple (45), ax (46), hat (52), bed (76), bell (77), hen (81), cape (85), cake (86), cane (87), tray (88), gate (89), nails (90), rake (91), vase (92); chairs

Have children arrange their chairs in a line to form the Long *a* Train. Distribute picture cards as tickets. Those with pictures whose names contain the long *a* sound may board the train. Others go to the end of the line. Continue distributing tickets until all children are aboard.

147

Phonograms/Rhyme

▶ **Say** the names of the pictures in each row.
Color the pictures whose names rhyme.

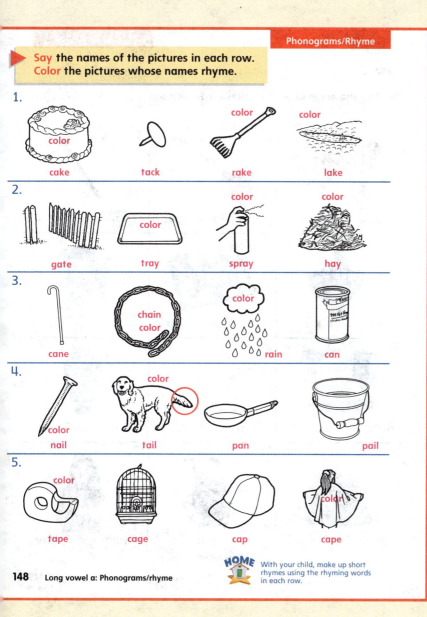

1. cake / tack / rake / lake
2. gate / tray / spray / hay
3. cane / chain / rain / can
4. nail / tail / pan / pail
5. tape / cage / cap / cape

 With your child, make up short rhymes using the rhyming words in each row.

148 Long vowel a: Phonograms/rhyme

CURRICULUM CONNECTIONS

SPELLING
Say each spelling word and then use it in a context sentence. Have children write each word as a spelling pretest.
1. **cane** Dan walks with a **cane**.
2. **hay** We can jump in the **hay**.
3. **lake** There are fish in that **lake**.
4. **rain** Gail got wet in the **rain**.
5. **tape** You can fix the rip with **tape**.
6. **vase** Place the **vase** on that tray.

WRITING
Ask children to draw a cake top and write a sentence telling what they might celebrate with it.

MATH
Materials: measuring cups and spoons, sand

Have children experiment with the measuring instruments to find 2 half cups = 1 cup, 4 quarter cups = 1 cup, 3 teaspoons = 1 tablespoon.

 **AstroWord** Long Vowels: *a, i*

Integrating Phonics and Reading

Shared/Guided Reading
Show the cover and read the title. Ask children if they like pancakes.
First Reading Each time you come to *pat-a-cake* or *pancakes*, point to the word. Have children say it along with you.
Second Reading Ask children to identify the long *a* words in the story. You might want to add these to the classroom Word Wall.
Comprehension
After reading, ask children the following questions:
- How does the boy in the story feel about pancakes? How do you know? *Recall/Details*
- Which part of the story would not really happen? Why not? *Recall/Fantasy and Reality*

ESL/ELL English Language Learners
Ask children to act out the following: mixing and pouring batter, flipping and catching pancakes in a pan, putting pancakes on a table.

AUDITORY LEARNERS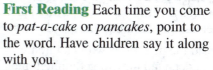
Say these word pairs and ask children to wave each time they hear a rhyming pair: gave, save; hay, day; plate, play; tape, tame; lake, take; mail, pail; sake, sail; main, pain; same, game; vase, vain; gate, wait.

CHALLENGE
Ask children to look at the pictures they did not color on page 148. Have them name the two pictures that contain the long *a* sound. (gate, cage) Challenge them to pick one of the words to make a word chain that will change *gate* into *cage* or *cage* into *gate*. One example is: Start with *gate*. Change *t* to *m*. (game) Change *g* to *c*. (came) Change *m* to *g*. (cage)

EXTRA SUPPORT/INTERVENTION
Materials: Phonics Picture Cards: apple (45), ax (46), hat (52), bed (76), bell (77), hen (81), cape (85), cake (86), cane (87), tray (88), gate (89), nails (90), rake (91), vase (92)

Mix up the cards and have the child say each picture name. After repeating the name several times, have the child tell whether the word contains a long *a* sound. *See Daily Phonics Practice, page 316.*

148

Lesson 70 — Pages 149–150

Long Vowel a

Skill Focus

Children will

★ recognize the sound of long a.

★ identify pictures whose names contain the sound of long a.

★ understand that ai, a_e, and ay can stand for long a.

★ apply what they have learned by reading and writing.

Teach

Phonemic Awareness: Phoneme Categorization Say the word *raise*, elongating the long *a* sound, and have children repeat the word. Tell children that the sound they hear in the middle of *raise* is long vowel *a*. Next, say these groups of words. Ask children to raise their hands when they hear a long *a* word.

- take   say   fast
- pal   wait hay
- stay   tap   page
- can   race sail

Sound to Symbol Display picture cards for gate (89), tray (88), and nails (90). Write each word on the board. Help children read the words aloud, listening for the vowel sound. Next, underline the vowels in each word. Ask volunteers to circle the vowel they hear with colored chalk. Help children conclude that the long *a* sound can be spelled *a_consonant_e, ai,* and *ay*.

Practice and Apply

Sound to Symbol As children complete page 149, encourage them to say each picture name softly to themselves, emphasizing the vowel sound.

For page 150, read the directions with children. Make sure they understand how to get through the maze.

Writing Note the long *a* words that children write on page 150 and check for correct spelling.

Reading Use *That Cat!*, MCP Phonics and Reading Long Vowel Skills Library, Level A, to provide practice in reading words with long *a* that have the *a_e* pattern.

FOCUS ON ALL LEARNERS

ESL/ELL ENGLISH LANGUAGE LEARNERS

- Before beginning page 149, draw a can and a cane on the board and print the words beneath the pictures. Have children name the objects. Then, ask which different vowel sounds they hear in each word. Underline the *a* in *can* and the *a* and *e* in *cane*. Remind children that the long *a* sound can be spelled *a_consonant_e, ai,* and *ay*.

- For page 150, ask volunteers to read the directions and explain them in their own words. Work together with the children to draw a line connecting the first two long *a* words. Have them finish the activity independently.

VISUAL LEARNERS

Materials: Phonics Picture Cards: cap (48), cat (49), ham (50), lid (57), mitt (58), pig (59), bug (61), cup (63), box (70), dog (71), doll (72), hen (81), ten (82), tent (83), cape (85), cake (86), cane (87), gate (89), nails (90), rake (91), vase (92)

Push the cards into the center of the table to form a haystack. Children can take turns drawing a card and naming the picture. If the name contains the long *a* sound, they may keep the card.

Sound to Symbol

▶ **Help** Jay get to the game. **Read** each word. **Draw** a line to join the long a words.

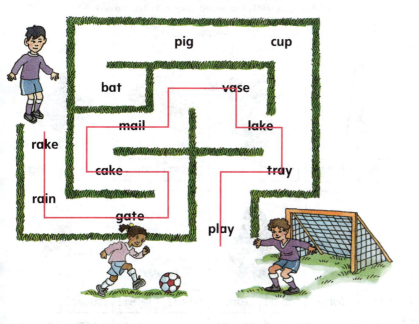

▶ **Use** some of the long a words to write a sentence.

_____
_____
_____

150 Long vowel a: Sound to symbol

 With your child, make up a story using some of the words along the path that leads to the soccer game.

CURRICULUM CONNECTIONS

SPELLING
Materials: spelling master (page 145l), crayons, index cards

Have children use the spelling master on page 145l to write each long *a* word on an index card. Have them draw a picture of the word on the back of the card. Save these cards for use in the next lessons.

WRITING
Assign each child a partner. Have children work together to choose a game they both like to play. Have them illustrate their game and write about it.

MATH
Materials: cutouts of circle, square, triangle

Write the word *shape* on the board and help children pronounce it. Ask children to identify the vowel sound they hear in this word. Using the cutouts, introduce the three shapes. Then, invite children to go on a shape hunt in the classroom.

 AstroWord Long Vowels: *a, i*

AUDITORY LEARNERS
Materials: strips of paper numbered 1 to 12, masking tape

Randomly write the words *cake, bake, game, name, cage, page, rain, grain, day, say, late,* and *state* on the board and cover each word with a numbered strip. Invite children to select two numbers and read aloud the words under the strips. Have children raise their hands if the words rhyme.

CHALLENGE
Working with a partner, have children take turns making up oral riddles for the long *a* words on pages 149 and 150. Each partner should give a riddle for the other to guess.

EXTRA SUPPORT/INTERVENTION
Materials: green and red markers

Help children read the three words under each picture on page 149. After reading each long *a* word, have them underline the vowel that they hear with a green marker and cross out the silent vowel with a red marker. **See Daily Phonics Practice, page 316.**

Integrating Phonics and Reading

Guided Reading
Show children the cover. Ask them to make predictions about the story based on the book's title and cover illustration.

First Reading Have children describe what the cat is doing in each picture.

Second Reading Have children identify the long *a* words in the story. List the words on the board or add them to the classroom Word Wall.

Comprehension
After reading, ask children the following questions:
• Why was Matt sad? *Recall/Character*
• Do you think Matt and Dad will keep the cat? *Reflective Analysis/Details*

ESL/ELL English Language Learners
Look at the words on the last page with children. Help them to express the same idea in a complete sentence, such as *Matt's new friend was that cat!*

Lesson 71 Pages 151–152

Long and Short vowel a

Skill Focus

Children will

★ distinguish between short *a* and long *a* picture names.

★ identify words that contain the sound of long *a*.

Teach

Phonological Awareness: Rhyme Tell children that you will say pairs of words. If the words rhyme, children should clap their hands.

- tail   sail
- cap   cape
- Sam   same
- lake   rake
- day   say
- tack   take

Sound to Symbol Draw a picture of rain coming from a cloud on the board. Underneath, write the words *ran* and *rain*. Ask children to say *rain* and tell if its vowel sound is long or short. Call on a volunteer to point to the word *rain* on the board. Repeat, using a picture of a cane and the words *can* and *cane*. Have children say the word *cane* and identify the vowel sound, then select the correct label.

Sound to Symbol Write the words *cap* and *cape* on the board. Ask volunteers to read the words and underline the vowels in each word. Then, have children circle the vowel they hear with colored chalk. Remind children that long *a* can be spelled with the letters *a_consonant_e*. The *e* is silent.

Practice and Apply

Sound to Symbol Help children identify the pictures on page 151 and help them read the names of the children on page 152. After they have completed the pages, remind children that the long *a* sound can be spelled *a_consonant_e*, as in *rake*, *ai* as in *rain*, and *ay* as in *pay*.

Reading Use *Making a Plate*, MCP Phonics and Reading Long Vowel Skills Library, Level A, to provide practice in reading words with long *a*.

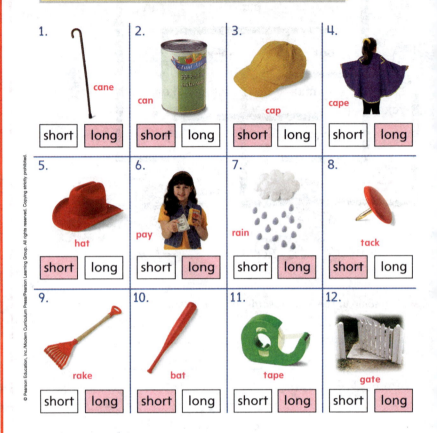

Phonemic Awareness

Name _____

> **Say** the name of each picture. If the vowel sound is short, color the box with the word **short**. If the vowel sound is long, color the box with the word **long**.

Long and short vowel a: Phonemic awareness **151**

FOCUS ON ALL LEARNERS

ESL/ELL ENGLISH LANGUAGE LEARNERS

- Before beginning page 151, display tape, a cap, a tack, a plate, and paste. Have children say the name of each object and identify the vowel sound as long or short. Then, write the words on the board. Have children hold each object up to the correct word. Use the worksheet activity on page 151 to check comprehension of long and short vowel sounds.

- Before beginning page 152, remind children that the long *a* sound can be spelled *a_consonant_e*, *ai*, and *ay*. On the board, write *cake, pay, pain, wait, safe, bay*. Have children identify the vowel they hear, the second (silent) vowel, and the initial and final consonant sounds for each word.

VISUAL LEARNERS

Materials: Phonics Picture Cards: apple (45), cap (48), cat (49), lamp (53), cape (85), cake (86), cane (87), tray (88), gate (89), nails (90), vase (92)

Display each picture. Have children say its name and identify the vowel sound.

151

Sound to Symbol

▶ Help Dave, Gail, and Ray find the long **a** words. Circle each one you find.

1. Dave

at	(ate)	(rake)	rack	(page)
(made)	(safe)	tap	(tape)	mad

2. Gail

(rain)	ram	(wait)	cat	(pail)
sat	(sail)	(main)	man	pal

3. Ray

(May)	man	(pay)	pat	(play)
(day)	hat	(say)	(way)	sand

HOME: With your child, think of sentences using words that rhyme with *Dave*, *Gail*, and *Ray*, such as *Ray wants to play today*.

152 Long vowel a: Sound to symbol

CURRICULUM CONNECTIONS

SPELLING
Materials: spelling cards made in Lesson 70, pages 149–150

Have partners work together to sort the words into three piles based on the different spellings of the long *a* sound.

WRITING
Write this slogan on the board: *Play safe.* Have children identify the vowels. Talk about safety rules to remember when playing. Then, ask children to draw a picture of someone playing safely.

FINE ARTS
Materials: paper, paints, brushes, crayons

Discuss with children how they could show rain in their artwork. Elicit words containing the long *a* sound such as *rainy* and *gray* that could be used to describe the scenes. Then, invite children to paint and draw their own rainy day scenes.

 TECHNOLOGY AstroWord Long Vowels: *a, i*

AUDITORY LEARNERS
Materials: red and green construction-paper bracelets

Have children slip a bracelet on each wrist. Say these words: *bag, ate, camp, cape, make, day, gas, sad, tax, lake, nail, date, man, came, tail, tap, van, gave.* Have children hold up the red bracelet if they hear short *a* and the green bracelet if they hear long *a*.

CHALLENGE
Write these words on the board: *hat, pal, pan, man, tap, ran*. Challenge children to transform these short *a* words into long *a* words by adding a vowel.

EXTRA SUPPORT/INTERVENTION
Materials: Phonics Picture Cards: apple (45), ax (46), bag (47), cap (48), cat (49), ham (50), hand (51), hat (52), lamp (53), cape (85), cake (86), cane (87), tray (88), gate (89), nails (90); two bags

Help children label one bag *Short a* and the other bag *Long a*. Have children say each picture name several times, listening for the vowel sound. Have them identify the sound and place the picture card into the appropriate bag. **See Daily Phonics Practice, page 316.**

Integrating Phonics and Reading

Guided Reading
Show the cover and read the title. Ask children if they know what the woman is using to make plates.

First Reading Offer children support as needed with reading the words *potter, kiln,* and *glaze*.

Second Reading Ask children to identify the long *a* words in the story. You might want to add these to the classroom Word Wall.

Comprehension
After reading, ask children the following questions:
- Is this a true or a made-up story? How can you tell? *Reflective Analysis/Fantasy and Reality*
- What do you think might happen if Mrs. Salas didn't bake the plate? *Inference/Details*

ESL/ELL English Language Learners
Before beginning the book, introduce the vocabulary words *potter, clay, kiln,* and *glaze*. Use appropriate actions or pictures to help demonstrate and explain the meanings.

Lesson 72   Pages 153–154

Long Vowel a

Skill Focus
Children will
- ★ identify picture names and words that contain the sound of long *a*.
- ★ identify rhyming long *a* words.

Teach

Phonemic Awareness: Medial Sound Isolation Say the word *can*, emphasizing the medial vowel sound: *caaan*. Ask children to identify the sound. Repeat the steps, using the word *cane*. Then, draw a can and a cane on the board. Say a group of words, such as *cap, last, fan, mat, cape, lake, pail, paint, wave, way*. Ask volunteers to point to the can if they hear the short *a* sound and point to the cane if they hear long *a*.

Phonological Awareness: Rhyme Tell children that you will say groups of three words. When you pause, children should repeat the two rhyming words.

- cape   tape   tap
- rain   ran   pain
- pig   pay   hay
- rake   rock   lake
- sail   tail   tall

Sound to Symbol Draw a lake on the board. Say the word *lake* and label the picture. Then, ask a volunteer to come up and underline the vowels using colored chalk.

Add items that have the long *a* sound to the picture: a boat with a *sail*, a sun with *rays*, and a *rain* cloud. As before, say each long *a* word and label the picture. Also have a volunteer highlight the vowels. Remind children that the long *a* sound can be spelled *a_consonant_e, ai,* and *ay*.

Practice and Apply

Sound to Symbol Help children identify the pictures on page 153. Suggest that they listen for the sound of long or short *a* in each name before circling the matching word.

For page 154, have volunteers read the words in each balloon. Remind children to color a balloon only if it has three rhyming words.

Reading Use *My Shadow*, MCP Phonics and Reading Long Vowel Skills Library, Level A, to provide practice in reading words with long *a*.

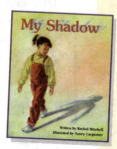

153

Sound to Symbol

Name _____

▶ Say the name of each picture. Circle its name.

1. (rat) rate	2. pain (pan)	3. tap (tape)
4. can (cane)	5. (can) cane	6. hate (hat)
7. cape (cap)	8. (cape) cap	9. ran (rain)
10. (bat) bait	11. (hay) hat	12. take (tack)

Long and short vowel a: Sound to symbol   **153**

FOCUS ON ALL LEARNERS

ESL/ELL ENGLISH LANGUAGE LEARNERS

- Before beginning page 153, remind children that the long *a* sound can be spelled *a_consonant_e, ai,* and *ay*. Model the spellings by writing *tape, rain, hay* on the board and underlining the *a_e, ai,* and *ay*.
- For page 154, remind children that rhyming words end with the same sound. Have children repeat these word pairs and clap when they hear rhyming words: *cake, bake; ray, ran; gain, pain; nail, name; pay, way; wave, cave.*

KINESTHETIC LEARNERS

Materials: Phonics Word Cards, Set 1: *ax* (5), *bag* (8), *cab* (10), *camp* (11), *gas* (16), *mad* (25), *wax* (33), *bake* (119), *cane* (122), *cape* (123), *date* (124), *lay* (127), *made* (128), *nail* (130), *safe* (135), *tame* (140)

Display the word cards on the chalkboard ledge. Read aloud a word and ask a child to stand and pronounce the word and identify the vowel sound.

Rhyming

Color each balloon that has three rhyming long **a** words.

1. game / tame / name — color
2. take / tape / ape
3. cane / lane / mane — color
4. sail / same / rail
5. cake / rake / lake — color
6. gate / date / late — color
7. fade / made / make
8. cave / wave / cake
9. bake / fake / fame
10. nail / mail / pail — color
11. rain / gain / pain — color
12. hay / day / pay — color

154 Long vowel a: Rhyming

HOME Pick a balloon with three rhyming words. Ask your child to name another word that rhymes.

CURRICULUM CONNECTIONS

SPELLING

Materials: spelling cards made in Lesson 70, pages 149–150

Have children work with a partner and take turns displaying the picture side of each spelling card. Ask the partner to name the picture and write its name. Have children check the spelling by comparing it to the word written on the back of the card.

WRITING

Have children use the words in the balloons they colored on page 154 to write silly rhyming questions. Start them off with this example: *Can you mail a nail that's in a pail?*

PORTFOLIO

SCIENCE

Materials: walnut shells, clay, toothpicks, index cards, straws, pan of water

Children can make toy sailboats using walnut shells. Show them how to cut a sail from an index card and attach it to a toothpick mast stuck into a small ball of clay inside the shell. Have them use drinking straws to investigate the power of wind by blowing on their sails.

TECHNOLOGY **AstroWord** Long Vowels: *a, i*

AUDITORY LEARNERS **GROUPS**

Write these words on the board: *tape, play, rake, mail.* Give oral clues such as *Use this to fix a rip.* Have children answer each riddle by circling the correct word.

CHALLENGE

Have children look at the words in the balloons that they did not color on page 154. Challenge them to cross out the word that does not rhyme with the others, and write a new rhyming word.

EXTRA SUPPORT/INTERVENTION

Materials: Phonics Picture Cards: apple (45), ax (46), bag (47), cap (48), cat (49), ham (50), hand (51), hat (52), lamp (53), cape (85), cake (86), cane (87), tray (88); self-stick notes

Write each picture name on a self-stick note. Then, display the pictures and the notes. Have children work with a partner to attach the self-stick notes to label the pictures. See Daily Phonics Practice, page 316.

Integrating Phonics and Reading

Shared/Guided Reading
Show the cover as you read the title. Invite children to tell what they know about shadows.

First Reading Invite children to join in as you read the words *When I ___, my shadow ___,* and *My shadow can be a ___.*

Second Reading Ask children to identify the long *a* words in the story. List these on the board or on the classroom Word Wall.

Comprehension
After reading, ask children these questions:
- Which shadow shape did you like best? Why? *Reflective Analysis/Opinion*
- What other shadow shapes do you think you can make? How? *Creative/Description*

ESL/ELL English Language Learners
Have children draw and label pictures to show these long *a* words from the story: *snail, whale, spaceship, plane, train.*

154

Lesson 73 Pages 155–156

Long Vowel a

Skill Focus

Children will

★ recognize the sound of long *a*.

★ identify and spell picture names that contain the sound of long *a*.

★ write words that contain the sound of long *a* to complete sentences.

★ recognize and read high-frequency words.

Teach

Phonemic Awareness: Phoneme Substitution Model for children how to solve a riddle by changing the first letter of a word. Say: *What rhymes with face and begins with the /r/ sound?* Then give the answer: *race*. Next, read these riddles and have children tell you the answers:

- What rhymes with *late* and begins with *g*? (*gate*)
- What rhymes with *nail* and begins with *p*? (*pail*)
- What rhymes with *pay* and begins with *d*? (*day*)

Sound to Symbol Write the following on the board: *Fay got up ___.* (lace late lame) Have children identify the correct answer and tell how they chose it. Ask a volunteer to underline the letters that stand for the vowel sound in each answer choice. Then, repeat with this sentence: *Gail came to town on a ___.* (tray trace train) Remind children that the letters *ay*, *a_e*, and *ai* can stand for the long *a* sound.

Practice and Apply

Blend Phonemes As children complete page 155, encourage them to say each picture name, blending together the beginning, middle, and ending sounds.

Writing For page 156, suggest that children try each word choice before writing a word. As they complete the activity, they will have the opportunity to read the following high-frequency words: *out, when*.

Critical Thinking For Talk About It, have children take time to picture themselves at a lake before naming things they might like to do.

Reading Use *The Best Birthday Mole Ever Had*, MCP Phonics and Reading Long Vowel Skills Library, Level A, to provide practice in reading words with long and short *a*.

155

Spelling

Name _____

▶ **Say** the name of each picture. **Print** the missing vowels on the line. In the last box, **draw** a picture of a long **a** word. **Print** the word.

1. cape   2. c a n   3. r a i n   4. v a s e
5. c a k e   6. l a k e   7. b a g   8. n a i l
9. g a m e   10. p a i l   11. g a t e   12.

Long and short vowel a: Spelling   155

FOCUS ON ALL LEARNERS

ESL/ELL ENGLISH LANGUAGE LEARNERS

- Before beginning page 155, read the directions with children. Complete item 2 together to ensure understanding. When children have completed the page, review answers aloud and ask volunteers to write each answer on the board.
- Before beginning page 156, write *lake, cave,* and *sail* on the board, and ask volunteers to read the words aloud. Use pantomime gestures if necessary to confirm children's understanding of the words.

VISUAL LEARNERS

Materials: drawing paper, crayons

Have small groups form teams to hunt for classroom objects whose names contain the sound of long *a*. Have them draw and label pictures of these objects.

KINESTHETIC LEARNERS

Assign each child a partner. Using the picture labels on page 155, have them take turns tracing a long *a* word on their partner's palm for the partner to guess.

Words in Context

Look at the picture. Circle the word that will finish each sentence. Print it on the line.

1. __Dave__ and Ray go out to play.
   Save / (Dave) / Sand

2. They go to the __lake__.
   (lake) / make / late

3. They play a __game__.
   gate / name / (game)

4. Ray sits by a __cave__.
   save / came / (cave)

5. Dave sees a boat with a __sail__.
   save / (sail) / mail

6. They go in when it __rains__.
   (rains) / cane / ran

Talk about it: What are some things you might do at a lake?

HOME Ask your child to use the words circled on this page in sentences.

156 Long a: High-frequency words, critical thinking

CURRICULUM CONNECTIONS

SPELLING

Materials: spelling cards made in Lesson 70, pages 149–150; bag

Have partners place a set of spelling cards in the bag, then take turns selecting a card and making up an oral clue for the word. Have the partner write the spelling word that fits the clue.

WRITING

After rereading the story on page 156, ask children to draw a picture of a day at the lake and write two sentences to go with the picture.

SOCIAL STUDIES

Help children locate on a map the largest lake in your state. Write its name on the board. Then, have children write three sentences about the lake. Suggest that they might write about its size, whether or not it is far away, and whether they would like to see it some day.

TECHNOLOGY **AstroWord** Long Vowels: *a, i*

AUDITORY LEARNERS GROUPS

Say silly sentences such as the following with an incorrect long *a* word: *The bus was lane.* (late) *We will bake a came.* (cake) *Let's play a board gate.* (game) Using the context of the sentence, have children supply the correct long *a* word.

CHALLENGE

Write the word *ate* on the board and say it aloud. Challenge children to add one or more letters to the beginning of this word to build new words. Possibilities include *date, late, fate, gate, hate, Kate, mate, Nate, rate, plate, slate, crate,* and *grate*.

EXTRA SUPPORT/INTERVENTION

Have children fold a piece of paper in half. Have them head one column *a_e* and the other *ai*. Have them write each long *a* word on page 155 under the heading that shows how the long *a* sound is spelled. See Daily Phonics Practice, page 316.

Integrating Phonics and Reading

Guided Reading
Show the cover as you read the title and explain that moles are small mammals that like to dig tunnels.
First Reading Have children look at each illustration and tell how they think the characters are feeling.
Second Reading Have children name the two characters whose names have the long *a* sound. (Snake, Ladybug) Then, have them find other long *a* words in the story.
Comprehension
After reading, ask children the following questions:
• What problem did Mole have at his party? *Recall/Problem and Solution*
• Was Mole's solution a good one? *Reflective Analysis/Details*

ESL/ELL English Language Learners
Have children look at the invitation on page 4. Talk about date, time, and place, using the current date and time and the location of your classroom as examples.

Lesson 74 Pages 157–158

Long Vowel a

Skill Focus

Children will

★ recognize the sound of long *a*.

★ identify and spell picture names that contain the sound of long *a*.

★ write words that contain the sound of long *a* to complete sentences.

★ recognize and read high-frequency words.

Teach

Phonemic Awareness: Phoneme Blending
Say the word *pail*, separating the beginning, middle, and ending sounds: /p/ /ā/ /l/. Have children repeat the segmented word and then say the word naturally. Help them identify each of the sounds. Repeat the procedure with *late, cave, pay, take,* and *rain*.

Sound to Symbol Write *date* and *late* on the board and read the words aloud. Have children tell how the words are alike and different. Then, add *say* and *tail* to the words on the board and read them aloud. Ask children to tell how all the words are alike and different. Remind them that the letters *a_e, ay,* and *ai* can all make the long *a* sound.

Next, elicit rhyming words for *late, say,* and *tail* and record them. Have volunteers identify the vowel sound in each word and use colored chalk to highlight the letters that stand for the vowel sound.

Words in Context: Decodable Words Write these words on the board: *mad, made*. Then, write and read the sentence below. Have children select the word that completes the sentence.

• I ____ a gift for you. (*made*)

Practice and Apply

Blend Phonemes As children complete page 157, encourage them to say each picture name, blending together each of the sounds.

Writing For page 158, suggest that children try each word choice before writing a word. As they complete the activity, they will have the opportunity to read the high-frequency word *home*.

Critical Thinking For Talk About It, encourage children to reread the story before telling why Mom was glad to be home.

Reading Use *The Name Is the Same*, MCP Phonics and Reading Long Vowel Skills Library, Level A, to provide practice in reading words with long *a*.

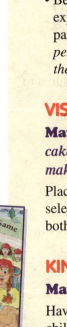

Spelling

Name _____

Say the name of each picture. Print the picture name on the line. In the last box, draw a picture of a long *a* word. Print the word.

1. rake
2. pail
3. hay
4. game
5. cake
6. rain
7. pay
8. nail
9. lake
10. vase
11. sail
12.

Long vowel a: Spelling 157

FOCUS ON ALL LEARNERS

ESL/ELL ENGLISH LANGUAGE LEARNERS

- For page 157, read the directions with children. Name the pictured objects, if necessary.
- Before beginning page 158, write *gave* on the board and explain that this word shows a past action for *give*. As you pantomime giving a pencil to a volunteer, say, *I give the pencil to [name]*. Then fold your arms and say, *I don't have the pencil now. I gave it to [name]*.

VISUAL LEARNERS

Materials: Phonics Word Cards, Set 1: *bake* (119), *cake* (120), *date* (124), *day* (125), *gate* (127), *lake* (130), *make* (132), *rain* (134), *same* (136), *sale* (138); paper bag

Place the word cards in a bag. Have each child in the group select two cards. Have the child read aloud the words and use both words in an oral sentence.

KINESTHETIC LEARNERS

Materials: clay

Have each child select a picture on page 157. Then, have children roll clay snakes and use them to form letters to write the picture name.

Words in Context

Circle the word that will finish the sentence. Print it on the line.

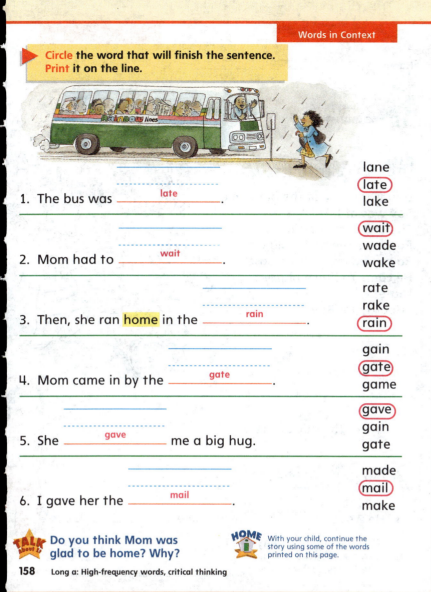

1. The bus was __late__. lane / (late) / lake
2. Mom had to __wait__. (wait) / wade / wake
3. Then, she ran home in the __rain__. rate / rake / (rain)
4. Mom came in by the __gate__. gain / (gate) / game
5. She __gave__ me a big hug. (gave) / gain / gate
6. I gave her the __mail__. made / (mail) / make

TALK About It Do you think Mom was glad to be home? Why?

HOME With your child, continue the story using some of the words printed on this page.

158 Long a: High-frequency words, critical thinking

CURRICULUM CONNECTIONS

SPELLING
Materials: red and green crayons
Have children write their spelling words, using a red crayon to print each vowel. Then, have them say each spelling word, listening for the vowel sound. Have them use a green crayon to underline the vowel they do not hear.

WRITING
Materials: toy telephone
PORTFOLIO
Have children recall why Mom was late in the story on page 158. Have children work with a partner to role-play Mom calling home and her child taking a message. Have them write a phone message based on the phone call.

SOCIAL STUDIES
Talk with children about bus safety, reminding them that the most dangerous areas around a bus are on the sides of the bus and directly in front of the bus.

TECHNOLOGY AstroWord Long Vowels: a, i

AUDITORY LEARNERS GROUPS
Read aloud these sentences.
Have children write a word that contains the sound of long *a* to complete each. *Use a hammer to pound a ___.* (*nail*) *Horses like to eat ___.* (*hay*) *Baseball is my favorite ___.* (*game*) *Those big gray clouds mean ___.* (*rain*)

CHALLENGE
Materials: picture dictionaries
Write these homophones on the board and help children read them: *sail, sale; tail, tale; pail, pale.* Help children use dictionaries to find the meaning of each word.

EXTRA SUPPORT/INTERVENTION
If children have difficulty spelling the words on page 157, suggest that they begin by spelling the beginning and/or ending consonant sounds first. Give help as needed with variant spellings of the long *a* sound. See Daily Phonics Practice, page 316.

Integrating Phonics and Reading

Guided Reading
Show the cover as you read the title. Ask children whom they think the story will be about.
First Reading Have children look at each illustration and tell which of the following characters they see: Coach Dan, the boy named Sam, the girl named Sam.
Second Reading Have children find three rhyming words in the story. (*name, game, same*) Then, have them find two other long *a* words. (*base, plate*)

Comprehension
After reading, ask children the following questions:
- Who has the same name? *Recall/Character*
- How else could the coach have solved the problem? *Creative/Problem and Solution*

ESL/ELL English Language Learners
Draw a simple map of a baseball field. Help children label these places: home plate; first, second, and third base; the pitcher's mound.

Lesson 75 Pages 159–160

Phonics and Reading / Phonics and Writing

Long Vowel a

Skill Focus

Children will

★ read words that contain the sound of long *a*.

★ write long *a* words to finish sentences.

★ build words with long *a* phonograms -*ay*, -*ail*.

Teach

Phonological Awareness: Rhyme Say *wave, save*. Ask children what they notice about the two words. Remind them that words that rhyme sound alike except for the beginning sound. Then, tell them you will say a group of words. Ask children to wave their hands when they hear a word that rhymes with *wave*. Use: *tent, gave, rag, shave, sand, ring, brave, pond, cave, dust, page, pave*.

Sound to Symbol Write *bake* on the board and read the word aloud. Tell children they will use it in a word relay. Demonstrate by saying *c*. Have a volunteer come up, change the first letter to *c*, and read the new word, *cake*. Continue with these letters: *f, l, m, r, s, t, w*. Then, ask volunteers to underline the vowels in the word *wake*. Remind children that long *a* can be spelled with *a_consonant_e*, and the *e* is silent. Add that long *a* can also be spelled *ay*, as in *day*, and *ai*, as in *rain*.

Read Words in Sentences Write these sentences on the board. Help children read them and underline the long *a* words.

- Gail plays in the game.
- She races to first base.
- The fans say she is safe!

Practice and Apply

Phonics and Reading After children have read the story, encourage them to identify words that have the long *a* sound.

Critical Thinking For Talk About It, discuss what it means to reach home plate in baseball.

Phonics and Writing For page 160, tell children to try each letter at the top to make a word with -*ay* or -*ail*. Remind them that not every letter will make a real word.

Reading Use *Save That Trash!* MCP Phonics and Reading Long Vowel Skills Library, Level A, to provide practice in reading words with long vowel *a*.

159

Name _____

Phonics & Reading — Read the story. Use long *a* words to finish the sentences.

Hooray For Ray!

It was the day of the big game.
Ray was at bat.
The ball came at him.
Ray gave the ball a big whack!
Ray raced around the bases.
He came to home plate.
"Safe!"
"Hooray for Ray!"

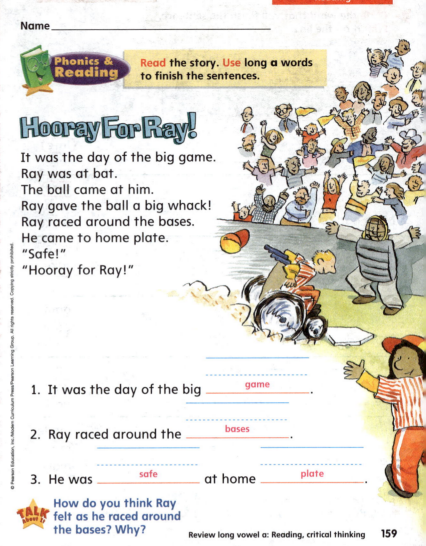

1. It was the day of the big ___**game**___.

2. Ray raced around the ___**bases**___.

3. He was ___**safe**___ at home ___**plate**___.

TALK About It How do you think Ray felt as he raced around the bases? Why?

Review long vowel a: Reading, critical thinking **159**

FOCUS ON ALL LEARNERS

ESL/ELL ENGLISH LANGUAGE LEARNERS

- As you and children read the story on page 159, have them list, name, or point to words with long *a*. Ask them to point to the two letters that make the long a sound (*a_e or ay*). Then, have them complete items 1 to 3.

- For page 160, read the directions aloud and ask children to explain in their own words what they are to do. Complete the first item together to verify understanding.

VISUAL/AUDITORY LEARNERS

Materials: index cards

Ask each child to find three long *a* words on pages 159–160 and write them on index cards. Have them place the cards face down on the table and take turns selecting a card, reading the word, and using it in a sentence.

AUDITORY/KINESTHETIC LEARNERS

Have children read the story on page 159 to partners. Have the partners raise their hands each time they hear a word that contains the sound of long *a*.

Phonics & Writing

Building Words

Use one of the letters to make a word with *ay* or *ail*. Write each real word on the lines.

d s p h v — ay
1. day
2. say
3. pay
4. hay

p m s y n — ail
5. pail
6. mail
7. sail
8. nail

▶ Write a sentence using one of the words you made.

HOME Help your child think of other long vowel *a* words, such as *race* and *grape*.

160 Review long vowel a: Phonograms

CURRICULUM CONNECTIONS

SPELLING
Dictate these spelling words and sentences and have children write the words as a spelling posttest.
1. **cane** That **cane** is made of wood.
2. **hay** Cows like to eat **hay**.
3. **lake** That **lake** is very deep.
4. **rain** The game stopped because of **rain**.
5. **tape** You can fix the rip with **tape**.
6. **vase** Dad filled the **vase** with water.

MATH
Say: *Ray's team scored 4 runs. Jane's team scored 1 run. How many more runs did Ray's team score?* Invite children to make up similar problems about the scores in different games.

FINE ARTS
Teach children the song "Take Me Out to the Ball Game." Have them raise a hand each time they hear a word that contains the sound of long *a*.

TECHNOLOGY
AstroWord Long Vowels: *a, i*

AUDITORY/KINESTHETIC LEARNERS *GROUPS*
Read the story on page 159 aloud to children. Have them pretend to swing at a baseball each time they hear a long *a* word.

CHALLENGE
Materials: tape or video recorder (optional)

Explain that TV sports programs often interview players after a big game. Working with a partner, have children plan an interview between Ray and a sports reporter. They can do the interview live or, if possible, tape record or videorecord it to share with the class.

EXTRA SUPPORT/INTERVENTION
Pair children with partners and have them read the story on page 159 aloud before they try to answer the questions. Before writing an answer, have them identify the sentence in the story that contains the information. See *Daily Phonics Practice, page 316.*

Integrating Phonics and Reading

Guided Reading
Show the cover as you read the title. Have children name the items they see and tell why someone might save them.

First Reading For each project, have children name the item that is saved and reused.

Second Reading Have children identify the long *a* words in the book. List them on the board or on the classroom Word Wall.

Comprehension
After reading, ask children the following questions:
- Which project did you like best? Why? *Reflective Analysis/Opinion*
- Why is it important to make less trash? *Inference/Cause and Effect*

ESL/ELL English Language Learners
Help children think of another way to say each of these words or phrases from the book: *trash, toss it out, make sure.*

160

Lesson 76 Pages 161–162

Take-Home Book

Review Long Vowel a

> **Skill Focus**
>
> Children will
> ★ read long *a* words in the context of a story.
> ★ review selected high-frequency words in the context of a story.
> ★ reread for fluency.

Teach

Build Background Remind children that the theme of this unit is "Let's Play." Ask them if they have ever put on face paint at a street fair or for a party, play, or other fun event. Encourage them to tell about the experience. What did the face paint look like? Who helped them put it on?

Phonemic Awareness: Phoneme Blending
Explain to children that you will say the parts of a word. Children should repeat the parts after you, orally blending the parts to make the word. Use these words, separating the sound of each phoneme, as in /p/ /ā/ /n/ /t/ (*paint*): *paint, race, made, say, plate, train, name, gate*. Explain that the sound heard in the middle of each word is long *a*.

Sound to Symbol Display the word cards for *make* (132), *paint* (133), and *shape* (251) on the chalkboard ledge. Then, write these word forms on the board: m_k_, p__nt, sh_p_. Pick a word card and ask a volunteer to read the word, then select letter cards *Aa*, *Ee*, or *Ii* to complete the word on the board. *Use letter cards*

Practice and Apply

Read the Book Help children tear out and fold the pages to make their Take-Home Books. Then, read the book together. Invite children to tell how the girl had fun.

Sound to Symbol Read aloud or have volunteers read the book. Have children identify the long *a* words (*make, face, paint, shapes, play*). Invite volunteers to write the words on the board and read them aloud.

Review High-Frequency Words Write the word *you* on the board. Have children spell the word, then say it, blending the sounds.

Reread for Fluency Have children reread the book to increase their fluency and comprehension. Children can take their books home to read and share with family members.

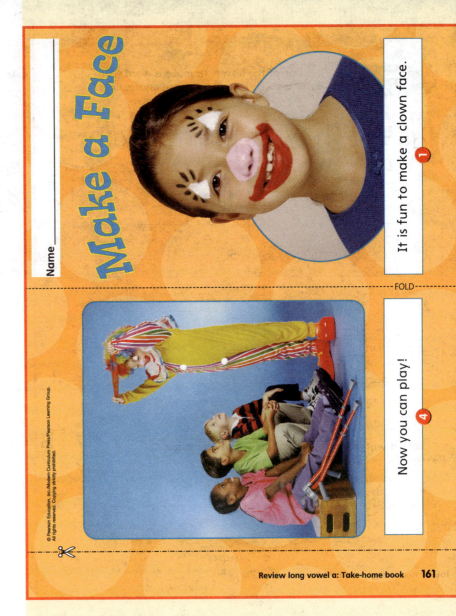

Review long vowel a: Take-home book 161

FOCUS ON ALL LEARNERS

ESL/ELL ENGLISH LANGUAGE LEARNERS
After assisting children with making the Take-Home Book, use the following activities to teach English language learners.

- Build background for the story by talking about where we can see clowns and what clowns do.
- Have children look through the story for words that contain the sound of long *a*. Keep a list on the board of the words they find.

VISUAL LEARNERS

Materials: large cutout of a clown face, index cards, masking tape

Attach the clown face to a bulletin board. Then, invite children to suggest words that have the sound of long *a*. Record the words on index cards. Attach the cards above the clown face.

KINESTHETIC LEARNERS

Materials: Phonics Picture Cards: apple (45), ax (46), hat (52), gate (89), nails (90), rake (91)

Hold up the picture cards one at a time at random and have children say the picture name softly to themselves. Have them pantomime the action of painting if the word has the long *a* sound.

161

2. You will need some face paint.

3. Start by making shapes.

162 Review long vowel a: Take-home book

CURRICULUM CONNECTIONS

ART/DRAMA
Materials: crayons, paper, craft sticks, glue or tape

Have children draw the funny faces they might make with face paint. Tell them to make their drawings about the same size as their own faces. Then, help them cut out the faces and attach them to the craft sticks to make masks. You might then invite groups of children to use their masks to put on a play about some funny clowns.

MATH
Materials: crayons, paper

Invite children to draw squares, triangles, circles, and other shapes they know. Then, help them label the shapes and assemble the drawings into a book.

WRITING
Work with children to brainstorm a list of words with a long *a* sound. Write the words on the board. Have children write and illustrate silly sentences using the words, such as *The ape in a cape skates.*

 **AstroWord** Long Vowels: *a, i*

AUDITORY/VISUAL LEARNERS
Materials: Take-Home Books

Pair children and have them take turns reading aloud each page of the story. Have the listening partner raise a hand each time he or she hears a word with the long *a* sound.

CHALLENGE
Challenge children to write and illustrate their own books called "Make a Face." Suggest that they show and write about happy faces, sad faces, and other kinds of facial expressions we can make.

EXTRA SUPPORT/INTERVENTION
Materials: Take-Home Books

Before asking children to read the story independently, read it aloud to them and have them follow along in their books. Then, pair children and have them alternate reading aloud each page. **See Daily Phonics Practice, page 316.**

Lesson 77   Pages 163–164

High-Frequency Words

Skill Focus

Children will

★ recognize and read the high-frequency words *they, where, out, two, were, your*.

★ use high-frequency words to complete sentences.

Teach

Analyze Words Write the words *they, where, out, two, were, your* on the board. Point to each word as you read it aloud. Have children repeat each word after you. Then:

- Have children use letter cards to spell each word. You may want to pair *where* and *were*, pointing out the different spellings and pronunciations.

- Slowly say each word as you point to the letters. Encourage children to listen for the consonant and vowel sounds in the word.

- Have children say each word, blending the sounds.

- Help children associate the sounds they hear in each word with a familiar word.

- You may wish to add the words to the class Word Wall so that children can use the words they learn to find similar spelling patterns and phonemic elements in new words.

Read Words in Sentences Write the following sentences on the board. Invite volunteers to read the sentences and underline the high-frequency words. Then, help children read the sentences.

- Where did the twins go?
- The two girls were not home.
- They just went out.
- They went to your house.

Practice and Apply

Write Words Have children turn to page 163. Read the directions aloud and make sure children understand what to do. Do the same for page 164. Encourage children to use the strategies they have learned to associate sounds with letters and blend words to help them read. Children can work with a partner to complete Checking Up.

Reading You may wish to use *Where Do They Live?* MCP Phonics and Reading Library, High Frequency Word Collection, Level A, to reinforce some of the high-frequency words.

163

High-Frequency Words

Name _____

▶ Read the words in the box. Write a word to finish each sentence.

They	Where
out	two
were	your

1. Kate and Jay ____**were**____ at the beach.

2. Dad took them ____**out**____ to play in the waves.

3. "I see ____**two**____ fish," said Kate.

4. "____**Where**____ are the fish?" Jay said.

5. Dad said, "They are by ____**your**____ feet."

6. ____**They**____ jumped in the waves all day.

High-frequency words   163

FOCUS ON ALL LEARNERS

ESL/ELL ENGLISH LANGUAGE LEARNERS

Materials: High-frequency word cards

English language learners may have difficulty pronouncing words with *r*-controlled vowels (*were, where, your*) or words with vowel pairs (*out*) and words with irregular spelling and pronunciation patterns (*they, two*).

To assess each English language learner's pronunciation of the high-frequency words:

- Hold up each word card.
- Say the word as you display it. Then, have children repeat it.
- Help children use the word in a sentence.

KINESTHETIC LEARNERS

Write each of the high-frequency words on an index card and tape the cards to the floor, leaving a few feet from one to the next. Have children pretend to swim from word to word, reading each word aloud as they reach it.

High-Frequency Words

▶ Look at the picture. Then, print words from the box to finish the story. The word shapes will help you.

> They   were   two
> out   Where your

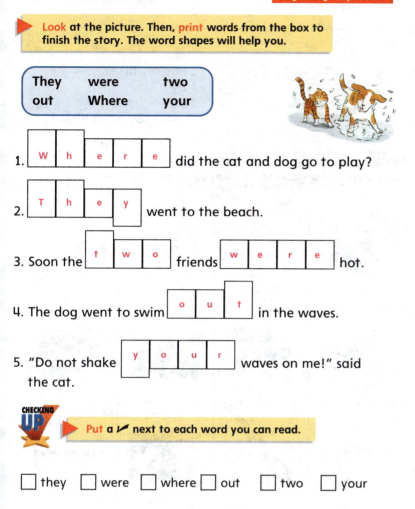

1. **W h e r e** did the cat and dog go to play?
2. **T h e y** went to the beach.
3. Soon the **t w o** friends **w e r e** hot.
4. The dog went to swim **o u t** in the waves.
5. "Do not shake **y o u r** waves on me!" said the cat.

CHECKING UP

▶ Put a ✔ next to each word you can read.

☐ they ☐ were ☐ where ☐ out ☐ two ☐ your

HOME Help your child retell the story, using some of the new words.

164 High-frequency words

CURRICULUM CONNECTIONS

ART/WRITING

Materials: fiction and nonfiction books featuring fish and other sea animals

Have each child choose a book to look at and read. Then, have children draw pictures and write sentences to tell what they liked about the books. Ask them to find and underline any high-frequency words they used.

SOCIAL STUDIES

Invite several volunteers who have visited seaside or lakeside beaches to come to the front of the room. Have the other children ask them questions about their experiences. Encourage both groups to use high-frequency words in their discussion.

VISUAL/AUDITORY LEARNERS

Write the following on the board:

A clock has ____ hands.	They
____ tell us the time.	Your
____ clock runs fast.	two
____ was Ed?	out
Why ____ Ned and Ted gone, too?	were
They went ____ for a walk.	Where

Read each incomplete sentence. Have a volunteer draw a line from the sentence to the word that will finish it, then read the completed sentence.

CHALLENGE

Challenge children to write questions and answers, using as many high-frequency words as possible. For example: *Where are your two hands? They are at the ends of your arms.*

EXTRA SUPPORT/INTERVENTION

Materials: high-frequency word cards

Say the high-frequency words aloud. Tell children to hold up the correct high-frequency word card as you say each word.

Integrating Phonics and Reading

Shared/Guided Reading
Show the cover as you read the title. Invite children to predict what they will learn about in the book.

First Reading Have children join in as you read each question that begins with *Where*.

Second Reading Encourage children to look for the words *where* and *they*.

Comprehension
After reading, ask children the following questions:
- How is the lion's home like the lamb's home? *Recall/Comparison*
- Which animal would you like to learn more about? Why? *Reflective Analysis/Opinion*

ESL/ELL English Language Learners
Look at page 8 and help children name the four different types of homes for people shown: farmhouse, townhouse, pueblo, and log cabin.

164

Lesson 78 Pages 165–166

Long Vowel i

Skill Focus

Children will

★ recognize the sound of long *i*.

★ identify picture names and words that contain the sound of long *i*.

★ identify rhyming long *i* words.

ESL/ELL Native speakers of Spanish may spell this vowel sound as *ai*. Practice with pairs of words like *rain, ride; tail, tire; fair, fire;* and so on.

Teach

Phonemic Awareness: Phoneme Categorization Hold up a dime and say the word *dime*. Have children repeat it with you several times. Explain that the vowel sound they hear in *dime* is long *i*. Then, say these groups of words. Have children name the two words in each group that have the long *i* sound. Use: *hide, lake, mine; pie, time, rake; cry, tame, line; pay, like, night; rail, bite, vine*.

Phonological Awareness: Rhyme Say *fine, line*. Point out that these words rhyme. Then, read aloud the sentences below. Ask children to tell you which two words in each sentence rhyme.

- She will ride at low tide. (*ride, tide*)
- I will get a white kite. (*white, kite*)
- Did you spill pie on your tie? (*pie, tie*)

Sound to Symbol Write the word *kite* on the board and read it aloud. Underline the *i* and *e*. Tell children that these letters stand for the long *i* sound in *kite*.

Practice and Apply

Phonemic Awareness Read aloud the rhyme on page 165. Have children listen for and name words with the long *i* sound. (*ride, bike, kite, hike, night*) You may want to explain that although *fly* sounds like a long *i* word, it is spelled with a *y*, not an *i*.

Sound to Symbol Help children identify the pictures on pages 165 and 166. Suggest that they say the picture names quietly to themselves as they complete each page.

Reading Use *Jim's Visit to Kim*, MCP Phonics and Reading Long Vowel Skills Library, Level A, to provide practice in reading words with long *i*.

165

Phonemic Awareness

Name _____

I ride my bike.
I fly a kite.
I take a hike.
Then, I say good night!

▶ **Ride** has the long sound of **i**. **Circle** each picture whose name has the long sound of **i**.

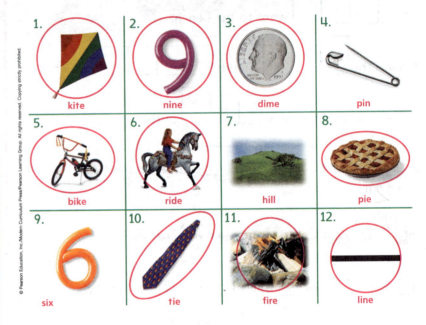

1. kite
2. nine
3. dime
4. pin
5. bike
6. ride
7. hill
8. pie
9. six
10. tie
11. fire
12. line

Long vowel i: Phonemic awareness **165**

FOCUS ON ALL LEARNERS

ESL/ELL ENGLISH LANGUAGE LEARNERS

- Before beginning page 165, display realia or pictures of a kite, a tie, a dime, a knife, and numerals 5 and 9. As you show each object, ask a volunteer to name it aloud, then print the word on the board.

- Read aloud the directions for page 166 and remind children that rhyming words sound alike except for the beginning sound. Then, ask a volunteer to name the pictures in item 1. Assist children in determining which picture names rhyme, and have them color the pictures. Have children work in pairs to complete items 2 to 6. Then review answers aloud.

VISUAL LEARNERS *INDIVIDUAL*

Materials: paper, crayons, discarded magazines, scissors, paste, fabric strips

Have children cut paper into kite shapes and decorate them with drawings or cutout pictures of objects whose names contain the sound of long *i*. Invite children to share the decorations on their kites.

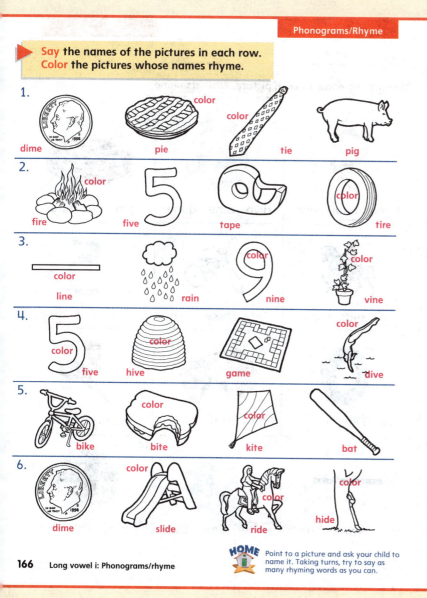

Phonograms/Rhyme

Say the names of the pictures in each row.
Color the pictures whose names rhyme.

166 Long vowel i: Phonograms/rhyme

CURRICULUM CONNECTIONS

SPELLING
Say each spelling word and then use it in a context sentence. Have children write each word as a spelling pretest.
1. **bike** I have a red **bike**.
2. **five** She has **five** dimes.
3. **kite** Will that **kite** fly?
4. **pie** Dad baked a **pie**.
5. **ride** We will go for a bike **ride**.
6. **tire** The **tire** on my bike is flat.

WRITING
Assign each child a partner. Explain that they will write an invitation asking their partner to fly kites. Discuss why an invitation should include the day, time, and place.

SOCIAL STUDIES
People around the world have flown kites for thousands of years. Have children hold their own kite festival by drawing or bringing in kites.

 **AstroWord** Long Vowels: *a, i*

Integrating Phonics and Reading

Guided Reading
Show the cover as you read the title. Ask children to tell what Jim would like to do during his visit.
First Reading Encourage children to talk about what is happening in each picture.
Second Reading Ask children to identify the long *i* words in the story. You might want to add these to the classroom Word Wall.
Comprehension
After reading, ask children the following questions:
- What did Jim want to do when he visited Kim? *Recall/Details*
- Did the story turn out the way you expected? *Reflective Analysis/Plot*

ESL/ELL English Language Learners
Point out the words *sometimes* and *someday* and talk about their meanings. Then, have students think of different ways to finish these sentences: *Sometimes I like to ____. Someday I will ____.*

AUDITORY/KINESTHETIC LEARNERS
Say the following word pairs: *kite, bike; cake, light; my, pie; cat, fine; sight, mate; tie, ripe; nail, nine*. Have children stand if the vowel sounds in both words are the same and remain seated if they are not.

CHALLENGE
Ask children to look at the pictures they did not color on page 166. Have them name the pictures that contain the long *i* sound. Challenge them to name as many long *i* words with the *i_consonant_e* pattern as they can.

EXTRA SUPPORT/INTERVENTION
To simplify the task on page 166, divide it into steps. Help children name the pictures in each row and circle those that contain the long *i* sound. Then, have them say the circled picture names aloud, listening for words that rhyme. **See Daily Phonics Practice, page 317.**

Lesson 79   Pages 167–168

Long Vowel i

Skill Focus

Children will

★ recognize the sound of long *i*.

★ understand that *ie* and *i_consonant_e* can spell long *i*.

★ identify pictures whose names contain the sound of long *i*.

★ apply what they have learned by reading and writing.

Teach

Phonological Awareness: Blending Onsets and Rimes Tell children that you will say the parts of a word. Children should repeat the parts after you and then blend them together to say the word. Use these words: /r/ide, /t/ie, /l/ight, /h/ive. Ask children what they notice about all the words. Help them conclude that they all contain the long *i* sound.

Sound to Symbol Draw a pine tree and a pie on the chalkboard. Label each picture and say the word. Ask children what vowel sound is heard in each word. Then, ask them to underline the vowels in each word with colored chalk. Explain that in some words the long *i* can be spelled *ie*, and in other words long *i* can be spelled *i_consonant_e*. The *e* is silent. Next, write the words *ride* and *tie* on the board and ask children to tell what vowel sound they hear in each word, then underline the vowels that make the sound.

Practice and Apply

Sound to Symbol As children complete page 167, encourage them to say each picture name quietly to themselves and listen for the beginning, middle, and ending sounds.

For page 168, read the directions with children. Make sure they understand how to complete the crossword puzzle. You might want to complete some of the items together.

Writing Note the long *i* words that children write on page 168 and check for correct spelling.

Reading Use *Six Fine Fish*, MCP Phonics and Reading Long Vowel Skills Library, Level A, to provide practice in reading words with long *i*.

Sound to Symbol

Name _____

▶ **Say** the name of each picture. **Circle** its name.

1.	2.	3.
mine (nine) vine	dive dine (dime)	pin (pie) pine
4.	5.	6.
(ride) hide ripe	bite (bike) kite	fine fire (five)
7.	8.	9.
tie ride (tire)	(bite) tide bike	like (kite) tile
10.	11.	12.
vine wine (line)	(dive) dime five	(hide) ride hit

Long vowel i: Sound to symbol   167

FOCUS ON ALL LEARNERS

ESL/ELL ENGLISH LANGUAGE LEARNERS

• Before beginning page 167, review with children that in some words the long *i* can be spelled *ie*, and in other words long *i* can be spelled *i_consonant_e*. Write *kite, dive, nine* on the board and say each word aloud. Work with children to circle the vowel they hear (long *i*) and the vowel that is silent (*e*). Then, ask children to underline the initial and final consonants. Repeat with *pie, tie, lie*.

• Adapt the crossword activity on page 168 by having children name the pictures for items 1 to 8, write each picture name, then use one of the words in a sentence.

KINESTHETIC LEARNERS

Materials: letter cards: *Ii, Ee, Pp, Ff, Vv, Dd, Mm*

Have children form "living words" from page 167 by standing and holding their cards for others in the group to read. Children will be able to form these words: *dime, pie, five, dive*.

▶ **Read** the words in the box. **Print** a word in the puzzle to name each picture.

tie	bike	ride	ice
kite	mice	pie	dime

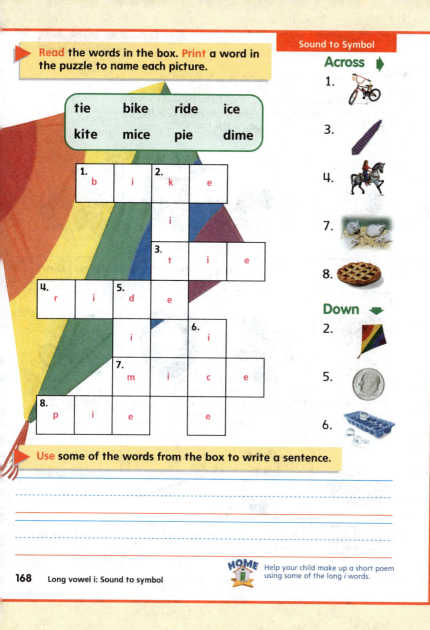

Sound to Symbol

Across ➡

1. [bike]
3. [tie]
4. [horse ride]
7. [mice]
8. [pie]

Down ⬇

2. [kite]
5. [dime]
6. [ice]

▶ **Use** some of the words from the box to write a sentence.

 Help your child make up a short poem using some of the long *i* words.

168 Long vowel i: Sound to symbol

CURRICULUM CONNECTIONS

SPELLING
Materials: spelling master (page 145l), crayons

Have children make word cards using the spelling master list. On the other side of the cards have them draw a picture to illustrate each word.

WRITING

Working with a partner, have children write a riddle for a word that contains the long *i* sound.

MATH
Materials: play dimes and pennies

Elicit from children that a dime is equal to ten pennies. Write these problems on the board and help children read them.

1. five dimes = _____ pennies
2. nine dimes = _____ pennies

Working with partners, have children use play money or other manipulatives to help them calculate each answer.

 **AstroWord** Long Vowels: *a, i*

Integrating Phonics and Reading

Guided Reading
Show children the cover illustration and read the title. Ask whether they think the book will tell facts or a made-up story.

First Reading Point out the labels on pages 5, 7, 9, 11, 13, and 15. Make sure children understand that these are kinds of real fish.

Second Reading Have children identify the long *i* words in the book. List the words on the board or add them to the classroom Word Wall.

Comprehension
After reading, ask children the following questions:
- Did you learn anything that surprised you? What was it? *Reflective Analysis/Details*
- Which fish would you like to learn more about? Why? *Reflective Analysis/Opinion*

ESL/ELL **English Language Learners**
Check comprehension of vocabulary from the book by having children draw: a fish with *stripes*, a fish with *spikes*, and a fish with *sharp teeth*.

AUDITORY LEARNERS
Materials: masking tape or chalk

Draw a line and have children stand along it. Then, read these words and have children "take a hike" by taking one step forward if the word contains the sound of long *i*: bike, game, made, mine, nine, pie, pin, dug, vine, wipe, tire, lie, pump, can, aid, pile, pine, pain.

CHALLENGE
Focus attention on the words in each box on page 167. Challenge children to work with a partner to use two of the three words in each box in an oral sentence.

EXTRA SUPPORT/INTERVENTION
Assign children partners and have them read aloud the words in each box on page 167. Before circling the word that names the picture, have children cross out any word that does not contain the sound of long *i*. See Daily Phonics Practice, page 317.

Lesson 80   Pages 169–170

Long and Short Vowel i

Skill Focus

Children will

★ distinguish between long *i* and short *i* picture names.

★ identify words that contain the sound of long *i*.

Teach

Phonological Awareness: Rhyme Read the following groups of words and have children repeat the two words in each group that rhyme. Then, have them identify the vowel sound in the rhyming words as long *i* or short *i*.

- bike   hide   hike
- hill   mint   fill
- pie   tie   pine
- like   lime   time
- side   ride   ripe
- spin   trip   sip

Sound to Symbol Draw a safety pin (see page 169, item 11) and a pine tree on the board. After children identify each object, label them. Discuss how the words are alike and different. Then, have a volunteer circle the vowels in each word with colored chalk. Next, write the following words on the board. Help children read each word and circle the vowels. Discuss how the *e* at the end of the words changes the vowel sound.

- rip, ripe
- hid, hide
- fin, fine
- dim, dime

Practice and Apply

Sound to Symbol Help children identify the pictures on pages 169 and 170. Suggest that they say each picture name quietly to themselves and listen for a long or short vowel sound as they do each activity. After they have completed the pages, review that in some words the long *i* can be spelled *ie*, and in other words long *i* can be spelled *i_consonant_e*.

Reading Use *Dinner by Five*, MCP Phonics and Reading Long Vowel Skills Library, Level A, to provide practice in reading words with long *i*.

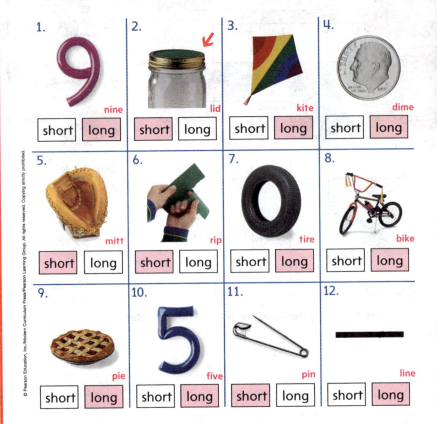

Phonemic Awareness

Name _____

Say the name of each picture. If the vowel sound is short, color the box with the word short. If the vowel sound is long, color the box with the word long.

Long and short vowel i: Phonemic awareness   169

FOCUS ON ALL LEARNERS

ESL/ELL ENGLISH LANGUAGE LEARNERS

- Before beginning page 169, practice aural discrimination of long *i* versus short *i* by saying pairs of words such as *kite*, *time* and *pin*, *right*. Have children say whether the vowel sounds are the same or different.

- Prepare for the sound-to-symbol activity on page 170 by writing long *a* and long *i* words such as *cape*, *rain*, *bite*, and *dive* on the board. Work with children to circle the vowel they hear and the vowel they do not hear. Then, ask children to underline the initial and final consonants. Repeat with short *i* words such as *pin*, *rip*, *lid*, asking children to circle the vowel and underline the initial and final consonants.

VISUAL LEARNERS

Materials: Phonics Picture Cards for short and long *i* (57–60, 98–101)

Place the picture cards so they are partially visible in different spots around the room. Then, play "I Spy" by giving clues about the picture cards and having volunteers find and name them.

169

Sound to Symbol

▶ **Say** the name of each picture. **Circle** its name.

1. rid (ride)
2. kit (kite)
3. (pin) pine
4. cap (cape)
5. dim (dime)
6. (rip) ripe
7. (lid) lied
8. ran (rain)
9. (fin) fine
10. bit (bite)
11. (Tim) time
12. slid (slide)

170 Long and short vowels a, i: Sound to symbol

HOME With your child, make up sentences using the short and long vowel words, such as *The shark's fin is fine.*

CURRICULUM CONNECTIONS

SPELLING
Materials: spelling cards made in Lesson 79, pages 167–168

Working with a partner, have children sort the words into two piles based on the spelling of the long *i* sound.

WRITING
Materials: drawing paper, crayons

Draw a smiling face on the board and label it with the word *smile*. Help children read the word. Then, have children draw pictures showing something that makes them smile.

PORTFOLIO

SOCIAL STUDIES
Materials: rice; rice cakes or crackers

Display some rice and have children identify it. Talk with children about rice dishes that they enjoy eating and list them on the board. Have cakes or crackers for children to taste. Encourage children to describe the flavors of each rice treat and take a class vote to see which is most popular.

TECHNOLOGY **AstroWord** Long Vowels: *a, i*

Integrating Phonics and Reading

Shared/Guided Reading
Show children the cover and read the title. Ask what they think the children will have for dinner.
First Reading As you read, alternate saying the lines of dialogue on pages 7, 9, and 13 with children.
Second Reading Have children identify the long *i* and short *i* words in the story. List both groups of words on the board or Word Wall.
Comprehension
After reading, ask children the following questions:
• What do Mike and Kim want to do by five? *Recall/Plot*
• What might have happened if they didn't clean up the mess? *Inference/Cause and Effect*
ESL/ELL English Language Learners
Write: *Mom likes pizza. I liked that. Mom will like this dinner.* Explain that the endings *-s, -ed* and the word *will* can change what a sentence tells us about when something happened.

AUDITORY LEARNERS   **GROUPS**
Materials: tape player, tape of marching music

Play some marching music. Then, point to each child and have him or her say a word that contains the sound of long *i* to join the line of marchers.

CHALLENGE
Introduce the concept of action words as words that tell what people or things do. Brainstorm a list of long *i* action words, for example *drive, dive, slide, hide, ride, bite, smile*. Have children write and illustrate each word to make a long *i* action word book.

EXTRA SUPPORT/INTERVENTION
Materials: Phonics Picture Cards 54–60, 93–102; two large envelopes; markers; masking tape

Label one envelope *short i words* and the other *long i words*. Tape each envelope to the board. Have children select a card, say the picture name, and deposit the picture in the appropriate envelope. **See Daily Phonics Practice, page 317.**

Lesson 81 Pages 171–172

Long Vowel i

Skill Focus

Children will

★ recognize the sound of long and short *i*.

★ identify and spell picture names that contain the sound of long and short *i*.

★ write words that contain the sound of long *i* to complete sentences.

★ recognize and read high-frequency words.

Teach

Phonemic Awareness: Phoneme Blending
Say the word *lime*, separating the sound of each phoneme: /l/ /ī/ /m/. Ask children what vowel sound they hear in the middle. (long *i*) Then, have them say the whole word, stretching the long *i* sound. Repeat, using *fine, life, mile, bite*.

Sound to Symbol Draw a first-aid kit and a kite on the board. Label the pictures and have children say *kit, kite*. Also have them identify the vowel sound in each word. Work with children to circle the vowel they hear (short *i* in *kit*, long *i* in *kite*). Then, cover and uncover the *e* at the end of *kite*. Discuss how the addition of this letter changes the vowel sound. Repeat with pictures of a fir tree (a pine cone shape) and fire, and the words *fir, fire*.

Practice and Apply

Blend Phonemes As children complete page 171, encourage them to say each picture name, blending together the beginning, middle, and ending sounds.

Writing For page 172, suggest that children try each word choice before writing a word. As they complete the activity, they will have the opportunity to read the high-frequency word *first*.

Critical Thinking For Talk About It, children might reach several conclusions. They might say that Jim liked riding on a carousel or that he did not have enough money to buy a kite or a pie.

Reading Use *The Bike That Spike Likes*, MCP Phonics and Reading Long Vowel Skills Library, Level A, to provide practice in reading words with long and short *i*.

Spelling

Name _____

▶ **Say** the name of each picture. **Print** the missing vowels on the line. **Trace** the whole word.

1. r_i_d_e_   2. p_i_g   3. d_i_m_e_   4. f_i_r_e_

5. l_i_n_e_   6. h_i_v_e_   7. l_i_d   8. k_i_t_e_

9. f_i_v_e_   10. b_i_k_e_   11. d_i_v_e_   12. s_i_x

Long and short vowel i: Spelling   **171**

FOCUS ON ALL LEARNERS

ESL/ELL ENGLISH LANGUAGE LEARNERS

- Review the picture names on page 171. Then, help children identify the beginning, middle, and ending sound in each word.
- Read the word choices on page 172 with children. Before children complete the page, help them use each word in context in an oral sentence.

VISUAL LEARNERS

Lead children on a "long *i* hike" around the school and its grounds. Make a list of the items you find. These might include fire alarms, bike racks, car tires, telephone wires, floor tiles, and file cabinets.

KINESTHETIC LEARNERS

Materials: chart paper, marker, beanbag

Draw a large pie on a piece of chart paper and divide it into 12 sections. In each section write one of these words: *bite, dime, dive, fire, tie, lie, like, lime, line, mile, pile, pipe*. Have children take turns tossing the beanbag and reading the word on which it lands.

171

Words in Context

► Look at the picture. Circle the word that will finish the sentence. Print it on the line.

1. Jim has ___five___ dimes.
   fine / file / (five)

2. He will not get a ___kite___.
   (kite) / bite / bake

3. He will not get a ___pie___.
   lie / (pie) / pile

4. **First**, Jim waits in ___line___.
   like / lied / (line)

5. He has fun on the ___ride___.
   rise / ripe / (ride)

6. He rides home on his ___bike___.
   take / (bike) / bite

TALK Why do you think Jim chose the ride?

HOME Help your child think of sentences using words from the page to continue the story.

172 Long vowel i: High-frequency words, critical thinking

CURRICULUM CONNECTIONS

SPELLING
Have children write their spelling words, leaving a blank for each vowel. Then, have them exchange lists with a partner and fill in the missing vowels. After completing each word, have them write the whole word.

WRITING
Have children reread the story on page 172. Then, ask them to pretend that they went on a trip to an amusement park, as Jim did. Have them write about the fun they had. Invite them to read their work aloud.

PORTFOLIO

MATH
Materials: play money, discarded magazines, scissors, self-stick notes

Have children cut out pictures of items whose names contain the sound of long *i* and use them to stock the shelves in a "long *i* store." Children can price each pictured object by writing its cost on a self-stick note and attaching it to the item. Once the store is set up, some children can take the role of cashiers while others act as customers.

AUDITORY LEARNERS **GROUPS**
Say these silly sentences with an incorrect long *i* word: *I ate a slice of apple pipe.* (pie) *Those green bananas are not ride.* (ripe) *We went for a five mile hide.* (hike) Using the context of the sentence, have children supply the correct long *i* word.

CHALLENGE
Working with a partner, have children write sentences telling what else Jim might do with his five dimes. Have them read the sentences and underline any words that contain the sound of long *i*.

EXTRA SUPPORT/INTERVENTION
Assign each child a partner and have them read aloud each sentence and the word choices on page 172. After writing their word choice on each line, have children take turns reading aloud each completed sentence. **See Daily Phonics Practice, page 317.**

Integrating Phonics and Reading

Shared/Guided Reading
Show the cover as you read the title. Ask children to tell where Spike is and what he is looking at.

First Reading Invite children to join in each time they see the words *the bike that Spike likes*.

Second Reading Have children identify the long and short *i* words in the story. List the words on the board in two columns.

Comprehension
After reading, ask children the following questions:
- What happened before the bike got to the store? *Recall/Sequencing*
- Who are the people who buy the bike at the end of the story? *Inference/Character*

ESL/ELL English Language Learners
Ask children to point out the pictures of the people who are named in the text. Have them tell what the people are doing.

The Bike That Spike Likes

172

Lesson 82 Pages 173–174

Long Vowel i

Skill Focus

Children will

★ recognize the sound of long *i*.

★ identify and spell picture names that contain the sound of long *i*.

★ write words that contain the sound of long *i* to complete sentences.

★ recognize and read high-frequency words.

Teach

Phonemic Awareness: Phoneme Substitution Remind children that sometimes they can make a new word by changing the first letter of a word. For example, if they change the first letter in *dime* to *t*, they will make the word *time*. Then, give the following directions and have children say each new word.

- Change the first letter in *hive* to *d*. (*dive*)
- Change the first letter in *tie* to *p*. (*pie*)
- Change the first letter in *night* to *l*. (*light*)

Ask children to identify the long vowel sound heard in all the words.

Sound to Symbol On the board, draw a curvy path with a large sign that says *bike path*. Ask a volunteer to read the sign aloud. Next, invite children to think of things containing the long *i* sound that they might see while on a bike ride. Have them draw and label items such as a bee hive, a pine tree, and a vine. Conclude by having children read aloud the long *i* words on the board and underline the vowels.

Practice and Apply

Blend Phonemes As children complete page 173, encourage them to say each picture name, blending together the beginning, middle, and ending sounds.

Writing For page 174, suggest that children try each word choice before writing a word. As they complete the activity, they will have the opportunity to read the high-frequency word *long*.

Critical Thinking For Talk About It, help children recall times when they won at a game or sport. Help them conclude that Mike would share the same feelings.

Reading Use *Dive In!* MCP Phonics and Reading Long Vowel Skills Library, Level A, to provide practice in reading words with long and short *i*.

FOCUS ON ALL LEARNERS

ESL/ELL ENGLISH LANGUAGE LEARNERS

- Help children identify each picture on page 173 by asking such questions as "What toy is that?" and "What number is that?"
- Work through page 174 with children. Read the first sentence together with each of the word choices. Then, have the children circle the word that will finish the sentence. Continue with items 2 through 6. Then, read the completed story together.

VISUAL LEARNERS

Materials: Phonics Word Cards: *bike* (143), *fine* (144), *hide* (146), *hike* (147), *kite* (148), *life* (149), *mine* (150), *pie* (152), *side* (154), *time* (155), *vine* (156), *tire* (157); masking tape

Draw a large clock face on the board. Cover each numeral with a word card. Have a child come up, read a word, and remove the card to reveal the numeral.

KINESTHETIC LEARNERS

Materials: mural paper, marker

Draw a vine on paper. In each large leaf, have children write a word that contains the sound of long *i*.

Words in Context

Circle the word that will finish the sentence. Print it on the line.

1. Mike likes his __bike__.
   bite
   (bike)
   bake

2. It has a nine on the __side__.
   (side)
   sale
   sand

3. It is the same size as __mine__.
   miss
   (mine)
   mitt

4. Mike will __ride__ it in the race.
   (ride)
   ripe
   rake

5. The race is six __miles__ long!
   miss
   mills
   (miles)

6. Last time it ended in a __tie__.
   (tie)
   tide
   tip

TALK About It How does it feel when you win a race?

HOME Help your child make up a sentence that uses any two circled words, then draw a picture that goes with it.

174 Long vowel i: High-frequency words, critical thinking

CURRICULUM CONNECTIONS

SPELLING
Materials: spelling cards made in Lesson 79, pages 167–168

Working with a partner, have children take turns displaying the picture side of each spelling card. Have their partners write the spelling word. Children can check this spelling by comparing it with the word written on the back of the card.

WRITING
Draw a trophy on the board and write the word *prize* under it. Help children read the word and explain that a trophy like this is often given as a prize. Ask children to design their own trophy and write about how they might win the prize.

SOCIAL STUDIES
Discuss bike safety with children. Elicit opinions on where and when children think it is safe to ride. Explore the importance of wearing a bike helmet at all times. Then, have children dictate a list of safety rules.

TECHNOLOGY **AstroWord** Long Vowels: *a, i*

Integrating Phonics and Reading

Shared/Guided Reading
Show the cover as you read the title. Ask children to tell where the children are and what they will do.
First Reading Invite half the class to read Rosa's words and half to read Mike's words as you narrate.
Second Reading Have children identify the long and short *i* words in the story. Add the words to your Word Wall.
Comprehension
After reading, ask children these questions:
• Why did Mike sit and watch while Rosa went sledding and riding? *Inference/Character*
• Were you glad when Rosa tried to get Mike to dive in? *Reflective Analysis/Judgments*
ESL/ELL English Language Learners
Explain that *slid* is the past-tense form of *slide*. Then, help children name the past-tense forms of these story words: *sit, watch, come, ride*. Remind children that to form the past tense of most words we add *-ed*, but we change some words to the past tense in other ways.

AUDITORY LEARNERS **GROUPS**
Have each child fold a sheet of writing paper in half. Label one column *long i words* and the other column *short i words*. Dictate these words and have children write each in the correct column: *dim, dime, kit, kite, fine, fin, rip, ripe, pine, pin, bite, bit*.

CHALLENGE
Using the following example, show children how to construct a word chain by changing one letter in a word to write a new word: *bike, like, line, fine*. Using words from page 173, challenge children to create their own word chains.

EXTRA SUPPORT/INTERVENTION
Encourage children who have difficulty spelling the picture names on page 173 to begin by writing the consonant sounds they hear. Give help as needed in writing the vowel sounds. **See Daily Phonics Practice, page 317.**

Lesson 83   Pages 175–176

Phonics and Reading / Phonics and Writing

Long Vowel i

Skill Focus

Children will

★ read words that contain the sound of long *i*.

★ write long *i* words to finish sentences.

★ build words with long *i* phonograms -*ide*, -*ine*.

ESL/ELL In many languages, such as Spanish and Khmer, each letter or symbol stands for one sound. Children may need support with pronouncing and spelling long versus short vowel sounds.

Teach

Phonemic Awareness: Medial Sound Isolation

Materials: Phonics Picture Cards for bike (93), hive (96), kite (98), nine (99)

Show the picture card for *bike* and have children identify it. Say the word, then /ī/. Tell children you are saying the word and then its vowel sound. Remind children that this is the sound of long *i*. Then, have children say these words and follow each one with its vowel sound: *hive*, *kite*, *tie*, *right*, and *nine*.

Read Words in Sentences Write these sentences on the board.

- Ray rides his bike.
- Kim runs with her kite.
- Mike likes to eat apple pie.

Help children read the sentences. Then, ask them to circle the words that have the long *i* sound.

Practice and Apply

Phonics and Reading After children have read the story, encourage them to identify words that have the long *i* sound.

Critical Thinking For Talk About It, encourage children to think about animals and machines that fly.

Phonics and Writing For page 176, tell children to try each letter at the top to make a word with -*ide* or -*ine*. Remind them that not every letter will make a real word.

Reading Use *Flip's Trick*, MCP Phonics and Reading Long Vowel Skills Library, Level A, to provide practice in reading words with long vowel *i*.

175

Name _____

 **Phonics & Reading**

Read the story. **Use** long *i* words to finish the sentences.

Flying a Kite

Children in many places like to fly kites.
In Japan, children fly kites on New Year's day.
The kites can come in many shapes and sizes.
Children tie on a string.
The kites dive and glide.
Hold on to the line!

1. Children in many places like to fly __**kites**__.

2. Children __**tie**__ on a string.

3. The kites __**dive**__ and glide.

TALK About It Can you think of more shapes and sizes for kites?

Review long vowel i: Reading   **175**

FOCUS ON ALL LEARNERS

ESL/ELL ENGLISH LANGUAGE LEARNERS

- As children read the story on page 175, have them find and identify words with long *i*. Ask them to point to the vowels in the words as well as the beginning and ending consonant sounds. Then, have them complete comprehension items 1 to 3.

- Read the directions for page 176 with children. Check comprehension by having volunteers use their own words to tell what they are to do.

VISUAL/AUDITORY LEARNERS

Materials: construction paper, marker, scissors

Cut out two kites. Label one *long a* and the other *long i*. Have children list words that contain the long *a* and the long *i* vowel sounds. As they dictate these words, record them on the corresponding kite. Then, ask volunteers to read them aloud.

KINESTHETIC/AUDITORY LEARNERS

Say these words and have children make their hands sail like a kite when they hear a word that contains the long *i* sound: *bike, game, dive, hike, mine, save, tail, line, wipe, tire, came, late, gate, lie, fire, pie, nail, vine.*

Phonics & Writing

Building Words

Use one of the letters to make a word with **ide** or **ine**. Write each real word on the lines.

r s w h y   n m b f l

___ide   ___ine

1. ride   5. nine
2. side   6. mine
3. wide   7. fine
4. hide   8. line

▶ Write a sentence using one of the words you made.

_____
_____
_____

HOME Help your child make up a sentence using as many long vowel *i* words as you can.

176 Review long vowel i: Phonograms

CURRICULUM CONNECTIONS

SPELLING
Dictate these spelling words and sentences and have children write the words as a spelling posttest.
1. **bike** I can ride a **bike**.
2. **five** There are **five** people in his family.
3. **kite** Can you fly a **kite**?
4. **pie** Kate loves cherry **pie**.
5. **ride** Tim will **ride** a horse.
6. **tire** Mom's car had a flat **tire**.

HEALTH
Tell children that people often have to run to get the kite to fly. Mention that running is good exercise. Then, ask children to suggest other ways to exercise when they are indoors.

SOCIAL STUDIES
Materials: globe or world map

Have children find the name of the country mentioned in the story on page 175. Then, using a globe or a world map, help them locate Japan.

TECHNOLOGY **AstroWord** Long Vowels: *a, i*

AUDITORY LEARNERS
Have children write long *i* words to answer these oral questions: *What can fly at the end of a string?* (kite) *A kite string is called this.* (line) *This kind of tall evergreen tree can wreck a kite.* (pine)

CHALLENGE
Materials: slips of paper, pencils

Have children write all the long *i* words found in the story on page 175, on separate slips of paper. Then, have them sort the words into piles based on the spelling of the vowel sound. Challenge them to write another word to add to each pile.

EXTRA SUPPORT/INTERVENTION
Read the story aloud and have children track the text with a finger to follow along. Then, help children read the sentences aloud and have them identify the word they will use to complete the sentence before writing it. See Daily Phonics Practice, page 317.

Integrating Phonics and Reading

Guided Reading
Show the cover as you read the title. Have children tell who they think Flip is and what kind of trick he might do.

First Reading For each page, have children look at the picture and describe what Flip is doing.

Second Reading Have children identify the long *i* words in the book. List them on the board or on the classroom Word Wall.

Comprehension
After reading, ask children the following questions:
• Is Flip good at sitting and jumping? Why or why not? *Inference/Character*
• Did the story turn out the way you expected? *Reflective Analysis/Plot*

ESL/ELL English Language Learners
Write the following on the board: *Come! Sit! Stay!* Explain that these are the most basic commands used in dog training. Have pairs of children act out each command.

Lesson 84 Pages 177–178

Take-Home Book

Review Long Vowels a and i

Skill Focus

Children will

★ read long *a* and long *i* words in the context of a story.

★ review selected high-frequency words in the context of a story.

★ reread for fluency.

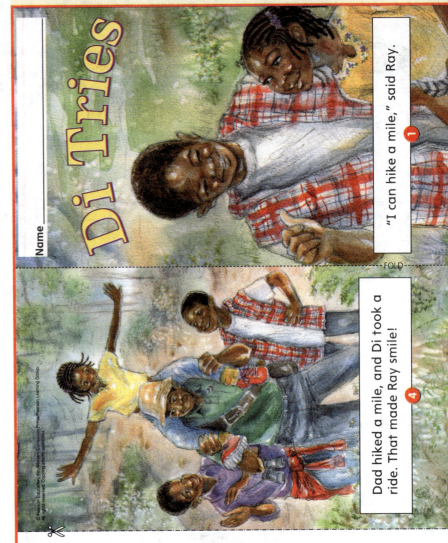

Review long vowels a, i: Take-home book

Teach

Build Background Remind children that the theme of this unit is "Let's Play." Ask them to listen to these tips for a certain outdoor activity and then try to guess what it is.

- Wear comfortable boots or shoes.
- Bring a map and a compass.
- Stay on the trail.

After children have guessed the answer, invite them to share any hiking experiences they have had.

Phonemic Awareness: Phoneme Blending Say the word *hike*, separating the sound of each phoneme: /h/ /ī/ /k/. Ask children to identify the vowel sound they hear. Next, say a series of words. Tell children to tap their feet each time they hear a word that has the long *i* sound. Use: *five, paint, race, high, pie, wait, white, ride, mice, tie.*

Practice and Apply

Read the Book Help children tear out and fold the pages to make their Take-Home Books. Then, read the book together. Invite children to tell what Di tried to do and what she ended up doing.

Sound to Symbol Read aloud or have volunteers read the book. Have children identify the long *a* and long *i* words. (*Ray, may, make, way; I, hike, mile, Di, fine, ride, smile*) You may want to point out that though *try* sounds like a long *i* word, it is not spelled with an *i*. Invite volunteers to write the words on the board and read them aloud.

Review High-Frequency Words Write the words *I, said,* and *you* on the board. Have children spell the words, then say them.

Reread for Fluency Have children reread the book to increase their fluency and comprehension. Children can take their books home to read and share with family members.

FOCUS ON ALL LEARNERS

ESL/ELL ENGLISH LANGUAGE LEARNERS

- Read the story together. Discuss what Di means when she says, "Make way!" Explain that she means "Step aside so that I can get through."
- Have children look at the illustrations. Ask them to tell what is happening in each one. Call attention to each character's facial expression and talk about how he or she feels.

VISUAL/AUDITORY LEARNERS

Materials: hiking boot cutouts

Give children hiking boot cutouts and have them write words that contain the long *i* sound on the boots.

KINESTHETIC LEARNERS

Materials: Phonics Word Cards, Set 1: long *a, i* (136–142, 151–157); backpack

Put the word cards in the backpack and have children take turns drawing a card, reading the word, and placing it into a long *a* or long *i* pile.

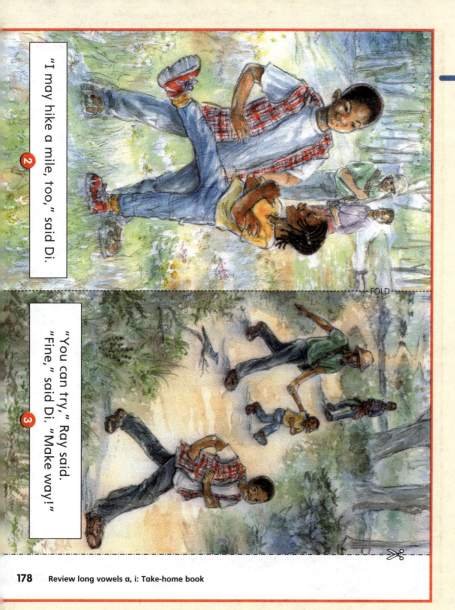

"I may hike a mile, too," said Di.

"You can try," Ray said. "Fine," said Di. "Make way!"

178 Review long vowels a, i: Take-home book

CURRICULUM CONNECTIONS

SCIENCE
Materials: chart paper, marker, mural paper, crayons

Talk with children about the living things Di and her family might see while hiking in a park or in the woods. Record children's ideas on chart paper. Then, have them draw a mural showing plant and animal life along a hiking trail. Encourage them to label the living things in the mural.

HEALTH
Materials: crayons, drawing paper

Lead children in a discussion of why hiking is good exercise. Discuss the importance of getting physical exercise at least three times a week. Have children name other activities that are considered good exercise. Have them draw pictures showing themselves engaged in these activities. Suggest that they write sentences to go with their pictures.

WRITING
Materials: crayons, drawing paper

Have children draw a place where they would like to go hiking. Then, have them write a description of the place. Suggest that they tell where it is, how it looks, and what is special about it.

 **AstroWord** Long Vowels: *a, i*

AUDITORY/KINESTHETIC LEARNERS
Materials: Take-Home Books

Read aloud sentences from the story, omitting a long *i* or long *a* word, for example, *That made Ray _____.* Ask children to supply the missing word. Then, have them check their responses against the story text.

CHALLENGE
Have children write sentences telling what they think Ray and Di might say after the hike. Challenge them to use at least one long *a* and one long *i* word in the writing.

EXTRA SUPPORT/INTERVENTION
Materials: Take-Home Books, tape recorder, audiotape

Record the story. Before children try to read the story independently, suggest that they listen to the tape as they follow along in their books.

See Daily Phonics Practice, pages 316–317.

178

Lesson 85   Pages 179–180

High-Frequency Words

Skill Focus

Children will

★ recognize and write the high-frequency words *long, there, why, little, could, about*.

★ use high-frequency words to complete sentences.

Teach

Analyze Words Write the words *long, there, why, could, little, about* on the board. Point to each word as you read it aloud. Have children repeat each word after you. Then:

- Have children use letter cards to spell each word.
- Slowly say each word as you point to the letters. Encourage children to listen for the consonant and vowel sounds.
- Have children say each word, blending the sounds.
- Help children associate the sounds they hear in each word with a familiar word.
- You may wish to add the words to the class Word Wall so that children can use the words they learn to find similar spelling patterns and phonemic elements in new words.

Read Words in Sentences Write the following sentences on the board. Invite volunteers to read the sentences and underline the high-frequency words. Then, help children read the sentences.

- Kate asked if we could play outside.
- We said we could not stay there long.
- We could play for about ten minutes.
- Kate asked us why.
- We said we had just a little time before lunch.

Practice and Apply

Write Words Have children turn to page 179. Read the directions aloud and make sure children understand what to do. Do the same for page 180. Encourage children to use the strategies they have learned to associate sounds with letters and blend words to help them read. Children can work with a partner to complete Checking Up.

Reading You may wish to use *Three Little Kittens*, MCP Phonics and Reading Library, High Frequency Word Collection, Level A, to reinforce some of the high-frequency words.

High-Frequency Words

Name _____

▶ **Read** the words in the box. **Write** a word to finish each sentence.

long	there
Why	little
could	about

1. __Why__ was Maya smiling?

2. She was thinking __about__ her pets.

3. She had two __little__ white mice.

4. The mice had __long__ tails.

5. Maya __could__ hold them in her hands.

6. The mice liked to be __there__ .

High-frequency words   179

FOCUS ON ALL LEARNERS

ESL/ELL ENGLISH LANGUAGE LEARNERS

Materials: High-frequency word cards

English language learners may have difficulty pronouncing some of the words, such as *the* and *with*. To assess each child's pronunciation of the high-frequency words, use the high-frequency word cards.

- Say a word as you display it. Then, have children repeat it.
- Help children use the word in a sentence.

VISUAL LEARNERS

Draw six mouse shapes on the chalkboard and write one of the high-frequency words inside each mouse. One at a time, have volunteers come up, read a word, and spell it. Then, have the volunteer add a tail to the mouse.

AUDITORY LEARNERS

Make sure children have the letter cards to spell the high-frequency words. Have each child make up riddles for the high-frequency words, such as, "It rhymes with song." Ask them to read their riddles aloud so that others can guess the answers. Then, ask children to use their letter cards to spell the words.

179

High-Frequency Words

► Look at the picture. Then, **print** words from the box to finish the story. The word shapes will help you.

long	Could	little
Why	there	about

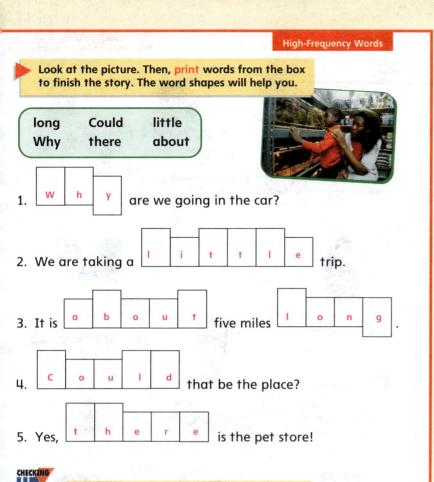

1. **Why** are we going in the car?
2. We are taking a **little** trip.
3. It is **about** five miles **long**.
4. **Could** that be the place?
5. Yes, **there** is the pet store!

CHECKING UP

► Put a ✔ next to each word you can read.

☐ long ☐ could ☐ little ☐ why ☐ there ☐ about

 Help your child use the boxed words to make up sentences, such as *The little mouse is nice.*

180 High-frequency words

CURRICULUM CONNECTIONS

ART/WRITING

Materials: picture books about mice

Share a few picture books in which mice are the main characters, such as *Frederick* by Leo Lionni or *Mouse Paint* by Ellen Stoll Walsh. Then, invite children to write and illustrate their own books about the adventures of a mouse or group of mice.

MATH

Materials: crayons, long strips of paper

Show children how to draw a simple mouse shape. Then, have them draw six mice in a row on the strips of paper. Have them use three different crayons to create a color pattern, coloring each mouse with one of the colors.

VISUAL/KINESTHETIC LEARNERS

Using twelve index cards, make two sets of word cards for the high-frequency words. Turn the cards face down. Have children take turns turning up two at a time, trying to make a match. Each time a match is made, the child reads the word.

CHALLENGE

Challenge children to write sentences about themselves, their pets, and their friends, using the high-frequency words.

EXTRA SUPPORT/INTERVENTION

Write the words *long, why, could, there, little, about* on the board. Then, write the following incomplete sentences: *Have I told you ____ my new puppy? She is very ____. ____ is she hiding? Where ____ she be? It may take a ____ time to find her. I will look over ____.* Read each sentence aloud and help children select the word that completes it.

Integrating Phonics and Reading

Guided Reading
Show the cover as you read the title. Ask children what they notice on or in the three kittens' hands. Then, invite them to make predictions about the story.

First Reading Have children describe what they see in each picture.

Second Reading Have children point to the word *little* each time it appears in the story.

Comprehension
After reading, ask children the following questions:
• How do the kittens feel when they lose their mittens? How do you know? *Inference/Character*
• Why were the kittens sad after their mittens were found? *Recall/Details*

ESL/ELL English Language Learners
Discuss the meaning of *first, second,* and *third.* Then, have children read the story and use picture clues to decide which is the first, second, and third kitten in pages 4 and 5 and 12 and 13.

Lesson 86 Pages 181–182

Long Vowel u

Skill Focus

Children will

★ recognize the sound of long *u*.

★ identify picture names and words that contain the sound of long *u*.

★ identify rhyming long *u* words.

ESL/ELL Children who speak Cantonese or Vietnamese may pronounce a "round," French-sounding *u*. Spanish speakers may have trouble with the /yōō/ sound of long *u* as in *cube* and *use* (pronouncing *coob, ooze*).

Teach

Phonemic Awareness: Phoneme Categorization Say the word *fruit*, elongating the long *u* sound. Then, say the word naturally and ask children to repeat the word. Repeat, using the word *cube*. Explain that the sound they hear in the middle of *fruit* and *cube* is long *u*. Tell children that long *u* may have two slightly different sounds, /ōō/ as in *fruit* and /yōō/ as in *cube*. Then, say these groups of words. Ask children to clap when they hear a word that has the sound of long *u*.

- fruit   suit   bug
- cube   cat   mule
- tin   tune   June

Sound to Symbol Draw a tub and a tube on the board. Say and label each picture name and underline the *u*. Ask children what things sound and look alike in the two words. (Both begin with the *t* sound and end with the *b* sound; both words begin with the letters *t-u-b*.) Then, say *tub, tube* again. Ask what things sound and look different in the words. (*Tube* has an *e* at the end. The vowel sounds are different.) Explain that *tub* has a short *u* sound and *tube* has a long *u* sound.

Practice and Apply

Phonemic Awareness Read aloud the rhyme on page 181. Have children listen for and name words with the long *u* sound.

Sound to Symbol Help children identify the pictures on pages 181 and 182. Suggest that they say the picture names quietly to themselves as they complete each page.

Reading Use *True or False?* MCP Phonics and Reading Long Vowel Skills Library, Level A, to provide practice in reading words with long and short *u*.

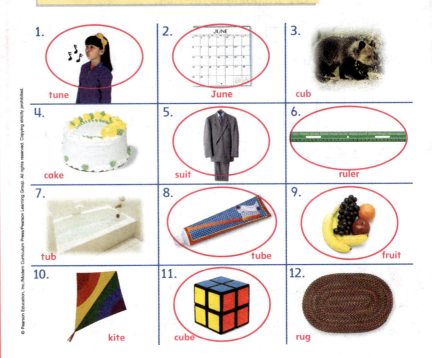

Phonemic Awareness

Name_____

Lu used a tube
Of strong white glue
To paste her cube
On top of Sue's.

▶ **Tube** has the long sound of **u**. Circle each picture whose name has the long sound of **u**.

1. tune   2. June   3. cub
4. cake   5. suit   6. ruler
7. tub   8. tube   9. fruit
10. kite   11. cube   12. rug

Long vowel u: Phonemic awareness   **181**

FOCUS ON ALL LEARNERS

ESL/ELL ENGLISH LANGUAGE LEARNERS

Materials: glue, a tube, a cube, a ruler

- Prepare children to identify words with the long *u* sound on page 181 by showing the objects listed above. Have a volunteer name each one. Repeat, emphasizing the sound of long *u*. Then, write each word on the board. Ask children to circle the *u* in each word.

- Before children begin page 182, practice identifying rhyming long *u* words. Say word pairs such as *hug, huge; use, fuse; nut, cube; suit, fruit; cube, tube*. Have children repeat the pairs that rhyme.

VISUAL LEARNERS

Materials: cardboard tubes, discarded magazines, scissors, paste

Invite children to look through magazines and cut out pictures of items whose names contain the sound of long *u*. Have them paste the pictures on the tubes to decorate them. Have them use these "long *u* tubes" as megaphones as they say the picture names.

Phonograms/Rhyme

▶ Say the names of the pictures in each row.
Color the pictures whose names rhyme.

182 Long and short vowel u: Phonograms/rhyme

HOME With your child, make up a sentence that rhymes for each row of rhyming pictures, such as *I sang a tune in June.*

CURRICULUM CONNECTIONS

SPELLING
Say each spelling word and then use it in a context sentence. Have children write each word as a spelling pretest.
1. **cube** The ice **cube** began to melt.
2. **fruit** Plums are one kind of **fruit**.
3. **glue** I got **glue** on my hands.
4. **mule** That **mule** likes to eat hay.
5. **tube** Where is the **tube** of glue?
6. **tune** I can play a **tune** on the flute.

WRITING
Have children work with a partner to select a picture on page 181 and write several words that rhyme with the picture name.

MUSIC
Materials: paper roll tubes

Write *music* on the board and have children read the word with you. Then, have children make their own music by humming through the tubes.

 **AstroWord** Long Vowels: *e, u*

Integrating Phonics and Reading

Shared/Guided Reading
Show the cover as you read the title. Explain that children will find more true or false questions about animals in the book.

First Reading As you read each page, have children join in for the question *True or False?* and the *True!* or *False!* that begins each answer.

Second Reading Ask children to identify the long *u* words in the story. You might want to add these to the classroom Word Wall.

Comprehension
After reading, ask children the following questions:
• Which questions and answers surprised you most? *Reflective Analysis/Opinion*
• Can you make up your own true or false question about an animal? *Creative/Fantasy and Realism*

ESL/ELL English Language Learners
Help children think of words and phrases that are close in meaning to *true* and *false*. Examples include *correct, right; incorrect, wrong.*

AUDITORY LEARNERS
Select a tune that children can hum. Then, say these words and ask children to hum the tune if they hear the long *u* sound in the word: *flute, mule, tug, pump, cube, suit, cub, tube, rude, ruler, flu, glue, dust, huge, rule.*

CHALLENGE
Ask children to name some two-part and three-part words that contain the long *u* sound. Possible words include *music, tuba, tuna, musician, uniform, united, unit,* and *universe.*

EXTRA SUPPORT/INTERVENTION
Materials: Phonics Picture Cards: cape (85), cake (86), cane (87), tray (88), bike (93), fire (94), five (95), hive (96), mule (103), ruler (104), suit (105), tube (106), uniform (107)

After saying each picture name, have children sort the cards into two piles: those pictures whose names contain the sound of long *u* and those pictures whose names do not. **See Daily Phonics Practice, page 318.**

Lesson 87 Pages 183–184

Long Vowel u

Skill Focus

Children will
★ recognize the sound of long *u*.
★ identify pictures whose names contain the sound of long or short *u*.
★ understand that *u_e*, *ue*, or *ui* can stand for the sound of long *u*.
★ use long *u* words in the context of a sentence.

Teach

Phonological Awareness: Blending Onsets and Rimes Tell children that you will say the parts of a word. Children should repeat the parts after you, orally blending the parts to make the word. Use these words.

- /r/ude
- /s/uit
- /m/ule
- /k/ube

Ask children if all the words have the sound of /o͞o/ or /yo͞o/ (*yes*). Tell them that the sound they hear in each word is the sound of long *u*.

Sound to Symbol
Materials: box with cube, glue, and fruit
Display the box and have children identify its contents. Then, write *cube, glue,* and *fruit* on the board. Have volunteers underline the vowels in each word with colored chalk. Discuss which vowel is heard and have a child circle it. Help children conclude that the long *u* sound can be spelled *u_consonant_e*, *ue*, and *ui*.

Sound to Symbol Write the words *cut* and *cute* on the board. Ask volunteers to read the words and underline the vowels. Have children circle the vowel they hear with colored chalk. Remind children that long *u* can be spelled with the letters *u_consonant_e*. The *e* is silent.

Practice and Apply

Sound to Symbol As children complete page 183, encourage them to say each picture name quietly and listen for the beginning, middle, and ending sounds.

For page 184, read the directions with children. Make sure they understand how to match each number to a letter to use the code.

Reading Use *Blue Sue*, MCP Phonics and Reading Long Vowel Skills Library, Level A, to provide practice in reading words with long and short *u*.

FOCUS ON ALL LEARNERS

ESL/ELL ENGLISH LANGUAGE LEARNERS

- To prepare children for the activity on page 183, write *nut, suit, cup, tube, fun,* and *glue* on the board. Identify the vowel sound in each word as long or short *u*. Then, identify the letters that represent the vowel sound in each word.
- Before children begin page 184, model how to use the code in the box at the top of the page. You can adapt the activity by providing a word list as reference. Then, have children select the best word to finish each sentence.

KINESTHETIC LEARNERS

Materials: number cubes, tape player, music

Invite children to sit in a circle and pass cubes around as the music plays. When it stops, have the children with cubes stand and say a word that has the long *u* sound.

Sound to Symbol

Read each sentence. Use the code to make each pair of words. Print them on the lines. Then, circle the word that finishes the sentence.

1 = a	2 = e	3 = i	4 = u	5 = b	6 = c
7 = f	8 = l	9 = m	10 = r	11 = s	12 = t

1. June plays the (t u b a)   r u l e .
            12 4 5 1   10 4 8 2

2. Luke will feed his   f l u t e   (m u l e) .
            7 8 4 12 2   9 4 8 2

3. Sue likes to eat   c u b e   (f r u i t) .
            6 4 5 2   7 10 4 3 12

4. Ben got a new   (s u i t)   c l u e .
            11 4 3 12   6 8 4 2

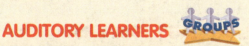
5. Duke's house is   t r u e   (b l u e) .
            12 10 4 2   5 8 4 2

HOME Make up riddles using the long vowel *u* words from the page. Ask your child to guess each word.

184   Long vowel u: Sound to symbol

CURRICULUM CONNECTIONS

SPELLING
Materials: spelling master (page 145l)
Have children use the master to make spelling cards. Have them illustrate the words on the back of the cards.

WRITING

Review the words to the traditional song "The Bear Went Over the Mountain," and then work with children to write a new verse about a mule who went over a sand dune.

MATH
Material: number cubes
Have partners answer these questions:
1. What is the highest number you can get when you roll two cubes?
2. What is the lowest number you can get when you roll the two cubes?
3. How many ways can you roll: 4, 5, 6, 7, 8, 9, 10?

TECHNOLOGY   **AstroWord** Long Vowels: *e, u*

Integrating Phonics and Reading

Guided Reading
Show children the cover illustration and read the title. Ask students to make predictions about why Sue is blue.
First Reading Have children use the illustrations to point out the things that are blue.
Second Reading Have children identify the long and short *u* words in the story. List the words on the Word Wall.
Comprehension
After reading, ask children the following questions:
• What strange things happened in the story? *Recall/Details*
• How would you explain the reason everything turned blue? *Inference/Cause and Effect*
ESL/ELL English Language Learners
Have children make up sentences to tell about things that are blue. For example: *The sky is blue. A lake is blue.*

AUDITORY LEARNERS   GROUPS
Materials: drawing paper, crayons
Assign each child a partner and explain that they will work together to draw a cute bug. Have the pair take turns saying words that contain the long *u* sound. After saying a word, have the child add another part to the bug.

CHALLENGE
Working with a partner, have children look for rhyming long *u* words on page 183. Have them list each set of words that they find.

EXTRA SUPPORT/INTERVENTION
Materials: blue crayons
Pair children and have them work together to read the three words under each picture on page 183. As they say each word, have them listen for the long *u* sound. If they hear it, have them underline the word in blue. See Daily Phonics Practice, page 318.

Lesson 88 Pages 185–186

Long Vowel u

Skill Focus

Children will

★ distinguish between short *u* and long *u* picture names.

★ identify words that contain the sound of long *u*.

★ apply what they have learned by reading and writing.

Teach

Phonological Awareness: Rhyme Ask these riddles and have children guess the answers. Then, have them say each pair of rhyming words.

- What word rhymes with *fruit* and means "something you wear"? (*suit*)
- What word rhymes with *rule* and means "an animal like a horse"? (*mule*)
- What word rhymes with *June* and means "something you can hum"? (*tune*)

Remind children that the vowel sound heard in each word is long *u*.

Sound to Symbol

Materials: Phonics Picture Cards for tub (68) and tube (106)

Show the picture cards and write *tub* and *tube* on the board as column headings. Have children repeat the words. Ask a volunteer to use colored chalk to underline the vowels in each word. Then, have children tell which word has the long *u* sound and which has the short *u* sound. Next, ask volunteers to say other words that contain the vowel sound they hear in each word, write the words in the correct column, and underline the vowel or vowels in each word. Remind children that the long *u* sound can be spelled *u_consonant_e*, *ue*, and *ui*.

Practice and Apply

Sound to Symbol Help children identify the pictures on page 185. Remind them to listen for a short or long vowel sound in each picture name. For page 186, make sure children understand that they are to color a bubble only if all the words in it have the sound of long *u*.

Writing Note the long *u* words that children write on page 186 and check for correct spelling.

Reading Use *A Hunt for Clues*, MCP Phonics and Reading Long Vowel Skills Library, Level A, to provide practice in reading words with long and short *u*.

185

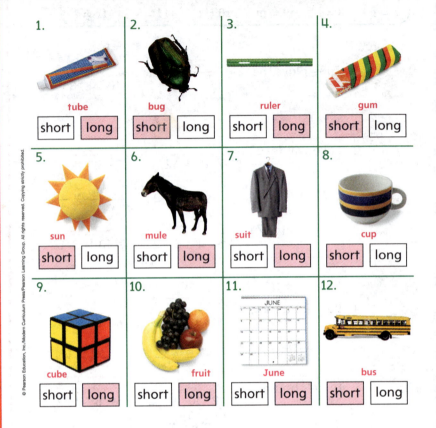

FOCUS ON ALL LEARNERS

ESL/ELL ENGLISH LANGUAGE LEARNERS

Materials: Phonics Picture Cards: mule (103), cup (63), jug (64), ruler (104), nuts (65), sun (67), suit (105), tube (106); letter cards *Aa, Ii, Uu*

- To prepare children for the activity on page 185, display picture cards and write the column headings *long* and *short* on the board. Ask children to tell whether each word has the long or short vowel sound of *u*. Have volunteers write the word under the correct heading.
- Before beginning the activity on page 186, display letter cards *Aa, Ii, Uu*. Say a series of words with long vowels and tell children to point to the correct letter card that stands for the long vowel sound. Use these words: *mail, mule, mile, cube, cave, kite, blue, safe, suit*.

VISUAL LEARNERS GROUPS

Materials: Phonics Picture Cards: bug (61), bus (62), cup (63), jug (64), nuts (65), mule (103), ruler (104), suit (105), tube (106), uniform (107); masking tape

Draw a tree on the board and tape on the picture cards to represent fruit. Children "pick" the fruit by naming a picture.

Phonemic Awareness

▶ **Color** the bubble blue if it has three long **u** words in it.

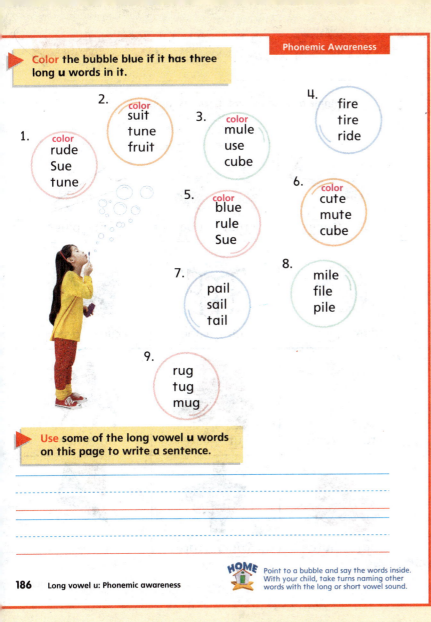

1. color — rude, Sue, tune
2. color — suit, tune, fruit
3. color — mule, use, cube
4. fire, tire, ride
5. color — blue, rule, Sue
6. color — cute, mute, cube
7. pail, sail, tail
8. mile, file, pile
9. rug, tug, mug

▶ **Use** some of the long vowel **u** words on this page to write a sentence.

_____
_____
_____

186 Long vowel u: Phonemic awareness

HOME Point to a bubble and say the words inside. With your child, take turns naming other words with the long or short vowel sound.

CURRICULUM CONNECTIONS

SPELLING
Materials: spelling cards made in Lesson 87, pages 183–184

Have children work with a partner to sort the words to show three different spellings of the long *u* sound.

WRITING
Ask children to name their favorite fruits. Make a list of the fruits they name. Have children draw pictures of favorite fruits and write about them.

SCIENCE
Materials: pictures of a mule, donkey, and horse

Share simple background information about mules with children. They may be interested to learn that a mule has a horse for a mother and a donkey for a father. Display the pictures of a mule, a donkey, and a horse and have children compare the animals to see how the mule is like both the donkey and the horse.

TECHNOLOGY AstroWord Long Vowels: *e, u*

Integrating Phonics and Reading

Guided Reading
Show children the cover illustration and read the title. Ask who will be hunting for clues in the story they are about to read.

First Reading Have children use the illustrations to point out the clues that True Blue finds.

Second Reading Have children identify the long and short *u* words in the book. List the words on the board or add them to the classroom Word Wall.

Comprehension
After reading, ask children the following questions:
• Who is True Blue looking for? *Recall/Plot*
• Do you think True Blue is better at finding clues or finding food? *Inference/Details*

ESL/ELL English Language Learners
Reread the last page with children. Then, have them use their own words to tell about the foods that were nearby as True Blue found each clue.

AUDITORY/KINESTHETIC LEARNERS

Play the "listen up" game by sharing oral sentences with short and long *u* words. Have children stand when they hear a long *u* word and sit when they hear a short *u* word. Sentences could include: *June ordered the fruit cup on the menu. Bud got gum on his blue suit.*

CHALLENGE
Write these words on the board: *hug, tub, cut, cub, us.* Challenge children to transform these short *u* words into long *u* words by adding a vowel. Then, have them use each word in an oral sentence.

EXTRA SUPPORT/INTERVENTION
Materials: Phonics Picture Cards: bug (61), bus (62), cup (63), jug (64), mule (103), ruler (104), suit (105), tube (106), uniform (107)

Have children say the word *true* and identify the vowel sound. Then, display each picture card and have children say the picture name. Have them nod their heads if it is true that this name contains the long sound of *u*. See Daily Phonics Practice, page 318.

Lesson 89 Pages 187–188

Long Vowel u

Skill Focus

Children will

★ identify words and pictures whose names contain short and long vowel sounds.

★ write words that contain the sound of long and short *u* to complete sentences.

★ recognize and read high-frequency words.

Teach

Phonemic Awareness: Phoneme Substitution Say the name *Jane*. Have children repeat it and identify the vowel sound. Then, tell children that they can make a new word by changing this vowel sound to long *u*. Say *June* and have children repeat the word. Then, ask children to change each of the following to a long *u* word: *tone* (*tune*); *role* (*rule*); *mile* (*mule*); *ride* (*rude*).

Sound to Symbol Write these words on the board, using colored chalk to highlight the vowels: *cute, suit, blue*. Call on volunteers to read the words. Ask children how the words are alike. Then, ask children to name other words that contain the sound of long *u* as you list them. Have volunteers come up and highlight the vowels in each one. Remind children that the long *u* sound can be spelled *u_consonant_e, ue,* and *ui*.

Sound to Symbol Write these words on the board: *cub, cube; hug, huge*. Have a volunteer underline the vowels in each word with colored chalk. Then, ask a volunteer to circle the vowel that is heard in the words *cube* and *huge*. Discuss how the *e* at the end of the word changes the vowel sound.

Practice and Apply

Sound to Symbol As children complete page 187, encourage them to say each picture name quietly to themselves and to listen for a long or short vowel sound.

Writing For page 188, suggest that children try each word choice before writing a word. As they complete the activity, they will have the opportunity to read the following high-frequency words: *from, too*.

Critical Thinking For Talk About It, point out the picture of the school bus as a clue.

Reading Use *Mrs. Tuck's Little Tune*, MCP Phonics and Reading Long Vowel Skills Library, Level A, to provide practice in reading words with long and short *u*.

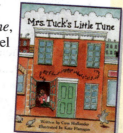

187

Sound to Symbol

Name _____

▶ Say the name of each picture. Circle its name.

1. tub (tube)
2. (tub) tube
3. (pin) pine
4. dim (dime)
5. cub (cube)
6. (cub) cube
7. ran (rain)
8. (cut) cute
9. rid (ride)
10. (hat) hate
11. (cape) cap
12. kit (kite)

Long and short vowels a, i, u: Sound to symbol 187

FOCUS ON ALL LEARNERS

ESL/ELL ENGLISH LANGUAGE LEARNERS

Materials: letter cards *Tt, Uu, Bb, Ee*

• To prepare for the activity on page 187, have children use the letter card to first spell *tub* and then add *e* to spell *tube*. Help them identify the vowel sound in each word as short or long. Point out that adding *e* changed the short vowel sound to a long vowel sound.

• Read the word choices on page 188 with children. Before children complete the page, help them use each word in context in an oral sentence. Then, help children to identify the picture clues.

KINESTHETIC LEARNERS

Materials: Phonics Word Cards: *bug* (61), *bump* (62), *buzz* (65), *cup* (67), *dug* (68), *jug* (71), *jump* (72), *luck* (73), *mud* (74), *rug* (77), *run* (78), *sun* (79), *tub* (80), *cube* (158), *fuse* (159), *June* (160), *rule* (161), *Sue* (162), *tune* (163), *use* (164)

Distribute the cards and have each child read one. Ask who has a long *u* word and have a child begin a "mule train." Children may join the mule train if their words contain long *u*.

Words in Context

▶ **Look** at the picture. **Circle** the word that will finish the sentence. **Print** it on the line.

1. Luke will __use__ a box. — us, (use), tune
2. The box looks like a __cube__. — cute, (cube), cub
3. He got it from __Sue__. — rule, (Sue), due
4. Luke has a __tube__ of glue in it. — tune, tub, (tube)
5. He will put a __ruler__ in it, **too**. — (ruler), rude, rubs
6. Luke will take it on the __bus__. — suit, bun, (bus)

TALK About It Where do you think Luke is taking the box?

HOME Help your child to think of a sentence that uses some of the long *u* words on the page.

188 Long and short vowel u: High-frequency words, critical thinking

---

CURRICULUM CONNECTIONS

SPELLING
Materials: spelling cards made in Lesson 87, pages 183–184

Have children work with a partner and take turns displaying the picture side of each spelling card. Ask the partners to name the picture and write its name. Have children check the spelling by looking at the back of the card.

WRITING

Have children recall the school supplies that Luke brought to school in a box. Then, have children make lists of some important school supplies that they use.

MATH
Materials: rulers, small objects, paper

Review with children how to use a ruler to measure objects. Have children fold their papers in half. Have them head columns with *Less Than 6 Inches* and *More Than 6 Inches*. Have children measure objects and list them in the appropriate column.

 **TECHNOLOGY** **AstroWord** Long Vowels: *e, u*

AUDITORY LEARNERS GROUPS
Give these hints for long *u* words. Have children draw pictures to answer them: *This animal can be very stubborn. This musical instrument looks like a silver tube. Toothpaste comes in this. A small block of ice is called this.*

CHALLENGE
Have children play a clue game. Have them think of an object whose name has a long *u* sound. Then, they should write three clues for the object. They can read their clues for partners to guess the object.

EXTRA SUPPORT/INTERVENTION
Point out the pictures on page 188 and explain that they can help children understand each sentence. Have children work in pairs to read aloud each sentence and the three words before completing the sentences. See Daily Phonics Practice, page 318.

Integrating Phonics and Reading

Guided Reading
Show the cover as you read the title. Ask children to tell what instrument Mrs. Tuck will use to play her tune.
First Reading Have children look at the illustrations and point out the people who are humming or hearing Mrs. Tuck's little tune.
Second Reading Have children identify the long and short *u* words in the story. Ask them to list the words on the board.

Comprehension
After reading, ask children the following questions:
- What was Mrs. Tuck doing one morning? *Recall/Plot*
- How did everyone in town end up humming the tune? *Recall/Cause and Effect*

ESL/ELL English Language Learners
Have children act out the following actions from the story: play a flute, hum a tune, get on a bus, get off a bus.

Lesson 90   Pages 189–190

Long Vowel u

Skill Focus

Children will

★ identify and spell picture names that contain the sounds of long u, a, and i, and short u.

★ write words that contain the sound of long u to complete sentences.

★ recognize and read high-frequency words.

Teach

Phonemic Awareness: Phoneme Blending
Say the word *mule*, separating the sound of each phoneme: /m/ /ū/ /l/. Ask children what vowel sound they hear in the middle of the word. (long u) Then, ask them to say the word, stretching the long u sound. Repeat the process using these long u, a, and i words: *tune, lace, night, game, dune, ripe, rude, paid.*

Sound to Symbol Write *cut, cub,* and *hug* on the board and have children read the words aloud. Add *e* to the end of each word and ask children to read the new words aloud. Work with children to circle the vowel they hear in each word. Then, cover and uncover the *e* at the end of *cute, cube,* and *huge.* Remind children that adding *e* to the end of these words changes the short u sound to long u.

Sound to Symbol Write *blue, cute,* and *fruit* on the board. Have volunteers underline the vowels. Then, have children read the words and identify the vowel sound they hear. Discuss the different ways to spell the long u sound.

Practice and Apply

Blend Phonemes As children complete page 189, encourage them to say each picture name, blending together the beginning, middle, and ending sounds.

Writing For page 190, suggest that children try each word choice before writing a word. As they complete the activity, they will have the opportunity to read the high-frequency word *want.*

Critical Thinking For Talk About It, encourage children to look at the picture at the top of the page.

Reading Use *Who's in the Jungle?* MCP Phonics and Reading Long Vowel Skills Library, Level A, to provide practice in reading words with long and short u.

Spelling

Name _____

▶ **Say** the name of each picture. **Print** the missing vowels on the line. **Trace** the whole word.

1. c u b e	2. _ a i _	3. J u n e	4. f i v e
5. _ a _ e	6. t u b e	7. k i t e	8. s u i _
9. g u m	10. c u p	11. m u l e	12. _ u n e

Long and short vowels a, i, u: Spelling   **189**

FOCUS ON ALL LEARNERS

ESL/ELL ENGLISH LANGUAGE LEARNERS

Materials: letter cards *Aa, Ii, Uu*

- Practice long vowel discrimination before having children complete page 189. Say a series of words with long *a, i,* and *u,* such as *mail, mule, mile, cube, cave, kite, blue, safe, suit.* Tell children to point to the correct letter card for each one.

- Read the directions for page 190 and ask children to restate them in their own words. Have children complete page 190 individually. Review answers aloud and have volunteers write each answer on the board for verification.

KINESTHETIC/AUDITORY LEARNERS

Materials: Phonics Word Cards: *bump* (62), *mud* (74), *pup* (76), *tuck* (81), *us* (82), *cute* (158), *fuse* (159), *June* (160), *rule* (161), *rude* (162), *use* (164)

Display one word at a time. Ask a volunteer to read it aloud. Then, have children bray like mules if the word contains the long u sound.

Words in Context

Circle the word that will finish the sentence. Print it on the line.

1. Sue has a __mule__.
   must / **mule** / mile

2. Is a mule a __cute__ pet?
   cute / cube / cut

3. Will she ride it in __June__?
   jug / tune / **June**

4. Does the mule like to eat __fruit__?
   fun / **fruit** / rule

5. I do not have a __clue__.
   cute / **clue** / cuts

6. I want to ask __Sue__.
   sun / **Sue** / suit

Talk about it: Where do you think Sue lives? Why do you think that?

Home: Help your child to continue the story using some of the circled words on the page.

190 Long vowel u: High-frequency words, critical thinking

CURRICULUM CONNECTIONS

SPELLING
Have children work with a partner to make up clues for their spelling words. To help them get started, you might wish to present this clue as a model: *This is what we call apples, oranges, and pears.* (fruit) Once the partners have completed their clues, have them share them with another pair.

WRITING
Material: Phonics Picture Card: mule (103)

Ask children to imagine that Sue's mule is missing! Have children make a sign to advertise Sue's lost pet.

SCIENCE
Materials: easy books about animals that work

Explain to children that before the invention of tractors, mules often were used to do heavy farm work. Have children consult simple reference materials to find out more about the work done by animals. Then, have them draw and caption a picture showing an animal helper.

TECHNOLOGY

AstroWord Long Vowels: *e, u*

AUDITORY LEARNERS
Read aloud the following sentences and explain that a long *u* word is missing in each sentence. Have children use context clues to guess the missing word: *June likes to whistle a _____.* (tune) *Interrupting a friend is ___.* (rude) *A six turned up when I rolled the number ___.* (cube)

CHALLENGE
Have children fold a paper into three columns. Head the first one *u_e as in mule*, the second one *ue as in clue*, and the third one *ui as in fruit*. Challenge children to list as many words with the different spellings as they can.

EXTRA SUPPORT/INTERVENTION
Before writing the missing vowels to complete the words on page 189, have children name each picture and identify the vowel sound heard in the picture name. **See Daily Phonics Practice, page 318.**

Integrating Phonics and Reading

Guided Reading
Show the cover as you read the title. Mention that another word for *jungle* is *rain forest*. Ask children what they know about jungle animals.

First Reading Invite children to describe the animal that is peeking out from behind the trees in each right-hand page.

Second Reading Have children identify the long and short *u* words in the story. List the words on the board.

Comprehension
After reading, ask children the following questions:
• What kind of place is a jungle? *Inference/Setting*
• Who or what can you find in a jungle? *Recall/Details*

ESL/ELL English Language Learners
Have children draw and label pictures of each of the animals named in the book: *monkey, tree frog, blue bird, lion, bug, parrot.*

Lesson 91   Pages 191–192

Long Vowel u

Skill Focus

Children will

★ identify and spell picture names that contain the sounds of long *u*, *a*, and *i*, and short *u*.

★ identify and write words that contain the sound of long *a*, *i*, and *u*.

▶ Teach

Phonemic Awareness: Medial Sound Isolation

Materials: Phonics Picture Cards: suit (105), mule (103)

Hold up the picture card for *suit* as you say its name, then its vowel sound: *suit*, /o͞o/. Tell children you are saying a word and then its vowel sound. Explain that the sound heard in the middle of the word is long *u*. Model the procedure again, using *mule*, /yo͞o/. Then, have children say these words and follow each one with its vowel sound: *fruit*, *tune*, *cube*, *rule*. Remind children that long *u* can have the sound of /o͞o/ or /yo͞o/.

Sound to Symbol Write this sentence on the board and ask a volunteer to read it aloud: *Kate will ride the mule.* Using three colors of chalk, ask volunteers to underline the long *a*, long *i*, and long *u* word in the sentence. Then, point to each underlined word and have children circle the vowels. Ask volunteers to draw a square around the vowel that is heard in each word. Explain that in each of these words, the long vowel is heard and the *e* is silent. Repeat the procedure with this sentence: *The duke ate a bit of rice.*

▶ Practice and Apply

Sound to Symbol As children complete page 191, encourage them to say each picture name, blending together the beginning, middle, and ending sounds.

For page 192, explain that the words in the puzzle are printed both across and down. You might want to model finding and circling *rain* and *ice* for children.

Reading Use *Blast Off!*, MCP Phonics and Reading Long Vowel Skills Library, Level A, to provide practice in reading words with long *a*, *i*, and *u*.

Spelling

Name _____

▶ **Say** the name of each picture. **Print** the name on the line. In the last box, **draw** a picture of a long *u* word. **Print** the word.

1. cube	2. cake	3. tune
4. nine	5. mule	6. bug
7. suit	8. tube	9. tire
10. cup	11. June	12.

Long and short vowels a, i, u: Spelling   **191**

FOCUS ON ALL LEARNERS

ESL/ELL ENGLISH LANGUAGE LEARNERS

• Help children identify the picture names on page 191 before they spell each word. Then, help them think of an additional long *u* word to write and draw for item 12.

• Work with children to complete the word search puzzle on page 192. Then, have them complete items 1 to 6 individually.

VISUAL/KINESTHETIC LEARNERS

Materials: index cards

Give each child two cards. Have them write a long *u* word on one card and another long vowel word on the other card. Mix up the word cards and stack them face down in a pile. Play "Slap the *u*" by having children take turns turning over one card at a time. If the word contains the long *u* sound, the first child to slap the card keeps it.

KINESTHETIC LEARNERS

Materials: letter cards *Uu, Ee, Bb, Cc, Ll, Mm, Nn, Rr, Tt*; chairs

Place four chairs in a row and display the letter cards. Have children take turns creating long *u* words by sitting in chairs and holding up cards.

Phonemic Awareness

▶ Circle the long **a**, long **i**, and long **u** words in the puzzle. The words in the box will help you.

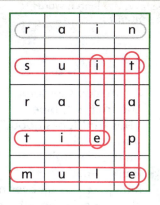

| rain | ice | tape |
| suit | tie | mule |

▶ Print the word from the box that names each picture.

1. rain
2. ice
3. mule
4. suit
5. tie
6. tape

Ask your child to use three of the words from the box in a sentence.

192 Review long vowels a, i, u: Phonemic awareness

CURRICULUM CONNECTIONS

SPELLING
Write these list words on the board: *cube, fruit, glue, mule, tune*. Then, say these words and ask volunteers to point to the list words that rhyme: *suit, dune, Sue, rule, tube*.

WRITING
Materials: small objects

Assign children partners and give each pair a small object to hide. Have the pair work together to write three clues that describe where the object is hidden. Have children share their clues with another pair and then use the hints to locate each other's objects.

SCIENCE
Materials: ice cubes, plastic glasses, water

Have children place an ice cube in a plastic glass, and then fill the glass to the rim with water. Have them predict what will happen to the level of the water in the glass when the ice cube melts. Have children compare their predictions with what actually happens. (*The water from the melted ice takes up less space than the ice cube itself.*)

 **AstroWord** Long Vowels: *e, u*

Integrating Phonics and Reading

Guided Reading
Show the cover as you read the title. Ask children if they think this book will tell a true or made-up story.
First Reading Encourage children to point out and talk about details in the photos.
Second Reading Point out these words in the book: *space, fly, blue, white*. Have children identify the vowel sound in each one.
Comprehension
After reading, ask children the following questions:
• Have you heard of the space shuttle? What do you know about it? *Reflective Analysis/Prior Knowledge*
• What are some of the things the astronauts saw from the space shuttle? *Recall/Details*

ESL/ELL English Language Learners
Write these action phrases from the story on the board. Then, help students act out each one: *climb aboard, take off, float around*.

AUDITORY LEARNERS
Ask one child in the group to think of a mystery long *u* word. Explain that others in the group may ask this child yes or no questions to help them guess the mystery word. Have children keep track of the number of questions asked before the word is guessed.

CHALLENGE
Challenge children to transform a *cake* into a *mule* by creating a word chain in which they change one letter in each word. (One chain is *cake, make, male, mile, mule*; others are possible.)

EXTRA SUPPORT/INTERVENTION
If children have difficulty spelling the words on page 191, suggest that they begin by spelling the beginning and/or ending consonant sounds. Give help as needed with variant spellings of the long vowel sounds.
See Daily Phonics Practice, page 318.

Lesson 92

Pages 193–194

Phonics and Reading / Phonics and Writing

Long Vowel u

Skill Focus

Children will

★ read words that contain the sound of long *u*.

★ write long *u* words to finish sentences.

★ build words with long *u* phonograms *-une*, *-ule*.

Teach

Phonemic Awareness: Phoneme Categorization

Materials: Phonics Picture Cards: rake (91), hive (96), mule (103), ruler (104), suit (105), tube (106)

Display the picture cards for *ruler*, *rake*, and *suit*. Have children identify each word and tell which two have the long *u* sound. Repeat, using the cards for *mule*, *hive*, and *tube*.

Sound to Symbol Write the words *cube*, *suit*, and *glue* in three columns on the board. Ask children how the words are alike. (*They all have the long* u *sound.*) Then, ask how the words are different. (*They have different spellings for the long* u *sound.*) Invite volunteers to come up to the board and write a word with the same long *u* spelling in one of the columns. Ask children to underline the vowels in each word.

Read Words in Sentences Write these questions on the board.

- Can Sue paint a blue cube?
- Can Duke make a suit?

Help children read the questions. Then, ask them to circle the words that have the long *u* sound.

Practice and Apply

Phonics and Reading After children have read the story, encourage them to identify words that have the long *u* sound.

Critical Thinking For Talk About It, give children this clue: *It's the fruit that has the word blue in its name.*

Phonics and Writing For page 194, tell children to try each letter at the top to make a word with *-une* or *-ule*. Remind them that not every letter will make a real word.

Reading Use *The Cat That Broke the Rules*, MCP Phonics and Reading Long Vowel Skills Library, Level A, to provide practice in reading words with long *u*.

193

Name _____

Phonics & Reading — Read the story. Use long *u* words to finish the sentences.

The Blue Suit

A cute cub saw some fruit.
The fruit was blue.
"This fruit looks good,"
said the cub.
He ate the fruit.
He hummed a tune.
Blue juice got all over him.
"Look!" said the cub's dad.
"You have a new blue suit!"

1. The _____ fruit _____ was blue.

2. Blue _____ juice _____ got on the cub.

3. The cub had a new _____ blue _____ suit _____.

Talk About It What kind of fruit did the cub eat?

Review long vowel u: Reading, critical thinking 193

FOCUS ON ALL LEARNERS

ESL/ELL ENGLISH LANGUAGE LEARNERS

- Talk about bears and bear cubs with English language learners before reading the story on page 193. Have volunteers tell what they know about bears. Talk about what bears eat: insects, honey, fish, fruit. Print *fruit* and *blueberries* on the chalkboard. Point out the sound of long *u*.

- Pair students with English-speaking partners for the word-building activity on page 194.

VISUAL/AUDITORY LEARNERS

Materials: chart paper, marker, blue crayons

Draw a large blueberry plant on chart paper. Draw some giant berries on the bush. Then, invite children to write long *u* words on the berries. Have them use a blue crayon to color the berries with long *u* words.

KINESTHETIC/AUDITORY LEARNERS

Create groups of three. Have one child act as the reader while the other two play the parts of the cub and his dad. Then, have children switch roles so all have a chance to read each part.

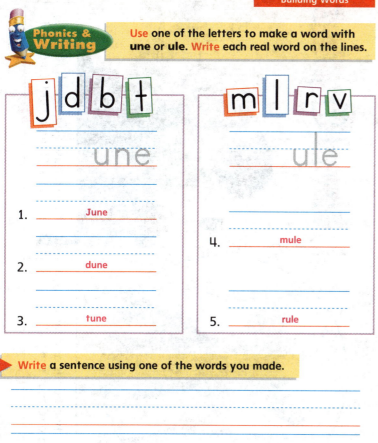

CURRICULUM CONNECTIONS

SPELLING
Dictate these spelling words and sentences and have children write the words as a spelling posttest.
1. **cube** You need a number **cube** to play that game.
2. **fruit** Apples are her favorite **fruit**.
3. **glue** That **glue** is very sticky.
4. **mule** A **mule** has very long ears.
5. **tube** Toothpaste comes in a **tube**.
6. **tune** Can you sing that **tune**?

HEALTH
Materials: illustration of the food pyramid, drawing paper, crayons

Help children find the category for fruits on the food pyramid. Discuss the number of recommended servings of fruit per day. Have children draw pictures showing fruits that they like to eat for breakfast, for lunch, for dinner.

TECHNOLOGY **AstroWord** Long Vowels: *e, u*

VISUAL/KINESTHETIC LEARNERS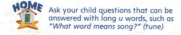
Write several long *u* words, such as *cube, rude, juice, mule, suit, June, cute, fruit, tube, Sue, use,* on sheets of paper. Tape the sheets to the floor to form a U-shaped path. Have children follow the path, reading aloud the words as they go.

CHALLENGE
Have children write a story in which they encounter a bear cub in a patch of blue fruit. Some children may wish to compare their stories to Robert McCloskey's well-known story *Blueberries for Sal*.

EXTRA SUPPORT/INTERVENTION
For page 194, suggest that children use a separate sheet of paper to write each initial letter followed by the phonogram shown. They can then circle the real words and write them on the page. See Daily Phonics Practice, page 318.

Integrating Phonics and Reading

Guided Reading
Show the cover as you read the title. Then, flip through the illustrations and invite children to predict how a cat might break a rule.

First Reading Have children point to the rug, Leo's food, and his library card.

Second Reading Point out these words in the book: *cute, huge, June, rules*. Encourage children to use them in sentences, such as *Leo is a cute cat*.

Comprehension
After reading, ask children the following questions:
- How did the people at the library feel about Leo? How do you know? *Inference/Character*
- If you were Leo, would you like the pet shop better or the library? *Creative/Comparison*

ESL/ELL **English Language Learners**
Remind children that the story takes place in a library. Discuss the different things they can find in a library, such as books, magazines, newspapers, and videotapes.

Lesson 93 Pages 195–196

Take-Home Book

Review Long Vowels a, i, u

> ### Skill Focus
> Children will
> ★ read long *a, i,* and *u* words in the context of a story.
> ★ review selected high-frequency words in the context of a story.
> ★ reread for fluency.

Teach

Build Background

Materials: large flashlight or other strong light source

Remind children that the theme of this unit is "Let's Play." Turn on the light source and tell children that indoors they might play a game with a light like this one. Shine the light against the wall and make a simple shadow shape with your hand.

Write the word *shadow* on the board and have children talk about how shadows are formed. Make sure they understand that shadows are caused when something solid, like a hand, blocks light.

Phonemic Awareness: Medial Sound Isolation Divide children into three teams: the *a*-team, the *i*-team, and the *u*-team. Then, say long vowel words in random order, stretching the long vowel sound each time. For example: *bike, face, five, June, cube, lake*. For each stretched word, have the team named for the vowel repeat the stretched word, then say the word naturally.

Practice and Apply

Read the Book Help children tear out and fold the pages to make their Take-Home Books. Then, read the book together. Invite children to make shadows as shown.

Sound to Symbol Read aloud or have volunteers read the book. Have children identify the long *a, i,* and *u* words. (*use, make, shine, light, cute, way, huge, white, like*) Invite volunteers to write the words on the board and read them aloud.

Review High-Frequency Words Write the words *you, your, one, two,* and *like* on the board. Have the children spell the words, then say them.

Reread for Fluency Have children reread the book to increase their fluency and comprehension. Children can take their books home to read and share with family members.

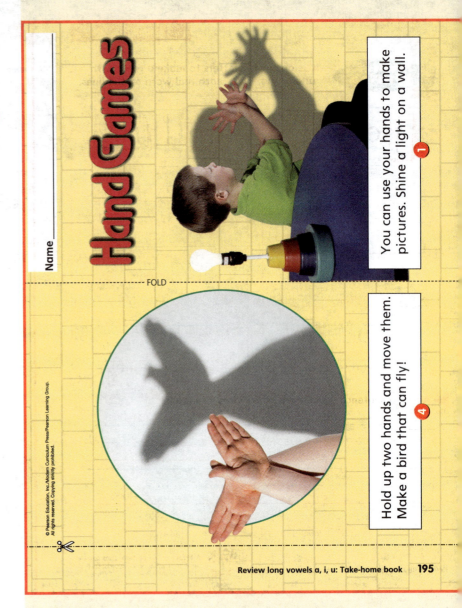

FOCUS ON ALL LEARNERS

ESL/ELL ENGLISH LANGUAGE LEARNERS

Materials: letter cards

- Read the text together and have children look at the photos. Review the shadow pictures and have children identify each animal.
- Provide a set of letter cards. Ask children to look through the book and, using the letter cards, spell out the long *a, i,* and *u* words.

VISUAL LEARNERS

Materials: Take-Home Books, writing paper

Have children fold their papers in three columns and head each column *Long a, Long i,* or *Long u*. Then, ask children to find words in the story with each long vowel sound. Have them record each word in the appropriate column.

KINESTHETIC/AUDITORY LEARNERS

Ask children to demonstrate how to make the letters *a, i,* and *u* by using their fingers. Then, have children take turns saying words that contain one of these long vowel sounds. Others in the group can make the letter that names the sound with their fingers.

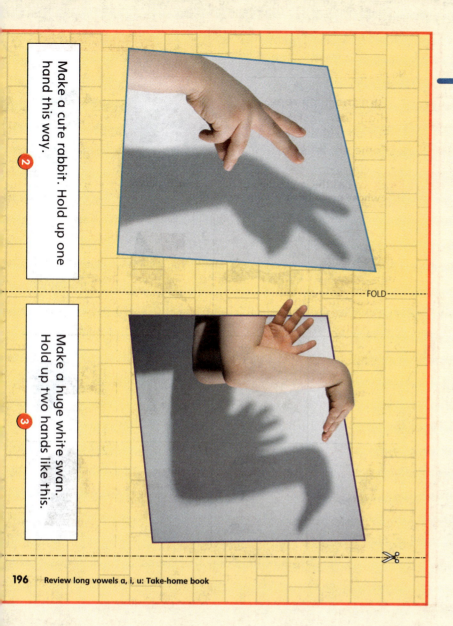

2. Make a cute rabbit. Hold up one hand this way.

3. Make a huge white swan. Hold up two hands like this.

196 Review long vowels a, i, u: Take-home book

CURRICULUM CONNECTIONS

FINE ARTS

Materials: light source, white and black construction paper, chalk, scissors, paste

Explain that before cameras were invented, people made shadow pictures of people's heads. This art form is called a silhouette. Show how to create a silhouette by using chalk to trace the shadow of a child's head and shoulders on black paper. Pair children and help them draw each other's silhouettes on black paper. Cut out the silhouettes and mount them on white paper.

PHYSICAL EDUCATION

On a sunny day, play a game of shadow tag. Explain that the person who is "it" can tag someone by touching his or her shadow.

SCIENCE

Materials: chalk

Have children pick a spot to stand on the playground and mark their shadows. Return at different times of day and have them observe what happens to the length of the shadow. Invite them to speculate why the length changes during the day.

TECHNOLOGY

AstroWord Long Vowels: *a, i;* Long Vowels: *e, u*

AUDITORY/VISUAL LEARNERS PARTNERS

Materials: Take-Home Books

Pair children and have them take turns reading aloud each page of the story. Have the listening partner raise a hand each time he or she hears a word with the long *u* sound. Repeat this activity listening for long *a* and long *i* words.

CHALLENGE

Have children experiment and then write two sentences telling how to make the shadow pictures bigger and smaller.

EXTRA SUPPORT/INTERVENTION

Materials: Take-Home Books

Before children read, help them identify each shadow picture and write the animal names on the board. Then, pair children with more competent readers and have them take turns reading each page.
See Daily Phonics Practice, pages 316–318.

Lesson 94 Pages 197–198

Long Vowel o

Skill Focus
Children will
★ recognize the sound of long o.
★ identify pictures whose names contain the sound of long o.

ESL/ELL Emphasize the difference between pronouncing and spelling long o versus short o. Have children say and write *cot, coat; hop, hope; not, note.*

Teach
Phonemic Awareness: Phoneme Categorization Say the words *home, coat,* and *rope.* Have children repeat the words and tell whether they all have the same vowel sound. Explain that the vowel sound heard in all three words is long o. Then, say the following groups of words. Have children identify the two long o words in each group. Use: *bone, box, toe; hope, stove, make; load, ride, soak; tune, tone, row.*

Phonological Awareness: Rhyme Say *nose, hose.* Point out that these words rhyme. Then, read aloud the sentences below. Ask children to tell you which two words in each sentence rhyme.

- She will row and wear a bow. (*row, bow*)
- Can a bone be shaped like a cone? (*bone, cone*)
- A goat does not wear a coat. (*goat, coat*)

Sound to Symbol Write the word *rope* on the board and read it aloud. Underline the *o* and *e*. Tell children that these letters stand for the long o sound in *rope.*

Practice and Apply
Phonemic Awareness Read aloud the rhyme on page 197. Have children listen for and name words with the long o sound. (*rope, low, slow, show, go*)

Sound to Symbol Help children identify the pictures on pages 197 and 198. Suggest that they say the picture names quietly to themselves as they complete each page.

Reading Use *Sparky's Bone,* The MCP Phonics and Reading Long Vowel Skills Library, Level A, to provide practice in reading words with long and short o.

Phonemic Awareness

Name _____

Turn the jump rope,
High, low, fast, slow!
Put on a show!
Come on, let's go!

▶ **Rope** has the long sound of **o**. **Circle** each picture whose name has the long sound of **o**.

1. rope 2. bone 3. kite 4. soap
5. cake 6. cone 7. toe 8. row
9. goat 10. nose 11. box 12. robe

Long vowel o: Phonemic awareness **197**

FOCUS ON ALL LEARNERS

ESL/ELL ENGLISH LANGUAGE LEARNERS
- Before beginning page 197, display realia or pictures of a bone, a bow, a robe, a rope, and soap. Help children to name each object. Correct mispronunciations and reinforce the sound of long o.
- Read aloud the directions for page 198. Then, ask a volunteer to name the pictures in item 1. Assist children in determining which picture names have the long o sound, and have them color the pictures. Have children work in pairs to complete items 2 to 4, then review answers aloud.

KINESTHETIC LEARNERS
Materials: jump rope

Have children form a circle. Give one child the end of a rope and toss the other end to another child. Have the children holding the ends of the rope each give a word that contains the long o sound like *rope.* Each child then passes the rope end to another child. Continue until all have had a turn.

Sound to Symbol

▶ **Say** the names of the pictures in each circle. **Color** the parts of the circle that have pictures with long **o** names.

1.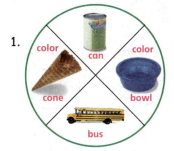
2.
3.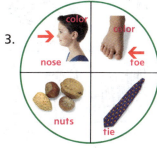
4.

▶ **Use** some of the long **o** words to write a sentence.

_____

HOME With your child, take turns saying all the long o words you can name.

198 Long vowel o: Sound to symbol

CURRICULUM CONNECTIONS

SPELLING
Say each spelling word and then use it in a context sentence. Have children write each word as a spelling pretest.
1. **bone** The dog ate a **bone**.
2. **bow** Sue tied a **bow** in her hair.
3. **robe** Did you hang up your **robe**?
4. **rope** We pulled the sled with a **rope**.
5. **soap** Wash your hands with **soap**.
6. **toe** Joe cut his **toe** on a rock.

WRITING
Ask children to share other jump rope jingles that they may know. Working with partners, have children write new jingles.

SOCIAL STUDIES
Invite children to ask their parents or older relatives to recall jump rope rhymes from their childhood. Suggest that children work with a family member to write these rhymes and bring them in to share.

TECHNOLOGY **AstroWord** Long Vowels: *i, o*

AUDITORY/KINESTHETIC LEARNERS
Say these words and have children tap their noses each time they hear a word that has the long *o* sound: *nose, hose, coat, dog, low, hoe, name, toes, tone, tile, loaf, boat, suit, jokes, soap, tape.*

CHALLENGE
Ask children to select four pictures whose names contain the long *o* sound from page 197. Challenge them to draw pictures of objects whose names rhyme with each picture they select.

EXTRA SUPPORT/INTERVENTION
Materials: Phonics Picture Cards: rake (91), bike (93), fire (94), five (95), mule (103), boat (108), bowl (109), coat (110), cone (111), goat (112), robe (113), hose (114), nose (115); short length of rope

Place the rope on a table and display the picture cards on the chalkboard ledge. Have children take turns selecting pictures whose names contain the long *o* sound like *rope* and place them along the rope. See Daily Phonics Practice, pages 318–319.

Integrating Phonics and Reading

Shared/Guided Reading
Show the cover and read the title. Invite children to tell what Sparky is like, based on the illustration.
First Reading Have children join in each time Sparky says, "Who stole my bone?"
Second Reading Ask children to identify the long *o* words in the story. You might want to add these to the classroom Word Wall.

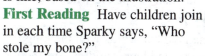

Comprehension
After reading, ask children the following questions:
- What did Sparky think happened to her first bone? *Recall/Plot*
- Why were there two bones in the second hole? *Inference/Drawing Conclusions*

ESL/ELL English Language Learners
Point to the book's title and explain that *'s* shows that the bone belongs to Sparky. Then, write *Cat, Frog, Cow, Mother* on the board. Ask children to add *'s* and say what each animal offered to Sparky.

Lesson 95 Pages 199–200

Long Vowel o

Skill Focus

Children will

★ identify picture names and words that contain the sound of long o.

★ identify rhyming long o words.

★ begin to recognize long o spelling patterns ow, o_consonant_e, oe, and oa.

ESL/ELL Children who speak Asian languages may confuse and assimilate long o with the sound of aw in awful. Practice low, law; so, saw.

Teach

Phonological Awareness: Rhyme Say *cone, bone*. Have children repeat the words. Ask them what they notice. Make sure they point out that the words rhyme and that both words have the long o sound. Then, say these silly sentences and have children complete each one with a rhyming long o word.

- The goat wore a _____.
- A dog named Joan buried a _____.
- The toad used a hose to water the _____.

Sound to Symbol Draw a bow, a rose, a toe, and a boat on the board and label each picture. Have volunteers read the words and identify the vowel sound in each one. Have volunteers underline the vowels in each word with colored chalk. Explain that the long o sound can be spelled different ways. In some words, long o can be spelled ow. In other words, long o can be spelled o_consonant_e; the e is silent. Long o can also be spelled with oe together, and with oa.

Ask children to name other words with the long o sound. List the words and have children sort them according to the letters that spell the long o sound.

Practice and Apply

Sound to Symbol As children identify the pictures on pages 199 and 200, encourage them to say each picture name softly to themselves and listen for the beginning, middle, and ending sounds. After they have completed the pages, review what they have learned about the different ways to spell the long o sound.

Reading Use *Lottie Goat and Donny Goat*, MCP Phonics and Reading Long Vowel Skills Library, Level A, to provide practice in reading words with long and short o.

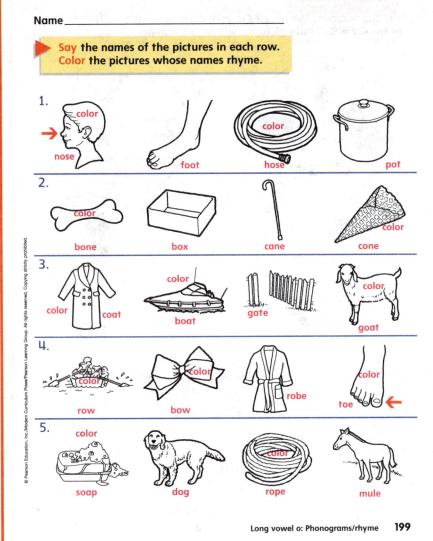

FOCUS ON ALL LEARNERS

ESL/ELL ENGLISH LANGUAGE LEARNERS

Materials: a bow, a rope, soap, picture of a toe

- To prepare for page 199, say a long o or short o word and have children supply a rhyming word. Use *coat, top, hole, cone,* and *hot*.
- Before children begin page 200, show the objects listed above. Label each one using a self-stick note. Read the labels with children and ask volunteers to underline the vowels in each word. Remind them that the long o sound can be spelled in different ways.

VISUAL/KINESTHETIC LEARNERS

Materials: Phonics Picture Cards: bike (93), fire (94), five (95), mule (103), ruler (104), suit (105), tube (106), boat (108), bowl (109), coat (110), cone (111), goat (112), robe (113), hose (114), nose (115); masking tape; toy car

Draw a road and tape cards along it. Children move the car along the road as they name pictures.

Sound to Symbol

▶ Say the name of each picture. Circle its name.

1. (coat) cat coal
2. ripe (rope) rip
3. name rose (nose)
4. sap (soap) sop
5. (boat) bat toad
6. (robe) rob bone
7. rain (cone) cane
8. doe hoe (toe)
9. gate (goat) got
10. row (bow) toe
11. (hose) hope hot
12. cone boat (bone)

Help your child think of other words that rhyme with the names of the pictures on this page, such as *nose, rose, toes.*

200 Long vowel o: Sound to symbol

CURRICULUM CONNECTIONS

SPELLING
Materials: spelling master (page 145I)

Have children make spelling word cards using the master list. Have them illustrate each word on the back of each card.

WRITING
Materials: black construction paper, white chalk

Write the word *snow* on the board and have children read it and identify the vowel sound. Have children describe snow. If you live where snow is a rarity, display pictures of people engaged in snow activities. Then, invite children to use chalk on black paper to draw snow scenes. Have them write sentences describing the snow games they would like to play.

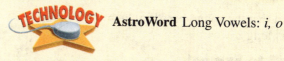 **AstroWord** Long Vowels: *i, o*

Integrating Phonics and Reading

Guided Reading
Show the cover and read the title. Tell children that Lottie Goat and Donny Goat will take a trip in this story. Ask children to tell how they will travel.

First Reading Have children point out each character in the illustrations and tell what the character is doing.

Second Reading Ask children to identify the long *o* words in the story. List the words on the board.

Comprehension
After reading, ask children these questions:
• How did Lottie Goat and Donny Goat solve their problem? *Recall/Problem and Solution*
• What do you think Lottie and Donny should do next? *Inference/Personal Response*

ESL/ELL English Language Learners
Look at the last page with children. Have them tell in their own words why the boat did not go very far. Also have them describe what the crow is doing and why.

AUDITORY/KINESTHETIC LEARNERS
Invite children to form a large circle. Explain that you will say two words. If the words rhyme and have the long *o* sound, have them tap their toes. Some word pairs are *slow, know; boat, coat; bone, boast; cone, king; hose, nose; soap, soup; bow, snow; dog, dock.*

CHALLENGE
Have children identify four different spellings of the long *o* sound on page 200 (*oe, ow, o_e,* and *oa*) and use these spellings as column heads. Challenge children to think of other long *o* words and record them in the correct column.

EXTRA SUPPORT/INTERVENTION
Materials: index cards, crayons

Write *coat, rope, bow,* and *toe* and have children identify four spellings of the long *o* sound. Have them record each spelling on an index card. Suggest that they refer to these cards as they complete page 200. See *Daily Phonics Practice, pages 318–319.*

Lesson 96   Pages 201–202

Long Vowel o

Skill Focus

Children will

★ identify words that contain the sound of long o.

★ identify different spellings for the sound of long o.

★ apply what they have learned by reading directions.

Teach

Phonological Awareness: Blending Onsets and Rimes Tell children that you will say the parts of a word. Have children blend the parts to say the word.

- /r/ope   /t/oe
- /n/ose   /r/ow
- /b/oat   /d/oe

Explain that the sound heard in the middle of each word is long o.

Sound to Symbol

Materials: Phonics Picture Cards: boat (108), bowl (109), robe (113)

Show the picture cards and write *boat*, *bowl*, and *robe* on the board. Have children read each word. Next, write these words on the board: *pole, rose, coat, hole, low, stone, bow, soap, road, note, slow*. Randomly point to a word and have children read it aloud. Ask a volunteer to write the word under the picture name that has the same spelling for the long o sound.

Practice and Apply

Sound to Symbol Help children identify the pictures on page 201. Tell them that they will be circling different spellings for the long o sound as they work through this page.

For page 202, make sure children understand that they will read and follow directions to make changes to the picture. You might wish to monitor their work as they complete the first two items.

Reading Use *When I Go See Gram*, MCP Phonics and Reading Long Vowel Skills Library, Level A, to provide practice in reading words with long and short o.

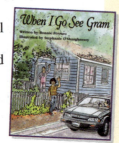

Spelling

Name _____

▶ **Say** the name of each picture. **Circle** the letters that make the long sound of **o**.

1. goat	2. bow	3. nose	4. cone
5. rope	6. boat	7. note	8. row
9. soap	10. hose	11. coat	12. bone

Long vowel o: Spelling   **201**

FOCUS ON ALL LEARNERS

ESL/ELL ENGLISH LANGUAGE LEARNERS

- Review spelling patterns for long *o* words before children complete page 201. Write *rose, loaf, low,* and *toe* on the board. Help children circle the letters in each word that stand for the long *o* sound.

- Complete page 202 together with children, working in small groups or pairs.

VISUAL LEARNERS

Materials: Phonics Picture Cards: 85–92, 103–115; tape

Draw trees on the board and tell children these are oak trees. Tape the cards to the trees as acorns. Have children pick only the acorns whose names have the long *o* sound.

KINESTHETIC LEARNERS

Materials: Phonics Picture Cards: boat (108), coat (110), cone (111), goat (112), robe (113), nose (115); corresponding word cards (165, 166, 167, 168, 176, 174)

Give half the children picture cards and half word cards. Then, have each child find the matching word or picture.

Reading

▶ Look at the picture. Then, follow the directions below.

Directions
1. Color the hose green.
2. Color the boat blue.
3. Circle the girl who will row.
4. Draw a toad on the stone.
5. Make an X on the hoe.
6. Color the roses red.
7. Draw a hole for the mole.
8. Draw a rope on the goat.

 With your child, make up a story about the picture using the long o words.

202   Long vowel o: Reading

CURRICULUM CONNECTIONS

SPELLING
Materials: slips of paper, markers

Have children write each spelling word on a slip of paper. Then, have them mix up the strips and sort the spelling words into four piles based on the spelling of the long *o* sound.

WRITING
Assign each child a partner and have them work together to write a riddle for a word that contains the long *o* sound. To help them get started, you might share this model: *I live on a farm. I have horns. I eat almost anything. What am I?* (a goat)

SCIENCE
Materials: objects with distinctive odors, paper bags

Introduce the word *odor* and explain that this word that contains the long *o* sound means "smell." Place items in bags. Have children close their eyes and take a sniff test.

TECHNOLOGY   **AstroWord** Long Vowels: *i, o*

AUDITORY/VISUAL LEARNERS   GROUPS
Write these words on the board: *Joe, loaf, hope, load, joke.* Say aloud sentences with a missing word, for example: *Bread comes in a __. Joan told a funny __. My friend's name is __. A truck has a heavy __. I __ to have pizza for lunch.* Have children select a word from the board to complete the sentence.

CHALLENGE
Materials: 1-inch grid paper

Have children write a long *o* word in the center of their grid paper with one letter in each box. Then, have them write other long *o* words using letters from the first word, as in a crossword puzzle. They can continue adding words, using letters from the new words. Challenge them to see who can construct a puzzle with the most long *o* words.

EXTRA SUPPORT/INTERVENTION
Pair children with a partner and have them work together to read aloud the words under the pictures on page 201. **See Daily Phonics Practice, pages 318–319.**

Integrating Phonics and Reading

Shared/Guided Reading
Show children the cover illustration and read the title. Ask them to describe the people they see on the cover and tell who they might be.

First Reading As you read, invite children to read aloud the words *Not ever?* and *No, never!* in speech balloons.

Second Reading Have children identify the long *o* words in the story. List them on the board or add them to the classroom Word Wall.

Comprehension
After reading, ask children the following questions:
• What are the things the girl has never done before her visit to Gram's? *Recall/Details*
• What kind of person is Gram? What makes you think so? *Inference/Character*

ESL/ELL **English Language Learners**
Explain that *Gram* is a short, affectionate way to say *Grandmother*. Help children think of other ways to say *Grandmother*, in English or in their first language.

202

Lesson 97 Pages 203–204

Long Vowel o

Skill Focus

Children will

★ distinguish between picture names with short o and long o sounds.

★ identify rhyming long o words.

Teach

Phonemic Awareness: Phoneme Substitution Remind children that they can sometimes make a new word by changing a word's beginning sound. Then, give them these sound clues and ask them to identify each new long o word.

- It rhymes with *bone* and begins like *coat*. (**cone**)
- It rhymes with *hoe* and begins like *toad*. (**toe**)
- It rhymes with *coat* and begins like *no*. (**note**)
- It rhymes with *low* and begins like *boat*. (**bow**)

Sound to Symbol Write the words *not* and *note* on the board and read them aloud. Discuss what happens to the vowel sound when *e* is added to the end of *not*. Then, write the words *rob, hop,* and *rod* on the board and read them aloud. Ask volunteers to add an *e* to the end of each word, using colored chalk. Ask what happens to the short vowel sound when *e* is added to the end of the word. Elicit that the silent *e* changes the short vowel sound to a long vowel sound.

Practice and Apply

Sound to Symbol Help children identify the pictures on page 203. Remind them to listen for a short or long vowel sound in each picture name.

For page 204, remind children to circle all the words that rhyme with the picture name. Also remind them that there are different ways to spell the long o sound.

Reading Use *A Stew for Egor's Mom*, MCP Phonics and Reading Long Vowel Skills Library, Level A, to provide practice in reading words with long and short o.

Say the name of each picture. If the vowel sound is short, color the box with the word **short**. If the vowel sound is long, color the box with the word **long**.

1. robe — short / long
2. mop — short / long
3. doll — short / long
4. boat — short / long
5. cone — short / long
6. goat — short / long
7. pot — short / long
8. coat — short / long
9. top — short / long
10. rope — short / long
11. bone — short / long
12. sock — short / long

Long and short vowel o: Phonemic awareness 203

FOCUS ON ALL LEARNERS

ESL/ELL ENGLISH LANGUAGE LEARNERS

- Before children begin page 203, practice discriminating between long and short o words. Say the following and have children point to their noses when they hear a long o sound: *hope, hop, sock, soak, cot, coat, note, not, rode, rod, mom, most.*

- To help children prepare for the activity on page 204, say a series of long and short o words and have children supply a rhyming word for each one. Use: *coat, top, hole, bone,* and *hot.*

VISUAL/AUDITORY LEARNERS

Materials: Phonics Picture Cards: box (70), dog (71), doll (72), mop (73), ox (74), top (75), boat (108), bowl (109), coat (110), cone (111), goat (112), robe (113), hose (114), nose (115); chart paper; marker

Draw a large tic-tac-toe grid on the chart paper. Have one child place pictures whose names contain the short o sound to mark moves while the other child uses only long o pictures. The first to place three pictures in a row wins.

Sound to Symbol

Say the name of each picture. Circle the words in the boxes that rhyme with the picture name.

1. cone

(bone)	cane	(loan)	(moan)	can
(Joan)	(tone)	run	(zone)	coat

2. goat

got	(boat)	(coat)	note	(vote)
rate	cute	(tote)	gate	(moat)

3. toe

(snow)	(doe)	tip	top	(slow)
(go)	tube	(row)	(foe)	tail

4. row

rope	(slow)	(blow)	rip	(snow)
(low)	ride	(bow)	(tow)	rock

204 Long vowel o: Sound to symbol

 Help your child to make up sentences using the rhyming words, such as *I wore a coat in the boat.*

CURRICULUM CONNECTIONS

SPELLING
Have children write their spelling words, leaving a blank for each vowel. Then, have them exchange lists with a partner and fill in the missing vowels.

WRITING
Materials: books on animals

Brainstorm a list of animals whose names contain the long *o* sound. These might include a toad, a mole, a goat, a boa, a foal, a goldfish, and a doe. Ask children to share what they know about each animal. Then, have pairs of children select an animal from the list and write several factual sentences about their animal.

MATH
Record on the board the names of animals that have the long *o* sound. (See writing activity for some suggestions.) Have children vote for their favorite animals. Record this information in a tally chart. Then, have children count the tally marks to determine which animal is the most popular.

 AstroWord Long Vowels: *i, o*

AUDITORY/KINESTHETIC LEARNERS
Tell children they will play "Top to Toe." Say these words and have children touch the tops of their heads if the vowel sound is short and touch their toes if the vowel sound is long: *soap, jokes, low, dog, fox, top, hose, boat, comb, rock, fox, pot, tone, toad.*

CHALLENGE
Materials: a snow globe or a picture of one, drawing paper, crayons

Help children identify the snow globe. Then, shake it and have children explain how snow globes got their name. Have children draw snow globes that contain scenes with objects whose names have the long *o* or short *o* sounds.

EXTRA SUPPORT/INTERVENTION
Have partners work together to read the words in each row on page 204 and underline all words with the long *o* sound. Then, have them say those words aloud, listening for those that rhyme with the picture name. **See Daily Phonics Practice, pages 318–319.**

Integrating Phonics and Reading

Guided Reading
Show children the cover illustration and read the title. Ask them to tell if they think the story they are about to read will be silly or serious.

First Reading Children may need support reading the words *stew, aren't,* and *fireplace.*

Second Reading Have children identify the long and short *o* words in the book. List the words on the board in two columns.

Comprehension
After reading, ask the following questions:
- What are some of the silly things that Egor did as he cooked the stew? *Recall/Details*
- Are you surprised that Mom liked the stew? *Reflective Analysis/Character*

ESL/ELL English Language Learners
Help students recall the things Egor put in his stew and discuss what is silly about them. Then, help them make a list of ingredients that they might put in a real stew.

Lesson 98   Pages 205–206

Long Vowel o

Skill Focus

Children will

★ identify words and pictures whose names contain the sounds of short vowel o and the sounds of long i, u, and o.

★ write words that contain the sound of long o to complete sentences.

★ recognize and read high-frequency words.

Teach

Phonemic Awareness: Medial Sound Isolation Draw an ice-cream cone on the board and help children name it. Then, say *cone*, followed by /ō/. Model the procedure again using *row*, then /ō/. Then, have children say these words and follow each one with its vowel sound: *nose, soak, toad*. Ask children to identify the vowel sound heard in all the words. (*long o*)

Sound to Symbol Write these words on the board, then call on volunteers to highlight the vowels with colored chalk: *road, hoe, joke, low*. After children read the words, ask how they are alike and how they are different. (*All have the long o sound; the sound is spelled with different letters in each word.*) Ask a volunteer to write another word under *road* that spells the long o sound with the letters *oa* together. Repeat with *hoe* (*oe*), *joke* (*o_consonant_e*), *low* (*ow*).

Practice and Apply

Sound to Symbol As children complete page 205, encourage them to say each picture name quietly to themselves and to listen for a long or short vowel sound.

Writing For page 206, suggest that children try each word choice before writing a word. As they complete the activity, they will have the opportunity to read the high-frequency word *goes*.

Critical Thinking For Talk About It, have children sort the animals named on the page into two groups: pets and wild animals. Then, have them tell how they made their choices for the pets group.

Reading Use *When Bob Woke Up Late*, MCP Phonics and Reading Long Vowel Skills Library, Level A, to provide practice in reading words with long and short o.

205

Sound to Symbol

Name _____

▶ Say the name of each picture. Circle its name.

1. cat (coat)	2. not (note)	3. (mop) mope	4. kit (kite)
5. bat (boat)	6. rob (robe)	7. got (goat)	8. cub (cube)
9. sap (soap)	10. (rat) rate	11. moan (man)	12. cute (cut)

Long and short vowels a, i, u, o: Sound to symbol

FOCUS ON ALL LEARNERS

ESL/ELL ENGLISH LANGUAGE LEARNERS

- Before children complete page 205, make sure that they can name each picture. Have children read both word choices to practice pronunciation, offering help as needed.

- Read the word choices on page 206 with children. Make sure they understand the meaning of each one. Have children work in small groups or pairs to complete the page.

VISUAL LEARNERS   INDIVIDUAL

Materials: construction paper, crayons, discarded magazines, paste

Have children draw large bowls on their papers and label them *long o bowls*. Then, ask children to cut out words and pictures whose names have the long o sound and paste them on their bowls.

KINESTHETIC/VISUAL LEARNERS

Materials: Phonics Picture Cards 85–115, paper

Distribute the cards. Direct children to different spots in the room, based on their long *a*, long *o*, long *i*, or long *u* picture name. For example, tell everyone with long *o* pictures to meet at the board.

Words in Context

Look at the picture. Circle the word that will finish the sentence. Print it on the line.

1. A mole hides in a __hole__. — hose / (hole) / hope
2. A fish swims in a __bowl__. — box / bone / (bowl)
3. A goat eats a __cone__. — bone / (cone) / cane
4. A cat goes up a __pole__. — poke / (pole) / loan
5. A dog begs for a __bone__. — (bone) / robe / boat
6. A fox cleans its __coat__. — cone / coal / (coat)

TALK About It Which animals make good pets? Why?

HOME Ask your child to use the words circled on this page in sentences.

206 Long vowel o: High-frequency words, critical thinking

CURRICULUM CONNECTIONS

SPELLING
Materials: spelling cards made in Lesson 95, pages 199–200

Have children work in pairs and take turns displaying the picture side of each spelling card. Have a partner write the spelling word. Children can check this spelling by comparing it to the word written on the back of the card.

WRITING
Materials: class pet or other animal, hand lenses

Allow time for children to observe a class pet or other animal such as an ant or a ladybug. Have children write several sentences describing their observations.

SCIENCE
Materials: mural paper, crayons

Have children work together to create a mural that shows different animal habitats and homes. Environments might include a forest, swamp, seashore, desert, jungle, and rain forest.

TECHNOLOGY
AstroWord Long Vowels: i, o

AUDITORY/VISUAL LEARNERS **GROUPS**
Materials: Phonics Word Cards: *bone* (165), *coast* (166), *foam* (167), *hole* (168), *home* (169), *load* (170), *loaf* (171), *joke* (172), *note* (174), *poke* (175), *oats* (176), *rode* (177), *rose* (178), *toe* (179); paper bag

Place the word cards in the bag. Have children select one card. Have them read the words on both sides of the card and use one or both of them in an oral sentence or two.

CHALLENGE
Have children recall other animals whose names contain the sound of long *o*. A doe, a foal, a goldfish, and a toad may be mentioned. Have each child select one of these animals and write a sentence with a missing long *o* word about this animal for a partner to complete.

EXTRA SUPPORT/INTERVENTION
Point out the pictures on page 206 and explain that these pictures can help them understand each sentence. Have children work in pairs to read aloud each sentence and the three words before completing the sentence. See Daily Phonics Practice, pages 318–319.

Integrating Phonics and Reading

Shared/Guided Reading
Show the cover as you read the title. Then, preview the illustrations. Ask children if they think Bob has a good day or a bad day in the story.

First Reading Invite children to read aloud each of the notes from Bob's mom.

Second Reading Have children identify the long and short *o* words in the story. Ask them to list the words on the board and to circle any words that rhyme.

Comprehension
After reading, ask children the following questions:

- What kind of day is Bob having in the story? *Recall/Summarize*
- Did you ever have a day like Bob's? *Reflective Analysis/Comparison*

ESL/ELL English Language Learners
Have children act out these story events: *Bob woke up late; tripped on a hose; dropped the note; went back home; got to school.*

Lesson 99 Pages 207–208

Long Vowel o

Skill Focus

Children will
* recognize the sound of long o.
* identify and spell picture names that contain the sound of long o.
* write words that contain the sound of long o to complete sentences.
* recognize and read high-frequency words.

Teach

Phonemic Awareness: Phoneme Blending
Say the word *home*, separating the sound of each phoneme: /h/ /ō/ /m/. Ask children what vowel sound is heard. (long o) Have children say the word, stretching the medial sound: *home*. Repeat with *goal, vote, rose,* and *foam*.

Sound to Symbol Say these words and write them on the board: *hop, not, mop, rob*. Have volunteers come up, add an *e* to each word, and read the new word. Discuss how adding *e* changed each of the words. Then, say the words *do* and *to* and write them on the board. Ask volunteers to add an *e* to each word to make a long *o* word, then read the word. (*doe, toe*) Discuss how the letters *oe* together can spell the long *o* sound.

Next, say and write these words: *cat, sap, bat*. Ask a volunteer to add an *o* to each word to make a long *o* word, then write the new word and read it aloud. (*coat, soap, boat*) Discuss how the letters *oa* together can also spell the long *o* sound.

Practice and Apply

Blend Phonemes As children complete page 207, encourage them to say each picture name, blending together the beginning, middle, and ending sounds.

Writing For page 208, suggest that children try each word choice before writing a word. As they complete the activity, they will have the opportunity to read the following high-frequency words: *blue, them*.

Critical Thinking For Talk About It, have children recall the items that were in the store and help them conclude that a store that sells many different items is called a department store.

Reading Use *The Hiccups Would Not Stop*, MCP Phonics and Reading Long Vowel Skills Library, Level A, to provide practice in reading words with long and short *o*.

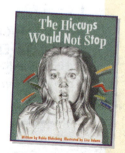

Spelling

Name_____

Say the name of each picture. Print the missing vowels on the line. Trace the whole word.

1. c o n e
2. h o s e
3. r o b e
4. t o p
5. r o p e
6. c o a t
7. n o t e
8. n o s e
9. s o a p
10. p o t
11. m o p
12. b o a t

Long and short vowel o: Spelling 207

FOCUS ON ALL LEARNERS

ESL/ELL ENGLISH LANGUAGE LEARNERS
* Review the picture names on page 207. Then, help children identify the beginning, middle, and ending sound in each word.
* Have children work in pairs to complete page 208. Review answers aloud in small groups.

VISUAL LEARNERS
Materials: drawing paper, crayons

Ask children to draw a picture of a large house with lots of windows. Tell them that inside the home there are many objects whose names have the long *o* sound. Have them draw some of these objects so they are visible through the windows.

KINESTHETIC LEARNERS
Materials: chart paper, marker, beanbag

Draw a target on chart paper and divide it into three sections. Write one of these words in each section: *rope, cube, bike*. Write an *o, u,* or *i* beside the appropriate word. Have children toss the beanbag to land on words with the long *o* sound. After a hit, have them read the word aloud. Wherever they land, have them suggest other words with the same long vowel sounds.

Words in Context

Circle the word that will finish the sentence. **Print** it on the line.

1. The store is up the __road__.
   - (road)
   - robe
   - role

2. Joan goes in and smells the __soap__.
   - song
   - soak
   - (soap)

3. It gets on her __nose__.
   - not
   - (nose)
   - hope

4. Joan sees a red __bow__.
   - boss
   - (bow)
   - row

5. She sees a blue __robe__, too.
   - (robe)
   - rob
   - ripe

6. She will pay and take them __home__.
   - hose
   - hole
   - (home)

THINK What kind of store did Joan visit?

HOME With your child, think of other sentences using these long o words.

Long vowel o: High-frequency words, critical thinking

CURRICULUM CONNECTIONS

SPELLING
Write two sets of the spelling words on cards, omitting the vowels in one set and the initial consonant in another set. Have children work with a partner to write the missing letter or letters on each card. Encourage them to say the words aloud as they write missing letters.

WRITING
Brainstorm a list of items children might buy. Be sure to include some words containing the long *o* sound. Then, have children select an item and write an advertisement for it.

PORTFOLIO

MATH
Materials: small objects whose names contain the sound of long *o*, self-stick notes, play money

Explain to children that they are going to set up a "long *o* store," where items whose names contain this vowel sound are for sale. Using self-stick notes, have children price and label the objects and then arrange them. Children can take turns acting as customers and cashiers in the long *o* store.

TECHNOLOGY
AstroWord Long Vowels: *i, o*

AUDITORY LEARNERS — GROUPS
Read aloud these silly sentences and have children replace the incorrect word with a long *o* word that makes sense in the context of the sentence: *Joan put on her slippers and rope.* (robe) *Wash your toes with soak.* (soap) *Joe dove off the side of the bowl.* (boat)

CHALLENGE
Give pairs of children these categories and challenge them to think of words containing the sound of long *o* that fit in each group: animals, articles of clothing, body parts, household objects, plants.

EXTRA SUPPORT/INTERVENTION
Point out the picture at the top of page 208 and tell children that it will help them understand the story. Have children work in pairs to read aloud each sentence and the three word choices before completing the sentence. **See Daily Phonics Practice, pages 318–319.**

Integrating Phonics and Reading

Shared/Guided Reading
Show the cover as you read the title. Ask children to tell about times that they had the hiccups and whether they did anything special to make them stop.

First Reading Invite children to join in each time you come to a sentence that has a "hic."

Second Reading Have children identify the long and short *o* words in the story. List the words on the board in two columns.

Comprehension
After reading, ask children the following questions:
- What did Jo try to make her hiccups stop? Which action worked? *Recall/Plot*
- What do you think Jo will do the next time she has hiccups? *Inference/Details*

ESL/ELL English Language Learners
Have children review the story. Then, work with them to make a list entitled "Three Ways to Stop Hiccups."

Lesson 100
Pages 209–210

Review Long Vowels
a, i, u, o

Skill Focus

Children will

★ recognize the sound of long o.

★ identify and spell picture names that contain the sound of long o.

★ identify and distinguish among words that contain the sounds of long a, i, u, and o.

Teach

Phonological Awareness: Rhyme Read aloud these rhyme riddles and invite children to tell you the answers.

- It rhymes with *tone* and is something dogs like to chew on. (*bone*)
- It rhymes with *take* and is something that is filled with water. (*lake*)
- It rhymes with *like* and is something you can ride. (*bike*)
- It rhymes with *cube* and is something that you squeeze to get toothpaste. (*tube*)

Sound to Symbol Write this sentence on the board and ask a volunteer to read it aloud: *Joan and Jake rode bikes to Blue Lake.* Ask children to underline the words that have long vowel sounds in the sentence. After the four vowel sounds are identified, label four columns on the board *Long a, Long i, Long u, Long o*. Have volunteers write words from the sentence under each column heading. Then, ask children to think of other words that contain these long vowel sounds and list them under the correct heading.

Practice and Apply

Blend Phonemes As children complete page 209, encourage them to say each picture name, blending together the beginning, middle, and ending sounds.

Sound to Symbol Before children begin the activity on page 210, review how to play tic-tac-toe. Remind children that they will be looking for three words in a row with the same long vowel sound.

Reading Use *Grandpa, Grandma, and the Tractor*, MCP Phonics and Reading Long Vowel Skills Library, Level A, to provide practice in reading words with long o.

209

Spelling

Name _____

▶ **Say** the name of each picture. **Print** the name on the line. In the last box, **draw** a picture of a long **o** word. **Print** the word.

1. bone	2. soap	3. rope
4. bow	5. hose	6. toe
7. coat	8. cone	9. boat
10. row	11. nose	12.

Long vowel o: Spelling **209**

FOCUS ON ALL LEARNERS

ESL/ELL ENGLISH LANGUAGE LEARNERS

- Before children begin page 209, review different spellings for the long *o* sound. Write the headings *o_e, oa, ow, oe* on the board. Work with children to list one or more words for each spelling.

- Complete page 210 with children, working in pairs or small groups. Have children say each picture name in a game board aloud before deciding which three have the same long vowel sounds.

VISUAL LEARNERS *INDIVIDUAL*

Materials: paper, discarded magazines, scissors, paste

Have children label each of four sheets of paper *Long a, Long i, Long u,* or *Long o*. Have children cut out words and/or pictures whose names have each of these vowel sounds. Then, have them paste these words and pictures on the appropriate sheet.

Sound to Symbol

▶ **Say** each picture name. **Draw** a line through the three pictures in a row that have the same long vowel sound.

1.
2.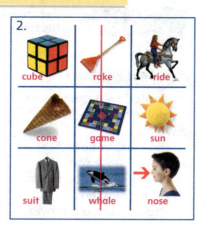
3.
4.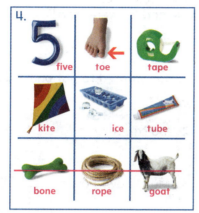

210 Review long vowels a, i, u, o: Sound to symbol

HOME Ask your child to think of more words using the long vowel a, i, u, or o that "won" in each puzzle.

CURRICULUM CONNECTIONS

SPELLING
Materials: letter cards: *Bb, Oo, Nn, Ee, Ww, Rr, Pp, Ss, Aa, Pp, Tt*

Have children work in pairs and take turns dictating the six long *o* spelling words for their partner to spell using the cards. After each word is spelled correctly, have both children write the word.

WRITING
Review the words to the traditional song "Row, Row, Row Your Boat" with children. Then, work with children to write some new verses to the song that incorporate other long *o* words: "Hold, Hold, Hold Your Toe" or "Grow, Grow, Grow Some Oats."

SCIENCE
Materials: flashlight

Dim the lights and, using a flashlight, project a shadow onto the classroom ceiling. Then, have children recall what causes a shadow, pointing out that a shadow is caused when light is blocked by an object.

TECHNOLOGY  **AstroWord** Long Vowels: *i, o*

Integrating Phonics and Reading

Guided Reading
Show the cover as you read the title. Ask children to tell where they think the story will take place.
First Reading Have children point out the tractor or other machines and describe the work they are doing.
Second Reading Have children identify the long *o* words in the story. Also ask them to find a word that has both a long *i* and a long *a*.
Comprehension
After reading, ask children the following questions:
• Why do Grandma and Grandpa stop using the tractor? *Inference/Cause and Effect*
• What new job does the tractor do at the end of the story? *Inference/Plot*

ESL/ELL English Language Learners
Write the word *farm* in the center of a semantic web and list these words around it: *tractor, dirt, planting, shed, plow*. Using the illustrations as a guide, discuss the meaning of each "farm word."

AUDITORY LEARNERS (GROUPS)
Talk with children about the meaning of the term *echo*. Then, say these words and have children echo a word only if it contains the sound of long *o*. Words are: *loaf, loan, lot, note, not, sod, soap, blow, bit, snow, sow, soak, sole, comb, coast, cod, coat, cone*.

CHALLENGE
Remind children that word chains are formed by changing one letter in a word to make a new word. Write these words on the board and have children work with a partner to write some word chains: *boat, row, coast, robe*. Suggest that children compare their chains.

EXTRA SUPPORT/INTERVENTION
When working on page 209, suggest that children begin by writing the letters that stand for the consonant sound in a word. Give help as needed in writing the letters that stand for the vowel sound. **See Daily Phonics Practice, pages 316–319.**

Lesson 101 Pages 211–212

Phonics and Reading / Phonics and Writing

Long Vowel o

Skill Focus

Children will

★ read words that contain the sound of long o.

★ write long o words to finish sentences.

★ build words with long o phonograms -ose, -old.

Teach

Phonemic Awareness: Phoneme Substitution Write the word *gold* on the board. Help children to read it aloud and have them identify the vowel sound they hear. Then, invite a volunteer to delete the *g* and add *c* to make a new word (*cold*). Continue, adding *b* (*bold*), *f* (*fold*), and *h* (*hold*). Have children identify the middle sound heard in all the words. You may wish to point out that these words do not follow the long *o* spelling patterns children have seen in previous lessons.

Sound to Symbol Write the words *no* and *go* on the board and ask a volunteer to underline the vowel in each word. Explain that if a word or syllable has one vowel and it comes at the end of the word or syllable, the vowel is usually long, as in *no* and *go*.

Words in Sentences Write these sentences on the board.
- Joan danced in an old coat.
- Joe told so many funny jokes.

Help children read the sentences. Then, ask them to circle the words that have the long *o* sound.

Practice and Apply

Phonics and Reading After children have read the story, encourage them to identify words that have the long *o* sound. Also, check their comprehension of these high-frequency words: *knows, over, how*.

Critical Thinking For Talk About It, have children recall the tricks mentioned in the story before responding.

Phonics and Writing For page 212, tell children to try each letter at the top to make a word with *-ose* or *-old*. Remind them that not every letter will make a real word.

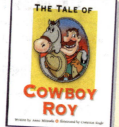

Reading Use *The Tale of Cowboy Roy,* MCP Phonics and Reading Long Vowel Skills Library, Level A, to provide practice in reading words with long *o* pattern o_e.

Name _____

Phonics & Reading — **Read** the story. **Use** long **o** words to finish the sentences.

Joe's Show

Joe wanted to put on a show.
"My dog Bo will be in the show," he said.
"Bo can catch a bone."
Joe's friend Rose came by.
"Can my dog Moe be in your show?" Rose asked.
"He knows how to roll over," she said.
"Yes," said Joe.
Moe and Bo were stars!

1. Joe wanted to put on a ____show____.

2. Bo can catch a ____bone____.

3. Moe knows how to ____roll____ over.

TALK About It What other tricks can pets do?

Review long vowel o: Reading, critical thinking 211

FOCUS ON ALL LEARNERS

ESL/ELL ENGLISH LANGUAGE LEARNERS

- Build background for the story on page 211 by inviting children to tell about tricks or clever things they have seen pets do. Discuss the illustration at the top to preview the story.
- Pair students with English-speaking partners for the word-building activity on page 212.

VISUAL/AUDITORY LEARNERS

Materials: chart paper, marker, crayons

On a piece of chart paper, have children draw the outline of a dog with a big bone. Have each child write words with the long *o* sound on the bone. Have children in the group take turns reading aloud each other's words.

KINESTHETIC/AUDITORY LEARNERS

Have the group make cutouts of Joe, Rose, Bo, and Moe. Then, have them use the cutouts to act out the story while group members read it aloud.

211

Building Words

Use one of the letters to make a word with **ose** or **old**. **Write** each real word on the lines.

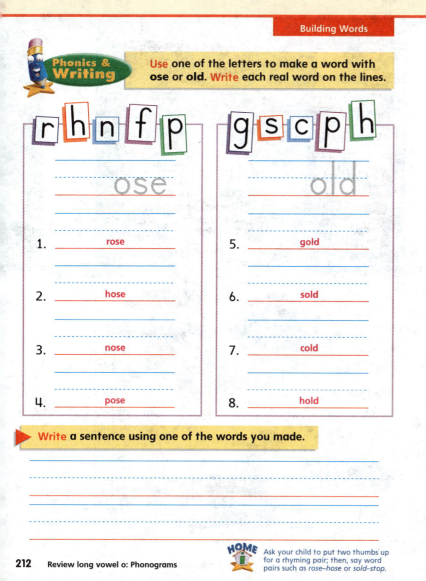

1. rose
2. hose
3. nose
4. pose
5. gold
6. sold
7. cold
8. hold

▶ **Write** a sentence using one of the words you made.

 Ask your child to put two thumbs up for a rhyming pair; then, say word pairs such as *rose–hose* or *sold–stop*.

Review long vowel o: Phonograms

CURRICULUM CONNECTIONS

SPELLING
Dictate these spelling words and sentences and have children write the words as a spelling posttest.
1. **bone** Bo likes to catch a **bone**.
2. **bow** She wore a **bow** in her hair.
3. **robe** I made a costume out of a **robe**.
4. **rope** We held the curtain up with **rope**.
5. **soap** The baby got **soap** in her eyes.
6. **toe** He scraped his **toe** on the rock.

FINE ARTS
Materials: oak tag, scissors, craft sticks, paste

Have children make cutout puppets and mount them on craft sticks. Have children use their puppets to put on a shadow show.

WRITING
Have children write about another pet owner and pet that might be in Joe's show. Invite them to share their stories with the class.

AstroWord Long Vowels: *i, o*

Integrating Phonics and Reading

Shared/Guided Reading
Show the cover as you read the title. Then, invite children to tell what they know about cowboys.
First Reading Have children read Roy's words as you narrate.
Second Reading Have children identify a long *o* word with the spelling pattern o_e and write it on the board. (rope)
Comprehension
After reading, ask children the following questions:
• How did Cowboy Roy really feel about the rattlesnake? *Inference/Character*
• Could Cowboy Roy do all the things he said he could? *Recall/Fantasy and Realism*

ESL/ELL English Language Learners
Point out the word *hiss* on page 9. Have children *hiss* these story words by exaggerating the *s* sounds: *this, it's, cows, miles.*

AUDITORY LEARNERS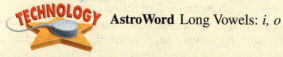
Have children take turns reading the story aloud to a partner. Suggest that the partner softly bark each time he or she hears a word that contains the long *o* sound.

CHALLENGE
Have children make a sign that tells about Joe's show. Suggest that they include long *o* words such as *go, open, over,* and *hope*.

EXTRA SUPPORT/INTERVENTION
Suggest that children underline the long *o* words in the story. They can then try out these words to see which one makes sense as they complete the sentences at the bottom. **See Daily Phonics Practice, pages 318–319.**

Lesson 102   Pages 213–214

Take-Home Book

Review Long Vowels
a, i, u, o

Skill Focus
Children will
* read long *a, i, u,* and *o* words in the context of a story.
* review selected high-frequency words in the context of a story.
* reread for fluency.

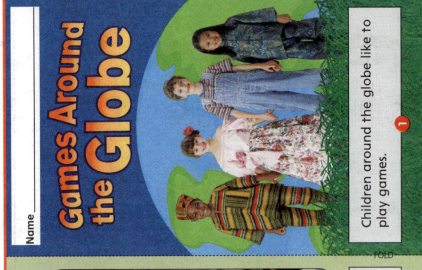

Review long vowels a, i, u, o: Take-home book   213

Teach
Build Background
Materials: globe

Help children recall that the theme of this unit is "Let's Play." Then, display the globe and help children identify it. Explain that the globe is a model of the world, and it shows all of the different countries. Help children find the United States on the globe. If you have children who have lived in or visited other countries, have them name these countries and help them point them out on the globe.

Phonological Awareness: Rhyme Say the following sentences and ask children to identify the rhyming words in each one. Also, have them identify the long vowel sound in the rhyming words.

* Miles would like to hike.
* What is the name of this game?
* Can you get this boat to float?
* The clown wore a cute blue suit.

Practice and Apply
Read the Book Help children tear out and fold the pages to make their Take-Home Books. Then, read the book together. Discuss which of the games children have played or would like to play.

Sound to Symbol Read aloud or have volunteers read the book. Have children identify the long *a, i, u,* and *o* words. (*play, games, places; like, kind; rules, tune; globe, know, rope*) Invite volunteers to write the words on the board, read them aloud, and underline the vowels.

Review High-Frequency Words Write the words *the, like, they, do,* and *you* on the board. Have children spell the words, then say them.

Reread for Fluency Have children reread the book to increase their fluency and comprehension. Children can take their books home to read and share with family members.

FOCUS ON ALL LEARNERS

ESL/ELL ENGLISH LANGUAGE LEARNERS
After assisting children with making the Take-Home Book, use the following activities to teach English language learners.

* Build background by inviting children to tell about favorite games from their cultures.
* Read the text together and discuss the photos. Ask questions such as "What does the soccer ball look like?"
* Review the story words *around, globe, ball, rules, clap, rope.* Have children use each word in an oral sentence.

KINESTHETIC LEARNERS

Materials: Phonics Word Cards; Set 1: *paint* (133), *safe* (135), *dime* (144), *fire* (146), *cube* (158), *rule* (161), *boat* (165), *hole* (168), *joke* (172); chalk or masking tape

Make a hopscotch grid on the floor with chalk or tape. Place cards in the corners of the squares. Have children hop through the squares, saying another word with the same vowel sound for each square.

213

2 Some children play ball games. They must know the rules of the game.

3 Some children like to play clapping games. They can clap and sing a tune.

214 Review long vowels a, i, u, o: Take-home book

CURRICULUM CONNECTIONS

HEALTH/SCIENCE
Materials: jump ropes (optional)

Show children how to find and feel their pulse, either at their wrist or at the side of their neck. If room allows, have them jump rope. If there is not room, have them "jump" pretend ropes. Then, have them feel their pulse again. Discuss what happens to their pulse when they exercise. Explain that the heart is a muscle, just like those in their arms and legs. Discuss why it is important to exercise muscles.

SOCIAL STUDIES
Materials: globe or world map

Ask students to imagine an international jump-rope championship that involves four different countries. Have them use the map or globe to choose the countries. Then, invite them to tell about the imaginary competition.

WRITING
Materials: drawing paper, crayons, construction paper, stapler

Ask children to draw pictures of themselves playing their favorite game. Help them fasten the picture to a larger piece of construction paper. Under the picture, have them write a sentence or two telling about the game.

 **AstroWord** Long Vowels: *a, i,*
Long Vowels: *i, o,*
Long Vowels: *e, u*

AUDITORY/VISUAL LEARNERS
Materials: Take-Home Book, tape recorder, blank tape

Pair children and have them work together to make a read-along audiotape of the story. Suggest that they come up with a signal that indicates when a page should be turned. Encourage them to invite others to enjoy their tape.

CHALLENGE
Have children work with a partner to select one of the games featured in the Take-Home Book. Then, have them write a brief set of directions telling how to play the game.

EXTRA SUPPORT/INTERVENTION
Materials: index cards

Write these story words on index cards: *game, globe, rules, like*. Help children read the words. Then, have them identify the long vowel sound in each one. **See Daily Phonics Practice, pages 316–319.**

214

Lesson 103 Pages 215–216

High-Frequency Words

Skill Focus

Children will

★ recognize and read the high-frequency words *from, them, their, which, because, want*.

★ use high-frequency words to complete sentences.

Teach

Analyze Words Write the words *from, them, their, which, because, want* on the board. Point to each word as you read it aloud. Have children repeat each word after you. Then:

- Have children use letter cards to spell each word.
- Slowly say each word as you point to the letters. Encourage children to listen for the consonant and vowel sounds in the word.
- Have children say each word, blending the sounds.
- Help children associate the sounds they hear in each word with a familiar word.

You may wish to add these words to the class Word Wall so that children can use the words they learn to find similar spelling patterns and phonemic elements in new words.

Read Words in Sentences Write the following sentences on the board. Invite volunteers to read the sentences and underline the high-frequency words. Then, help children read the sentences.

- We got two cards from Grandma.
- Which do you want to open first?
- You can tell them apart by their size.
- I picked this one because of the pretty stamp.

Practice and Apply

Write Words Have children turn to page 215. Read the directions aloud and make sure children understand what to do. Do the same for page 216. Encourage children to use the strategies they have learned to associate sounds with letters and blend words to help them read. Children can work with a partner to complete Checking Up.

Reading You may wish to use *Steve's Room*, MCP Phonics and Reading Library, High Frequency Word Collection, Level A, to reinforce some of the high-frequency words.

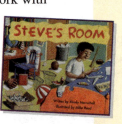

High-Frequency Words

Name _____

▶ Read the words in the box. Write a word to finish each sentence.

from	which
them	because
Their	want

1. Joe could not go out ___**because**___ of the rain.

2. "Do you ___**want**___ to call Cody or Flo?" Mom said.

3. Joe did not know ___**which**___ friend to call.

4. Mom said Joe could call both of ___**them**___.

5. They played a game ___**from**___ Mexico.

6. ___**Their**___ game was fun!

High-frequency words **215**

FOCUS ON ALL LEARNERS

ESL/ELL ENGLISH LANGUAGE LEARNERS

Materials: High-frequency word cards

English language learners may have difficulty pronouncing the /th/ in *them* and *their* and the vowel pair *au* in *because*.

- Use the high-frequency word cards. As you show children a word, read it aloud.
- Have children say the word and trace each letter in the air. Then, ask them to use the word in a sentence.

VISUAL LEARNERS

Materials: number cube or spinner with numbers 1 to 6

Number the high-frequency words from 1 to 6 and write them on the board. Have each child roll the cube or spin the spinner to get a number. The child then says the word that goes with that number, spells it, and uses it in a sentence.

VISUAL/AUDITORY LEARNERS

Write each of the high-frequency words on an index card. Put the cards in a paper bag. Have each child draw a card, read the word aloud, and use it in a sentence.

High-Frequency Words

Look at the picture. Then, print words from the box to finish the story. The word shapes will help you.

from   their   because
them   Which   want

1. Lin and Lola know Joel **f r o m** school.
2. They **w a n t** him to be **t h e i r** friend.
3. Joel used to say, "**W h i c h** twin is which?"
4. Now he can tell **t h e m** apart.
5. He knows **b e c a u s e** Lin has a gold cap.

CHECKING UP

Put a ✓ next to each word you can read.

☐ them   ☐ want   ☐ because   ☐ which   ☐ from   ☐ their

 Help your child to make up a sentence using some of the words in the box.

216 High-frequency words

CURRICULUM CONNECTIONS

SOCIAL STUDIES
Review the story about the game on page 215 and point out the picture. Explain that the children are playing with a piñata, a colorful toy that is popular in Mexico. At birthday parties and other celebrations, children hit the piñata with a stick so that it breaks open and candy or other prizes spill out. Then, invite children to tell about their favorite games to play at parties and celebrations.

LANGUAGE ARTS
Materials: books of riddles and jokes

Remind children that telling jokes and riddles is one way to play and have fun. Invite them to look through the books and to point out any high-frequency words they find.

KINESTHETIC LEARNERS GROUPS
Materials: chalk

Draw a line on the floor and have six children stand along it. As you say each high-frequency word, have a child spell the word aloud and take one big step forward for each letter. When all the words have been spelled, ask children which has the most letters, based on the number of steps taken.

CHALLENGE
Challenge children to write a set of sentences, leaving a blank for each of the high-frequency words. Then, have them exchange papers and fill in the blanks.

EXTRA SUPPORT/INTERVENTION
Materials: high-frequency word cards

Suggest that children practice the words by holding the high-frequency cards up one at a time while a partner reads the words.

Integrating Phonics and Reading

Shared/Guided Reading
Show the cover as you read the title. Ask children to tell what they see in the room and whether they think it is messy or neat.

First Reading Invite half the class to join in as you read Dad's words and the other half to join in as you read Steve's words.

Second Reading Have children point to the word *from* each time it appears in the story.

Comprehension
After reading, ask children the following questions:
- What did Dad want Steve to do? *Recall/Plot*
- Do you think Steve got rid of the mess? Why or why not? *Reflective Analysis/Opinion*

ESL/ELL English Language Learners
Have children draw and label each of these objects found in Steve's room: shell, bird's nest, toy jet, butterfly net.

216

Lesson 104 Pages 217–218

Long Vowel e

Skill Focus

Children will

★ recognize the sound of long e.

★ identify pictures whose names contain the sound of long e.

★ identify rhyming long e words.

ESL/ELL Children who speak Asian languages or Spanish may confuse long e and short i. Practice saying *feet, fit; Pete, pit; heal, hill.*

Teach

Phonological Awareness: Blending Onsets and Rimes Explain to children that you will say the parts of a word. Ask children to blend the parts together to say a word. Use these words.

- /b/ee   /f/eed   /n/eat
- /s/eal   /m/eat   /p/eel

Explain that the vowel sound heard in each word is long *e*.

Sound to Symbol On the board, draw a bee and a leaf and label both pictures. Ask children to say the picture names and identify the vowel sound that is heard in each word. Underline the vowels in each word. Tell children that the letters *ee* together and the letters *ea* together can stand for the long *e* sound.

Practice and Apply

Phonemic Awareness Read aloud the rhyme on page 217. Have children listen for and name words with the long *e* sound. *(here, tree, be, see, green, leaves, me)*

Sound to Symbol Help children identify the pictures on pages 217 and 218. Suggest that they say the picture names quietly to themselves as they complete each page. You might also tell children that the number of rhyming words on page 218 may vary from row to row.

Reading Use *Dee and Me*, MCP Phonics and Reading Long Vowel Skills Library, Level A, to provide practice in reading words with long and short *e*.

Phonemic Awareness

Name _____

Here in my tree
Is the best place to be.
I can see down,
But the green leaves
Hide me!

▶ **Tree** has the long sound of e. **Circle** each picture whose name has the long sound of e.

1. bee
2. leaf
3. feet
4. ten
5. gate
6. heel
7. cube
8. jeep
9. seal
10. fire
11. jeans
12. seat

Long vowel e: Phonemic awareness **217**

FOCUS ON ALL LEARNERS

ESL/ELL ENGLISH LANGUAGE LEARNERS

- Before beginning page 217, work with children who need practice differentiating between long *e* and short *i*. Model the sound of long *e* and have children repeat after you. Then, say word pairs such as *sit, seat; ship, sheep;* and *hit, heat*. Have children repeat the words and identify the ones that have the long *e* sound.

- Prepare children for page 218 by practicing the pronunciation of long *e* rhyming words such as *me, see; bead, seed;* and *sheep, leap.* Have children complete the page in pairs, then review answers.

VISUAL/KINESTHETIC LEARNERS

Materials: Phonics Picture Cards: cake (86), cane (87), bike (93), fire (94), ruler (104), tube (106), coat (110), cone (111), beads (116), bee (117), eagle (118), jeep (119), leaf (120)

Have children stand by their desks. Display each picture and have a volunteer name it. Have children tap their feet if the picture name contains the long *e* sound.

217

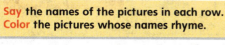

Phonograms/Rhyme

▶ **Say** the names of the pictures in each row.
Color the pictures whose names rhyme.

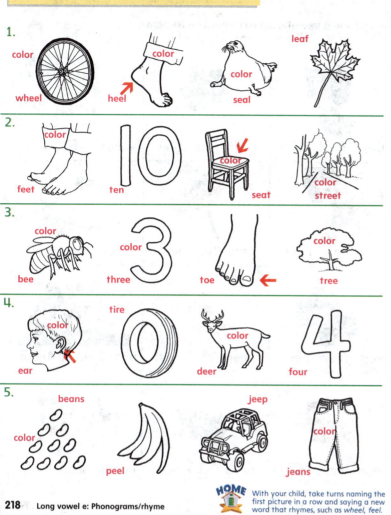

218 Long vowel e: Phonograms/rhyme

 With your child, take turns naming the first picture in a row and saying a new word that rhymes, such as *wheel, feel*.

CURRICULUM CONNECTIONS

SPELLING
Say each spelling word and then use it in a context sentence. Have children write each word as a spelling pretest.
1. **bean** Jean planted a **bean** seed.
2. **feet** My **feet** got wet.
3. **jeep** Her dad has a green **jeep**.
4. **peel** Will you **peel** that apple?
5. **seal** We saw a **seal** at the zoo.
6. **seat** Please sit in that **seat**.

WRITING
With children, make a list of body parts that contain the long *e* sound. The list might include the words *feet, heel, ear,* and *knee*. Have children work in pairs using these words to write directions for a simple exercise routine. For example: *Stamp your feet. Click your heels. Touch your ears. Bend your knees.*

 **AstroWord** Long Vowels: *e, u*

AUDITORY LEARNERS
Materials: letter card: *Ee*
Say these words and have children hold up the letter card when they hear a word that contains the long *e* sound: *bean, leak, ten, cube, men, feed, peek, get, peel, bee, jeep, peas, seed, seal, hem, tree.*

CHALLENGE
Have children review the rhyming pictures in each row on page 218. Challenge them to think of another word that rhymes with those picture names.

EXTRA SUPPORT/INTERVENTION
To assist children who have difficulty identifying rhyming words, say the first picture name in each row. Then, have the child respond by repeating this word and naming the next picture to check for rhyming sounds. **See Daily Phonics Practice, pages 319–320.**

Integrating Phonics and Reading

Guided Reading
Show children the cover as you read the title. Invite them to tell what each of the girls is doing.
First Reading Have children use the pictures to tell about what happens whenever Dee does things by herself.
Second Reading Ask children to identify the long *e* words in the story. You might want to add these to the classroom Word Wall.
Comprehension
After reading, ask children the following questions:
• What is the main thing that Dee wants to do? *Recall/Summarize*
• Why does she usually need a little help when she tries to do all the things her sister does? *Inference/Cause and Effect*

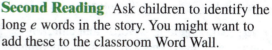 **English Language Learners**
Say or write: *I can _____; I need help when I _____.* Have children think of different ways to complete each sentence.

Lesson 105 Pages 219–220

Long Vowel e

Skill Focus

Children will

★ identify picture names and words that contain the sound of long e.

★ understand that ee and ea can stand for long e.

★ apply what they have learned by reading and writing.

Teach

Phonemic Awareness: Phoneme Categorization Model the sound of long e: eee. Have children repeat the sound and identify it. Then, say the following groups of words. Ask children to identify the two words from each group that have the long e sound.

- bell   bee   beam
- feet   foot   feel
- team   tea   tip
- seal   sea   sock
- lemon   leave   leaf

Sound to Symbol Draw a picture of a beanstalk on the chalkboard. Include several large leaves and some beans. Next to the beanstalk, draw a tree with leaves and a bee. Label the pictures using the words *leaf, bean, tree, bee*.

Help children read the words and identify the long vowel sound. Underline the vowels in each word, then ask volunteers to circle the vowel they hear with colored chalk. Remind children that the long e sound can be spelled ea and ee.

Practice and Apply

Sound to Symbol Help children identify the pictures on page 219. For page 220, make sure children understand that they are to join only the long e words to get through the maze.

Writing Note the long e words that children write on page 220 and check for correct spelling.

Reading Use *Where Is the Queen?* MCP Phonics and Reading Long Vowel Skills Library, Level A, to provide practice in reading words with long e.

Sound to Symbol

Name _____

▶ Say the name of each picture. Circle its name.

1. beet feed (feet)
2. (leaf) lead feel
3. meat (seat) seed
4. feel (heel) heat
5. see tea (bee)
6. real seat (seal)
7. (jeep) Jean peep
8. beep (peel) reel
9. beam seem (team)
10. bead jeans (bean)
11. need (seed) seal
12. (beads) bean beep

Long vowel e: Sound to symbol   219

FOCUS ON ALL LEARNERS

ESL/ELL ENGLISH LANGUAGE LEARNERS

- To prepare children for page 219, write the phrase *green leaf* on the board. Circle the *ee* and *ea*. Remind children that many long *e* words are spelled with these letters.

- Adapt the maze activity on page 220 by having children read each word, circle the words with long *e*, then connect the circled words.

VISUAL/AUDITORY LEARNERS

Materials: Phonics Picture Cards: rake (91), nine (99), mule (103), uniform (107), coat (110), cone (111), beads (116), bee (117), eagle (118), jeep (119), leaf (120)

Draw a tree on the board and tape the cards to it as leaves. Have children say each picture name and pick those pictures whose names have the same long *e* sound as *leaf*.

Phonemic Awareness

▶ **Help** Jean and Lee find the seals at the zoo. **Read** each word. **Draw** a line to join the long e words.

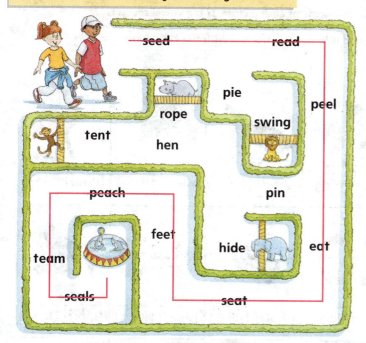

▶ **Use** some of the long e words to write a sentence.

_____
_____
_____

220 Long vowel e: Phonemic awareness

HOME Help your child to use some of the words along the path to make up a short story.

CURRICULUM CONNECTIONS

SPELLING
Material: spelling master (page 145l)
Have children make spelling word cards, illustrating each word on the back of a card.

WRITING
Write this team cheer on the board and help children read it aloud. *Our team is really neat! Our team is the team to beat!* Have children identify the long *e* words. Then, have them brainstorm a list of other long *e* words that could be used in a cheer and write them on the board. Possibilities include *dream, beat, lead, seem,* and *leap*. Working in small groups, have children write team cheers to share with the class.

PORTFOLIO

FINE ARTS
Materials: cardboard; dried peas, lentils, and other beans; white glue
Invite children to create mosaics using beans. Have them draw a simple picture of an object, then glue the beans in and around the picture.

TECHNOLOGY **AstroWord** Long Vowels: *e, u*

AUDITORY/KINESTHETIC LEARNERS **GROUPS**
Read these sentences aloud and have children tap their feet when they hear words with the long *e* sound: *See the seal eat its meal. She cooks beans with meat. Jean has a bag of neat beads. Will we see the team this week? The horn on the jeep went beep, beep.*

CHALLENGE
Have children identify the pictures of foods with the long *e* sound on page 219. Then, challenge children to work with a partner to create a meal made up only of foods that contain the long *e* sound. Possibilities might include peas, beans, meat, peaches, and iced tea.

EXTRA SUPPORT/INTERVENTION
On page 219, have children say each picture name and then read aloud the words. Ask them to underline all words with the long *e* sound. Then, have them circle the word that names the picture. **See Daily Phonics Practice, pages 319–320.**

Integrating Phonics and Reading

Guided Reading
Show children the cover illustration and read the title. Invite them to tell where they think the story takes place.

First Reading Have children use the illustrations to tell how people are preparing for the ball or enjoying themselves at the ball.

Second Reading Have children identify the long *e* words in the story. List the words on the board or add them to the classroom Word Wall.

Comprehension
After reading, ask children the following questions:
- What happened after the queen worked hard all day long? *Recall/Cause and Effect*
- Were you surprised when the king found the queen sleeping? Why or why not? *Reflective Analysis/Personal Response*

ESL/ELL English Language Learners
Explain the two meanings of *ball* (a fancy party; a round toy). Have children draw and label pictures showing each meaning.

220

Lesson 106   Pages 221–222

Long Vowel e

Skill Focus

Children will

★ distinguish between short vowel e and long e picture names.

★ understand that ee, ea, and e at the end of a word or syllable can spell long e.

★ identify rhyming long e words.

Teach

Phonological Awareness: Rhyme Read aloud the following sentences. Have children identify the rhyming words in each one.

- Plant the seeds far away from the weeds.
- Have you seen my bean patch?
- I see a bee near your knee.

Have children identify the long vowel sound heard in all the rhyming words.

Sound to Symbol Write these words on the board and underline the vowels: *bee, beet, beat*. Ask children what is the same about the words. (They all begin with *be*; all have the long vowel e sound.) Then, ask what is different about the words. (Two words have a *t* at the end; two are spelled with *ee* and one is spelled with *ea*.) Remind children that the long e sound can be spelled with *ee* and with *ea*.

Then, write these words on the board: *be, he, me, we*. Ask a volunteer to underline the vowel in each word. Explain that the letter *e* can sometimes spell the long *e* sound without being followed by a vowel. Remind children that if a word or syllable has one vowel that comes at the end of the word or syllable, the vowel is usually long.

Next, ask volunteers to add a consonant to the end of each word. Possible answers include *bed, beg; hem, hen; men, met; wed, wet*. Ask children what happened to the vowel sound when the consonant was added. (It changed from long e to short e.)

Practice and Apply

Sound to Symbol Help children identify the pictures on page 221. Remind them to listen for a short or long vowel sound in each picture name.

After children have completed page 222, have them review their answers. Discuss the different spellings for each set of long e rhyming words.

Reading Use *Eve Shops*, MCP Phonics and Reading Long Vowel Skills Library, Level A, to provide practice in reading words with long and short e.

Phonemic Awareness

Name _____

▶ Say the name of each picture. If the vowel sound is short, color the box with the word **short**. If the vowel sound is long, color the box with the word **long**.

Long and short vowels a, i, e: Phonemic awareness   221

FOCUS ON ALL LEARNERS

ESL/ELL ENGLISH LANGUAGE LEARNERS

- Before children begin page 221, practice differentiating between long and short vowel sounds. Say *seat, lap, tree, nest, feet, three, tell, wheel, pit*. Have children clap when they hear the long e sound.

- Before beginning page 222, ask children to explain what rhyming words are. Then, say a word and have children supply a rhyming word. If supplying a word is difficult, name two words and ask children to say whether they rhyme. Have children complete the activity in pairs, then review answers.

VISUAL/AUDITORY LEARNERS

Materials: Phonics Picture Cards: bed (76), bell (77), eggs (80), tent (83), beads (116), bee (117), eagle (118), jeep (119)

Place the cards randomly around the room so the pictures are partially visible. Then, play "I Spy" by giving hints about the pictures. Once the correct picture name is identified, have a child hold up the picture and identify the vowel sound.

221

Phonograms/Rhyme

➤ **Say** the name of each picture. **Circle** the words in the boxes that rhyme with the picture name.

1. bee	(me)	team	(see)	met	bean
	(he)	(we)	(fee)	(tea)	seed
2. heel	(feel)	(seal)	sell	deep	(deal)
	men	(meal)	(real)	leaf	help
3. meat	(feet)	(beat)	bet	(heat)	set
	(seat)	net	(neat)	(peat)	wet
4. peas	(please)	pegs	feet	meats	(fleas)
	seals	(teas)	begs	deep	team

222 Long vowel e: Phonograms/rhyme

HOME Ask your child to clap for a rhyming pair; then, say word pairs from the page, such as *me, see* and *tea, met*.

CURRICULUM CONNECTIONS

SPELLING
Materials: self-stick notes
Have children write their spelling words on self-stick notes. Then, have them sort the words into two piles based on the spelling of the vowel sound.

WRITING
Share the expression "busy as a bee" with children, and invite them to tell what they think it means. Then, suggest that they think of some things they would like to get done before the end of the day. Have children write lists of the things they would like to accomplish if they were busy as bees. Invite several "bees" to get together to share their lists.

PORTFOLIO

HEALTH
Talk with children about what to do if a bee lands on them. Make the point that swatting the bee can often result in a bee sting as the bee tries to defend itself.

TECHNOLOGY **AstroWord** Long Vowels: *e, u*

AUDITORY LEARNERS GROUPS
Give the following commands, stressing the underlined word. Have children follow them only if the emphasized word has the long *e* sound: *The word* see *says clap. The word* bee *says cover your eyes. The word* ice *says jump. The word* me *says sit quietly in your seat.*

CHALLENGE
Have children study the words on page 222 to find three different spellings for the long *e* sound. Have them use these spellings as column heads and add a fourth column for short *e*. Then, have them write each word on page 222 under the correct spelling of the long or short *e* sound.

EXTRA SUPPORT/INTERVENTION
Before children identify rhyming words on page 222, have them read aloud the words in each numbered row. Then, have them repeat each word and the picture name, checking to see if the two words rhyme.
See Daily Phonics Practice, pages 319–320.

Integrating Phonics and Reading

Shared/Guided Reading
Show the cover as you read the title. Ask children what kind of store Eve will shop in. Then, have them name some of the items she might buy there.

First Reading Invite children to join in each time they see the words *So she did.*

Second Reading Have children identify the long and short *e* words in the book. List the words on the board in two columns.

Comprehension
After reading, ask children the following questions:
• How did Eve help with the shopping? *Recall/Plot*
• Where did she put all the things Ken gave her? How do you know? *Inference/Details*

ESL/ELL English Language Learners
Help children point out and name grocery items shown in the illustrations, such as peaches and paper plates.

Eve Shops

222

Lesson 107 Pages 223–224

Long Vowel e

Skill Focus

Children will

★ identify picture names that contain the sounds of short e and long e, i, u, and a.

★ write words that contain the sound of long e to complete sentences.

★ recognize and read high-frequency words.

Teach

Phonemic Awareness: Medial Sound Isolation Say the word *red* with children, encouraging them to stretch the middle sound and then blend it with the rest of the word: *reeed, reeed, red*. Ask children to identify the vowel sound. Then, repeat the procedure, using the long *e* word *read*. Have children identify the vowel sound. Continue, using these pairs: *fed, feed; pep, peep; net, neat; Ben, bean; wed, weed*.

Sound to Symbol Draw a large circle on the board and say that it is a plate. Then, help children name foods whose names contain the long *e* sound. Possibilities include *peas, beef, beets, meat, green beans, cheese, cream,* and *peaches*.

As children say each word, write it on the plate. Ask volunteers to circle words in which the long *e* sound is spelled *ee* and to underline the words in which the sound is spelled *ea*. Conclude by pointing to the words at random and having children read them.

Practice and Apply

Sound to Symbol As children complete page 223, encourage them to say each picture name quietly to themselves and to listen for a short or long vowel sound.

Writing For page 224, suggest that children try each word choice before writing a word. As they complete the activity, they will have the opportunity to read the following high-frequency words: *more, after*.

Critical Thinking For Talk About It, help children recall the foods that were mentioned in the story before naming their favorite foods.

Reading Use *Eyes Are Everywhere*, MCP Phonics and Reading Long Vowel Skills Library, Level A, to provide practice in reading words with long and short *e*.

FOCUS ON ALL LEARNERS

ESL/ELL ENGLISH LANGUAGE LEARNERS

- Work through page 223 with children. Ask students to use the words they read on the page in sentences.
- Have children work in pairs to complete page 224. Review answers aloud in small groups.

VISUAL LEARNERS

Materials: drawings of two pies, cut into eight pieces

To play the "easy as pie" game, write long *e* words on the slices of one pie and short *e* words on the slices of the other pie. Mix up the pieces and give them to a small group. Have them work together to sort the pieces to reassemble a long *e* and short *e* pie.

KINESTHETIC LEARNERS

Materials: Phonics Picture Cards: bed (76), bell (77), desk (79), eggs (80), cape (85), tube (106), coat (110), beads (116), bee (117), eagle (118), jeep (119)

Have two lines of children stand about 20 feet apart. Display a picture card and have it named. If the picture name contains the long *e* sound, have a child take one leap forward. Continue until a child from one group reaches the opposite line.

Words in Context

► Look at the picture. Circle the word that will finish the sentence. Print it on the line.

1. I sit in my __seat__.
   - seal
   - seed
   - (seat)

2. It feels nice to rest my __feet__.
   - (feet)
   - feel
   - feed

3. Dean heats up the __meat__.
   - met
   - team
   - (meat)

4. Mom piles on more __peas__.
   - peak
   - (peas)
   - pens

5. Can I eat a heap of __beans__?
   - beds
   - (beans)
   - beads

6. After I eat I brush my __teeth__.
   - (teeth)
   - team
   - ten

TALK What food do you like best? Why?

HOME Help your child make up a story using some of the circled words on the page.

224 Long vowel e: High-frequency words, critical thinking

CURRICULUM CONNECTIONS

SPELLING
Materials: green crayons

Have children write their spelling words. Ask them to use a green crayon to trace over the vowels. Then, have them underline the silent vowel in each word.

WRITING
Write the words *breakfast, lunch,* and *dinner* on the board. Discuss the importance of eating nutritious foods at each meal. Have children choose a meal and copy its name on their papers. Then, have them write and draw a menu of their favorite foods for this meal.

PORTFOLIO

HEALTH
Talk about healthy foods and list them on the board. Challenge children to include food whose names contain the long *e* sound. Possibilities include *wheat bread, peaches, beans, beets, peas, cheese,* and *beef.*

TECHNOLOGY **AstroWord** Long Vowels: *e, u*

AUDITORY LEARNERS
GROUPS

Materials: paper plates, crayons

Name these foods and have children draw those whose names contain the long *e* sound on their plates: *potatoes, beef, plums, peaches, green beans, squash, beets, fish, lemons, peas, carrots, cheese, ice cream.*

CHALLENGE
Point out the word *teen* on page 223 (item 5) and have it read aloud. Ask children to name numbers that end with the word part *-teen*. Then, challenge children to write all the numbers that end in *teen*.

EXTRA SUPPORT/INTERVENTION
PARTNERS

Point out the picture clues on page 224 and remind children that these pictures can help them read the sentence. Then, pair children with partners and have them read aloud the sentence and word choices before they respond. **See Daily Phonics Practice, pages 319–320.**

Integrating Phonics and Reading

Guided Reading
Show the cover as you read the title. Invite children to name the animals in the illustration.

First Reading Call attention to the pictures on pages 8 to 15. Have children use their own words to compare what we see with what the animals see.

Second Reading Have children find one short *e* word and four long *e* words in the book. List the words on the board.

Comprehension
After reading, ask children the following questions:
- Does this book tell facts or a made-up story? *Inference/Fact and Fantasy*
- Which part of the book did you find the most interesting? *Reflective Analysis/Personal Opinion*

ESL/ELL English Language Learners
Have children point to their eyes. Then, have them point to and name other parts of their faces.

224

Lesson 108   Pages 225–226

Long Vowel e

Skill Focus

Children will

★ identify and spell picture names that contain the sounds of long and short e.

★ write words that contain the sound of long e to complete sentences.

★ recognize and read high-frequency words.

Teach

Phonemic Awareness: Phoneme Substitution Ask children these riddles:

- What word would be made if the *h* in *heat* changed to a *b*? (*beat*)
- What word would be made if the *m* in *me* changed to a *w*? (*we*)
- What word would be made if the *s* in *seal* changed to an *m*? (*meal*)

Then, ask children to identify the vowel sound heard in all the words. (long *e*)

Sound to Symbol Write these sentences on the board and have volunteers read them aloud: *I fed the dog. Pam will feed the cats.* Ask children to identify the word with the short *e* sound and the word with the long *e* sound. Then, have volunteers underline the vowels in *feed* and *fed*. Ask what happens to *fed* when you add another *e* (the short *e* sound changes to long *e*). Repeat, writing: *I sat on my bed. Where is that bead?* Discuss what happens to *bed* when you add an *a*. Remind children that *ee* and *ea* are two of the ways to spell the long *e* sound.

Practice and Apply

Blend Phonemes As children complete page 225, encourage them to say each picture name, blending together the beginning, middle, and ending sounds.

Writing For page 226, suggest that children try each word choice before writing a word. As they complete the activity, they will have the opportunity to read the high-frequency word *many*.

Critical Thinking For Talk About It, have children tell which part of the story helped them decide which team will win.

Reading Use *Steve's Room*, MCP Phonics and Reading Long Vowel Skills Library, Level A, to provide practice in reading words with long and short *e*.

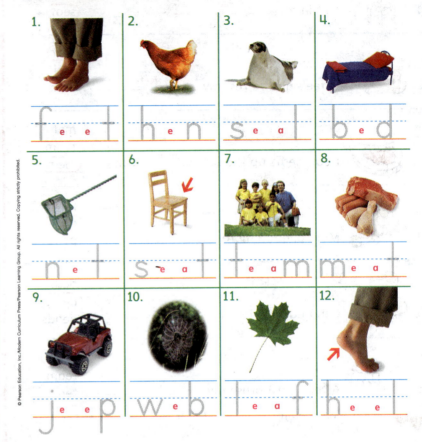

Long and short vowel e: Spelling 225

FOCUS ON ALL LEARNERS

ESL/ELL ENGLISH LANGUAGE LEARNERS

- Review the picture names on page 225. Then, help children identify the beginning, middle, and ending sound in each word.
- After children have completed page 226, review the answers aloud. Ask volunteers to write the answers on the board.

VISUAL/AUDITORY LEARNERS

Write the words *sent, leap, sea,* and *team* on the board and have them read. Then, read these sentences aloud and ask children to select the word that belongs in each sentence: *I _____ a letter to Steve. The Lions are my favorite _____. Fish live in the _____. Goats like to run and _____.*

KINESTHETIC LEARNERS

Materials: caps with team logos, tape player, music

Invite children to sit in a circle on the floor. Then, pass out the caps and have the team logos identified. As the music plays, have children pass the caps around the circle. When it stops, have children holding the team caps say words containing the long *e* sound.

Words in Context

Circle the word that will finish the sentence. Print it on the line.

1. We rode to Lee's game in the ___jeep___.
   - jeans
   - (jeep)
   - peep

2. We sat in a row with many ___seats___.
   - (seats)
   - seals
   - seems

3. The Seals beat the Bees last ___week___.
   - well
   - (week)
   - keep

4. The Bees are in the ___lead___.
   - (lead)
   - leap
   - leak

5. The Seals ___need___ to win.
   - neat
   - (need)
   - seed

6. Will Lee's ___team___ win the game?
   - tent
   - tame
   - (team)

TALK About It Which team do you think will win?

HOME With your child, make up a silly sentence using some of the circled words.

226 Long vowel e: High-frequency words, critical thinking

CURRICULUM CONNECTIONS

SPELLING
Materials: spelling cards made in Lesson 105, pages 219–220

Have children work with a partner and take turns displaying the picture side of each spelling card. Have their partners write the spelling word. Children can check this spelling by comparing it to the word written on the back of the card.

WRITING

Write these headlines on the board and have children read them aloud: *Bees Beat Seals; Seals Beat Bees.* Working with a partner, have children choose one of these two headlines. Then, have them write some sentences about the team victory.

SOCIAL STUDIES
Encourage children who come from other cultures to talk about favorite games they know about. Then, invite children to draw pictures showing favorite games.

TECHNOLOGY AstroWord Long Vowels: *e, u*

AUDITORY LEARNERS
Say these sentences with a silly word. Have children replace the word with a long *e* word that makes sense. *We get wool from a sleep.* (sheep) *The king sat next to the key.* (queen) *I ate franks and bees for lunch.* (beans) *These boots keep my knees dry.* (feet).

CHALLENGE
Have children reread the story on page 226. Then, have them work in pairs to write several more sentences to report on the outcome of the game. Children can share their story conclusions in a small group.

EXTRA SUPPORT/INTERVENTION
Pair children and have them work together to read the sentences and the word choices on page 226. Remind children that the word they choose must make sense in the sentence. **See Daily Phonics Practice, pages 319–320.**

Integrating Phonics and Reading

Guided Reading
Show the cover as you read the title. Have children preview the illustrations and then tell who they think the story's characters are.

First Reading Have children tell what Dad is doing in the illustrations on pages 7, 9, 11, 13, and 14.

Second Reading Have children find another word besides *Steve* with the long *e* sound in the story. Have them find six short *e* words.

Comprehension
After reading, ask children the following questions:
- What is Steve's room like at the beginning of the story? *Recall/Setting*
- What is it like at the end? *Inference/Setting*

ESL/ELL English Language Learners
Give children a few items such as books, papers, and toys. Working at a desktop, the children can use the items to show the meanings of *make a mess* and *get rid of the mess.*

Lesson 109   Pages 227–228

Review Long Vowels
a, i, u, o, e

Skill Focus

Children will

★ recognize the sound of long *e*.

★ identify and spell picture names that contain the sound of long *e*.

★ distinguish among the sounds of long *a*, *i*, *u*, *o*, and *e*.

Teach

Phonemic Awareness: Phoneme Blending

Say the word *jeep*, separating the sound of each phoneme: /j/ /ē/ /p/. Ask children to say the word naturally, and ask what vowel sound they hear in the middle. (long *e*) Then, have them say the word, stretching the long *e* sound: *jeeep*. Repeat the procedure, using *meal*, *seat*, and *reef*. Conclude by asking children how the words are alike and different. (They all have the long *e* sound; they have different beginning and ending sounds.)

Sound to Symbol

Materials: letter cards *Aa, Ee, Ii, Oo, Uu*

Ask children to recall the names of the five vowel letters and identify each one by holding up a letter card. Then, have children look around the room to find words that contain long vowel sounds. As each is identified, write the word on the board.

Have children identify the long vowel sound in each of the words you wrote. Invite volunteers to underline the letters that stand for the vowel sound in each word. You may wish to review the different spelling patterns for each long vowel sound.

Practice and Apply

Blend Phonemes As children complete page 227, encourage them to say each picture name, blending together the beginning, middle, and ending sounds.

Sound to Symbol Help children identify the pictures on page 228. Remind them to listen for a different vowel sound in each row.

Reading Use *Ice Fishing*, MCP Phonics and Reading Long Vowel Skills Library, Level A, to provide practice in reading words with long vowels *a*, *i*, *u*, *o*, and *e*.

Spelling

Name _____

▶ **Say** the name of each picture. **Print** the name on the line. In the last box, **draw** a picture of a long *e* word. **Print** the word.

1. heel	2. bee	3. leaf
4. bed	5. seed	6. team
7. seat	8. men	9. feet
10. peas	11. jeep	12.

Long and short vowel e: Spelling   **227**

FOCUS ON ALL LEARNERS

ESL/ELL ENGLISH LANGUAGE LEARNERS

- Before children complete page 227, have them name each picture and say whether the vowel sound is long *e* or short *e*. Remind them that there are different ways to spell the long *e* sound.
- Complete page 228 with children, working in pairs or small groups. Have children say each picture name in each row before deciding which ones have the target vowel sound.

VISUAL/AUDITORY LEARNERS   PARTNERS

Materials: Phonics Picture Cards: cake (86), rake (91), bike (93), kite (98), mule (103), tube (106), boat (108), cone (111), beads (116), bee (117)

Mix up the cards and spread them out face down. Have children take turns selecting two cards. If the picture names have the same vowel sound, the player keeps the cards. If not, return the cards face down.

227

Phonemic Awareness

▶ **Look** at the vowel sound. **Color** the pictures in each row whose names have that vowel sound.

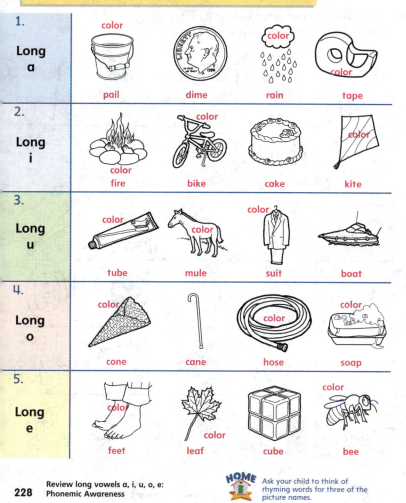

1. Long a — color pail, dime, color rain, color tape
2. Long i — fire (color), color bike, cake, color kite
3. Long u — color tube, horse (color mule), color suit, boat
4. Long o — color cone, cane, color hose, color soap
5. Long e — color feet, color leaf, cube, color bee

228 Review long vowels a, i, u, o, e: Phonemic Awareness

HOME Ask your child to think of rhyming words for three of the picture names.

CURRICULUM CONNECTIONS

SPELLING
Materials: index cards, markers

Have children copy their spelling words on index cards. Then, tell them to cover their eyes and imagine a picture of the word as you or a partner spells it aloud. Have them spell the word aloud as they keep a picture of the word in their minds.

WRITING
Materials: drawing paper, crayons

 PORTFOLIO

Begin by brainstorming long *e* words and recording them on the board. Have children draw a scene with some of these objects and write descriptions of their pictures.

MATH
Assign each of five groups a long vowel sound. Have the groups work to list words that contain their long vowel sound. One child in each group should act as recorder. Then, have groups exchange lists to tally the words. Help children use the results to make a bar graph. Which letter has the most words? Which has the fewest?

TECHNOLOGY **AstroWord** Long Vowels: *e, u*

AUDITORY LEARNERS GROUPS
Materials: letter cards *Aa, Ee, Ii, Oo, Uu*

Say these words and have children hold up the letter that stands for the long vowel sound heard in each word: *plate, five, cane, mule, cone, robe, jeep, tune, side, tail, joke, toe, weep, lime, game, rule*.

CHALLENGE
Challenge pairs of children to write sentences that contain only words with the same long vowel sound. For example for long *a*, children might write: *Kate ate Lane's date cake.*

EXTRA SUPPORT/INTERVENTION
Materials: coat, plate, beads, dime, tube

Display each object and have it identified. Then, have children identify the vowel sound heard in each name. Display each object once more and ask children to say words that have the same long vowel sound as the object's name. *See Daily Phonics Practice, pages 316–320.*

Integrating Phonics and Reading

Shared/Guided Reading
Show the cover as you read the title. Ask children to tell what they think ice fishing is.

First Reading Have half the class read the part about ice fishing and the other half read about regular fishing.

Second Reading Write the headings *Long a, Long i, Long u, Long o,* and *Long e* on the board. Ask students to find one or more words that you can list under each heading.

Comprehension
After reading, ask children the following questions:
- How is ice fishing like the kind of fishing most people do? *Recall/Comparisons*
- How is it different? *Recall/Comparisons*

ESL/ELL English Language Learners
Explain that the word *fish* can be used in different ways. Help children make up sentences in which it means "an animal that lives in water" and "to catch fish."

Lesson 110 Pages 229–230

Review Long and Short Vowels

Skill Focus

Children will
★ orally blend phonemes.
★ orally blend word parts.
★ identify picture names and spell words that contain the sounds of long and short *a, i, u, o,* and *e*.

Teach

Phonemic Awareness: Medial Sound Isolation

Materials: Phonics Picture Cards: rake (91), five (95), suit (105), coat (110), bee (117)

Show the picture card for *rake* and have children identify it. Say the word, then /ā/. Tell children you are saying a word and then its middle sound. Ask children to identify the vowel sound they hear. Then, have children say the other words as you hold up the picture cards, following each one with its vowel sound.

Sound to Symbol On the board, draw an arrow like the one on page 229 and write *seal* along it. Using your hand to track the letters, slide across the arrow, pronouncing the word *seal* by blending the sounds together. Invite volunteers to read the word in the same way.

Next, ask nine children to draw similar arrows on the board. Print these long and short vowel words along the arrows as children observe: *cap, send, fit, hop, rub, gate, dive, suit, hope.* Then, ask children to blend the letter sounds to read the words.

Practice and Apply

Sound to Symbol Help children identify the pictures on pages 229 and 230. For page 230, make sure children understand that they will write each blended word and then draw a line to the correct picture.

Reading Use *Cat's Trip*, MCP Phonics and Reading Long Vowel Skills Library, Level A, to provide practice in reading words with short and long vowels.

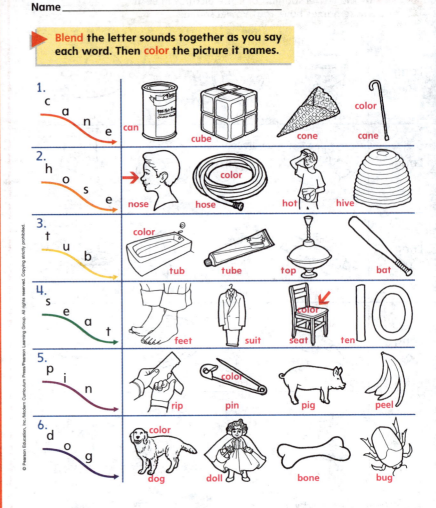

FOCUS ON ALL LEARNERS

ESL/ELL ENGLISH LANGUAGE LEARNERS

Materials: letter card *Ee*

• Before children begin page 229, confirm that they can recognize and say short and long vowel sounds. Print *pin, tub, can,* and *not* on the board. Have children read each word aloud. Then, hold up an *e* card at the end of each word and ask children to read the new words. Review the picture clues on page 229 together.

• For page 230, have children print all the words before doing the matching task.

KINESTHETIC LEARNERS

Materials: index cards, pencils, tapes, crayons

Have children write *long vowel* on one card and *short vowel* on the other. Show them how to tape the cards to pencils to make flags. Say these words and have them wave the correct flag for each one: *fat, cup, bike, fuse, mix, peep, tap, fuss, jet, box, mud, hop, rag, dime, rule.*

Blending

> Blend the letter sounds together as you say each word.
> Print the word on the line. Draw a line to the picture it names.

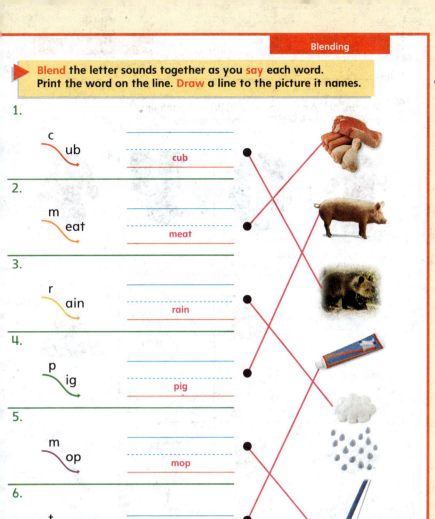

1. c ub — cub
2. m eat — meat
3. r ain — rain
4. p ig — pig
5. m op — mop
6. t ube — tube

Review vowels: Blending phonograms

HOME Help your child make up silly rhymes for picture names, such as *Hop on a mop.*

CURRICULUM CONNECTIONS

SPELLING
Have children draw six arrows and print their spelling words, separating the initial letter from the rest of the word. Ask them to take turns reading the words aloud to a partner. Then, have them close their eyes and try to visualize the letters in each word as they spell the word aloud.

WRITING

Materials: milk or lemon juice, cotton swab, white paper, lamp

Assign partners and have them write each other a secret message using lemon juice or milk and a cotton swab. Once the "ink" has dried, children can exchange messages and read them by holding them by a warm lightbulb.

FINE ARTS
Explain that a collage uses different materials to make a design. Have children pick a short and a long vowel. Then, have them make a collage of pictures and words that contain the vowels.

 **AstroWord** Long Vowels: *i, u;*
Long Vowels: *e, u;*
Long Vowels: *a, i*

AUDITORY LEARNERS
Materials: Phonics Picture Cards: cane (87), vase (92), five (95), kite (98), mule (103), tube (106), boat (108), nose (115), jeep (119), leaf (120)

Display the pictures. Then, say a picture name, separating it into discrete phonemes, such as /j/ /ē/ /p/. Have children blend the sounds together and select the picture whose name you have given.

CHALLENGE
Materials: letter cards *Aa, Ee, Ii, Oo, Uu*

Assign partners. Have one child think of a long vowel word and say it. Have the other find and hold up the letter that is heard in the word. Have children switch roles and continue the game.

EXTRA SUPPORT/INTERVENTION
Check to make sure children can successfully blend the letter sounds to read the words, giving assistance if necessary. If children attempt to pronounce silent vowels in the long vowel words, suggest that they cross them out. **See Daily Phonics Practice, pages 316–320.**

Integrating Phonics and Reading

Guided Reading
Show the cover as you read the title. Ask children to look closely at the illustration and explain how they can tell that Cat is going on a trip.
First Reading Call attention to the thought bubbles in the illustrations. Invite children to tell what they show.
Second Reading Ask children to find a word in the story for each short and long vowel.

Comprehension
After reading, ask children these questions:
- What does Cat tell Duck at the beginning of the story? *Recall/Details*
- Why does Pig think that Cat is taking her for a ride at the end? *Inference/Summarizing*

ESL/ELL English Language Learners
Show children a set of quotation marks and explain that these mark words spoken by a story character. Invite children to read the words spoken by various characters using different voices.

Lesson 111   Pages 231–232

Review Long Vowels

Skill Focus

Children will
★ identify and spell the names of pictures that contain long vowel sounds.
★ distinguish between short and long vowels.

Teach

Phonemic Awareness: Phoneme Categorization Say these groups of words and ask children to identify the word that does not contain the same vowel sound.

- cube   cake   cute
- bike   bite   bell
- desk   deer   deep
- bake   bark   paid
- loaf   lost   load

Sound to Symbol Review some of the ways children have learned to spell long vowel sounds.

- Write the words *pin* and *pine* on the board. Discuss what letter was added to change the short vowel sound into a long vowel sound.
- Write *leaf*, *feet*, and *be* and discuss three ways of spelling the sound of long *e*.
- Review the special spelling of long vowel sounds in *hay*, *nail*, *coat*, and *suit*.

Practice and Apply

Sound to Symbol Help children identify the pictures on page 231. Review the directions on page 232, making sure that children understand that the word in each box is the word they will change. Explain that there can be more than one correct answer for some of the blanks in the short vowel column; students should choose one word to write.

Reading Use *Summer at Cove Lake*, MCP Phonics and Reading Long Vowel Skills Library, Level A, to provide practice in reading words with short and long vowels.

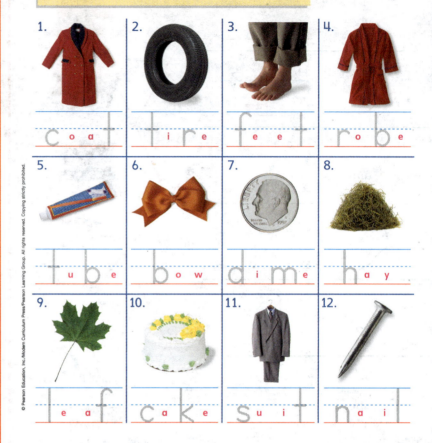

FOCUS ON ALL LEARNERS

ESL/ELL ENGLISH LANGUAGE LEARNERS

- Before children complete page 231, work with them to name each picture and identify the long or short vowel sound.
- For page 232, some children might supply rhyming words for the "Short Vowel" portion of the activity instead of doing vowel substitution. Offer additional assistance and support by completing the page with children, working in pairs or small groups. Model how to try out each vowel to see if it forms a real word.

VISUAL LEARNERS

Have children write these words in one column: *cake, top, tie, bow, road, suit, nail, ray, bent, feet*. In a second column, have children write these words: *mop, take, say, load, fruit, pie, pail, sent, meet, low*. Have them connect rhyming words and identify the vowel sound in each pair.

Spelling

▶ Read the word in the box. Add an e to make a long vowel word. Write it on the first line. Then change the vowel of the word in the box to make a short vowel word. Write it on the second line.

	Long Vowel	Short Vowel
1. tap	tape	top
2. pin	pine	pan, pen, pun
3. cut	cute	cat, cot
4. hop	hope	hip
5. not	note	nut, net
6. pan	pane	pin, pen, pun
7. hid	hide	had

HOME Help your child think of sentences using short and long vowel word pairs, such as *I did not get a note.*

232 Review long and short vowels

CURRICULUM CONNECTIONS

SPELLING
Dictate these spelling words and sentences and have children write the words as a spelling posttest.
1. **feet** I put my **feet** in the water.
2. **seat** Please sit down in your **seat**.
3. **peel** A banana has a **peel**.
4. **jeep** Let's take a ride in the **jeep**.
5. **bean** I like to eat **bean** soup.
6. **seal** I saw a **seal** at the zoo.

WRITING

Invite children to choose a long vowel and to make a list of words with that long sound. Challenge them to write and illustrate a sentence, such as *Three bees sit in a tree*, using three words from the list.

TECHNOLOGY **AstroWord** Long Vowels: *i, o;*
Long Vowels: *e, u;*
Long Vowels: *a, i*

AUDITORY/VISUAL LEARNERS
Materials: index cards, marker

Write these words on index cards: *bake, take, lie, pie, cube, tube, nose, rose, jeep, leap*. Place the cards face down and have each child select two cards. Have the child read the words, identify the vowel sounds, and use them in a sentence that contains both words.

CHALLENGE
Materials: primary dictionary

Have children investigate the different meanings of the word *note*. Then, have them pick two of the meanings and draw and caption pictures to illustrate them.

EXTRA SUPPORT/INTERVENTION
Materials: letter cards *Aa, Bb, Cc, Ee, Ii, Kk, Oo, Pp, Rr, Tt, Uu*

Before beginning page 232, have children use letter cards to form these words: *cap, kit, tub, rob*. Have them add an *e* to each to make a new word. Have them read the new word and identify the change in the vowel sound. **See Daily Phonics Practice, pages 316–320.**

Integrating Phonics and Reading

Guided Reading
Show the cover as you read the title. Ask children to predict some of the things the girl might do during the summer at Cove Lake.
First Reading Ask children to find the words *fish, frog,* and *bug* and to find these animals in the art.
Second Reading For each of the long and short vowel sounds, have a pair or small group of students find one or more words.
Comprehension
After reading, ask children these questions:
• Did Rose enjoy the summer? How do you know? *Inference/Details*
• What is special about the way this story is told? *Reflective Analysis/Comparison*

ESL/ELL English Language Learners
Explain that the letters "*P.S.*" added to the end of a letter introduce something the writer forgot to say in the main part of the letter. Then, reread one or more of Rose's letters. Discuss the information in the P.S.

232

Lesson 112
Pages 233–234

Phonics and Spelling / Phonics and Writing

Long Vowels

Skill Focus
Children will
★ spell and write words with long vowels *a, i, u, o, e.*
★ write a letter using words with long vowels *a, i, u, o, e.*

Teach
Phonics and Spelling On the chalkboard, make a chart with the following headings: *a, i, u, o, e.* Then, say the following words and have a volunteer come up and write each one under the correct heading: *soak, meal, day, suit, tie, nail, sweet, rope, blue, five.* Discuss the different spellings of each long vowel sound.

Practice and Apply
Phonics and Spelling Point out the heading for each long vowel sound on page 233. Have children read the list words aloud to hear the vowel sounds before they write the words beside the correct headings.

Phonics and Writing Before children write a letter on page 234, encourage them to recall a fun event they have participated in at school. Have them dictate a class letter including the greeting, body, and signature. Then, as children write their own letters, remind them to use some of the spelling words listed on the page.

Reading Use *Never Say Never*, MCP Phonics and Reading Long Vowel Skills Library, Level A, to review long vowels.

Name _____

Phonics & Spelling

Say and spell each long vowel word. Print each word on a line in the box that shows its long vowel sound.

| fruit | rain | pie | bean | bike |
| bone | hay | soap | seal | glue |

Long a	hay	rain
Long i	bike	pie
Long u	fruit	glue
Long o	bone	soap
Long e	seal	bean

Review long vowels a, i, u, o, e: Spelling **233**

FOCUS ON ALL LEARNERS

ESL/ELL ENGLISH LANGUAGE LEARNERS
- Before children begin page 233, copy the word list onto the chalkboard. Help children read the words aloud.
- For page 234, write a sample letter on chart paper for children. Then, draw names and have children write letters to each other. Pair them to read their letters aloud.

VISUAL/KINESTHETIC LEARNERS INDIVIDUAL
Materials: index cards or slips of paper, marker

Have children write the spelling words on separate index cards or slips of paper. Then, have them sort the words into piles according to the long vowel sound. Have them read the words in each group.

KINESTHETIC LEARNERS PARTNERS
Materials: list of unit spelling words

Have children take turns, one acting out a spelling word and the other writing the word. Once the spelling word is written, have them switch roles.

Writing

Write a letter to a friend. Tell about a game, sport, or hobby you like. The words in the box may help you.

| kite | rope | feet |
| bike | flute | day |

Dear _____,

_____

_____

_____

_____

_____

Your friend,

_____

You may want to help your child address an envelope and mail the letter to a friend.

234 Review long vowels a, i, u, o, e: Writing

CURRICULUM CONNECTIONS

SPELLING

Cumulative Posttest Review Unit 3 spelling words by using the following words and dictation sentences.
1. **lake** They swam at the **lake**.
2. **rain** Gray clouds often bring **rain**.
3. **kite** We flew the **kite** yesterday.
4. **pie** Dad baked an apple **pie**.
5. **fruit** Apples are my favorite **fruit**.
6. **glue** Use **glue** to mend that toy.
7. **robe** We gave Mom a warm **robe**.
8. **bow** I put a **bow** on the gift.
9. **seat** Please take a **seat** before class starts.
10. **peel** We will **peel** apples for dessert.

WRITING

Have children work in small groups to create a pass-along story about a game that the class likes to play. Have each member of each group contribute a sentence or two to the story. Then, have the groups share their finished stories with the class.

TECHNOLOGY   **AstroWord** Long Vowels: *i, o;*
Long Vowels: *e, u;*
Long Vowels: *a, i*

Integrating Phonics and Reading

Guided Reading
Show the cover and read the title. Flip through the pages to preview the art and invite children to predict who the characters will be.
First Reading Ask how the characters feel, based on their expressions in the illustrations.
Second Reading Have children find two long *a* words, two long *o* words, and two long *e* words. Ask how the long vowel sound is spelled in each.
Comprehension
After reading, ask children these questions:
• What does Mother Rabbit tell Little Bunny when he says he will never get the carrots? *Recall/Character*
• How does Little Bunny finally get the carrots? *Recall/Plot*

ESL/ELL **English Language Learners**
Ask children what the opposite of *never* is. Then, help them name the opposite of each of these story words: *little, outside, laughed, asleep, quietly*.

AUDITORY/VISUAL LEARNERS

Materials: list of unit spelling words from page 145I

Have children take turns giving oral clues about a spelling word. Once the word is successfully guessed, have each child in the group write the word. Then, have the child giving the clue spell the word aloud so that others can check their spelling.

CHALLENGE

Challenge children to write a rhyming word for each spelling word in the box on page 233. Have them circle any pairs of rhyming words whose spellings of the vowel sound differ; for example, *soap* and *rope*.

EXTRA SUPPORT/INTERVENTION

Materials: letter cards *Aa, Ee, Ii, Oo, Uu*; index cards; marker

Write spelling words on index cards, omitting one or more of the vowels. Have children pronounce each word after you. Then, have them use the letter cards to supply the missing vowel or vowels. **See Daily Phonics Practice, pages 316–320.**

Lesson 113 Pages 235–236

Take-Home Book

Review Long Vowels
a, i, u, o, e

Skill Focus

Children will

★ read long *a, i, u, o, e* words in the context of a story.

★ review selected high-frequency words in the context of a story.

★ reread for fluency.

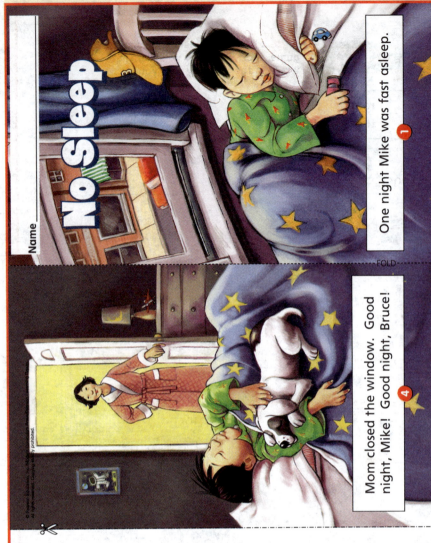

Review long vowels a, i, o, u, e: Take-home book **235**

Teach

Build Background Help children recall that the theme of this unit is "Let's Play." Ask them to describe how they feel after a long day of play. Remind children that it's important to get a good night's sleep after playing hard. Then, invite them to share what they do at bedtime before going to sleep.

Phonemic Awareness: Phoneme Categorization Have children listen to these groups of words and identify the two words with the same vowel sound, and that sound.

- sleep   seal   fun   (long *e*)
- pay   sit   take   (long *a*)
- true   suit   pan   (long *u*)
- rice   bed   tie   (long *i*)
- hot   snow   home   (long *o*)

Practice and Apply

Read the Book Help children tear out and fold the pages to make their Take-Home Books. Then, read the book together. Invite children to tell what happened one night after Mike fell asleep.

Sound to Symbol Read aloud or have volunteers read the book. On the board, write: *Long a, Long e, Long i, Long o, Long u.* Have children identify the long vowel words. (*night, Mike, asleep, Bruce, face, woke, came, blue, jeep, made, beep, closed, window*) Invite volunteers to write the words on the board in the correct columns. You may wish to point out the *-igh* spelling for long *i* in *night*.

Review High-Frequency Words Write *the* and *one* on the board. Have children spell the words and then say them.

Reread for Fluency Have children reread the book to increase their fluency and comprehension. Children can take their books home to read and share with family members.

FOCUS ON ALL LEARNERS

ESL/ELL ENGLISH LANGUAGE LEARNERS

After assisting children with making the Take-Home Book, use the following activities to teach English language learners.

- Build background by discussing what might wake up someone who had fallen asleep.
- Teach/review these expressions: *fast asleep, woke up, closed the window.*
- To check comprehension, give specific phonemic and vocabulary-related tasks: circle the words that are names of people or pets, underline the long *e* words, and so forth.

KINESTHETIC/VISUAL LEARNERS

Materials: Phonics Picture Cards: cape (85), cake (86), nails (90), bike (93), kite (98), tie (101), mule (103), suit (105), tube (106), boat (108), bowl (109), nose (115), bee (117), jeep (119), leaf (120); blanket or piece of fabric

Place the picture cards on the blanket or fabric like quilt squares. Have children take turns selecting a card, saying the picture name, and then identifying the vowel sound.

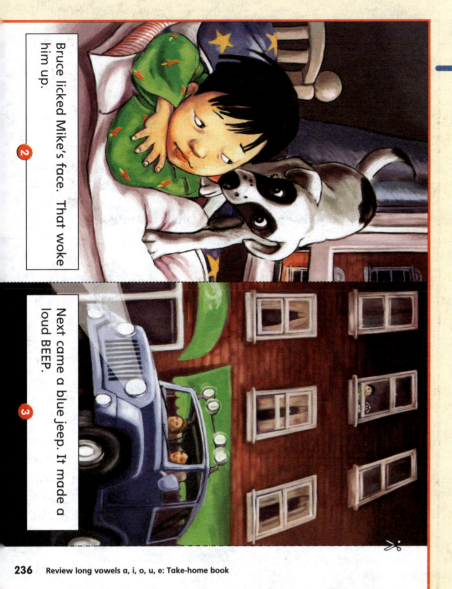

2 Bruce licked Mike's face. That woke him up.

3 Next came a blue jeep. It made a loud BEEP.

236 Review long vowels a, i, o, u, e: Take-home book

CURRICULUM CONNECTIONS

SCIENCE
Materials: classroom objects

Remind children that Mike heard a noise outside and he knew it was a car horn. Challenge children to use their ears to identify some sounds. Have them close their eyes as you make sounds of bells, scissors, stapler, closing a door, chalk on chalkboard, hitting blocks together.

HEALTH
Materials: drawing paper, crayons

Talk with children about the importance of getting a good night's sleep. Explain that having a routine, doing the same things at bedtime each night, can help them relax and fall asleep more easily. Suggest that they illustrate things to do at bedtime.

LANGUAGE ARTS

Invite children to bring in books of stories, poems, or songs that they like to hear at bedtime. Take time to read aloud several of these books over the next few days.

AstroWord Long Vowels: *a, i;*
Long Vowels: *i, o;*
Long Vowels: *e, u*

AUDITORY/VISUAL LEARNERS
Materials: letter cards *Aa, Ee, Ii, Oo, Uu;* Take-Home Books

Have one child slowly read aloud one page of the story. Have the partner listen for words with long vowel sounds. For each long vowel word, have the partner display the appropriate letter card.

CHALLENGE

Invite children to write a continuation to this story. What might make Mike wake up again? What might help him go back to sleep? Suggest that they illustrate their ideas.

EXTRA SUPPORT/INTERVENTION
Materials: index cards

Write these words on the board: *night, asleep, jeep, woke, closed, face, blue*. Pronounce one word at a time and have children find it on the board. Then, have children use the word in an oral sentence. **See Daily Phonics Practice, pages 316–320.**

236

Lesson 114 Pages 237–238

Unit Checkup

Review Long Vowels/High-Frequency Words

> **Skill Focus**
>
> Children will
> - identify picture names that contain long vowel sounds.
> - distinguish between words that contain long and short vowel sounds.
> - write words that contain long and short vowel sounds to complete sentences.
> - read high-frequency words.

Teach

Phonemic Awareness: Phoneme Blending
Say the word *bake*, separating the individual phonemes: /b/ /ā/ /k/. Ask children to say the word naturally, then identify the long vowel sound. (long *a*) Repeat, using these words: *glue, dive, seal, soap, rain*.

Sound to Symbol Write these words on the chalkboard: *blue, bone, line, road, gate, feet, tire, tube, fruit, pie, hoe, leaf, nail*. Name a long vowel sound and ask a volunteer to touch and read a word that has that sound. Then, point to each word and have children identify the letters that stand for the long vowel sound. Discuss what spelling patterns tell them that a word has a long vowel sound.

Practice and Apply

Assess Skills Help children identify the pictures on page 237. Review the directions for both pages, making sure children know to fill in the circle by the correct word on page 237. You may want to have children read the story aloud when page 238 is completed.

Assess High-Frequency Words Read aloud the directions above the list of high-frequency words. Stress that children should put a check mark in a box only if they can read the word. If they cannot read the word, they should leave the box empty. You may wish to have children work in pairs to complete the exercise or have individual children read the words aloud to you. The words are also assessed orally on the pretest and posttest for Unit 3, pages 145e–145h.

UNIT 3 CHECKUP

Name_____

> Say the name of each picture. Fill in the bubble beside the picture name.

1. ● cake ○ rake ○ coat ○ keep
2. ○ mile ○ mail ○ ruler ● mule
3. ○ wave ○ vase ● five ○ dive
4. ○ bone ● cone ○ cane ○ tune
5. ○ jeans ● jeep ○ deep ○ game
6. ○ sail ○ seem ○ rose ● suit
7. ● tie ○ toe ○ lie ○ tire
8. ○ rail ○ road ○ read ● rain
9. ○ bait ○ goat ● boat ○ toad
10. ○ tile ● tube ○ tape ○ time
11. ○ mate ○ moat ○ boat ● meat
12. ● rope ○ soap ○ pole ○ robe

Long vowels: Assessment 237

FOCUS ON ALL LEARNERS

ESL/ELL ENGLISH LANGUAGE LEARNERS

- Have children work with partners to complete items 1 to 6 on page 237. Then, have them complete items 7 to 12 individually.

- After children have finished the sentence completion activity on page 238, further review long vowels by having them underline all the words on the page that contain long vowel sounds. Go over the answers, asking children to explain the difference between a correct answer and an incorrect choice.

KINESTHETIC/AUDITORY LEARNERS

Materials: five button cutouts, each labeled with a vowel; cassette player; music tape

Have children sit in a circle with one child, with closed eyes, in the center as "it." As the music plays, have children pass the buttons around the circle. Stop the music and have "it" guess which children have the buttons. A child who is identified must say a word for the vowel.

UNIT 3 CHECKUP

▶ Circle the word that will finish the sentence. Print it on the line.

1. Sue had a ____neat____ blue kite.   net (neat)

2. The kite did ____not____ have a tail yet.   (not) note

3. Joe ____cut____ up rags to make a tail.   (cut) cute

4. Then they sailed the ____kite____.   kit (kite)

▶ Can you read each word? Put a ✓ in the box if you can.

☐ long ☐ their ☐ where ☐ want ☐ out ☐ little
☐ your ☐ could ☐ about ☐ two ☐ from ☐ why
☐ they ☐ which ☐ them ☐ were ☐ there ☐ because

Long vowels and high-frequency words: Assessment

ASSESS UNDERSTANDING OF UNIT SKILLS

STUDENT PROGRESS ASSESSMENT
You may wish to review the observational notes you made as children worked through the activities in the unit. Your notes will help you evaluate the progress children make with identifying long vowel sounds and spellings.

PORTFOLIO ASSESSMENT
Review the materials children have collected in their portfolios. You may wish to have interviews with children to discuss their written work and the progress they have made since the beginning of the unit. As you review children's work, evaluate how well they use phonics skills.

DAILY PHONICS PRACTICE
For children who need additional practice with long vowels, quick reviews are provided on pages 316–320 in Daily Phonics Practice.

PHONICS POSTTEST
To assess children's mastery of long vowels and high-frequency words, use the posttest on pages 145g–145h.

AUDITORY/VISUAL LEARNERS
Materials: Phonics Word Cards: *late* (126), *pie* (152), *cube* (158), *boat* (165), *jeep* (185)

Display the word cards. Then, give an oral sentence, leaving out one of the card words, such as *Do you want a piece of __?* Have the group decide which word makes sense in the sentence and then identify its vowel sound.

CHALLENGE
Assign partners and ask each child to write a question about the story on page 238. Have partners exchange and then answer each other's questions.

EXTRA SUPPORT/INTERVENTION
Materials: letter cards *Aa*, *Ee*, *Ii*, *Oo*, and *Uu*

Print long vowel words on the board, leaving out the vowels. Some words to use are *l_n_, g_t_, l__f, c_k_, t_r_*. (*line, gate, leaf, cake, tire*) Touch an incomplete word and have children use the cards to complete the word. See Daily Phonics Practice, pages 316–320.

Teacher Notes

UNIT 4

Consonant Blends, Y as a Vowel

THEME: EVERYBODY EATS

CONTENTS

UNIT 4 RESOURCES 239b
Assessment Options 239c
Administering & Evaluating the Pretest/Posttest 239d
    Unit 4 Pretest 239e–239f
    Unit 4 Posttest 239g–239h
    Unit 4 Student Progress Checklist 239i
English Language Learners 239j
Spelling Connections 239k–239l
Phonics Games, Activities, and Technology 239m–239o
BLM Unit 4 Activity 239p
Home Connections 239q

TEACHING PLANS
    Unit Opener/ Home Letter 239–240
    Lessons 115–116: *r* blends 241–244
    Lessons 117–118: *l* blends 245–248
    Lessons 119–120: *s* blends 249–252
    Lesson 121:   Final blends 253–254
    Lesson 122:   Review initial/final blends 255–256
    Lesson 123:   Review consonant blends:
                      Phonics & Reading 257
                      Phonics & Writing: Building Words 258
    Lessons 124–125: *y* as a vowel 259–262
    Lesson 126:   Review consonant blends and
                      y as a vowel:
                      Phonics and Spelling 263
                      Phonics & Writing: A Shopping List 264
    Lesson 127:   Take-Home Book: "Pizza Feast" 265–266
    Lesson 128:   Unit Checkup: Consonant blends/
                      y as a vowel 267–268

Student Performance Objectives

In Unit 4, children will be introduced to consonant blends and the sounds of *y* as a vowel within the context of the theme "Everybody Eats." As children begin to understand and learn to apply the concept that when two or more consonants come together in a word, the sound of each consonant is usually heard and that the letter *y* can represent a vowel sound, they will be able to

▶ Identify the sounds of consonant blends containing *r*, *l*, or *s*

▶ Identify the sounds of consonant blends *mp*, *sk*, *nk*, *st*, and *nd* at the ends of words

▶ Identify the sound of letter *y* when it represents the long *e* or long *i* vowel sounds

Overview of Resources

LESSON	MCP PHONICS AND READING LIBRARY, LEVEL A PROGRAM	TITLE	PICTURE CARDS	LETTER CARDS/ WORD CARDS	DAILY PHONICS PRACTICE
115: *r* blends	RR, Stg Two Bk 28	*Roll Out the Red Rug*	121–122, 124–128, 130–131		320
116: *r* blends	RR, Stg Two Bk 29	*At the Track*	121, 124, 126, 128, 129, 131	Rr	320
117: *l* blends	RR, Stg Two Bk 25	*Glenda the Lion*	133–134, 136, 138–140		321
118: *l* blends	RR, Stg Two Bk 26	*Planting a Garden*	133–136, 138–139	Bb, Cc, Ff, Gg, Ll, Pp 205–208, 211–216	321
119: *s* blends	RR, Stg Two Bk 23	*Sally's Spaceship*	140, 143–145, 147, 149, 151–152	Ll, Kk, Nn, Mm, Pp, Tt, Ww	321
120: *s* blends	RR, Stg Two Bk 31	*The River Grows*			321
121: Final blends	RR, Stg Two Bk 37	*That Pig Can't Do a Thing*		Mm, Pp, Ss, Kk, Nn, Tt, Dd	321–322
122: Review initial/ final blends	RR, Stg Two Bk 41	*Stan Packs*	3, 7, 14, 25, 39, 78–79, 86, 121, 128–129, 151		321–322
123: Review consonant blends	RR, Stg Two Bk 24	*My Lost Top*			320–322
124: *y* as a vowel	VFC, Set 1	*Kermy and Pepper*	7, 47, 137		322
125: *y* as a vowel	VFC, Set 3	*Mystery at Fairly Field*	7, 42, 137, 169	Yy	322
126: Review consonant blends and *y* as a vowel	RR, Stg Two Bk 27	*A Fun Place to Eat*	121–122, 124–127, 130–131	Complete Set	320–322
127: Take-Home Book: "Pizza Feast"					320–322
128: Unit Checkup: Consonant blends/ *y* as a vowel			121, 136, 137, 140, 149	Ll, Pp, Rr, Ss, Tt	320–322

VFC–Very First Chapters   RR–Ready Readers   Stg–Stage   Bk–Book

Assessment Options

Throughout Unit 4, assess children's ability to identify and write words with consonant blends and *y* as a vowel. Use the Unit Pretest and Posttest for formal assessment. For ongoing informal assessment, you may wish to use children's work on the Review pages, Take-Home Books, and Unit Checkups. You may also want to encourage children to evaluate their own work and to participate in setting goals for their own learning.

ESL/ELL Some students may require additional assessment strategies to meet their special language needs. For additional support for English language learners, see page 239j.

FORMAL ASSESSMENT

Use the Unit 4 Pretest, on pages 239e–239f, to help assess a child's knowledge at the beginning of the unit and to plan instruction.

ESL/ELL Before administering the Pretest, preview the picture clues on page 239e so that children are familiar with the picture names. Then, they can focus on matching the answer choices to the picture clues.

Use the Unit 4 Posttest, on pages 239g–239h, to help assess mastery of unit objectives and to plan for reteaching, if necessary.

ESL/ELL Some English language learners may have difficulty reading directions. Read them aloud to the group and model how the test is to be completed.

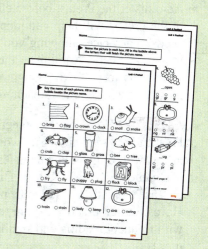

INFORMAL ASSESSMENT

Use the Review pages, Unit Checkup, and Take-Home Books in the student book to provide an effective means of evaluating children's performance.

Unit 4 Skills	Review pages	Checkups	Take-Home Books
r blends	255–258, 263–264	267–268	265–266
l blends	255–258, 263–264	267–268	265–266
s blends	255–258, 263–264	267–268	265–266
Final blends	255–258, 263–264	267–268	265–266
Initial blends	255–258, 263–264	267–268	265–266
y as a vowel	263–264	267–268	265–266

STUDENT PROGRESS CHECKLIST

Use the checklist on page 239i to record children's progress. You may want to cut the sections apart to place each child's checklist in his or her portfolio.

PORTFOLIO ASSESSMENT

This logo signals opportunities for collecting student work for individual portfolios. You may also want to include the Pretest and Posttest, the Review pages, the Unit Checkup, Phonics & Reading, and Phonics & Writing pages.

PHONEMIC AWARENESS AND PHONICS ASSESSMENT

Use PAPA to obtain an itemized analysis of children's decoding skills.

PAPA Skills	MCP Phonics Lessons in Unit 4
Blending sounds	Lesson 122
Deleting sounds	Lessons 116, 118, 120–122
Consonant blends	Lessons 115–123
Long vowels	Lessons 124–126

239c

Pretest and Posttest

DIRECTIONS

To help you assess children's progress in learning Unit 4 skills, tests are available on pages 239e–239h.

Administer the Pretest before children begin the unit. The results of the Pretest will help you identify each child's strengths and needs in advance, allowing you to structure lesson plans to meet individual needs. Administer the Posttest to assess children's overall mastery of skills taught in the unit and to identify specific areas that will require reteaching.

ESL/ELL Note that the objective of the Unit 4 Pretest and Posttest is to read and write words with consonant blends and *y* as a vowel. English language learners, especially speakers of Vietnamese, Korean, Khmer, Hmong, and Cantonese, may confuse *r* blends and *l* blends, pronouncing them the same way. Have children practice saying the picture clues aloud; reinforce with frequent reading and spelling opportunities throughout the unit.

PERFORMANCE ASSESSMENT PROFILE

The following chart will help you identify specific skills as they appear on the tests and enable you to identify and record specific information about an individual's or the class's performance on the tests.

Depending on the results of the tests, refer to the Reteaching column for lesson-plan pages where you can find activities that will be useful for meeting individual needs or for daily phonics practice.

Answer Keys

Unit 4 Pretest, page 239e (BLM 21)
1. flag
2. clock
3. snail
4. crab
5. glass
6. tree
7. fly
8. puppy
9. block
10. train
11. lamp
12. sink

Unit 4 Pretest, page 239f (BLM 22)
13. clap
14. penny
15. sled
16. grapes
17. sink
18. swim
19. play
20. fly

Unit 4 Posttest, page 239g (BLM 23)
1. cr
2. sk
3. nd
4. gr
5. sw
6. sl
7. dr
8. nk
9. tr
10. y
11. sk
12. pl

Unit 4 Posttest, page 239h (BLM 24)
13. puppy
14. sniffs
15. soft
16. play
17. try
18. slid
19. flopped
20. funny

Performance Assessment Profile

Skill	Pretest Questions	Posttest Questions	Reteaching: Focus on All Learners	Reteaching: Daily Phonics Practice
r blends	4, 6, 10, 16	1, 4, 7, 9, 17	241–244	320
l blends	1, 2, 5, 7, 9, 13, 15, 19, 20	6, 10, 12, 16, 18, 19	245–248	321
s blends	3, 15, 18	5, 6, 11, 14, 18	249–252	321
Final blends	11, 12, 17	2, 3, 5, 8, 11, 15	253–258, 263–266	321–322
Initial blends	1, 2, 3, 4, 5, 6, 7, 9, 10, 13, 15, 16, 18, 19, 20	1, 4, 5, 6, 7, 9, 10, 11, 12, 14, 16, 17, 18, 19	255–258, 263–266	321–322
y as a vowel	7, 8, 14, 20	1, 10, 13, 17, 20	259–262	322

Unit 4 Pretest

Name _____

> Say the name of each picture. Fill in the bubble beside the picture name.

1.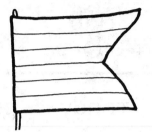
   ○ brag   ○ flag

2.
   ○ crown   ○ clock

3.
   ○ snail   ○ snake

4.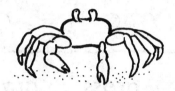
   ○ crab   ○ clap

5.
   ○ glass   ○ grass

6.
   ○ bee   ○ tree

7.
   ○ fry   ○ fly

8.
   ○ puppy   ○ plug

9.
   ○ flock   ○ block

10.
    ○ train   ○ stain

11.
    ○ lady   ○ lamp

12.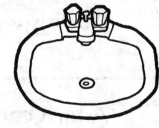
    ○ sink   ○ swing

Go to the next page. →

BLM 21 Unit 4 Pretest: Consonant blends and *y* as a vowel

Unit 4 Pretest

Name _____

▶ **Read the hint. Fill in the bubble below the correct word.**

13.	Do this with your hands.	cap ○	clap ○	lap ○
14.	Spend this.	sunny ○	candy ○	penny ○
15.	Ride this in the snow.	sled ○	slip ○	snap ○
16.	You can eat these.	capes ○	grass ○	grapes ○
17.	Wash the dishes here.	milk ○	sink ○	sing ○
18.	Do this in a pool.	swing ○	sting ○	swim ○
19.	Do this with a ball.	plan ○	play ○	stay ○
20.	A bird can do this.	fly ○	sky ○	flag ○

Possible score on Unit 4 Pretest is 20. Number correct _____

BLM 22 Unit 4 Pretest: Consonant blends and *y* as a vowel

239f

Unit 4 Posttest

Name _____

▶ Name the picture in each box. Fill in the bubble above the letters that will finish the picture name.

1. __y	2. ma__	3. ha__	4. __apes
○ cl ○ sk ○ cr	○ sk ○ nk ○ nt	○ nt ○ nd ○ mp	○ gl ○ gr ○ g
5. __ing	6. __ed	7. __um	8. si__
○ sw ○ sl ○ sr	○ sw ○ sl ○ st	○ dr ○ gr ○ br	○ ng ○ nt ○ nk
9. __ack	10. fl__	11. __unk	12. __ug
○ st ○ tr ○ cr	○ y ○ e ○ i	○ st ○ sl ○ sk	○ gl ○ pr ○ pl

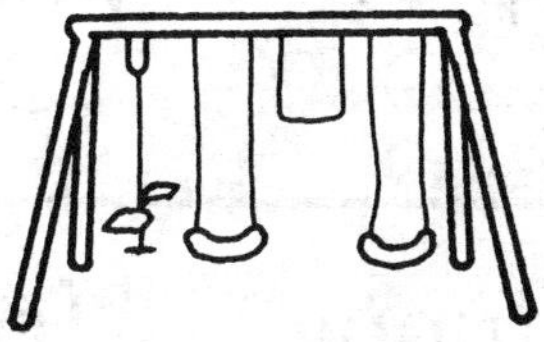

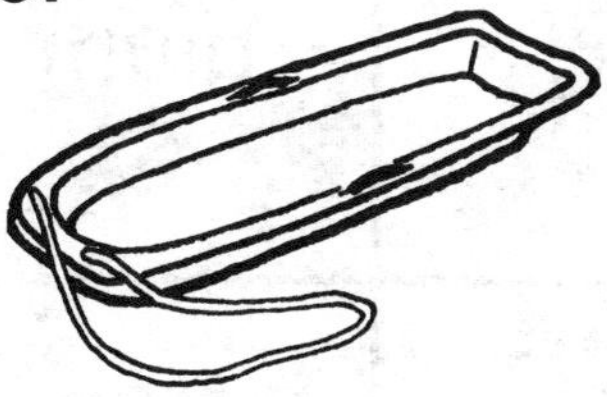

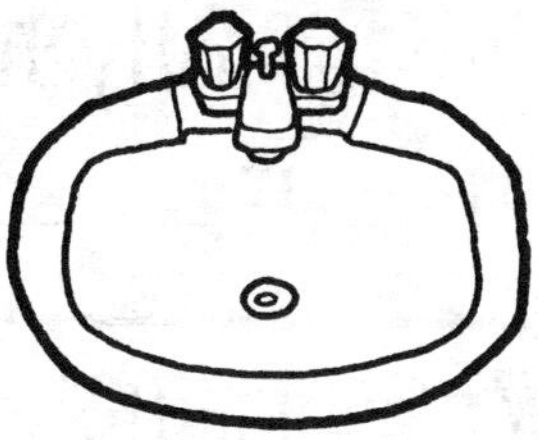

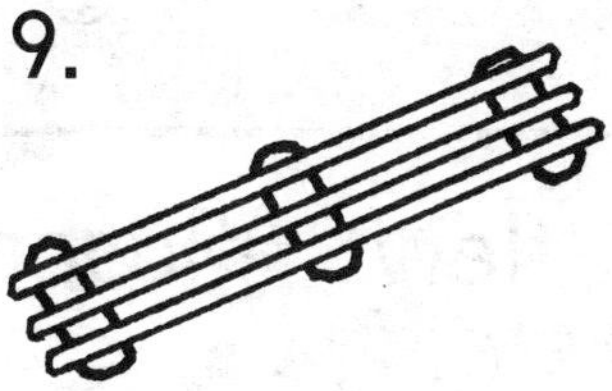

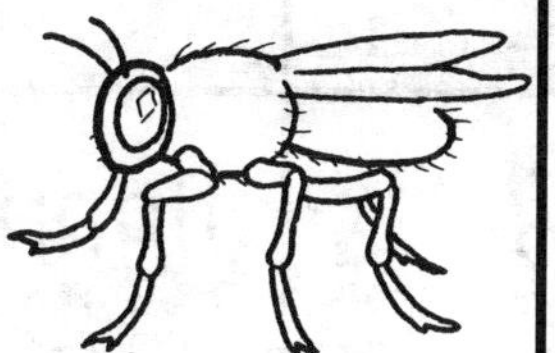

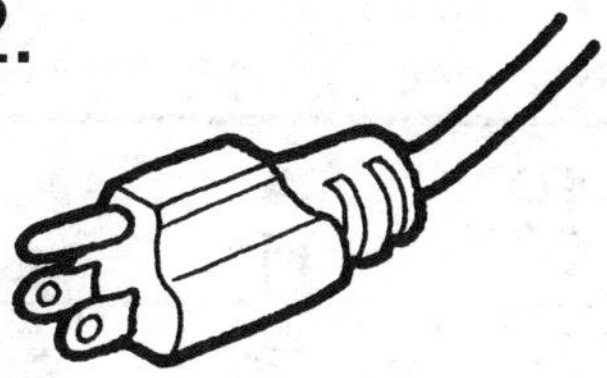

Go to the next page. →

BLM 23 Unit 4 Posttest: Consonant blends and *y* as a vowel

Unit 4 Posttest

Name _____

> Fill in the bubble under the word that will finish each sentence.

13.	Holly has a new _____.	puppy ○	sunny ○	sleepy ○
14.	It _____ her hand.	snips ○	sniffs ○	snakes ○
15.	Its fur is very _____.	sift ○	soft ○	stuff ○
16.	Holly likes to watch it _____.	plum ○	plow ○	play ○
17.	Holly saw it _____ to run fast.	tree ○	funny ○	try ○
18.	It _____ on the slick tile.	sled ○	slid ○	slim ○
19.	It _____ down on the floor.	flopped ○	flew ○	flashed ○
20.	Holly thinks her puppy is _____.	bunny ○	funny ○	lazy ○

Possible score on Unit 4 Posttest is 20. Number correct _____

BLM 24 Unit 4 Posttest: Consonant blends and *y* as a vowel

Student Progress Checklist

Make as many copies as needed to use for a class list. For individual portfolio use, cut apart each child's section. As indicated by the code, color in boxes next to skills satisfactorily assessed and insert an *X* by those requiring reteaching. Marked boxes can later be colored in to indicate mastery.

Student Progress Checklist

Code: ■ Satisfactory   ☒ Needs Reteaching

Student: _____

_____

Pretest Score: _____

Posttest Score: _____

Skills
- ☐ *r* Blends
- ☐ *l* Blends
- ☐ *s* Blends
- ☐ Final Blends
- ☐ *y* as a Vowel

Comments / Learning Goals

Student: _____

_____

Pretest Score: _____

Posttest Score: _____

Skills
- ☐ *r* Blends
- ☐ *l* Blends
- ☐ *s* Blends
- ☐ Final Blends
- ☐ *y* as a Vowel

Comments / Learning Goals

Student: _____

_____

Pretest Score: _____

Posttest Score: _____

Skills
- ☐ *r* Blends
- ☐ *l* Blends
- ☐ *s* Blends
- ☐ Final Blends
- ☐ *y* as a Vowel

Comments / Learning Goals

Student: _____

_____

Pretest Score: _____

Posttest Score: _____

Skills
- ☐ *r* Blends
- ☐ *l* Blends
- ☐ *s* Blends
- ☐ Final Blends
- ☐ *y* as a Vowel

Comments / Learning Goals

BLM 25 Unit 4 Checklist

ESL/ELL English Language Learners

Throughout Unit 4 there are opportunities to assess English language learners' ability to read and write words with consonant blends and with *y* as a vowel. Blends may be especially problematic for English language learners. Some children may confuse *r* blends and *l* blends, while others may have trouble with initial *s* blends that do not exist in their home languages. Native speakers of Spanish may confuse the sound of *j* in English with the sound of *y* in Spanish. Monitor difficulties with pronunciation and provide ample practice opportunities.

Lesson 115, pages 241–242 Speakers of Vietnamese, Hmong, Korean, Khmer, and Cantonese may confuse *r* blends and *l* blends. Initial *r* blends are relatively common in Spanish, Tagalog, and Russian. Monitor pronunciation for the "tap *r*" sound. Be sure children do not separate the two consonants with an intervening schwa sound (where *froze* might sound like *for Rose*).

Lesson 117, pages 245–246 Korean, Khmer, Hmong, Cantonese, and Vietnamese speakers may confuse *l* blends and *r* blends. Spanish-speaking children may pronounce a short *e* before *sl* words since Spanish lacks this initial blend.

Lesson 119, pages 249–250 Children whose home languages are Vietnamese, Cantonese, Khmer, Hmong, or Korean may have trouble with initial *s* blends, since they do not exist in these languages. Spanish-speaking children may pronounce a short *e* before all *s* blends, while Russian speakers may pronounce a voiced *z* sound in some blends (*zboon* for *spoon*).

Lesson 121, pages 253–254 Children who speak Cantonese, Khmer, or Korean may have difficulty with final blends. Learners whose home language is Tagalog or Spanish may "clip" the blends, pronouncing only the first consonant of each.

Lesson 122, pages 255–256 Native speakers of Spanish may be more familiar with initial consonant blends, which are more common in that language.

Lesson 124, pages 259–260 Native speakers of Spanish will have little trouble with the sounds of *y*, since *y* functions as a consonant and vowel in Spanish as well. However, they may confuse the sound of *j* in English with the sound of *y* in Spanish.

Spelling Connections

INTRODUCTION

The Unit Word List is a comprehensive list of spelling words drawn from this unit. The words are grouped by letter patterns. To incorporate spelling into your phonics program, use the activity in the Curriculum Connections section of each teaching plan.

ESL/ELL It is recommended that English language learners reach the intermediate fluency level of English proficiency before focusing on spelling.

Introduce the words in each group in the Unit 4 Word List separately and have English language learners focus on the pattern itself as a spelling key. Have children sound out the words, then underline or highlight the consonant blend or use of *y* as a vowel.

The spelling lessons utilize the following approach for each phonics element.

1. Administer a pretest of six words (seven words for *s* blends) that have not yet been introduced. Dictation sentences are provided.
2. Provide practice.
3. Reassess. Dictation sentences are provided.

A final review is provided at the end of the unit on page 263.

DIRECTIONS

Make a copy of Blackline Master 26 for each child. After administering each pretest, give children a copy of the appropriate word list.

Children can work with a partner to practice spelling the words orally and identifying the blend or the vowel sound in each word. They can also use their letter cards to form the words on the list. You may want to challenge children to make new words by substituting consonant blends. Children can write words of their own on *My Own Word List* (see Blackline Master 26).

Have children store their list words with the letter cards in the envelope in the back of their books. You may want to suggest that students keep a spelling notebook, listing words with similar patterns. Another idea is to build Word Walls with children and display them in the classroom. Each section of the Word Wall can focus on words with a single phonics element. The Word Walls will become a good resource for spelling when children are writing.

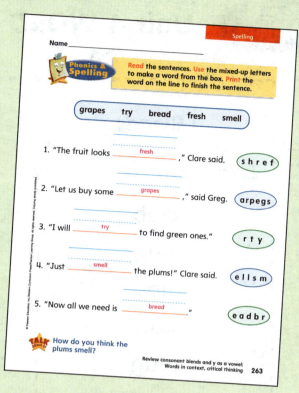

Unit Word List

r Blends
frame
dress
prize
train
bride
crown

l Blends
block
club
flag
glass
plant
plug

s Blends
skate
smoke
snake
spoon
square
star
swing

Final Blends
desk
list
lamp
mask
sink
trunk

y as a Vowel
baby
cry
fly
lady
penny
sky

Name _____

 Unit 4 WORD LIST

r Blends

frame
dress
prize
train
bride
crown

l Blends

block
club
flag
glass
plant
plug

s Blends

skate
smoke
snake
spoon
square
star
swing

Final Blends

desk
list
lamp
mask
sink
trunk

y as a Vowel

baby
cry
fly
lady
penny
sky

My Own Word List

BLM 26 Unit 4 Spelling Words

Phonics Games, Activities, and Technology

The following collection of ideas offers a variety of opportunities to reinforce phonics skills while actively engaging children. The games, activities, and technology suggestions can easily be adapted to meet the needs of your group of learners. They vary in approach so as to consider children's different learning styles.

WORD WHEELS

Make word wheels for words ending with *y*. For *y* representing the long *i* sound, write consonant blends on the larger wheel. For *y* representing the long *e* sound, write the first part of the words on the larger wheel. Write *y* on the smaller wheels. Have children read the words as the letters are lined up.

ESL/ELL This game can be simplified for English language learners by adding picture clues of words containing the long *i* and *e* sounds to the wheels for children to pronounce. When they have mastered this version, pair English language learners to play the game, using the Unit 4 Word List as a reference.

"PUT THE SOUNDS TOGETHER" SONG

Use the words on the right with the tune for "Frère Jacques" ("Are You Sleeping?") to help children focus on blending sounds together to form a word. Use words with initial and final blends, pronouncing the blend as one sound.

> Listen to the sounds I say:
> /gr/ /i/ /n/, /gr/ /i/ /n/
> Put the sounds together,
> And then say the word for:
> /gr/ /i/ /n/, /gr/ /i/ /n/

SWITCH

Write initial and final blends on cards or slips of paper, making sure there are two cards for each blend. Have children sit on their chairs in a circle and each choose a card. Select a child to be "it" to stand in the middle of the circle. Remove that child's chair. Say a word that begins or ends with a blend. The two children holding that blend should stand and change places. "It" tries to take one of the chairs. The child who does not get a seat is "it." Continue giving other words.

ESL/ELL This game relies on quick recognition and comprehension of blends for success. Have English language learners work together in a group and eliminate the child who is "it."

BLEND CHAINS

Provide strips of colored paper and paste. Write a word that begins or ends with a blend on a strip and paste the ends together to form a loop. Have children write other words with that blend on strips and link the words together in a chain. Have children make a chain for each blend.

TREASURE WORD HUNT

Make available newspaper advertising supplements, particularly those from grocery stores. Have children look for words that have initial and final blends. Suggest that they cut out the words they find and paste them to a poster titled "Treasure Words" or make a model of a treasure chest out of a box. You might decorate the poster with a large treasure chest and make cardboard yellow-gold "coins" for children to paste their words onto.

ESL/ELL This game can be completed successfully by having English language learners work in pairs. Have one child find the words and the partner verify them before they cut out and paste their "treasures."

USING DESCRIBING WORDS

Work with children to generate a list of describing words that end in *y*, such as *sleepy, lazy, happy, funny, pretty, busy, sunny*. List the words on a chart and display it where children can refer to it. Encourage them to use more describing words in their writing. As they become aware of descriptive words, have them add new words they find to the chart.

BLENDING OBJECTS

Place several objects whose names begin or end with blends, such as a slipper, a plate, a glove, a stamp, or a flag, on a table with a sheet of paper for each object. Challenge children to write words that begin or end with the same blends as the objects on the sheets of paper.

Y BOOKS

Have children write and illustrate words that end in *y* for pages for a book. Gather the pages into a picture dictionary of words with *y* representing the long *i* sound and *y* representing the long *e* sound.

STOP SIGN

Make a stop sign by writing *stop* on a card and fastening it to a craft stick. Write action words with blends or with *y* as a vowel on separate cards. Show one word card at a time and have children read the word and perform the action until you show the stop sign. Some action words to use include *blink, jump, stand, stamp, clap, cry, skip, stoop,* and *bend*.

ESL/ELL This game works best by introducing the action words on several occasions before conducting the activity. Write the words on tagboard and, next to them, provide a visual clue of each action. Post so children can see as they play the activity.

BLEND SHUFFLE

On each of eight cards write an initial consonant blend: *cr, dr, fl, sl, pl, st, sp,* or *br*. Shuffle the cards and place them in a pile face down. Children take a card and say a word that begins with the blend on the card.

ADD A LETTER

Write the following word parts on cards or on a chart: *lum, rum, lap, tan, rin, lim, rus,* and *win.* Have children use letter cards to add one or more letters at the beginning or at the end to make words that begin or end with blends. Have them write the words they make. Some word parts can have letters added both at the beginning and at the end.

TOSS A WORD

Duplicate Blackline Master 27. The top portion may be cut out and folded to make a cube. The bottom portion may be cut apart into cards. Each player has a cube and a set of cards. The cards are placed in front of each child, face up. To play, one child tosses the cube, then selects a card that can make a word with the blend on the cube. The child pronounces the word and turns the card face down. The next child repeats the action. If a word cannot be made, no cards are turned over and the play moves to the next child. The game continues until one child has turned over all his or her cards.

ESL/ELL This game and Sneaky Snakes require that English language learners have the ability to recognize and spell words containing specific blends. Allow children to use picture clues, word lists, or their personalized picture dictionaries as references for these activities.

SNEAKY SNAKES

Show children how to cut out a circle. Then, starting at the outside edge of the circle, show them how to cut around and around in a spiral. They can draw a face in the center of the resulting spiral to make a snake. Ask them to write on the snakes *s*-blend words that describe their snakes.

The following software products reinforce children's understanding of letter recognition and consonant sounds.

Reading Blaster™ Ages 5–7
Through fun activities such as stories and word searches, children increase their vocabulary and practice reading skills that include recognizing beginning and ending sounds. The activities are offered at five levels.

** Sunburst Technology
   1900 South Batavia Ave.
   Geneva, IL 60134
   (800) 321-7511
   www.sunburst.com

Turbo "Twist"™ Spelling
This program, intended for ages six and up, covers a wide range of phonics including consonant blends and digraphs and short and long vowels. The program assesses each player's skill level and adjusts accordingly.

** Leapfrog
   6401 Hollis St., Suite 150
   Emeryville, CA 94608
   (800) 883-7430
   www.leapfrog.com

Name _____

Toss a Word

(Cube net with faces: us, fl, st, sl, bl, fr)

| ack | op | ame | ow |
| ake | ip | ock | ump |

Home Connections

The Home Connections features of this program are intended to involve families in their children's learning and application of phonics skills. Three effective opportunities to make connections between home and school include the following.

- **HOME LETTER**
- **HOME NOTES**
- **TAKE-HOME BOOKS**

HOME LETTER

A letter is available to be sent home at the beginning of Unit 4. This letter informs family members that children will be learning to identify blended consonant sounds and the sounds of *y* as a vowel within the

context of the unit theme, "Everybody Eats." The suggested home activity focuses on drawing a picture of a favorite food and writing a sentence about it. This activity promotes interaction between child and family members while supporting children's learning. The letter, which is available in both English and Spanish, also suggests books related to the theme of food that family members can look for in a local library and enjoy reading together.

HOME NOTES

Whenever the Home logo appears within the student book, a phonics activity is suggested to be done at home. The activities are simple to do, requiring little or no preparation or special materials, and are meant to reinforce the targeted phonics skill.

TAKE-HOME BOOKS

The student book contains a number of Take-Home Books that can be cut out and assembled. The story language in the books reinforces the phonics skills. In each book, children are asked to respond by finishing the book. The books can then be taken home and shared with family members. In Unit 4, one Take-Home Book is available. It focuses on consonant blends and on *y* as a vowel and is related to the theme "Everybody Eats."

Home Notes in Spanish are also available for both teachers and parents to download and use from our website, www.PlaidPhonics.com.

UNIT 4

Pages 239–240

Consonant Blends and y as a Vowel

Skill Focus

Assess Prior Knowledge
To assess children's prior knowledge of consonant blends and *y* as a vowel, use the pretest on pages 239e–239f.

Unit Focus

Build Background

- Write the theme "Everybody Eats" on the board. Read the words and help children find them on page 239. Invite children to name some of their favorite foods, eliciting *bread* as one response. Write their suggestions in a chart headed "Foods We Like to Eat."

- Read the text aloud. Then, discuss the article with children. Ask them what the main idea is. Also have them describe the three different kinds of bread the article tells about.

Introduce Consonant Blends and y as a Vowel

- Print this sentence on the board and read it aloud: *We made long, skinny loaves of bread.* Underline the word *bread* and tell children that when we say *bread* we pronounce both the sound of *b* and the sound of *r*. The two consonants together are called a blend.

- Next, underline the word *skinny* and point out that it begins with a consonant blend, *sk*. Ask children to say the word *skinny*. Then, point out the *y* at the end of the word and explain that the letter *y* can sometimes have a vowel sound. Pronounce the word with children and identify the vowel sound as the sound of long *e*. Explain that children will learn more about consonant blends and *y* as a vowel in this unit.

Critical Thinking Read aloud the Talk About It question at the bottom of page 239. Encourage children to describe their favorite kinds of bread.

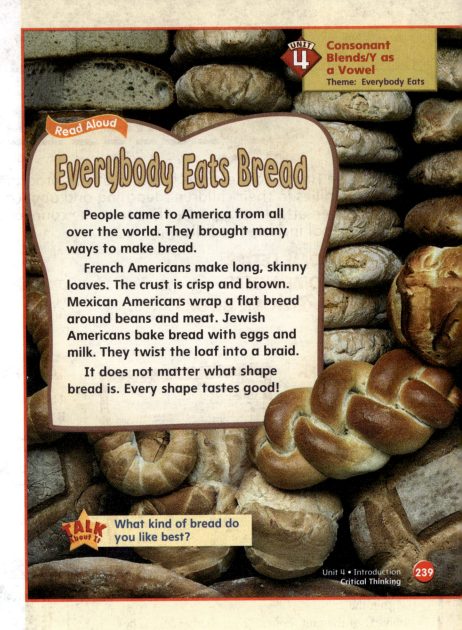

UNIT 4 Consonant Blends/Y as a Vowel
Theme: Everybody Eats

Read Aloud

Everybody Eats Bread

People came to America from all over the world. They brought many ways to make bread.

French Americans make long, skinny loaves. The crust is crisp and brown. Mexican Americans wrap a flat bread around beans and meat. Jewish Americans bake bread with eggs and milk. They twist the loaf into a braid.

It does not matter what shape bread is. Every shape tastes good!

TALK about It What kind of bread do you like best?

Unit 4 • Introduction
Critical Thinking **239**

THEME FOCUS

A PLACE IN THE PYRAMID
Materials: a food pyramid chart

Show children the food pyramid and explain that it shows different food groups. It also shows how much of each kind of food we should eat each day. Help children find bread in the largest group at the bottom. Explain that we need to eat plenty of bread, along with cereal, rice, and pasta, to stay healthy.

THE LUNCH LOG
Materials: construction paper, crayons, yarn for binding

For each of five days after lunch, have children talk about what they ate, why it was good for them, how it helps them to work and play well. Have them draw and label pictures for a log.

FOOD CHANT
Teach children this chant. *I eat things that help me grow. Apples, lettuce, a tomato.* Then, have children substitute favorite healthy foods or drinks for *apples* and *lettuce*.

Dear Family,

In this unit called "Everybody Eats," your child will learn about words that begin and end with consonant blends and words with **y** as a vowel. Many food names, such as **gr**apes, **pl**um, **str**awberry, m**ilk**, and **ch**erry, begin or end with consonant blends or end with **y** as a vowel. As your child becomes familiar with consonant blends and words with **y** as a vowel, you might try these activities together.

▶ Talk with your child about a favorite food. Have him or her draw a picture of the food. Then, help him or her to write a sentence about the food.

▶ Read the article on page 239 together. Ask your child to identify words with consonant blends and **y** as a vowel.

▶ Your child might enjoy reading these books with you. Look for them in your local library.

The Giant Carrot by Jan Peck
Blueberries for Sal by Robert McCloskey

Sincerely,

Estimada familia:

En esta unidad, titulada "Todos comemos" ("Everybody Eats"), su hijo/a estudiará palabras en inglés que comienzan y terminan con combinaciones de consonantes y palabras con y como una vocal. Muchos nombres de alimentos, como por ejemplo, **gr**apes (uvas), **pl**um (ciruela), **str**awberry (fresa), m**ilk** (leche) y **ch**erry (cereza), comienzan o terminan con grupos de consonantes o terminan con **y** como una vocal. A medida que su hijo/a se vaya familiarizando con los grupos de consonantes y las palabras con **y** como una vocal, pueden hacer las siguientes actividades juntos.

▶ Conversen con su hijo/a sobre una comida favorita. Pídanle que haga un dibujo de dicha comida y después, con su ayuda, que escriba una oración que describa la comida.

▶ Lean juntos el artículo en la página 239. Pidan a su hijo/a que identifique palabras con combinaciones de consonantes e **y** como una vocal.

▶ Ustedes y su hijo/a disfrutarán leyendo estos libros juntos. Búsquenlos en su biblioteca local.

The Giant Carrot de Jan Peck
Blueberries for Sal de Robert McCloskey

Sinceramente,

HOME CONNECTIONS

- The Home Letter on page 240 is intended to acquaint family members with the phonics skills children will be studying in the unit. Children can tear out page 240 and take it home.
- You may want to suggest that children complete the activities on the page with a family member. Encourage children to look in the library for the books suggested and read them with family members.

LEARNING CENTER ACTIVITIES

WRITING CENTER
Provide materials for children to draw and write menus for role-playing a restaurant scene. Have them work in groups to set up a pretend restaurant. Children can take the roles of customers, wait staff, cashier, and cooks.

SCIENCE CENTER
Provide water and cornstarch for children to experiment with mixing materials and with liquids and solids. Have children record how the mixture becomes liquid when held in their hands and solid when away from their body heat. Then, have children add paints and create food pictures with the mixture.

MATH CENTER
Provide measuring cups, measuring spoons, and unpopped popcorn, dried beans, rice, or salt for children to measure quantities.

BULLETIN BOARD
Throughout the unit, invite children to add to a bulletin board titled "Everybody Eats." Magazine cutouts, parts of food packages, and children's drawings might be displayed. Children may also write picture captions in which they underline phonetic elements from the unit—for example, *My f<u>r</u>iend and I like b<u>r</u>ead.*

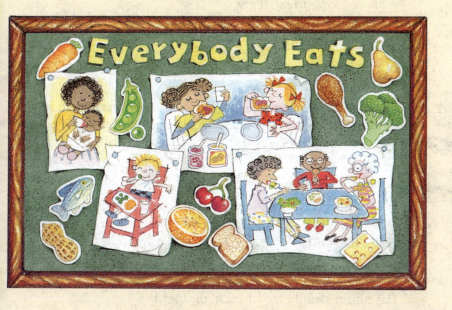

Lesson 115 Pages 241–242

r Blends

Skill Focus

Children will

★ recognize the sounds of *r* blends.

★ identify picture names that contain *r* blends.

ESL/ELL Speakers of Vietnamese, Hmong, Korean, Khmer, and Cantonese may confuse *r* blends and *l* blends. Initial *r* blends are relatively common in Spanish, Tagalog, and Russian. Monitor pronunciation to make sure children do not separate the two consonants with an intervening schwa sound (where *froze* might sound like *for Rose*).

Teach

Phonological Awareness: Blending Onsets and Rimes Say the word *grapes*, emphasizing the initial blend: *gggrrrapes*. Repeat the word naturally and have children say it, then ask if they hear one or two sounds at the beginning. (*two*) Explain that /gr/ is a blend of two consonants, *g* and *r*. Their sounds blend together, but each sound is heard.

Sound to Symbol Write *green* on the board. Point to the word and say it, emphasizing the initial blend, and have children repeat. Circle the beginning blend and explain that in the word *green*, the letters *gr* blend to make the beginning sound. Follow the same procedure for *tray, brown, crust, press, freeze*. Ask volunteers to circle the letters that blend to make the beginning sound of each word.

Practice and Apply

Phonological Awareness Read aloud the rhyme on page 241. Have children listen for and name words that begin with *r* blends.

Sound to Symbol Help children identify the pictures on pages 241 and 242. Draw their attention to the words shown in the first columns on pages 241 and 242, and explain that the underlined letters show the consonant blend at the beginning of each word. Make sure children understand that they are to circle the pictures in each row that have the same beginning blend as this word.

Reading Use *Roll out the Red Rug*, MCP Phonics and Reading Library, Super Skills Collection, Level A, to provide practice in reading words with *r* blends.

Sound to Symbol

Name _____

I love to munch
Fresh fruit for brunch
And have a bunch
Of grapes with lunch.

▶ **Say** the name of the first picture in the row.
Circle each picture in the row whose name begins with the same blend.

1. g**r**apes — groceries, bridge, cry, grasshopper
2. **t**ree — bride, truck, train, triangle
3. b**r**ush — bread, broom, track, brick
4. c**r**ib — crown, pretzel, crab, crane

R blends: Sound to symbol   241

FOCUS ON ALL LEARNERS

ESL/ELL ENGLISH LANGUAGE LEARNERS

- To prepare for page 241, have children focus on initial *r* blends by practicing these blend + vowel sound words: *grow, tree, brew, cry, play, free, dry*.
- Before beginning page 242, help children differentiate *r* blends from *l* blends. Help them pronounce *grow, glow; braid, blade; fright, flight*.

VISUAL LEARNERS

Materials: Phonics Picture Cards: bread (121), crib (124), fruit (128), train (130)

Place the pictures in a pile face down. Call on two children at a time to take the top card, name the picture, and then name another word that begins with the same *r* blend.

KINESTHETIC LEARNERS

Materials: Phonics Picture Cards: bread (121), bridge (122), crib (124), crown (125), dress (126), drum (127), train (130), tree (131)

Display the picture cards along the chalkboard ledge. Have children match pairs of pictures with the same beginning blend. Have them identify the letters in the blend.

Sound to Symbol

Say the name of the first picture in the row.
Color each picture in the row whose name begins with the same blend.

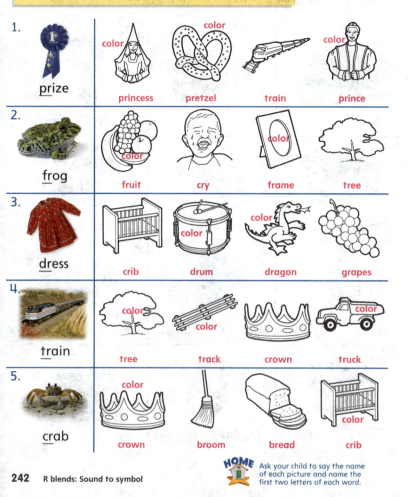

242 R blends: Sound to symbol

Ask your child to say the name of each picture and name the first two letters of each word.

CURRICULUM CONNECTIONS

SPELLING
Dictate the following words and read the sentences. Have children write the words for a spelling pretest.
1. **frame** — The picture is in a **frame**.
2. **dress** — The **dress** is red.
3. **prize** — The best speller won a **prize**.
4. **train** — The **train** runs on a track.
5. **bride** — The **bride** carried flowers.
6. **crown** — The queen wears a **crown**.

WRITING
Have children illustrate and write about a fruit snack they might enjoy.

SOCIAL STUDIES/FINE ARTS
Have children draw pictures to show the variety of fruits and vegetables a greengrocer would sell. Then, have children use their pictures to set up their own produce department. Children can take turns playing the roles of grocer and shoppers.

TECHNOLOGY **AstroWord** Consonant Blends & Digraphs

Integrating Phonics and Reading

Shared/Guided Reading
Show the cover as you read the title. Ask children if they think this story takes place today or long ago.
First Reading As you read, invite half the class to join in for the words *Roll out the red rug*. Have the other half join in for *Here comes the new king!*
Second Reading Ask children to identify the words with *r* blends. List these on the board or add them to the classroom Word Wall. Have children identify the letters in each blend.

Comprehension
After reading, ask children these questions:
• What do the people do to greet the new king? *Recall/Details*
• Why will the people have to roll the rug back up at the end? *Inference/Cause and Effect*

ESL/ELL English Language Learners
Invite children to act out the following story actions: *Roll out the red rug. Tap on the drum. Grab the flag.*

AUDITORY/KINESTHETIC LEARNERS
Play "Cross Your Arms." Tell children that you are going to say some words. If they hear an *r* blend at the beginning of the word, they should cross their arms. If the word does not begin with an *r* blend, their hands are to remain in their laps. Use these words: *bread, cake, dog, truck, room, crown, train, grass, dragon*.

CHALLENGE
Have partners choose an *r* blend and create silly tongue twister sentences they can teach to the class.

EXTRA SUPPORT/INTERVENTION
Have children form a train by standing in a line and placing their hands on the waist of the person in front of them. Have the train move each time children hear a word that begins with an *r* blend. Some words to say are *train, table, track, crab, goat, grass,* and *fruit*. See Daily Phonics Practice, page 320.

242

Lesson 116
Pages 243–244

r Blends

Skill Focus
Children will
★ identify picture names and spell words that contain *r* blends.

Teach

Phonological Awareness: Categorization
Ask children to listen carefully as you say groups of three words. Have them identify the two words in each group that begin with *r* blends.

- green   grow   go
- brain   basket   branch
- can   crash   crunch
- print   pin   prove

After children identify the words, ask them to name the two consonants in the blend.

Sound to Symbol Tell children you will ask a question and give them two possible answers. They should pick the word that answers the question. When children identify the correct answer, write the word on the board.

- Can someone catch a *fog* or a *frog*?
- Do leaves grow on a *tree* or a *tea*?
- Do you mow *gas* or *grass*?
- Can you sweep with a *boom* or a *broom*?
- Which is an animal: a *cab* or a *crab*?
- Do you *drive* a car or do you *dive* it?
- If you win a game, do you get a *prize* or *pies*?

Reread the list of answers with children. Ask volunteers to underline the two letters that make the sound they hear at the beginning of each word.

Practice and Apply

Sound to Symbol Help children identify the pictures on pages 243 and 244. Remind them to look carefully at each word on page 243 before choosing an answer.

Blend Word Parts As children complete page 244, encourage them to say each picture name, blending the beginning, middle, and ending sounds of each word. Remind them that they will be printing the beginning blend to complete each word.

Reading Use *At the Track*, MCP Phonics and Reading Library, Super Skills Collection, Level A, to provide practice in reading words with *r* blends.

Sound to Symbol

Name _____

▶ Say the name of each picture. Circle its name.

1. free (tree)
2. trick (brick)
3. (prize) cries
4. (frog) frame
5. crab (crib)
6. drive (dress)
7. braid (bride)
8. (grapes) grass
9. crane (crown)
10. (drum) drip
11. frown (frame)
12. (grass) grab

R blends: Sound to symbol   243

FOCUS ON ALL LEARNERS

ESL/ELL ENGLISH LANGUAGE LEARNERS

- Before beginning page 243, help children say the names of the pictures and the words so that they pronounce both consonants of the blend. Point out that *r* is always the second letter in each blend.
- Before beginning page 244, write the seven consonant blends (*cr, tr, br, fr, br, dr, pr*) on the board. Then, have children look through pages 243–244 and identify a picture clue for each initial *r* blend. Ask them to name the picture and point to the blend on the board.

VISUAL LEARNERS

Write the sentences below on the board. Ask children to read the sentences together and to list the words with *r* blends on a sheet of paper.

- Brett broke his brown crayon.
- Grace ate some green grapes.
- Fred's frog won a prize.
- Try not to drop the drum.
- The crab crossed the creek.

Spelling

▶ **Say** the name of each picture. **Print** its beginning blend on the line. **Trace** the whole word.

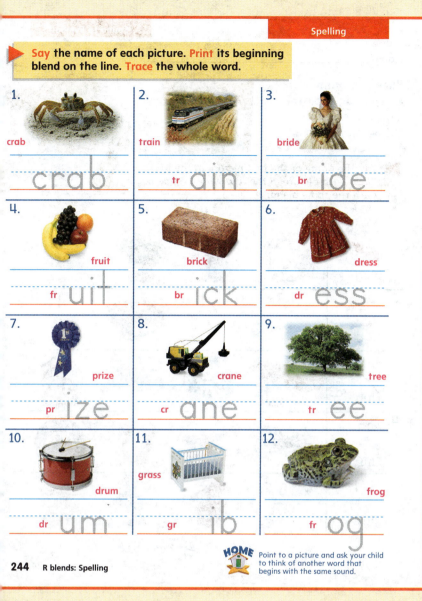

1. crab — cr ab
2. train — tr ain
3. bride — br ide
4. fruit — fr uit
5. brick — br ick
6. dress — dr ess
7. prize — pr ize
8. crane — cr ane
9. tree — tr ee
10. drum — dr um
11. grass — gr ass
12. frog — fr og

HOME Point to a picture and ask your child to think of another word that begins with the same sound.

244 R blends: Spelling

CURRICULUM CONNECTIONS

SPELLING

Materials: spelling master (page 239I), index cards

Together, read the spelling words for *r* blends from the master. Have children write each word on a card and underline the two letters for the blend in each word. Have children illustrate each word on the back to make practice spelling cards.

WRITING

Have children illustrate and write about how a frog prince found a crown.

FINE ARTS

Materials: colored construction paper; paste; objects for decorating, such as pasta, buttons, sequins, beans, yarn, or fabric scraps

Have children make and decorate a frame for a favorite drawing. Show them how to fold a sheet of construction paper and cut out the center, leaving a frame.

TECHNOLOGY

 **AstroWord** Consonant Blends & Digraphs

AUDITORY/KINESTHETIC LEARNERS

Materials: letter card *Rr*

Ask children to listen as you say some words. They should hold up the letter *r* when they hear a word that begins with an *r* blend: *potato, pretzel, bread, toast, cranberry, gravy, banana, grapes, meat, broccoli, lettuce, drink, fruit, dressing*.

CHALLENGE

Challenge children to write and draw a story with a surprise ending and have the story include three words with *r* blends.

EXTRA SUPPORT/INTERVENTION

Materials: Phonics Picture Cards: bread (121), crib (124), dress (126), fruit (128), grapes (129), tree (131)

Hold up one picture at a time. Have a child name the picture and say another word that begins with the same consonant blend. **See Daily Phonics Practice, page 320.**

Integrating Phonics and Reading

Guided Reading
Show the cover as you read the title. Have children use the cover to predict what the story will be about.

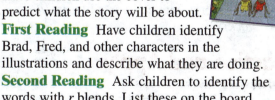

First Reading Have children identify Brad, Fred, and other characters in the illustrations and describe what they are doing.

Second Reading Ask children to identify the words with *r* blends. List these on the board or add them to the Word Wall. Have children identify the letters in each blend.

Comprehension
After reading, ask children these questions:
• Why do Fred and Brad race each other? *Recall/Character*
• What happens in the race? Who wins? *Recall/Summarize*

ESL/ELL English Language Learners
Point to the picture on page 9 and ask, *Who hops faster here?* (Fred) Repeat with pages 10, 12, and 13.

244

Lesson 117 — Pages 245–246

l Blends

Skill Focus

Children will
- ★ recognize the sounds of *l* blends.
- ★ identify picture names and words that contain *l* blends.

ESL/ELL Korean, Khmer, Hmong, Cantonese, and Vietnamese speakers may confuse *l* blends and *r* blends. Spanish-speaking children may pronounce a short *e* before *sl* words, since Spanish lacks this initial blend.

Teach

Phonological Awareness: Alliteration Say this sentence and write it on the board: *Blair blows blue bubbles.* Ask children what sound they hear at the beginning of *Blair, blows,* and *blue.* (bl) Remind them that sometimes two consonant sounds are blended together at the beginning of a word. Help children identify the blend at the beginning of *blue* as /bl/. Continue by having children identify the blends found at the beginning of the words in these sentences.

- Glenn's globe glides.   *(gl)*
- Flat flutes fly.   *(fl)*
- Clean class clocks click. *(cl)*

Point out that all the blends have the sound of *l*.

Sound to Symbol Write the word *plum* on the board and have children read it with you. Ask them what two letters are blended together to make the beginning sound. Have a volunteer underline the letters *p* and *l*. Next, write *gl, fl, cl, bl,* and *pl* on the board and write the phonogram _ock. Challenge children to add different blends to the phonogram to make real words with consonant blends. (*flock, clock, block*)

Practice and Apply

Phonemic Awareness Read aloud the rhyme on page 245. Have children listen for and name words that begin with *l* blends.

Sound to Symbol Help children identify the pictures on pages 245 and 246. Draw their attention to the words shown in the first column on page 245, and explain that the underlined letters show the consonant blend at the beginning of the word. Make sure children understand that they are to circle the pictures in each row that have the same beginning blend as this word.

Reading Use *Glenda the Lion,* MCP Phonics and Reading Library, Super Skills Collecion, Level A, to provide practice in reading words with *l* blends.

Sound to Symbol

Slice the plum.
Place it on a plate.
You take some.
I'll be glad to wait.

▶ **Say** the name of the first picture in the row. **Circle** each picture in the row whose name begins with the same blend.

1. plug — plate, prize, plant, crib
2. block — blouse, pliers, blanket, broom
3. club — sled, clock, crib, clown
4. flag — fly, flashlight, frame, flat
5. glass — grapes, glove, globe, groceries

L blends: Sound to symbol 245

FOCUS ON ALL LEARNERS

ESL/ELL ENGLISH LANGUAGE LEARNERS

- Before beginning page 245, practice differentiating *l* blends from *r* blends. Help children pronounce *play, pray; crown, clown; flea, free; glass, grass; broom, bloom.*
- Offer support before children begin page 246 by printing a series of consonant blends on paper: *bl, fl, gl, cl, pl.* Say a word and have English language learners point to or say the correct blend.

VISUAL LEARNERS

Write the *l* blends *bl, cl, fl, gl,* and *pl* as headings on the board. Invite children to look around the room and identify objects whose names begin with an *l* blend, such as a globe or a flag. As children name things, they should tell you under which heading to write the word. When the chart is complete, read it as a group.

KINESTHETIC LEARNERS

Materials: clay

Let children shape the *l* blends *bl, cl, fl, gl,* and *pl* out of clay. Encourage children to spell out *l* blend words with clay.

Sound to Symbol

➤ Say the name of each picture. Circle its name.

1. (block) flock
2. grape (plate)
3. (class) glass
4. drag (flag)
5. clue (glue)
6. (plug) plum
7. crack (clock)
8. (plant) plan
9. (flat) float
10. grass (glass)
11. (club) clap
12. (fly) cry

HOME Play a word game with your child by saying, "I say *fly*, you say fl___." Your child supplies a word with the blend.

246 L blends: Sound to symbol

CURRICULUM CONNECTIONS

SPELLING
Dictate the following words and read the sentences. Have children write the words for a spelling pretest.
1. **block** The **block** is made of wood.
2. **club** Hit the ball with a **club.**
3. **flag** The **flag** has stars.
4. **glass** I can see through the **glass.**
5. **plant** The **plant** needs sun.
6. **plug** We will **plug** the hole.

WRITING
Have children work in pairs to write a grocery list. Ask them to try to include items that begin with *l* blends. They may include real items or make up brand names, such as Slippery Soap.

MATH
Work with children to make a list of five foods children like. Take a survey to see which foods are most favored by having children sign their name on a line under their favorite. Help children interpret the resulting graph.

TECHNOLOGY **AstroWord** Consonant Blends & Digraphs

Integrating Phonics and Reading

Shared/Guided Reading
Show the cover as you read the title. Flip through the pages to show children the animal characters.
First Reading Invite children to join in each time you come to this sentence: *But the [animal name] was sleeping.*
Second Reading Ask children to identify the words with *l* blends in the story. List these on the board or add them to the Word Wall. Have children identify the letters in each blend.
Comprehension
After reading, ask children these questions:
- Why can't Glenda get any of the animals to play with her? *Recall/Cause and Effect*
- Why does Glenda roar? *Inference/Cause and Effect*

ESL/ELL **English Language Learners**
Using the picture on pages 12 and 13, point to each animal and say, *Glenda roars at the ___.* Children should complete the sentence to name each animal in the picture.

AUDITORY/KINESTHETIC LEARNERS **GROUPS**
Materials: Phonics Picture Cards: block (133), clock (134), flag (136), glass (138), plant (139), sled (140); cube-shaped blocks; masking tape

Write *bl, cl, fl, gl, pl,* and *sl* on separate pieces of masking tape and attach a piece to each side of the block. Display the picture cards. Let children roll the block, call out the letters that are facing up, and choose a picture whose name begins with that blend.

CHALLENGE
Challenge children to look through books to find *l* blend words. Ask them to list the words they find.

EXTRA SUPPORT/INTERVENTION
Materials: Phonics Picture Cards: block (133), clock (134), flag (136), glass (138), plant (139), sled (140); tape

Write *bl, cl, fl, gl, pl, sl* on the board. Have children select a picture and say its name. Then, have them tape it under the letters that spell its initial *l* blend. **See Daily Phonics Practice, page 321.**

246

Lesson 118   Pages 247–248

l Blends

Skill Focus

Children will

★ identify and spell picture names that contain *l* blends.

★ write words that contain *l* blends to complete sentences.

★ recognize and read high-frequency words.

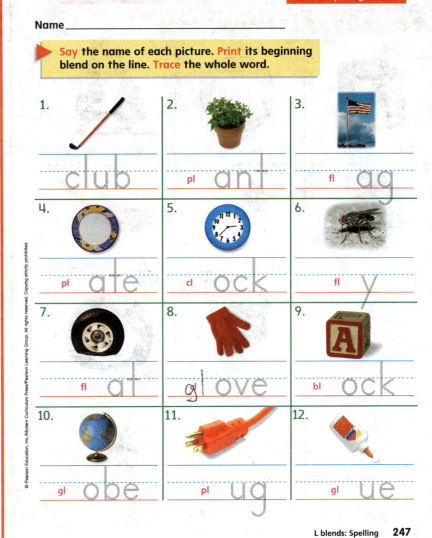

Teach

Phonological Awareness: Initial Sound Isolation Say the word *block,* emphasizing the beginning blend, and have children repeat the word. Then, say *block,* /bl/, and have children repeat. Explain that the sound they hear at the beginning of *block* is the sound of *bl.* Ask children to say these words, then identify the beginning blend: *glass, play, clock, flower.*

Sound to Symbol Write the words *lock, late, lass, lap,* and *low* on the board and have children read each one. Then, add *c* in front of *lock* and have children read the new word. Have children identify the blend heard at the beginning of *clock,* and ask a volunteer to underline the letters that stand for that sound. Continue, adding *p* to *late, g* to *lass, f* to *lap,* and *b* to *low.*

Next, write these blends on the board as column headings: *cl, pl, gl, fl, bl.* Ask children to name words that begin with these blends. Write the words under the appropriate column headers and ask volunteers to circle the letters that stand for the consonant blend heard at the beginning of each word.

Practice and Apply

Blend Word Parts As children complete page 247, encourage them to say each picture name, blending together the beginning, middle, and ending sounds.

Writing For page 248, suggest that children try each word choice before writing a word. As they complete the activity, they will have the opportunity to read the following high-frequency words: *into, grow.*

Critical Thinking For Talk About It, have children recall what Bruce and Fran did before responding.

Reading Use *Planting a Garden,* MCP Phonics and Reading Library, Super Skills Collection, Level A, to provide practice in reading words with *l* blends.

FOCUS ON ALL LEARNERS

ESL/ELL ENGLISH LANGUAGE LEARNERS

Materials: Phonics Picture Cards: block (133), clock (134), clown (135), glass (138), plant (139)

- Before beginning page 247, have children name the pictures as you point to each one. Monitor pronunciation, helping children to pronounce both consonants of the blend. Point out that *l* is always the second letter in each blend.

- Use Phonics Picture Cards for block, clock, clown, glass, and plant to reinforce *l* blends before beginning page 248. Point to each card and ask a volunteer to name the card. Then, write the picture name on the board, using colored chalk to highlight the letters that make the *l* blend.

KINESTHETIC LEARNERS   GROUPS

Materials: Phonics Word Cards: *grin* (205), *pride* (206), *track* (207), *train* (208), *blade* (211), *blocks* (212), *clock* (213), *flat* (214), *glass* (215), *plan* (216); chart paper; marker

Draw a planter box on the chart paper. Players pick a card, read the word aloud, and if the word begins with an *l* blend, plant a flower by drawing one in the box.

Words in Context

▶ Say the name of each picture. Circle the word that will finish the sentence. Print it on the line.

1. Take a peek into my ___class___ .
   clap / (class) / grass

2. Bruce draws a funny ___clown___ .
   clock / (clown) / frown

3. Fran makes a clock from a paper ___plate___ .
   (plate) / prank / plum

4. Mr. Glen lets us grow ___plants___ .
   plans / plates / (plants)

5. We play with clay and ___blocks___ .
   braids / drives / (blocks)

6. We look at the ___globe___ .
   (globe) / glass / grape

Talk About It: Would you like to do what Bruce and Fran did in school? Why?

Home: Point to the words Bruce, Fran, Glen, grow, play, clay and ask your child to think of more words that begin with the same sounds.

248 L blends: High-frequency words, critical thinking

CURRICULUM CONNECTIONS

SPELLING
Materials: spelling master (page 239l), index cards

Have children use the *l* blend spelling words on page 239l to make practice spelling cards. Have them illustrate each word on the back of the card.

WRITING
Have children illustrate and write about a favorite classroom game they like to play.

PORTFOLIO

MATH
Have children make clocks out of paper plates. Discuss the parts of a clock, where the numbers belong, which hand tells the minutes, and which hand tells the hour. Have children practice reading time with their clocks.

TECHNOLOGY **AstroWord** Consonant Blends & Digraphs

AUDITORY/KINESTHETIC LEARNERS   GROUPS
Materials: red, green, orange, yellow, black, and blue crayons; glue; tape; glitter; buttons; paper plates; pencil; block; clay

Display the materials on a table. Ask children to select an object whose name begins with a blend. Have them name the object and identify the blend they hear at the beginning of the word.

CHALLENGE
Challenge children to list at least 10 objects whose names contain *l* blends.

EXTRA SUPPORT/INTERVENTION
Materials: Phonics Picture Cards: block (133), clock (134), flag (136), glass (138), plant (139); letter cards *Bb, Cc, Ff, Gg, Ll, Pp*

Display the picture cards on the chalkboard ledge. Have one child name a picture. Then, have the group use letter cards to form the blend they hear at the beginning of the picture name. **See Daily Phonics Practice, page 321.**

Integrating Phonics and Reading

Guided Reading
Show the cover as you read the title. Invite children to share what they know about gardens.

Planting a Garden

First Reading Have children look at the thought bubbles and tell what the girls are thinking.

Second Reading Ask children to identify the words with *l* blends in the story. List these on the board or add them to the classroom Word Wall. Have children identify the letters in each blend.

Comprehension
After reading, ask children these questions:
• What grew at the end of the story? Did this surprise you? *Reflective Analysis/Opinion*
• What would you like to plant in a garden? *Reflective Analysis/Personal Experience*

ESL/ELL English Language Learners
Invite children to act out each of these actions from the story: *plant the seed, pat it flat, water the plant.*

Lesson 119 Pages 249–250

s Blends

Skill Focus

Children will

★ recognize the sounds of s blends.

★ identify picture names and words that contain s blends.

ESL/ELL Children whose home languages are Vietnamese, Cantonese, Khmer, Hmong, or Korean might have trouble with initial s blends, since they do not exist in these languages. Spanish-speaking children might pronounce a short e before all s blends.

Teach

Phonemic Awareness: Phoneme Addition
Tell children you will say a word. They can make a new word by adding the s sound to the beginning. Use these words: *lip, low, top, peak, trap, nap*. Conclude by pointing out that all the words children made have consonant blends that begin with the sound of s.

Sound to Symbol Write *top, low, wing, nap,* and *pin* on the board and help children read each word. Ask volunteers to add s to the beginning of each word and to read the new word. Point out that when each word is pronounced, both beginning consonants can be heard. Ask children to underline the blend at the beginning of each word.

Next, write the words *trap* and *cream* on the board. Add s to form the words *strap* and *scream* and help children read each word. Explain that some s blends have three consonants. Have volunteers underline the blends *str* and *scr*.

Practice and Apply

Phonemic Awareness Read aloud the rhyme on page 249. Have children listen for and name words that begin with s blends.

Sound to Symbol Help children identify the pictures on pages 249 and 250. Draw their attention to the words shown in the first column on page 249, and explain that the underlined letters show the consonant blend at the beginning of the word. Make sure children understand that they are to circle the pictures in each row that have the same beginning blend as this word.

Reading Use *Sally's Spaceship*, MCP Phonics and Reading Library, Super Skills Collection, Level A, to provide practice in reading words with s blends.

FOCUS ON ALL LEARNERS

ESL/ELL ENGLISH LANGUAGE LEARNERS
Materials: index cards

- Before beginning page 249, discuss the different meanings of the homophones *steps, stamp, store,* and *slide*.
- Before beginning page 250, write the blends *sl, sp, st, sk, sw, sc, sm, sn, sk, scr, sq,* and *str* on index cards. Hold up a card and ask children to identify pictures whose names begin with that blend. Provide help as needed. Children can then complete the page individually or in pairs.

VISUAL/KINESTHETIC LEARNERS
Materials: Phonics Picture Cards: sled (140), skates (143), smoke (144), snail (145), spoon (147), stamp (149), strawberry (151), swing (152); string

Display the pictures along the chalkboard ledge and give each child a piece of string. One at a time, write each s blend—*str, st, sl, sp, sk, sn, sm,* or *sw*—on the board. Have children hold the string to connect the picture that begins with the blend to the letters.

Sound to Symbol

Say the name of each picture. Circle its name.

1. (sled) slide
2. stops (steps)
3. (spill) spade
4. (skunk) spunk
5. spin (swim)
6. scrap (scrub)
7. sweet (street)
8. (smoke) spoke
9. (square) scare
10. (swing) string
11. (snake) skate
12. spot (spoon)

HOME Say "s-l, sl." Ask your child to name a word that begins with the sl sound. Repeat for st, sp, sk, sw, sm.

250 S blends: Sound to symbol

CURRICULUM CONNECTIONS

SPELLING
Dictate the following words and read the sentences. Have children write the words for a spelling pretest.
1. **skate** I can **skate** really fast.
2. **smoke** **Smoke** comes from the fire.
3. **snake** The **snake** is long and thin.
4. **spoon** I eat cereal with a **spoon.**
5. **square** A **square** has four sides.
6. **star** I see a **star** in the sky.
7. **swing** I fly high on my **swing.**

WRITING
Have children draw a picture and write about foods a squirrel might store for the winter.

PORTFOLIO

SCIENCE
Help children make a K–W–L chart about strawberries with these column headings: *What We Know, What We Want to Know,* and *What We Learned.* Help children record their facts and questions. Then, help them find answers to their questions before filling in the third column.

TECHNOLOGY   AstroWord Consonant Blends & Digraphs

KINESTHETIC LEARNERS   GROUPS
Materials: letter cards: *Ll, Kk, Nn, Mm, Pp, Tt, Ww*

Print the letter *s* on the board. Tell children to listen as you say some words with *s* blends. Have a volunteer come to the board and place the letter card by the letter *s* to make the blend. Then, they can pantomime the word. Use the following words: *skip, spin, swim, smile, stamp, sleep, sweep, skate, snap.*

CHALLENGE
Challenge children to draw or write things that are sold in stores and have names that begin with *s* blends. They might use newspaper ads to find words.

EXTRA SUPPORT/INTERVENTION
Materials: Phonics Picture Cards: sled (140), skates (143), smoke (144), snail (145), spoon (147), stamp (149), swing (152)

Display the pictures and ask children to name each one. Then, shuffle the pictures and turn them over. Have children select one card at a time, name it, and name the letters they hear in the *s* blend at the beginning of the picture name. **See Daily Phonics Practice, page 321.**

Integrating Phonics and Reading

Shared/Guided Reading
Show the cover as you read the title. Invite children to describe Sally's spaceship.

First Reading Invite half the class to read the words spoken by Sally and the other half to read the words spoken by her mother while you read the narrator's part.

Second Reading Ask children to identify the words with *s* blends in the story. List these on the board or add them to the Word Wall. Have children identify the letters in each blend.

Comprehension
After reading, ask children these questions:
- Why did Sally make a spaceship? *Recall/Cause and Effect*
- Do you think Sally's spaceship really worked? Why or why not? *Reflective Analysis/Opinion*

ESL/ELL English Language Learners
Using the pictures on pages 7, 9, and 11, ask children to answer the question, *What did Sally take on her spaceship?* Encourage them to use complete sentences in their answers.

Lesson 120 Pages 251–252

s Blends

Skill Focus
Children will
★ identify and spell picture names that contain *s* blends.
★ write words that contain *s* blends to complete sentences.
★ recognize and read high-frequency words.

Teach

Phonological Awareness: Initial Sound Isolation Say the word *snail,* stretching the beginning *sn* blend: *sssnnnail.* Have children repeat the word in this way several times. Ask children to identify the blend they hear at the beginning of the word *snail.* Then, have children suggest another word that begins with the same blend. Repeat the procedure, using these words: *stop, smart, skate, spot, squash, street.*

Sound to Symbol Write these words on the board: *send, spend, say, stay, sip, slip.* Have children read the words and identify those that begin with consonant blends. Ask volunteers to underline each consonant blend.

Next, write __ __ *ell* on the board. Ask children what *s* blends they might add to make words with this ending. *(spell, smell, swell)* Repeat, using the word endings *-eet, -ill, -oke,* and *-ate.* Each time, have volunteers come up to the board and make as many *s* blend words as they can. Have the class read the words on the board together, emphasizing the beginning sounds.

Practice and Apply

Blend Word Parts As children complete page 251, encourage them to say each picture name, blending together the beginning, middle, and ending sounds.

Writing For page 252, suggest that children try each word choice before writing a word. As they complete the activity, they will have the opportunity to read the high-frequency word *each.*

Critical Thinking For Talk About It, have children recall the safety rules cited in the sentences before naming additional rules.

Reading Use *The River Grows,* MCP Phonics and Reading Library, Super Skills Collection, Level A, to provide practice in reading words with *s* blends, *r* blends, and *l* blends.

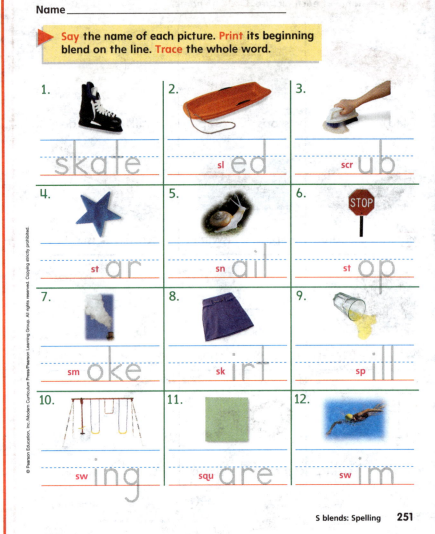

S blends: Spelling 251

FOCUS ON ALL LEARNERS

ESL/ELL ENGLISH LANGUAGE LEARNERS

- Before beginning pages 251 and 252, have children say the names of the pictures and the words. Monitor pronunciation, making sure they pronounce both or all the consonants of the blend. Point out that *s* is always the first letter in each blend.

- Offer support before children begin page 252 by printing a series of consonant blends on paper: *st, sl, sw, sn, str, sw.* Say a word and have English language learners point to or say the correct blend.

VISUAL LEARNERS
Materials: books

Have pairs of children look through books to find words with initial *s* blends. Have them list each word and circle the blend. Invite children to share their lists and group the words by their initial blends.

KINESTHETIC LEARNERS

Write the words *scrub, stop, sleep, swing, slide, swim, smile,* and *skate* on the board. Ask one child at a time to secretly select a word and act it out. Have others in the group guess the word, point to it on the board, and identify the initial consonant blend.

Words in Context

▶ **Say** the name of the picture. **Circle** the word that will finish the sentence. **Print** it on the line.

1. Be sure to __stop__ and read each rule!
   - spill
   - (stop)
   - star

2. Take turns on the __slide__.
   - (slide)
   - sling
   - slip

3. Do not run near the __swing__.
   - sting
   - (swing)
   - swim

4. Please do not pet the __snake__.
   - (snake)
   - spoke
   - snail

5. Look before you cross the __street__.
   - steps
   - (street)
   - stamp

6. Always __swim__ with a pal.
   - sweep
   - snake
   - (swim)

TALK ABOUT IT What other safety rules do you know?

HOME Help your child to think of new sentences using some of the circled words.

252 S blends: High-frequency words, critical thinking

CURRICULUM CONNECTIONS

SPELLING
Dictate the following *r*, *l*, and *s* blend words and read the sentence. Have children write the words for a posttest.
1. **train** — I rode on a **train**.
2. **glass** — The **glass** has milk in it.
3. **star** — My prize was a gold **star**.
4. **crown** — Does the king wear a **crown**?
5. **plant** — Please water that **plant**.
6. **square** — A **square** has four sides.

WRITING
Have children draw and write two sentences about a snail or a snake.

SOCIAL STUDIES
Have children work with you to make a list of school safety rules. Then, ask them to choose a rule and make a poster to remind others of the rule. Display the posters.

AstroWord Consonant Blends & Digraphs

AUDITORY LEARNERS
Play a version of "Simon Says." Give directions to children and have the children perform them only if the first word begins with an *s* blend. Directions to give include *Speak fast; Stand up; Jump; Smile and wave; Clap your hands; Spin around.*

CHALLENGE
Challenge children to write three direction sentences using *s* blend words, such as *Spin like a top; Skip to the globe; Swing your arms.* Then, have them exchange lists with a partner and each perform the other's directions.

EXTRA SUPPORT/INTERVENTION
Materials: paper, pencil, magazines, scissors, glue

Ask children to draw a large square on a piece of paper. Then, have them look through magazines to cut out pictures of things whose names begin with an *s* blend. They can paste their pictures in the square. See **Daily Phonics Practice, page 321.**

Integrating Phonics and Reading

Guided Reading
Show the cover as you read the title. Invite children to name rivers they have heard about.
First Reading Have children look at the photos and relate what they see to the facts and descriptions in the text.
Second Reading Ask children to identify the words with *s* blends in the story. List these on the board or add them to the Word Wall. Have children identify the letters in each blend.
Comprehension
After reading, ask children these questions:
- What did you learn about rivers that you didn't know before? *Reflective Analysis/ Prior Knowledge*
- What else would you like to know about rivers? *Reflective Analysis/Personal Experience*

ESL/ELL English Language Learners
Point to photos and ask children questions such as: *On page 4, does the water slip or crash down? On page 6, is the river slow or fast?*

Lesson 121 Pages 253–254

Final Blends

Skill Focus

Children will

★ identify picture names and spell words that contain final *mp, sk, st, lk, nk, lt,* and *nd* blends.

ESL/ELL Children who speak Cantonese, Khmer, or Korean may have difficulty with final blends. Learners whose home language is Tagalog or Spanish might "clip" the blends, pronouncing only the first consonant of each.

Teach

Phonological Awareness: Rhyme Remind children that rhyming words are words that sound alike except for the beginning sound. Say the rhyming words *blink, wink.* Ask volunteers to name other words that rhyme with these words. (*pink, sink, rink*) Repeat with the following words.

- jump, stump   (*lump, pump*)
- bunk, trunk   (*junk, dunk*)
- hand, land   (*sand, band*)
- nest, best   (*rest, pest*)

Sound to Symbol Write the words *jump, mask, fast, wink,* and *sand* on the board. Help children read the words aloud. Explain that two consonant sounds may be blended together at the end of a word. Have volunteers underline the final blends.

Next, ask children to suggest words that rhyme with the words on the board. Record the words under each rhyming word and read the lists with the class. Point out the consonant blend at the end of each word.

Practice and Apply

Sound to Symbol Help children identify the pictures on pages 253 and 254. After they have completed the activities, encourage them to identify all the final blends they found on the pages. (*mp, sk, nk, st, nd, lk, lt*)

Blend Word Parts As children complete page 254, encourage them to say each picture name, blending together the beginning, middle, and ending sounds. Remind them that each picture name ends with a blend.

Reading Use *That Pig Can't Do a Thing,* MCP Phonics and Reading Library, Super Skills Collection, Level A, to provide practice in reading words with final blends.

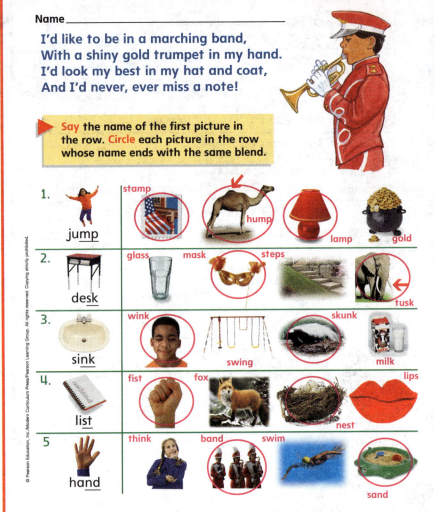

FOCUS ON ALL LEARNERS

ESL/ELL ENGLISH LANGUAGE LEARNERS

Materials: letter cards *Mm, Pp, Ss, Kk, Nn, Tt, Dd*

- Before beginning page 253, verify recognition of final blends by pointing to a picture clue on the page. Help children identify the picture, then have them arrange letter cards that stand for the final blend.
- Before beginning page 254, have children say the names of the pictures, making sure that they pronounce both consonants of each final blend.

VISUAL LEARNERS

Say a word. Invite children to come to the board and write the ending blend of the word. Then, have them use the word in a sentence. Words to give are *stand, wink, list, limp, lost, ask, think, camp,* and *risk.*

KINESTHETIC LEARNERS

Have children listen for final blends in the action words you say. If the word ends with a final blend, they are to perform the action. Use the following words: *wink, dig, stamp, swim, jump, run, slide, hop, land.*

Spelling

Say the name of each picture. Print its ending blend on the line. Trace the whole word.

1. trunk
2. la**mp**
3. de**sk**
4. mi**lk**
5. li**st**
6. wi**nk**
7. ne**st**
8. si**nk**
9. ma**sk**
10. be**lt**
11. ju**mp**
12. ha**nd**

HOME Ask your child to point to a picture, name a word that rhymes, and then name the letters in the final blend.

254 Final blends: Spelling

CURRICULUM CONNECTIONS

SPELLING
Dictate the following words and read the sentences. Have children write the words for a spelling pretest.
1. **desk** There are pens in the **desk.**
2. **list** Where is my shopping **list**?
3. **lamp** I read near the **lamp.**
4. **mask** I wear a **mask** on Halloween.
5. **sink** Pour that water in the **sink**.
6. **trunk** The car has a **trunk** in back.

WRITING
Have children invent a delicious snack to sell at a food stand called Best Foods. Ask them to name their snack and to illustrate its package. Encourage them to use words that have final consonant blends, such as *Best Pink Berry Lumps*.

TECHNOLOGY **AstroWord** Consonant Blends & Digraphs

AUDITORY/KINESTHETIC LEARNERS
Materials: Masking tape, paper, crayons or markers

Write these words on the board: *stamp, desk, mask, toast, nest, sink, skunk, hand, pond*. Read the words with the class and invite children to choose a word to illustrate. When children have finished their drawings, erase the words. Have children show their pictures for the group to guess the word. Call on volunteers to write the word on the board.

CHALLENGE
Write *mp, sk, nk, st,* and *nd* on the board. Challenge children to write at least three words that end with each blend. Then, ask them to write three sentences, using words from their lists.

EXTRA SUPPORT/INTERVENTION
Ask children to help you spell the words *stump, ask, band, fast, wink, felt,* and *silk*. Write each word on the board and underline the final blend. Have children use these key words to help them write the final consonant blends on page 254. **See Daily Phonics Practice, pages 321–322.**

Integrating Phonics and Reading

Guided Reading
Show the cover as you read the title. Invite children to name some things pigs can and can't do.

First Reading Have children look at the illustrations and describe what the pig is doing.

Second Reading Ask children to find three final *nk,* one final *nt,* and one final *mp* word in the story. List the words on the board or add them to the classroom Word Wall.

Comprehension
After reading, ask children these questions:
- Do the girl and the father feel the same way about the pig? *Recall/Comparison*
- What is funny about the story's ending? *Reflective Analysis/Cause and Effect*

ESL/ELL English Language Learners
Make a list of words that describe the pig and write them on the board. (*fat, pink, a ham*) Then, explain the two meanings of *ham:* "a kind of pork" and "someone who loves to perform."

Lesson 122   Pages 252–256

Review Initial and Final Blends

Skill Focus

Children will

★ orally blend word parts.

★ identify picture names and spell words that contain initial and final blends.

ESL/ELL Native speakers of Spanish may be more familiar with initial consonant blends, which are more common in that language.

Teach

Phonological Awareness: Initial and Final Sound Isolation Say the word *crunch*, stretching the initial *r* blend: *cccrrunch*. Ask children to repeat the word, stretching the *c* and *r* sounds. Help them to identify the beginning sound as the *cr* blend. Continue with *drag, please, flat,* and *slow*. Next, say a series of words with children, this time stressing the final blend in each one. Use *last, silk, raft,* and *pump*. Ask children to identify the consonants that make the ending sound heard in each word.

Sound to Symbol Draw a curved arrow and write *sl, e,* and *d* above it, as shown on page 255. Pronounce the word *sled* by blending the sounds together as you move your hand across the arrow. Have volunteers come to the board and blend the word in the same way.

Draw another curved arrow and write *sl-i-p*. Have children blend the word with you. Make new words by changing the letters on the left to *tr, sn, fl, gr*. Repeat the procedure for words with final blends. Use *wink, rust, mask,* and *lamp*.

Practice and Apply

Sound to Symbol Help children identify the pictures on pages 255 and 256. For page 256, make sure children understand that they will write each blended word and then draw a line to the correct picture.

Reading Use *Stan Packs*, MCP Phonics and Reading Library, Super Skills Collection, Level A, to provide practice in reading words with initial and final blends.

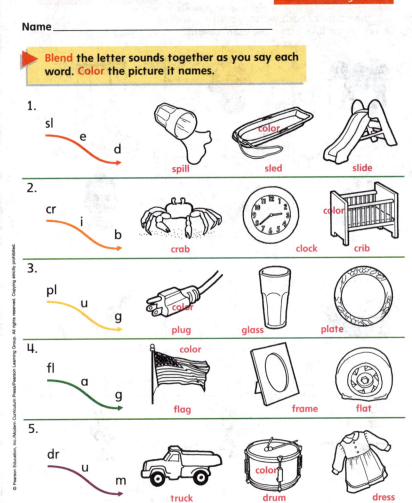

Blending

Name _____

▶ **Blend** the letter sounds together as you say each word. **Color** the picture it names.

1. sl → e → d   spill   sled (color)   slide
2. cr → i → b   crab   clock   crib (color)
3. pl → u → g   plug (color)   glass   plate
4. fl → a → g   flag (color)   frame   flat
5. dr → u → m   truck   drum (color)   dress

Review initial blends   **255**

FOCUS ON ALL LEARNERS

ESL/ELL ENGLISH LANGUAGE LEARNERS
Materials: index cards

- Before children begin page 255, review the skill of identifying initial blends by preparing cards with these consonant blends: *sl, cr, pl, fl, dr*. Write one blend on each card. Then, have children select cards and name two words that contain the blend. Allow children to use the page to find words containing the blends.

- Repeat the activity before children begin page 256, using these final blends: *nk, st, lk, ft, mp, sk*.

KINESTHETIC LEARNERS

Materials: Phonics Picture Cards: book (3), daisy (7), glove (14), moon (25), plant (38), belt (78), desk (79), cake (86), bread (121), fruit (128), grapes (129), strawberry (151); paper plate

Play "Fill the Plate." Place the picture cards face down. Have children pick a card and name it. If the word has a beginning or an ending blend, they put the picture on the plate. When all the cards have been identified, review each card on the plate.

255

Blending

▶ Blend the letter sounds together as you say each word. Then **print** the word on the line. **Draw** a line to the picture it names.

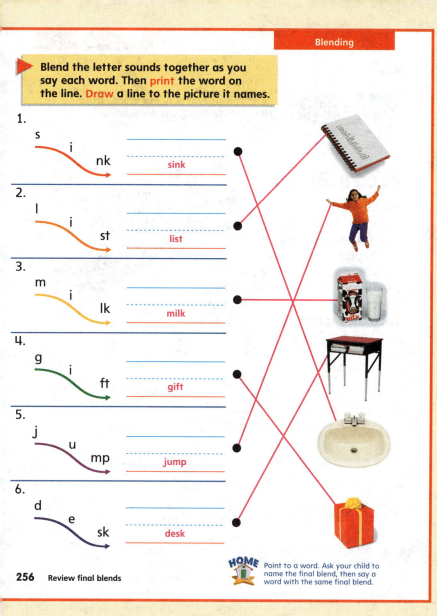

1. s-i-nk — sink
2. l-i-st — list
3. m-i-lk — milk
4. g-i-ft — gift
5. j-u-mp — jump
6. d-e-sk — desk

Review final blends

HOME Point to a word. Ask your child to name the final blend, then say a word with the same final blend.

CURRICULUM CONNECTIONS

SPELLING
Materials: spelling master (page 239l), index cards

Have children use the words with final blends on page 239l to make practice spelling cards. Have them illustrate each word on the back of the card.

WRITING
Have children illustrate a triple-scoop ice-cream cone. Have them write on the cone about the three fantastic flavors. Encourage them to use words with initial and final blends.

PORTFOLIO

SCIENCE
Demonstrate how the sense of smell affects the way things taste. Have children put on blindfolds and invite them to identify some foods and flavorings by smell. Then, have them hold their nose and taste some of the foods. Is it easier to identify them by taste or by smell? Some foods or flavorings to use include lemon, vanilla, cinnamon, mint, bread, onion, and banana.

TECHNOLOGY AstroWord Consonant Blends & Digraphs

AUDITORY/KINESTHETIC LEARNERS
Have children stamp their feet if they hear a word that has a beginning or an ending blend. Use the following words: *round, pink, food, fame, frame, train, rain, blow, low, milk, jam, tar, star, fist, fit, square, band.*

CHALLENGE
Write the following words on the board. Challenge children to add one or more letters to each word to make a word with a consonant blend. Encourage them to compare their final lists to see how many words they made. Words are *lip, rip, pan, cat, lap, den, lock, rain,* and *ten.*

EXTRA SUPPORT/INTERVENTION
Draw an arrow similar to those on pages 255 and 256. Write *p* on the left and *ill* on the right. Help children blend the word. Then, add *s* in front of the *p* and help them blend the new word. Do the same with *d-en*. Add *t* to the end to help children blend a word with a final blend.
See Daily Phonics Practice, pages 321–322.

Integrating Phonics and Reading

Guided Reading
Show the cover as you read the title. Invite children to identify the items in Stan's suitcase.
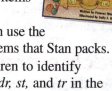
First Reading Have children use the illustrations to point out the items that Stan packs.
Second Reading Ask children to identify words with initial blends *bl, dr, st,* and *tr* in the story. Ask which of these words has the final blend *mp*.
Comprehension
After reading, ask children these questions:
- What kinds of things did Stan pack instead of clothes? *Recall/Details*
- What kind of trip would you like to take? What would you pack? *Creative/Personal Experience*

ESL/ELL English Language Learners
Work with children to list the items that Stan packed on the board. Talk about what each one is and whether it would be useful on a short trip.

Lesson 123 Pages 257–258

Phonics and Reading / Phonics and Writing

Consonant Blends

Skill Focus

Children will

★ read words that contain initial and final consonant blends.

★ write words containing initial and final consonant blends to finish sentences.

★ build words with initial blends and phonograms -ick, -ay.

Teach

Phonemic Awareness: Phoneme Blending
Say a word, segmenting the individual phonemes. Have children repeat the segmented word and say the complete word. Then, ask children to identify the consonant blend heard at the beginning of the word. Use /k/ /l/ /a/ /p/ (clap); /b/ /r/ /i/ /k/ (brick); /s/ /m/ /a/ /l/ (small); /s/ /t/ /ō/ /n/ (stone); /g/ /r/ /ā/ /p/ (grape); /s/ /l/ /ē/ /p/ (sleep); /f/ /l/ /i/ /p/ (flip); /s/ /k/ /r/ /ē/ /n/ (screen).

Sound to Symbol Write these words on the board: *fruit, breeze, list, most, band, brain, lend, free, broke, past, fry.* Point out that each word contains a beginning or ending blend. Ask a volunteer to underline the blend in each word in the column and say whether it is a beginning blend or an ending one.

Read Words in Sentences Write these sentences on the board.

- Hank and Brad are best friends.
- Glen will toast the bread.

Help children read the sentences. Then, ask them to circle the words that have initial or final blends.

Practice and Apply

Phonics and Reading After children have read the story, encourage them to identify words that have initial or final blends.

Critical Thinking For Talk About It, remind children that yeast helps bread dough to rise.

Phonics and Writing For page 258, tell children to try each blend at the top to make a word with -ick or -ay. Remind them that not every blend will make a real word.

Reading Use *My Lost Top,* MCP Phonics and Reading Library, Super Skills Collection, Level A, to provide practice in reading words with initial and final blends.

257

Name _____

Reading

Phonics & Reading Read the story. Then, use words from the story to finish the sentences.

Fred's Bread

Fred made some bread.
He mixed flour, water,
and too much yeast.
The bread grew and grew.
Now Fred had too much bread!
He asked his friends to stop by.
They sliced the soft bread and made toast.
Then they spread jam on the toast.
They had a feast!

1. Fred made some _____**bread**_____.

2. Fred asked his friends to _____**stop**_____ by.

3. He and his friends had a _____**feast**_____.

⭐ **Talk About It** Why did Fred end up with so much bread?

Review consonant blends: Reading, critical thinking 257

FOCUS ON ALL LEARNERS

ESL/ELL ENGLISH LANGUAGE LEARNERS

- Build background for the story on page 257 by talking about how bread is made. List and discuss the basic ingredients, including flour, water, and yeast. You may want to bring these ingredients into the class to show children. Invite children to relate any experiences they have had with bread making.

- Pair students with English-speaking partners for the word-building activity on page 258.

VISUAL LEARNERS

Write the blends *st, nt, tr,* and *mp* on the board. Have children work with a partner to list words that have each blend.

KINESTHETIC LEARNERS

Have small groups of children act out the story "Fred's Bread." Suggest that they add a second scene in which Fred goes shopping for fresh fruit and buys too many strawberries.

Building Words

Add the word part to each of the blends in the boxes. Say the word. If it is a real word, write it on the line.

| tr | sm | br | cl | sl |

ick

1. trick
2. brick
3. click
4. slick

| pl | gr | gl | cl | st |

ay

5. play
6. gray
7. clay
8. stay

▶ Write a sentence using two of the words you made.

 Ask your child to make up a sentence using two more of the words he or she wrote.

258 Review consonant blends: Phonograms

CURRICULUM CONNECTIONS

SPELLING
Dictate the following words and read the sentences. Have children write the words for a spelling posttest.
1. **sink** Put the dises in the **sink**.
2. **lamp** Read by the **lamp**.
3. **mask** I am wearing my cat **mask**.
4. **trunk** The elephant has a **trunk**.
5. **list** Make a **list** of ingredients.
6. **desk** The paper is on your **desk**.

HEALTH
Materials: a traditional flat bread (matzoh, pita, tortillas) and a piece of yeast bread

Explain that *yeast breads* rise because yeast is added to the dough, and *flat breads* are not made with yeast and do not rise. Show children the two kinds of bread and ask them to describe how they think each kind of bread was made.

WRITING
Materials: chart paper

Have children write step-by-step directions for making their favorite sandwiches.

TECHNOLOGY **AstroWord** Consonant Blends & Digraphs

Integrating Phonics and Reading

Guided Reading
Show the cover as you read the title. Invite children who have played with tops to tell about how they work.
First Reading Have children use the illustrations to track the movement of the top.
Second Reading Ask children to identify words with initial blends *sl, sn,* and *st* and final blend *st* in the story.

Comprehension
After reading, ask children these questions:
• How did the boy feel about his top? How do you know? *Inference/Character*
• What did the top do one day? *Recall/Summarize*

ESL/ELL English Language Learners
Explain that the word *past* can mean both "a time gone by" and "in a direction that goes in front of and beyond." Help children make a list of the things the top slid past. Encourage them to list some things that are not named in the text, such as the table, door, and dog.

AUDITORY LEARNERS

Read these animal riddles aloud and have children respond orally. Write the answers on the board, then have children identify the beginning or ending blend in each answer. The word <u>trunk</u> has both a beginning and ending blend.

• Does a <u>snake</u> or a <u>snail</u> have a shell?
• Does a parrot <u>squeak</u> or <u>squawk</u>?
• Do we get <u>milk</u> or <u>silk</u> from cows?
• Does an elephant have a <u>trunk</u> or a <u>tank</u>?

CHALLENGE
Write the words *blend* and *stamp* on the board and point out that these words have both a beginning and an ending blend. Ask children to make a list of other words that have blends both at the beginning and at the end. Challenge them to write a sentence using at least three words from their list.

EXTRA SUPPORT/INTERVENTION
Work with children to read aloud the story of Fred's bread, one sentence at a time. Then, have children reread the story with a partner. See *Daily Phonics Practice*, pages 320–322.

Lesson 124
Pages 259–260

y as a Vowel

Skill Focus

Children will

★ discriminate between the consonant and vowel sounds of y.

★ identify picture names and words that contain the vowel sounds of y.

ESL/ELL Native speakers of Spanish will have little trouble with the sounds of y, since y functions as a consonant and vowel in Spanish as well. However, they may confuse the sound of j in English with the sound of y in Spanish.

Teach

Phonological Awareness: Rhyme Tell children that you will say pairs of words. Ask them to clap if the words rhyme. Use: *fry, shy; cry, yard; sky, my; handy, candy; shady, shiny; lady, shady.*

Sound to Symbol Write on the board: *Henny Penny will try to fly.* Read the sentence, emphasizing and underlining each y. Explain that the letter y sometimes has a vowel sound and sometimes has a consonant sound. Then, use the words *Henny, Penny, try,* and *fly* to point out the following:

- The letter y has a long i sound when it is found at the end of a one-syllable word and when it is the only vowel in the word.

- The letter y usually has a long e sound if it comes at the end of a word with more than one syllable.

Practice and Apply

Phonemic Awareness Read aloud the rhyme on page 259. Help children listen for and name words in which y has the sound of long i or long e. (long i: *try, my, shy, cry*; long e: *berry, flaky*) Write the words on the board.

Sound to Symbol Help children identify the pictures on pages 259 and 260. Before they begin page 259, remind them that y can have either a consonant or a vowel sound.

Reading Use *Kermy and Pepper*, MCP Phonics and Reading Library, Super Skills Collection, Level A, to provide practice in reading words with y as a vowel.

Sound to Symbol

Name _____

Won't you try my berry pie?
The crust is flaky, my, oh my.
Come on, have some.
Don't be shy.
If you won't try it, I may cry!

Say the name of the picture. **Circle** the words in the boxes with the same sound of y as the picture name. Then, **circle** the pictures whose names have the vowel sound of y.

1. (fly)	(by)	lazy	yellow	(dry)	yet
	(my)	(sky)	yoke	(cry)	yarn
2. (yo-yo)	(yes)	fry	(you)	(yard)	funny
	(yellow)	puppy	sly	(yell)	windy
3. (20)	fly	(candy)	yams	(lady)	(penny)
	pry	(fairy)	(baby)	try	(pony)

Y as a vowel: Sound to symbol **259**

FOCUS ON ALL LEARNERS

ESL/ELL ENGLISH LANGUAGE LEARNERS

Materials: Phonics Picture Cards: daisy (7), yo-yo (47), fly (137)

- Before beginning page 259, help children review the three sounds that the letter y stands for. Display the picture cards one at a time. Have children name them. Then, print the words on the board. Identify the sound that the letter y stands for in each word.

- Have children identify the picture clues on page 260 before they complete the page. Remind them to listen for and identify the beginning sounds as well as the sound of y to determine the correct spelling of each picture's name.

AUDITORY/VISUAL LEARNERS

Materials: Phonics Picture Cards: daisy (7), fly (137)

Display the pictures on the chalkboard ledge and write the picture name above each picture. Ask volunteers to name other words that end in y, like *daisy* or *fly*. Then, write the word above the appropriate picture. Have children read the lists with you.

Sound to Symbol

Say the name of each picture. Circle its name.

1. (puppy)   buggy
2. fry   (fly)
3. lady   (baby)
4. (penny)   funny
5. (pony)   penny
6. (cry)   try
7. spy   (sky)
8. fifty   (twenty)
9. sly   (fry)

260 Y as a vowel: Sound to symbol

 Point to each picture and help your child think of a word or name that rhymes, such as *puppy-guppy*.

CURRICULUM CONNECTIONS

SPELLING
Dictate the following words and read the sentences. Have children write the words for a spelling pretest.
1. **baby**   The **baby** was just born.
2. **cry**   I hear the baby **cry.**
3. **fly**   I **fly** my kite.
4. **lady**   The **lady** is singing.
5. **penny**   I found a **penny** and a dime.
6. **sky**   There is a star in the **sky.**

WRITING
Ask children to work with a partner to write about a puppy that tries to catch a fly. Have them illustrate their story.

MATH
Ask children to name as many kinds of berries as they can. Record the names of the berries on the board. Then, make a graph listing these berries as column headings. Have each child select a favorite berry. Then, record the results on the graph and help children interpret the graph.

TECHNOLOGY **AstroWord** Consonant Blends & Digraphs

Integrating Phonics and Reading

Shared/Guided Reading
Show the cover as you read the title. Ask children to tell who Kermy and Pepper are, based on the illustration.
First Reading Read the book aloud, one chapter at a time, as children follow along. As you finish each chapter, invite children to retell what happened.
Second Reading Have children review Chapter 2 to find words in which *y* has the sound of long *i* or long *e*. (*carefully, shiny, Tabby; fly*) Repeat for other chapters.

Comprehension
After reading, ask children these questions:
- What does Kermy say when he finally talks? *Recall/Plot*
- How does this show that Kermy is a smart bird? *Inference/Plot*

ESL/ELL English Language Learners
Pair students with English-speaking partners to select a chapter to read and discuss.

AUDITORY LEARNERS   GROUPS
Write the sentences below on the board and read them as a group. Have volunteers circle each word that ends with the sound of long *i* and underline the words that end with the sound of long *e*.
- The fly will try to land on the jelly.
- It is a dry, windy day.
- Pry the lid off the empty jar.
- Billy is acting silly.

CHALLENGE
Challenge children to look through books to find words that end with *y* as a long *e* sound and as a long *i*. Have them make two lists of words. Then, ask them to use their words to write three sentences.

EXTRA SUPPORT/INTERVENTION
Work with children to read each word on page 259 before you have them circle the words in which *y* has the same sound as that of the first picture word. Ask them to notice where the letter *y* appears in each word. **See Daily Phonics Practice, page 322.**

Lesson 125 Pages 261–262
y as a Vowel

Skill Focus
Children will
- write words that contain *y* as a vowel to complete sentences.
- recognize and read high-frequency words.
- identify and spell picture names that contain *y* as a vowel.

Teach
Phonemic Awareness: Phoneme Categorization Tell children that you will say groups of three words. Ask them to identify the two words that have the same vowel sound of *y* and the word that has a different sound.

- bunny   try   baby
- my   why   story
- penny   pony   by
- dry   happy   cry

Sound to Symbol
Materials: Phonics Picture Cards: daisy (7), yo-yo (42), fly (137), cherry (169)

Write the words *yes, try,* and *twenty* on the board as column heads. Ask children what sound *y* stands for in each word. Then, hold up each picture card. Ask volunteers to identify the picture name and say if the word has *y* as a consonant, as a long *e* sound, or as a long *i* sound. Have children come up to the board and write each word where it belongs.

Practice and Apply
Writing For page 261, suggest that children try each word choice before writing a word. As they complete the activity, they will have the opportunity to read the high-frequency word *only*.

Blend Word Parts As children complete page 262, encourage them to say each picture name, blending together the different sounds that make up each word.

Critical Thinking For Talk About It, suggest that children think about what a baby can eat, the sounds a baby can make, and what a baby does for fun.

Reading Use *Mystery at Fairly Field,* MCP Phonics and Reading Library, Super Skills Collection, Level A, to provide practice in reading words with *y* as a vowel.

Words in Context

Name _____

Say the name of each picture. Circle the word that will finish the sentence. Print it on the line.

1. Wendy can not ride a _____ pony _____ .
   bony / (pony) / penny

2. She is too small to feed a _____ puppy _____ .
   puffy / poppy / (puppy)

3. She can not draw the _____ sky _____ .
   (sky) / sly / spy

4. Mom will not let her eat _____ candy _____ .
   sandy / (candy) / funny

5. I feel sad if she starts to _____ cry _____ .
   my / (cry) / try

6. Wendy is only a _____ baby _____ .
   bunny / (baby) / buggy

Talk About It What can a baby do?

Y as a vowel: High-frequency words, critical thinking 261

FOCUS ON ALL LEARNERS

ESL/ELL ENGLISH LANGUAGE LEARNERS
Materials: Phonics Picture Cards: daisy (7), fly (137); pennies

- Before beginning page 261, talk with children about babies they may know. Encourage them to talk about things a baby can and cannot do. Then, write the words *baby* and *cry* on the board, using colored chalk to write the *y*. Discuss the different sound of *y* in each word.

- To prepare for the activity on page 262, review the sounds of *y*. Hold up each picture card and have children use the pennies to cover all the words on the page that contain the same sound of *y*.

KINESTHETIC LEARNERS GROUPS
Materials: letter card *Yy*

Write the word parts *fl, sh, cand, pupp, sk, penn, budd,* and *cr* on the board. Have children hold their letter card at the end of a word part and read their word. Ask them to identify the sound the letter *y* stands for in the word.

261

Spelling

▶ **Say** the name of each picture. **Print** the picture name on the line. In the last box, **draw** a picture of a word in which *y* is a vowel. **Write** the word.

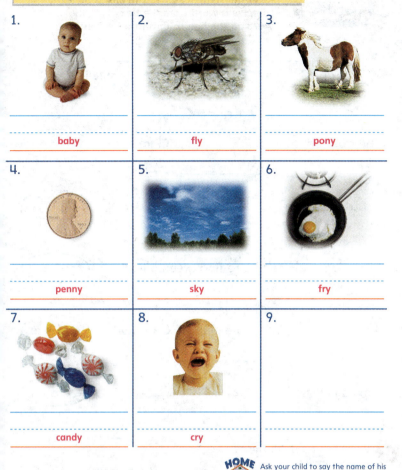

1. baby
2. fly
3. pony
4. penny
5. sky
6. fry
7. candy
8. cry
9.

 Ask your child to say the name of his or her picture and spell the word.

262 Y as a vowel: Spelling

CURRICULUM CONNECTIONS

SPELLING
Materials: spelling master (page 239l), index cards

Have children use the *y* words on page 239l to make practice spelling cards. Have them illustrate each word on the back of the card.

WRITING
Ask children to illustrate and write about things that might fly in the sky. Collect their pictures to make a book titled *What's in the Sky?*

MATH
Help children learn to count by tens. Write the number words *ten, twenty, thirty, forty, fifty, sixty, seventy, eighty, ninety,* and *one hundred.* Have children copy the words and write the corresponding numerals.

VISUAL/KINESTHETIC LEARNERS
Materials: sand trays

Write one word at a time on the board and read it. Have children trace an *i* or *e* in the sand to show what sound the *y* stands for in the word. Words to use include *pony, lucky, fly, funny, cry, sky, story, my, happy.*

CHALLENGE
Challenge children to draw a picture and write a silly sentence about a pony that wants to fly.

EXTRA SUPPORT/INTERVENTION
Work with the children to read all the answer choices on page 261. Help them identify the beginning and ending sounds of each picture on page 262 before they try to spell each word. **See Daily Phonics Practice, page 322.**

Integrating Phonics and Reading

Shared/Guided Reading
Show the cover as you read the title and ask children what sport the characters in the story play.

First Reading Read the book aloud, one chapter at a time, as children follow along. As you finish each chapter, invite children to retell what happened.

Second Reading Review Chapter 3 with children. Help them identify two names in which *y* has the sound of long *e* and one word in which *y* has the sound of long *i*.

Comprehension
After reading, ask children these questions:
• What mysterious thing happens at Fairly Field? *Recall/Summarize*
• How does Lisa solve the mystery? *Recall/Summarize*

ESL/ELL English Language Learners
Pair students with English-speaking partners. Have the partners read and discuss a chapter.

Lesson 126
Pages 263–264

Phonics and Spelling / Phonics and Writing

Consonant Blends and y as a Vowel

Skill Focus

Children will

★ spell and write words that contain initial and final consonant blends.

★ write a shopping list using words that contain initial and final consonant blends.

Teach

Phonics and Spelling Write this scrambled word on the board: *atesk*. Then give this clue: *This is what you might do at an ice rink.* Ask children to unscramble the word and write it on the board. Also have them identify the consonant blend at the beginning of *skate*.

Repeat the procedure using the scrambled word *ryd* and the clue *opposite of wet*. Have children identify the vowel sound of *y* in *dry*.

Practice and Apply

Phonics and Spelling Read the directions for page 263 with children. Make sure they understand that they are to unscramble the letters in each oval and that the unscrambled word will make sense in the sentence next to the letters.

Phonics and Writing
Materials: chart paper, marker

Write *Shopping List* at the top of a chart and read the title with children. Discuss how lists help people remember things. Explain that children can use the lines on page 264 to write a list of things they might like their family to buy at the grocery store. Together, read the directions at the top of the page and the words in the box. Then, have children complete the writing activity on their own.

Reading Use *A Fun Place to Eat*, MCP Phonics and Reading Library, Super Skills Collection, Level A, to review initial and final blends and *y* as a vowel.

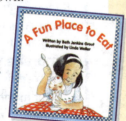

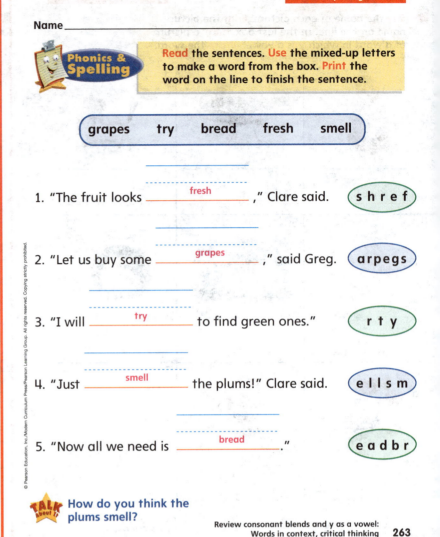

FOCUS ON ALL LEARNERS

ESL/ELL ENGLISH LANGUAGE LEARNERS

- Before beginning page 263, review consonant blend sounds. Print *freeze, gray, small, broom, fist* on index cards and ask volunteers to read the words aloud. Explain the meanings of words as needed. Then, cut the words apart and scramble the letters. Prompt responses with incomplete sentences for each word, such as *I see a cat that is ____.* Have children work in pairs to complete the activity on page 263.

- You might wish to work with children to complete the writing activity on page 264. Review the words in the box. Encourage children to add words to name items such as *green grapes* or *sweet peas*. Write the names of the items on the board while children write them on their shopping lists.

KINESTHETIC LEARNERS

Materials: drawing paper, crayons with labels

Ask children to look at crayon labels to find color names that contain consonant blends, such as *gray, green,* or *blue*. Ask them to draw a picture using the colors whose names have such blends and to write the color names on the page.

263

Phonics & Writing

Writing

Write a shopping list for your family's next trip to the store. List things to buy. Look at the words in the box for help.

| bread | drink | sweet | fruit |
| plums | grapes | milk | berry |

SHOPPING LIST

 Talk with your child about what items could be added to the list.

264 Review blends and y as a vowel: Writing

CURRICULUM CONNECTIONS

SPELLING

Cumulative Posttest Review Unit 4 spelling words by using the following words and dictation sentences.

1. **crown** The queen wears a **crown.**
2. **glass** I poured a **glass** of milk.
3. **skate** I like to ice **skate.**
4. **spoon** I eat soup with a **spoon.**
5. **star** The **star** shines brightly.
6. **desk** I write at my **desk.**
7. **trunk** We put the clothes in the **trunk.**
8. **baby** The **baby** is smiling.
9. **fly** The bird can **fly.**
10. **penny** I found a **penny.**

WRITING

Have children write a list of the foods they like to eat for breakfast. Encourage children to circle beginning blends and underline final blends in the words on their lists.

PORTFOLIO

TECHNOLOGY **AstroWord** Consonant Blends & Digraphs

AUDITORY LEARNERS

Materials: Phonics Picture Cards: bread (121), bridge (122), crib (124), crown (125), dress (126), drum (127), train (130), tree (131)

Place the cards for bread, crib, dress, and train along the chalkboard ledge. Put the other pictures in a pile face down. Have children select a picture from the pile and name it. Then, have the child place the card by the picture whose name begins with the same blend on the chalkboard ledge.

CHALLENGE

Materials: newspaper grocery ads

Challenge children to look through grocery store ads for products and brand names that have consonant blends. Have them compile a list of these words and then group the words by initial or final blend.

EXTRA SUPPORT/INTERVENTION

Materials: letter cards

Have children use their letter cards to spell one of the boxed words on page 263. Then, have them scramble the letters and give them to a partner to unscramble and spell the word. See Daily Phonics Practice, pages 320–322.

Integrating Phonics and Reading

Shared/Guided Reading
Show the cover and read the title. Invite children to offer their own ideas about what a fun place to eat would be like.
First Reading As you read, have children join in to finish sentences beginning with *I want to* and *I got to.*
Second Reading Ask children to identify words with initial blends *cl, fl, pl, sp,* and *st* in the story. Ask which of these words has the final blend *mp.* Also point out the blend *nd* in *hands.*

Comprehension
After reading, ask children these questions:
- What can the girl do in the fun place to eat? *Recall/Details*
- What does this place turn out to be? How do you know? *Inference/Setting*

ESL/ELL **English Language Learners**
Review the actions named in the story, including *spin in my chair, clap my hands,* and *stamp my feet.* Invite children to act out each one.

264

Lesson 127   Pages 265–266

Take-Home Book

Review Consonant Blends and y as a Vowel

Skill Focus

Children will
★ read words with initial and final consonant blends and *y* as a vowel in the context of a story.
★ review selected high-frequency words in the context of a story.
★ reread for fluency.

◆ Teach

Build Background Recall with children that the theme of this unit is "Everybody Eats." Ask children to name some of the foods they learned about. Write any words with consonant blends and *y* as a vowel on the board. Next, print the word *pizza* on the board and read it aloud. Ask children to share what they know about pizza. Help them describe pizza as a food that is made with bread dough, tomato sauce, cheese, and different kinds of toppings.

Phonological Awareness: Substitution
Present these oral riddles for children to answer.

- What word rhymes with *Fred* and begins with the blend *br*? (bread)
- What word rhymes with *tapes* and begins with the blend *gr*? (grapes)
- What word rhymes with *pass* and begins with the blend *gl*? (glass)

◆ Practice and Apply

Read the Book Help children tear out and fold the pages to make their Take-Home Books. Then, read the book together. Encourage children to tell what they learned about making pizza.

Sound to Symbol Read aloud or have volunteers read the book. Have children identify the beginning and ending consonant blends in the words *try, crust, press, flat, spread, crisp, plate,* and *great.* Also have them identify the vowel sound of *y* in *try.* Invite volunteers to write the words on the board.

Review High-Frequency Words Write the words *you* and *the* on the board. Have children spell each word and then say it, blending the sounds.

Reread for Fluency Have children reread the book to increase their fluency and comprehension. Children can take their books home to read and share with family members.

Review consonant blends and y as a vowel: Take-home book   265

FOCUS ON ALL LEARNERS

ESL/ELL ENGLISH LANGUAGE LEARNERS
Materials: index cards

After assisting children with making the Take-Home Book, use the following activities to teach English language learners.

- Read the text together.
- Have children look at the photos and talk about the ingredients and/or steps that they show.
- Prepare a set of cards with the blends *tr, st, cr, pr, fl, spr, pl,* and *gr.* Have each child pick a card and scan the story for a word that begins or ends with that blend.

KINESTHETIC LEARNERS
Materials: construction paper, scissors, paste

Draw and cut out a large circle to represent a pizza. Invite children to draw and cut out "toppings" for the pizza. Have them write a word with a blend or with *y* as a vowel on each topping and paste it on the pizza shape.

2. Press the crust in a pan. Make it round and flat.

3. Spread the sauce and cheese all over.

266 Review consonant blends and y as a vowel: Take-home book

CURRICULUM CONNECTIONS

SOCIAL STUDIES
Materials: world map

Explain that the first pizza came from Italy and show children where Italy is on the map. Brainstorm with children a list of other favorite foods that come from other countries. Help them find the countries on the map. Examples include tacos from Mexico, egg rolls from China, spaghetti from Italy, sweet potatoes from Africa.

MATH
Materials: carry-out pizza menu

Make available pizza menus or make up one of your own. Have groups of children work together to select a pizza they might like to order, including at least two extra toppings. Then, have them write out their order and add up the cost of their pizza.

LANGUAGE ARTS
Materials: crayons, construction paper

Invite children to make their own how-to cookbook using recipes for things they know how to make, such as fruit salad, peanut butter and jelly sandwiches, a vegetable salad, and so on.

 **AstroWord** Consonant Blends & Digraphs

VISUAL/AUDITORY LEARNERS
Materials: Take-Home Books

Have children take turns reading the Take-Home Book with a partner. Partners can then ask each other questions about the book.

CHALLENGE
Children can use the Take-Home Book as a model for writing directions for making their own favorite pizza. Have them include their favorite toppings.

EXTRA SUPPORT/INTERVENTION
Materials: Take-Home Book

Read the story aloud to children as they follow along in their books. Then, invite them to reread the story with you. See Daily Phonics Practice, pages 320–322.

Lesson 128 — Pages 267–268

Unit Checkup

Consonant Blends and y as a Vowel

Skill Focus

Children will

★ identify picture names that contain consonant blends.

★ write words that contain consonant blends and *y* as a vowel to complete sentences.

Teach

Phonological Awareness: Blending Onsets and Rimes Say the following word parts. Have children orally blend the parts to say the word, then identify the initial blend.

- /st/ep   /cr/y
- /bl/end   /fl/ake
- /sk/y   /br/ush
- /gl/ow   /tr/y

After children have blended the words, repeat them. Have children clap when they hear a word in which *y* has the sound of long *i*.

Sound to Symbol Draw these pictures on the board: a star, a fly, a train, a snake. Call on volunteers to label each picture with its name. Ask children to identify the blends heard in each word.

Point to the word *fly*. Ask children what vowel sound the *y* stands for. Then, have them name some other words with *y* as a vowel. List the words on the board. Be sure to include words such as *daisy* and *penny*, in which *y* has the sound of long *e*.

Practice and Apply

Assess Skills Help children identify the pictures on page 267. You may wish to demonstrate how to fill in the bubble to mark the correct answer. For page 268, remind children to try each word choice before circling and writing their answer.

UNIT 4 CHECKUP

Name _____

▶ **Say** the name of each picture. **Fill in** the bubble beside the picture name.

1. ○ trip ○ prize ● train ○ drain
2. ○ snail ● snake ○ skate ○ string
3. ○ clock ○ braid ○ blouse ● block
4. ○ crab ○ grab ○ club ● crib
5. ● flag ○ glass ○ flat ○ blank
6. ○ green ● dress ○ drum ○ desk
7. ○ deck ○ drive ● desk ○ jump
8. ○ clap ● plant ○ plug ○ plate
9. ● stamp ○ steps ○ stop ○ spill
10. ○ glue ● globe ○ drive ○ glove
11. ● frame ○ lamp ○ fly ○ frog
12. ○ glass ○ spot ● spoon ○ smoke

Consonant blends: Assessment   267

FOCUS ON ALL LEARNERS

ESL/ELL ENGLISH LANGUAGE LEARNERS

- Before beginning page 267, review the names of the picture clues aloud as a group. You may wish to pair less proficient English language learners with more proficient children on items 1 to 6. Review together; then ask them to complete items 7 to 12 individually. Check answers orally as a class.

- Reviewing the word choices on page 268 will greatly facilitate English language learners' completion of the worksheet. After children complete items 1 to 6 independently or in pairs, have them underline any consonant blends in the distractors. As you review answers, ask children to read aloud the answers they chose and the distractors.

VISUAL LEARNERS GROUPS

Materials: Phonics Picture Cards: bread (121), flag (136), fly (137), sled (140), stamp (149)

Place the picture cards face down. Have children take turns drawing a card and giving clues to the group until someone guesses what the picture is. Have a volunteer write the word on the board and have the group read the word.

 CHECKUP

▶ Circle the word that will finish each sentence. Print it on the line.

1. __Start__ the day with a good meal.
   Stop
   (Start)
   Star

2. Corn __flakes__ and milk are great.
   flags
   frames
   (flakes)

3. __Try__ adding some fruit.
   Fry
   (Try)
   Why

4. __Drink__ a glass of juice.
   (Drink)
   Trunk
   Dress

5. Some __toast__ is good, too.
   float
   test
   (toast)

6. Stay away from __sweet__ things.
   (sweet)
   smoke
   square

268   Consonant blends and y as a vowel: Assessment

ASSESS UNDERSTANDING OF UNIT SKILLS

STUDENT PROGRESS ASSESSMENT
You may wish to review the observational notes you made as children worked through the activities in the unit. Your notes will help you evaluate the progress children made with blends and *y* as a vowel.

PORTFOLIO ASSESSMENT
Review the materials children have collected in their portfolios. You may wish to have interviews with children to discuss their written work and progress they have made since the beginning of the unit. As you review children's work, evaluate how well they apply phonics skills.

DAILY PHONICS PRACTICE
For children who need additional practice with blends and *y* as a vowel, quick reviews are provided on pages 320–322 in Daily Phonics Practice.

PHONICS POSTTEST
To assess children's mastery of blends and *y* as a vowel, use the Posttest on pages 239g–239h.

KINESTHETIC LEARNERS

Materials: letter cards *Ll, Pp, Rr, Ss, Tt*

Say a word. Have children use letter cards to spell the blend they hear at the beginning or end of the word. Words to say are *stop, plan, truck, spin, melt, slip, prize, last, help.*

CHALLENGE
Ask children to think of a favorite animal and what that animal likes to eat. Have them name their animal, then write a recipe for an imaginary dish their animal might eat, such as Freddy Frog's Fabulous Flyburgers. Suggest that they try to use words with blends. Have them illustrate their work.

EXTRA SUPPORT/INTERVENTION
Write these words on the board and have children read them: *top, rip, lap, rib, pin, plan, hum, care.* Have children add *s* before *top, t* before *rip, c* before *lap, c* before *rib, s* before *pin, t* after *plan, p* after *hum,* and *s* before *care.* Have children read each new word. See Daily Phonics Practice, pages 320–322.

268

Teacher Notes

Endings, Digraphs, and Contractions
THEME: WHATEVER THE WEATHER

CONTENTS

UNIT 5 RESOURCES 269b
Assessment Options 269c
Administering & Evaluating the Pretest/Posttest 269d
    Unit 5 Pretest 269e–269f
    Unit 5 Posttest.................................. 269g–269h
    Unit 5 Student Progress Checklist 269i
English Language Learners 269j
Spelling Connections 269k–269l
Phonics Games, Activities, and Technology 269m–269o
BLM Unit 5 Activity 269p
Home Connections 269q

TEACHING PLANS

	Unit 5 Opener/ Home Letter......................	269–270
Lessons 129–130:	Inflectional endings *-ed* and *-ing*	271–274
Lesson 131:	Consonant digraph *th*	275–276
Lesson 132:	Consonant digraph *wh*	277–278
Lesson 133:	Consonant digraph *sh*	279–280
Lesson 134:	Consonant digraph *ch*	281–282
Lesson 135:	Consonant digraph *kn*	283–284
Lessons 136–137:	Review consonant digraphs...........	285–288
Lesson 138:	Review endings, digraphs:	
	Phonics & Reading	289
	Phonics & Writing: Building Words.....	290
Lesson 139:	Take-Home Book: "Clouds"...........	291–292
Lesson 140:	Contractions with *will*	293
	Contractions with *is*.................	294
Lesson 141:	Contractions with *am* and *are*	295
	Contractions with *not*	296
Lesson 142:	Review Contractions	297–298
Lesson 143:	Review endings, consonant digraphs, contractions:	
	Phonics & Spelling	299
	Phonics & Writing: A Personal Description	300
Lesson 144:	Take-Home Book: "It's Raining".....	301–302
Lesson 145:	Unit Checkup: Endings, digraphs, contractions	303–304

Student Performance Objectives

In Unit 5, children will be introduced to words with inflectional endings, consonant digraphs, and contractions in conjunction with the theme "Whatever the Weather." As children begin to understand and learn to apply the concept that inflectional endings are added to a base word, that a consonant digraph represents a single sound, and that two words can be shortened to form a contraction, they will be able to

▶ Add the endings *-ed* and *-ing* to familiar base words

▶ Identify the sounds of consonant digraphs *th*, *wh*, *sh*, *ch*, and *kn* in words

▶ Identify contractions formed with *will*, *is*, *am*, *are*, and *not*

▶ Distinguish among contractions formed with *will*, *is*, *am*, *are*, and *not*

Overview of Resources

LESSON	MCP PHONICS AND READING LIBRARY, LEVEL A PROGRAM	TITLE	PICTURE CARDS	LETTER CARDS	DAILY PHONICS PRACTICE
129: Inflectional endings -ed and -ing	VFC, Set 1	Very Unusual Pets			323
130: Inflectional endings -ed and -ing	VFC, Set 3	Mystery at Fairly Field			323
131: Consonant digraph th	RR, Stg Two Bk 34	Five Little Dinosaurs	36–37, 82–83, 101, 154–156		323
132: Consonant digraph wh	RR, Stg Two Bk 36	Humpback Whales	40–41, 84, 90, 120, 154–160, 164		324
133: Consonant digraph sh	RR, Stg Two Bk 33	Silvia's Soccer Game	33–35, 67, 105, 164–166		324
134: Consonant digraph ch	RR, Stg Two Bk 35	Cat Chat	4, 6, 168–169		324
135: Consonant digraph kn	RR, Stg 0/1 Bk 19	Rabbit Knits			325
136: Review consonant digraphs	RR, Stg Two Bk 40	Rush, Rush, Rush	154, 157, 164, 167		323–325
137: Review consonant digraphs	RR, Stg Two Bk 41	Stan Packs		Aa, Cc, Ee, Hh, Ii, Ll, Kk, Nn, Oo, Pp, Ss, Tt, Ww	323–325
138: Review endings, digraphs	RR, Stg Two Bk 38	Something to Munch			323–325
139: Take-Home Book: "Clouds"			154–155, 157–158, 164–165, 168–169		323–325
140: Contractions with will and is	RR, Stg Three Bk 1	That Cat		Ee, Hh, Ii, Ll, Oo, Ss, Tt, Uu, Ww, Yy	325
141: Contractions with am, are, and not	RR, Stg Two Bk 35	Cat Chat		Complete Set	325
142: Review contractions	RR, Stg Three Bk 8	When I Go See Gram			325
143: Review endings, consonant digraphs, contractions	RR, Stg Two Bk 39	Dragon's Lunch			323–325
144: Take-Home Book: "It's Raining"					323–325
145: Unit Checkup: Endings, digraphs, contractions			153, 156, 158–161, 163, 164, 167–168		323–325

VFC–Very First Chapters   RR–Ready Readers   Stg–Stage   Bk–Book

Assessment Options

In Unit 5, assess children's ability to identify and write words with inflectional endings, consonant digraphs, and contractions. Use the Unit Pretest and Posttest for formal assessment. For ongoing informal assessment, you may wish to use children's work on the Review pages, Take-Home Books, and Unit Checkups. You may also want to encourage children to evaluate their own work and to participate in setting goals for their own learning.

ESL/ELL Note pronunciation difficulties, but assess children's work based on their abilities to distinguish endings, digraphs, and contractions when pronounced by a native speaker. For additional support for English language learners, see page 269j.

FORMAL ASSESSMENT

Use the Unit 5 Pretest, on pages 269e–269f, to help assess a child's knowledge at the beginning of the unit and to plan instruction.

ESL/ELL Before administering the Pretest, preview picture clues on page 269e so that children are familiar with the picture names.

Use the Unit 5 Posttest, on pages 269g–269h, to help assess mastery of unit objectives and to plan for any reteaching.

ESL/ELL Some English language learners may understand a concept but have difficulty with directions. Read the directions aloud and model how to complete the worksheets.

INFORMAL ASSESSMENT

Use the Review pages, Unit Checkup, and Take-Home Books in the student book to provide an effective means of evaluating children's performance.

Unit 5 Skills	Review pages	Checkups	Take-Home Books
Inflectional endings -ed, -ing	289–290, 299–300	303–304	291–292 301–302
Consonant digraph th	285–290, 299–300	303–304	291–292 301–302
Consonant digraph wh	285–290, 299–300	303–304	291–292 301–302
Consonant digraph sh	285–290, 299–300	303–304	291–292 301–302
Consonant digraph ch	285–290, 299–300	303–304	291–292 301–302
Consonant digraph kn	285–290, 299–300	303–304	291–292 301–302
Contractions with will, is	297–300	303–304	301–302
Contractions with am, are, not	297–300	303–304	301–302

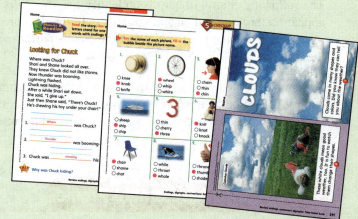

STUDENT PROGRESS CHECKLIST

Use the checklist on page 269i to record children's progress. You may want to cut the sections apart to place each child's checklist in his or her portfolio.

PORTFOLIO ASSESSMENT

 This logo signals opportunities for collecting student work for portfolios. You may also want to include the Pretest and Posttest, the Review pages, the Unit Checkup, Phonics & Reading, and Phonics & Writing pages.

PHONEMIC AWARENESS AND PHONICS ASSESSMENT

Use PAPA to obtain an itemized analysis of children's decoding skills.

PAPA Skills	MCP Phonics Lessons in Unit 5
Blending sounds	Lesson 137
Deleting sounds	Lessons 131, 132, 133, 134, 137
Consonant digraphs	Lessons 131–137

269c

Pretest and Posttest

DIRECTIONS

To help you assess children's progress in learning Unit 5 skills, tests are available on pages 269e–269h.

Administer the Pretest before children begin the unit. The results of the Pretest will help you identify each child's strengths and needs in advance, allowing you to structure lesson plans to meet individual needs. Administer the Posttest to assess children's overall mastery of skills taught in the unit and to identify specific areas that will require reteaching.

ESL/ELL Note that the objective of the Unit 5 Pretest and Posttest is to correctly use words with inflectional endings, consonant digraphs, and contractions. English language learners may find that some structures in English are not customary in their native languages, especially Asian languages. Have children practice both saying the picture clues aloud as you stress the target sound aloud and matching contractions to the complete words that make up the contractions.

PERFORMANCE ASSESSMENT PROFILE

The following chart will help you identify specific skills as they appear on the tests and enable you to identify and record specific information about an individual's or the class's performance on the tests.

Depending on the results of the tests, refer to the Reteaching column for lesson-plan pages where you can find activities that will be useful for meeting individual needs or for daily phonics practice.

Answer Keys

Unit 5 Pretest, page 269e (BLM 28)
1. sheep
2. chain
3. whale
4. three
5. knot
6. chicks
7. wheel
8. thorn
9. shell
10. knob
11. ship
12. cheese

Unit 5 Pretest, page 269f (BLM 29)
13. We're
14. wanted
15. fixing
16. he'll
17. he's
18. spilled
19. wasn't
20. I'm

Unit 5 Posttest, page 269g (BLM 30)
1. wh
2. th
3. ch
4. sh
5. ch
6. kn
7. th
8. sh
9. wh
10. ch
11. th
12. kn

Unit 5 Posttest, page 269h (BLM 31)
13. I'm
14. going
15. doesn't
16. looked
17. You'll
18. worked
19. Won't
20. She's

Performance Assessment Profile

Skill	Pretest Questions	Posttest Questions	Reteaching	
			Focus on All Learners	Daily Phonics Practice
Consonant digraph *th*	4, 8	2, 7, 11	275–276, 285–292 299–302	323, 324
Consonant digraph *wh*	3, 7	1, 9	277–278, 285–292, 299–302	324
Consonant digraph *sh*	1, 9, 11	4, 8	279–280, 285–292 299–302	324
Consonant digraph *ch*	2, 6, 12	3, 5, 10	281–282, 285–292 299–302	324
Consonant digraph *kn*	5, 10	6, 12	283–292, 299–302	325
Contractions with *is, will*	16, 17	17, 19, 20	293–294, 297–302	325
Contractions with *am, are, not*	13, 19, 20	13, 15, 19	295–302	325
Endings *-ed, -ing*	14, 15, 18	14, 16, 18	271–274, 299–302	323

Unit 5 Pretest

Name _____

▶ Say the name of each picture. Fill in the bubble beside the picture name.

1. 
○ sleep
○ sheep
○ ship

2. 
○ chain
○ share
○ hair

3. 
○ wade
○ thank
○ whale

4. 
○ tree
○ teeth
○ three

5. 
○ cot
○ knit
○ knot

6. 
○ chicks
○ kicks
○ tricks

7. 
○ wheel
○ heel
○ weed

8. 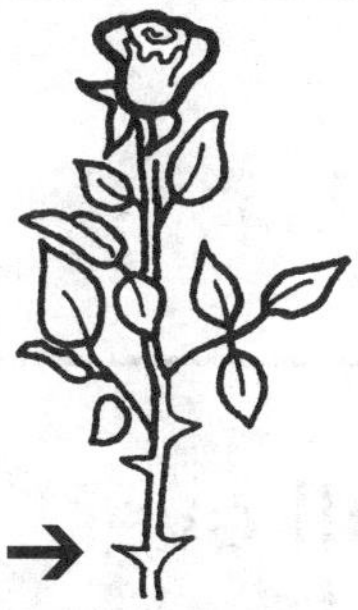
○ horn
○ torn
○ thorn

9. 
○ sell
○ shed
○ shell

10. 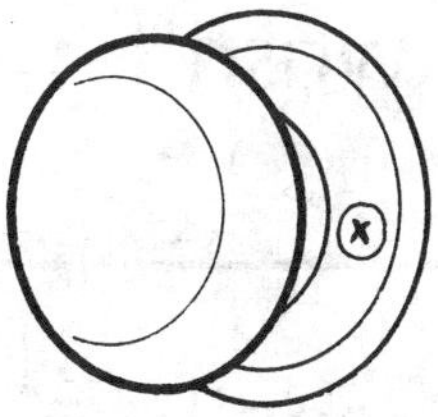
○ knot
○ knob
○ nose

11. 
○ sip
○ chip
○ ship

12. 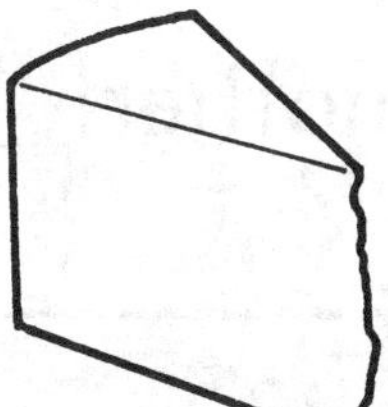
○ knees
○ cheese
○ cheek

Go to the next page. ➔

BLM 28 Unit 5 Pretest: Consonant digraphs *th, wh, sh, ch, kn*

269e

Unit 5 Pretest

Name _____

> Read each sentence. Fill in the bubble under the word that best completes the sentence.

13.	____ waiting for Matt.	We're ○	We'll ○
14.	He ____ to have lunch.	wanting ○	wanted ○
15.	He is ____ a sandwich.	fixing ○	fixed ○
16.	Next ____ fill a glass.	he's ○	he'll ○
17.	I hope ____ careful.	he's ○	he'll ○
18.	Last week he ____ milk all over.	spilling ○	spilled ○
19.	His mother ____ very happy.	won't ○	wasn't ○
20.	If he spills, ____ not going to clean up.	I'm ○	she'll ○

Possible score on Unit 5 Pretest is 20. Number correct _____

BLM 29 Unit 5 Pretest: Contractions with *is, will, am, are, not*; endings *-ed, -ing*

Unit 5 Posttest

Name _____

▶ Name the picture in each box. Fill in the bubble above the consonant digraph that will complete the picture name.

1. __eel	2. __ree	3. __ain	4. __ell
○ th ○ wh ○ kn	○ sh ○ wh ○ th	○ ch ○ sh ○ th	○ sh ○ ch ○ th
5. pea__	6. __ot	7. __orn	8. __elf
○ kn ○ sh ○ ch	○ kn ○ wh ○ th	○ wh ○ th ○ sh	○ sh ○ ch ○ wh
9. __ale	10. __air	11. __umb	12. __ob
○ th ○ sh ○ wh	○ sh ○ ch ○ th	○ th ○ ch ○ wh	○ wh ○ th ○ kn

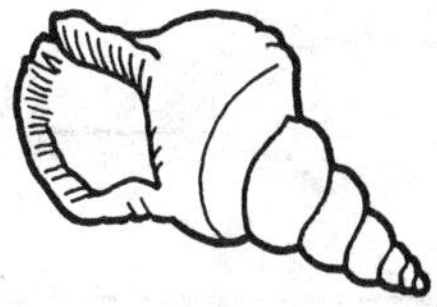

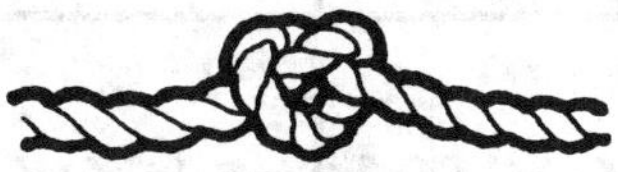

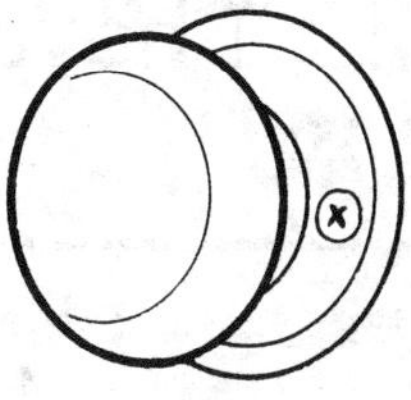

Go to the next page. ➔

BLM 30 Unit 5 Posttest: Consonant digraphs *th, wh, sh, ch, kn*

Unit 5 Posttest

Name _____

> Read each sentence. Fill in the bubble under the word that will finish each sentence.

13.	____ cleaning my room.	I'll ○	I'm ○
14.	Mom is ____ to be very happy.	going ○	goes ○
15.	She ____ like a messy room.	isn't ○	doesn't ○
16.	Last night she ____ at my room.	looking ○	looked ○
17.	"____ have to clean this up," she said.	You're ○	You'll ○
18.	I have ____ hard.	working ○	worked ○
19.	____ Mom be surprised?	Wasn't ○	Won't ○
20.	____ going to smile.	She's ○	She'll ○

Possible score on Unit 5 Posttest is 20. Number correct _____

BLM 31 Unit 5 Posttest: Contractions with *is, will, am, are, not*; endings *-ed, -ing*

Student Progress Checklist

Make as many copies as needed to use for a class list. For individual portfolio use, cut apart each child's section. As indicated by the code, color in boxes next to skills satisfactorily assessed and insert an *X* by those requiring reteaching. Marked boxes can later be colored in to indicate mastery.

Student Progress Checklist

Code: ■ Satisfactory ☒ Needs Reteaching

Student: _____

_____

Pretest Score: _____

Posttest Score: _____

Skills

- ☐ Inflectional Ending -ed
- ☐ Inflectional Ending -ing
- ☐ Consonant Digraph th
- ☐ Consonant Digraph wh
- ☐ Consonant Digraph sh
- ☐ Consonant Digraph ch
- ☐ Consonant Digraph kn
- ☐ Contractions with will
- ☐ Contractions with is
- ☐ Contractions with am
- ☐ Contractions with are
- ☐ Contractions with not

Comments / Learning Goals

Student: _____

_____

Pretest Score: _____

Posttest Score: _____

Skills

- ☐ Inflectional Ending -ed
- ☐ Inflectional Ending -ing
- ☐ Consonant Digraph th
- ☐ Consonant Digraph wh
- ☐ Consonant Digraph sh
- ☐ Consonant Digraph ch
- ☐ Consonant Digraph kn
- ☐ Contractions with will
- ☐ Contractions with is
- ☐ Contractions with am
- ☐ Contractions with are
- ☐ Contractions with not

Comments / Learning Goals

BLM 32 Unit 5 Checklist

ESL/ELL English Language Learners

Throughout Unit 5 there are opportunities to assess English language learners' ability to read and write words with inflectional endings, consonant digraphs, and contractions. These skills may be challenging to English language learners, who may confuse sounds such as initial *h* and digraph *wh* or *ch* and *sh*. Other English language learners may be unfamiliar with the wide use of contractions in English. Note which phonics concepts children are struggling with and monitor performance.

Lesson 129, pages 271–272 Native speakers of Spanish, Russian, Chinese, and many other languages may mispronounce /n/ for /ng/ and /ed/ for /d/. Practice the following pairs with children who demonstrate pronunciation difficulty: *kin, king; thin, thing; win, wing; sun, sung*.

Lesson 131, pages 275–276 Some English language learners may have difficulty distinguishing the initial unvoiced *th* of *thin* and *f* (*fin*), or voiced *th* (*then*) and *d* (*den*). Offer listening and speaking practice with specific word pairs such as *three, free* and *than, fan*. Speakers of some Asian languages won't pronounce the *th* since it doesn't exist in these languages.

Lesson 132, pages 277–278 Native speakers of Japanese, Korean, Spanish, Tagalog, and Vietnamese may confuse the digraph *wh* with the initial *h* sound. Have them practice with word pairs such as *when, hen; wheel, heel;* and *white, height*.

Lesson 133, pages 279–280 Children whose first language is Spanish or Tagalog may assimilate *sh* and *ch*. Native speakers of Cantonese, Khmer, Vietnamese, Hmong, or Korean may confuse *sh* with *s, ch,* or the /zh/ sound of *s* in *measure*. Practice with *cheap, sheep; chew, shoe; chair, share;* and *chip, ship*.

Lesson 134, pages 281–282 Children who speak Cantonese, Vietnamese, Khmer, Korean, or Hmong may confuse *ch* with *sh* or initial *j*. Offer additional practice, having them clearly pronounce *chair, share; chip, ship; chilly, jelly;* and *cheap, jeep*.

Lesson 135, pages 283–284 Children whose home language is Spanish, Cantonese, or Haitian Creole may be unfamiliar with the digraph *kn*. Stress that the *k* is silent; it is part of the written word, but it stands for no sound.

Lesson 140, pages 293–294 Many character-based languages, such as Chinese, do not form contractions with subject + verb/modal, while native speakers of Spanish will understand the concept. Look for pronunciation difficulties between long and short vowel sounds in contractions. Practice *she'll, shell; I'll, ill;* and *we'll, well*.

Lesson 141, pages 295–296 Some English language learners may be unfamiliar with the wide use of contractions in English. Spanish speakers, however, may recognize contractions *del* and *al* (*de el* and *a el*); French speakers will note *j'ai* (*je* and *ai*).

Lesson 142, pages 297–298 Native speakers of Chinese, Japanese, Korean, or Vietnamese who had difficulty pronouncing /l/ versus /r/ may need additional support and oral/aural practice with the pairs *you'll, you're; we'll, we're;* and *they'll, they're*.

Spelling Connections

INTRODUCTION

The Unit Word List is a comprehensive list of spelling words drawn from this unit. The words are grouped by inflected ending, consonant digraph, and contraction patterns. To incorporate spelling into your phonics program, use the activity in the Curriculum Connections section of each teaching plan.

ESL/ELL It is recommended that English language learners reach the intermediate fluency level of English proficiency before focusing on spelling.

The words in the Unit 5 Word List are grouped by inflectional endings, consonant digraphs, and contractions. Introduce the words and their meanings in each group separately, a few at a time, through visuals or realia. Provide ample practice over time and contextual background when introducing the words.

The spelling lessons use the following approach for each pattern.

1. Administer a pretest of five or six words that have not yet been introduced. Dictation sentences are provided.
2. Provide practice.
3. Reassess. Dictation sentences are provided.

A final review is provided at the end of the unit on page 299.

DIRECTIONS

Make a copy of Blackline Master 33 for each child. After administering the pretest for each element, give each child a copy of the appropriate word list.

Children can work with a partner to practice spelling the words orally and identifying the ending, the consonant digraph, or the two words that were shortened in each word. They can also use their letter cards to form words on the list. You may want to challenge children to make new words by substituting sounds or endings. Children can write words of their own on *My Own Word List* (See Blackline Master 33).

Have children store their list words with the letter cards in the envelope in the back of their books. You may want to suggest that students keep a spelling notebook, listing words with similar patterns. They may want to contribute to Word Walls to display in the classroom. Each section of the Word Wall can focus on words with a single element. The Word Walls will become a good resource for spelling when children are writing.

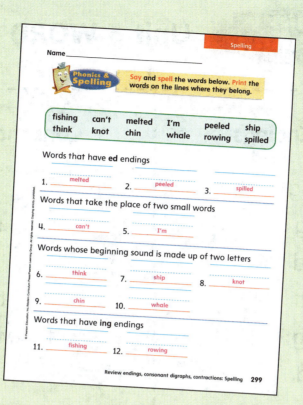

Unit Word List

Inflectional Endings
cooking
fishing
melted
peeled
rowing
spilled

Consonant Digraphs
chin
knot
ship
think
whale

Contractions
can't
he's
I'm
we'll
you're

Name _____

Unit 5 WORD LIST

Inflectional Endings

cooking
fishing
melted
peeled
rowing
spilled

Consonant Digraphs

chin
knot
ship
think
whale

Contractions

can't
he's
I'm
we'll
you're

My Own Word List

Phonics Games, Activities, and Technology

The following collection of ideas offers a variety of opportunities to reinforce phonics skills while actively engaging children. The games, activities, and technology suggestions can easily be adapted to meet the needs of your group of learners. They vary in approach so as to consider children's different learning styles.

YESTERDAY

Say a sentence with a verb in the present tense. Have children repeat the sentence, adding the word *yesterday* and changing the sentence to past tense. For example, if you say *I jump rope*, children should respond *Yesterday I jumped rope*.

SNEAKY H

Write the words that follow on the chalkboard, on a chart, or on cards. Have a child select a word and read it. Then have the child rewrite the word, adding "Sneaky H" after the first letter. Have the child read the new word. Words to use are *tin, sip, tick, sack, ten, cop, seep, tree, camp*.

CONTRACTION SLIDES

Make word slides featuring contractions. To reinforce the theme "Whatever the Weather," you might make the slides in the shape of a cloud or the sun. For contractions with *will*, write *'ll* beside the "window" and put the first word of the contraction on the slide. Make slides for contractions with *will* (*'ll*) and *not* (*n't*).

ESL/ELL This game and Contraction Action (page 269n) are practical activities for English language learners, most of whom are unfamiliar with contractions. Encourage English language learners to use these manipulatives whenever they need to check their own work.

ALLITERATIVE SENTENCES

Work with children to generate lists of words for each consonant digraph. Have them use words from a list and words of their own to write alliterative sentences. Ask them to illustrate their sentences and share them with the group.

SPECIAL WORD WALL

Provide a sheet of chart paper for each consonant digraph and write the digraph at the top. As children read on their own, or as your class works on a unit in science or social studies, list on the appropriate chart any digraph words they find.

CONTRACTION ACTION

Write words that can be combined into contractions on slips of paper to make Contraction Action cards. Have children work with a partner. One child chooses a card and reads the words. The second child says the contraction and writes it. Then the partners change roles. Continue until all the words have been read and written as contractions.

CH SANDWICHES

Provide bun shapes cut from construction paper and a supply of different-colored strips of paper. Have children paste the bottom of a bun to the bottom of a sheet of construction paper. Then, have them write different *ch* words on colored strips and paste them on the bun. Finish the sandwich by adding the top bun.

ESL/ELL This game, Digraph Necklaces, and SH Shelf can be completed successfully by having English language learners work in pairs. Have children take turns using reference materials, such as the Unit Word List, personalized dictionaries, or journals as sources for words containing the target consonant digraphs.

WORD CLUES

Have children respond to clues like the following for words that rhyme: *What sounds like keep but starts with /sh/? What sounds like hair but starts with /ch/? What sounds like sing but starts with /th/?*

DIGRAPH NECKLACES

Provide pieces of pasta (large size, such as rigatoni), yarn or string, and fine-tipped markers. Have children write words with consonant digraphs on pieces of pasta and string them to make digraph necklaces. Suggest that children have words with each digraph on their necklace. Have them read one another's necklaces.

SH SHELF

Cut a "shelf" from construction paper and attach it to a bulletin board or to chart paper. Have children write and illustrate words or phrases with the *sh* sound to put on the shelf.

FLIP MY LID

Duplicate Blackline Master 34 and distribute to children. Help children cut apart the word cards. Make a flipper by writing *-ed* and *-ing* on opposite sides of a plastic margarine tub lid or cardboard disk. Shuffle the cards and place them face down in a pile. Children play the game by choosing a card and flipping the lid. They must add the ending to the word and use the word in a sentence.

ACTION WORDS

Work with children to generate a list of action words ending in *-ing*. Have children select a secret word from the list and pantomime it. Have classmates guess and spell the word. You might have children select a word to illustrate. Have them write the word on the illustration. Collect the pages into a class book of actions.

ESL/ELL This game requires that English language learners have a strong vocabulary of action verbs. Prompt with flashcards and picture clues cut out from magazines or photos that model actions. To reinforce meanings, take turns acting out the action words they generate as the group says, "____" is "____."

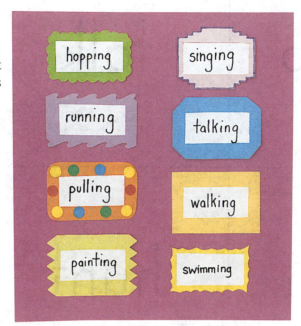

The following software products reinforce children's understanding of word structure.

Curious George® Learns Phonics
Games and activities help children learn about letter names, phonemic awareness, and phonics as children travel to the circus with Curious George.

** Simon & Schuster, Inc.
   1230 Avenue of the Americas
   New York, NY 10020
   (888) 793-9972
   www.simonsays.com

Reader Rabbit's® Learn to Read with Phonics™
This CD-ROM combines word recognition, phonics, and progressively challenging stories to develop phonemic awareness and sight vocabulary and to build recognition of letter patterns.

** Riverdeep The Learning Company
   500 Redwood Blvd.
   Novato, CA 94947
   (800) 825-4420
   www.learningcompanyschool.com

Name _____

Flip My Lid

jump	talk	dream
clean	hunt	camp
plant	paint	push
lift	play	crunch

BLM 34 Unit 5 Activity

Home Connections

The Home Connections features of this program are intended to involve families in their children's learning and application of phonics skills. Three effective opportunities to make connections between home and school include the following.

- **HOME LETTER**
- **HOME NOTES**
- **TAKE-HOME BOOKS**

HOME LETTER

A letter is available to be sent home at the beginning of Unit 5. This letter informs family members that children will be learning to identify words with endings, consonant digraphs, and contractions

within the context of the unit theme, "Whatever the Weather." The suggested home activity focuses on creating a chart showing the weather for each day of the week. This activity promotes interaction between child and family members while supporting children's learning. The letter, which is available in both English and Spanish, also suggests books related to the theme of weather that family members can look for in a local library and enjoy reading together.

HOME NOTES

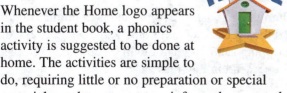

Whenever the Home logo appears in the student book, a phonics activity is suggested to be done at home. The activities are simple to do, requiring little or no preparation or special materials, and are meant to reinforce the targeted phonics skill.

TAKE-HOME BOOKS

The student book contains a number of Take-Home Books that can be cut out and assembled. The story language in the books reinforces the phonics skills. In each book, children are asked to respond by finishing the book. The books can then be taken home and shared with family members. In Unit 5, two Take-Home Books are available. They focus on endings, consonant digraphs, and contractions while extending the theme "Whatever the Weather."

Home Notes in Spanish are also available for both teachers and parents to download and use from our website, www.PlaidPhonics.com.

269q

Pages 269–270

Inflectional Endings, Consonant Digraphs, and Contractions

Skill Focus

Assess Prior Knowledge
To assess children's prior knowledge of inflectional endings, consonant digraphs, and contractions, use the pretest on pages 269e–269f.

Unit Focus

Build Background

- Write the theme "Whatever the Weather" on the board. Read the words and help children find them on page 269. Talk about the meaning of the phrase and the kinds of weather in your area.

- Point to the picture and ask what kind of weather it shows. Then, read the text aloud. Ask children if the weather in your area is like the weather in Chicago or Florida, or if it is somewhere in between.

Introduce Inflectional Endings, Consonant Digraphs, and Contractions

Print these sentences on the board and read them aloud with children: *We looked out the window. "It's snowing!" we yelled.* Underline the words *looked, snowing,* and *yelled* and circle the *-ed* and *-ing* endings. Tell children that they will be learning more about words with these endings in this unit. Then, circle *It's* and explain that this word is a contraction, or shortened word, that stands for *it is.* Let children know they will learn more about contractions in this unit, too. Next, print these sentences and read them aloud: *The thunder boomed. The wind whirled.* Point to the words *thunder* and *whirled.* Have children pronounce the words, listening to the beginning sounds. Identify these sounds as digraphs and explain that children will also learn about the sounds and spellings of five consonant digraphs.

Critical Thinking Read aloud the Talk About It question at the bottom of page 269. Encourage children to discuss ways to predict weather.

THEME FOCUS

ALL KINDS OF WEATHER

Recall that the theme for this new unit is "Whatever the Weather." Direct children's attention to the picture of snow on page 269. Invite children to talk about other kinds of weather. Lead a discussion about the kind of weather children like best and why.

SOUNDS OF WEATHER

Have children in pairs use classroom items to mimic sounds of weather and then present them to others to guess the sound. For example, dripping sand on glass might be rain and crumpled paper might be wind in the trees.

WEATHER LOGS

Materials: construction paper, writing paper, staplers

Have children make and decorate small booklets to use as weather logs. They can use these logs to keep a record of the weather by writing sentences describing each day's weather in these logs.

Dear Family,

In this unit, "Whatever the Weather," your child will learn about contractions, words ending with **ed** and **ing**, and consonant digraphs. A consonant digraph is formed with two letters that stand for one sound. For example, the **sh** in **sheep** and the **th** in **thermometer** are digraphs. As your child becomes familiar with these concepts, you might try these activities together.

▶ Help your child to create a weather chart. For each day of the week, he or she can draw a picture of that day's weather. At the end of the week, ask your child to tell you what the weather was each day.

▶ With your child, read the article on page 269. Help him or her to identify the words with consonant digraphs and contractions and words that end in **ed** or **ing**.

▶ Your child might enjoy reading these books with you. Look for them in your local library.

The Snowy Day
by Ezra Jack Keats
Let's Count the Raindrops
by Fumi Kosaka

Sincerely,

Estimada familia:

En esta unidad, titulada "Pronósticos del tiempo" ("Whatever the Weather"), su hijo/a estudiará en inglés contracciones, palabras que terminan en **ed** y en **ing** y digramas de consonantes. Un digrama de consonantes está formado por dos letras que representan un sonido. Por ejemplo, la **sh** en **sheep** (oveja) y la **th** en **thermometer** (termómetro) son digramas. A medida que su hijo/a se vaya familiarizando con estos conceptos, pueden hacer las siguientes actividades juntos.

▶ Ayuden a su hijo/a a crear un mapa meteorológico. Para cada día de la semana, su hijo/a puede hacer un dibujo sobre el tiempo que hubo ese día. Al final de la semana, pídanle que les explique cuál fue el tiempo en cada día.

▶ Lean juntos el artículo en la página 269. Ayuden a su hijo/a a identificar las palabras con contracciones, los digramas de consonantes y las palabras que terminan en **ed** o en **ing**.

▶ Ustedes y su hijo/a disfrutarán leyendo estos libros juntos. Búsquenlos en su biblioteca local.

The Snowy Day de Ezra Jack Keats
Let's Count the Raindrops de Fumi Kosaka

Sinceramente,

HOME CONNECTIONS

- The Home Letter on page 270 is intended to acquaint family members with the phonics skills children will be studying in the unit. Children can tear out page 270 and take it home.

- You may want to suggest that children complete the activities on the page with a family member. Encourage children to look in the library for the books suggested and read them with family members.

LEARNING CENTER ACTIVITIES

WRITING CENTER

Materials: gray construction paper, paste

Teach children to sing these words to the tune of "Row Your Boat."

Snow, snow, snow and wind,
What a stormy day!
When the snow stops falling down,
We'll go out and play!

Then, have them write or dictate their own version of the song, describing a rainy day. Have them mount their songs on gray paper cut in the shape of clouds.

SCIENCE CENTER

Materials: sponges, water, ball of string

As an introduction to the water cycle, consider the case of the disappearing rain puddle. Have children create rain puddle spots on the chalkboard. Have them measure the circumference of each spot with string as it slowly disappears. Talk about where the water goes.

MATH CENTER

Materials: temperature and rainfall measurements gathered from the classroom weather center or from a daily newspaper

Help children create vertical bar graphs to record the daily temperature and rainfall measurements gathered in the classroom weather station. Have children use the graph to identify the high and low temperature and the day with the most rainfall. They can also compare the number of days with rain to the number of dry days.

BULLETIN BOARD

Help children make cutout figures and dress them appropriately for various types of weather. Drawing paper and crayons can be used to create weather backdrops on which to display the figures. Lead the class in a discussion of how weather affects the way people dress.

Lesson 129   Pages 271–272

Inflectional Endings -ed and -ing

Skill Focus

Children will

★ form new words by adding -ed or -ing to base words.

★ identify base words in words with inflectional endings -ed and -ing.

ESL/ELL Native speakers of Spanish, Russian, Chinese, and many other languages may mispronounce /n/ for /ng/ and /ed/ for /d/. Practice the following pairs with children who demonstrate pronunciation difficulty: *kin, king; thin, thing; win, wing; sun, sung.*

Teach

Introduce Inflectional Endings -ed and -ing Say: *rained, raining.* Ask children to repeat the words and listen for the ending sounds. Help children use each word in a sentence. Then, write the words *rain, raining,* and *rained* on the board and help children read them. Underline the base word *rain* in *raining* and *rained.* Explain that *rain* is the base word and -ed and -ing are endings added on.

Say this incomplete sentence: *It is ___ outside today.* Ask which word completes the sentence. When children identify the word *raining,* point out that the ending -ing is used to tell about something that is happening now. Next, say: *It ___ yesterday.* Ask which word completes this sentence. Explain that the ending -ed is used to tell about the past.

Practice and Apply

Phonemic Awareness Read aloud the rhyme on page 271. Have children identify words with the -ed and -ing endings. Write each word on the board and underline the ending -ed or -ing.

Sound to Symbol Help children identify the pictures on pages 271 and 272. Read the directions for each page aloud. Make sure children understand that they are to add the ending shown to each word on page 271; on page 272 they are to circle base words.

Reading Use *Very Unusual Pets,* MCP Phonics and Reading Library, Super Skills Collection, Level A, to provide practice in reading words with the -ed and -ing endings.

Inflectional Endings

Name _____

It rained and poured all week.
Now it's raining again.
The puddles are growing so big!
I'm jumping and playing in them.

▶ **Say** the name of each picture. **Print** the ending you see in the corner of the box to finish its name. **Trace** the whole word.

1. ed	2. ed	3. ing
spilled	melt ed	eat ing
4. ing	5. ed	6. ing
rain ing	boil ed	fish ing
7. ed	8. ed	9. ing
row ed	peel ed	cry ing

Inflectional endings -ed and -ing   271

FOCUS ON ALL LEARNERS

ESL/ELL ENGLISH LANGUAGE LEARNERS

* Before beginning page 271, demonstrate jumping and ask: *What am I doing?* Then, stop and ask: *What did I do?* Have children jump and take turns asking and answering the questions. Do the same for *hop, pour, ask,* and *hum.*

* Model the activity on page 272 by printing the cue words (*jumped, reading, melted, cooking*) on the board. Cover the endings one at a time with an index card as you circle the base words.

VISUAL LEARNERS PARTNERS

Write these words on the board: *yelled, pumped, rained, saying, flying, landed, floated, melting, rowing, fishing.* Have children take turns selecting a word, reading it aloud, and using the word in a sentence.

KINESTHETIC/AUDITORY LEARNERS GROUPS

Write these words on the board: *yelling, yelled, mixing, mixed, loading, loaded, rowing, rowed, spilling, spilled.* Have children take turns pantomiming a word for others to guess. To clue the tense, children can ask: *What am I doing?* or *What did I do?*

Inflectional Endings

▶ **Read** the word below each picture. Each picture name has a base word and an ending. **Trace** the circle around the base word. Then, **read** the words beside each picture. **Circle** each base word.

1. **jump**ed — (ask)ed, (yell)ed, (fix)ed, (play)ed; (mix)ed, (rock)ed, (bump)ed, (rain)ed
2. **read**ing — (go)ing, (tell)ing, (sail)ing, (mix)ing; (ask)ing, (wait)ing, (rest)ing, (boat)ing
3. **melt**ed — (wait)ed, (seat)ed, (heat)ed, (land)ed; (mail)ed, (load)ed, (float)ed, (end)ed
4. **cook**ing — (row)ing, (cry)ing, (fly)ing, (fish)ing; (pick)ing, (say)ing, (eat)ing, (melt)ing

272 Inflectional endings -ed and -ing: Base words

HOME With your child, hunt for words with endings in favorite storybooks.

CURRICULUM CONNECTIONS

SPELLING
Say each spelling word and then use it in a context sentence. Have children write each word as a spelling pretest.
1. **cooking** — Dad is **cooking** dinner.
2. **fishing** — Sandy is going **fishing**.
3. **melted** — The snow **melted** in the sun.
4. **peeled** — Mom **peeled** a banana for me.
5. **rowing** — They are **rowing** the boat.
6. **spilled** — Who **spilled** the milk?

WRITING
Materials: drawing paper, crayons

PORTFOLIO

Have children fold their papers in half. On the left, have them draw a picture showing yesterday's weather; on the right, have them draw today's weather. Have them write a sentence about each picture. Encourage them to use words ending with *-ed* to tell about yesterday's weather and words ending with *-ing* to tell about today's weather.

TECHNOLOGY **AstroWord** Base Words and Endings

AUDITORY LEARNERS GROUPS
Materials: index cards, crayons

Have children write *-ed* and *-ing* on each side of a card. Say these words: *landed, talking, rested, waiting, mailed, cooked, peeled, raining, fishing*. Have children display the *-ed* or *-ing* side of the card to indicate the ending they hear. Ask them to repeat the word and to identify the base word.

CHALLENGE
Have children select two words with each ending from page 272. Then, have them write a sentence using each word. After sharing the sentences with a partner, have the partner identify whether the sentence tells about something that is happening now or happened in the past.

EXTRA SUPPORT/INTERVENTION
Before circling the base words on page 272, have children underline the *-ed* ending with a red crayon and the *-ing* ending with a blue crayon. Guide children to see that the base word is made up of the remaining letters. **See Daily Phonics Practice, page 323.**

Integrating Phonics and Reading

Shared/Guided Reading
Show the cover as you read the title. Ask children to predict what some of the unusual pets in the book will be.
First Reading Read the book aloud, one chapter at a time, as children follow along. As you finish each chapter, invite children to tell what they learned.
Second Reading Point out the following words with the *-ing* and *-ed* endings: *eating* (page 13); *called* (page 15); *trained* (page 18); *lived* (page 19); *swimming* (page 22). Have children use each word in a sentence about pets.

Comprehension
After reading, ask children these questions:
- What unusual pets does the book tell about? *Recall/Details*
- Which of the pets is your favorite? Why? *Personal Response/Opinion*

ESL/ELL English Language Learners
Pair students with English-speaking partners. Have the partners read and discuss a chapter.

Lesson 130 Pages 273–274

Inflectional Endings -ed and -ing

Skill Focus

Children will

★ write words with the endings -ing and -ed to complete sentences.

★ recognize and read high-frequency words.

Teach

Review Inflectional Endings -ed and -ing Ask children to repeat after you: read, reading. Tell them you will say a word and that they should say the word with the -ing ending. Say these words: fix, pull, cook, spill, paint, jump, work, play. Write each word on the board as children say it. Repeat, using -ed and the same list of words.

Next, write these headings on the board: Base Word, + ed, + ing. Then, write these base words in the first column and call on volunteers to read them: rain, snow, jump, play. Ask other volunteers to add -ed and -ing to these base words and to write the new words under the corresponding headings. Randomly point to the words in the columns. Have children read them aloud and use them in oral sentences.

Words in Context: Decodable Words Write these words on the board: cooked, cooking. Then, write and read the sentence below. Have children select the word that completes the sentence.

• Mom _____ dinner early today. (cooked)

Practice and Apply

Writing For page 273, suggest that children try both word choices before writing a word to complete a sentence. As children complete the activities on pages 273 and 274, they will have the opportunity to read the following high-frequency words: most, other.

Critical Thinking For Talk About It on page 273, suggest that children reread the sentences before responding. For the question on page 274, make sure that children know that "raining cats and dogs" means "raining very hard."

Reading Use *Mystery at Fairly Field*, MCP Phonics and Reading Library, Super Skills Collection, Level A, to provide practice in reading words with the -ed and -ing endings.

Words in Context

Name _____

▶ Circle the word that will finish the sentence. Print it on the line.

1. We were __waiting__ to eat. — (waiting) / waited

2. Dad was __cooking__ the ham. — (cooking) / cooked

3. Mom was __asking__ for help. — (asking) / asked

4. She and I __dressed__ the baby. — dressing / (dressed)

5. Sandy __peeled__ the fruit. — peeling / (peeled)

6. I __helped__ the most! — helping / (helped)

Talk About It: How does this family help each other?

Inflectional endings -ed and -ing; High-frequency words, critical thinking

---

FOCUS ON ALL LEARNERS

ESL/ELL ENGLISH LANGUAGE LEARNERS

• If children are challenged by the activity on page 273, teach them the rule that -ing words are used with is, are, was, and were. Have them look for those clues in each sentence.

• Before beginning page 274, explain the meaning of the idiomatic expression raining cats and dogs. Invite children to use the expression in their own oral sentences.

KINESTHETIC LEARNERS

Materials: oak tag strips, crayons, scissors

Children can make word puzzles by writing words with inflectional endings on strips and leaving a small space between the word and the ending. Show them how to cut the strip between the base word and the ending. Encourage them to cut in zigzags or curves to make puzzle pieces. Have the group mix up the pieces and solve the puzzles, reading each word.

VISUAL LEARNERS

Materials: index cards, self-stick notes

Write -ed and -ing on separate self-stick notes. Have each child select a base word from pages 273 and 274 and write it on a card. Have each child read his or her word with each ending.

Words in Context

▶ **Circle** the word that will finish the sentence. **Print** it on the line.

1. Dad was _____going_____ fishing.
   go / (going)

2. I _____asked_____ him to take me to Mary's home.
   asking / (asked)

3. We were _____kicking_____ a ball to each other.
   kicked / (kicking)

4. Then we _____started_____ to get wet.
   (started) / starting

5. It was _____raining_____ cats and dogs.
   rain / (raining)

6. We _____waited_____ for the rain to stop.
   waiting / (waited)

7. Then we _____played_____ on Mary's swing set.
   (played) / playing

TALK About It What does "raining cats and dogs" mean?

HOME Using words with endings, take turns telling what you did today.

Inflectional endings -ed and -ing; High-frequency words, critical thinking

274

CURRICULUM CONNECTIONS

SPELLING
Materials: spelling master (page 269l)

Have children use the -ed and -ing spelling words on page 269l to make practice spelling cards. Have them write the base word on the back of each card.

WRITING
Materials: drawing paper, crayons

PORTFOLIO

Invite children to draw pictures showing themselves playing outside. Have them write about their pictures. Encourage them to use words ending with -ed and -ing.

PHYSICAL EDUCATION

Work with children to brainstorm a list of games that can be played indoors when rainy weather prevents them from going outdoors to play. Be sure to include traditional games such as "Simon Says." The next time weather keeps them indoors, suggest that children consult the list. Have volunteers take turns leading the games.

TECHNOLOGY AstroWord Base Words and Endings

AUDITORY LEARNERS (GROUPS)

Share oral sentences like these for *play* and *bake* and have children supply the missing word: *This afternoon I will ___ baseball. Yesterday I ___ baseball. Right now, I am ___ baseball. Tomorrow I will ___ a cake. Yesterday I ___ a cake. Now I am ___ a cake.*

CHALLENGE

Have children pick three words from pages 273 and 274 and write sentences using the word *yesterday*. Have them do the same to write three sentences using the words *right now*.

EXTRA SUPPORT/INTERVENTION

Help children read aloud the sentences before they complete the pages. Have them tell the story for each page in their own words and then complete some of the sentences together. **See Daily Phonics Practice, page 323.**

Integrating Phonics and Reading

Shared/Guided Reading
Show the cover as you read the title. Ask children if they like to watch or play baseball and why.

First Reading Read the book aloud, one chapter at a time, as children follow along. As you read, have children relate what is happening in the illustrations to the story.

Second Reading Turn to page 6 and ask children to find three words with the -ed ending. On page 10, have them identify three words with the -ing ending.

Comprehension
After reading, ask children these questions:
• Who solves the mystery of the missing bats? *Recall/Character*
• Who sent a bag of new bats to the Fairly Falcons? Why? *Recall/Character*

ESL/ELL English Language Learners
Pair students with English-speaking partners. Have the partners work together to find more words with the -ing and -ed endings.

274

Lesson 131 — Pages 275–276

Consonant Digraph th

Skill Focus

Children will

★ identify picture names and spell words that begin with the digraph *th*.

★ distinguish between the sounds of *th* and *t* in picture names.

ESL/ELL Some English language learners may have difficulty distinguishing the initial unvoiced *th* of *thin* and *f* (*fin*), or voiced *th* (*then*) and *d* (*den*). Practice with word pairs such as *three, tree; ten, then; thin, fin*. Speakers of some Asian languages won't pronounce the *th* since it doesn't exist in these languages.

Teach

Phonemic Awareness: Phoneme Categorization Ask children to listen for the beginning sound as you say the word *thick*. Have them repeat after you, *thick,* /th/. Then, say the following groups of three words. Have children identify the two words in each group that begin with the same sound as *thick*.

- thumb   thin   table
- this   zoo   that
- thirty   day   think

Sound to Symbol Write *thumb* and have children say the word with you. Point to the *t* and ask if they hear the *t* sound heard at the beginning of *top*. (no) Underline *th* and tell children that together these letters are pronounced /th/. Explain that when two consonants come together to make a new sound, we say the consonants form a digraph.

Practice and Apply

Phonemic Awareness Read aloud the rhyme on page 275. Have children listen for and name words that begin with *th*. Write them on the board.

Sound to Symbol Help children identify the pictures on pages 275 and 276. Remind them to listen carefully for the beginning sound as they complete each activity.

Blend Phonemes As children complete page 276, encourage them to say each picture name, blending together the beginning, middle, and ending sounds. Remind them that they will be printing *th* or *t* to finish each word.

Reading Use *Five Little Dinosaurs*, MCP Phonics and Reading Library, Super Skills Collection, Level A, to provide practice in reading words that begin with *th* and *t*.

275

Phonemic Awareness

Name_____

My soft mittens are thick, not thin.
My fingers and thumbs stay warm in them.
When the thermometer says thirty-three,
Outside with my mittens is where I'll be.

▶ **Thumb** begins with the sound of **th**. Circle each picture whose name begins with the sound of **th**.

1. thumb
2. three
3. two
4. tiger
5. thorn
6. think
7. thirty
8. thermometer
9. train
10. thread
11. tie
12. thirteen

Consonant digraph th: Phonemic awareness **275**

FOCUS ON ALL LEARNERS

ESL/ELL ENGLISH LANGUAGE LEARNERS

Materials: Phonics Picture Cards: tiger (36), ten (82), tie (101), thermometer (154), thimble (155), thumb (156)

- Before beginning page 275, practice distinguishing words that begin with the *th* sound. Display the picture cards face up and make sure children know the name of each card. Then, ask children to sort the cards into two piles according to beginning sounds.

- Use page 276 to verify that children can pronounce *th* clearly and spell *t* versus *th* words correctly. Have children complete the page in pairs; review answers aloud.

KINESTHETIC LEARNERS GROUPS

Materials: Phonics Picture Cards: tiger (36), turkey (37), ten (82), tent (83), thermometer (154), thimble (155), thumb (156); mural paper; marker

Draw a long thermometer on the paper and place it on the floor. Randomly place the pictures near the temperature markings. Have children "raise the temperature" by naming each picture and identifying the initial /th/ or /t/ sound of the picture name.

Say the name of each picture. **Print** **th** or **t** to finish each word. **Trace** the whole word.

Spelling

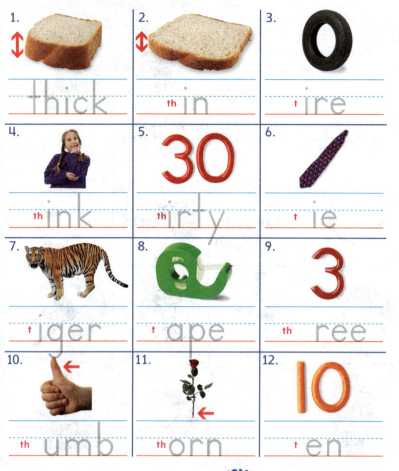

1. thick
2. th in
3. t ire
4. th ink
5. th irty
6. t ie
7. t iger
8. t ape
9. th ree
10. th umb
11. th orn
12. t en

276 Discriminating between th and t: Spelling

HOME Help your child to make up a sentence using words with *t* and *th*, such as *Thirty tigers had thick tails.*

CURRICULUM CONNECTIONS

SPELLING
Say each spelling word and then use it in a context sentence. Have children write each word as a spelling pretest.
1. **chin** He has a cut on his **chin**.
2. **knot** I have a **knot** in my shoelace.
3. **ship** We took a cruise on a big **ship**.
4. **think** I will **think** of the answer.
5. **whale** A **whale** lives in water.

WRITING
Long ago, people made up stories to explain thunder. Have children illustrate and write their own stories about thunder's origin.

MATH/SCIENCE
Materials: unbreakable thermometers, plastic cups of warm, lukewarm, and cold water

Have children measure the water temperatures and record the data for each cup. Repeat after an hour. Help them to determine why all the water reaches the same temperature.

TECHNOLOGY  **AstroWord** Consonant Blends & Digraphs

Integrating Phonics and Reading

Shared/Guided Reading
Show the cover as you read the title. Have children count and describe the dinosaurs in the illustration.
First Reading Invite children to join in as you read pages 2, 4, 6, 8, 10, and 12. Also invite them to roar as you read page 14.
Second Reading Ask children to identify the words beginning with *th* and *t* in the story. List the words on the board in two columns.

Comprehension
After reading, ask children these questions:
• How do you think the little dinosaurs feel when they are sitting all alone at the end of the day? *Inference/Character*
• Who roars at the end of the story? Why? *Inference/Character*

ESL/ELL English Language Learners
Point out that the story counts down from five to one little dinosaurs. Then, practice counting forward from 1 to 5 and back from 5 to 1 with children.

AUDITORY LEARNERS
Have children hold up three fingers every time they hear you say a word with /th/. Use these words: *thing, table, thirteen, tea, thorn, time, thick, thank, tank, think, thin, tube, ten, thermos, tire, thimble.*

CHALLENGE
Direct attention to the rhyme on page 275 and challenge children to find a word that begins with *th* that has a different beginning sound than *thumb*. When they identify *them*, challenge them to name other words that contain this voiced sound of *th*. (*than, then, theirs, that, the, there,* etc.)

EXTRA SUPPORT/INTERVENTION
Materials: index cards, small self-stick notes

Print the words *tin, tank, tree, tick,* and *torn* on the cards, one word on each card. Have children write *th* on a self-stick note. Have them cover the initial *t* in each word with *th* and read the new word. **See Daily Phonics Practice, page 323.**

276

Lesson 132   Pages 277–278

Consonant Digraph wh

Skill Focus

Children will

★ identify picture names and spell words that begin with the digraph *wh*.

★ distinguish between the *th* and *wh* digraphs.

ESL/ELL Native speakers of Japanese, Korean, Spanish, Tagalog, and Vietnamese may confuse the digraph *wh* with the initial *h* sound.

Teach

Phonological Awareness: Blending Onsets and Rimes Tell children that you will say the parts of a word. Children should repeat the word parts, then orally blend them to say the word.

- /hw/ite   /hw/ale   (white, whale)
- /hw/eel   /hw/istle   (wheel, whistle)

Sound to Symbol Whistle and have children identify the action. Write *whistle* on the board. Underline the *wh* and explain that this is another consonant digraph. Write *win* and say the word several times with *whistle*, emphasizing the beginning sound to show the difference between /w/ and /hw/.

Next, say some words and have children whistle when they hear a word that begins like *whistle*. Write those words. Use: *whale, when, wheat, thimble, window, where, thick, thin*.

Practice and Apply

Phonemic Awareness Read aloud the rhyme on page 277. Have children listen for and name words that begin with *wh*. Write the words on the board.

Sound to Symbol Help children identify the pictures on pages 277 and 278. Explain that some of the words begin with the sound of *wh* and others begin with the sound of *th*. On page 277, they will circle only the pictures whose names begin with *wh*.

Blend Phonemes As children complete page 278, encourage them to say each picture name, blending together the beginning, middle, and ending sounds. Remind them that they will be printing *wh* or *th* to finish each word, then tracing the word.

Reading Use *Humpback Whales*, MCP Phonics and Reading Library, Super Skills Collection, Level A, to provide practice in reading words that begin with *wh*.

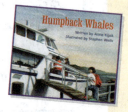

Phonemic Awareness

Name_____

The wind whines and whistles.
It whips through the tree.
It whirls around wildly,
And takes my white cap from me!

▶ **White** begins with the sound of **wh**. Circle each picture whose name begins with the sound of **wh**.

1. wheel
2. thumb
3. whale
4. three
5. white
6. thorn
7. wheelchair
8. whistle
9. wheat
10. thermometer
11. wheelbarrow
12. think

Consonant digraph wh: Phonemic awareness   277

FOCUS ON ALL LEARNERS

ESL/ELL ENGLISH LANGUAGE LEARNERS

Materials: Phonics Picture Cards: thimble (155), thumb (156), whale (157), wheat (158)

- Before beginning page 277, practice distinguishing words that begin with the *wh* sound. Say these words and have children raise a hand when they hear a word that begins with /hw/: *while, height, wide, heel, wheel, when, hen, heat, week, hi, why*.

- Review the sounds of *wh* and *th* before completing page 278. Hold up each picture card. Say the picture name followed by the beginning digraph, and have children repeat after you.

KINESTHETIC LEARNERS

Materials: Phonics Picture cards: wagon (40), web (84), whale (157), wheat (158), wheel (159), whistle (160)

Display the pictures on the chalkboard ledge. Ask children to be the wind. Have them take turns whistling and whirling their way up to the board to select a picture whose name begins with /hw/. Have them pick up the card, name it, and "blow away."

277

Spelling

Say the name of each picture.
Print **wh** or **th** to finish each word.
Trace the whole word.

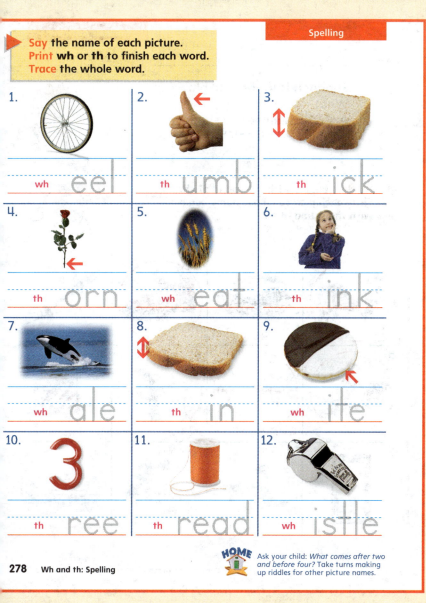

1. wh eel
2. th umb
3. th ick
4. th orn
5. wh eat
6. th ink
7. wh ale
8. th in
9. wh ite
10. th ree
11. th read
12. wh istle

278 Wh and th: Spelling

HOME Ask your child: *What comes after two and before four?* Take turns making up riddles for other picture names.

CURRICULUM CONNECTIONS

SPELLING
Materials: Spelling master (page 269I)

Have children use the consonant digraph spelling words to make practice spelling cards. Have them draw a picture illustrating each word and write the word on the back of the card.

WRITING
Write these question words on the board and help children read them aloud: *What? Where? Why? When?* Have children work with a partner to use these words to write four questions they might ask a friend.

SCIENCE
Materials: chart paper, crayons, markers

Tell children it is possible to get an idea about how hard the wind is blowing by looking at objects such as the school flag. Help children develop an informal wind-scale chart using the flag. Possibilities include showing a limp flag for a calm day, a slightly unfurled flag for a breeze, and a flag straight out for a strong wind.

AstroWord Consonant Blends & Digraphs

Integrating Phonics and Reading

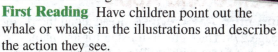

Guided Reading
Show the cover as you read the title. Ask children what the girl in the illustration is doing.

First Reading Have children point out the whale or whales in the illustrations and describe the action they see.

Second Reading Ask children to identify the words beginning with *wh* in the story. List the words on the board or add them to the classroom Word Wall.

Comprehension
After reading, ask children these questions:
- What kind of animals are the people in the story watching? *Recall/Main Idea*
- Would you like to go on a boat trip to look at whales? Why or why not? *Reflective Analysis/Opinion*

ESL/ELL English Language Learners
Have students reread the story aloud, taking turns to read the questions and answers.

AUDITORY/VISUAL LEARNERS
Materials: Phonics Picture Cards: whale (157), wheat (158), wheel (159), sheep (164), nails (90), leaf (120)

Say riddles and ask children to select the picture that shows the answer: *What word do you get if you add /hw/ to eat?* (wheat) *To eel?* (wheel) *To ale?* (whale)

CHALLENGE
Materials: picture books with simple text

Have children look for questions and list any *wh* words they find, such as *who, what, where, why,* and *when*.

EXTRA SUPPORT/INTERVENTION
Materials: Phonics Picture Cards: wagon (40), windmill (41), web (84), thermometer (154), thimble (155), thumb (156), whale (157), wheat (158), wheel (159)

Have children say each picture name and sort the pictures into three piles: words beginning with /hw/, /w/, and /th/. See Daily Phonics Practice, page 324.

Lesson 133 Pages 279–280

Consonant Digraph sh

Skill Focus

Children will

★ identify picture names and spell words that begin with the digraph *sh*.

★ distinguish between the sounds of *sh* and *s* in picture names.

ESL/ELL Children whose first language is Spanish or Tagalog may assimilate *sh* and *ch*. Native speakers of Cantonese, Khmer, Vietnamese, Hmong, or Korean may confuse *sh* with *s*, *ch*, or the /zh/ sound of *s* in *measure*.

▶ Teach

Phonemic Awareness: Initial Sound Isolation
Materials: flashlight
Use the flashlight to cast a shadow of your hand on the chalkboard. Have children identify your action. Then, say *shadow*, /sh/, and have children repeat. Explain that you are saying a word and then its first sound. Continue by saying these words for children to repeat, identifying the inital /sh/: *shade, show, shop, share*.

Sound to Symbol Write *shadow* on the board and underline the *sh*. Remind children that when two consonants come together to make a whole new sound, they are called a digraph. Explain that the digraph *sh* stands for /sh/. Ask children to suggest other words that begin with /sh/. List their words on the board. Invite volunteers to "shadow" the letters *sh* in each word by tracing over them. Read the list of words with the group.

▶ Practice and Apply

Phonemic Awareness Read aloud the rhyme on page 279. Have children listen for and name words that begin with *sh*. Write them on the board.

Sound to Symbol Help children identify the pictures on pages 279 and 280. Remind them to listen carefully for the beginning sound and to circle only the words that begin with /sh/ as they complete page 279.

Blend Phonemes As children complete page 280, encourage them to say each picture name, blending together the beginning, middle, and ending sounds. Remind them that they will be printing *sh* or *s* to finish each word.

Reading Use *Silvia's Soccer Game*, MCP Phonics and Reading Library, Super Skills Collection, Level A, to provide practice in reading words that begin with *sh* and *s*.

Name _____

Shannon is in the sunlight.
What does she see?
A shiny, shimmering shadow.
She says, "You can't catch me!"

▶ **Shadow** begins with the sound of **sh**. **Circle** each picture whose name begins with the sound of **sh**.

1. sheep
2. skunk
3. shoe
4. spoon
5. shell
6. shelf
7. shadow
8. stamp
9. shade
10. seal
11. slide
12. ship

Consonant digraph sh: Phonemic awareness   279

FOCUS ON ALL LEARNERS

ESL/ELL ENGLISH LANGUAGE LEARNERS

- Before beginning page 279, practice discriminating between /sh/ and /ch/. Have children repeat these word pairs, making the "quiet sign" by holding a finger up to their mouths for each word that begins with /sh/: *ship, chip; show, chose; chop, shop; shame, chain; cherry, Sherry*.

- Reinforce sound-to-spelling distinctions of *s* versus *sh* words with the activity on page 280. Have children say each picture name. Correct pronunciation if necessary. As a group, have children print *sh* or *s* and trace the whole word.

KINESTHETIC LEARNERS

Materials: mural paper on which you have traced around a shoe to make footsteps

In each shoe shape, write a word beginning with *sh* or *s*. Possible words are: *shoe, ship, shame, shin, sheep, sail, sort, sink, save*. Have children read each word and then step on only the words beginning with the *sh* digraph.

> **Say** the name of each picture.
> **Print** sh or s to finish each word.
> **Trace** the whole word.

Spelling

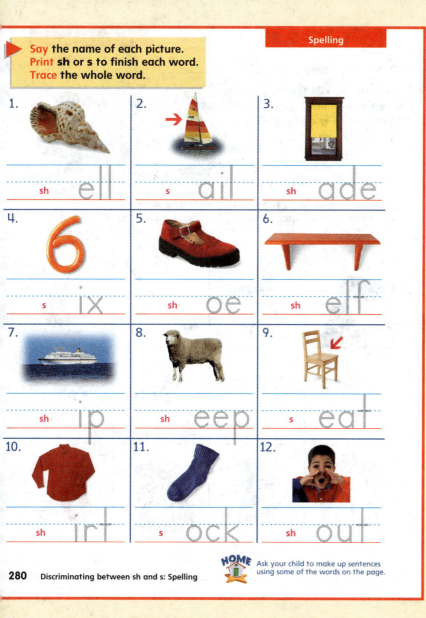

1. sh ell
2. s ail
3. sh ade
4. s ix
5. sh oe
6. sh elf
7. sh ip
8. sh eep
9. s eat
10. sh irt
11. s ock
12. sh out

 Ask your child to make up sentences using some of the words on the page.

280 Discriminating between sh and s: Spelling

CURRICULUM CONNECTIONS

SPELLING
Materials: List of spelling words with blanks for digraphs

Give children a list of the spelling words with blanks replacing the initial consonant digraphs. Have them complete each word.

WRITING
Invite children to create a story about a runaway shadow. Before they begin writing, discuss: *Whose shadow is it? Why did the shadow decide to run away? How did the person or thing get its shadow back?*

SCIENCE
Materials: transparent, translucent, and opaque objects, such as acetate sheets, plastic wrap, clear plastic bags, waxed paper, plastic cups, blocks, craft sticks; flashlight

Working with partners or in small groups, have children use the flashlight to see which materials create shadows. Have them record their findings.

TECHNOLOGY **AstroWord** Consonant Blends & Digraphs

VISUAL LEARNERS **PARTNERS**
Materials: tic-tac-toe grids, 10 squares for markers

Have one child write *sh* on five markers and on the others write *s*. Then, have children play a game of tic-tac-toe. To place markers, one child gives words beginning with /sh/ while the other child gives words beginning with /s/.

CHALLENGE
Have children work with a partner to generate a list of at least 10 words that begin with the *sh* sound. Then, have them write tongue twisters such as: *She should show her shells. Six shells share the shelf.*

EXTRA SUPPORT/INTERVENTION
Materials: Phonics Picture Cards: scissors (33), seven (34), soap (35), sun (67), suit (105), sheep (164), shirt (165), shoe (166); paper bag labeled with the digraph *sh*

Have children mix up the picture cards and take turns selecting one. Have them say the picture name. If it begins with the *sh* digraph as in *shadow,* have them place the card in the bag. **See Daily Phonics Practice, page 324.**

Integrating Phonics and Reading

Guided Reading
Show the cover as you read the title. Invite children to share experiences they have had with soccer.

First Reading Invite children to describe the action in each photo. Remind them to identify the team the players belong to.

Second Reading Ask children to identify the words beginning with *sh* and *s* in the story. List the words on the board in two columns.

Comprehension
After reading, ask children these questions:
• Which two teams play in the big soccer game? *Recall/Details*
• What happens in the game? *Recall/Summarize*

ESL/ELL English Language Learners
Ask children to find the names of the two teams in the story. (*Super Sports* and *Blue Stars*) Point out that each word of each name begins with a capital letter. Then, help students name more sports teams. Write the names on the board.

280

Lesson 134 — Pages 281–282

Consonant Digraph ch

Skill Focus

Children will

★ identify picture names and spell words that begin with the digraph *ch*.

★ distinguish between the sounds of *ch* and *c* in picture names.

ESL/ELL Children who speak Cantonese, Vietnamese, Khmer, Korean, or Hmong may confuse *ch* with *sh* or initial *j*.

Teach

Phonemic Awareness: Phoneme Identity
Read this tongue twister aloud, stressing the initial /ch/ sounds: *Chip used a chunk of chalk to make a check on the chalkboard.* Have children identify the words that have the same beginning sound.

Sound to Symbol Draw a picture of a chair on the board and ask children to identify it. Write *chair* under the picture and have children say the word with you, emphasizing the beginning sound.

Next, ask children to suggest other words that begin with the same sound as *chair*. List their words on the board. Underline the initial *ch* in each one and explain that this digraph spells the sound /ch/.

Practice and Apply

Phonemic Awareness Read aloud the rhyme on page 281. Have children listen for and name words that begin with *ch*. Write the words on the board.

Sound to Symbol Help children identify the pictures on pages 281 and 282. Remind them to listen carefully for the beginning sound and to circle only the words that begin with /ch/ as they complete page 281.

Blend Phonemes As children complete page 282, encourage them to say each picture name, blending together the beginning, middle, and ending sounds. Remind them that they will be printing *ch* or *c* to finish each word.

Reading Use *Cat Chat*, MCP Phonics and Reading Library, Super Skills Collection, Level A, to provide practice in reading words that begin with *ch* and *c*.

FOCUS ON ALL LEARNERS

ESL/ELL ENGLISH LANGUAGE LEARNERS

Materials: Phonics Picture Cards: camel (4), cookies (6), chair (168), cherry (169)

- Before beginning page 281, practice distinguishing words that begin with *ch*. Say a series of words. Tell children they should cheer if they hear the sound of *ch* at the beginning of a word. Use: *chin, jet, check, share, chalk, child, chair, sheet, cheese, jog,* and *cherry*.

- Review the sounds of *ch* and *c* before completing page 282. Hold up each picture card. Say the picture name and have children repeat after you. Then, write the word on the board and ask children to identify the letter or letters that stand for the beginning sound.

VISUAL LEARNERS   INDIVIDUAL

Materials: construction-paper strips, old magazines, crayons, scissors, paste, stapler

Have children draw or cut out and paste pictures of objects whose names begin with *ch* on construction paper strips. Then, have them staple or paste the strips together to form a *ch* chain.

Spelling

Say the name of each picture. Print **ch** or **c** to finish each word. Trace the whole word.

1. ch __in
2. ch __eck
3. c __oat
4. ch __eese
5. c __ube
6. ch __ick
7. ch __alk
8. c __at
9. ch __ain
10. ch __erry
11. c __ow
12. ch __air

Ask your child to identify common household items whose names begin with *ch* or *c*, such as *chair* and *comb*.

282 Discriminating between ch and c: Spelling

CURRICULUM CONNECTIONS

SPELLING
Materials: index cards, crayons

Have children write each spelling word on an index card. Then, pair children and have them turn their 10 cards face down and mix them up. Have pairs play "Concentration," taking turns turning over two cards to match the words.

WRITING
Discuss that a champion is a person who is the best at something. Discuss the things children do well. Suggest that they illustrate and write about themselves as champions.

PORTFOLIO

SCIENCE
Materials: picture books about chimpanzees

Encourage children to draw a chimpanzee and write one fact about it to share. They may want to look through books or in an encyclopedia to find a fact.

TECHNOLOGY   **AstroWord** Consonant Blends and Digraphs

AUDITORY LEARNERS
Pose these oral riddles and have children respond with words that begin with the /ch/ sound. What goes with a table? *(chairs)* What goes with crackers? *(cheese)* What goes with an eraser? *(chalk)* What goes with a checkerboard? *(checkers)* What goes with a fireplace? *(chimney)*

CHALLENGE
Write these words on the board and help children read them: *chin, teacher, peach*. Discuss the position of the *ch* digraph in each word. Have children work with partners to list other words with *ch* in the initial, medial, and final position.

EXTRA SUPPORT/INTERVENTION
Materials: index cards, markers

Have children write *ch* on a card. Then, read aloud these words and have children display the card when they hear a word beginning with this digraph: *chain, cane, cheer, crane, clear, cheese, camp, chin, chick, champ, camel, chalk*. See Daily Phonics Practice, page 324.

Integrating Phonics and Reading

Shared/Guided Reading
Show the cover as you read the title. Preview the illustrations and ask children whom the cat might chat with in the story.

First Reading Invite children to read the cat's words while you read the parts of the narrator and the other animals.

Second Reading Ask children to identify the words beginning with *ch* and *c* in the story. List the words on the board in two columns.

Comprehension
After reading, ask children the following questions:
- What does the cat want to do? ***Recall/Plot***
- Is it easy or hard for the cat to do this? Why? ***Recall/Summarize***

ESL/ELL English Language Learners
Have children draw a farmyard scene that includes each animal from the story. Help them label each farm animal.

282

Lesson 135   Pages 283–284

Consonant Digraph kn

Skill Focus

Children will

★ identify picture names and words that begin with the digraph *kn*.

★ identify sentences that describe pictures.

ESL/ELL Children whose home language is Spanish, Cantonese, or Haitian Creole may be unfamiliar with the digraph *kn*. Stress that the *k* is silent; it is part of the written word, but it stands for no sound.

Teach

Phonemic Awareness: Phoneme Blending
Knock on the door or a wall and say the word *knock*, segmenting the individual phonemes: /n/ /ô/ /k/. Have children repeat the segmented word and then say the word naturally. Repeat the activity, using these words: *knew, knee, mine, knot, knife*.

Sound to Symbol Write the word *knock* on the board and ask what sound children hear at the beginning of this word. Then, ask what letter they see at the beginning of *knock*. When children identify the *k*, explain that *kn* forms a digraph that spells the *n* sound in some words. The *k* is silent.

Next, write the words *knot, knife, knee,* and *know* on the board and read each one. Have volunteers underline the digraph at the beginning of each word.

Practice and Apply

Blend Word Parts As children complete page 283, encourage them to say each picture name, blending together the beginning sound and the rest of the word. Remind them to trace the whole word, then circle only the pictures whose names begin with *kn*.

Sound to Symbol For page 284, suggest that children look at the picture and carefully read both sentences before circling the one that tells about the picture.

Reading Use *Rabbit Knits,* MCP Phonics and Reading Library, Super Skills Collection, Level A, to provide practice in reading words that begin with *kn*.

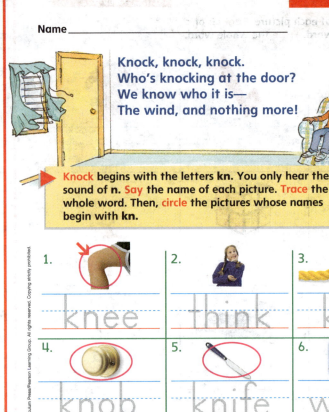

Name _____

Knock, knock, knock.
Who's knocking at the door?
We know who it is—
The wind, and nothing more!

▶ **Knock** begins with the letters **kn**. You only hear the sound of **n**. **Say** the name of each picture. **Trace** the whole word. Then, **circle** the pictures whose names begin with **kn**.

1. knee
2. think
3. knot
4. knob
5. knife
6. whale
7. chin
8. knock
9. knit

Consonant digraph kn: Spelling   283

FOCUS ON ALL LEARNERS

ESL/ELL ENGLISH LANGUAGE LEARNERS

- Begin page 283 as a group, reading words aloud, tracing letters, and circling the pictures whose names begin with *kn*. Have children finish the activity individually. Then, have children rewrite all the *kn* words to reinforce spelling.

- Children may be unfamiliar with the meaning of the word *knight* on page 284. Write the words *knight* and *night*. Help children read each word and identify the difference in their spellings. Then, discuss the meaning of each word.

VISUAL/AUDITORY LEARNERS

Write these word forms on the board: __ife, __ock, __it, __ot, __eel, __ee. Have children complete each word with the digraph *kn*. Then, have them take turns reading the words to their partners and using them in oral sentences.

KINESTHETIC/VISUAL/ AUDITORY LEARNERS

Materials: index cards, marker, paper bag

Write these words on cards and place them in a bag: *knee, knife, knit, knock, knot*. Have children take turns selecting a card and acting out the word for the group to guess.

Words in Context

▶ **Circle** the sentence that tells about the picture.

1. The tire is black and white.
   (Chad tied a knot in the rope.)

2. Randy did not skin his knee.
   (Kelly kneels down on the mat.)

3. (Did you hear a knock at the door?)
   Did Nick knock over the vase?

4. I fed the bread to the chicks.
   (I used a knife to slice the cheese.)

5. (Chuck knows where his watch is.)
   Kate turned the knob to the left.

6. (Susan knits a sweater for her sister.)
   Jenny ties a knot with her shoe strings.

7. The knight does not ride a horse.
   (The knight rides a horse with spots.)

HOME Ask your child to point to and read each *kn* word.

Consonant digraph kn: Words in context

CURRICULUM CONNECTIONS

SPELLING
Materials: index cards, crayons, glue, rice

Have children use crayons to write each spelling word on a card. Then, have them trace over the consonant digraph with glue and sprinkle the glue with rice. Let dry.

WRITING
Write the following story starter on chart paper: *I turned the knob. The secret door opened.* Have children copy the story starter and finish the story.

SOCIAL STUDIES
Materials: yarn, knitting needles, sweater, picture of sheep

Display the objects and discuss with children how they go together. Explain that sheep grow a heavy coat each winter. In the spring the thick, woolly coat is cut off. The wool is cleaned and spun into yarn. The yarn can be knitted into sweaters and other objects.

TECHNOLOGY
AstroWord Consonant Blends & Digraphs

Integrating Phonics and Reading

Shared/Guided Reading
Show children the cover as you read the title. Ask if they can guess what Rabbit is knitting.

First Reading As you read, have children join you after you say the words *Rabbit can . . . .*

Second Reading Ask children to identify the word beginning with *kn* in the story. Write it on the board or add it to the classroom Word Wall.

Comprehension
After reading, ask children these questions:
• What things can Rabbit knit? *Recall/Details*
• Why did Rabbit's parents say "Stop"? *Inference/Details*

ESL/ELL English Language Learners
Point to the scarves in the picture on page 6 and write on the board *scarf, scarves*. Point out that most words ending in *f* form the plural by changing *f* to *v* and adding *es*.

AUDITORY LEARNERS **GROUPS**
Read aloud these words and have children knock on their desks each time they hear a word that begins with the sound that *kn* stands for: *know, shadow, whip, knuckle, knit, shop, knight, wheat, knob, cane, knack.*

CHALLENGE
Write these homophones on the board and have children read them: *knot, not; knew, new; knight, night.* Talk with children about the meaning of each word. Then, have them write pairs of sentences that illustrate the different meanings.

EXTRA SUPPORT/INTERVENTION
Materials: red crayons

Write the following words on the board: *knee, knight, knife, knob, knot, knit.* Have children underline the digraph *kn* in each word. Tell them that the *k* is silent before the letter *n*. Then, have them cover the *k* in each word and read the word aloud. *See Daily Phonics Practice, page 325.*

284

Lesson 136

Pages 285–286

Review Consonant Digraphs

Skill Focus

Children will

★ write words with the digraphs *th*, *wh*, *sh*, *ch*, and *kn* to complete sentences.

★ recognize and read high-frequency words.

Teach

Phonemic Awareness: Phoneme Substitution Tell children you will say a word. They can make a new word by changing the beginning sound to /sh/. Then, give these words: *well, fin, cake*. Do the same with these digraphs: /th/ *(kick, pan, rose)*; /wh/ *(bite, tale, rip)*; and /ch/ *(bat, sip, fill)*.

Sound to Symbol Write the consonant digraphs *th*, *wh*, *sh*, *ch*, and *kn* on the board. Remind children that consonant digraphs are two letters that come together to make a new sound.

Next, write *thin, shell, know, wheel, lunch, dish, with, chair,* and *mother* on the board and have children read each word. Point out that a digraph may be found at the beginning, middle, or end of a word. Then, say a sentence, leaving out one of the words. Have children select the correct word and repeat the complete sentence. For example, *The ice is too ___ to skate. It is time to eat ___. Please sit down in your ___.*

Practice and Apply

Writing For page 285, suggest that children try each word choice before writing a word to complete a sentence. For page 286, have them read the words in the box at the top aloud. Point out that each word is the answer to one of the riddles.

As children complete the activities on pages 285 and 286, they will have the opportunity to read the following high-frequency words: *finds, people*.

Critical Thinking For Talk About It on page 285, suggest that children recall what Chuck and Beth did at the beach before responding.

Reading Use *Rush, Rush, Rush*, MCP Phonics and Reading Library, Super Skills Collection, Level A, to provide practice in reading words with consonant digraphs.

Review Consonant Digraphs

Name _____

▶ Circle the word that will finish the sentence. Print it on the line.

1. Chuck __knows__ about a sunny beach.
   - (knows)
   - knob
   - knock

2. We catch the bus at __three__.
   - thick
   - (three)
   - thorn

3. Beth puts a __white__ sheet down.
   - (white)
   - wheat
   - whip

4. Chuck finds __shells__ in the sand.
   - sheets
   - shades
   - (shells)

5. I __teach__ Beth a new game.
   - (teach)
   - reach
   - cheat

6. Then we sit and look at the __ships__.
   - shape
   - (ships)
   - shake

Talk About It: What else can people do at the beach?

Review consonant digraphs: High-frequency words, critical thinking

---

FOCUS ON ALL LEARNERS

ESL/ELL ENGLISH LANGUAGE LEARNERS

- Read the incomplete sentence and word choices on page 285 as a group. Identify each correct choice. Then, have children circle and write the words.

- For English language learners who are unfamiliar with riddles, change each item on page 286 to a direct question, such as *What has hair called wool and can be white, brown, or black?*

VISUAL LEARNERS

Materials: paper, magazines, catalogs, glue, scissors

Have children cut out pictures of items whose names begin or end with *th, wh, sh,* and *ch*. Then, have them use the pictures to make a consonant digraph collage.

KINESTHETIC LEARNERS

Materials: Phonics Picture Cards: thermometer (154), whale (157), sheep (164), chain (167); marker; masking tape; four chairs

Label each chair back with one digraph: *wh, th, sh, ch*. Have four children each select a picture card and sit in the chair that is labeled with the digraph heard in the picture name. Each child says the picture name and identifies the digraph.

Words in Context

▶ Read each clue. Print the answer to each riddle on the line. Use the cloud pictures if you need help.

| three | sheep | wheel | cherry |
| ship | chick | whale | knife |

1. My hair is called wool.
   I can be white, brown, or black.

   I am a ___sheep___.

2. I hatch out of an egg.
   My mother is a hen.

   I am a ___chick___.

3. I live in the sea.
   I am much bigger than a fish.

   I am a ___whale___.

4. I sail across the sea.
   People ride in me.

   I am a ___ship___.

5. I come after two and before four.

   I am ___three___.

6. I am round. I help cars and bikes go.

   I am a ___wheel___.

7. I am round and red.
   I am good to eat.

   I am a ___cherry___.

8. I am very sharp. People use me to cut things.

   I am a ___knife___.

286 Review consonant digraphs: High-frequency words

HOME Ask your child to read the riddles to you so you can guess the answers.

CURRICULUM CONNECTIONS

SPELLING
Materials: drawing paper, crayons

Have children fold their papers to divide the paper into six boxes. In each box, invite children to draw a cloud picture of one of the spelling words. Have partners trade papers and label each picture.

WRITING
Materials: drawing paper, crayons, construction paper, stapler, marker

Help children brainstorm a list of other words containing consonant digraphs that could be used to write riddles similar to those on page 286. After children share their riddles with the class, photocopy them and bind the pages together to create a class book of riddles.

MUSIC
Share the traditional song "I Gave My Love a Cherry." Have children identify the many words containing consonant digraphs in the song.

TECHNOLOGY

AstroWord Consonant Blends & Digraphs

AUDITORY LEARNERS

Read these riddles and have children identify each word: What word rhymes with *block* and begins like *knot*? (knock) What word rhymes with *whip* and begins like *shake*? (ship) What word rhymes with *meat* and begins like *white*? (wheat)

CHALLENGE
Write this traditional riddle on the board and help children read it.
*Thirty white horses on a red hill,
Now they tramp, now they champ, now they stand still.*
Have children identify the digraphs and guess the riddle. (teeth)

EXTRA SUPPORT/INTERVENTION
Write these words on the board: *ship, three, chick, sheep, whale, wheel, knife, cherry.* Help children read each word and match it to one of the cloud pictures on page 286. See Daily Phonics Practice, pages 323–325.

Integrating Phonics and Reading

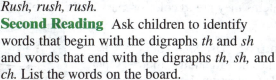

Shared/Guided Reading
Show the cover as you read the title. Ask children what the people in the illustration are rushing to do.

First Reading Invite children to join in each time they see the words *Rush, rush, rush.*

Second Reading Ask children to identify words that begin with the digraphs *th* and *sh* and words that end with the digraphs *th, sh*, and *ch*. List the words on the board.

Comprehension
After reading, ask children these questions:
- What are some of the things the family rushes to do? *Recall/Details*
- Why does the family rush to do these things? *Recall/Cause and Effect*

ESL/ELL English Language Learners
Point out the phrase *catch a fish* on page 8. Discuss what this phrase usually means. (to go fishing; to catch a fish with a fishing rod) Then, have students look at the illustration and tell what it means in the story.

Lesson 137   Pages 287–288

Review Consonant Digraphs

Skill Focus

Children will

★ orally blend word parts.

★ apply what they have learned about consonant digraphs *th, wh, sh, ch,* and *kn* by reading directions.

Teach

Phonemic Awareness: Initial Sound Isolation Say the word *shout,* emphasizing the beginning sound, and have children repeat the word. Then, say *shout,* /sh/, and have children repeat. Ask them what letters spell the sound heard at the beginning of *shout.* Repeat, using these words: *chin, knife, shade, whale, thank.* Have children say the word, say the beginning digraph, and identify the letters in the digraph.

Sound to Symbol Draw a curved arrow on the board and write the word *chin,* as shown on page 287. Blend the sounds together as you move your hand from left to right. Invite several volunteers to come to the board and read the word in the same way.

Draw similar arrows for the following words: *wheel, knew, thorn, shine.* Have children blend the letter sounds together as you move your hand from left to right. Then, ask volunteers to circle the consonant digraph in each word. Challenge children to think of other words that begin with each digraph.

Practice and Apply

Sound to Symbol Help children identify the pictures on page 287. Make sure they understand that they will write each blended word and then draw a line to the correct picture.

Before children work on page 288, read each numbered direction line together. Help children find the items they are to color or mark in the large picture.

Reading Use *Stan Packs,* MCP Phonics and Reading Library, Super Skills Collection, Level A, to provide practice in reading words with consonant digraphs.

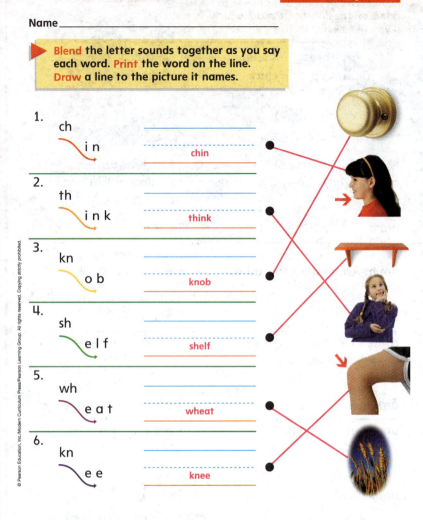

FOCUS ON ALL LEARNERS

ESL/ELL ENGLISH LANGUAGE LEARNERS

- Have children identify the two body parts, chin and knee, shown on page 287. Review these and other body parts containing consonant digraphs by having children say the name and point to each. In addition to *chin* and *knee,* include *knuckle, thumb, shoulder, mouth, teeth, cheek.*

- Have children work with partners or in small groups to complete the activity on page 288.

VISUAL LEARNERS

Materials: cube, masking tape

Place masking tape on each surface of a cube and write a digraph *wh, th, sh, ch, kn* on five sides. Draw a star on the sixth. Have children toss the cube and say a word that begins with the digraph shown. If the star shows, the child may name a digraph and have another child say a word that contains it.

KINESTHETIC LEARNERS

Materials: chart paper, marker, beanbag

Draw a target of five parts. Print a digraph in each part: *ch, th, sh, wh, kn.* The child must toss the beanbag, then say and spell a word that begins with the digraph on which the beanbag lands.

Look at the picture. Then **follow** the directions.

Reading

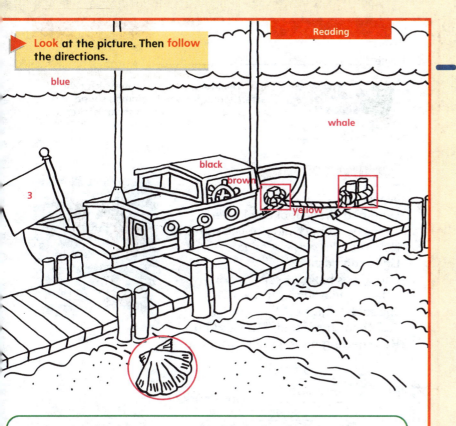

1. Color the ship black.
2. Circle the shell on the beach.
3. Write a three on the flag.
4. Color the wheel brown.
5. Color the thick rope yellow.
6. Draw a whale in the water.
7. Draw a box around each knot.
8. Color the sky blue but keep the cloud white.

 With your child, make up a story to go with the picture.

Review consonant digraphs: Reading

CURRICULUM CONNECTIONS

SPELLING
Materials: letter cards *Aa, Cc, Ee, Hh, Ii, Ll, Kk, Nn, Oo, Pp, Ss, Tt, Ww*

Have children dictate each spelling word *(chin, knot, ship, think,* and *whale)* for a partner to spell with letter cards. Then have the partners exchange roles.

WRITING
Materials: large index cards or half sheets of paper

Ask children to imagine that they are visiting the spot shown in the picture on page 288. Have them use a large index card or half-sheet of paper to make a postcard to send to a friend. Show them how to put a picture on the front and a message on the back.

PHYSICAL EDUCATION
Lead children in a game of "Sheldon says." Children should only follow a command that has a consonant digraph, such as *Sheldon says touch your cheek.*

 **AstroWord** Consonant Blends & Digraphs

Integrating Phonics and Reading

Guided Reading
Show the cover as you read the title. Invite children to name some items that they would pack for a trip.

First Reading Discuss the items that Stan packs. Ask children if they would choose to bring each one on a trip.

Second Reading Ask children to identify words that begin with the digraphs *ch, sh, th,* and *wh.* Also have them find a word that has *th* in the middle. Write the words on the board.

Comprehension
After reading, ask children these questions:
• What did Stan forget to pack? *Recall/Details*
• Which item would you tell Stan to unpack to make room for his clothes? Why did you pick this item? *Reflective Analysis/Opinion*

ESL/ELL English Language Learners
Point to these pictures and ask children to name them: drum, stamps, blocks, shells. For each word, have children think of more words that begin with the same sound.

AUDITORY LEARNERS
Read sentences and have children identify the word that does not fit. Have them replace it with a word containing a digraph: *Zebras are black and wheat.* (white) *I fell down and scraped my knot.* (knee) *We get wool from a shadow.* (sheep) *We ate crackers and chin.* (cheese)

CHALLENGE
Materials: drawing paper, crayons

Have children draw a picture that contains sheep, wheat, thorns, a chipmunk, chicks, and cherry trees. Then, have them write directions about their picture similar to those found on page 288 and give them to a partner to follow.

EXTRA SUPPORT/INTERVENTION
Write these words on blending arrows like those found on page 287: *white, shell, chain, thank, child, knot, knight, whale, shape.* Have children blend the sounds to read each word aloud. **See Daily Phonics Practice, pages 323–325.**

288

Lesson 138
Pages 289–290

Phonics and Reading / Phonics and Writing

Endings and Digraphs

Skill Focus
Children will
- read words that contain inflectional endings and digraphs.
- write words that contain inflectional endings and digraphs to finish sentences.
- build words with initial digraphs and phonograms *-in, -ip*.

Teach

Phonemic Awareness: Phoneme Identity
Read each of the following sentences aloud. Have children repeat each one. Then, have them identify the words that have the same beginning sound.
- Charlie chopped cherries for the cheesecake.
- Shelby shopped for shoes and shirts.
- Theo thinks he has three thermometers.

Sound to Symbol Write the words *child, shape, think, wheel,* and *knob* on the board. Have volunteers read the words aloud and underline the consonant digraph in each one.

Words in Sentences Write these sentences on the board.
- We opened the door and walked out.
- Soon the rain was pouring down.
- We rushed back home and closed the door.

Help children read the sentences. Then, ask them to circle the words that end in *-ed* or *-ing*.

Practice and Apply

Phonics and Reading After children have read the story, encourage them to identify words that have consonant digraphs or the ending *-ed* or *-ing*.

Critical Thinking For Talk About It, encourage children to find a sentence in the story that will help them answer the question.

Phonics and Writing For page 290, tell children to try each letter at the top to make a word with *-in* or *-ip*. Remind them that not every letter will make a real word.

Reading Use *Something to Munch*, MCP Phonics and Reading Library, Super Skills Collection, Level A, to provide practice in reading words with consonant digraphs.

289

Name _____

Read the story. **Use** words in which two letters stand for one beginning sound and words with endings to finish the sentences.

Looking for Chuck

Where was Chuck?
Shari and Shane looked all over.
They knew Chuck did not like storms.
Now thunder was booming.
Lightning flashed.
Chuck was hiding.
After a while Shari sat down.
She said, "I give up."
Just then Shane said, "There's Chuck!
He's chewing his toy under your chair!"

1. __**Where**__ was Chuck?

2. __**Thunder**__ was booming.

3. Chuck was __**chewing**__ his toy.

 Why was Chuck hiding?

Review endings, digraphs: Reading, critical thinking   289

FOCUS ON ALL LEARNERS

ESL/ELL ENGLISH LANGUAGE LEARNERS

- Build background for the story on page 289 by talking about what happens during a thunderstorm. Use the following words from the story: *storm, thunder, lightning, flash, boom.* Encourage children to tell how they feel about such storms.
- Pair students with English-speaking partners for the word-building activity on page 290.

VISUAL LEARNERS

Materials: writing paper, crayons

Have children make five column heads for these digraphs: *ch, sh, th, kn, wh.* Then, have them find words beginning with these digraphs in the story on page 289 and record each under the correct heading. Encourage them to add other words to each list.

KINESTHETIC LEARNERS

Divide children into groups of three. Have one child read the story while the other two act out the parts of Shari and Shane. Have children switch roles so that each child has an opportunity to read the story.

Building Words

Add the word part to each of the letter pairs in the boxes. Say the word. If it is a real word, write it on the line.

| th | ch | kn | wh | sh |

___in

1. thin
2. chin
3. shin

| th | ch | wh | sh | kn |

___ip

4. chip
5. whip
6. ship

Write a sentence using two of the words you made.

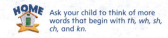

Ask your child to think of more words that begin with *th, wh, sh, ch,* and *kn*.

290 Review consonant digraphs: Phonograms

CURRICULUM CONNECTIONS

SPELLING

Dictate these spelling words and sentences. Have children write the words as a posttest.
1. **chin** — Dad cut his **chin** while shaving.
2. **knot** — I can't untie this **knot**.
3. **ship** — The **ship** sank on the rocks.
4. **think** — Can you **think** of a game to play?
5. **whale** — The **whale** looked for food underwater.

SCIENCE/LANGUAGE ARTS

Materials: children's book about Benjamin Franklin

Read the book to children. Then, invite them to tell what they learned about Franklin's inventions and other accomplishments. Call particular attention to the experiment in which he used a kite and a key to prove that lightning was a form of electricity.

 AstroWord Base Words and Endings

AUDITORY/KINESTHETIC LEARNERS

Have children take turns reading the story on page 289 to their partners. Have partners clap each time they hear a word containing a consonant digraph. Have them raise their hands each time they hear a word ending in *-ed* or *-ing*.

CHALLENGE

Ask children what they think might happen after Shari and Shane find Chuck. Suggest that they write a continuation of the story. Encourage them to include what the children might say to try to make Chuck come out from under the chair. Also encourage them to use words with endings and digraphs in their stories.

EXTRA SUPPORT/INTERVENTION

Pair children and have them read aloud the story on page 289 before answering the questions. Have them identify the sentence in the story that contains the information they need to answer each question. See Daily Phonics Practice, pages 323–325.

Integrating Phonics and Reading

Shared/Guided Reading
Show the cover as you read the title. Then, preview the illustrations and invite children to make predictions about what will happen in the story.
First Reading Invite children to join in when they see the words *Slam! Bam! Crash!*
Second Reading Ask children to identify words that end with the digraphs *sh, ch,* and *th*. Also have them find a word that has *th* in the middle. List the words on the board.

Comprehension
After reading, ask children these questions:
- How would you describe the cook in the story? *Inference/Character*
- What kinds of foods have you helped to make? Were you messy or neat? *Reflective Analysis/Personal/experience*

ESL/ELL English Language Learners
Invite children to act out these words from the story: *mash, wash, munch, crunch*.

Lesson 139 Pages 291–292

Take-Home Book

Review Endings and Consonant Digraphs

> **Skill Focus**
> Children will
> ★ read words with inflectional endings and consonant digraphs in the context of a story.
> ★ review selected high-frequency words in the context of a story.
> ★ reread for fluency.

◆ Teach

Build Background Recall with children that the theme of this unit is "Whatever the Weather." Display page 291 and explain that clouds form when water evaporates and turns into an invisible gas called water vapor. When the water vapor cools, it turns into tiny droplets of water that form clouds. Tell children that they will be reading a book about different kinds of clouds.

Phonemic Awareness: Phoneme Substitution Present these oral riddles for children to answer.

- What word rhymes with *mine* and begins with the digraph *sh*? *(shine)*
- What word rhymes with *fill* and begins with the digraph *ch*? *(chill)*
- What word rhymes with *rock* and begins with the digraph *kn*? *(knock)*

◆ Practice and Apply

Read the Book Help children tear out and fold the pages to make their Take-Home Books. Then, read the book together. Help children read the labels that identify the different kinds of clouds.

Sound to Symbol Read aloud or have volunteers read the book. Have children identify the base word and ending in *showing*. Then, have them identify the consonant digraphs in the words *shapes, know, weather, showing, thunder, thin, white, watch,* and *change*. Invite volunteers to write the words on the board.

Review High-Frequency Words Write the words *come, you, they, about, the, are, of,* and *them* on the board. Have children spell each word and then say it, blending the sounds.

Reread for Fluency Have children reread the book to increase their fluency and comprehension. Children can take their books home to read and share with family members.

Review endings, consonant digraphs: Take-home book **291**

FOCUS ON ALL LEARNERS

ESL/ELL ENGLISH LANGUAGE LEARNERS
Materials: index cards

After assisting children with making the Take-Home Book, use the following activities to teach English language learners.

- Read the text together. Discuss the meaning of any unfamiliar words. Have children look at the photos and talk about the shapes and colors of the different clouds they see.
- Prepare a set of cards with the digraphs *th, wh, sh, ch,* and *kn*. Have each child pick a card and scan the story to find one or more words that begin with that blend. *(they, these, that, thunder, thin, weather; white; shapes, showing; change; know)*

KINESTHETIC LEARNERS
Materials: Phonics Picture Cards: thermometer (154), thimble (155), whale (157), wheat (158), sheep (164), shirt (165), chair (168), cherry (169); mural paper; marker

Draw eight clouds on the paper. In the corner of each shape, place a picture card. Then, have children do a "sky walk" by hopping from cloud to cloud, saying the picture name, and identifying the digraph.

Cumulonimbus Clouds

② These clouds are showing that bad weather is near. Rain and thunder will come soon.

- - - - - FOLD - - - - -

Cirrus Clouds

③ These thin clouds are made of ice. They tell us that the weather will be good.

292 Review endings, consonant digraphs: Take-home book

CURRICULUM CONNECTIONS

ART/SCIENCE
Materials: blue or gray construction paper, chalk, cotton, paste, crayons

Have children explore different materials to create pictures of different types of clouds. Have them label the pictures based on the information presented in the Take-Home Book.

WRITING
Materials: drawing paper, crayons

Invite children to pretend that they are clouds. Ask questions like these: *What type of cloud would you be? Where would you go? What would you see?* Have children illustrate and write about their adventures as a cloud.

SCIENCE
Materials: wide-mouth plastic jars, plastic wrap, rubber bands

Children can make rain by filling a jar with an inch of warm water and then tightly covering it with a piece of plastic wrap. Have them place the jar on a sunny windowsill and observe what happens.

AstroWord Consonant Blends & Digraphs

AUDITORY/VISUAL LEARNERS
Tell children you will name some images that they might see formed by clouds. Have them raise their hands each time they hear a word that contains a consonant digraph. You might say: *whale, fish, boat, ship, chipmunk, knock, cow, bird, thimble, sheep.*

CHALLENGE
Using information presented in the Take-Home Book, have children look out the window on several cloudy days and identify the types of clouds they see in the sky. Encourage them to write in their weather logs sentences describing the clouds.

EXTRA SUPPORT/INTERVENTION
Materials: Take-Home Books, cassette recorder, tape

Make an audiotape of the Take-Home Book and have children follow along in their books as they listen to the tape. Then, have children read the story on their own. **See Daily Phonics Practice, pages 323–325.**

Lesson 140   Pages 293–294

Contractions with will and is

> **Skill Focus**
>
> Children will
> - identify contractions for word pairs with *will* and *is*.
> - write contractions with *will* and *is* to complete sentences.
> - recognize and read high-frequency words.
>
> **ESL/ELL** Many character-based languages, such as Chinese, do not form contractions with subject + verb/modal. Native speakers of Spanish will understand the concept.

▶ Teach

Introduce Contractions with *will* and *is* Say these sentences: *He will go sledding. He'll go sledding.* Encourage children to tell what is the same and what is different about them.

Then, write the sentences on the board. Underline the words *He will* and *He'll*. Explain that *He'll* is a shortened form of the words *He will*. Tell children that this kind of shortened form is called a *contraction*. Identify the apostrophe in *He'll* and tell children that it replaces the letters that were left out of the contraction. Discuss what letters were left out of *He will* to make *He'll*. Follow the same procedure for these sentences: *She is my friend. She's my friend.*

▶ Practice and Apply

Phonological Awareness Read aloud the rhyme on page 293. Have children identify the contractions they hear. Write each one on the board. Then, have children listen to the rhyme again and identify the words that stand for the two contractions. Write *They will* and *I will* on the board.

Writing Before children begin pages 293 and 294, go over the contractions in the box at the top of each page. As children complete the activities, they will have the opportunity to read the following high-frequency words: *no, water*.

Critical Thinking For Talk About It on pages 293 and 294, have children review what the children in the stories do before naming other things to do when the weather is cold and while at the park.

Reading Use *That Cat!*, MCP Phonics and Reading Library, Super Skills Collection, Level A, to provide practice in reading contractions.

Contractions

Name _____

They'll slide down the hill.
They will go very fast.
I'll slide down, too.
I will be the last.

I will = I'll	you will = you'll	they will = they'll
he will = he'll	she will = she'll	we will = we'll
	it will = it'll	

▶ **They'll** is a short way to say **they will**. Read each sentence. Circle the short way to write the underlined words.

1.	It will be fun to go for a ride on a sled.	You'll / **(It'll)**
2.	I will get on the sled.	We'll / **(I'll)**
3.	You will get on the sled with me.	**(You'll)** / She'll
4.	They will all get on the sled, too.	**(They'll)** / It'll
5.	Oh, no! Get off or we will fall!	he'll / **(we'll)**

What are some other things to do outside when the weather is cold?

Contractions with will: Words in context, critical thinking   293

FOCUS ON ALL LEARNERS

ESL/ELL ENGLISH LANGUAGE LEARNERS

Before beginning pages 293 and 294, provide additional practice with the contractions children are learning.

- On the board, write the column heading *Word Pairs* and write these words underneath: *I will, you will, he will, she will, it will, they will, we will*. Next to the words, label a second column *Contractions*. Ask volunteers to write the contraction next to each word pair.
- Repeat with word pairs *he is, she is, it is*.

VISUAL LEARNERS

Materials: index cards, markers

Have one child write on index cards the contractions found in the word banks on pages 293 and 294. Have the other child write the uncontracted form of these words. Then, have children combine the two sets of cards and use them to play "Contraction Concentration."

AUDITORY LEARNERS

Say sentences such as *Do you think it will snow?* and *She is playing outside*. Have children say the same sentences using contractions.

293

Contractions

She's is a short way to say **she is**. **Look** at each picture. **Read** the sentence. **Print** the short way to write the underlined words. **Use** the words in the box to help you.

> she is = she's   it is = it's   he is = he's

1. It is a nice day to play in the park.
   __It's__ a nice day to play in the park.

2. He is going down the slide.
   __He's__ going down the slide.

3. She is having fun in the water.
   __She's__ having fun in the water.

4. He is playing on the swings.
   __He's__ playing on the swings.

5. It is full of things to do!
   __It's__ full of things to do!

TALK About It What else can you do at the park?

HOME Ask your child what words form the contractions *they'll*, *we'll*, and *you'll*.

294 Contractions with is: Words in context, critical thinking

CURRICULUM CONNECTIONS

SPELLING
Say each spelling word and then use it in a context sentence. Have children write each word as a spelling pretest.
1. **can't** — I **can't** pick up this heavy box.
2. **he's** — He says **he's** almost ready to go.
3. **I'm** — **I'm** too tired to watch a movie.
4. **we'll** — Do you think **we'll** win the game?
5. **you're** — Stop when **you're** done.

WRITING
Have children write about what they enjoy doing at a park. To help them get started, lead the class in a brainstorming session. Record this information in a word web around the word *park*. Children can illustrate their work and share it with the group.

PORTFOLIO

SCIENCE
Materials: modeling clay, paper clips, plastic pan full of water

Point out the floating inner tube on page 294. Then, invite children to perform floating and sinking experiments by making little boats out of clay and loading them with paper clips. Encourage them to find out how the size and shape of the boat affect the load the boat can carry.

Integrating Phonics and Reading

Guided Reading
Show the cover as you read the title. Point out the word *moving* on the cartons. Invite children to make predictions about the story.
First Reading Have children point out the cat in the illustrations and tell what it is doing.
Second Reading Point out the contractions *It's* and *you'll* on page 9. You might also point out these contractions in the story and discuss the words they stand for: *didn't*, *let's*, *I've*.
Comprehension
After reading, ask children these questions:
- How did Matt feel about moving? Why?
  Recall/Character
- How did the cat make Matt feel better?
  Recall/Character

ESL/ELL English Language Learners
Ask children to find the word *moving* on page 3. On the board, write *move* + *ing* = *moving* and explain that silent *e* is dropped from the end of a word before the ending *-ing* is added.

AUDITORY/VISUAL LEARNERS   GROUPS
Materials: index cards, marker
Make word cards for the contractions in the boxes at the top of pages 293 and 294 and give each child a card. Then, say the uncontracted form of each word and have the child holding the corresponding contraction stand.

CHALLENGE
Challenge children to write five sentences using the contractions that they did not circle as responses on page 293. Have them share their sentences with a partner and have the partner identify the two words that make up each contraction.

EXTRA SUPPORT/INTERVENTION
Materials: letter cards: *Ee, Hh, Ii, Ll, Oo, Ss, Tt, Uu, Ww, Yy*; macaroni
Form the words *you will* with letter cards. Using a piece of macaroni as an apostrophe, have the child form the contraction *you'll* by removing the letters *w* and *i*. Repeat this procedure with other contractions on pages 293 and 294. **See Daily Phonics Practice, page 325.**

Lesson 141
Pages 295–296

Contractions with am, are, and not

Skill Focus

Children will

★ identify contractions for word pairs with *am*, *are*, and *not*.

★ write contractions with *am*, *are*, and *not* to complete sentences.

★ recognize and read high-frequency words.

ESL/ELL Some English language learners may be unfamiliar with the wide use of contractions in English. Spanish speakers, however, may recognize contractions *del* and *al* (*de el* and *a el*); French speakers will note *j'ai* (*je* and *ai*).

◆ Teach

Introduce Contractions with am, are, and not Write these words on the board and have children identify them as contractions: *she's, it's, they'll, I'll*. Ask children to identify the word pair that forms each contraction and have them identify the letters replaced by the apostrophe.

Explain that contractions can also be formed with the words *am*, *are*, and *not*. Write these word pairs and contractions in two columns.

- I am   they're
- you are   we're
- they are   I'm
- we are   you're

Read the words aloud and have volunteers draw lines to match each word pair with its contraction. Repeat the matching activity, using *can not–can't, does not–doesn't, will not–won't, is not–isn't*.

◆ Practice and Apply

Writing Before children begin pages 295 and 296, go over the contractions in the box at the top of each page. As children complete the activities, they will have the opportunity to read the following high-frequency words: *love, says*.

Critical Thinking For Talk About It on page 295, have children review the animals in the story before naming other zoo animals. For page 296, encourage children to point out the sentence in the story that helped them answer the question.

Reading Use *Cat Chat*, MCP Phonics and Reading Library, Super Skills Collection, Level A, to provide practice in reading contractions.

Contractions

Name_____

▶ **I'm** is a short way to say **I am**. **Look** at each picture. **Read** the sentence. **Print** the short way to write the underlined words. **Use** the words in the box to help you.

I am = I'm	we are = we're
you are = you're	they are = they're

1. You are going to the zoo.

   You're going to the zoo.

2. I am going with you.

   I'm going with you.

3. We are going to see the seals.

   We're going to see the seals.

4. They are fun, and the cubs are, too.

   They're fun, and the cubs are, too.

5. I think we are going to love the zoo!

   I think **we're** going to love the zoo!

TALK About It What other animals can you see at the zoo?

Contractions with am and are: Words in context, critical thinking   **295**

FOCUS ON ALL LEARNERS

ESL/ELL ENGLISH LANGUAGE LEARNERS

- Use pages 295 and 296 as a practice and assessment opportunity. Have children complete each page individually, asking for assistance if needed. Review answers as a group.

- Before beginning page 296, you might wish to provide extra practice with *won't*, an irregularly formed contraction.

VISUAL/AUDITORY LEARNERS

Materials: index cards, markers

Make word cards for these contractions: *I'm, we're, you're, they're, can't, doesn't, won't, isn't*. Say the two words that make up each contraction and have children go to the board to select the contracted form.

KINESTHETIC LEARNERS

Materials: several complete sets of letter cards; index card with an apostrophe

Say each of these contractions: *I'm, we're, you're, they're, can't, doesn't, won't, isn't*. Have children in the group select the letter and apostrophe cards needed to spell each contraction. Then, have them stand, holding the cards to form the contraction.

Contractions

▶ **Can't** is a short way to say **can not**. **Read** the sentences. **Circle** the short way to write the underlined words. **Use** the words in the box to help you.

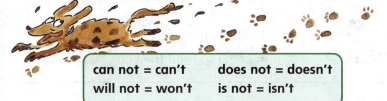

| can not = can't | does not = doesn't |
| will not = won't | is not = isn't |

1. Wags <u>is not</u> clean. He is a muddy mess!	can't doesn't (isn't)
2. Mom <mark>says</mark> he needs a bath. Wags just <u>will not</u> get into the tub.	(won't) isn't doesn't
3. Wags <u>does not</u> like baths. He runs away.	isn't can't (doesn't)
4. I <u>can not</u> catch him. Mom will help me.	(can't) doesn't won't
5. Wags <u>is not</u> muddy now. I am the one who needs a bath!	(isn't) can't doesn't

TALK About It Who needs a bath now and why?

HOME Using the contractions, take turns making up other sentences about Wags.

296 Contractions with not: Words in context

CURRICULUM CONNECTIONS

SPELLING
Materials: spelling master (page 269l), index cards

Have children make a word card for each spelling word. Then, challenge children to come up with different ways to sort the words. Possibilities include sorting by the number of letters, by the number of letters replaced by the apostrophe, and by the number of vowels. Have children write other words with the same contracted ending.

WRITING
Materials: puppets (optional)

PORTFOLIO

Have groups of three write a play about the child and his or her mom trying to give Wags a bath. Before children begin to write, suggest they try to include contractions.

SOCIAL STUDIES
Materials: mural paper, crayons

Zoos, parks, playgrounds, libraries, houses of worship, shops, town pools, beaches, and schools are all important community resources. Discuss what children might see or do at each place and draw it on a mural.

AUDITORY/VISUAL LEARNERS **PARTNERS**
Have partners play a game of "Contraction Ping-pong." To play, one child says a word pair that can be contracted, such as *is not*. The other child responds with the contracted form. After several rounds, children can reverse the game by beginning with the contraction.

CHALLENGE
Challenge children to think of other contractions that contain the word *not*. These might include *don't, aren't, shouldn't, wouldn't, haven't, hasn't,* and *hadn't*. Have them make a chart like the one at the top of page 296, listing the word pairs and the contractions.

EXTRA SUPPORT/INTERVENTION
Many children have difficulty remembering that *won't* is the contracted form of *will not*. Give sentences containing *will not*, such as *I will not be late*. Have children repeat the sentence, using the contracted form. **See Daily Phonics Practice, page 325.**

Integrating Phonics and Reading

Shared/Guided Reading
Show the cover as you read the title. Flip through the illustrations and invite children to make predictions about what will happen in the story.

First Reading As you read, have small groups of children take the parts of the narrator and each of the animals.

Second Reading Point out the contractions *I'm* and *can't* and have children reread the sentences in which they appear.

Comprehension
After reading, ask children these questions:
- Did the cow, duck, chick, and ant have good reasons for not wanting to chat? *Reflective Analysis/Character*
- What do you think the cat would have done if the horse didn't want to chat? *Inference/Plot*

ESL/ELL English Language Learners
Draw children's attention to the sentences beginning "I'm too busy. . . ." on pages 3, 4, 5, and 6. Have them restate each one using *I am*.

296

Lesson 142   Pages 297–298

Review Contractions

Skill Focus

Children will

★ identify sentences that describe pictures and contain contractions.

ESL/ELL Native speakers of Chinese, Japanese, Korean, or Vietnamese who had difficulty pronouncing /l/ versus /r/ may need additional support and oral/aural practice with the pairs *you'll, you're; we'll, we're;* and *they'll, they're.*

Teach

Review Contractions Write the words *will, is, am, are,* and *not* to head five columns on the board. Ask children to recall contractions that include each of these words and have volunteers write them in the correct column.

Point to each contraction and ask children to identify the word pair that makes up the contraction. Then, point to contractions at random and ask volunteers to use each one in an oral sentence.

Words in Context: Decodable Words Write these words on the board: *isn't, can't.* Then, write and read the following sentence. Have children select the word that completes the sentence.

• I ____ come and play with you. (can't)

Practice and Apply

Sound to Symbol Tell children to look carefully at the pictures on pages 297 and 298 and to select the sentence that best tells about each picture. Suggest that they think about the two words that make up each contraction before choosing a sentence. Remind them that on page 297 they will be circling the sentence; on page 298 they will be filling in the bubble next to the sentence.

Reading Use *When I Go See Gram,* MCP Phonics and Reading Library, Super Skills Collection, Level A, to provide practice in reading words with contractions.

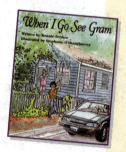

Review Contractions

Name _____

▶ **Circle** the sentence that tells about the picture.

1. I'll eat the hot dog.
   (I'm going to read the book.)

2. (It's in the bag.)
   She'll sleep in the tent.

3. We won't go on the ride.
   (We're on the ride.)

4. She's going to play on the swing.
   (They're going to like my painting.)

5. (You're going to rake the yard.)
   We'll drive up to the lake.

6. (I can't skate very well on the ice.)
   He doesn't like ice cream on his cake.

Review Contractions: Words in context   297

FOCUS ON ALL LEARNERS

ESL/ELL ENGLISH LANGUAGE LEARNERS

• Ask children to take turns reading aloud to the group the sentences on pages 297 and 298. Have them say each contraction and tell which two words form it, then highlight the contractions with a marker.

• Have children complete page 297 working with a peer partner. Have them complete page 298 individually.

VISUAL/AUDITORY LEARNERS

Write *is, are, will,* and *not* on the board. Say a contraction and have a child repeat it. Then, have the child come forward and point to the word that is part of the contraction. Some contractions to use are *we're, you're, he's, can't, she's, she'll, we'll,* and *didn't.*

KINESTHETIC LEARNERS

Materials: small slips of paper, egg carton, beans

Have children write these contractions and place each in an egg cup: *I'll, you'll, it'll, he's, there's, it's, I'm, you're, we're, can't, doesn't, won't.* Have children take turns tossing a bean into the carton, reading the contraction where it lands, and using the contraction in a sentence.

297

Review Contractions

▶ **Fill in** the bubble beside the sentence that tells about the picture.

1. ● It's a dog.
   ○ It can't be a dog.
   ○ They're dogs.

2. ● He's on a bike.
   ○ She's in a jet.
   ○ I'm on the bus.

3. ● It won't rain today.
   ○ It'll rain all day.
   ○ I'll play in the rain.

4. ○ We don't like bugs.
   ● She'll eat a hot dog.
   ○ We're eating the fruit.

5. ○ They'll go for a ride.
   ● We'll go for a swim.
   ○ You're up a tree.

6. ○ She can't find her shoes.
   ○ He doesn't want to ride his bike.
   ● She's trying to catch a fish.

HOME Ask your child to use contractions such as *I'll, I'm,* and *won't* to tell about himself or herself.

298 Review Contractions: Words in context

CURRICULUM CONNECTIONS

SPELLING
Dictate these spelling words and sentences and have children write the words as a spelling posttest.
1. **can't** — I **can't** hear you.
2. **he's** — I think **he's** going to be late.
3. **I'm** — **I'm** packed and ready to go.
4. **we'll** — She says **we'll** go outside.
5. **you're** — I think **you're** tired.

WRITING
Have children review the pictures on pages 297 and 298 and identify three activities that they might do on a single day. Have children write sentences about the activities, using *first, next,* and *last*.

SCIENCE
Materials: balloon

Blow up a balloon and then let the air out. Use this to explain *expand* and *contract* and have children tell what it has to do with contractions.

AUDITORY LEARNERS
Say these sentences, emphasizing the underlined words. Have children repeat the sentence using a contraction. *I am cold. She will come. We will be late. It is early. They are happy. We are eating. He is going. I can not see. They will not come. She does not care.*

CHALLENGE
Materials: drawing paper, crayons

Have children select three sentences that do not tell about pictures on pages 297 and 298. Have them draw pictures to illustrate each sentence. Ask them to exchange pictures with a partner to identify and write the sentence that goes with each picture.

EXTRA SUPPORT/INTERVENTION
Assign partners and have them work together to read the sentences on pages 297 and 298. Have them discuss which sentence tells about each picture. See Daily Phonics Practice, page 325.

Integrating Phonics and Reading

Shared/Guided Reading
Show the cover as you read the title. Tell children that in the story a girl visits her grandmother. Have them predict some things they might do.
First Reading Let half the class read the words spoken by the girl and the other half read the words spoken by Gram as you narrate.
Second Reading Have children find the contractions *it's* and *we'll* and read aloud the sentences in which they appear.

Comprehension
After reading, ask children these questions:
- Does the girl enjoy her visit to Gram's house? Why? *Inference/Character*
- Imagine that the girl and Gram went to the park together. What might they do there? *Creative/Character*

ESL/ELL English Language Learners
Review vocabulary by having children find each of these words in the story and tell what they mean: *cereal, robe, roses, hose.*

Lesson 143 Pages 299–300

Phonics and Spelling / Phonics and Writing

Endings, Consonant Digraphs, Contractions

Skill Focus

Children will

★ spell and write contractions and words with endings and consonant digraphs.

★ write a description of their favorite kind of weather using contractions and words with endings and consonant digraphs.

▶ Teach

Phonics and Spelling Write these spelling words, using blanks to stand for the missing letters:

- peel_ _   row_ _ _   _ _ ot
- _ _ ale   _ _ n't   _ 'm

Say each word, having children pronounce it after you: *peeled, rowing, knot, whale, can't, I'm*. Ask volunteers to fill in the missing letter or letters.

▶ Practice and Apply

Phonics and Spelling Have volunteers read the words on the cloud on page 299. Then, review the directions.

Phonics and Writing Remind children that they have been reading and learning about the weather. Explain that they will use the lines on page 300 to write about their favorite kind of weather. Read the directions at the top of the page and the words in the box together. You may want to brainstorm together about different kinds of weather and write the ideas on the board. Then, have children complete the writing activity on their own.

Reading Use *Dragon's Lunch,* MCP Phonics and Reading Library, Super Skills Collection, Level A, to review contractions and words with endings and consonant digraphs.

299

Spelling

Name _____

Say and **spell** the words below. **Print** the words on the lines where they belong.

fishing	can't	melted	I'm	peeled	ship
think	knot	chin	whale	rowing	spilled

Words that have **ed** endings

1. melted   2. peeled   3. spilled

Words that take the place of two small words

4. can't   5. I'm

Words whose beginning sound is made up of two letters

6. think   7. ship   8. knot

9. chin   10. whale

Words that have **ing** endings

11. fishing   12. rowing

Review endings, consonant digraphs, contractions: Spelling   299

FOCUS ON ALL LEARNERS

ESL/ELL ENGLISH LANGUAGE LEARNERS

- Before children begin page 299, check their understanding of the spelling words by having them use each one in a sentence.
- To help children get started with the writing activity on page 300, brainstorm ideas aloud. Then, encourage children to write sentences that express the ideas they discussed. Have them read their descriptions aloud to the group.

VISUAL/AUDITORY LEARNERS   INDIVIDUAL

Materials: index cards or slips of paper

Have children write the spelling words from page 299 on cards or slips of paper. Have them mix up the words, then sort the words into three piles: words with endings, words with consonant digraphs, and words that are contractions.

KINESTHETIC LEARNERS

Materials: pieces of chart paper taped together, marker

Lay the paper on the floor and divide into a 5-by-5 grid. In each square, write a letter of the alphabet, placing *x* and *z* in the same square. Say a spelling word and have a child spell it by hopping from letter to letter on the grid.

Writing

What kind of weather do you like best? **Write** a description of your favorite kind of weather. **Use** describing words to tell about what you see, hear, or feel. The words in the box may help you.

know	I'm	playing	walking
rained	what	that	it's

 Ask your child to forecast tomorrow's weather.

300 Review endings, digraphs, contractions: Writing

CURRICULUM CONNECTIONS

SPELLING

Cumulative Posttest Review Unit 5 spelling words by using the following words and dictation sentences.

1. **cooking** — What are you **cooking**?
2. **peeled** — Ann **peeled** the banana.
3. **spilled** — She **spilled** the hot soup.
4. **knot** — The string has a big **knot**.
5. **ship** — The **ship** sailed out of sight.
6. **think** — What do you **think**?
7. **whale** — We saw a huge **whale**.
8. **can't** — I **can't** eat a whole cake.
9. **you're** — He said that **you're** late.
10. **I'm** — **I'm** in first grade.

WRITING

Materials: cassette recorder or video camera (optional), chart paper, markers

Working with partners, have children write their own pretend weather report. If possible, video or audiotape the forecasts so that children can share them.

 **AstroWord** Base Words and Endings

AUDITORY/VISUAL LEARNERS

Materials: list of unit spelling words

Have children take turns giving clues about a spelling word from page 299. Once the word is successfully guessed, have each child in the group write the word. Then, have the child giving the clue spell the word aloud so that others can check the spelling.

CHALLENGE

Introduce the concept of alphabetical order with children. Then, have them write in alphabetical order the spelling words on the cloud on page 299.

EXTRA SUPPORT/INTERVENTION

Materials: individual slates

Say each spelling word. Have children work with a partner to write the word on a slate. See Daily Phonics Practice, pages 323–325.

Integrating Phonics and Reading

Guided Reading
Show the cover and read the title. Ask children if they think they will be reading a true story or a make-believe story and how they know.
First Reading Have children describe what is happening in the illustrations. Encourage them to notice humorous details, such as the words on Dragon's bib.
Second Reading Challenge children to find two words with the ending -ed, one contraction, and nine words with consonant digraphs.
Comprehension
After reading, ask children the following questions:
- What did Dragon want? *Recall/Summarize*
- How do you think the family felt after Dragon left? Why? *Inference/Character*

ESL/ELL English Language Learners
Point out the words that Dragon says before he leaves: *Now I am done.* Explain that this is another way of saying, *Now I am finished.*

Lesson 144   Pages 301–302

Take-Home Book

Review Endings, Consonant Digraphs, Contractions

Skill Focus

Children will
- ★ read contractions, words with endings, and consonant digraphs in the context of a story.
- ★ review selected high-frequency words in the context of a story.
- ★ reread for fluency.

◆ Teach

Build Background Help children recall the theme of this unit, "Whatever the Weather." Discuss how we can know what the weather is. Conclude by telling children that they will read a story about two children who are tricked by the weather.

Phonemic Awareness: Phoneme Categorization Say the following groups of words. Ask children to identify the word that does not contain the same beginning digraph.

- knit   chin   kneel
- shoe   shop   chance
- shy   why   wheat
- think   ship   thirty

◆ Practice and Apply

Read the Book Help children tear out and fold the pages to make their Take-Home Books. Read the book together. Ask children if they were surprised by the ending.

Sound to Symbol Read aloud or have volunteers read the book. Have children find the following: four words with endings; four contractions; and seven words with digraphs. Invite volunteers to write the words on the board.

Review High-Frequency Words Write the words *out, said, there, with, them,* and *the* on the board. Have children spell each word and then say it, blending the sounds.

Reread for Fluency Have children reread the book to increase their fluency and comprehension. Children can take their books home to read and share with family members.

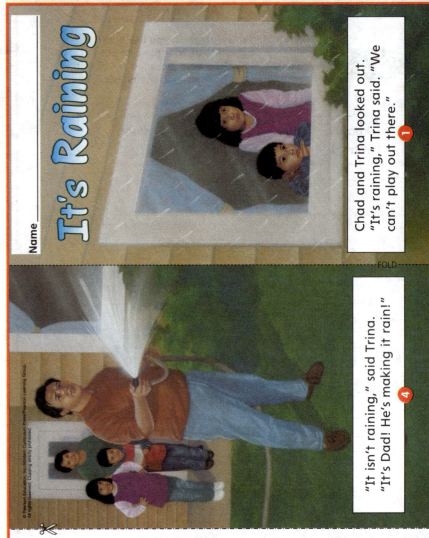

Review endings, digraphs, contractions: Take-home book   301

FOCUS ON ALL LEARNERS

ESL/ELL ENGLISH LANGUAGE LEARNERS

After assisting children with making the Take-Home Book, use the following activities to teach English language learners.

- Prepare activity sheets for children to practice verb endings. Divide the sheet into three columns: *base word, -ed,* and *-ing.* Have children work together in pairs to find the words *looked, raining,* and *opened* in the story. Have them print the words in the appropriate column and then supply the other two forms, e.g., *looked, look, looking.*

- Have children find and write the four story words with contractions *(it's, can't, isn't, he's),* then write the two words that make up the contraction.

KINESTHETIC/AUDITORY LEARNERS

Assign children to work in groups of five and have them take the parts of a narrator, Trina, Chad, Mom, and Dad. Have them act out the story as they read aloud.

301

2. Mom looked out with them. "It isn't raining today," she said.

3. "I know it was raining," Chad said. Trina opened the door and looked outside.

302 Review endings, digraphs, contractions: Take-home book

CURRICULUM CONNECTIONS

SCIENCE
Materials: hose, drawing paper, crayons

You can use a hose on a sunny day to create a rainbow for children to observe. Turn on the hose full force and place your thumb over the end of the hose to scatter the water into tiny droplets. Have children observe the spray with their backs facing the sun. As the drops fall, they act as tiny prisms separating the sunlight into a rainbow. Help children identify the colors as red, orange, yellow, green, blue, indigo, and violet. When you return to the classroom, suggest that they make drawings of their observations.

WRITING
Materials: drawing paper, crayons

Have children write and draw what they think Chad and Trina will do now that they know they can go outside to play.

SOCIAL STUDIES
Have children recall what work Dad is doing. Talk with children about jobs that they do at home to help out. Then, have each child write a brief note to a parent, offering to do one of these jobs to help out around home.

 **AstroWord** Consonant Blends & Digraphs

AUDITORY/VISUAL LEARNERS
Materials: Take-Home Book

Have children share questions about the story with a partner. For example, they might ask why Chad and Trina can't play outside or why Dad is using the hose. When children respond, ask if they found the information in the text or illustrations.

CHALLENGE
Discuss what children think Trina and Chad will tell their dad about this funny mix-up. Suggest that children write a conversation between the children and their father. Invite them to share their conversation with a small group.

EXTRA SUPPORT/INTERVENTION
Go through the story page by page and discuss what is happening in each picture. Then, help children read the page aloud. **See Daily Phonics Practice, pages 323–325.**

Lesson 145   Pages 303–304

Unit Checkup

Endings, Consonant Digraphs, and Contractions

Skill Focus

Children will

★ identify picture names that contain consonant digraphs.

★ write words that contain inflectional endings, consonant digraphs, and contractions to complete sentences.

Teach

Phonological Awareness: Blending Onsets and Rimes Say the following word parts. Have children orally blend the parts to say the word.

- /ch/eese   (cheese)
- /n/ock   (knock)
- /sh/eep   (sheep)
- /th/umb   (thumb)
- /hw/ite   (white)

After children have blended the words, point out that each one begins with one of the digraphs they have learned about. Write the digraphs *ch, kn, sh, th,* and *wh* on the board as column headings and ask children to name other words that begin with each digraph. Have volunteers write the words on the board.

Sound to Symbol On the chalkboard, print these column headings: *Endings -ed* and *-ing, Consonant Digraphs, Contractions.*

Ask volunteers to print each of the following words under the correct heading as you read them aloud: *shine, can't, raining, snowed, we're, think.* Have new volunteers use colored chalk to underline the endings and the consonant digraphs. Ask other volunteers to write the two words that each contraction stands for.

Practice and Apply

Assess Skills Help children identify the pictures on page 303. You may wish to demonstrate how to fill in the bubble to mark the correct answer. For page 304, remind children to try each word choice before circling and writing their answer.

Name _____

UNIT 5 CHECKUP

▶ **Say** the name of each picture. **Fill in** the bubble beside the picture name.

1.
○ knee
● knob
○ knife

2.
● wheel
○ whip
○ white

3.
○ chain
○ thin
● chin

4.
○ sheep
● ship
○ chip

5.
○ thin
○ cherry
● three

6.
● knit
○ knot
○ knock

7.
● chair
○ shame
○ chat

8.
○ while
○ throat
● whale

9.
○ throne
● thumb
○ shade

Endings, digraphs, contractions: Assessment   303

FOCUS ON ALL LEARNERS

ESL/ELL ENGLISH LANGUAGE LEARNERS

- Before beginning page 303, review the skill by having children find each of the following objects in the classroom and identifying the beginning digraph: *chair,* the numeral *3, shelf, knob, white* chalk. Write each word on the board and ask volunteers to underline the digraph. Have children name more words that begin with the digraphs *ch, th, sh, kn,* and *wh,* and write them on the board.

- Build background for the story on page 304 by talking about activities that take place on a snowy day, such as sledding, shoveling, and making snowmen.

KINESTHETIC/VISUAL/AUDITORY LEARNERS

Materials: large paper bags or sheets of paper and masking tape, scissors, markers

Have children work together to act out the forming of a contraction. Group members can decide on a word pair they wish to contract. They can make letter vests out of paper bags as costumes, or they can write letters on paper and attach them to their clothing with tape. Have each group present its dramatization to the class.

UNIT 5 CHECKUP

▶ Look at the picture. Circle the word that will finish the sentence. Print it on the line.

1. How deep do you ___think___ it is?
   - (think)
   - knew
   - chase

2. She's ___trying___ to find out.
   - rowing
   - spilled
   - (trying)

3. It's up to his ___chin___!
   - knot
   - (chin)
   - whale

4. She ___can't___ get it out.
   - isn't
   - don't
   - (can't)

5. ___They're___ happy that it snowed.
   - (They're)
   - I'll
   - It's

6. The snow has all ___melted___!
   - peeled
   - spilled
   - (melted)

304 Endings, digraphs, contractions: Assessment

ASSESS UNDERSTANDING OF UNIT SKILLS

STUDENT PROGRESS ASSESSMENT

You may wish to review the observational notes you made as children worked through the activities in the unit. Your notes will help you evaluate the progress children make with reading and writing words with inflected endings, digraphs, and contractions.

PORTFOLIO ASSESSMENT

Review the materials children have collected in their portfolios. You may wish to have interviews with children to discuss their written work and the progress they have made since the beginning of the unit. As you review children's work, evaluate how well they use phonics and word study skills.

DAILY PHONICS PRACTICE

For children who need additional practice with endings, digraphs, and contractions, quick reviews are provided on pages 323–325 in Daily Phonics Practice.

PHONICS POSTTEST

To assess children's mastery of endings, digraphs, and contractions, use the Posttest on pages 269g–269h.

VISUAL LEARNERS GROUPS

Have children locate the sentences containing contractions on page 304. Then, have them rewrite each sentence, substituting the two words from which the contraction is formed.

CHALLENGE

Materials: Phonics Picture Cards: teeth (153), thumb (156), wheat (158), wheel (159), brush (161), fish (163), chain (167), chair (168)

Place the pictures in the chalk ledge. Have each child select a picture and use its name to write a sentence that also contains either a contraction or a word with the ending *-ed* or *-ing*.

EXTRA SUPPORT/INTERVENTION

Materials: Phonics Picture Cards: thumb (156), wheel (159), chair (168)

Display each picture card and have children say its name. Then, have them look at the responses found on page 303 and point out the word that names each picture. See Daily Phonics Practice, pages 323–325.

304

Teacher Notes

Daily Phonics Practice

Contents

UNIT 1 (LESSONS 1–29)

Letters *Ss, Tt, Bb, Hh, Mm, Kk*	308
Letters *Jj, Ff, Gg, Ll, Dd, Nn,* and Review	309
Letters *Ww, Cc, Rr, Pp, Qq, Vv,* and Review	310
Letters *Xx, Yy, Zz,* and Review	311

UNIT 2 (LESSONS 30–68)

Short *a* and Review	312
Short *i* and Review	312
Short *u* and Review	313
Short *o* and Review	314
Short *e* and Review	315

UNIT 3 (LESSONS 69–114)

Long *a* and Review	316
Long *i* and Review	317
Long *u* and Review	318
Long *o* and Review	318
Long *e* and Review	319

UNIT 4 (LESSONS 115–128)

r Blends	320
l Blends	321
s Blends	321
Final Blends and Initial Blends	321
Consonant and Vowel Sounds of *y* and Review of Blends	322

UNIT 5 (LESSONS 129–145)

Inflectional Endings *-ed* and *-ing*	323
Consonant Digraph *th*	323
Consonant Digraph *wh* and Discriminating Between *wh* and *th*	324
Consonant Digraph *sh* and Review	324
Consonant Digraph *ch* and Review	324
Consonant Digraph *kn* and Review	325
Contractions and Review	325

Daily Phonics Practice

UNIT 1 LESSONS 1–9, 26–29

Letters Ss, Tt, Bb, Hh, Mm, Kk

- Pass out letter cards for *A–Z*. Have children line up in alphabetical order as you sing the Alphabet song.

- Have children choose a favorite nursery rhyme. Ask them to recite their rhyme and clap whenever they come to a rhyming word. Use "Simple Simon," "Three Blind Mice," and "Jack Be Nimble."

- Pass out uppercase and lowercase letters *Ss, Tt, Bb, Hh, Mm, Kk* to 12 children. Have children hold their letters in front of their chests, find their partners, and make an uppercase/lowercase pair.

- Build an *S* Sandwich. Draw two slices of bread on the chalkboard. On the chalkboard ledge, set up picture cards including many that begin with the *s* sound. Have children come up to the board and choose a picture card whose name begins with the sound of *s* to put in the sandwich.

- Have children make the timeout sign with their hands and say *Timeout!* each time they hear a word that begins or ends with the sound of *t*.

- Ask children to answer riddles by saying a word that begins or ends with the sound of *s, t,* or *b*. Say *What word rhymes with* mop *and begins with* t? *What word rhymes with* mat *and begins with* b? *What word rhymes with* clock *and begins with* s?

- Take an imaginary bike ride through the neighborhood. Invite children to name objects to look for on their ride whose names begin with the sound of *b*, such as *bus, bush, bakery, ball, boat,* and *building*.

- Have children hop on one foot each time they hear you say a word that begins with the sound of *hop*. Use these words: *hat, horse, hobby, jump, book, hold, hand, heart, hot, hen*.

- Write the letters *Ss, Tt, Bb, Hh, Mm,* and *Kk* on paper grocery bags or small boxes. Have children toss a beanbag into one of the containers and name a word that begins with that sound.

- Set up a post-office box in front of the classroom. Hand out an index card to each child. Ask children to write *M* and *m* on their cards, say a word that begins with the sound of *m*, and then "mail the message."

- Say short easy rhyming words. Ask children to repeat the word you say and then say a rhyming word that begins with the sound of *k*—for example, *tea, key, bite, kite, mitten, kitten, sick, kick, beep, keep, sting, king*.

- Place letter cards for *s, t, b, h, m, k* on the chalkboard ledge. Invite children to pick a letter, say a word that begins with that sound, and use the word in a sentence.

- Hold up classroom objects whose names begin with a consonant sound. Ask children to find other objects whose names have the same beginning consonant sound.

Daily Phonics Practice

UNIT 1 LESSONS 10–17, 26–29

Letters Jj, Ff, Gg, Ll, Dd, Nn, and Review

◆ Place picture cards on the chalkboard ledge. Say a word that begins with the same sound as that of one of the picture names. Ask a volunteer to come to the board and select the picture whose name has the same beginning sound.

◆ Put picture cards for letter sounds *j, f, g, l, d,* and *n* in a box. Have children select a card, name the picture, and say a sentence using the word.

◆ Divide the class into two groups. Have one group of children cut out from magazines and newspapers uppercase letters *J, F, G, L, D,* and *N*. Ask the second group to cut out lowercase letters *j, f, g, l, d,* and *n*. Have children pair up to make letter partners.

◆ Play "be the judge." Have each child write *Jj* on an index card. As you display picture cards, many with the sound of *j*, ask children to hold up their letter card if the name of the picture begins with the sound of *j*.

◆ Hold up picture cards one at a time. Ask children if the picture name has the same sound as that of the beginning of *fence*. If so, tape the picture card on the board to create a fence with the cards.

◆ Set out a gift-wrapped box. Line up picture cards, many with the sound of *g*. Ask children to choose a card whose name has the same sound as that of the beginning of *gift* and put the card in the gift box.

◆ Place picture cards of *j, f,* and *g* words in random order on the chalkboard ledge. Say the word *gift*. Ask volunteers to select a picture card whose name begins with the same sound. Have children hold up the cards and name the pictures. Repeat with *farmer* and *jacket*.

◆ Ask children to fold a sheet of paper into four sections. Then, give them four clues for words that begin with the sounds of *s, t, b,* and *h*. Have them draw a picture and write one letter in each block for the answers to your clues.

◆ Have children listen carefully for words you say that begin with the same sound as that of *lion*. When they hear that sound, invite children to roar like a lion. Use *long, girl, like, jacks, fast, look, list, fall, lake,* and *left*.

◆ Have children listen carefully for words that begin like the word *dog* as you read some sentences. Ask them to hold up fingers to indicate how many *d* words they hear and then have them name the words. Say these sentences: *A fox lived in a den. The den was dark and damp. It had a dirt floor.*

◆ On the chalkboard ledge, display picture cards whose names have the sound of *n*. Have children identify each picture as you print the word above the card. Ask volunteers to come up and underline the *n* in the word.

◆ Display picture cards of *S, T, B, H, M, K, J, F, G, L, D,* and *N* in random order. Say a child's name that begins with one of the consonant sounds. Ask a volunteer to select a card, hold it up, and identify the picture whose name has the same sound.

Daily Phonics Practice

UNIT 1 LESSONS 18–23, 26–29

Letters Ww, Cc, Rr, Pp, Qq, Vv, and Review

◆ Play tic-tac-toe on the chalkboard. Divide the class into two teams: *C* and *P*. Explain that three picture cards whose names begin with their team letter must be in a row going down or across. The list may include *pig, pie, pot* and *cat, cot, cow*.

◆ Display all of the consonant letters studied so far. Say the word *bat*. Ask volunteers to hold up the cards with the letters that stand for the beginning and ending sounds of *bat*. Also use *jug, fun, sail, ham,* and *kid*.

◆ Play "Concentration" with uppercase and lowercase letter cards for *Ww, Cc,* and *Rr*. Ask children to mix up the letter cards and pick two to see if they match.

◆ Ask a child to put on a paper headband. Slip the bottom part of a letter card, facing out, inside the headband so that the letter can be seen. Have the child guess the mystery letter by having classmates name words that have the same beginning letter sound.

◆ Create a *W* wall. Have children come up to the chalkboard and write a *W* or *w* anywhere on the board as they name a word that starts with the sound of *w*. Continue until the board is covered with *Ww*'s.

◆ Have children choose a partner. Hand out a letter card to each pair. Say some words and have each pair hold up its letter card if the letter on it matches the beginning sound of the word. Use *seal, month, goose, wallet, loop, wave,* and *kiss*.

◆ *Am I a cat, a cow, or a camel?* Describe an aspect of one of the three animals and have children respond with the correct animal. Use *I give milk; I have soft fur and say meow;* and *I live in the desert*.

◆ Hang picture cards for these on the board: *book, cap, goat, horn, fan,* and *hand*. Ask a volunteer to name a word that rhymes with a picture name. Write responses under the card. Have children use the rhyming words in sentences.

◆ Ask a volunteer to call out a word with the beginning sound of *r*. Write the word on the board and have children repeat it. After a second word is called, have children repeat both words. Have children repeat each word on the entire list as it grows.

◆ Use picture cards of words beginning with *t, s, b, h, m, k, j, f, g, l, d, n,* and use the corresponding letter cards. While children cover their eyes, place the picture cards around the room. Ask volunteers to find a picture card and match it with its letter card.

◆ Demonstrate a clap-snap-snap rhythm. Say some words and ask children to think of two words that rhyme with each word you say. Have them chant the words to the clap-snap-snap rhythm. Use *rake-take-make, goat-coat-note, box-fox-ox*.

◆ Make a large paper pocket from construction paper. Have children cut out pictures from magazines whose names have the beginning sound of *p* and put them in the paper pocket.

◆ Place picture cards of a *sock, lock, boat, goat, key, bee, snail, whale, nose,* and *hose* on the chalkboard ledge. Ask volunteers to select the pictures whose names rhyme with the word *dock*. Repeat, using the words *coat, tree, tail,* and *rose*.

Daily Phonics Practice

- Display letter cards for *w, c, r, p, q, v*. Ask children to identify the letters that stand for the beginning and ending sounds in these words: *quarter, car, pop, camp, rip, cow, water, purr, vinegar*.

- Suspend a quilt or blanket by hooking it to the backs of four chairs. Invite children to tiptoe quietly under the quilt as they name a word that begins with the sound of *q*. Repetitions are acceptable, since there are few *q* words.

- Pass out picture cards whose names begin with the sound of *v*. Ask children to name their picture and say a sentence using the word.

UNIT 1 LESSONS 24–29

Letters Xx, Yy, Zz, and Review

- Name a classroom object. Have children walk around the room, placing a self-stick note on any item whose name has the same beginning sound.

- Say a word and invite children to name words that rhyme with it. Offer easy rhyming words such as *wet* (*bet, jet, pet, net, set*) or *cat* (*fat, mat, pat, sat*).

- Say *x*, *y*, and *z* words. Ask children to cross their index fingers when they hear a word that has the sound of *x*, yawn when they hear a word that begins with the sound of *y*, and say *ZAP!* when they hear a word that begins with the sound of *z*. Use *zing, extra, x-ray, yes, yellow, zoo, yak, fox*, and *box*.

- Ask children to listen for the ending sound of the words you say. Invite them to name a word that begins with that same sound. Write both words on the board and ask a volunteer to come up to the board and circle the ending and beginning letters of the two words.

- Write the letters *m, n, b, t, d, f, l, p*, and *s* on the board. Ask a volunteer to listen for the ending sound in the word you say, then come to the board and circle the letter. Use *hum, sob, elf, ten, mat, bed, miss, bell*, and *nap*.

- Distribute one letter card to each child. For each word you say, have the child with the beginning-sound letter hold that letter up and the child with the ending-sound letter hold that letter up. Use *fork, pet, bed, car, tub, ball, quiet, jam*, and *miss*.

- Draw a series of letter-labeled dots in a circle on the chalkboard. Ask a volunteer to draw a line from one dot to the next by matching the beginning sounds of two words you say. Dots may be labeled with these letters: *b, f, s, h, d, l, p, r, t*, and *m*.

- Set out alphabet cards for both uppercase and lowercase consonants. Have each child come to the board, take a letter, and pair up with a partner who has the opposite-case letter. Then, ask partners to line up in alphabetical order.

- Have children choose one of these letters and write it on a sheet of paper: *g, m, d, v, k, p, l, n, b*. Say some words and have children decide whether they hear the sound of their letter in the middle of the word. Use *tiger, seven, yellow, lemon, cookies, tunnel, ladder, zipper*, and *rubber*.

- Play "I spy" with classroom objects whose names begin and end with consonant sounds. For example: *I spy something that begins with the sound of* p *and ends with the sound of* n. (*pen*) *I spy something that begins and ends with the sound of* r. (*ruler*)

Daily Phonics Practice

UNIT 2   LESSONS 30–36, 40, 44, 48, 55, 59, 63, 66–68

Short a and Review

- On the chalkboard ledge, display alphabet cards for all the consonants and the letter *a*. Ask the class to choose a consonant and think of a short *a* word that begins with that letter. Have a volunteer "write" the word by arranging the letter cards in the proper sequence.

- Say a short *a* word, such as *fat*. Have children brainstorm one or more rhyming words (*bat, sat, cat, mat*). Repeat, using *sad, map,* and *tan*.

- Pass out the following letter cards to nine children: *b, t, c, t, f, t, a, a, a*. Ask children to come to the front of the classroom and arrange themselves so that the letters form short *a* words. (*bat, cat, fat*)

- Display picture cards of objects whose names have the short *a* sound. Add a few that do not. Point to a picture and ask children to raise their hands and say *meow* if the picture name has the same vowel sound they hear in *cat*. Ask them to be "quiet as a mouse" if the picture does not contain the short *a* sound.

- Write ten words on the chalkboard, six of which have the short *a* sound. Have volunteers circle the words with a short *a* sound.

- Ask children to close their eyes as you distribute flash cards with the medial short *a* sound. Have children stand and read their card to the class. Ask volunteers to use the word in a sentence. Use *mad, ham, am, hand, bat, bad, cab, camp, cat,* and *can*.

- Play a word-scramble game. Mix up two consonant cards and one vowel *a* card that make a three-letter short *a* word. Ask children to rearrange the cards to form a word. For example: *a-p-m* becomes *map*; *t-c-a* becomes *cat*.

- Say three words in a row, one of which has the short *a* sound. Ask children to stand up and repeat the short *a* word. Use *cup, bed, bat* or *sit, hat, pet* or *ram, lid, sun*.

UNIT 2   LESSONS 38–42, 44, 55, 59, 63, 66–68

Short i and Review

- Make alphabet cards for all the consonants and for the vowels *a* and *i*. Put the consonant cards on the chalkboard ledge and have volunteers select two cards and place them on each side of a vowel to make a c-v-c word. Reuse vowel cards.

- Ask children to stand when they hear a word with the short *i* sound. Say three words, one of which has the short *i* sound. Use *bed, sit, can, pin, map,* and *toy*.

- Write sentences with short *i* words on the chalkboard. Ask a volunteer to circle the short *i* words. Write *Jim will win. That is a big tin can. Fix the rip with a pin.*

- Write c-v-c words on the chalkboard, leaving a space for each missing vowel. Ask volunteers to come to the board and fill in *a* for the missing vowel. After all vowels are filled in, have children replace the *a* with *i*. Use *l_p, f_n, p_n, w_g, b_t, l_d, b_g*.

Daily Phonics Practice

- Display the picture cards for wig, pin, fist, ring, sink, lip, fist, bib, gift, and milk in random order on the chalkboard ledge. Say the word *big*. Ask volunteers to come to the board and select a picture whose name rhymes with *big*. Repeat, using other rhyming words.

- Say a short *i* word. Ask children to say the word and name a word that rhymes. Use *sit, big, win, Bill, dip, fist, bib, sink,* and *ring*.

- Play "pig, pig, pen" (instead of duck, duck, goose). Have a volunteer name a short *i* word and have the child who is "pen" name another short *i* word.

- Place picture cards whose names have short *a* and *i* sounds on the table along with a bag, labeled *a*, and a bin, labeled *i*. Ask volunteers to choose a picture card, name it, and toss it in the bag if it has the short *a* sound, and in the bin if it has the short *i* sound.

- Race to the "finish line." Put a strip of masking tape on the floor at one end of the room. Place picture cards and word cards with the short *i* sound around the classroom. Have children pick up three cards and say the words as they cross the finish line.

UNIT 2 LESSONS 46–52, 55, 59, 63, 66–68

Short u and Review

- Tape picture cards whose names contain the short vowels *a, i,* and *u* to the board. Draw three large circles on the board and write the letter *a, i,* or *u* above each one. Ask a volunteer to choose a card, say the picture name, identify the vowel, and tape it in the correct circle.

- Distribute index cards and have children write *u* on their cards. Ask children to hold up their cards when they hear a word that has the short *u* sound. Say words such as these: *rag, rug, rig*.

- Have children play a game of "I spy." Invite them to take turns giving clues to objects in the room. For example, *I spy something that you can pour water in and drink from.* (*cup*) Continue with short *a* and *i* words.

- Write c-v-c words on the chalkboard. Ask volunteers to come to the board, say a word, erase the vowel, and replace it with a different vowel—*a, i,* or *u*. Use *hat, jug, nip, zap, bad, hid, cup, pit,* and *bag*.

- Write these sentences on the board: *The little bug ran in the bag. Sid can fix that big sink. Sam, Gus, and Liz sat in the bus.* Have children copy them to make "rainbow" sentences by using a red crayon for words with the same vowel sound as that of *cat*, blue for *pig*, and green for *fun*.

- Have children take turns making word ladders by changing the medial vowel letter in words. Demonstrate, for example, by writing on the board *cap*, then writing *cup* below it.

Daily Phonics Practice

- Have pairs of children select letters for *a, i, u, t, b, n, r, p, s*. Have them take turns selecting a vowel and two consonants to make three-letter short vowel words. Encourage them to keep a list of the words they make.

- Ask pairs of children to spread out a set of consonant letter cards and a set of vowel letter cards. Say a word and have one child hold up the letter that stands for the word's beginning sound while another child holds up the letter that stands for the ending sound. Then, both children should find and hold up the card that stands for the vowel sound. Use *sand, men, bend, ramp, hum, web, pen, camp, pond, dad, dump, fin, jug, hiss, pig,* and *fox*.

- Tape c-v-c picture cards on the board in random order. Under each card, write the beginning and ending consonants, leaving a blank for the vowel. Call on volunteers to select a card, say the picture name, and fill in the vowel to complete the word.

UNIT 2 LESSONS 53–59, 63, 66–68

Short o and Review

- Display picture cards of short *o* words. Ask volunteers to select a card whose name has the same vowel sound they hear in *top* and place their card on top of the one before. Continue, making a tower with each card on top of the other.

- Recite "Pop, Goes the Weasel" together. Sing the rhyme several times and have children replace the word *pop* with a word that has the same short *o* sound they hear in *pop*.

- Ask children to fold a sheet of paper into four sections. Then give them four clues for words that begin with the sounds of short *a, u, i,* and *o*. Have them draw a picture and write one letter in each block for the answers to your clues. For example: *In the first box, draw a red and shiny fruit. In the second box, draw something that keeps you dry when it rains.*

- Distribute word cards, several of which have the short *o* sound. Ask children with a short *o* sound word card to come to the front of the classroom. Ask volunteers to make a sentence with the word.

- Ask four volunteers to stand in front of the room. Give each one a letter card for *a, i, u,* or *o*. Distribute c-v-c picture cards to the rest of the class. Have children line up behind the letter that stands for the vowel sound in the name of their picture.

- Write these words on the board, leaving a blank for the vowel: c_t, m_g, t_p, r_p, h_t, s_d, d_d, f_n. Call on volunteers to select a word and write in the vowel *a, i, u,* or *o*. Have children say the completed word and use it in a sentence.

- Recite the familiar nursery rhyme "Hickory, Dickory, Dock." Have children clap on the rhyming words. Then ask children to rhyme words for clock-face numbers one through ten.

- Have small groups work together to make collages of pictures of objects whose names have the short *a, i, u,* and *o* sounds, such as *cat, pig, rug, tub, top, mop, can, lips*. You may want to provide old magazines and catalogs for children to cut out pictures or have them draw pictures. Help children label each picture with its name.

Daily Phonics Practice

- Display vowel cards for *a, i, o, u* on the chalkboard ledge and draw a picture of a large suitcase on the board. Have children "take a trip" by packing something that has one of the short vowel sounds in its name. Write the words in the suitcase. You may want to display consonant letter cards as well to help children think of words.

UNIT 2 LESSONS 61–68

Short e and Review

- Write ten words on the chalkboard, six of which have the short *e* sound. Have volunteers circle the words with the short *e* sound. Use *bed, wet, man, pen, fig, but, egg, men, jet,* and *box*.

- Write the word *but* on the chalkboard. Ask children to erase the vowel and replace it with an *e*. Have children read the new word (*bet*). Repeat, using these words: *man, jot, log, pan, bid, nut,* and *ham*.

- Pass out the following letter cards to nine children: *b, d, p, t, t, n, e, e, e*. Ask children to come to the front of the classroom and arrange themselves so that the letters form short *e* words. Examples are *bed, pet, ten*.

- Write sentences with short *e* words on the board. Ask volunteers to circle the short *e* words. Use these sentences: *The hen laid an egg. Put the pen and pencil on the desk. The men set up the tent.*

- Create a "clean slate." Write these words on the board: *cap, ham, hill, dog, kit, bag, ten, rock, jump, pin, run, desk, bus, bed,* and *mop*. Have a volunteer come to the board, read a word, name the vowel sound, and then erase the word. Continue until all words have been identified and erased.

- On the chalkboard ledge, line up alphabet cards for all the consonants. Print a large *e* on the board. Have volunteers select two consonant cards and hold them in place on each side of the *e* to make a c-v-c word.

- Pair children, then pass out a picture card and an index card to each child. Ask children to write the picture name on the index card. Have partners exchange cards and write a word that rhymes with the partner's word. Ask the partners to say their words together.

- Demonstrate a tap-tap-clap rhythm. Say two words and ask children to think of a third word that rhymes with the words you say. Have them clap as they call out a rhyming word for every two you tap. Use *bed-head-red, dog-log-fog, den-pen-hen, pat-mat-sat, wig-fig-pig*.

- Write *a, e, i, o,* and *u* on the chalkboard. Have children identify any vowels that are in their names. Ask volunteers to come to the board and write the vowel or vowels under the ones that are already written on the board. Continue, creating a column of letters under each vowel.

- Write common vowel-consonant word endings such as *-an, -it, -un, -og,* and *-en* on the board. Ask volunteers to form words by selecting a consonant alphabet card and holding it in front of a vowel-consonant ending.

Daily Phonics Practice

UNIT 3 LESSONS 69–76, 84, 93, 100, 102, 109–114

Long a and Review

- Ask children to wave their hands when they hear a word with long *a*. Then, say three words, one of which has the long *a* sound, for example, *lake, pole, bike*.

- Invite children to participate in a scavenger hunt for long *a* words. Allow them ten minutes to search the classroom for objects whose names have the long *a* sound (for example, *game, table, tape, paper, plate*). Print their words on the board.

- Draw a cap and a cape on the board. Use flashcards and ask children if the words on the cards have the same *a* sound as that in *cap* or in *cape*. Ask a volunteer to write the flashcard word below the word with the same *a* sound. Use *can, last, fan, mat, ham, pal, cane, fake, pail, paint, wave,* and *way*.

- Pass out cards on which are written action words with the long *a* sound. Have each child choose a card and pantomime the action. Write action words on the board after they have been acted out. Use *skate, paint, sail, rake, bake, wave, wake, race,* and *pay*.

- Ask children to say long *a* words. Write the words on the board, then ask for a rhyming word.

- Have children play a game of "change it." Write these words on the board: *cap, mad, can, tap, pan, Jan, man, fad*. Ask children to add *e* to the end of each word and read the new word they make.

- Mix up flashcards of short *a* and long *a* words and place them face down on a table. Invite a volunteer to pick a card, read the word aloud, and identify the vowel sound.

- Play "animal farm." Say the name of an animal and ask a volunteer to come to the board and write the letter that stands for the beginning sound of the name. Encourage children to make the sound of their animal. Use *bird, cow, hen, tiger, goose, zebra, seal, dog, lion, rat, wolf, fox, mouse, parrot*.

- Assign children to four groups: short *a*, long *a* with the spelling *ay*, long *a* with the spelling *ai*, long *a* with the spelling *a_e*. Have each group think of a word that matches their vowel sound or spelling. Ask a volunteer to write the word on the board.

- "Bake a cake!" Encourage children to fill the cake with "ingredient" words that have the long *a* sound in the middle of the word, such as *baking powder, raisins, dates, grapes*. Continue with nonsense answers.

- On the chalkboard, write sentences containing words with the long *a* sound. Ask a volunteer to circle the sound of long *a* in the word. Write: *Please don't be late. Stay on the trail. Make a dog out of clay. Ray will sail the boat. Put the game away.*

- Hold up picture cards. Have children wave if the vowel sound in the picture name is the same as the vowel sound in *wave*, or clap if the vowel sound in the picture name is the same as the vowel sound in *clap*. Use cards for *apple, bag, cap, cat, hand, hat, cake, cane, gate, rake, vase,* and *skates*.

Daily Phonics Practice

UNIT 3   LESSONS 78–84, 93, 100, 102, 109–114

Long i and Review

◆ Read sentences with short and long *i* sounds. Have half the class stand when they hear a short *i* sound and the other half stand when they hear a long *i*. Use these sentences: *Mike got a bit of mud on the side of his white pants. It happened when his bike tire went through a big puddle. "You should ride on the sidewalk," said Tim. The next time he rode his bike, that's just what Mike did.*

◆ Write "Simple Simon" on a sheet of chart paper and recite it with the class. Ask volunteers to underline the long *i* words in the rhyme. Read it again as a class and have children raise one arm each time they say a word with the long *i* sound.

◆ Play "a dime every time." Ask children to listen carefully as you read these words: *five, time, nine, pin, tide, mitt, white, vine, hid,* and *ice.* Have them put a plastic coin in a box each time they hear a word that has the same sound as the *i* in *dime.*

◆ Place picture cards and corresponding letter cards of c-v-c words on the chalkboard ledge. Ask a volunteer to select a picture card and "write" the word by arranging the letter cards. This can be a group activity with three children "writing" one word.

◆ Pronounce sets of three words, two with long vowel *i* and one with short vowel *i*. Ask children to identify the two words whose vowel sounds are the same. Use these sets: *dime, tie, lid; ride, vine, six; pie, kite, fin; fire, five, hill; bike, dive, gift; bike, nine, pig.*

◆ Display picture cards on the chalkboard ledge. Ask children to name each picture and identify the vowel sound they hear in the word. Encourage them to use that word and one of the other picture names in a sentence. Use *bib, king, lid, mitt, pig, six, bike, fire, five, kite, nine, pie, tie,* and *tire.*

◆ Line up flashcards that have words with long *a* and long *i* sounds. Ask a volunteer to select a card, read the words aloud, and identify the vowel sound. Use *gate, lay; gave, made; same, rake; make, paid; five, dive; hike, lie; vine, ripe; mine, lime.*

◆ Write sentences on the board and have one volunteer circle words with the long *a* sound and another underline words with the long *i* sound. Use these sentences: *James will ride his bike to the lake. Kay ate the nine dates on her plate. Mice like to hide in the hay. Dave had a slice of Kate's lime pie.*

◆ Write these words on the chalkboard: *mane, lake, Dave, bake, lane, Kate,* and *tame.* Ask a volunteer to erase the *a* and substitute it with an *i*. Have children read the new words.

◆ Place picture cards and word cards for short and long *i* words around the classroom. Have children pick up three cards and say the words on the cards.

Daily Phonics Practice

UNIT 3 LESSONS 86–93, 100, 102, 109–114

Long u and Review

- Have children cut out words from newspapers and magazines that have the vowel sound they hear in *glue*. Ask them to glue those words to a sheet of paper. Explain that the following letter combinations can stand for the long u sound: *ui, ue, u__e*.

- Play "true or false." Hold up labeled picture cards and ask the class to say *true* if the card has a picture whose name contains the long u sound, and *false* if the name does not.

- Have children copy the words *short* and *long* on opposite sides of an index card. Ask them to hold up the side of their card that describes the vowel sound in these words: *dog, ice, cute, cap, it, red, cape, pond, bake, sun, line, pup, suit, ten,* and *dime*.

- Make a long u cube with six labeled pictures. Invite a volunteer to roll the cube, name the picture, and spell the word. Use these words: *fruit, mule, ruler, tube, suit,* and *glue*.

- Write ten words on the chalkboard, six of which have the long u sound. Have a volunteer circle a word with the long u sound. Then, have the entire class read the circled words. Use *suit, clue, tub, juice, cube, tune, sun, cute, gum,* and *bus*.

- Display picture cards whose names have the long u sound. Have children make up a nonsense tune using these long u words.

- Say a long u word, such as *cube*. Have children name a rhyming word. Use *mule, rule; suit, fruit; tune, dune; true, clue; fuse, muse, excuse*.

- Have children fold a sheet of paper in four sections. Say the following unfinished sentences: *Toothpaste comes in a ___. Ten pennies equals one ___. Use an umbrella in the ___. Can you whistle a ___?* Ask children to draw a picture in each section of the paper to answer the sentences. Have children write the picture name and underline the letters that stand for the vowel sound.

- On the chalkboard ledge, place picture cards whose names have long *a, i,* and *u*. Say a word that has the long *a, i,* or *u* sound. Ask a volunteer to come to the board and select a picture whose name has the same vowel sound.

- Play "just one clue." Tell students that you are thinking of something whose name has the long u sound. Give just one clue to see if someone can guess. Use these clues: *I make beautiful music. I am what holds toothpaste. I am a stubborn animal. I am white and very sticky. I am clothing worn in a business office.*

UNIT 3 LESSONS 94–102, 109–114

Long o and Review

- Have children brainstorm lists of words that rhyme with each of the following: *goat, low, nose, cone*. Write the words on the board and then help children make up sentences that contain words from one or more of the lists. (*A goat in a coat ate a bone all alone.*)

- Play "boat float." Set up a small tub of water and a container of tiny plastic foam balls as boats. Ask volunteers to name a word that has the same sound that they hear in the word *boat* and put a ball in the water.

Daily Phonics Practice

- Display picture cards that have the short *o* and long *o* sounds. "Stack the deck" so that there are many more long *o* words than short *o* ones. Have each child choose a card, identify the vowel sound, and join children with the short or long vowel sounds in a line. (*The long vowel line will be long; the short vowel line will be short.*)

- Sing "Old King Cole" together. Have children cup their hands around their mouths to make an *O* every time they recite a word that has the same sound as *o* in *old*.

- Write the phrase *"Oh, give me a home, where the buffalo roam…"* on the board. Invite volunteers to make up nonsense rhymes and change the words *home* and *roam* to other words that have the long *o* sound. Try *Oh give me a boat, where the buffalo float….*

- Go "around the world." Draw a picture of Earth on the board with the letters *h, m, s, t, b* around the circle. Invite children to travel the world by naming a word that begins with each consonant and has the short *a* sound. Continue with words that have the short *i, u,* and *o* sounds.

- Play "guess what I have." Ask a volunteer to choose a picture card and keep it hidden. Have him or her say to the class, *I am thinking of a word that has the long* o *sound and is an animal* (or *is something in the classroom, is a toy to play with, is seen outside*, and so on).

- Display flashcards and identify words with short *a, i, u,* and *o*. Then, distribute the cards randomly. Tell children who have words that contain the short *a* sound to stand together. Do the same for children with short *i, u,* and *o* cards.

- Let two teams play "chalkboard baseball." Draw a baseball diamond on the board and print *o* and *i* in the middle. Each team takes a letter. Batters advance by naming long *o* or long *i* words, with an incorrect word being an out. After three outs, the second team takes over. Repeat for long vowels *a* and *u*.

UNIT 3 LESSONS 104–114

Long e and Review

- Play "Morse code." Ask children to write a dot for a word that has the sound of short *e* or a dash for a word that has the sound of long *e*. Use *bet, beet, please, ten, ear, tree, seat, bed, bell, street, three,* and *egg*.

- Write *ee* and *ea* on the chalkboard. Have children select a word card with one of two long *e* sound spellings. Ask children to say the word they select and display it on the chalkboard ledge under *ee* or *ea*.

- Make a tic-tac-toe game on the board and write a long *e* word in each square. Then, divide the class into *X*'s and *O*'s. Have *X*'s begin by reading one word in any box and, if correct, putting an *X* in the square. *O*'s take a turn, say a word and, if correct, put an *O* in the square. Play until a row of *X*'s or *O*'s is made.

- Ask children "long *e* animal riddles." Say, *What insects buzz and give honey?* (bees) *What birds fly together in a shape like a V?* (geese) *What animal looks like a horse with stripes?* (zebra) *What animal has wool and says "baa"?* (sheep)

Daily Phonics Practice

- Say words with long *e* and short *e* sounds. Ask volunteers to say a rhyming word. Use these words: *ten, leg, pen, men, jet, hen, egg, nest, bell, wheel, seat, heel, seal, leaf, three, tree, eat, jeep,* and *beans*.

- Display picture cards and word cards for the long *e* sound. Have children match a word card with a picture card. Then, ask them to use their word in a sentence.

- Explain to children that the letter *e* at the end of a word changes the short vowel sound to the long vowel sound. Give some pair examples and then ask children to name a long vowel word when they hear the short vowel word. Use *tub, tube; cut, cute; man, mane; mat, mate; bit, bite; pin, pine; dim, dime; hop, hope; tot, tote*.

- Play "same or different." Say some word pairs and ask children to raise both hands if the words end with the same sound. Have them keep their hands down if the ending sounds are different. Use *deal, meal; man, bat; gum, hum; cat, yet; fill, roll; wake, fake; rap, tape; some, team; pal, pat; feet, meet*.

- Write ten words on the chalkboard, eight of which have the long *e* sound. Have volunteers come up to the board, circle the long *e* words, and underline the letters that stand for the long *e* sound. Use *peel, bean, leaf, seat, heel, three, ear, tree, hole,* and *cube*.

Daily Phonics Practice

UNIT 4 LESSONS 115–116, 123, 126–128

r Blends

- Draw five hills on the chalkboard. Write a different vowel in the middle of each hill. Display picture cards one at a time and ask a volunteer to name each picture and write its name on the hill, adding the beginning and ending consonant letters. Encourage children to pronounce the words by blending the sounds together.

- Display letter cards for *b, c, f, g, d, p, t,* and *r*. Have children listen for consonant sounds that are blended together at the beginning of a word. Pronounce the blended words and have children use their letter cards to "spell" the beginning *r* blend. Use *cream, group, brand, truth, drag, frost, press, brake, tree, crumb, great,* and *pride*.

- Write a story on the chalkboard. Ask volunteers to name and circle the words that begin with *r* blends. Use this story: *Brenda is a funny dragon. She wears a crown on her head. She sits under a tree all day and eats grapes. Her best friend is a frog. They like to cry over sad stories about a prince and princess.*

- Have children crawl like crabs as they say words that begin with an *r* blend.

- Play "freeze frame." Write a series of *r*-blend words on the chalkboard. Ask volunteers to hold up a small picture frame to freeze-frame the *r* blend in a word on the board. Use *crab, brick, free, bride, grass, frown, drip, prize, drive,* and *crown*.

Daily Phonics Practice

UNIT 4 LESSONS 117–118, 123, 126–128

l Blends

- Ask children to put their heads down on their desks as you randomly distribute these picture cards: block, clock, fly, clown, glass, plant, broom, crown, drum, fruit, grapes, tree. If a child receives a card, have him or her stand, say the picture name, and identify the letters that represent the beginning blend.

- Review *r* and *l* blends by playing a rhyming game. Use these clues: *begins with* br *and rhymes with* pick *(brick); begins with* cl *and rhymes with* sock *(clock); begins with* gl *and rhymes with* mad *(glad); begins with* pl *and rhymes with* gate *(plate)*.

- Write these word endings on the board: *-ub, -ant, -ag, -ate, -ock, -at, -obe, -us, -ue*. Hold up an *l*-blend card—*cl, pl, fl, bl, gl*—and ask a volunteer to choose a card and combine it with one of the word endings on the board. Have children say the new word.

UNIT 4 LESSONS 119–120, 123, 126–128

s Blends

- Have children fold a sheet of paper into four sections. Have them listen to these sentences and answer them by drawing a picture whose name begins with an *s* blend: *This animal carries its house on its back (snail). You eat cereal with this (spoon). In winter we shovel this (snow). To mail a letter, put this on an envelope (stamp).* Have them circle the *s* blend in their picture label.

- Distribute six *s* letter cards and letter cards for *l, k, n, m, p,* and *t*. Have children with an *s* card pair with another consonant. Ask them to use their *s* blend in a word and say it in a sentence. Display picture cards of a sled, skates, a snake, a smile, a spider, and a star and other *s*-blend pictures for reference.

- Play "I smell a skunk." Write *r*-, *s*-, and *l*-blend words on the chalkboard, using mostly *s* blends. Invite volunteers to say *I smell a skunk* as they circle the words that begin with *s* blends.

- Hold up a picture card and ask a volunteer to name it. Have children identify the letters that stand for the beginning blend. Then, ask children to use the word in a sentence. Use *skates, smoke, snail, snowman, spoon, spring, star,* and *swing*.

UNIT 4 LESSONS 121–123, 126–128

Final Blends and Initial Blends

- Play "stop the music." Put picture cards of final-blend words in a bag and start the music. Have children pass the bag around a circle until the music stops. Ask the child holding the bag to choose a picture card, say its name, and identify the letters that stand for the final blend.

Daily Phonics Practice

- Say these words as you write them on the chalkboard: *hand, skim, dusk, cast, story, brim, pink, snail, lamp, spin, sleep, club, think, camp, plane, frog, green.* Invite volunteers from the front of the room to come to the board and underline initial blends and volunteers from the back of the room to circle final blends.

- Write the following word endings on the chalkboard: *-ing, -um, -own, -ant, -unk, -ar, -ay.* Call on volunteers to write a beginning consonant blend in front of each ending to form a word. Have the class say the words aloud.

- Play "rhyme time." Read a word and name three beginning blends. Ask children to identify words that begin with these blends and rhyme with the word you say. Use words that rhyme with *rake* and begin with *st, sn, fl*; that rhyme with *date* and begin with *cr, pl, sl*; that rhyme with *sing* and begin with *sw, br, fl.*

UNIT 4 LESSONS 124–128

Consonant and Vowel Sounds of y and Review of Blends

- Distribute word cards with short and long vowel sounds. Ask volunteers with word cards that contain a short vowel sound to come to the front of the room. Encourage each child to say the word and identify the short vowel sound. Repeat the activity with long vowel sounds. Use *ask, time, coat, hit, mule, up, team, stop,* and *cane.*

- Display a picture card of a yo-yo. Ask children to name the picture and the consonant sound they hear at the beginning of the word *yo-yo*. Write the letter *y* on the board. Invite children to brainstorm words that begin with the consonant sound of *y*.

- Pronounce these pairs of words: *too, you; yellow, fellow; mess, yes; yell, bell; card, yard; yet, net; yam, ram.* Encourage children to say the word from each pair that begins with the consonant sound of *y*.

- Say words with the consonant sound of *y* and some blend words. Have children yell YES! when they hear the consonant sound of *y*. Use *yellow, prize, yard, yam, brick, yes, you, drive, cry, yell,* and *yo-yo.*

- Have children use a yellow crayon to trace the beginning sound of *y* in words they find in magazines and newspapers.

- Pronounce the following words: *pony, bunny, sky, dry, happy,* and *jelly*. Ask children what vowel sound they hear at the end of each word. (long *e* or long *i*) Write each word on the board without its last letter. Call on volunteers to write the letter at the end of each word that makes the vowel sound. (*y*)

- Display word cards with *y* endings. Ask volunteers to select a word with the long *e* sound and say its name. (Variation: Have children select a word with the long *i* sound.)

- Write these beginning blends on the board: *cr, dr, sl, fr, sk, fl, sp, tr.* Ask a volunteer to take a *y* card and combine it with a blend to make a word. Have children say the new word.

Daily Phonics Practice

UNIT 5 LESSONS 129–130, 138–139, 143–145

Inflectional Endings -ed and -ing

♦ Give one third of the class cards with words such as these on them: *heat, fold, test, add, paint, float, need.* Make cards with *-ed* and *-ing* endings on them for the rest of the class. Have each child with a word card find two children holding cards with endings, put them together, and read the new words formed.

♦ Write these words on the chalkboard: *camp, jump, rain, fix, peel, cook,* and *mix.* Have children add *-ed* or *-ing* to each word and use each base word and the new words in sentences.

♦ Write these words on the chalkboard: *mailing, cooking, needing, mixing, playing,* and *telling.* Have children erase the *-ing* ending from each and then read the base word.

♦ Have children erase the ending from each of these words and then read the base word: *rocked, floated, melted, rained, jumped.*

♦ Write these words on the chalkboard: *jump, play, cook, paint.* Use the pattern _____ is _____. Have children write their own names in the first blank. Then, ask them to choose a word from the list, add the correct ending, and write the new word in the second blank. (Variation: Use the pattern *Yesterday,* (name) _____.)

♦ In this sentence pair, have children add the *-ed* ending to the action word to form a new word that tells about the past: *I cook the beans. Last week I _____ the beans.* Repeat with other sentence pairs.

UNIT 5 LESSONS 131, 136–139, 143–145

Consonant Digraph th

♦ Have children fold a sheet of paper into four sections. Have children draw a picture of something in each section that begins like the word *think.* Give clues such as these: *It is part of your hand . . . something that shows the temperature . . . the number after 12.*

♦ Have children listen carefully for words you say that begin with the same sound as the beginning sound of *thump.* Suggest that children thump their fist on the desk or floor when they identify a word. Say the words *thing, fence, left, thirsty, school, right, thirteen, twenty, sister, thanks.*

♦ Choose a child to name a word that begins with the same sound as that of *thin.* Have the next child say that word plus another *th-* word. Continue around the circle, with each child saying the previous word and a new one.

Daily Phonics Practice

UNIT 5   LESSONS 132, 136–139, 143–145

Consonant Digraph wh and Discriminating Between wh and th

- Write the following on the chalkboard: __ite, __ale, __eel, __eat, __en. Have children write *wh* in each blank and then read the word.

- Have children whistle when you say a word that begins like *whistle*. Use *wish, wheat, water, wheel, win, whine, whir, worry, what, work, white,* and *whiz*.

- Write *th* on one side of the chalkboard and *wh* on the other. Ask children to point to the letters that stand for the beginning sound in these words: *think, what, white, thin, thank, whale, when,* and *thick*.

UNIT 5   LESSONS 133, 136–139, 143–145

Consonant Digraph sh and Review

- Ask children to put a finger to their lips and say *sh* when you say a word that begins like *sheep*. Use these words: *shake, show, sink, shore, sack, sing, share, shock, stick,* and *shadow*.

- Display picture cards for *sh, th,* and *wh* words. Say *shake, thump,* or *whistle*. Have a child choose a card whose picture name starts with the same sound and name the initial consonant digraph.

- Play "whistle and shake." Have children whistle when you say a word that begins with *wh* and shake if it starts with *sh*. Use *whine, shine, shower, whip, shop, what, shook, sheep, ship,* and *whisk*.

- Have children write *th* and *sh* on opposite sides of an index card. Have them hold up the side that stands for the ending of each of these words: *wash, bath, wish, both, teeth, lash, with, math, stash, fish,* and *mash*.

UNIT 5   LESSONS 134, 136–139, 143–145

Consonant Digraph ch and Review

- Have each child point to his or her chin when you say a word that begins with the same sound as that in *chin*: *chop, cherry, shop, cheap, show, cheat, chill, chat, share,* and *cheese*.

- Have children fold a sheet of paper into four sections. Have them label each section with one of the consonant digraphs—*ch, wh, th, sh*—and illustrate it with a picture of something that begins with that sound.

- Display picture cards for four consonant digraphs: *ch, wh, th,* and *sh*. Divide the class into four teams for a relay race. Assign a digraph to each team. Have team members run to pick up cards with their sound on it.

- Have children pantomime each of these words and then name its initial digraph: *chop, whistle, cheer, think, shake, thump, chase, whine,* and *shower*.

Daily Phonics Practice

UNIT 5 LESSONS 135–139, 143–145

Consonant Digraph kn and Review

◆ Say these incomplete sentences and have children fill in an appropriate *kn* word to finish them: *Jane can ___ a sweater. I fell and scraped my ___. Tie a ___ in the shoelace. Cut the cheese with a ___.*

◆ Write these consonant digraphs on the board: *kn, sh, ch, wh, th*. Have children pick a digraph and then say a word that begins with that sound. Invite a second child to use that word in a sentence.

UNIT 5 LESSONS 140–145

Contractions and Review

◆ Give children cards with these words on them: *I will, I'll, you will, you'll, we will, we'll, she will, she'll, he will, he'll, they will, they'll.* Have each child pair up with the person who has a card that means the same as theirs. Switch cards and repeat.

◆ Write these sentences and have children identify and give the full meaning of each contraction: *It's a hot day. He's going to swim. He'll float in the water. He'll be cooler there.*

◆ Have children write these short sentences on a sheet of paper, leaving a space between each one: *Jack is late. He will run. He will be on time.* Discuss which words can be shortened. Have children underline those words and then write the sentences again, this time with the contractions.

◆ Write these word pairs on the board: *I am, you are, we are, they are.* Have volunteers pick a phrase, write the contraction for it, and then use the contraction in a sentence.

◆ Pass out cards with these words on them to four children: *is, does, can, will.* Distribute cards with the word *not* on them to four others. Have each child in the first group find a *not* card and then write the contraction for his or her word.

◆ List the following on the chalkboard without apostrophes: *Ill, youll, shell, itll, well, theyll, hes, shes, its, Im, youre, were, theyre, isnt, cant, doesnt, wont.* Ask children to add apostrophes to make each a contraction.

Teacher Notes

Teacher Notes

Teacher Notes

Teacher Notes

Teacher Notes

Teacher Notes

Teacher Notes

Teacher Notes

Enhance MCP Phonics With These Additional Programs

MCP Phonics & Reading Libraries, K–3

Phonemic Awareness & Phonics Assessment (PAPA), K–4

Spelling Workout, 1–8

Astroword, K–3

MCP Phonics & Reading Libraries, K–3

Motivate success with on-level storybooks matched to specific decoding and reading skills with the *MCP Phonics & Reading Libraries*. A model for integrating phonics with each title is found at point-of-use throughout the *MCP Phonics Teacher Resource Guides*.

Phonemic Awareness & Phonics Assessment (PAPA), K–4

Phonemic Awareness & Phonics Assessment (PAPA) helps identify decoding strengths and needs, and guides instruction for students needing additional support. A correlated list of *PAPA* skills matched to specific lessons in *MCP Phonics* is presented within each Unit of the *MCP Phonics Teacher Resource Guide*.

Continued on reverse side

Return this card today for:
- ✔ Production Registration
- ✔ Free Gift

Title of the Product/Program You Purchased: _____
Grade Level: _____ Date of Purchase: _____
Your Name: _____ Date: _____
School Name: _____ County: _____
Your School/Home Address (circle one): _____
_____
Your E mail Address: _____
Your School/Home Phone Number (circle one): (____) _____

1. **I am a:** (check all that apply)
   - ☐ Teacher (T)
   - ☐ Curriculum Supervisor (V)
   - ☐ Principal/Administrator (N)
   - ☐ Department Chair (C)
   - ☐ Home School Teacher (H)
   - ☐ Federal Funds Supervisor (F)

2. **I teach level(s):**
   - ☐ K–2
   - ☐ 3–6
   - ☐ 7–12
   - ☐ College /Adult Education
   - ☐ Other _____

3. **Areas of Instruction:**
   - ☐ Early Literacy/Phonics
   - ☐ Reading/Language Arts
   - ☐ Social Studies
   - ☐ Staff Development
   - ☐ Special Education
   - ☐ ESL/ELL
   - ☐ Math
   - ☐ Science
   - ☐ Gifted
   - ☐ Assessment
   - ☐ Family Literacy
   - ☐ Other

4. **How will you use *MCP Phonics* overall?**
   - ☐ As a primary phonics program
   - ☐ As a supplement to a primary/core reading program
   Please list your primary/core reading program_____ Copyright_____
   - ☐ As a supplement for use in a summer school/after school program

   More specifically, how will you use this product in your classroom?
   - ☐ Student material for classroom instruction
   - ☐ Student material for homework assignments
   - ☐ Student supplement for review or practice
   - ☐ Remediation/Intervention
   - ☐ Teacher Resource

5. **How did you first hear about *MCP Phonics*?**
   - ☐ Sales Rep
   - ☐ Online Store
   - ☐ Catalog/Brochure
   - ☐ Other _____

6. **Please rank in order of importance the features that prompted you to purchase *MCP Phonics*:**
   - ☐ Systematic skills instruction & practice
   - ☐ Alignment to current research
   - ☐ Flexibility to support any reading program/methodology
   - ☐ History of program success
   - ☐ Other: _____

7. **What time of year does your school place orders for consumable classroom materials?**
   - ☐ January–March
   - ☐ April–June
   - ☐ July–September
   - ☐ October–December

8. **How much money does your school spend a year on supplemental materials?**
   - ☐ Less than $500
   - ☐ Between $500–$1,000
   - ☐ Between $1,000–$2,000
   - ☐ Over $2,000

9. **Did you purchase *MCP Phonics* through a Grant?**
   - ☐ Yes   Please list Grant: _____
   - ☐ No

10. ☐ **Yes, I would like more information about the following programs:**
    - ☐ MCP Phonics & Reading Libraries
    - ☐ Phonemic Awareness & Phonics Assessment (PAPA)
    - ☐ Spelling Workout
    - ☐ Astroword

11. ☐ **Yes, I am interested in participating in studies to determine program effectiveness.**

To complete mailer, fold twice and seal with adhesive tape. Do not staple. *Thank you.*

Thank you for purchasing *MCP "Plaid" Phonics*.

Please see the side panels for information regarding these related phonics programs!

Additional Programs, Continued

Spelling Workout, 1–8

Using the same scope and sequence found in *MCP Phonics*, *Spelling Workout* provides research-based spelling instruction that just makes sense. By using both programs, students hear and read the sounds, then write words as they progress from simple, letter-sound relationships to more complex spelling patterns.

Astroword, K–3

Astroword helps students practice and apply essential phonemic awareness, phonics, structural analysis, vocabulary, and spelling skills. A built-in management system also provides individual or class-summary performance measures. Correlated activities are referenced at point-of-use in the *MCP Phonics Teacher Resource Guides*.

BUSINESS REPLY MAIL
FIRST-CLASS MAIL   PERMIT NO. 315   PARSIPPANY NJ

POSTAGE WILL BE PAID BY ADDRESSEE

PEARSON LEARNING GROUP
MCP PHONICS PRODUCT REGISTRATION
299 JEFFERSON RD
PARSIPPANY NJ 07054-9026

NO POSTAGE NECESSARY IF MAILED IN THE UNITED STATES

Return the attached Product Registration Card or call today for more information about any of these programs.

Modern Curriculum Press
Globe Fearon
Celebration Press
Dale Seymour Publications
Good Year Books

Return This Card Today For:

✓ **Product Registration**
Be the first to know of product updates and improvements as soon as we develop them.

✓ **Free Gift**
To thank you for registering, we'll send you a special gift, while supplies last!

Visit Our Web site to register online: www.pearsonlearning.com.

Modern Curriculum Press
Globe Fearon
Celebration Press
Dale Seymour Publications
Good Year Books

www.pearsonlearning.com
Customer Service
1-800-321-3106